NO

D1236611

Boeing Airc

The Evolution of the Airplane. The first plane of the Wright brothers (inset) in 1903 weighed 750 pounds. The Stratocruiser, forty-two years later, weighs 135,000 pounds. Still larger planes are in process of construction. The airplane has evolved in many other traits than size, of course. The process is still dynamic, with prediction in many respects limited to only a few years in the future. (*Chapter 2, A New Transportation System.*)

The Social Effects of

AVIATION

WILLIAM FIELDING OGBURN

WITH THE ASSISTANCE OF

JEAN L. ADAMS AND S. C. GILFILLAN

HOUGHTON MIFFLIN COMPANY

BOSTON · NEW YORK · CHICAGO · DALLAS · ATLANTA · SAN FRANCISCO

The Riverside Press Cambridge

The Riverside Press
Cambridge · Massachusetts
Printed in the U.S.A.

★ ★ ★

Foreword

SOCIAL SCIENCE has profited less from the study of technology than it has from the study of geography, biology, or psychology, for few social scientists have written on the influence of technology. However, society has been revolutionized several times by technology, for most modern social changes are precipitated by mechanical invention and scientific discovery. Indeed, all major transportation systems, like those based on the boat, the horse, the railroad, and the automobile, have had profound effects upon society. How the new transportation based on aircraft is changing civilization, as reported in this book, reveals processes which are probably quite general. Hence other discoveries — for instance, the use of atomic energy — will conceivably follow similar procedures.

This book is unusual in that it is an attempt to foresee the changes that are coming because of aviation. The theory is that, since there is a time sequence between an invention and its social effects, we should, knowing the invention, be able to anticipate the consequent changes. Such an attempt has seldom been made, though there has been research to find out the effects of inventions that have already taken place, notably the effects of the Industrial Revolution. Because of the interrelated nature of our culture, a wide range of social institutions are covered — almost as many as were dealt with in *Recent Social Trends*, an extensive study a dozen years ago. However, the reader will note a conspicuous omission, the effect of aviation on the future of wars.

There is so much secrecy in this field, and the technological changes so rapid and revolutionary that the author could not make a satisfactory study.

The information in this book, though viewed as a contribution to social science, should be of value to all who look ahead and want to know how their lives, their businesses, their institutions, and their plans will be affected by this great new transportation invention.

Our first acknowledgment is to William A. Patterson, President of United Air Lines, and to its Board of Directors, whose generous financial aid made this work possible. The grant was an outright gift to the University of Chicago with no other expectation than that the research cover the field in which Mr. Patterson and the members of the Board naturally were greatly interested, and that it be as objective as possible. Mr. Patterson, a staunch believer in scientific research, is head of a business organization which has built up an exceptionally competent research staff and knows the value of scientific conclusions. This staff has been generous in supplying data upon our request, but has had nothing to do with the conduct of the research.

The work was done by a small, expert staff consisting of S. C. Gilfillan, who brought to his valuable work in the investigation a store of knowledge of technological processes and their social consequences, and of Jean L. Adams, who contributed much from beginning to end with her careful pen and her critical judgment. Assisting also were Gwen A. Williams and, for part of the time, Joseph B. Gittler. It was, further, necessary to seek the aid of specialists outside the University from such fields as shipping, railroads, and newspapers. Acknowledgment for their assistance is made at appropriate places in the text. Also, co-operative and helpful aid has been given by many leaders in aviation, specialists in the various areas covered, and government agencies concerned with aviation.

WILLIAM F. OGBURN

CHICAGO, ILLINOIS
September, 1945

★ ★ ★

Contents

1. INTRODUCTORY

2. USES

3. SOCIAL EFFECTS

★ ★ ★ ★   # I. INTRODUCTORY

1

Technology Brings Social Changes

THE PRESENT VOLUME is concerned with the problem of predicting the social effects of aviation in the modern world. It is based on the thesis that inventions, such as the railroad, the automobile, or the airplane, make certain changes in customs and social institutions. But before we proceed to our main task of trying to discover what changes the airplane will bring about, it will be profitable for the sake of analogy to review the changes which resulted from an earlier invention whose development and social effects are now familiar.

Let us take, for example, the automobile. We know that society is different because of it. Its widespread effect is visible on a vast number of institutions, industries, customs, and even personal values. It revolutionized, first of all, the methods of transportation, eliminating to a large extent the use of horses and mules, thereby affecting the industries which made wagons, buggies, and harness. The use of buses and trucks reduced both the passenger and freight traffic of the railroads. In fact, the competition of gasoline-driven vehicles on the highways is generally considered one of the chief causes of the bankruptcy of many railroad companies. In modern warfare, the tank has superseded the cavalry, with truly remarkable results.

Furthermore, the bus and automobile affected the distribution of population. Originally, when there was no local transportation except by horse-drawn vehicles, cities were confined to the small districts around railroad stations. Later, the electric streetcar somewhat extended the city limits. But, with the development of rapid-transit lines and the automobile, dwelling places spread out at a wider radius from the center of the city. The economic

3

city became much larger in area than the political city. In contra-distinction to the city with its political boundaries, the larger community came to be known as the metropolitan area. Naturally, the extension of the residential districts around the cities profoundly affected urban and suburban real-estate values.

Not only did the manufacture of the automobile itself create a large new industry, but it stimulated other industries as well. The production, refining, and distribution of oil, the laying of roads, the manufacture of rubber and cotton goods felt the impetus of a new demand. Other businesses, too, felt the stimulus of the automobile: small hotels and tourist houses rose by the side of the highway. The development of the chain store from city to city was greatly facilitated by the truck, which could carry uniform products over wide territories.

Domestic institutions also felt the impact of the new invention. In rural districts, the bus made it possible to form consolidated grammar and high schools which children could more easily attend. Many small rural churches were abandoned in favor of larger ones. On the other hand, rural ministers who owned automobiles could serve larger areas. Driving became a Sunday recreation for the whole family. Some families even instituted various household economies in order to pay the installments on their automobiles. The younger people found a new way to amuse themselves. As more families came to own cars, they changed the structure of their homes to include garages and driveways.

National and local governments, too, were modified by the automobile. Easy, rapid transportation by car helped to centralize governmental activities in Washington. In some instances, it influenced the transference of local functions to the national government. It favored the expansion of federal and state police, and widened the area of activity of the Federal Bureau of Investigation; it also facilitated the delivery of rural mail, the activities of rural county agents, and the fighting of forest fires. The national park system became more highly developed, partly through the encouragement of automobile tourists. Civic administration was faced with many new problems. Taxpayers on realty moved outside the city's tax jurisdiction, thereby decreasing the city's revenues; the law had to provide new traffic regulations and decide on the punishment for crimes rising from the misuse of automobiles. As mentioned above, the inconsistency between the metropolitan and economic area of the city presented a new political problem. Interstate commerce by truck also reduced the economic significance of state boundary lines, as the railroad had done, although the Supreme Court sometimes did not recognize the change in their status.

The customs and *mores* of the nation were likewise affected. Traveling on week-ends and during vacations brought people of various sections of the country closer together. It became customary to travel north in the summer and south in the winter. The social pressures in small towns were modified through the wider range of the citizens' contacts. The use of private automobiles and buses affected race relations in that it was difficult to discriminate in regard to such things as passing on the highway, or to adapt the "Jim Crow" laws to the bus.

The automobile changed the habits of courtship and extended the environment of young people. When the self-starter was invented, it became possible for a woman to drive a car without having to crank the engine, and another step was taken toward the emancipation of woman. The automobile modified the ideologies of the nation in other ways as well. People became less used to walking and more dependent upon the mechanized comforts of life. Certainly, in the twenties the automobile emphasized the pursuit of pleasure as opposed to the more puritan virtues. Even now, the automobile's emphasis upon speed has led to a general social attitude which puts more value upon rapidity and activity than it does upon the contemplative life.

The preceding sketch makes it clear that the invention of the automobile has influenced civilization in a vast number of ways. The study of its influence illustrates two general facts: first, that in order of time, the invention comes first and the changes in society follow; and, secondly, that these changes frequently require considerable time before they develop into real readjustments to the demands of the invention. It took some time, for instance, for the railroads to adjust to the traffic of the bus and truck. And in the case of city boundaries, although these have not yet been greatly changed, the time may come when political boundaries will be adjusted to the areas of economic activities. When that happens, it will be another step in the direction of the complete adjustment of urban governments to the invention of the private car.

But now, since we have arrived at the general rule that the invention comes first and its social effects follow, it is appropriate to ask whether or not the social effects of any given invention can be foreseen. Could we, for example, in 1905, when the automobile was first coming into use, have predicted the various consequences, some of which we have listed in the preceding paragraphs? Hindsight is notably better than foresight, and the process would certainly not have been simple; but neither would it seem to have been completely impossible. How it might have been done will be discussed in succeeding chapters on methods of prediction.

The problem of foreseeing the social effects of the automobile would not have been merely an intellectual exercise or an illustration of method. It would have yielded very practical and profitable results. Had we known in 1910 what the automobile was going to do to society, we might presumably have prepared better to meet its impact and to achieve an earlier adjustment. If city planners could have anticipated the movement of urban dwellers away from congested areas, they might have met the traffic issue before it came by laying out wider roads and express superhighways. Real-estate brokers might have made money instead of losing it. The railroads themselves could have forestalled overexpansion and consequent bankruptcies, or they might have met the competition of the gasoline engine by some new type of local service. There are innumerable ways in which foresight of what was going to happen could have mitigated the impact of the automobile on our society. We could not, of course, have completely removed the pains of adjustment, for, clearly, the very existence of the automobile implied the failure of some industries and the curtailment of others. The makers of buggies, wagons, and harness would have had to give up their business in any case, and the railroads would still have had to recognize and meet the new competition. But anticipation would have made all these adjustments come sooner and in a more satisfactory way.

The individual, as well as society as a whole, profits from the foreknowledge of approaching change. In the case of the automobile, the development of local transportation caused a drop in the real-estate values of houses near the business district, and families living in these houses moved to the edge of the city and beyond, where living was more pleasant. An alert resident who anticipated the autombile's coming would have moved out early and realized more on the sale of his property, while one less alert would have lost greatly by keeping his property until it was surrounded by cheap boarding houses. Hence it is clear that the actions of an individual can be greatly implemented by the prediction of social change.

A new invention, it should be noted, is a very common upsetter of plans. The investment banker's definition of an invention is "that which makes my securities insecure," and it would be to the advantage of anyone who is planning anything to adopt this definition. We have already shown how the newly invented automobile upset the plans of railroad companies and real-estate dealers. In 1905, the planning movement was still undeveloped, and city planning in the United States was just beginning, although there had been some planning of cities in general, and of a few in particular. If there had been any city planning before 1905, based solely on horses and streetcars as transportation, the effect of the automobile on such plans would have been very upsetting. Foreknowledge of the social consequences of an invention is therefore of incalculable advantage to planners.

The analogy between the airplane in 1945 and the automobile in 1905 is obvious. The statistical evidence is strong that the use of the airplane will be widespread in the postwar world. In 1905, the world stood on the threshold of the automobile age; at present we appear to stand on the threshold of the airplane age. Before World War II, there were some twenty-five thousand private planes and three hundred and fifty air liners carrying passengers along air routes in the United States. In 1910, before World War I, there were 459,000 automobiles in existence. The war has speeded the general evolution of the airplane even more than World War I influenced the evolution of the automobile. The general civilian population is probably not yet aware of the advantages which will be made available to potential plane-owners.

The question naturally arises, Can we foresee the changes that the wide adoption of airplanes will bring in the postwar decades? To try to answer this question is something of a venture, especially since there is very little adequate measurement on which to base predictions. The technique for the measurement of social phenomena has yet to be fully developed. In future years the method for predicting the effects of an invention will no doubt be more accurate. Our present purpose, however, is to make a responsible and useful study of a problem which immediately confronts us rather than to develop prediction as a scientific method, although it is hoped that the practice of looking ahead with confidence will be advanced. The problem of prediction in social science and of the forecast of the social effects of an invention will be discussed at greater length in the chapters on method.

It may seem that what we have said thus far implies that the effects of aviation on our society are predetermined and inevitable, that the airplane is going to do something to us or for us whether we like it or not, and that our part in the matter is merely to accept and adjust. Such an interpretation is not quite correct.

The question of how far the results of aviation on our society will be inevitable and how far they will be controllable involves the philosophic question of free will versus determinism. We need not, however, address ourselves in these immediate paragraphs to this problem in general, or even to its particular effect on the airplane, in order to achieve our end. It is enough to say that for the present the following chapters, as they consider the conditions of each particular effect, will illlustrate a relative freedom of choice which is man's to exercise. What is meant by "relative freedom" in regard to the use of inventions will perhaps be clearer if we summarize the two sides of the controversy.

Partisans of the optimistic view, that invention is the servant of mankind, note that the energy performed by power-making machines renders service which in human energy units would require one hundred slaves per individual in the United States. Electronics does his bidding in flooding the air with music, in carrying his voice across the oceans, in operating machines in his factory, or in transforming raw materials into useful daily implements. Hence, man's freedom to act and enjoy a good life seems greatly enlarged through scientific invention.

On the other hand, there are those who see the machine as a giant Frankenstein that enslaves mankind. The machine maims and kills, pollutes water and air, causes industrial diseases, quickens the tempo of life, creates cities which foster crime, increases divorce, breaks up the home, and makes war ever more disastrous. Workers, in their resentment, have tried to destroy by force the factories that have become their masters. The machine seems to be the dictator and man's rôle one of submission. It is from these instances that some believe there is a sort of inevitability of social effects brought by the machine.

There is, of course, truth in both these attitudes. The paradox of man's being both master and slave at the same time lies largely in the difference between the use of invention and its social effect. Man appears to be the master in the particular use he makes of the machine, but he seems not to be able to control all the derivative results of its creation and manufacture. The railroad is wonderfully obedient in taking us where we want to go, but once we build the railroad, the very act has the consequences of encouraging the growth and founding of cities, which in their turn lead to the results of city life — crime and broken homes. Similarly, in the case of the airplane, if a man wants to fly from New York to London overnight, he can do so. It is his to choose. The airplane is his to command. But once he chooses to do so, the United States and Great Britain are brought into closer contact. He may have some choice in making that contact one of co-operation or friction, but it is beyond his power thereafter to keep the United States isolated from Great Britain. His act is not merely an individual matter, for the airplane itself has brought the two nations socially nearer. Man may, therefore, exercise a relative freedom in choosing how to use an invention, but if he uses it at all, it will entail its own social effect of which he is necessarily the servant.

Whatever the axis of reference, it is our primary objective in this volume to study and anticipate with varying degrees of probability the kinds of impacts of aviation and their results on society — its customs, institutions, groups, and communities. Aviation will play a major rôle in the culture of tomorrow. It becomes our task to foresee with as great a degree of accuracy as possible just what this rôle will be. It is to be hoped that this book may help in the problems and adjustments that lie before us in an age of aviation.

2

A New Transportation System

THE EVOLUTION OF CIVILIZATION is speeded up because of transportation. There are two reasons for this. One is that transportation carries ideas and inventions to the people in all parts of the world. Use of the wheel spread over the earth from the place of its invention; the ideas of ancient Greece have influenced the whole of western civilization. The stagnant cultures are those in isolated mountains or islands with few links with the outside world. The second reason why transportation speeds the growth of our social heritage is that it helps to build an efficient size of the state, and of social organizations within it. At one time no political organization in the United States extended further than the area now encompassed in a county. Indeed, the community in early times consisted of a few families living in a camp. Modern factories and great universities could not have existed in such societies. Today, the United States is a closely knit country of three million square miles, one-sixteenth of the land area of the earth. Of the many influences that are making our forty-eight states into a single efficient social organization, railroad and automobile systems of transportation are basic.

Now comes a new transportation system — aviation. To chart its probable influence on civilization is the undertaking of this book. But first, the factors that inaugurated the new system of transport should be described. These factors are technology, business, and government, all of which are closely interwoven in the early history of aviation, as they were in the development of the railroads, though in somewhat different proportions.

11

The Beginnings

The basis for aviation as we know it now was laid by the flight of the Wright brothers at Kitty Hawk, North Carolina, on December 17, 1903. Samuel Langley had designed a heavier-than-air machine driven by a steam engine in 1896, which flew but carried no passengers. The automobile had become a practical machine a little earlier, but the automobile industry expanded more rapidly than did the production of airplanes. The delay in the development of aviation was largely technological, for the technical problems of flying were much greater than those for developing a land auto-car. Until World War I, airplanes were large box kites in design, driven through the air by the force of the motor. Stability and safety were the major concerns in those early days. In the few flights made before July 1, 1912, 158 persons had been killed in the United States and Europe.[1] At the beginning of 1911, there were only 541 certified pilots in all countries of the world. Flying was dangerous.

Governmental aid and sponsorship of aviation during World War I was important in stimulating the development of the airplane. The great value of the plane was recognized then for observing the movement of the enemy behind the lines, and also later for dropping bombs on his troops. Research during the war made the engine more efficient and lighter. The weight per horsepower was reduced from six pounds in 1909 to about 2.2 pounds during the war.

Lift and Drag

One of the most important aviational developments of the war was the all-metal monoplane which solved some of the most troublesome aerodynamic problems of that time.

A plane is kept in flight by lift, which is the upward suction of the air on the wings. The wing of a plane is flatter on the bottom and more curved on the top, as shown in Figure 1. When air rushes over such a surface, the pressure is less on the top of the

[1] M. J. Bernard Davy, *Air Power and Civilization*. London: George Allen and Unwin, Ltd., 1941, p. 75.

wing than on the bottom. In the widely used DC-3 transport plane, for instance, the pressure of air on the bottom of the wing is 14.7 pounds per square inch, and on the upper surface the pressure in flight is 14.523 pounds. The difference of .177 pounds per square inch amounts to a lift of 25.5 pounds per square foot.[2] The surface of the wings consists of 987 square feet; hence the total lift for the DC-3 is 25,200 pounds. The licensed gross weight of the DC-3 is 25,200 pounds.

But the air, in addition to giving lift to the plane, creates resistance. One can observe the resistance of the air by walking down the street on a windy day carrying a large, framed picture. If the picture faces in the direction in which the walker is going, it becomes a considerable obstacle to movement, which almost disappears as the edge of the picture is pointed into the wind. In a fast airplane it is surprising how a slight obstacle increases drag. Lowering the landing gear of the DC-3 decreases the speed eighteen miles an hour.

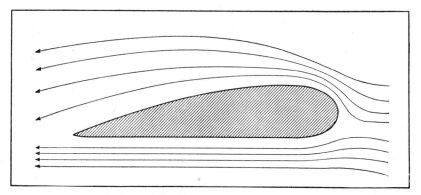

Figure 1. Lift on an Air Foil

This drawing shows the flow of air along the top and bottom of an airplane wing when in motion. At sea level, the air pressure on the under surface of the wing is 14.7 pounds per square inch. When the plane is in motion, the pressure upon the top surface may be only 14.523 pounds per square inch. This difference of .177 pounds per square inch furnishes a lift of 25.3 pounds per square foot of wing area. The DC-3, with a wing area of 987 square feet, thus has a total lift of 25,200 pounds. The licensed gross weight of the DC-3 is 25,200 pounds.

[2] The Association of American Railroads, *Initial Study of Air Transportation,* January, 1944, p. 6.

Early designers knew that the biplane was deficient in lift and high in drag, but they could not find a way to dispense with supporting wires and struts between the two wings, or to design the wing as an airfoil with greater lift. The problem was solved when duralumin, an alloy of copper and aluminum, was invented and used to cover the plane. Wings of planes had previously been constructed of wood and linen. The strength of the new light metal made it possible for the wing to be internally braced so that exterior trusses were no longer necessary. The increased speed also increased the lift. The all-metal monoplane was first produced by the Germans, copied in the United States in 1921, and further developed by 1924 into the Ford Tri-Motor.

Although this all-metal monoplane was a great advance, it still created a great deal of resistance to the air. The motors of the Ford plane were placed beneath the wing, and thus were in a poor position aerodynamically. Aeronautical engineers are still working on the problem of reducing drag. The flying wing, much discussed for the future, is an attempt to further reduce drag by using a new, differently shaped wing.

The wing loading — that is, the pounds carried per square foot of wing — is an index of how much the plane can lift and carry through the air, and shows the progress of aeronautical designing. The biplane of the Wright brothers had a wing loading of one and a half pounds as compared with the wing loadings today of forty pounds and above.

It required some time for the new type of streamlined plane to be developed to the point of extensive use. By the late 1920's, the fruits of the Ford Tri-Motor all-metal monoplane, capable of carrying eight passengers much longer distances than ever before, became evident. But first there was a recession in aviation's rate of development, due to the withdrawal of governmental aid.

Recession

These technological achievements were not put to the nation's use without governmental assistance. Governmental wartime aid to aviation in the United States ceased with the coming of peace in 1918. Private business enterprise in the United States tried to

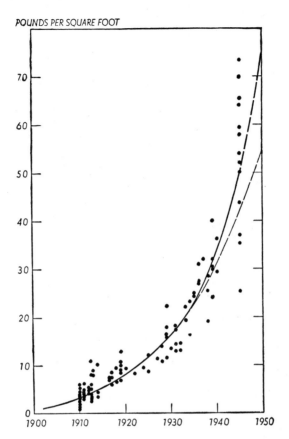

POUNDS PER SQUARE FOOT

Figure 2. THE WING LOADING TREND

With the development of aeronautics the wings of a plane carry a heavier
and heavier load. Wing loading is measured by dividing the area of the
wings in square feet into the gross weight of the plane in pounds. It is
obviously significant because it is an indication of the carrying power of
the plane. It is achieved because of speed and other aerodynamic improvements and for these reasons a heavier wing loading requires a longer landing
space, other things being equal.

The dots represent kinds of transport airplanes in the United States and
the two diverging free-hand trend lines suggest two possible trends up to
1950. In the early years, all planes, whether transport or not, were used.
Since 1930, only U.S. planes are included. The chart and data are from
W. W. Davies of the United Air Lines. These same sources and limitations
apply to other similar charts which follow.

take over. Land for airports was bought and investments for production were made. But the technological basis for aviation as a private business was not yet ready. Pilots, returned from the war, made exhibition flights, took passengers up on sightseeing trips, and did various heroic feats. The first trans-Atlantic flight was made in 1919. The enthusiasm for aviation which came out of the war led to the expectation of much private flying and a great development of passenger transportation. These hopes soon waned, however, despite the rather good economic conditions of the period, and were not revived until the second half of the 1920's.

Government Flies the Mail

In the early postwar years, government again gave aid to aviation by pioneering in the transportation of mail by air. The service over the first route, between New York and Washington, D.C., began on May 15, 1918. In 1919, scheduled air mail was flown by government-owned and operated planes between Chicago and New York, and a transcontinental service was soon to be established.

The coast-to-coast air mail service, which started in 1920, did not provide much saving of time over ground methods of transportation because the planes could fly only during the daytime. It was obvious that the time-saving benefits of air mail could be secured only if night flying were made practical. Tests and plans for night flying were begun in 1923, and after fifteen months of work, twenty-four-hour flying between the Atlantic and Pacific Coasts began on July 1, 1924. This important event in the history of aviation was made possible by the government with its own finances, equipment, and personnel.

Private Business Takes Over

The second half of the 1920's may be signalized as the period of the entry of private business into aviation. Air mail flights night and day proceeded with precision, and were a distinct success. The new equipment, with modern airfoil, all-metal construction and light, powerful engines, was coming into use. It was

decided, then, in 1925, to turn the air service over to private companies, but private enterprise was not yet ready to carry the
load unassisted. Governmental aid was continued through generous mail contracts. The authorization of the air mail contract
service for private companies was passed by Congress in February, 1925, but it was not until 1927 that private companies
actually flew mail from coast to coast. In that year, the east and
west sections of the transcontinental air route were turned over
to two private companies.

The number of operators increased rapidly; by 1927, there were
sixteen companies, which were increased to thirty-eight by 1930,
and nearly all of them were carrying passengers. Many small
companies came into existence; but even mail contract payments
were not enough to sustain some of them which operated for a
short time and failed.

Interest in aviation revived, particularly as a result of the historic Lindbergh flight from New York to Paris, a distance of 3600
miles, in a single-engined monoplane, in 33½ hours. Engine speeds
and performance were improving. Large amounts of private
capital became available. Cities began to show competitive
rivalry in obtaining air service. Businessmen realized the value
of air mail to them.

Aviation, through the new technological developments, had
reached a maturity by the middle 1920's which enabled businessmen to foresee a profitable air transportation business. Government, which had formerly actively participated in aviation, now
changed to regulation, though governmental aid still continued.
The Air Commerce Act of 1926 laid out an organization for
aviation. While the Post Office was to remain the all-important
financial support of the airlines, the Department of Commerce
was charged with the responsibility of fostering air commerce, of
establishing safeguards, and encouraging various facilities for
navigation. The Department of Agriculture provided the weather
reports, while the municipal governments were to be responsible
for the construction of local airports.

Government Provides Airports and Airways

No airports were built in the first decade of aviation. Open fields or the encircled area of a race track were often used. During the war the military forces provided landing places, and with the wartime development of flying there was a corresponding improvement in landing and take-off facilities. After the war, the cities along the air mail routes between the two coasts provided the necessary landing fields. Private fields were also built. In 1920, of the 271 airfields, 145 were municipal.

The development of night flying required many airport and airway aids from the federal authority. By 1927, there were 2000 miles of lighted airways. The number of rotating beacon lights was increased sixfold by 1930, to 1290. The government was also responsible for the radio range beam, developed in part by scientists in the Bureau of Standards of the Department of Commerce. With these radio beams, instruments in the plane give a steady hum as long as the pilot is on his course. Departure to the right or left brings warning signals on his instruments which direct him back to his route, enabling the pilot to fly a set course no matter what the visibility. By 1930, there were 33 such radio range beacon stations. The government also established radio stations to report weather conditions and to send messages to airplanes in flight. There were 17 such stations in 1927, and twice that number by 1930.

A Bench Mark in Aviation

We may look upon the middle 1920's as a bench mark in aviation. In 1926, the government began systematically to collect annual statistics on the numbers of passengers, miles flown, planes in operation, and so on. In that year, nearly 6000 passengers were carried by the airlines and 4,000,000 revenue plane-miles were flown over the 8000 miles of air routes in the United States. In 1925, there were 310 municipal airports, 225 commercial fields, and 63 intermediate fields on air mail routes. On the technical side of aviation, planes were able to carry much larger loads. By 1926, each square foot of wing could carry 12 pounds of gross weight because of the achievement of engineers in getting lift and

POUNDS PER HORSEPOWER

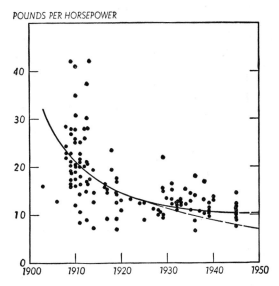

Figure 3. THE POWER LOADING TREND

There has not been very much change in recent years in the number of pounds a plane weighs per unit of horsepower. It remains about 12 or 13 pounds of gross weight per horsepower. As the planes get bigger, the total horsepower of the engines increases accordingly.

overcoming drag. The number of pounds per horsepower had been reduced from 19 at the end of the first decade of flying to 12 or 13 pounds in 1926. Thus, the power loading was cut in half. Planes were faster, too. The cruising speed had increased from forty miles an hour in 1910, which was not much different from that of the railroads, to one hundred miles an hour. The horsepower had moved up to a maximum of 350, as compared to 100 just prior to World War I. Nearly a quarter of a century of technological development was required after the flight of the Wright brothers before aviation had developed to the point of becoming a business in the United States for the transportation of passengers. Still greater achievements were to come by the middle 1930's.

Still More Technical Improvements

The technological evolution in flying continued into the 1930's,

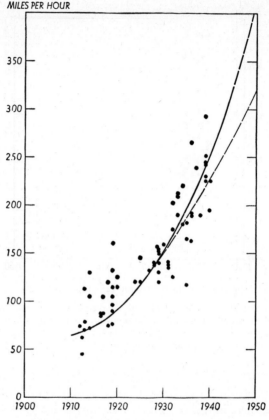

Figure 4. MAXIMUM SPEED TREND

The trend lines in the above diagram show a very marked upward trend
in speeds — a general fact that is well-known. The projection of these trend
lines upward indicates even faster speeds. This increase in the speed of
transport planes is foreshadowed by the speed of the new fighters and
bombers used in World War II and those projected for future military use.

and even today shows no indication of much slackening. What
were some of these improvements which made possible the
further expansion of aviation?

The attack on the problems of drag and lift, which had been
most encouraging in the 1920's, was given a powerful stimulus
by the improvement of an invention that placed the study of these
problems on an experimental basis — not of trial and error, but of

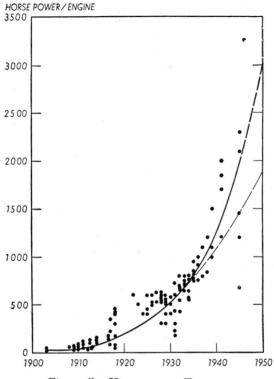

Figure 5. HORSEPOWER TREND

The data in this chart show the horsepower per engine per plane. The increase in the power of the engine in the past decade has been phenomenal.

exact measurement. It was now possible to tell from the design of a plane exactly what it could and could not do. This new invention was the large wind tunnel, small models of which had been known for many years. The Langley Field Wind Tunnel of the National Advisory Committee for Aeronautics has proved to be a very effective instrument in improving the designing of planes.

By using the wind tunnel it was possible to find exactly the amount of drag occasioned by the placement of the engine on the plane. In the planes of the 1920's, the engines had been located, most inefficiently, below the wings. It was the wind tunnel which showed the lessened drag when the engine was set on the wing chord. It also demonstrated the great resistance created by the head of the engine. The solution of this problem was a rounded, conoidal cowl placed over the air-cooled engine. This caused a much smoother flow of air over the nose of the plane, and reduced drag by half. Flush riveting and retractable landing gear also reduced drag. These improvements were incorporated into the planes of 1934 and 1935.

It was also well known that the thinner air of the higher altitudes permitted faster speeds if the planes could fly at such heights, since the less dense the air the less resistance it would provide for the plane. But it was found that the propeller needed to have a higher pitch, preferably an almost edge-on angle, in the thin air of high altitudes, even though traveling at greater speed. Ingenious hydraulic or electric devices were worked out and located in the hub of the propeller blades to adjust them to different pitches. This improvement was installed in the planes of the middle 1930's.

Not only were improvements being made in the design of the airframe, but the power plant was also undergoing an evolutionary development. The engine was made more dependable by duplicate ignition systems and an intricate carburetor which gave the proper mixture of gas and air at different altitudes and in all positions of the plane. Since the speed of an engine cylinder is limited to about 2400 revolutions per minute, greater power was obtained by increasing the number of cylinders in the radial engines. By the middle of the 1930's the horsepower had increased from 350 to 800, and the weight of an engine was approximately 1.3 pounds per horsepower. The engine which the Wright brothers had built for their plane, because there were none light enough at that time, weighed twelve pounds per horsepower. Most of these improvements in engines and in streamlining the frame for greater lift and lessened drag were worked out in experiments financed by the government.

The chief advantage of the foregoing gains in engine power, in lift, and in drag reduction was the attainment of greater speeds — the airplane's attribute of greatest social significance. The cruising

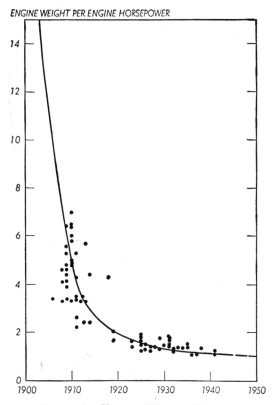

Figure 6. ENGINE WEIGHT TREND

The early engines were very heavy but the weight of the modern reciprocating engines seems to be becoming stabilized at near one pound per horsepower.

speeds in the middle 1930's were around 175 miles an hour, 75 per cent greater than in the middle 1920's, with block speeds, of course, much less. The plane's advantage in speed over the railroad was becoming more apparent when a trip could be made from New York to Chicago in about six hours, and from New York to San Francisco in about twenty-six hours.

However, the fast speeds of the new planes presented landing difficulties. As the aerodynamic efficiency of the plane increased, the gliding angle became flatter and flatter, making necessary much longer distances for landing. An invention was needed

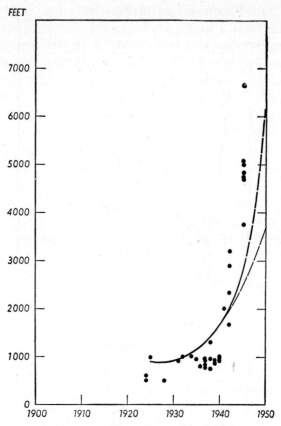

Figure 7. TAKE-OFF DISTANCE TREND

Fast planes with heavy wing loading require long take-off distances. Such requirements affect the size of the airport, which in turn is related to the distance of the airport from the center of the city.

which would slow down the plane as it came in to land and keep it from running out of the airport. To reduce the speed of the plane, part of the rear edge of the wing was bent downward, as a flap, at a sharp angle. This flap acted as an air brake, and at the same time cushioned the landing by increasing lift. Later planes were equipped with the Fowler flap, by which the wing is extended rearward before the flap becomes an air brake.

The planes were not only speedier, but they were becoming

bigger. The domestic planes of the 1930's had a gross weight between 10,000 and 40,000 pounds on the average, and those built for overseas service weighed 50,000 or 60,000 pounds. At the same time, the wing-loading was approaching 30 pounds per square foot as compared with 13 pounds for the planes of the middle 1920's. These larger planes with higher wing-loadings could, of course, carry more passengers and goods. Useful load was around 35 or 40 per cent of the gross weight; but in passenger planes much of this useful load consists of equipment. A plane of 25,000 pounds gross weight would possibly have 9000 or 10,000 pounds of useful load. In addition to fuel and some cargo, it might carry 4000 or 5000 pounds of passengers. If the average weight of a passenger and his baggage were estimated as two hundred pounds, these planes could carry twenty to twenty-five passengers.

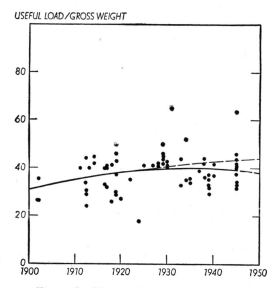

Figure 8. Useful Load Ratio Trend

There has been very little change in the ratio of the useful load to the gross weight. Useful load includes crew, passengers, cargo, oil and fuel. The bigger planes do not, therefore, have very much more useful load than the smaller ones relative to size. It tends to be around 40 per cent or under. The advantages of the larger planes are more marked in other characteristics.

In 1936, all these technological developments were combined to produce the DC-3, which became the most common passenger plane, even during the years of World War II, when ten thousand of them were built.

The Intermeshing of Business and Government

While technology provided the basis for the progress of aviation in the 1930's, the forces of business and government were intermingled in its development. The business organization of air transportation was settling down. From thirty-eight companies in 1930, the number decreased to twenty-one in 1936, and to seventeen in 1939. This consolidation was facilitated by the Watres Act of 1930, which empowered the Postmaster General to unify the industry. This he did by granting extensions much longer than the original routes through granting contracts without competitive bidding. This tendency toward concentration has persisted to the present. There are now sixteen domestic companies, five of which do between 80 and 90 per cent of the business.

The Watres Act provided that mail payments to airline companies were to be made on the basis of space, rather than the volume of mail carried, in an attempt to encourage passenger operations. In 1934, the government charged that the airline companies had engaged in abuses and collusion. Mail contracts were canceled and the government turned air mail operations over to Army pilots. Several accidents occurred during the bad flying weather of the winter months, and the transportation of mail was returned to the private companies. Under the Air Mail Act of 1934, companies were restricted to payments of forty cents a mile for the carriage of mail, and mail contracts were awarded by competitive bidding. Provisions of the act were intended to prevent monopolistic combinations and create an air transport system made up of competing air carriers.

By 1938, Congress had become fully aware of the difficulties of administration of the Air Mail Act of 1934, and the carriers were exerting pressure to get a new set of regulations. The result was the Civil Aeronautics Act of 1938, which created a governmental

Roadable Plane. Making the plane roadable will greatly increase its usefulness to the consumer since the plane can proceed on the ground from the landing field to the garage near the home or place of work. The plane in the picture above has a controllable wing and flies at various inclines with the body of the plane parallel to the ground. (*Chapter 5, Technological Trends in Aviation.*)

Delivery and Pick-up Without Stop. The pole under the plane carries a hook which catches the rope stretched between the two posts. Then the container, attached to the rope, is lifted into the body of the plane. Since 1939, mail and express have been carried to 118 small towns over several eastern states by this method. During the war the Army used this technique for lifting gliders filled with troops or supplies. (*Chapter 7, Carrying the Mail.*)

C. A

Roadable Aircraft. An autogiro was built which could travel along crowded streets with its rotors folded back — perhaps a forerunner of the roadable helicopter. The above roadable autogiro is now housed in a museum. (*Chapter* 11, *Private Flying.*)

Aviation and Natural Barriers. The plane transcends barriers of nature as does no other method of transportation. The plane in this picture is above snow-capped Mount McKinley. Indeed, there is some evidence to indicate that political barriers are more difficult for the airplane to cross than natural ones. (*Chapter* 12, *Air Routes.*)

U. S. A.

agency, the Civil Aeronautics Authority, empowered to regulate, promote, and control the entire air transportation system. In 1940, the name of this agency was changed to the Civil Aeronautics Board, and it was transferred to the Department of Commerce, but in general structure it remains today as the regulating agency of the air transport system.)

During this period the government continued its aid in the form of approximately 200 weather-reporting airway and airport stations, 100 radio range beacon stations, 60 radio marker beacons, and 22,000 miles of lighted airways. The municipal governments furnished 738 airports by 1936, charging, however, a rental fee to the airlines which used them. In addition, there were 451 commercial airports, 300 intermediate, and 235 military airports.

On the Eve of War

Under the combined influences of technology, government, and business, the record of the airlines in 1936 was impressive. The numbers of passengers and the volumes of air express carried increased by large percentages over previous years. During the early 1930's, the number of passengers carried each year was between 400,000 and 500,000. These were years of depression and confused relations with government on mail contracts. After the Act of 1934, the revival of business, and the use of new equipment, the number of passengers increased to 1,000,000 in 1936, which was about one-sixth of the number of railroad sleeping-car passengers. The air mail postage rate was lowered in 1934 to six cents per ounce, and the payment per plane-mile to the carriers dropped steadily from $1.09 in 1929 to about 28 cents in 1935. The number of pounds of domestic air express and freight increased from 788,000 pounds in 1931 to 6,900,000 pounds in 1936.

Not the least of the achievements of aviation was the attainment of greater safety through the use of more reliable engines, radio guides, weather reporting, and landing directions. The passenger fatalities per 100,000,000 miles flown on domestic lines were reduced from 28.6 in 1930 to 10 in 1936 and only 5 in 1935. At the same time the average passenger fare was reduced from

12 cents in 1926 to 5.7 cents per mile in 1936. Commercial transportation by air had become well established.

Private Flying

In contrast to commercial aviation, private flying had made little progress. In the development of the automobile, private cars came first and then commercial bus lines were established. But the first use of the airplane was principally for commercial transportation. There were only about 9000 small private planes in 1936, as compared with 24,000,000 automobiles. Still, there were 26,500,000 plane-miles flown in 1936 in non-scheduled pleasure flying, as compared with about 64,000,000 plane-miles flown by domestic, common-carrier planes. In addition to private flying for pleasure, there were 13,000,000 plane-miles of private flying for business purposes, and 23,000,000 plane-miles of non-scheduled commercial flying — that is, for hire. Perhaps the progress of private flying only appears to be slight. Those who think of it as slight are probably measuring the achievement against that of the automobile, and in terms of their expectations either of family planes for the population or of a large airplane manufacturing industry like that of the automobile.

International Aviation

International flying across large stretches of water has been slower in developing than domestic flying. One of the first American international lines was a service between Key West, Florida, and Havana, Cuba, established in 1927. The early years of the 1930's saw a great extension of air routes across the Caribbean and down the east and west coasts of South America. These routes were made possible by the development of planes capable of carrying a considerable payload, of landing on water or land, and having an adequate range. The government provided subsidies in the form of mail contracts at rates of $3.35 a plane-mile. Through these payments, one American airline was able to develop the difficult international routes, design planes able to fly them, and meet the competition of other nations in the areas to the south of us.

In Europe, aviation was considered an agency of na policy, and in most countries it became a governmental ꜱᴛᴇᴘ. prise. British airlines reached India in 1929, while the Dutch, in 1930, established a service to the Dutch East Indies, which was the first line to the Orient. In 1931, the French established scheduled service to Indo-China.[3] By 1935 and 1936, the British airlines had reached Singapore, Australia, and South Africa; the French, South America and Madagascar; the Italians, East Africa; and the Germans in 1934 had an air service to South America.

In the United States, an airline spanning the Pacific was made possible in the late 1930's by the new four-engined planes weighing eighteen or twenty tons. San Francisco to Hawaii, one of the longest non-stop flights, a distance of 2400 miles, was served in 1935. The route had been flown several times before by individuals; but fourteen lives had been lost in the various attempts in less adequate planes. In 1939, American flag lines flew from New York to Lisbon, using forty-two-ton seaplanes whose four engines could be repaired en route. Their flying range was 4000 miles and their cruising speed, 165 miles an hour. Scheduled service on international routes was disrupted by the war, but military planes began to fly new and longer routes. Wartime experience will be used in setting up more extensive international routes after the war.

Observations

This outline of the beginnings of aviation has been sketched to acquaint the reader with a background for the succeeding discussion of the future uses and social effects of aviation. The accompanying charts show the technological trends in speed, weight, power, and other factors. Since relatively smooth lines can be drawn through the course of these factors in the past, extrapolation for a few years in the future seems to be reliable. Yet the particular inventions on which these trends rest are not easily predicted. For instance, the all-metal, thick wing, or the

[3] Oliver J. Lissitzyn, *International Air Transport and National Policy* (Studies in Foreign Relations, No. 3). New York: Council on Foreign Relations, 1942, pp. 5-8.

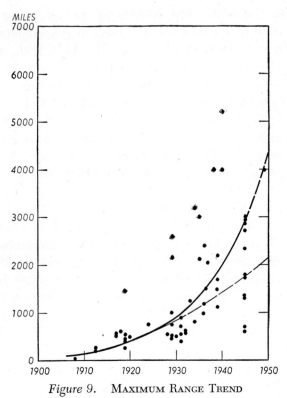

Figure 9.   MAXIMUM RANGE TREND

For most passenger traffic there is no need for ranges over 2500 miles. The actual utilization of this range capacity is restricted for most planes by the costs of carrying a large load of fuel.

engine cowl could not have been foreseen specifically much in advance of their actual invention, but it might have been predicted that some kind of inventions would be made that would accomplish the same general functions. It is easier to foresee future functions than the technical bases for their accomplishment. This point is important for a study of the social effects of the airplane, for the social effect of an invention is dependent upon its function, which may be achieved by several different inventions. Thus, in making a study of social effects, one is freed somewhat from forecasting particular inventions.

In this chapter there have been considered three factors in

establishing the new transportation system of aviation: technology, business, and government. The functions contributed by technology were seen to be predictable. The part played by business would certainly have been expected in the United States with its tradition of private initiative. Such may not have been the case with government. For in the United States, with its tradition that the government which governs least governs best, the tremendously important rôle of the government in aviation would probably not have been easily foreseen.

We may also observe that the great dynamic forces back of aviation, so evident in its first third of a century of growth, have by no means ceased, or even slowed up appreciably. World War II has also been a great impetus. With the war have come the great technical achievements of helicopters, gliders, nonstop pick-up devices, superchargers, turbine engines, jet-propulsion planes and rockets. These are bringing almost unimaginable speeds, flights at high altitudes, and large vehicles of great carrying power over enormous distances. These various achievements will be discussed later in the text, particularly in a following chapter on future technological developments, in so far as they can be foreseen.

3

On Predicting the Future

THE STUDY set forth in this book is concerned with the future. Therefore, the method is one of forecast. There are various other names which are used to characterize such a procedure, such as prediction, estimation, or prophecy. We shall approach it on the basis of prediction, which is the scientific term for gauging in advance what will happen. Everyone who tries to look into the future has prediction as his goal, but as he falls short of such a goal, his effort is described by the various other terms mentioned above.

The Popular Idea of Prediction in Social Phenomena

There is a popular conception that prediction is impossible in human and social affairs; at least, one often hears this opinion expressed, particularly among individuals who admire wisdom and conservatism and deplore recklessness. The person who essays to predict social events readily becomes the butt of criticism of wise elders.

There are various sources of this popular belief. One lies in the fact that we all can see the unexpected happen. What seems certain does not occur. Forecasts go wrong. We gamble on the future and lose. The truth is that reliable prediction is often not possible. Another source is the popular belief in luck and chance. The movement of the stock market or the success of a theatrical production is believed to be due to chance or luck. Disasters come from the hands of Fate. In some religious groups, God's way is held unpredictable and His hand is often seen manifested in the affairs of men. This conception of luck or fate denies causation or inevitability, which is the basis for scientific prediction.

Another source of disbelief in prediction of social affairs is the idea of freedom of the will. In some intellectual groups, it is admitted that prediction about the stars can be made because they are unaffected by human effort. But in society everything that is done is influenced by human will, and therefore is neither inevitable nor predictable.

Finally, there is the cautious person, interested in his reputation for good judgment, who does not wish to undertake the hazard of forecasting the future; and, having a reputation to protect, he speaks impressively about the futility of trying to look into the future.

Much Prediction in Actual Practice

In spite of this popular disbelief in prediction, there is a substantial amount of forecasting of the future being used as the basis for human action. In life, we are really forced to make some kinds of predictions. A merchant who buys a supply of goods for sale for the coming year is trying to predict the future demand for his goods. The fact that there are fewer merchants failing than there are not failing is evidence that these estimates are reasonably accurate. When a company buys a site for a factory, the officers must consider the future of the community, the market, the transportation system, the supply of raw materials, and the availability of a labor supply in the future. There are some things which we have learned to predict quite accurately. Life insurance companies can foretell how many will die in a given year, and they set their rates accordingly. We can make a fairly accurate estimate as to what the population of the United States will be in 1950.

Instead of thinking that either we can or cannot predict the future, we should admit into our thinking the idea of approximations; that is, that there are varying degrees of accuracy and inaccuracy of estimate. In addition we should break down the category of "human and social affairs" into the variety of types which compose it. In some of these categories it is not very difficult to make predictions, as, for instance, the birth rate next year. In other cases, such as when a war will end or what will be the future style of clothing, prediction is not so successful. In short, everyday experience tells us that accuracy of prediction varies according to the field.

Objection may be made that not all of the instances cited can be called prediction. The businessman who rents a store in a small town probably makes few measurements or calculations as to the growth of the town or the future volume of the market which could be called scientific prevision. He has a hunch that the town will grow, and he buys his merchandise on the basis of general experience. This type of anticipating the future is un-formulated, and should be called an art rather than a science, because the procedures used cannot be transmitted to other persons. For instance, the men who tell the quality of wool by feeling it, or of tea by tasting it, may be able to make quite accurate estimates of its durability or its selling quality without ever going through extensive calculations. But they cannot readily transmit their abilities to other people, for they do not know fully and clearly how they do it. In a somewhat similar manner, a father may predict accurately what the reaction of his son will be in a certain situation, but he probably does not know how he does it. Repetition and experience develop skills without full knowledge as to processes. This art of forecasting is not very useful in predicting about social organizations in a society where conditions are changing rapidly.

The work of the average university professor is very little concerned with the future. The professor is dealing with the present, or describing the past, or imparting knowledge accumulated long ago. Not needing usually to deal with the uncertain future, having rather high standards, and being sensitive to his reputation, he is reluctant to venture into the future. The businessman and the farmer in their work have to deal much more with the future than does the college teacher, and are less hesitant about doing so.

Planning Depends upon Prediction

Much of our present behavior is based on the plans for the future which the exigencies of life in a changing society force us to make. All of us make plans regarding personal problems. But planning, as the term is currently used, generally applies to the activity of institutions or organizations. For example, cities, states, and industry make plans for the future. Nearly all of us are now engaged in making plans for the postwar years. The extent of our planning is evidence of our effort to read the future. If we believed that predictions of the future were futile or impossible, we should not be engaged in planning for it.

Rough Approximations Are Sometimes Adequate for Practical Purposes

Scientific prediction in academic work is expected to be very accurate; and if it is slightly inaccurate, we expect to be advised as to the size of the error of the estimate. But in the practical world, the demand for accuracy varies. If a community builds a courthouse, it is not necessary to know accurately the population of the county year by year for a hundred years in the future. Only a rough idea of the future size of the county may be called for. If it errs by underestimation, an additional building or a new courthouse can be erected later. In fact, it might be unfair to take the money of the existing population and tie it up in a courthouse that was too large, even though it were suitable for the population a hundred years hence. Also a new courthouse might then be needed to utilize new building inventions. A more accurate prediction is needed as to the numbers of air passengers and planes in the near future if we are to plan an adequate system of airports. However, there would seem to be no great need for the Board of Foreign Missions to know the probable amount of international passenger traffic after the war in order to plan for the supplying and supervision of their foreign missions. Nor is it necessary for the universities to know with precision the future development of aviation in order to introduce new material in their geography courses; though aviation will affect both foreign missions and the teaching of geography. Planning, therefore, calls for varying degrees of accuracy, depending upon the nature of the organization doing the planning and the type of activity being planned.

Varying Approximations in This Study

One part of this book is concerned with the future of aviation, and another part with the future effects of aviation upon our society. We shall use many different devices in figuring out the future of aviation and its effects. The purpose of this chapter is to make explicit the methods we shall use. We are not attempting in this book to demonstrate a highly successful method in exact prediction in the field of social phenomena, but rather to make a study which will be useful, using the best methods that the data permit. In some fields, we think we can see the course of aviation clearly and with precision for a few years. In other cases, estimates become highly speculative. But it is thought that a high degree of accuracy is not necessary for much of the preparation for what is ahead, and in such situations the exposition of developments which are problematical will be useful.

PREDICTION BY MEASUREMENT

Prediction as a scientific method can be much better done where there is measurement, though the existence of measurement does not guarantee predictability.

Prediction by Extrapolation

A very common method of prediction is to plot the occurrence of the phenomena in the past and then extend the curve forward. If the occurrence follows some exact law, such as the curve of an ellipse, then prediction can be quite accurate from the course of the ellipse. That is the way in which the behavior of astral bodies is predicted. But social phenomena seldom follow such a law. Even when a known law describes the past course of social phenomena, it is not known how long that course will be followed in the future. A second-degree parabola may describe the growth of air mail over the past fifteen years in the United States, but it may not follow the projected parabolic curve in the future. However, projecting curves forward does give some indication of the trend. Such projections are usually more accurate for the immediate than for the distant future.

The projection of a curve which has had very little fluctuation in the past, and only a slow change in direction, is more reliable than for a curve which has changed direction frequently. The curve of the population of the United States is this type of steady curve, and its projections forward in the past have been quite close to the course it has later followed. On the other hand, the curve of the average length of journey by airplane has had some significant fluctuations in the past, and the average length of journey for the next two or three years is not so easily foretold by extending the curve forward.

A curve is thought of as having two components: a trend and a fluctuation around the trend. In extrapolating a curve that has fluctuations, it is the trend of the curve that should be projected forward rather than the last fluctuation. The trend is a line, sometimes straight but usually curving gently, drawn through the middle of the fluctuations of the data. The carrying-forward of a curve of fluctuating data is best done by first projecting the trend, and then weaving the probable fluctuations of the future around the projected trend. This second step can be done only if the rhythm of the oscillations is known. For instance, we know to a certain extent probable business fluctuations. If the law of the fluctuations is not known, it is probably better not to attempt to put in future fluctuations, but to rest content with the projected trend line. The projection is somewhat more accurate on a natural than on a logarithmic scale.

It is difficult to project the curve of the early periods of a rapidly growing phenomenon with any degree of certainty. Growth curves on a natural scale often show a very slow growth at the beginning, then a remarkably rapid growth in the early periods of development, and finally come to a relatively stable period in which little change occurs. Eventually they may, of course, decrease.[1] The curve is almost flat at first and then curves upward rather rapidly, until sometimes it appears to be going almost straight up. Such rapid growth cannot continue in a real world, but it is difficult to tell exactly in advance when the curve

[1] S. C. Gilfillan, *The Sociology of Invention.* Chicago: Follett Publishing Company, 1935, pp. 32-43.

will begin to flatten out. Many aviation curves are of this class, for aviation is young. For instance, the growth in the number of passenger-miles flown on scheduled airlines, when plotted for the last decade, moves very sharply upward, since the growth has been rapid. The rate of growth will surely slacken sometime, but exactly when this will happen is uncertain. Growth curves in their later stages can often be more reliably projected, for the rate of change is slow, and the curve is a gentle slope. The growth of rapidly expanding industries, such as the automobile or moving-picture industries, was more difficult to predict in their early years than at present, for they have now reached a stage of relative maturity. The same will be true of the growth curves of aviation.

Factors Influencing Projection

Carrying curves forward is not an objective method even when it is done by means of a mathematical equation. The person doing the projecting must always take into consideration the factors that may bend the curves in ways not indicated in the past and hence not a part of the mathematical equation, which is based on past data. For instance, the trend of the curve for passenger fares on airlines has been downward during the 1930's and 1940's from twelve cents a mile to five cents a mile. A projection of the curve of fares downward would very soon have us traveling by plane free of charge. It can be reasoned then that the precipitous downward course of fares must soon stop sharply and flatten out. So also it could have been reasoned that the rapid increase in the curve of automobile production in the 1920's could not have been extended forward very far at the same rates because of the limiting factor of population. After the distribution had reached, say, one car for seven families, it could have been guessed that the production of private automobiles would increase less rapidly each year because of the limiting number of families, particularly when it was known that the average income per family was around twelve hundred dollars per year.

The knowledge about various other factors which push or pull a curve one way or another is not as certain as the knowledge about the factors mentioned above; that is, that passenger fares must cost something or that not every family can have an automobile. For instance, in the prediction of the number of future crimes, such factors as broken homes, slum conditions, school systems, playgrounds, growth of cities, amount of neurosis, and the economic plane of living must be taken into consideration. Since the amount of influence which each of these factors has on the crime rate is not known and since the course of each of these factors in the future is not precisely predictable, taking them into consideration in modifying the projection of the curve of crime rates becomes a rather subjective process. Similarly, in projecting curves showing air passenger traffic between nations, there are many factors bearing on the future of such traffic that are highly variable, such as frequency of schedules, rates, business conditions, vacationing habits, international amity, and so on. We can see that the projection of a curve involves not merely a mechanical extrapolation of the curve, but such modification of the curve as familiarity with the factors influencing it in the future indicates.

A very important check on the extrapolation of some curves is the economic factor of price or cost, where it is involved. In extrapolating curves for air mail, it is well to allow for changes in rates. If we know that the Post Office may raise or lower the rate for air mail, we may not be able to predict the rates exactly, but we shall allow for a great error in future estimates. A useful device in this case is to assume various rates and work out estimates for each.

Errors of Extrapolation

The difficulties of extrapolation described in the previous paragraphs may tend to destroy the reader's confidence that extrapolation is of any value whatsoever. That there is some value can be shown by a test of this kind. Examine the curve of the early years of growth (first fifteen or twenty-five years) of some phenomenon, extrapolate the curve, and compare the extrapolation with what actually occurred. This experiment was carried out by three persons, using ten curves. The extrapolation was purely mechanical, since the experimenters did not know what material had been plotted except that they were data for the early years of the sales or production of some inventions. For a ten-year projection there were sixteen overpredictions with an average error of 74 per cent, and fourteen underpredictions with an average error of 43 per cent.[2] These are very large errors, but they very likely could have been reduced if the experimenters had known what materials they were dealing with. Also, the error would probably have been less if the extrapolation had been compared with the trend of the given data rather than with the actual fluctuation around the trend. Finally, the curves were the most difficult to extrapolate. They presented the early production of inventions like aluminum, electric power, dynamite, steel, etc., which had great fluctuations and steep slopes in the curves of their early years.

The extrapolation of a trend is most accurate for the first few periods for which it is projected; and the further it is projected, the greater the possible error. This observation is based on the fact that most trend lines are gently curving. More confidence can be placed upon the mechanical projection of a trend for three or four years hence, if the year is the unit concerned, than for ten or fifteen years in the future. The actual occurrence — that is, the fluctuation two or three years hence — may be missed, but not by very much unless the curve has violent fluctuations.

When the projection is carried forward for longer periods of time, it is sometimes good practice to carry forward two projections based on two assumptions: one, that the trend will bend rather rapidly; and the other, that it will bend more slowly. This is a precautionary measure to indicate that there is a possible error and that it becomes larger the farther the projection is carried. These errors may be enough to make the projection worthless for some uses. An estimate of the population of the sections of a town fifteen years in the future would not be accurate enough to permit a telephone company to know how many employees it will need, but it might be accurate enough to lay out trunk lines.

---

[2] For underprediction the limit of error is 100 per cent, but for overprediction there is no limit; that is, the error may be 2000 per cent, 5000 per cent, etc.

Familiarity with statistical series may help in extrapolation. For instance, some knowledge about the difference between trends and the fluctuations about trends enables one to attempt to project the trend first, rather than the fluctuation about the trend. If one knows that the trends in the past have been slow in changing, more confidence can be put in their projection than if the trends had changed more rapidly. Knowledge about cycles is also helpful. Many growth curves go through something like a cycle in that they begin slowly and haltingly, then shoot up at a very rapid rate for a short time and then tend to level off into a gentle slope of some duration. If it is known at what stage of the growth cycle a particular series occurs, the projection can be made with more assurance. For example, the growth of automobile production could have been projected more reliably in the period of maturity of the 1930's than in its period of rapid growth around 1920. Growth cycles may be disturbed, of course, by outside phenomena. The curve of the growth in numbers of railroad passengers was disturbed by the invention of the motor bus and the private automobile, which caused a decrease in the number of railroad passengers. These large, outside disturbing factors, such as the effect of the automobile on railroads, almost change the universe in which the prediction occurs. The logic of prediction is that the universe of the future will be much like the universe of the past. If some greatly upsetting factor occurs, such as a war or a revolutionary invention, the conditions are so changed that extrapolation is hardly worth trying.

Prediction by Correlation

We have been discussing a type of prediction that consists of projecting a trend line without aid from the measurement of any other factor to which it is related. In some cases, the curve being studied, Curve A, may be closely related to another curve, B. If we know the course of Curve B, the course of Curve A can be estimated. A very good illustration of this type of prediction is the method used in forecasting business conditions. It has been observed that the curve of business prosperity or depression is closely related to the curve of prices of certain selected stocks listed in the stock exchange, but that the changes in stock prices normally preceded changes in business conditions by several months. By plotting the price of these stocks, the course of business can be foretold. Great accuracy is not assured, however, because the curves of business and the stock market do not follow each other exactly. The correlation is only around .8, which means that only about two-thirds of the factors influencing the course of business are accounted for by the curve of the stock prices. As a result, the prediction is right only about two-thirds of the time. Since business demands a rather exact forecast of the future in the interest of business planning, there has grown up a distrust of this method of business forecasting. What business wants is a curve having a perfect correlation with the curve of business conditions, one which would give the right forecast every time.

In aviation there are several series which are related to one another, but ordinarily one does not precede the other in time enough to help in a forecast. Moreover, in the few cases where one series does precede another to a sufficient extent, the correlation is not particularly high. For instance, the growth in the number of airports does precede the transportation of passengers, but the curve of the construction of airports does not foretell the number of passengers except in very broad limits. The curves of the amount of mail and the number of passengers have some relation, since passengers and mail are often carried on the same plane. But the correlation is not very close, since some planes carry only mail, while other planes carry many passengers and only a small amount of mail. There is also some relation between passenger fares and the number of passengers. As the fare per mile over the last twenty years has gone down, the number of passengers has increased, but the correlation is not very close because there are so many other factors affecting the number of passengers, such as conveniences on the plane, fear of flying, frequency of schedule, business conditions, and so on. Indeed, with an unchanging fare from year to year, there may still be a great increase in the number of passengers.

If the correlated curve is more mature and there is more knowledge concerning its fluctuations than there is concerning the curve with which one is working, the correlated curve may be helpful in making a more reliable projection of the given curve. For instance, the fluctuations in the number of air passengers is correlated with the curve of intercity passenger traffic and with the index of production. A large amount of work has been done by researchers on the curves of intercity passenger traffic and that of the index of production, and a considerable amount of knowledge has been accumulated about their fluctuations and their projections. Hence they are helpful in extending the curve of air passengers.

The fact that the many different series do have some correlation and that they all fit together in a pattern means that a wide knowledge of the various series for which data exist does have a safeguarding influence against extreme statements.

As was mentioned in a previous paragraph, successful prediction is based upon the assumption that the environment, statistically called the "universe," does not change a great deal or suddenly. In tossing coins for heads or tails, the universe does not change, and from the law of probability the prediction of heads or tails can be determined with an exact error. The conditions affecting the growth of population year by year for a country as large as the United States do change from year to year, but not much, and population growth can be forecast quite accurately. On the other hand, the universe of the airplane may change violently and quickly because of the appearance of some new invention. For instance, the invention of jet-propulsion planes changes the universe in which predictions of speed are made. Meticulous statistical predictions of speed in the propeller plane are transcended by jet propulsion. However, as shown in the preceding chapter, the function of a structure or organization follows a trend even though there is a radical change in the form due to a new invention. Hence the function can be forecast from a trend somewhat better than might be thought from a consideration only of the radical change in the form. Thus, the introduction of the jet plane will increase the slope of the trend of speed, but hardly with a violent break.

We can see that the prediction of the growth of aviation may be changed by the appearance of new and startling technological advances in this field. Fortunately, it is possible to foresee somewhat in advance many new inventions, as will be discussed in later paragraphs. It takes a long time to develop an invention, although to the general public its appearance is often startling. However, the general proposition is still true that careful prediction by statistical measurement of a series is likely to be upset by some new invention or by major social changes.

Prediction of the Unique Event

Up to this point the discussion of forecasting on the basis of measurement has been concerned with the prediction of quantities or of averages based upon statistics. In such analysis the degree is being predicted; that is, the smallness or the largeness of the number of passengers who will be carried in airplanes. Likewise, we have not been concerned with whether mail will or will not be carried by plane, but rather with the amount or degree to which it will be transported. Where degree is not concerned, prediction is on the appearance or non-appearance of the phenomenon, sometimes referred to as the "all-or-none" principle. For instance, we might be concerned with predicting whether or not planes that pick up and deposit mail without landing will carry passengers. In such a prediction, we are not concerned with how many passengers will be carried, but whether they will carry any passengers — *all* they can get *or none*. The unique event to be predicted is the carrying of passengers by mail pick-up planes.

Most efforts to foresee unique events are not based upon measurement, for generally the measurements are not available. These unique events are the results of the coming-together of a number of factors. But in some cases these factors are measurable, and under such circumstances forecasting of the unique event is based upon measurement. Forecasting as to whether a particular prisoner will violate a parole if he is granted one is a prediction of a unique event. Many of the factors which produce this event are measurable and can be tabulated, such as the traits and experience of the prisoner as to his home life, his record in school, his prior prison experience, and so on. The parole records of individuals with various combinations of experiences and traits are then observed. Predictions as to whether a particular, that is, unique, prisoner will break parole are based upon these prior calculated percentages. In a similar way, the success or failure of a unique marriage may be estimated.

Much prediction of individual behavior that takes place every day by any one of us is based upon similar observations, except that we usually do not record and tabulate them on paper, but only preserve impressions of past experiences with the individual concerned, or individuals like him, in our memories. If an individual has shown courage repeatedly (statistically) in the face of danger, we readily say he will be brave in the future in a certain unique situation that involves danger.

In the study of the future influences of the airplane upon civilization, there is little occasion for forecasting unique events based upon measurement, for the measurements do not exist. Likewise, in anticipating technological improvements in aviation, we are dealing with unique events with little statistical measurement that can be used. In forecasting degrees of use of airplanes for different purposes, there is, fortunately, a good deal of measurement.

Prediction Not Based on Measurement

We have been considering forecasts based upon statistical measurement, such as the amount of air-borne express to be carried in future years. But statistical measurements are available for only a few of the many social phenomena. Yet we desire to know about the future whether or not there are statistics. We may want to know, for example, in what ways the airplane will or will not be used in agriculture, whether in sowing grain, fighting grasshoppers, or hunting coyotes. At this time, statistical series do not exist for such uses and may not be available for some time, if ever. Yet we may wish to know, in general, what uses farmers may make of aviation on the "all-or-none" principle, irrespective of degree.

Different Procedures

The reason for dividing our discussion into sections on measurement and non-measurement is that there are great differences in method between the two. One difference is that where measurement is not available, variation in degree cannot be computed. If amounts are of interest, reliance must be placed on the use of adjectives poorly suited to indicate exact quantities, adjectives such as large or small, fast or slow. Another difference is that for forecasts without measurement the demand for exact accuracy is often not very great, at least at a particular time. If we are interested in ascertaining whether the airplane will make the small nation weaker in international competition, we are perhaps satisfied at the present with a statement such as, on the average, small nations will be much weaker, or only a little weaker. Our curiosity is not so much for a statistical measure of weakness as it is for the kinds of small nations that will be weaker, or the situations that will make them weaker. Also, we may not need to have exact estimates of time. We may be content to say that small nations will be weaker as the danger of war approaches or that, if there is confidence that war is abolished, then small nations will not be weaker.

Since prediction without measurement is often unsuccessful and usually not explicit, some critics prefer to call it an art rather than a science. Such criticism is admitted; indeed, one is hardly justified in calling scientific the major part of prediction in the social sciences, even when it is based on measurement. However, we remind ourselves that our problem in studying aviation is not to be extremely exact, but rather to be as helpful as we can in trying to figure out the future of aviation and how it is likely to change our civilization. We must act in practical life before all the evidence is in or before a proof is rendered.

In the following paragraphs we shall set down the procedures that have proved helpful in the past. It is desired to make these methods explicit and thus to take the mysterious, which is incompatible with knowledge, out of whatever art there may be in trying to see ahead.

Same Patterns for Non-Measurement as for Measurement

There are certain assumptions we may make about non-measurable data even though we cannot demonstrate them with certainty. We often do this. For instance, before 1930, for the United States, we did not have any statistics on crimes committed because they were not being collected, but we might have inferred that there were certain regularities. Now that we have the statistics on crime, we can see the regularities by season, by sex, in reference to the business cycle, according to the type of crime, by size of locality, and so on. Since we do not have measurement in many fields of social science — due mainly to the cost and trouble of collecting data rather than to the inapplicability of the method — we must often make similar assumptions.

One assumption of general importance is that unmeasured data, over a series of time units, follow a trend. Since we find such a pattern in measurable data, it is natural to assume that we should find a trend in unmeasured data over a period of time if they were measured, and perhaps, also, fluctuations around the trend. For instance, the family as a social organization has been losing functions and becoming of less organizational significance for a very long time. This decline has not been measured; yet we speak of it as a trend. There is, of course, a good deal of data on changes in family organization, but much of it is not in the form of a statistical series which would show a mathematical curve with a trend and fluctuations. Nevertheless, we may use the statistical pattern of thinking for the degree of family change and say that the family has been losing functions and is likely to continue to lose them in the near future, provided the analysis of factors leads to the same conclusion. In other words, we assume trends for non-statistical data and try to make the best of these assumptions. In aviation there are miscellaneous data to show that the contacts of the communities of the Pacific Coast with the populations east of the Mississippi River have been increasing. We assume that there has been a trend, with fluctuations due to the business cycle and to war, toward making closer connections between the two coasts and that this trend will continue with more and faster air flights.

Another pattern found in measurement of growth that may be assumed for data not yet measurable is the form of the growth curve. The growth curve shows very little actual growth at the beginning — though the rate of growth may be great — then a period of rapid growth, followed by a period of less rapid growth or none at all, making the curve an elongated S. This form of growth is determined, of course, by the conditions in which the phenomena occur. Phenomena which occur under similar conditions, but whose actual data of growth are unknown and hence not subject to plotting, may be assumed to follow the pattern just described and would be so shown were measurements available. For instance, if the result of aviation is to encourage the fashion of making objects, such as luggage, tableware, casing, etc., light in weight, then we may assume without measurement that the total amount of light-weight objects will grow according to the pattern of a growth curve, though we should not know where the turning-points on such an imagined curve would occur.

Complexity of Social Factors

Another assumption that may be made for non-statistical data is that the phenomenon will be affected by many factors rather than by only one. For example, when a person becomes sick with a common cold, the cause of the cold may lie in a variety of factors, such as subjection to an unusual number of germs, fatigue, shortage of vitamin A, a drop in temperature, exposure to a motion of cold air on a part of the body, and increased acidity. In the physical sciences — physics, chemistry, astronomy, geology — the number of factors producing a phenomenon are generally considered to be much fewer than in the biological and social sciences. The complexity of factors in social phenomena is remarkable, as is shown by the many studies which have used partial correlation. In fact, in the social sciences, two variables with a correlation of one — that is, where all of the variation in one factor is accounted for by change in the other — have never been reported so far as is known.

There are many factors that must be taken into account in considering the various aspects of aviation. If we are dealing with the extension of air service to the small towns and villages, we must take into consideration such factors as the number of daily passengers in a small town, the fare charged and the ability to pay the fare, the existence of other means of transportation, the nearness to another airport, the demand for air mail, the willingness of the government to pay a subsidy for such air service, the political influence of the small town and the small businessman, and the maintenance of facilities for an airport. Some of these factors have more importance than others, but a good rule is to look around rather diligently for a large number of factors. If one is interested, for instance, in what effect the airplane will have on the relations between Great Britain and the United States, it will be seen at once that the relations will be affected by such factors as trade rivalries, tariff policies, war rumors, fiscal policies, propaganda developments, lend-lease adjustments, any one of which may overshadow the influence of the airplane. Furthermore, while the airplane service of perhaps ten hours between London and New York at a reasonable fare may increase the number of contacts between the two peoples and hence their familiarity, yet the airplane also brings rivalry for air bases as well as competition between the international airlines of the two nations. Where many powerful factors exist, the direction of the airplane's influence may be reversed by these other factors. The net influence of the plane may be to increase the friendship between the British and the Americans, yet economic or political factors may make the final result one of less friendliness. A search for the many factors affecting a situation reduces the probability of errors.

Bias

Scientific thinking is best assured when many data are available. When we do not have abundant data, our thinking is likely to be directed by subjective factors, variously characterized by such terms as bias, prejudice, emotion, and wishful thinking. Thinking without much evidence gives more opportunity for wishful thinking, which is, of course, quite unrealistic. The problem of bias becomes more important the less the evidence, the rarer the measurement, and the more numerous the factors involved. Anything that can be done to eliminate bias clears the way for better thinking.

We shall not go into the psychology of biased thinking here. There is a considerable literature on this complex subject which sets forth the important theories of the rôle of emotion and desire in the thinking process. Rather, we shall point out in the succeeding paragraphs a few common instances of how bias makes forecasting rather hazardous.

Wishful Thinking

Hope is a notoriously bad forecaster, though it may help to create the morale necessary to bring about the future condition desired. Students often think they are going to get higher grades in their class work than they actually get. We overestimate the chances of our favorite team's winning. Obviously, in prediction we need to be on our guard when our hopes are involved, and try to discard them. If possible, it is desirable to get in a mood of detachment, as if the result meant nothing at all to us. But usually we cannot detach our desires in a manner so cold-blooded.

In gathering estimates of the future from interested persons, we should watch out for the bias of self-interest. The predictions of aircraft manufacturers, who naturally want a good market, may be too high, on the average. So also the expectations of airline officials may be for a brighter future than will occur, though there will be exceptions. On the other hand, rival transportation systems, such as railroads and ocean steamship companies, which may lose business by virtue of the growth of air transportation, would be expected to predict a less rosy future for aviation than would the airline companies. Of course, railroad and aviation companies do not give opinions without data, and, since they both have much data, the distortion due to desires cannot be too great. But, certainly, an investigator collecting opinions and estimates should consider the possible biases of the sources of his information. In some cases this bias can be very large, as is illustrated by an experience which a mediator had in an attempt to learn the number on strike the first morning of a disturbance in a steel mill. The union leader said the number out was ten thousand to fifteen thousand; the manager of the plant said three hundred or four hundred. Each predicted according to his wishes in a period of great excitement, and each no doubt felt that his prediction, if widely known, would influence the number to go out on strike. The actual number on strike was about seven thousand.

The theory of the rôle of bias in prediction, as stated above, is greatly oversimplified. In the first place, the nature of an opinion depends to a great extent on the sense of responsibility of the renderer of an opinion at the time he gives it. If the opinion is given in casual conversation over cocktails, it may be quite different from what it would be if he were on the point of making a large investment of money on the basis of his opinions.

Furthermore, most intelligent businessmen are quite familiar with the danger of optimism based on their hopes and desires and learn to correct for it by undercutting their optimism. Indeed, some of them swing to the extreme and give a pessimistic judgment in order to safeguard themselves.

Then, too, not every individual is an optimist and allows his wishes to bias his estimates. Apparently there are pessimists as well as optimists. There is probably fixed in us in our early years a pattern of adjustment of our feeling into our thinking which becomes more or less constitutional in us as adults. This psychological set works out in many of us in such a way as to justify the term "optimist," while in others it works out in such a way as to call for the term "pessimist." However, there are not just two classes, without variations. There are all degrees of optimism and pessimism.

An attempt was once made to make a crude estimate of the number of optimists and pessimists in the following manner.[3] Students were asked to predict their grades, the arrangement being that the person who gave the grade could not know the prediction made by the student. Students who predicted that they would get a higher grade than they actually received in each of all their courses were labeled optimists, while those who pre-

[3] William F. Ogburn, "Studies in the Prediction and Distortion of Reality," *Social Forces*, vol. 13, no. 2, December, 1934, pp. 227-228.

dicted that they would have a lower grade in all of their courses than they actually got were called pessimists. It was interesting to note that there was an excess of both optimists and pessimists over a random expectation and that the excess of optimists was eight times as great as the excess of pessimists. These results seem to bear out the common observation that hope or fear swings estimates more than they should, but that the hopeful outnumber the fearful.

Try as we may to prevent wishful thinking, there is nothing so effective as plenty of data to correct it. But in cases of scarcity of data, one way of trying to reduce the error is to reduce the emotional element in thinking.

Influence of Fashion

Another bias in thinking when the data are few is the influence of the prevailing opinion, which has an element of fashion about it in the sense that it may be one thing today and another tomorrow. This may be illustrated by the changeable opinion about the future of the helicopter. When the helicopter was first flown successfully, it received an enthusiastic reception from the daily press and from the magazines. The tone of opinion was one of great optimism. It was predicted that the helicopter would become the family aircraft and that its production would furnish employment after the war. But afterward the climate of opinion about the helicopter changed. It became the fashion to decry its prospects. To say a good word about its promise was to be considered a careless thinker; to be skeptical was an index of good judgment. The prevailing wind had changed. Obviously, when opinion changes radically with little new evidence, it is quite different from a scientific conclusion which is valid from year to year.

Observers should be aware of their susceptibility to the influence of the prevailing opinion. This susceptibility is due in part to the fact that we pick up our ideas from others rather than basing them on our own research, and in part to the social pressure that gets us in the habit of conforming. Those who live on Main Street tend to think like Main Streeters. It is very difficult to see beyond the contemporary environment. In the late 1920's, businessmen were talking of permanent prosperity and of having licked forever business depression. During the depression of the early 1930's, the gloom was so thick that many businessmen thought that it was not a phenomenon of the business cycle, but that capitalism had failed. The winds of opinion have not the reliability of science.

During the war, there was a phenomenal development of aviation. Our sons became aviators and our daughters worked in airplane factories. Magazines carried large airplane advertisements, while the daily press reported the achievements of our military aircraft. It was a period of boomtime psychology for aviation. Peacetime conditions are bringing a great decrease in this air activity and, if there is a business depression, aviation may even fall below prewar levels. The expansionist attitude toward aviation will be severely restricted. Forecasts then will not be so bright as now. We conclude that somehow or other, when we cannot rely wholly on data in forecasting, some consideration must be made of the changeability of opinion on the subject.

The Danger of Being Too Conservative

Continuing our discussion of what to do about forecasting when data are meager, it may be observed that there is often a fear of making too extreme a forecast and an attitude of timidity or caution which leads to an underestimate. For example, the forecasts of the scores of winning football teams have been shown to be only about half as large as the actual scores.[4] Seldom was a very large score predicted, yet very large scores occur from time to time.

Simon Newcomb, the cautious dean of science, wrote the following negative forecast regarding the airplane in 1903:

> There are many problems which have fascinated mankind ever since civilization began which we have made little or no advance in solving. The only satisfaction we can feel in our treatment of the great geometrical problems of antiquity is that we have shown their solution to be impossible. The mathematician of today ad-

[4] *Ibid.*, p. 225.

mits that he can neither square the circle, duplicate the cube, or trisect the angle. May not our mechanicians, in like manner, be ultimately forced to admit that aerial flight is one of that great class of problems with which man can never cope, and give up all attempts to grapple with it? [5]

Yet in exactly eight weeks after this forecast was published, the Wright brothers made their memorable flight in a heavier-than-air machine at Kitty Hawk.

But extreme predictions are sometimes made. Writing at about the same time as Newcomb, H. G. Wells, the imaginative novelist and thinker, made an astounding number of successful predictions of the radical changes that were to take place during the following twenty-five years. There are, of course, plenty of extreme predictions made in the sensational Sunday supplements of certain newspapers by writers who are paid for catching the reader's attention through strange and dramatic statements. Also, poets have sometimes predicted coming events, such as flying. But such predictions are not highly responsible and are made more for psychological effects than for reliability.

Our thesis is that responsible forecasters, in the absence of many good data, err on the side of underprediction more often than overprediction and that they rarely foresee the exceptional. One reason for this may be that there is a certain prestige in being conservative. Conservativism is believed to denote soundness and good judgment rather than fear. Another reason is that a missed prediction on an extreme prophecy is more glaring than is a less extreme one. A responsible predictor feels ashamed of making a bad miss.

Forecasting in the social sciences is so difficult and inaccurate that few venture it. One type of prediction that is used is the so-called "slide-rule" prediction which deals with many data, with statistics, with costs and prices, and which predicts for only a few years ahead. The slide-rule prediction does not get very far into the future, for then there is more opportunity for new factors to come in. There this method breaks down, since it is based on

<hr>

[5] Simon Newcomb, "The Outlook for the Flying Machine," *The Independent,* October 22, 1903, p. 2509.

measurement. What little prestige there is to prediction lies with slide-rule prediction today.

Another type of predictor goes farther into the future and depends on more intangible procedures. The believed superiority of the slide-rule predictors reflects by reverse action on those who venture into the future without measurement. They are believed to be "wild" and unreliable, as they no doubt are when compared to the slide-rule predictors. Since no one wants to be a "wild" forecaster, this type of forecasting is disapproved. So social pressure operates to prohibit forecasters from making extreme forecasts and encourages the conservative type of prediction. It is very probable that a good forecaster with a slide-rule method would be a poorer forecaster for years farther into the future, where his slide-rule method does not work, than would be a person who never used the slide-rule type of prediction, but who had a wide general knowledge and was accustomed to finding his way around with imagination and without dependence on measurement.

Many Results from a Single Cause

Sometimes we are curious to know the many different phenomena that will occur rather than any particular one. For instance, many planners want to know the ways in which society will be different after World War II. They want to know the many different results flowing chiefly from one cause, war. This is a legitimate curiosity. Naturally, it is more difficult to foresee many results than one. But usually such a broad curiosity is satisfied with naming the changes rather than measuring the amounts and locating these varying amounts in time. In such situations, we are interested in the scope of the vision rather than in focusing on a single point. There is a certain interest in merely listing one hundred and fifty different uses and effects of the radio, even if these effects are not measured in time and degree. In such an inquiry, an omission may be more serious than a failure to observe an item meticulously. In forecasting for a particular change, there is sometimes a contempt for any estimate that does not predict for quantity and time; but if the limitations of time and quantity are removed, successful predictions may not be particularly difficult. It is much easier to predict successfully the wide use of the helicopter at some time in the future than it is to predict the number of them, their price, and the date of their successful use.

The degree of accuracy necessarily depends on the use of the prediction. There are many persons who want to know only whether divorces are likely to increase or decrease after the war, rather than to know the exact divorce rates. It would be better to predict the exact number of divorces within a small error, but a reliable forecast that divorce will increase after the war is better than no orientation at all. If a publisher is interested in shipping magazines by air after the war, he is interested in exact routes, schedules, and particularly rates. But a reader of magazines may be interested only in the general development of aviation in the postwar decade and what effects it will have on our way of life and our institutions. As far as he is concerned, a wide range of predictions on the "all-or-none" principle, without predictions as to rates for transporting magazines by air and so on, will be of interest. There is a desire on the part of many people to have an extensive picture of the influence of aviation on our civilization, and this desire may be satisfied in large part without estimates of degrees and of years.

Concern with the broad perspective of impending changes attributable to aviation necessitates a considerable familiarity with many societal factors. Society is an interlocking of many parts — institutions, customs, attitudes, traditions, etc. — just as is a complicated piece of machinery. The attainment of a broad perspective of impending changes is of distinct aid in forecasting the particular, since the particular is dependent upon many factors, such as price, business conditions, governmental policy, political influences, demand, and social attitudes. The rule of getting the general picture in order to know the particular is a familiar one in sociology and anthropology. A field worker, for instance, is advised not to study the family or religion of a strange culture without knowing the whole of the culture and how the family or religion is tied in with it. Likewise, in aviation, the question of whether there will be one or many airline companies of a single nation flying transoceanic routes and the extent of governmental regulation and aid depends in part on a knowledge of the political system, the economic policy, and social attitudes. A question of this kind is difficult to handle statistically. A descriptive knowledge of the many societal factors is needed.

In this particular book an attempt is made to obtain a general picture of how our daily life, our social organizations, and our customs will be modified by aviation. The success of the undertaking is dependent to an important degree on the range of vision. In view of the scope of the undertaking and of the general audience to whom it is addressed, there will be many instances where the "all-or-none" type of forecast will be used. In addition, there will be many particularistic forecasts. A number of studies have already been published making forecasts of the volumes of passengers, mail, and express at different rates. Planners in particular fields will also make more detailed estimates of the future as the need arises.

The discussion of method in regard to forecasting up to this point has been of a general nature with some illustrations from the field of aviation. We will next consider the special problems of predicting in the field of technology and the effects of inventions.

4

On Predicting the Social Effects of Invention

THE INVENTION of the airplane is an accomplished fact and does not need to be predicted, but there are many new inventions ahead in aviation. A "big invention" such as the airplane is a cluster of inventions of a smaller nature; that is, inventions on different parts of the main invention or the complex of inventions that go with the main one. There may also be new inventions on other types of aircraft such as the rocket or the helicopter. We may look, therefore, at the problem of anticipating inventions.

Technological Developments in General

It is possible to predict in a general way something about new inventions. The record of patents issued by the Patent Office gives some rough indication of the number of new inventions, although many patents are issued for minor changes or improvements of a mechanical nature which hardly conform to the general idea of an invention. And some rather important devices that have been made or discovered have never been patented. In the early years of the Patent Office, the number of patents grew much like an exponential curve, but of recent years the annual number granted either has been stationary or declining. Patents have been assigned, however, at the rate of between 40,000 and 50,000 per year in the United States during the 1930's and 1940's. The long continuation of this curve of patents leads us to think that much technological progress lies ahead and that no dramatic decline is in sight.

We can also expect a continuation of technological development from an analysis of the causes of invention. Invention is a

58

function of three variables: (1) mental ability, (2) demand, and (3) existing knowledge of earlier inventions and science out of which to make the new invention. The first factor, mental ability, is plentiful in a large country like the United States, if it is defined as being hereditary ability. This plentiful hereditary gift must, of course, be educated and trained, which is in part a function of the second factor, demand. The demand for invention is often quiescent, but it can be aroused, as, for instance, a demand in wartime for devices to prosecute the war. The third factor, existing knowledge, has often been absent in the past, making invention difficult or impossible, since a new invention is a combination of existing inventions and knowledge. Leonardo da Vinci, for example, did not have the gasoline engine and could not invent the airplane, despite his mental ability. Today we have such an enormous accumulation of scientific knowledge and mechanical invention with which to make new inventions that there is not likely to be a shortage of scientific knowledge to hinder future developments, though, of course, there may be in particular cases. In fact, the material out of which to make inventions is so plentiful that some optimists have been led to declare that we could invent anything we wanted to, provided we gave it our attention and brought our knowledge to bear upon it. Such a statement is an exaggeration, for we could not discover, let us say, how to remain young forever, even though there were a great demand for it. Nor have we yet succeeded in discovering a sure cure for cancer, although a great deal of research has been done and there is a great demand for it. A great discovery or invention often requires many years of effort, usually by several inventors and the contributions of many inventions.

We conclude, then, after a quick analysis of the factors producing inventions, that the situation ahead is favorable, in general, for continuing technological progress.

Predicting a Particular Invention

To the average person, a new invention seems to appear unexpectedly. It is not impossible, however, to foresee an invention at least a short time ahead of its appearance. Inventions have been forecast many times. The question arises as to whether these forecasts were lucky guesses or reliable predictions. S. C. Gilfillan shows [1] that by 1936 A. C. Lescarboura, writing in 1920, had 78 per cent of his predictions apparently right and 22 per cent probably wrong. He also claims that T. Baron Russell, writing in 1906, was 70 per cent apparently right in his predictions of inventions, with 21 per cent erroneous and 9 per cent doubtful. Charles P. Steinmetz, in 1915, is claimed to have been 76 per cent right and 24 per cent doubtful, with none wrong. George Sutherland, in 1900, is claimed to have been 64 per cent right, 33 per cent erroneous, and 3 per cent doubtful.

Inventions can be anticipated somewhat in advance of their maturity because of the fact that they have a life history. The idea of an invention is born and develops through childhood and adolescence into adulthood, and is not born full-grown as Minerva in mythical history is reported to have been. Gilfillan writes: [2]

> Taking 19 inventions voted most useful, introduced in 1888-1913, the average intervals were: between when the invention was first merely thought of, and the first working model or patent, 176 years; thence to the first practical use, 24 years; to commercial success, 14 years; to important use, 12 years, or say 50 years from the first serious work on the invention. Again, in the study of the most important inventions of the last generation before 1930, in *Recent Social Trends,* a median lapse was found of 33 years, between the "conception date" corresponding to the second above, and the date of commercial success.

Thus, the span of years in recent times from birth to maturity of an important invention averages around thirty-five to fifty years.

To make use of the life development of an invention in forecasting, it is necessary to learn about the early years of an invention. Reporting on inventional development in the United States or elsewhere is not very extensive or complete. A few specialists and laboratory workers know something about inventions

---

[1] S. C. Gilfillan, "The Prediction of Inventions," in *Technological Trends and National Policy,* National Resources Planning Board, 1937, p. 15.
[2] *Ibid.,* p. 19.

in progress, but, in general, the public knows little about them. However, the records of the Patent Office are open to the public except in wartime when secrecy conceals the patent applications that might give aid to the enemy.

But once knowledge is acquired about a patent or a young invention, there remains the question of whether it will successfully develop, or die out. The pitfalls and obstacles to the successful development of an invention to the stage of practical use are many, and the death rate is high. An invention, like a chain which is no stronger than its weakest link, will not work technically if there is a single missing item. In addition, an economic organization is required for the production and marketing of the invention after it is a technical success. This calls for the investment of funds, which must show a profit. That the birth of an invention is not good proof that it will live and be successful is shown by the high death rate in French patents. Before World War I, when French patents ran for fifteen years, only one out of twenty patents was kept in force for the full period by the payment of a small renewal fee. Of the patents on which payments were kept up, it is not known that all of these were commercial successes.

The death rate is lower for those inventions for which there is a strong demand. Most patents are for inventions for which there is probably not much demand. The demand is greatest for those inventions which, if successful, would have considerable social effect. Therefore, it should be somewhat less hazardous to predict the important inventions when we know of their existence and the beginning of their life.

The important rôle of demand in creating an invention, if there is sufficient mental ability and an abundance of scientific knowledge and equipment, is demonstrated by Gilfillan in the case of an invention to overcome fog.[3] The demand to overcome fog was tremendously increased with the coming of aviation. Successful landing of planes was impossible or hazardous in fog. So abundant was our knowledge and material on this subject that twenty-five different methods of conquering fog were being worked on

3 *Ibid.*, p. 22.

in 1936. Since then, several new methods have been made known, notably radar. One might have predicted that, with so great a demand and so much mental ability at work on the problem, it would be solved, as indeed it has been. We might not have been able to predict which of the approximately twenty-five methods would be successful, but it seemed probable that one of them would succeed. In this illustration, demand is the basis for the prediction of an invention, but not the particular one; nor would the demand justify a prediction as to when the successful invention would occur.

One reason why it is difficult to predict an invention with certainty or to predict the time of its success is the fact that inventions often require the completion of many different steps in the process before the end result is achieved. A new invention is the combination of many elements into one, and sometimes several of the elements that are to be combined into the new one must be themselves created. For instance, the invention of a successful incandescent electric light required the contributions of inventional elements by eight different scientists, including Edison.

The problem of forecasting the success of an invention in its early stages may be seen from consideration of the invention of the jet-propelled airplane. The idea of propelling an object rapidly through the air by the emission of compressed gases from a rear exhaust is as old as the rocket. The first patent for a jet-propelled plane (by steam) was issued to Golightly in England in 1849, but there was then no practicable airplane. A jet-propelled small model helicopter had been demonstrated in Paris in 1842. The first jet-propulsion flight in a full-sized aircraft with pilot was made in a glider propelled by a rocket in Germany in 1928, after experiments with models. The efficiency was less than 1 per cent. It was realized that the successful application of jet propulsion would demand a plane of great speed, which was not then in existence. From 1920 on, much work was done on power plants for jet propulsion, particularly in France and Germany around 1930. It was not until 1940 that an Italian, Campini, with the firm of Caproni, built a plane that would fly with jet propulsion. But the engine was complicated and heavy and the weight badly distributed. In England, Whittle, from an idea conceived in 1933, successfully developed his jet-propelled engine in 1937, and made his first successful flight in a plane with such an engine in 1941. In 1944, the invention became practicable.

Prediction with any certainty about jet propulsion would have been difficult prior to the few years preceding the Campini-Caproni flight in 1940. Even then, the successful achievements of 1944 might not have been attained had it not been for the war, which created a great demand for fast flights at high altitudes, to which the jet-propelled plane is peculiarly suited. Even now, we are somewhat hesitant about prediction of the peacetime future of jet propulsion with its heavy loads of fuel and great speed. The rôle of demand has been and will be very important. The strength of demand is not subject to measurement in the case of inventions, and it is not possible to do much in locating the time when demand will make a young invention a success.

In cases where major inventions have been achieved, but certain lesser improvements are needed to perfect the inventions, directors of laboratories concerned with inventions can sometimes predict that the inventions will be ready within an approximate time.

It may be concluded that, although sometimes an invention may be predicted with a high degree of probability and also sometimes the date of its perfection, in general there is considerable uncertainty as to whether an invention will or will not be made, or whether it will be made within a given era. On the other hand, the coming of an invention is not a matter of complete surprise; and speculation about achieving an invention can become quite realistic.

Predicting the Adoption and Uses of an Invention

An invention may be perfected technically and yet not be adopted. For instance, the magnetic wire recorder was achieved as far back as 1896. Yet it has never been put to much commercial use, although it had increased application in military operations during the war.

One of the reasons a mechanically successful invention may not be adopted is high price. In some cases, the cost may not prohibit everyone from purchasing the invention, but it restricts its use to the income classes that can afford it. If it is a producers' good, its high price may raise the cost of the finished product to prohibitive heights. The cargo rates on airplanes have been too high in the past for much use in carrying freight. So also the cost of an individual plane was too high in the 1920's for all but a few incomes. However, inventors, in contrast to researchers in pure science, usually have the cost factor in mind and are not likely to work much on an invention when they think the price is likely to be prohibitive.

A second important factor in restricting the use of an invention is the existence of a substitute which is available at a lower price or which is simpler or more workable. Perhaps one reason why the sound film, separate from pictures, is not used for producing music in homes is the fact that phonographs and records may be used instead. For similar reasons, the airplane finds a quicker use for cargo in Alaska and parts of Canada and South America, where there are few substitute methods of transportation, than in the United States which already has an extensive and varied system of transportation.

The lack of such qualities as simplicity, durability, and repairability may prevent the adoption of an invention. Most statistical machines for computing correlation coefficients are too complex for much use. Machines that break rather easily and that can be repaired only by experts who live in another area are not suitable for marketing. Sometimes there are objectional qualities that prevent use. For example, waterproofing chemicals for men's and women's clothing have existed for a long time, but they have not been used, partly because these chemicals did not withstand dry-cleaning processes and, in some cases, appearance was affected. Perhaps also the demand was not very great or there were adequate substitutes.

Manufacturers who acquire an invention in its early stages often find a large number of improvements necessary before it becomes suitable for marketing. When the General Electric Company took over the fluorescent lamp, an invention already made in several countries, many improvements were needed affecting price, breakability, simplicity, durability, and quality of performance before the invention was available for marketing. The cost of improvements for the fluorescent light amounted to many millions of dollars and many years of work by scientists and technicians. Even after the invention was put on the market and widely used, improvements continued to be made.

In general, whether an invention will or will not be used can often be foretold, after it is known that the major achievement of the invention has been accomplished, by taking into consideration such factors as price, substitutes, simplicity, dependability, repairability, etc.

The discussion on this point has concerned forecasting inventions with a limited use. But often an invention may be used for many different purposes and there is the problem of forecasting these many uses. The radio is used in broadcasting programs, in guiding ships to port, and in piloting airplanes. The broadcasts are used for musical entertainment, for dramatic presentation, for education, for news reporting, for advertising, and for many other purposes. The X-ray, likewise, has many different uses. Forecasting the variety of uses of an invention depends on much searching and imagination on the part of the predictor, plus a generous use of critical faculties and a wide knowledge of the fields considered. If one wishes to list only the variety of uses, then the problem is to cover as wide a range as possible. Even a slight use for a particular purpose justifies its listing. In 1919, the Curtiss Aeroplane and Motor Corporation, for example, listed ninety-one future uses of the airplane,[4] most of which have proved to be true. The problem of prediction becomes more difficult if the assignment is to measure the quantity of each use. The method of predicting the uses of a multiple-purpose invention is the same as that of predicting the use of a single-purpose invention except that there are more uses for which quantities must be predicted.

[4] The Curtiss Aeroplane and Motor Corporation, "Everyday Uses of An Aeroplane," December 26, 1919. Printed circular.

The method of forecasting the degree of use of an invention, once it has been adopted, differs in cases where statistical records are available from those where they are not. The employment of measurement from time records has already been discussed in the preceding chapter, especially in connection with projection and correlation with various factors. If the forecast is to be made before any records are available, the uncertainty becomes very great and speculation rests upon general knowledge of the field concerned. A prediction might be made that the helicopter will be used in killing coyotes. If it were desired to know how much use of the helicopter for this purpose there would be, the size of the sheep industry could be shown and the loss of sheep from coyotes estimated. Then the number of large sheep-owners, who might be able to pay high costs, could be ascertained. From then on, factors of cost, dependability, etc., would need to be known to make even a rough estimate. But the need for information as to how many helicopters would be used in killing coyotes would probably not arise unless such helicopters required some special construction feature. In any case, such quantitative information would not be needed in the early stages of helicopter development and not until salesmen were ready to go into this particular field. Even then, approximate estimates would probably serve this purpose very well.

In forecasting the extent of use of an invention when statistical time records are not available and are not likely to be kept, quantitative estimates may not be needed. Such might be true of the use of aircraft by physicians. There may be little demand for precise knowledge as to the extent of use of aircraft by doctors. Recourse is had again to general knowledge, facts about the situation, price, conceptions of human nature, and the availability of substitutes.

Resistance to the Use of Inventions

The discussion of the adoption of inventions ought not to be concluded without consideration of the actual resistances to their adoption. The difficulties of a successful invention, so far discussed, have concerned largely the technological and economic aspects of invention, but there are also other factors involved.

One of the most widespread and powerful oppositions to the adoption of an invention is that of "vested interests"; that is, people or institutions who stand to lose a preferred position if the invention is accepted. The saloon interests opposed the adoption of the rural free mail delivery, which, it was thought, would lessen the number of visits of farmers to the towns. Sometimes the vested interests are not free to make overt resistance, as, for instance, when the popularity of the invention is very great. With an invention as popular as the airplane, other transportation systems are not likely to engage in active opposition, except by improving their own competitive position through improved service or lower rates. However, in appraising the factors that speed or slow the adoption of inventions, a thorough search for opposition by vested interests is recommended.

Another obstacle to be considered is habit, which creates an inertia that many inventions must overcome. For example, a new food or a new drink must win its way over existing food habits, which resist change. Another illustration is simplified spelling, which would reduce office and printing expense and shorten the learning time of youth, but it meets with the resistance of habit. Some readers can recall how the habits of travel with the horse and buggy caused for a time the postponement of the purchase of the automobile by various individuals. It is not clear, however, that habit as such will play an unusual part in resistance to the use of the airplane. The war has given it such advertising that there already is great familiarity with it.

Fear may be a more effective resistant to the use of the plane. Flying through the air seems dangerous, especially when accompanied by reports of airplane accidents. Fear may also play a part in preventing the acquisition of aircraft by individuals and families for personal use.

Sometimes there are mechanical obstacles to the adoption of inventions. The short summers of the North operate somewhat against the adoption of air-conditioning in dwellings in the summer time. The weather has been an obstacle to the use of the airplane for travel, since the cancellation of scheduled flights due to bad weather causes uncertainty and annoyance on the part of the traveler. This difficulty is not so noticeable now, since only 6 per cent of the scheduled flights were canceled in 1943, and a greater reduction is expected. However, in personal flying, it is quite likely that weather difficulties and hazards will somewhat discourage non-scheduled and private flying.

Many of these obstacles of fear, habit, and concern about the weather in flying have been broken down by the national effort to boost aviation in wartime and the participation by a large part of the population in military flying. It is thought particularly that the introduction of aviational materials into the curriculum at the elementary- and secondary-school levels has been effective in diminishing any reluctance to fly on the part of the young.

Predicting the Social Effects of an Invention

Inventions are chiefly interesting to sociologists for their social influences, either in the habits of the users, or for what they do to our social organizations, customs, and ideologies. Our interest in this book is in what effects aviation will have on our daily lives and on civilization in general.

An invention is essentially something to use, and this use affects civilization in many ways. For instance, the discovery that plants could be made to grow from seed and cultivated by man changed not just food production from hunting to agriculture but many social institutions as well. The inventions of ironmaking, gunpowder, printing, and the steam engine affected so many parts of our culture that we say they changed civilization to some degree. Of course, there are some inventions, such as the safety razor, which have very little social influence. A great invention, such as the airplane, is likely to have such an extensive and far-reaching influence as to be uncountable and untellable. The immediate problem before us is, How can we go about trying to see in advance the changes in our society that will be brought about by a very significant complex of inventions such as the airplane?

The Difference Between Uses and Social Effects

It is useful to make a distinction between the uses of an invention and its social effects. One distinction has to do with the time element. The uses of an invention occur simultaneously with its adoption, whereas the social effects result after varying losses of time. For example, after the invention of the steam engine, it was used in factories, but the changes in the family due to workers going outside the home and the changing economic duties of the household did not occur until later. Thieves used automobiles to get from one place to another, but the changes in the courts because of this did not occur until later.

The uses of an invention change individual habits or the practices of the institutions immediately concerned. Social effects are usually considered to apply to social organizations or organized habits, such as family activities, governmental functions, city life, rural practices, recreation, and criminal behavior. In addition, there are changes in manners, morals, laws, customs, and attitudes which are more or less formalized. These organized habits and customs are not so quickly and readily modified as are the personal habits of individuals who use an invention.

Foreseeing the Habits of Using Inventions

The new habits and customs that accompany the uses of an invention are essentially direct. Hence, if we know what the uses are, it is not difficult to read off new habits. The truck requires a driver. The time clock is accompanied by an increase in the habit of punctuality. The radio means hearing more music.

Of very similar nature are the habits associated with the production of an invention. These are similar because they are very closely and directly associated with the invention. Automobile production brought many new occupations having to do with rubber, glass, paint, welding, etc. Television will bring a new set of habits, as did the radio. Aviation will bring new customs, as did the automobile. The method of foreseeing these is to make a study of the various steps in production and also of the different uses.

Correlated industries and occupations often grow up around

an important invention. These are a necessary part of the invention complex. Gasoline filling stations are a correlate of the automobile industries. Meteorology is an occupation which is integrally a part of aviation, although meteorologists do not make or fly airplanes.

There are other classes of customs associated directly and immediately with the use of an invention. If owners of automobiles use them frequently for pleasure driving on Sunday, for weekends or summer vacations, then the habits of recreation and vacationing of the users are changed. The airplane is also likely to change vacationing habits. If such vacationing becomes extensive and later is institutionalized into parks, resorts, hotels, etc., then these individual habits of users eventually become social effects through creating and influencing social institutions.

In studying the impact of an invention on society, then, the first step in dealing with social influences is to study habits and customs directly associated with the production and use of the invention.

Primary and Derivative Influences

The immediate changes in production, personal habits and closely connected institutions arising from the uses of an invention are called the primary effects. They are immediate and direct. The derivative influences are more often delayed, and concern institutions and socially organized habits. These derivative influences are somewhat like the distribution of forces in a billiard game. The cue ball strikes ball A, which in turn imparts its derivative force to ball B. The direct influence of the airplane, for example, is to increase the travel between the United States and the Orient. These contacts create a derivative influence, the study of the culture of the Orient, which in turn will impart to American culture the influence of, say, Chinese art and philosophy.

Another illustration might be the cotton gin, which had the primary effect of increasing the speed of removing the seed from the boll. This function led to the increased production of cotton (in conjunction with the strong market demand for cotton goods).

Increased cotton production was thus a secondary influence. The increased production in turn created a greater demand for slaves and raised their price. This was another derivative influence and might be called tertiary. The increased wealth of the South in slaves and in their products magnified the influence of the Southern economy on the political life of the nation — still another derivative influence.

Successive Diminution of Derivative Influences

The direct influence of an invention is stronger than its derivative influence, if we think of strength as the amount of change effected by virtue of the impact. The amount of change in habits of travel to and from the Orient attributable to the airplane is likely to be greater than the change in the habits of studying Oriental culture. The next derivative influence, namely, the reaction of Oriental culture on America, would seem to be still weaker. Indeed, the airplane's part in contributing to the influence of Oriental culture on the West appears to be very slight. Similarly, the influence of the cotton gin in causing the Civil War in 1861 may have been very slight. We do not know. But if there had been no cotton gin, can we be certain that the Civil War would have occurred or that it would have occurred at the time that it did? So, also, without air travel between the United States and China in the future, perhaps the influence of Chinese culture on American culture would have been less than it will be.

In studying the social influences of inventions, we look for the derivative influences. These influences may be very powerful or they may be attenuated to so great a degree as to be hardly worth mentioning. For instance, the influence of the cotton gin may have affected, in microscopic degree, wages, immigration, shipping, the tariff, and so on. Which of these may be worth while mentioning is a matter of emphasis. If social planning is the test of selection, then only major influences need to be noted. However, if we are interested in the extent of influence of an invention, or seeking explanations of changes taking place in our culture, then consideration must be taken of the many derivative influences.

Derivative Influences of Inventions Fan Out

Important inventions radiate influences in many different directions. The airplane affects railroads, agriculture, recreation, international relations, and so on. The procedure is to make a census of the variety of different influences.

The first derivative influences are more numerous than the direct ones; and the second derivative influences more numerous than the first. For example, one direct influence of the X-ray is to take pictures of the roots of teeth. From this one influence there are a number of first derivative influences, such as the employment of X-ray technicians, the increase of the capital equipment of dentists, creation of a new branch of dental education, etc. These in turn are followed by more derivative influences, such as the increase in expenditures for care of teeth, the maintenance of better teeth and better breath, the writing of books associated with X-rays, new classifications in libraries, and new salesmen.

The derivative influences continue to fan out until they are lost. The effect of dental X-rays on the average health of the population may be quite small when all the other factors affecting health are taken into consideration. If the influences of improved health on increased production are considered, the influences of the X-ray become so thinned out that they are not discernible.

Joint Influences of Many Inventions

The changes accompanying an invention are often either wholly or largely the direct influence of the particular invention. The present increased activity in meteorology is attributable to the airplane, although some increase may be due to the growth of scientific agriculture, and ocean transportation may also account for some of the growth of meteorology. But when it comes to the derivative influences of a particular invention, rather than the direct influences, we find important causes other than those of the invention under study. For instance, one influence of the immigration acts of the 1920's — social inventions — was to draw Negro labor from the Southern states to the Northern industrial cities in place of European immigrants who were restricted to limited quotas. A derivative influence was to raise the wages of the Negroes in the South. But there were other influences operating to raise the wages of Negroes in the South, such as the use of the tractor on the farms, the falling birth rate in the cities, the improved education of Negroes, and their membership in labor unions.

In cases of this sort it is not easy to measure influences. It would be difficult to say how many Negroes came North because of the restriction of immigration. We do not know how many would have migrated from the South to the big cities if immigration had not been restricted. There are various ways in which it can be demonstrated that the shortage of immigrants led to an increase in Negro laborers. Extended investigation would yield estimates.

But it would be even more difficult to measure the proportion of the increase in wages of Negroes which could be attributed to restricted immigration. Such a conclusion is reached by a few samples of wage data, an analysis of the situation, and the making of inferences. We can reason from the data that such and such an influence follows. If the phenomenon is found, the conclusion is drawn that the invention had that influence. But, theoretically, the higher wages of Negroes could have been because of other factors than the restriction of immigration. Indeed, it might be argued that the needs for labor from restricted European immigration were met by immigrants from Mexico and Canada and not by Negroes. It is easier to reason that an influence follows a certain situation than to demonstrate that it does.

A check on this inference is to move from the effect to the cause rather than from the cause to the effect. For instance, by inference from cause to effect, it is to be expected that a restriction of immigration would raise the wages of Negroes (and whites too). To move from effect to cause, one would take the fact of higher wages in the 1920's and try to figure out the many different causes.

It has been shown that the derivative influences of an invention join with other influences to produce an effect. This principle is in conformity with accepted ideas of causation in cultural phenomena, namely, that there are often several variables operating to produce a result. The increase in divorce is believed to be due to the many factors of declining birth rate, growth of city life, the employment of women, the weakening of religious forces, and the transfer of occupations from the home to industry. Sometimes, however, the factors do not all co-operate toward one result. Some factors operate to produce a certain result, others to prevent it. Certain factors lessen divorce, such as religion, education, particular habits of child rearing, etc. The phenomenon of divorce is a resultant of all these forces.

Sometimes the influence of an invention becomes invisible or negligible because the influence of other factors outweighs it. The influence of electrical goods for the home, such as the refrigerator, radio, telephone, and the electric light, is to make the home attractive and to keep the members of the family at home. On the other side, however, are the influences of the motion picture, commercial recreation, employment, advertising, the growth of restaurants, automobiles, and government activities, which tend to take the members of the family away from the home. The net result of both sets of forces may be less time at home. Hence the influence of electrical inventions on the home may not be visible. It is operating but obscured by other forces.

These observations are of significance for method. They mean that we should separate the impact of invention into two conceptions. One is of the influence of the invention that would be manifest if all other factors were constant. This influence is sometimes referred to as a tendency or trend. Since all other factors are never constant, such an influence must be estimated or deduced rather than measured or described in actuality. For instance, we would deduce the conclusion that the radio kept members of the family at home from the fact that some members of the family will stay at home at times to enjoy the radio rather than go out. This might be described as an influence, even though the increased sale of radios from year to year was accompanied by an increased amount of time spent away from home. Great care should be taken in such cases lest erroneous reliance is placed on such deductions. For example, in the late 1920's it was deduced that the automobile was causing a decline in the population of villages, for it was argued that farmers with fast automobiles and good roads were going farther away to bigger and better markets where there were also other activities. They would thus pass by the village without stopping. However, in the census of 1930, a representative sample of 8900 villages showed that they had increased in about the same proportion as the general population.[5] On second thought, observers recalled that if a farmer went past a small village to a larger town, more money must be spent for gasoline. So, as in all cases where there is not an abundance of evidence, great care must be used in making inferences as to the influences of inventions.

The second conception of significance for method is that a result sometimes attributed to an invention is, in reality, not due to the invention alone, but to the invention in conjunction with several other influences. For example, we may say that the isolation of the farmer is broken down by the automobile. But this statement does not mean that all of his loss of isolation is attributable solely to the automobile; it has also been due to such factors as the telephone, the radio, rural mail delivery, and the printing press. Not many social effects are the result of one invention exclusively, though the popular language often seems to imply it.

In looking for the social effects of the airplane, many effects will be shown, but few will be due solely to the airplane. This will be particularly true of the more remote derivative effects.

Convergence and Demand

The joined effects of many inventions may be said to converge on a particular situation. Many different inventions, such as the automobile, tractor, farm machines, and agricultural science, converge to make farming a commercial business. Sometimes these inventional influences are additive. For instance, the suburb is the sum of a number of inventional influences flowing from the steam railroad, electric railway, auto bus, private automobile, telephone, motion picture, chain store, etc.

[5] J. H. Kolb and E. de S. Brunner, "Rural Life," in *Recent Social Trends,* Chap. X, p. 512.

One hypothesis to explain this concentration is that the convergence is due to demand. For example, there is a demand for dwellings with yards, trees, fresh air, and located near to cities; and various inventions are bent to produce the suburb. It is as though inventional influences flow into channels dug by demand. The demand for some means of overcoming fog created a channel into which many inventions flowed. There appear to be many more inventions than there are channels of demand. Hence their influences become channelized into a few social effects.

The relevance of this point for method of prediction lies in the fact that we can be more certain that an invention will produce a particular effect if we know that many other inventions or factors have similar additive or converging influences. If we find a strong demand which channels these inventional influences on the particular objective, then the probabilities of the prediction are still further increased. We may forecast that the airplane will lessen the significance of boundary lines between states, counties, and cities in the United States. This result seems probable in view of the speed and altitude of plane travel. Geographical barriers, such as mountains, deserts, and water, which were obstacles to surface transportation, do not hinder the airplane. We observe that the railroad and the automobile also have the effect of weakening boundary lines. Trade tends to flow between states, counties, and cities rather than being confined within a single unit. The demand is to trade freely and to get the material goods we want no matter where they are produced. Thus, the prediction that the airplane will weaken boundary lines is strengthened because of the convergence of these influences.

Social Trends

The converging of inventional and other influences into channels created by demand is steady and continuous over considerable periods of time. When any group of converging factors change more or less steadily for some time in the same general direction, we have a social trend.

Let us connect this idea of trend with the conception of derivative effects of inventions. We have noted that these derivative influences do not operate alone, but join with other influences, and that the derivative influence of any one invention seems to thin out and lose force. Furthermore, these derivative influences fan out in various directions. It therefore becomes rather difficult to isolate, trace out, and measure the derivative influences of an invention. But these influences are real and produce social changes, despite the fact that they are difficult to measure.

Yet there is a method of dealing with any one of this mesh of influences which is effective for many practical purposes. This is the method of relating derivative influences with trends. Suppose that the problem is to find the derivative effects of the airplane on religious missionary policies. The procedure would be to describe first the trends in the missionary movement, and then inquire whether aviation's influences were in harmony with, opposed to, or indifferent to these trends with regard to the particular matter under consideration. The trend in foreign missions has been to be concerned less and less with the various customs of the people which differ from those of the people from whom the missionaries come, but rather to focus attention on religion as such and on certain essential matters, as health practices. There is a growing appreciation for the different customs of other people by missionaries and less insistence upon conformity to the daily practices of the homeland. The influence of aviation is expected to reinforce this trend, since more frequent contacts with out-of-the-way places through air travel will tend in general to bring greater understanding and more tolerance of the customs of other people. Contacts break down strangeness and often bring understanding. Hence the influence of the airplane would be to increase tolerance of the attitudes of foreign peoples. Since airplanes make access to the lands of foreign missions easier, the influence might be to lessen the desire of foreign missionaries to change the non-religious customs of the people among whom they work. This tendency of aviation may, of course, be very slight, perhaps negligible. But the influence is in line with social trends and, however slight, will be added to them, and thus has that much more chance of making itself felt.

Similarly, the influence of aviation on the public schools may be considered. The trend in the curriculum of the schools is toward the practical and perhaps toward the vocational. Aviation leads to shop work in the school, practical physics, and even some ground training for flying; so its influence is in line with the trend toward utilitarianism in the curriculum.

As has been said, when the inventional influence is in line with social trends, its influence is more likely to be effective in producing practical results than if it were opposed to the trends. This point is, therefore, of pragmatic importance for planners. If we are concerned chiefly with what is likely to result, rather than with scientific analysis of influences as such, then a comparison of inventional influences with the trends is a good working rule.

Importance of Coverage

If an investigation is concerned with how civilization is likely to be different because of the coming of an important invention, then it must be concerned with social effects as well as uses. It is often the piling-up of many derivative effects that accounts for the changes in civilization. An account of the social influences of an invention calls for an extensive survey into perhaps many different customs and organizations, and a considerable coverage of the parts of civilization is needed. Now each particular influence of an invention in a segment of civilization could be studied intensively in order to reach as exact a scientific conclusion as possible. For instance, the influence of the airplane on foreign missions could be studied intensively and the results made into a monograph if there were such a need and if there were time available. But if coverage is needed, then many such influences must be studied. It is obvious that some sort of selection is necessary. If range is needed, then intensive study must be sacrificed. If intensive investigation is called for, then coverage must be slighted.

One practical way out of the dilemma is to consider planning the selective factor and to choose for emphasis those influences that ought to be considered in making plans, and to signalize the others rather than to study them intensively.

In thinking of the effects of an invention as matters with which planners should be concerned, an interesting question arises as to what point in time in the evolution of an invention, or of an inventional influence a planner should take hold. Newspapers may not consider it worth while to make plans in regard to the helicopter at this early stage in its development. They may think it best to make no plans until the helicopter has become "foolproof" and until it is known what the original cost and the upkeep will be. The same problem arises as to when it is desirable to purchase real estate and hold it against the day when it will be needed for an airport. Money so invested will be held idle when the property might be making a financial return. An additional factor is the uncertainty of what size of airport will be needed. If the size and nature of the airport of the future and its needed location could be reliably predicted, then some of the gamble in planning would be removed. But to buy and hold land for an uncertain airport may mean planning too far ahead.

Therefore, even if the selection for study of the many social effects of an important invention is made in the interests of planning, the fact exists that the time is ripe for some plans but not ripe for others, or at least for very definite plans. A wide survey of the social effects of an invention will be helpful in indicating what plans may be called for in the future in those cases where the time is not yet ready for planning.

The problem for this book is to tap wide ranges of information and to utilize all the imagination available. The information over extensive areas may come from libraries, current literature, or from contacts with persons in the various fields.

The value of imagination lies in getting what the researcher calls "hunches." It is valuable to get suggestions from many persons, since it is surprising how limited the imagination of any one person may be. An openmindedness toward new ideas is rather essential at this stage of the investigation — even to a negation of the critical faculties. This hospitality to new suggestions may even go so far as to welcome and consider the wildest of possibilities.

There comes a time in the investigation, however, when this entertaining of fanciful possibilities must be restricted and the critical faculty must be used with all techniques available. Judgment and appraisal must be made of the many suggestions previously collected.

A Forecast of Forecasting

The following study is a somewhat pioneer effort. Not many social scientists have seriously tried to find out in advance what an important invention will do to society. Indeed, most social scientists prefer to be historians and are less willing to venture an estimate of the future than the businessman or the ordinary citizen. The ability to look ahead with some success is particularly important in a changing society. The best way to learn to do anything is to go ahead and try it. That is what the Wright brothers did with the airplane. We learn by doing. What is needed is many social scientists working at the problem of forecasting the future as well as social scientists writing histories of past events. With many social scientists working on the future, we should gradually accumulate a set of useful procedures. The need for such a body of procedure is the reason for writing the section on method in this pioneer undertaking. In the course of time, with others working on forecasting, a tradition of usages will be built up, and we shall know better how to do it.

★ ★ ★ ★   **II. USES**

5

Technological Trends in Aviation

THE FUTURE SOCIAL EFFECTS of the airplane depend upon what the airplane in the future will be, not on what it is today. No great inventions are static in the early years of their history. The airplane has changed greatly during the past twenty-five years and it would be irrational to assume that these changes will stop as of today. It is desirable, then, that some consideration be given to the probable technological developments of aircraft and the various other inventions that are correlated with flying.

It is not easy to foresee the new inventions of the future, even when they are modifications of an existing invention. For instance, jet propulsion of airplanes burst suddenly on the aeronautical world in the 1940's, though it had been a subject of experimentation for a long time. Yet no one was very certain in the 1930's if or when these experiments would become practical.

The beginnings of new inventional developments are very often known, but the time of their success or failure can be predicted only with varying degrees of probability. The far distant inventions can hardly be foreseen at all, and certainly not with accuracy as to time. It would have been difficult to predict radio broadcasting in the nineteenth century. There are special difficulties in learning about new developments in aviation at the time of this writing because of the war. Aeronautical developments wear a cloak of secrecy in wartime. Still, admitting all these obstacles and difficulties, it seems imperative in a treatment of the effects of aviation on the future of our civilization to try to see the inventions in aviation that lie ahead in the visible future.

Since our primary interest is in the use of aviation and its social effects rather than in the technical mechanics of the inventions themselves, the discussion will be presented according to the social characteristics of the technologies. Indeed, it is often not necessary to predict the particular invention or improvement itself in order to predict the social effect, as was shown in the closing paragraphs of Chapter II. The increasing speed of airplanes might have been forecast from the trend line of speed increases in the past, with only a general knowledge of demand and of the fact that greater speed could be had from better streamlining, superior fuels, more horsepower, lighter engines, and travel in thinner air. What is needed is prediction of function rather than of form, and from function we may read the social implications. Nevertheless, a knowledge of the structure of particular inventions is useful.

ADAPTABILITY

Aviation, like transportation on land or on water, has a great variety of vehicles. Man's needs in air transportation are varied, and aviation is making the adaptation with many different kinds of aircraft. Outstanding classifications are those for war and those for peace; those for scheduled transportation and for personal flying; those for transportation of passengers, of mail, and of cargo; and, finally — by type — the airplane, rotor craft, dirigible, glider, and rocket.

Passenger Planes for Average Distances

Aside from those for purposes of war, the adaptations of aviation which are likely to have the most extensive social effects are those for transportation of passengers, cargo, and mail, and those smaller planes to be used for personal, business, and governmental uses. With regard to the transportation of passengers, the needs vary according to the distances to be traveled. The average distance traveled in domestic passenger aviation is about 500 miles. This average distance has been increasing nearly 20 miles per year, so that, in the latter part of the postwar decade, the average distance traveled may be 650 miles, unless a large development of "feeder" or local mileage pulls the average downward. Hence the type of airplane most suited to such an average distance is likely to be widely used. The DC-3, extensively used in civil passenger transportation today, carries two engines, seats twenty-two passengers, has a crew of three, and a gross weight of 12.6 tons. Its wing loading is 25.6 pounds per square foot and its cruising speed, 180 miles per hour. Specifications have been set up for the future short-haul plane by the Aircraft Requirements Committee of the Air Transport Association,[1] calling for a seating capacity of from twenty-five to thirty persons, convertible partially or fully in not more than twenty minutes into a cargo plane, with seats folded back, to carry 7000 pounds of cargo. Its maximum range is to be 800 miles, with a cruising speed of at least 200 miles an hour. Tricycle landing gear is specified and a runway of minimum length of 2500 feet. In the years following, improvements are likely in the direction of greater speed, higher wing loading, improved brakes, a larger ratio of disposable load to gross weight, lighter engines, and improved propellers, leading to greater efficiency and more economical operation.

For distances of 1000 or 1500 miles, there will also be a considerable amount of travel in the United States, as from Chicago to New York, or New Orleans to Minneapolis, or St. Louis to Denver. For these distances, a larger plane, built to carry forty to sixty passengers at cruising speeds of some three hundred miles an hour or more, is most suitable. Planes of this type have been ordered by the major airlines and a few are already flying. Some of these planes, equipped with pressurized cabins, will fly at 20,000 feet. While such planes are particularly well adapted to the above-mentioned distances, they are also appropriate in load and economy for distances as short as one-third or one-half the above figures. Since these planes are suitable for the whole range from 400 to 1800 miles, they are likely to carry a great deal of the traffic that travels the modal distance of 500 miles, unless a smaller plane of the general type of the A.T.A. specifications is found to be extraordinarily efficient or a large number of passengers are flying the relatively shorter distances.

[1] Charles Froesch, "Short Haul Transports," *Air Transport*, September, 1943, pp. 33, 34.

Planes for Local Traffic

Another type of needed adaptation is aircraft for stops at short distances, those of less than two hundred miles. Such carriers are at present frequently referred to as "feeder" planes, since they feed traffic into the main trunkline routes from near-by territory. These planes are seen as small ones carrying from six to twenty passengers, or the equivalent in cargo. Since air traffic under, say five hundred miles, is more expensive when the air journey is shorter and the plane is smaller, the technological developments needed for feeder planes are those that will make for economy of operation. Low costs for local air transportation are of great importance, since the success and extension of feeder air service is contingent upon exceptional economy. Cheaper operation could be obtained with single-motored planes and a crew of one person. On some routes over flat terrain and with emergency landing fields, these will be sufficiently safe. For other routes, twin engines will be safer. Another improvement is a landing gear that will bring the plane down on a one-way landing strip, no matter what the direction of the wind. The tricycle gear, which is expected to become widely used, will aid landing on such strips.

Another technical development may be the adaptation to the passenger feeder planes of the non-stop pick-up and delivery mechanism for mail and express. The adaptation to passenger planes is said to be technically possible with no discomfort or undue risk to passengers. The pick-up device is quite simple, requires no landing field, and the ground equipment for a town costs only around $150. For passenger planes, landings would be necessary. Even with non-stop, pick-up apparatus, the carrying of mail is expensive, but the total costs could be reduced if, in addition, passengers were carried between stations where there are landings. The plane could descend on signal and stop for passengers if there were any.

These feeder lines may also be serviced by helicopters if rotary aviation becomes cheap enough. The greatest utility of a helicopter bus will be within the limits of the more thickly populated areas surrounding or within a great metropolis. The marked advantage of the helicopter is that it can land closer to the center of a town than can a plane, representing a saving of time, which is quite necessary for short-distance travel if competition with the cheaper fares of the auto bus is to be successful. Sikorski, inventor of the earliest used helicopter in America, has testified that a helicopter bus for fifteen persons is feasible within two years after the end of the war. One has already been flown, carrying nine passengers. Still larger buses may not be needed, at least until there has been much further evolution of the helicopter. The prospect for the helicopter for "feeder" transportation is very good indeed.

The Very Large Planes

There will also be a demand for planes to fly non-stop from the Atlantic to the Pacific Coast, from America to London, or from San Francisco to Hawaii, distances of around 2500 miles. Such non-stop distances call for still larger planes which can carry an adequate payload in addition to the great amount of fuel needed. It is in the field of very large planes that the development of aeronautical engineering has been extraordinarily rapid. In 1910, the planes averaged around 800 pounds. A decade later, a trend line indicates a gross weight of 2500 pounds. In 1930, the gross weight was 13,000 pounds, and in 1940, around 38,000 pounds.[2] In 1943, a seaplane weighing 160,000 pounds and a land plane weighing 90,000 pounds were built; and, in 1945, a plane of 130,000 pounds, which will carry 100 passengers, flew across the American continent. The largest plane on regular order by the airlines is one of 320,000 pounds, suitable for 204 passengers. Orders for fifteen such planes are said to have been placed. During the war, an experimental wooden plane of 400,000 pounds, capable of transporting 700 soldiers, was in the process of construction. Producers and designers talk of even larger planes. De Seversky speaks of a plane of 750,000 pounds, and Glenn Martin of one of 600,000 pounds, while Sikorski says that a monster of 1,000,000 pounds could be built by 1950, but doubts that it ever will be.

Indeed, one does not speak of limits in the face of such con-

[2] From figures supplied by W. W. Davies, United Air Lines.

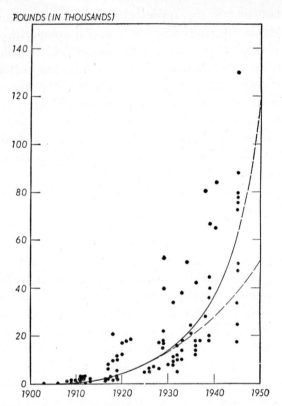

Figure 10.   GROSS WEIGHT TRENDS IN AIRPLANES

The planes are getting larger as shown by the gross weights, which represent the weight of the empty plane plus a full load.

The dots represent kinds of transport planes in the United States and
the two diverging free-hand trend lines suggest two possible trends up to
1950. The chart and the data are from W. W. Davies of the United Air
Lines, as is the next chart in this chapter.

tinuing rapid increases in size. Yet, practically, there will be
limits to the size of planes, just as the height of skyscrapers or the
size of ocean steamships have reached limits. Such limits may be
set by economics rather than by technology. In the case of airplanes, a definite limitation of the capacity of planes and of the
numbers of large planes is the preference of the public for more
frequent schedules with smaller planes rather than fewer trips
in very large planes.

Small Planes for Private Flying

An adaptation of aviation equal in importance to the passenger transport is that of making the light plane really useful to many individuals, families, businesses, and government. The development of such planes has received less attention from engineers and manufacturers than has the passenger transport plane. These aircraft are discussed further in the chapter on private flying, where it is indicated that there will be a demand for aircraft that will also travel on the ground like an automobile. Because of this great demand, the achievement of a combination automobile and aircraft is to be expected, since the engineering obstacles are not insuperable. For the plane, a pusher propeller in the rear appears to be more suited for a vehicle that is to move along the crowded highways.

A possible but more remote development for some small planes is the use of jet propulsion.[3] Of the many advantages of jet planes, an important one is the economy at relatively high altitudes, where the speed may be very great. But, at the same time, rather large loads of fuel are required, although improvements may be made in this regard. Even now, it would seem that jet-propelled planes suitable for distances of one thousand or fifteen hundred miles' range are practicable. The mechanism of the small turbojet engine is simpler, more easily processed, while the plane gives a smoother, noiseless ride. A variety of small planes for private flying will be demanded, and it is not improbable that there will be some demand for a jet-propelled private plane.

There are other novel suggestions, not yet adequately tested. One is the controllable wing, which serves also as rudder, elevator, and ailerons, with the result that the body of the plane is parallel to the earth, irrespective of the angle of ascent or descent. Such a wing might be more readily adaptable to a roadable plane, since it could be swung to take the direction of the road, instead of being perpendicular to it.

Any inventions that would enable the small plane to take off and land on shorter runways would be a distinct aid in its adapta-

[3] Hall L. Hibbard, "Jet Propulsion — for War and Peace," lecture at the University of California, May 15, 1945, p. 67.

tion to personal use, especially in congested areas. Since the demand may be strong for such properties, there will be some devices forthcoming to this end. Present thought on this problem is concerned with the changeable pitch and braking of propellers, with wing flaps and three- or four-wheeled landing gear with wheels swiveling for cross-winds.

The further adaptation of the small plane for private use involves no startling inventions except roadability, but rather the improvement of its qualities, following known lines of progress. The desiderata are freedom from stall and spin, radio and other instrumentation, especially an absolute altimeter. Still other desired qualities are those for safety, simplicity, ease of learning, cheapness, durability, small-landing-field requirements, vision, noise reduction, and speed. Such improvements are easy to make singly, but difficult to reconcile with each other; for instance, most of them militate against cheapness, simplicity, and speed.

The Helicopter

Of the rotor craft, the autogiro seems destined to be superseded by the helicopter, which is yet in its early developmental stages. Its adaptability to the needs of private flying is discussed in the chapter on private flying. Of outstanding importance in its further development is the perfection of an engine against stoppage of power and a device which will break the speed of descent as the helicopter nears the ground when the power is off. The helicopter should also be roadable for adequate adaptation to the needs of the user; and since an earlier autogiro was constructed to travel forty miles an hour on the highway, it seems reasonable to forecast that the helicopter will also have power applied to its wheels. Roadability, though, may wait upon the solution of various other problems of development. These are the simplification of the controls, reduction of vibration, and choice of methods of eliminating torque. The elimination of torque by co-axial rotors driven in opposite directions on the same axis yields a short and compact craft that appears to be best suited of the models yet presented for highways, yard landings, and family garages, though little has been published about the other characteristics and limitations of this type.

Gliders

During the war, the tow-plane with detachable gliders was used to transport large numbers of soldiers in areas where there were no adequate landing fields for the usual plane. The adaptation of the glider to general peacetime use is not certain. Cost, as always, is important. Since a glider is much cheaper than a plane, a glider and its tow-plane may be cheaper to construct than a plane of equivalent capacity; but the cost of operation, involving an additional pilot for the glider, less speed, and greater drag, may be greater than the cost of operation of a plane alone. The usefulness of a glider exists mainly in its flexibility and in the saving of time by not having to land the tow-plane. Just as it is adapted to some military operations, so it might be useful in such special peacetime functions as transporting men and supplies to unexplored regions, to forests in time of fire, or in special cargo operations for certain types of shippers. A more general use probably implies a well-organized and extensive transportation of cargo by air.

The technical developments that will occur with its possible wider use are an articulation in design of the glider with that of the tow-plane and the perfection of non-stop, pick-up machinery, as well as a device for wheeling the glider into suitable positions for loading and picking up. These technical developments will be easily made if there is demand for the glider. Obviously, the use of gliders could be much more widespread if they could be flown and landed without a pilot in the glider. While such a possibility may be seen theoretically, it is not at present in the realm of realism.

Amphibians

An adaptation of aviation that is needed is the plane that will land on water or on land. Such an amphibian would be very useful in undeveloped countries where there are lakes, rivers, and flat terrain. Also, transportation liners may, in some cases, need the capacity to land in harbors or seaports or at airports of inland cities. Such were the early planes of the Pan American Airways Company. However, amphibians are not very efficient planes. One of the main difficulties is that to land on water the propellers must be high enough not to strike the water. For this reason seaplanes have required a deep and bulky body, which has meant a great deal of drag. With the advent of the jet plane, operating without propellers, it seems possible to avoid the type of fuselage which seaplanes now have. Likewise, a plane with turbo-driven propellers for middle altitudes that could rise from the water by jet propulsion, with propellers temporarily feathered and still, could have a lower body with less drag.

The helicopter is particularly well suited to alighting on water or land. This is made possible by the use of inflated rubber bags, which enable the helicopter to land on snow or ice, and, if the ice is thin, the inflated rubber will remain afloat on water. No vehicle ever invented has so great an adaptability in landing as the helicopter.

Rockets

From jet-propelled planes to rockets is not a great step. The chief difference is that the jet plane depends upon air taken in from the atmosphere for combustion, while the rocket carries all its oxygen and fuel inside and is hence independent of the atmosphere and can travel at any altitude. For a long while, work with rockets was considered a fanciful hobby, but their use by the Germans as a war weapon in 1944 and 1945 proved that they had become very practical indeed. The German V-2 rocket, weighing twelve tons, is said to have carried a ton of explosives two hundred miles, at a speed of probably three thousand miles per hour; that is, four times the speed of sound at sea level. With such spectacular success in the early stages of the rocket, one hesitates to consider its increase in size and range as unlikely, particularly in view of the impetus that preparation for war may give to their development. Some rockets are without wings and so are not airplanes, but many do have wings, and an airplane may be driven by a rocket. Eventually, the rocket may be used for the transportation of cargo or persons. Before this is possible, however, it will be necessary to be able accurately to direct the rocket to a given locality, to solve the problem of heat caused by friction from the air, and to devise some method of slowing up the descent of the rocket as it nears its destination. These requirements are considered theoretically possible, even to the extent of making feasible the transporting of human beings.[4] The high speeds of the rocket are not believed to be harmful to man.

Not much can be said about the degree of development of the rocket in the near future, but, even though there is little to make us think that they may be put to practical use other than in carrying explosives, still, in any perspective of technological trends in aviation, the future of rockets ought to have mention. However, it is only their improvement as an explosive weapon of warfare that is foreseen with any degree of certainty in the visible future. The civilian demand for them would seem to be only for urgencies requiring great speed, and in most such instances other devices, such as telephone, telegraph, radio, facsimile transmission, etc., can be used.

Miscellaneous Adaptations

That there will be many miscellaneous specializations of aircraft other than those previously mentioned is certain. For instance, the helicopter principle may lead to the use of these craft for elevator purposes in connection with construction work, in forestry, in conflagrations, etc. Aircraft may also be equipped with gun mounts for shooting predatory animals. Similarly, special equipment will be needed for spraying fruit trees and various crops. Already the helicopter of the Coast Guard carries special apparatus for rescue work. These adaptations are, in general, to be viewed as minor ones from the point of view of technology and do not require any great changes in the existing or projected types to perform these multiform functions.

In addition to these general adaptations of various types of aircraft and their possible technical evolution, there remain to be

[4] G. Edward Pendray, "Passenger Flights by Rocket," *Harper's Magazine*, March, 1945, pp. 353-358.

discussed certain specializations of aviation in particular functions, such as safety, speed, economy, and comfort.

SAFETY

Technological developments to insure safety in flight are obviously of greatest importance, both for scheduled passenger flights
and for private flying. In scheduled flights most accidents occur
in landing, in leaving the ground, and in flying into obstacles
en route. As with the automobile, few accidents occur because
of defects in the machine, so careful is the workmanship and so
good the testing. Rather, the causes are due to the weather or to
pilot error, which is the source of well over 50 per cent of accidents. In the future many accidents may occur due to the effort
to reduce to as few as possible the canceled flights and to lessen
the number of unfinished scheduled flights by flying in all kinds
of weather. This goal cannot be achieved without technical aids,
for neither the airlines nor the controlling authorities will sanction
flights in bad weather unless mechanisms which increase safety
are used.

Electronics

Of these safety developments, great promise is expected from
the device popularly known as radar, so effective during the
war in locating as small an object as a distant enemy plane and
measuring its speed and distance on the principle of reflection
applied to radio waves. Radar is expected to be very useful in
warning of mountains and of other planes, into which pilots sometimes crash. This echo principle of the radio wave will also measure the altitude of a plane, not above sea level, as other instruments do now, but above the underlying ground, no matter what
the altitude of the land surface may be, a service of great value in
flying over mountains.

Planes should be able to land at airfields with a high degree of
safety, more or less irrespective of rain and fog. Proper radio in-
stallations will land a plane without the aid of a pilot and may
be used in some cases at some time in the future. Such installa-

tions are expected in civilian aviation, but some years will be required to make the adaptations. Pilots of planes which are equipped with radar may also see through a blanket of clouds. An outline of a city or an airport covered by a fog appears sketched on a panel in the plane. It has been with this device that bombers have been able to locate targets which were otherwise invisible. Accidents due to lack of visibility or to striking obstructions on descent should be progressively eliminated. It is not unreasonable to expect that these radar aids will be used in connection with television apparatus, giving much clearer vision. Indeed, some experimentation has been done along these lines.

Landings and Wind

Wind has never been a great problem in landing at airports with an adequate number of runways, so that the pilot may land into the wind no matter in what direction it blows. Difficulties with wind may become more frequent if small airports are increasingly used which have fewer runways, giving less choice of direction for landing into the wind. The problem of wind is not so great if these small fields have two runways perpendicular to each other. The demand is always for landing fields closer in to the resident population of a city, and the smaller the field, the closer in it can be built. Also it is desirable for a plane in transit to shorten its time in and around an airport. Taxiing time is lessened on airfields with one runway.

The tricycle landing gear, which enables a plane to land in cross-winds, is becoming more common. Some device is needed which will enable the airframe to point into the wind while the plane proceeds on the runway. One suggestion is to land in a cradle on wheels, the plane having no landing gear. This would have the additional advantage of saving that much weight. The plane could be guided to the cradle automatically. The problem is important, since its solution would mean smaller airports and hence more convenient ones.

Weather

Violent winds have at times proved dangerous in some flights off the regular routes for scheduled transports, particularly where adequate weather reports were not available. The perils of extreme weather conditions are not conquered yet for aviation, although high-altitude flying offers generally a very appreciable reduction. Such hazards are sure to be guarded by extensions of weather reporting and of research in this field.

Students of weather forecasting tell us that aviation, particularly during the war, has made weather research a three-dimensional enterprise. Hitherto, little was known of the movements of air high above the earth, especially over 35,000 feet, and of their influence on determining barometric pressures, wind movements, and fog near the earth's surface. Much more knowledge is to be expected which will make weather forecasting even more accurate. Good weather reporting is a most important ally of flying; hence an extensive network of weather-reporting stations is necessary in all areas where planes fly.

Icing is still one of the weather hazards. Icing on any part of the plane is bad, since it adds weight and increases drag. Heat can be applied successfully to prevent freezing in the carburetor, and some carburetors are so constructed that icing is avoided without heat. Icing in the carburetor is not a problem in the jet-propelled plane, for it burns fuel directly. The Germans have also used, in planes with the reciprocating engine, the direct injection of fuel into the air stream. Icing may be prevented to some extent on the propellers, where it is a very serious problem, by rubber shoes along the edge, and there are proposals to pipe heat to the edges of the whole propeller. It is said that icing does not occur over the United States at altitudes above 30,000 feet, or 20,000 feet in the cold of winter, so that high-altitude flying may be helpful in preventing icing.

Fire

Another danger in modern flying is fire, a peril which will be accentuated by the new very high-octane fuels with a low flash point. However, the making of fuels with more than 100-octane values with a high flash point is now quite practical. Indeed, some very great successes have been reported in this field, and the adoption of such fuels will greatly reduce the fire hazard. Oil is another source of fire, since oil sprayed on an object with a temperature of 330° Centigrade will ignite but not explode. Loss of life in plane crashes is caused by fire as well as by the fall. However, fire in airplanes is a rare occurrence.

Reducing Pilot Error

With the extension of private flying by amateurs, the problem of safety becomes much greater, since it will not be possible to exercise careful supervision over the many private fliers. Nor will the average skill among private fliers be as great as among professional pilots on the airliners. Even though private aircraft are mechanically perfect, the failure of human beings as pilots in private flying will cause many deaths. Realizing this, designers are working on devices to reduce pilot error.

All planes, except a few of the new safety types of light planes, have a stalling speed below which the plane suddenly falls out of control. Remedies, which have proved feasible but not widely accepted, are either instruments to warn of the approach of a stall, or a design of the plane so that it will automatically nose down to regain the necessary speed.

Since planes must land at considerable speeds, from thirty to over a hundred miles an hour, it is very easy for them to topple over on landing, especially if they have only two wheels. A base of three wheels, or four, is much safer, even though they add to wind resistance and weight to be lifted. The tricycle landing gear is expected to be rapidly adopted for large planes as well as for small ones. If the small planes become roadable, they will have four wheels.

The helicopter would seem to present fewer hazards than the small plane. With a helicopter, instead of landing at great speed, the pilot, like an automobile driver, comes to a stop slowly. The danger, however, in a helicopter lies in involuntary stoppage of the engines. Engines may stop for want of gas, but it is possible to make some sort of warning signal when the gas gets below a certain point. Engines also stop from failures in the mechanism. These will be much more serious than failures in an automobile engine. The problem of safety for the helicopter is further discussed in the chapter on private flying.

In conclusion, we may note that the record of increasing safety in aviation is phenomenal. The projected curves of diminishing accident rates give great confidence for the future. However, there remains much to be done, and new hazards arise. These new hazards may be due to the pressure to maintain schedules irrespective of weather, the demand to extend flying to the general public, and the desire to use small airfields. But, with each hazard, suggestions of new inventions and new developments are made to overcome the new dangers. Perhaps the most difficult problem to solve is that of reducing pilot error, but signals and other aids will be developed.

SPEED

The supreme achievement of aviation is speed. It may seem that we have been traveling fast enough, but, as more speed becomes available, it is used. There seems to be no limit to our demand for speed. Then, too, speed is efficient in aviation because of the greater use of the crew and capital investment in planes in a given amount of time — though there is a most economical speed for any specific plane. At any one time, the average speed used is far less than the fastest possible, but peak speeds in one decade may become average speeds in another decade.

In 1910, the average cruising speed of airplanes was 45 miles per hour. The average was 72 miles per hour in 1920. By 1930, it had become 145. In 1940, the unweighted average cruising speed of the different planes was about 220 miles, though passenger planes commonly cruised at around 180 miles per hour.[5] During the war, speed, particularly for fighter planes, was all-important in attacking and in escaping. Their speeds were well above 400 miles an hour. Horizontal speeds of between 500 and 600 miles an hour are supposed to have been attained by some army planes. A jet plane, the P-80, in 1945, flew 545 miles in 62 minutes from Dayton, Ohio, to La Guardia Field, and this has been referred to as a slow

5 From figures supplied by W. W. Davies, United Air Lines.

MILES PER HOUR

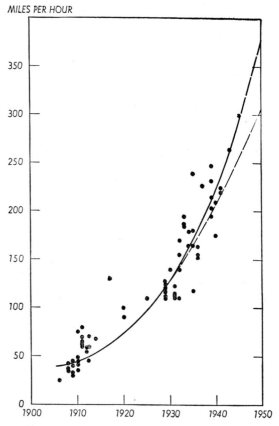

Figure 11.   THE CRUISING SPEED TREND

The trend of the cruising speed like the maximum speed is sharply upward. The cruising speed is usually around 15 per cent below the rated
R.P.M. and is approximately 60 per cent of the rated horsepower.

flight. In a few cases, planes are said to have traveled at 780 miles
an hour in a dive, or faster than the speed of sound, which at sea
level is 760 miles per hour. That the war experience in producing
speed will be transferred to civilian planes is certain. The new big
planes cruise at around 300 miles per hour, and some of them at
nearly 350 miles. One airline is said to be planning for world
tours with a cruising speed of 425 miles per hour.[6] It may well

[6] *Aviation News*, November 13, 1944, p. 12.

be that, in the second decade after the war, cruising speeds will be even greater, especially if jet passenger transports are used to fly at very high altitudes.

Speed is gained through improvements in either the power plant or the airframe of the plane. Probably the development of airplane engines has gone ahead of the improvements in the body of the plane. At least the structure seems to be more of a limiting factor on speed than the engine as it exists today, or as it is almost certain to be in the very near future.[7]

The Airframe

Of first importance in the design of the body of the plane is the smooth flow of air over the surfaces, especially when it is flying at higher speeds. The "laminar-flow" technique, just coming into use, refines the curves of the airframe and the propeller blade and smooths the surface until even dust is objectionable; in one case, the use of military paint instead of waxed metal reduced the speed by twelve miles per hour. A wing was invented in 1937 at Langley Field which preserved the laminar flow from becoming turbulent, almost to the back edge of the wing, reducing drag 67 per cent, which should raise the speed 30 per cent, if practical. A great help to laminar flow is the application of the power behind rather than before the wing, through pusher screws or jet propulsion. Turbine engines are much more neatly housed than the reciprocating type and hence are easier to bury in the rear of the wing. One of the new big civilian transport planes already announced is expected to have six of these engines placed in the rear of the wing.

A difficulty encountered with laminar flow at great speeds is that the light, thin metal covering the wing tends to wrinkle, causing a certain amount of turbulence and reducing speeds. This type of drag may be overcome with new materials, such as other metals, plastics, or even glass. It is also possible that lighter materials than the present metal alloys may be found. A sub-

---

[7] Sir A. H. Roy Fedden, *Aircraft Power Plant — Past and Future*, a Wilbur Wright Memorial Lecture for 1944. London: Aeronautical Reprint no. 99, pp. 100-101, 113.

stance like glass would have greater tensile strength and enable the construction of a wing which is thinner near the edges.

The fuselage and tail cause nearly half the drag in an airplane; hence there have always been designs for eliminating them as far as possible. While the "flying wing" presents great opportunities for lessened drag and greater speed, it has not been well adapted to transport use because of the great size needed to provide vertical space for human beings. It is also very delicate of balance. However, planes are now reaching the requisite size, and there are also compromise designs, widening the fuselage. Flying wings are expected to be very large even for cargo, and hence best adapted to long flights with large loads.

Propellers

The smooth flow of air around the propeller blades is another desideratum for speed, the achievement of which has already attained a high degree of success. As engine power increases, the propeller tips travel faster, approaching the sonic limit. This speed can be kept down by providing increased blade area through more blades or broader ones, and by increasing the pitch. Two propellers contrarotating on one axis also eliminate torque and some wasted rotation of the slipstream.

Jet Propulsion

Propeller problems are eliminated in the invention of the airplane propelled by a jet of escaping gas instead of by whirling propeller blades. These planes were used as pursuit and fighter planes during the war, especially for high-altitude flying. Their speed is discussed in terms of its approximation to the speed of sound, which is 650 miles per hour in the sub-stratosphere, 110 miles less than at sea level. The speed of sound has loomed like a blank wall against further progress of air speeds, and already has become a hampering factor. At that point the air ceases to be easily pushed aside and is piled up in a heated compression wave somewhat like the breaking wave at the bow of a boat, which has the effect of practically stopping an ordinary plane. Furthermore, the effect begins long before the plane has reached the speed of sound — even at 350 miles per hour — in corners where the airflow is crowded and hence hurried, and at the propeller tips. The increase in resistance is particularly rapid after 500 miles per hour. There is some indication that the coefficient of resistance reaches its maximum at the speed of sound, and falls thereafter until some 1500 miles per hour is reached, at which it levels off.[8]

But the remedies are obvious: substitute jet propulsion for the propeller, eliminate the corners, thin the surfaces, and sharpen the leading edges. Speeds a little faster than sound appear already to have been achieved in military diving; but how much can be accomplished in level flying in transport planes remains to be seen. A great deal of research has been carried on under military secrecy and will be continued in the future. One problem is to overcome the buffeting which the pilots and passengers may experience at these tremendous speeds. In addition, there is the problem of the heat generated by the friction of the air. The V-2 rockets are reported to have traveled at four times the speed of sound, high in the stratosphere, and, upon descending, they were heated red-hot externally by air friction.

Jet planes have certain other advantages. One is the low specific weight of the engines, perhaps half that of a reciprocating engine of the same power. This compensates largely for the greater weight of fuel required. The simplicity of the unit makes it much easier to install, remove, repair, and recondition. Especially important is the unit's smaller bulk, permitting well-streamlined inclusion within a wing or fuselage.

The jet-propulsion plane has been found most appropriate for high-speed, high-altitude flying in war planes, with ranges up to about fifteen hundred miles. The first step for their use in civil aviation will be carrying relatively small payloads of great time-utility for hops of a thousand or fifteen hundred miles, at somewhat lower speeds than the jet fighters have reached. Beyond such a use our vision of possibilities is not clear. But since the evolution of the jet plane is just beginning, we should not be blind to possible greater adaptability to civil uses.

[8] Hibbard, *op. cit.*, p. 12.

Jet propulsion may be combined with the internal combustion or gas turbine, and the proportions and ways of combining may be various. Any jet engine requires for efficiency some means of compressing the feed air and forcing it into the combustion chamber, and, except in the buzz-bomb, this is always accomplished by installing a gas turbine in the exhaust jet, which drives, on the same shaft, a rotary blower to compress the feed air. One could also fit on the same shaft a propeller to drive the plane at lower speeds and altitudes. There would be no gain of engine power, but there would be an advantage due to the fact that the propeller is more efficient than jet propulsion at the lower speeds and altitudes. One good form of the combination is proposed by Sir A. H. Roy Fedden.[9] He suggests a 100-ton transport with a fuselage but no tail surfaces, with four gas turbines buried in its wings, and with air ducts from the leading to the trailing edges of the wings. Each develops about three-fourths of its power through turbines and co-axial propellers, and about one-fourth from the exhaust jet; but it seems probable that the proportions could be varied according to the altitude.

The advantages of jet propulsion, gas turbines, and combinations of them are that the mechanism is simple, reliable, light, of small bulk, and adapted to streamlining into a wing. Further advantages of both, but more particularly of the jet form, are an almost complete elimination of vibration and noise, the ability to use cheaper fuel, and possible lowering of the wing level, when propellers are eliminated. A disadvantage of both new engines, at least in their present state of development, is a higher rate of fuel consumption, requiring heavier loads of fuel and cutting down the payload, particularly on long, over-ocean hops. A principal obstacle to both new motors, especially for small types, but one which is being progressively overcome, is the difficulty of finding suitable metals for the blades of the gas turbines necessary in both; that is, metals that can keep their shape and fit in close clearances, and resist corrosion and abrasion, while constantly red-hot. The main opportunity for heightened efficiency seems to lie in metals which are able to stand greater heat and bright, hard alloys like stainless steel and stellite.

9 Fedden, op. cit., p. 110.

Fuel

Every engine is designed for a certain kind of fuel, and vice versa. A continuing modification of gasoline for higher-octane numbers — that is, ability to resist detonation under ever higher compression — has brought, with the addition of an exhaust gas turbine for supercharging, greater efficiency to the reciprocating engine. Hundred-octane gasoline has become standard in military flying, and blends with triptane run up to 150-octane. All these will be available for civilian aviation, in so far as the reciprocating engine continues in use, and where motors are built to utilize the high compression. With the new engines — gas turbine, jet, and rocket — these expensive gasolines are useless, since there is no detonation possible, but only steady burning, and cheaper fuels, such as kerosene, petroleum, or others yet to be proved, will give the speeds possible with the turbo-jet planes.

Small Planes

The foregoing discussion has in the main been concerned with the speeds of transport passenger planes. Some or much of this speed may also work its way down to the light plane. Most of these now fly at low speeds, around a hundred miles an hour. Such slow speeds are not useful for covering long distances, and the traveler could often go more quickly by airliner or day-and-night express train, and far more cheaply, easily, safely, and dependably. There is the possibility that the jet engine may be used in the small personal plane, not only for its speed, but also for its other qualities, such as increased vision, quietness, simplicity, and lack of vibration. A jet engine flying easily two hundred miles an hour at ten thousand feet would have but half the weight of a reciprocating engine, and so could carry twenty-five or thirty more gallons of fuel. The adaptation of the turbine to the small plane presents problems because of the very little space between the rotating and the stationary blades, but presumably it can be achieved. So, also, improvement in fuel economy is related to the degree of heat the blade metal can stand. The turbo-jet small plane would probably be used, at least for a time, only by pilots wishing to travel at great speeds and heights for medium distances.

With regard to the helicopter, there is much.debate about how fast it may fly. The limiting factor is the speed of the rotor-blade tips, supposedly limited practically near the speed of sound. To achieve greater speed in the rotors and to meet the problem of torque, an idea long experimented with is propulsion by tangential jets from each blade tip. At present the idea seems to be little developed, though H. L. Hibbard, Lockheed engineer, predicts a helicopter driven by jets within a decade after the war.[10] The problem of speed of the helicopter has as yet not been a great concern of the engineers, who are more bothered with other matters, such as torque, controls, and vibration. When more attention can be given to speed, it is reasonable to expect considerably higher speeds than the present rates of around a hundred miles an hour, at least in helicopters for commercial transportation.

Lessening of Delays

Speed, so far in the discussion, has been viewed as a function exclusively of the aircraft in flight. Speed to the consumer, however, is also a function of time involved in stopping at an airport, and of forces other than the plane's speed. Delays *en route* are caused by frequency of stops, circling the airport, planes stacked up awaiting their turn to land, taxiing, loading and unloading, and flights canceled or diverted in bad weather. Most of these can be reduced by devices using radar and other electronic inventions, which, in fog or cloudy weather, can produce outlines on instrument screens in the plane, not only of other aircraft, but of objects on the ground. Similarly, electronics can give pictures to the control tower of approaching planes and measure their distances away. Much can be done to decrease the over-all time by better planning without any inventions of note. For instance, at the smaller airports, by better layout, the time of taxiing may be reduced. The loading of passenger planes could be speeded if each person carried his own luggage. For cargo, various known devices, such as movable bins and tie-down platforms, conveyor belts, and so on, can speed the loading and unloading.

[10] *C. A. A. Journal*, June 15, 1945, p. 67.

ECONOMY

A widespread adoption of flying depends upon cost; and the more people that fly, the greater will be the impact of aviation on society. There are many ways in which costs may be reduced. Foremost among these are large markets, enabling mass production and greater utilization of airline facilities. Other gains in economy may be had through better organization and increased efficiency in production, loading, scheduling, and tie-in with surface transport, especially through the helicopter bus. Lower costs can also be had by simpler accommodations for cheaper-class travelers. Our inquiry here does not concern these social and business types of economies, but rather those that technical invention may bring. It is difficult, however, to say much in general about the economies to come from invention, because, in the nature of the case, little is known about the costs of the devices to come. It is when improvements have matured and are adopted and marketed in great numbers that we can speak most authoritatively about costs. However, a few conclusions can be drawn definitely about some improvements, while others are so suggestive that some comment should be made.

Plane Design and Power Plant

In the preceding paragraphs dealing with the possibilities of increased speed, it was shown that design of planes for less resistance and achievement of laminar flow increases speed. Such better designing in general costs little, if any, more. This reduction of drag gets more distance out of a given amount of fuel, labor, and equipment, and hence assures economies. Other factors of design relate to heavier wing loading, improved engines, the better adaptation of the size of plane to the range required, etc. Economies from these changes are discussed in some detail in the chapters dealing with passenger and cargo rates.

This subject was treated by Edward Warner in his Wilbur Wright Memorial Lecture of 1943, when the turbo-jet plane was not yet flying. In Table 1 are listed economies in percentage reductions on DC-3 performance of operating costs for different degrees of technical improvements in the various parts of a transport plane. These percentages are not additive. The table shows that the technological improvements that are realizable will bring substantial economies.

TABLE 1.* ECONOMIES RESULTING FROM SPECIFIC IMPROVEMENT IN PLANES, BASED UPON STUDIES OF THE DC-3.

Assumed Change in Characteristics	Resultant reductions in percentages of operating costs (same cruising speed before as after change) at 10,000 feet.	
	At 200 m.p.h.	At 300 m.p.h.
1. Reduction of 33% in profile drag of wing, together with 20% reduction in parasite drag excluding wing.	10	20
2. Increase of 5% in propulsive efficiency.	3	10
3. Reduction of 10% in specific fuel consumption.	3	10
4. Reduction of 10% in unit weight of power plant.	4	15
5. Reduction of 10% in structural weight.	6	12
6. Reduction of 10% in weight of passenger accommodation.	3	3
7. Reduction of 50% in accident hazard.	3	3

* Edward Warner, "Post-War Transport Aircraft," 31st Wilbur Wright Memorial Lecture, reprinted in Aeronautical Engineering Review, October, 1943, p. 33

Technological development in aviation has been so rapid, especially during the war, that better designs appear every year, and great improvements have been made in economy, speed, and safety. However, demand for standard planes has kept flying many types a decade or more old. Improvements in the airframe are correlated with those in the power plant. The present type of engine is becoming enormously complicated and is not losing much weight per horsepower. But if the turbine and/or jet engines are used, as is now expected, their simplicity may not only save weight and space and promote speed and safety, but also is likely to save over-all costs. This prospect is not known, but the new engines' tested qualities justify such speculations. Further in the future we may have mail rockets of supersonic speed, perhaps unmanned, and the employment of atomic power.

Assisted Take-Offs

Inventions that may lead to substantial economies are devices to assist a plane in its take-off, particularly planes driven by reciprocating engines. These engines can carry a bigger load at full speed through the air than they can lift off a field of any reasonable length and approach-slope. There are various devices for assisting a plane into the air with its heavy load. During the war, rockets proved very useful. Rocket cartridges are inserted below the wing, and these give a strong lift to the plane for a few seconds, until they are spent and dropped off. In wartime, costs were not so significant as the shortage of big airports at the desired locations. Another useful method of assisting the take-off is the injection of water into the engine, reducing the very great heat and gaining more power. The take-off is said to be smoother with the water injection attachments than with the rocket. Not much can be said about the economies of such inventions without price figures; but presumably large planes of highest wing-loading may find appreciable savings by assisted take-offs. Indeed, it is thought that the extra payload carried by rocket-assisted take-offs might not only more than pay the cost of the rockets, but also permit lower cargo rates, because of the larger payload carried. This point is somewhat important in the transportation of cargo, where low rates are particularly needed for its development.

There are also varieties of other means which have been tried for helping a plane off the ground, such as a cable catapult; and, if substantial savings can be made through such aids, there will be a great demand for them, which should lead to the working-out of some methods that will be advantageous economically.

Other Possibilities

Of the various other miscellaneous modifications that may bring economies, the plane's equipment presents possibilities for lower costs, provided the public foregoes its demand for luxurious treatment. Upholstering can be sacrificed, making a saving in weight and in cost of seating. A well-designed seat without padding is more comfortable than a badly fitting chair with thick upholstery. Then, too, research on light materials, such as magnesium, may yield notable savings in weight. That such changes may be expected is indicated by proposals for varying classes of service. The equivalent of second- or third-class service in planes would embody the aforementioned economies.

As to planes constructed from other materials than aluminum and magnesium alloys, such as steel, plastics, or plywood, there seems to be little movement for radical changes. A few stainless-steel cargo planes were constructed during the war, and there have always been numerous plywood and fabric types of material. It seems doubtful that these materials will be used in future transports, and, if used, their economies will not be great.

While there are assured economies due to future technological developments in aviation, particularly in airframe design and larger size, and probably in engines, some of the improvements add to costs. Such is the case with radar equipment, radio services, various other instruments to aid in navigation, pressurizing, and air-conditioning. But the balance is probably much on the side of greater economy.

COMFORT

Anything new in technics that increases the comfort of the air passenger is surprisingly important, for comfort, as well as speed and safety, affects the amount of use of a vehicle, especially by first-class passengers.

High Altitudes

Of interest in this connection are the inventions that affect flight at high altitudes. There are a number of reasons for flying at high altitudes, such as less air resistance; avoidance of high mountains, clouds, plane collisions, storms, and icing; availability of celestial navigation; and choice of dependable winds, some of which are very fast. The large amount of high-altitude flying in the war has yielded experience of importance. The low barometric pressure and decreased oxygen has led to the use of oxygen masks and special clothing (not suitable for civil use), and exhaust-turbine-driven superchargers which compress air for the engine, and also of pressurized cabins. Then, too, the demand for altitude flying in combat speeded the production of·jet-propelled and rocket planes, which are well suited to flying at great altitudes. How do these inventions leading to high flying affect the comfort of the passenger? As yet, there has been very little flying of passengers at high altitudes, although a few pressurized transports have been built, and many placed on order.

In flying at altitudes of 15,000 to 20,000 feet or over, a great gain in comfort as well as in safety is effected because of the avoidance of storms and the bumpiness which is encountered when flying closer to the earth's surface and which is caused by the variations in the contour of the land, especially in mountainous regions. In fact, flying is said to be smoother the higher one goes. On the other hand, when traveling at high altitudes, fliers have encountered, in some latitudes, very strong winds moving more or less horizontally. Those who flew in the pressurized B-29 bomber over Japan reported, at times, winds of very high velocities which greatly impeded the progress of the missions. Varying the altitude makes possible some choice in winds and the direction in which they blow. It seems, then, that the inventions which achieve flying at high altitudes make for a more comfortable journey most of the time, provided, of course, that the cabins are air-conditioned and pressurized.

Vibration, Room, and Noise

High-altitude flying will be the practice only on long journeys, which generally mean large planes. In turn, large planes present opportunities for less crowding, more conveniences, and freer moving about on the part of the passengers, all of which are much appreciated by travelers on long trips. To remain seated in a small and cramped seat for many hours is not appealing to travelers who are accustomed to large steamships and Pullmans.

The discomfort due to vibration is very slight in modern transport planes. However, the propellerless types have no vibration at all. We do not know what the vibration or buffeting will be at sonic speeds, perhaps considerable. The problem of vibration has been a serious one in some helicopters, but has been greatly reduced in the later models. There is reason to think that in the future it may not be a bother.

The problem of noise in the interior of passenger planes has been rather satisfactorily solved in the passenger transports, at the cost of much weight carried. At least, there is little complaint. On the other hand, in the smaller planes used for private flying at low costs, it is not so practical to pad the interiors against noise which comes from the propeller, engine, and poor streamlining. Muffling the exhaust lessens the noise, but reduces the efficiency of the engine. The jet and gas turbine planes will be much quieter, but it is a question how soon these power plants will be available for light planes.

Travel in airliners already means very little discomfort, except in very rough weather. The problem is, therefore, not great, and there are many solutions in sight for the future.

CONCLUSION

Inventions as new and as significant as aircraft are likely to evolve rapidly. Most changes can probably be foreseen fairly well for a decade or so. However, beyond the improvements of existing models, there are many radical suggestions for more profound changes and additions, such as rocket transportation, jet-propelled flight at supersonic speeds, the application of jet propulsion to the rotors of the helicopters, gliders, methods of aiding take-off, and even atomic energy, which at present does not appear to be practical because of the weight of the protecting shield. The future of these improvements cannot at present be predicted with great assurance. However, a considerable variety of types of aircraft is already foreseen, which should enable adaptation to a diversity of needs. Much development is expected in the production of small aircraft for the personal flier and for short-haul passenger aircraft, though no radical departures are foreseen except in the helicopter. This is the aircraft with the most novel effects, because of its unique landing and take-off powers. The building of larger and larger planes for the future is a most dynamic process now. But equally active is the process of attaining ever higher speed and altitude. Achievements in the latter are precipitated by the turbine and jet engines, and have come so suddenly that they raise an acute problem of designing an airframe for the airplanes which will permit the sonic or supersonic speeds which the new and projected power plants are capable of producing. Greater safety is promised, particularly from electronic devices which permit landing in fog and avoiding collisions. Research in weather forecasting and the organization of weather-reporting services will also safeguard air travel. Of the inventions most active and promising, we may list turbo-jet engines, helicopters, electronics, laminar flow, and rockets.

6

Scheduled Transportation
of Passengers

NEARLY ALL NEW INVENTIONS have encountered opposition to their adoption before they have come into common use.
Some farmers objected to using the cast-iron plow because they
believed that the iron would poison the soil. The use of the
revolver was opposed by the army at one time. John Ruskin and
others like him, who protested against the mounting spirit of industrialism, resisted the railroad. We, in America, made fun of
the automobile and were reluctant to give up horses. There have
been many and varied oppositions to the airplane. These factors
have kept the number of passengers smaller than they would
otherwise have been, but the little oppositions are gradually decreasing.

Factors Affecting the Volume of Passenger Travel

Perhaps the greatest opposition to air travel in the past has
come from the fear of accidents, but this fear has now been pretty
well overcome. Most people nowadays are not afraid to ride in a
scheduled passenger plane. The accident record of airlines has
been improved so much that the future should see a safety record
of perhaps only one fatality per 100,000,000 passenger-miles, as
compared with an average of ten per 100,000,000 passenger-miles
for 1930-40.

Another obstacle to the growth of air travel has been the percentage of canceled flights. The traveling public wants dependable service and, if there is considerable uncertainty as to whether
the plane will start or complete the journey, the public will choose
the form of transportation on which they can depend. The number of canceled flights has been decreasing. In flying the mail in

1942, over 95 per cent [1] of the miles of service scheduled were actually flown. Of scheduled passenger flights, 89 per cent were completed in 1942.[2] Obviously, an improvement of the record would be of advantage in encouraging air travel. The fact that more than one in ten flights are canceled and a larger number not completed on time indicates that air schedules are not yet as dependable as the schedules of railroads and bus lines. But better meteorological service and electronics hold out great promise for nearly perfect performance in the future.

A small percentage of travelers by air suffer some discomfort from the motion of the ship, resulting in airsickness similar to seasickness on the ocean. One major airline reports that for the six years from 1938 to 1943, inclusive, only 1.9 per 1000 passengers were airsick. Since the advent of modern airliners the rate of airsickness has always been less than 1 per cent of the passengers carried.[3] Even fewer people will become airsick when planes are larger and improved in design and fly in the substratosphere where there is less air bumpiness. Considerable research was done on remedies for airsickness during the war, but no drug has yet been reported which is successful in more than 50 per cent of the cases.[4]

The long distance between the airport and the homes of the passengers is a hindrance to the growth of short-distance travel by air. The median distance from the airport to the center of the city was 4.8 miles in 1939 for all airports used by scheduled air carriers. For cities of over 100,000 population, the median distance was 7.2 miles.[5] For cities of 10,000 inhabitants, the one-way trip to the airport requires about 25 minutes, and for cities of 500,000, about 45 minutes.[6] Raymond,[7] of Douglas aircraft,

---

[1] Howard Mengos, editor, *Aircraft Yearbook*, Aeronautical Chamber of Commerce of America, 1943, p. 688.

[2] *C. A. A. Journal*, vol. 2, no. 13, p. 163.

[3] André Bernière, "Why You Get Airsick," *Flying*, February, 1945, p. 39.

[4] *Ibid.*, p. 130.

[5] John H. Frederick, *Commercial Air Transportation*, 1943, p. 64. Based on data from a survey made by the Civil Aeronautics Authority in 1939.

[6] A. E. Raymond, "An Adequate Transport System for the United States," in *Prospects and Problems in Aviation*, edited by L. S. Lyon and L. C. Sorrell, Chicago Association of Commerce, 1945, p. 50.

[7] *Ibid.*, p. 50.

figures that time will be saved when traveling in a DC-3 for distances beyond 80 miles, and that by 1950, with new equipment, a traveler will gain time in going by air on distances beyond 60 miles. This location of airports increases the total door-to-door time on very short trips so that a trip by air takes about the same amount of time as by railroad, or not a great deal less. It does not appear likely that the big airports will be moved physically closer to the center of the city, but non-stop highways to the airport will reduce the time required to reach them. Another possible solution is the use of helicopters, but such a service is not likely to be widespread in the first few years after the war. Improvements in regard to shortening the time necessary to reach the airport from the city center are to be expected in the future.

Of the possible obstacles to the growth of air passenger traffic, perhaps the most important is the competitive effort that is likely to be made by the railroads. Cheaper railroad fares, more speed, better seats, and more conveniences can do much to keep railroad passengers from traveling on airplanes. Should sleeping-space on a Pullman be offered for less than hotel accommodations and be available to those paying only coach fares, the railroads will be able to hold much of their traffic. It is not to be inferred that all the passengers on airplanes are taken from railroads. The planes develop an amount of travel over and beyond the numbers who travel the railroads, as the automobile developed passengers beyond the numbers using horses and railroads.

The popularization of aviation during the war has perhaps been the most important factor in breaking down opposition to aviation. Only with the coming of the war did the public realize the national importance of aviation and the possible effects of its widespread civilian use on the life of the average man. The development of traffic in the prewar years depended to an extraordinary degree on selling aviation to the public. Although this kind of promotion will have to continue in the future, it has been made incomparably easier by the war. In the first years of peace there will be dismantling of airplane factories and, with business depressions, there will be slumps in aviation, but still the war's service will be lasting in familiarizing the population with this new means of transportation, once held to be very dangerous.

The Amount of Passenger Travel

Before attempting to forecast the amount of air passenger travel after the war, it is desirable to show how much of the total domestic passenger travel in the United States is by air, as compared with other forms of travel. The best year for comparing the amounts of passenger travel on the various forms of transportation is in the last full year of peace. Passenger traffic in the war years was highly abnormal and has little predictive value for the postwar years. It is abnormal in that (1) private automobile transportation was greatly reduced because of tire and gasoline shortages, much of it being transferred to buses and railroads; (2) airplanes for scheduled passenger service were taken from the airlines by the government and there were not enough planes to permit the expansion that would otherwise have occurred; and (3) there is always an unusual amount of travel in wartime.

The passenger-miles flown by the domestic air carriers in the United States in 1940 were 1,147,000, whereas the passenger-miles on the railroads, not including commuters, were 19,800,000.[8] Air passenger travel was, then, about 6 per cent of railroad travel as measured in passenger-miles. At the same time, there were about 12,000,000 passenger-miles of travel on buses between cities. Thus, in 1940, this new system of air travel, hardly two decades old, carried only 3.5 per cent of the total intercity passenger transportation in the United States. We are interested in knowing what the growth of passenger traffic by air is likely to be during the next decade and following decades.

Limiting Factors in the Growth of Passenger Traffic

One way of approaching the problem of estimating the future passenger traffic is to assume that the trend of growth in the past will continue in the future. Before making such an assumption, however, it is desirable to ask whether there are any obvious factors which will operate to prevent or otherwise change greatly the extension of past rates of growth into the future. In the case of automobile production in the 1920's, there were discernible

[8] Association of American Railroads, *Initial Study of Air Transportation*, pp. 22, 27.

forces that would restrict production in the future. It was clear that the size of the population would be a limiting factor and that automobile production could not grow in the future as it had grown in the past. There would not have been enough people to buy the cars.

In the case of the airplane, the size of the population will not be a limiting factor in the immediate postwar years. There are still a large number of potential travelers, as is seen from the figures of rail passengers that may be shifted in part to the air, and there are still others who will travel more than they have in prior decades. The country is large and not yet covered with air routes. New routes will tap new areas of population. The demand for speed, which is largely responsible for air traffic, will not be greatly different in postwar years from what it was in prewar years. Air travel will continue for some time to improve in safety, regularity, and quality of service.

Possible factors which might depress the rate of growth of passenger transportation would be lowered rates and improved service by the railroads and the difficulty of the airlines in reducing costs. Another factor might be the development of private flying. The rates of growth of the passenger travel on the railroads and buses might have been much higher if there had not been a tremendous growth of transportation in private automobiles. However, private flying is not expected to increase to this extent in the immediate postwar decade.

Projection of Past Trends

In considering the future of passenger traffic, we shall depend a good deal on the projection of past trends. This can be done logically only if (1) there are no unusual or insuperable obstacles ahead and (2) if the various factors affecting the trends in the past, such as improvement in the quality of service, etc., are likely to be continued in the future. These observations indicate that all factors affecting the growth in the past are expected to continue their growth, except that, first, there may be rather more effective competition from the railroads than in the past, and, secondly, the stimulation of the war period may wane somewhat.

In the late 1920's, there was very little passenger traffic on the airlines. The airlines performed essentially a mail service, and it was the payment for mail that kept the planes going. But, in the 1930's, the growth in the number of passengers was, in general, rapid — slow during the severe depression years in the first part of the decade, and rapid during the latter part. Thus, 375,000 passengers were carried in 1930, 747,000 in 1935, 2,959,000 in 1940, and 4,081,000 in 1944. The annual rate of growth in passenger-miles flown was 30 per cent for the decade — a decade of depression. Airplane passenger traffic, then, began slowly in the 1920's, but the amount was greatly increased in the 1930's, particularly in the latter part of the decade. This behavior of the curve of air travel is like that of the beginnings of many other growth curves. The curve is long, rising slowly, and later becomes concave, rising rapidly.

Estimate of Future Passenger Traffic

There is something to be said logically for extending growth curves forward, though the further the projection, the greater the inaccuracy. The rate of growth of air passenger-miles between 1930 and 1940 averaged 30 per cent a year. This high rate of annual growth is not expected to continue in the future. Beginning with the number of passenger-miles in 1943 and projecting them forward to 1953 at this rate yields a result of 30,000,000,-000 passenger-miles. Since this is approximately equal to the total scheduled intercity passenger travel on buses, railroads, and airlines combined in the immediate prewar years, it is an unrealistic estimate. There are several other possible projections. We may take a look at several and see what sort of predictions they yield for 1953.

A straight line fitted to the years from 1936 to 1944, when the curve of growth of passenger-miles looked as though it were ceasing to be concave and approaching a more or less straight-line trend, yields an estimate of about 4,000,000,000 passenger-miles in 1953. It may be that the growth of aviation, when more planes are available in the postwar years, will be somewhat faster than indicated by this straight line.

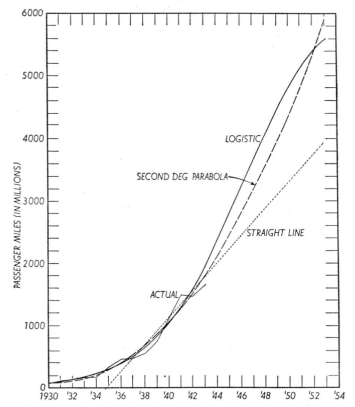

Figure 12. FUTURE PASSENGER-MILES ON UNITED STATES
DOMESTIC AIRLINES

Three different mathematical equations were fitted to the past data and
then projected to 1953. The straight line was determined from only that
recent portion of the curve that seemed to be moving upward with a
straight line trend.

A second-degree parabola, fitted by the method of least squares
to the available data, does not increase as rapidly as the usual
exponential curve with constant rate of increase. This parabola
forecasts 6,000,000,000 passenger-miles in 1953.

The curve of air passenger-miles may be expected to exhibit the
characteristics of the growth curve often observed in economic
and social phenomena, as well as in biological functions. The
logistic curve represents such a growth curve. It is concave at its

beginning, straightens out, and then becomes convex, like an elongated and distorted letter S. To fit a logistic curve, the data should extend past the inflection point. It is questionable whether the statistics of air passenger-miles have been in existence long enough to give this curve much predictive value. The curve of air passenger-miles reaches an inflection point only if the war years are included. This decreasing rate of growth would probably not have occurred had it not been for the wartime restrictions on air travel. The result is that the logistic projection almost reaches the upper asymptote in 1953. The estimate for 1953 is about 6,000,000,000 passenger-miles. Six billion passenger-miles might be considered a reasonable estimate for 1953, but obviously the curve of air passenger-miles is not expected to reach the upper limit of its growth in 1953.

Another type of growth curve, similar to the logistic curve, is the Gompertz curve. Fitting this curve to the data of air passenger-miles, we obtain an estimate of 13,000,000,000 passenger-miles for 1953. This curve fits the given data for 1930-44 somewhat better than the logistic curve. It has the added asset that it does not reach the upper limit of air passenger-miles in 1953. On the other hand, the upper asymptote which it does project is an astronomical figure which is obviously impossible. Yet the Gompertz curve may give some idea about the early part of a curve, about the latter part of which we have no information. The 13,000,000,000 passenger-miles which the Gompertz curve projects is more than twice as much as those given by the projections of the logistic and the parabola.

Since these mathematical equations give differing results, we must fall back on the logic supporting these equations. Perhaps the second-degree parabola, a combination of the straight line and the usual exponential curve, is most reasonable. The logistic curve could be used if the data were sufficient for a reasonable projection. The indications point to somewhat more than 6,000,-000,000 passenger-miles.

Future Passenger-Miles Indirectly Estimated

When curves are exceptionally uncertain as to their courses, such as the very early years of a growth series, resort may be had to comparisons with curves of more mature series that presumably have more stability and regularity. One curve frequently considered to have these characteristics is the curve of total intercity scheduled passenger traffic, including the passengers on airplanes, railroads, and buses. It has been discovered that this curve of total intercity passenger-miles conforms quite closely to the curve of the national income in its cyclical fluctuations, a curve which is also regarded to be relatively free from violent and erratic rates of growth. A good deal of work has been done on predicting the postwar national income. From national income predictions, the total intercity passenger traffic can be estimated and from this figure the portion going to aviation can, in turn, be estimated. This last step involves, it is true, a highly uncertain estimate; but, since it involves a percentage, there is a check on the possibility of violent overestimates possible in certain exponential projections. It should be further noted that the national income curve and the intercity passenger curves do have unusual fluctuations, but the rationality of them is pretty well understood and so can be taken into account. It may be of some value to see what is yielded by this method, even though it is indirect and involves several assumptions.

During the 1930's, for every dollar of national income, there was from 33 to 40 per cent of a passenger-mile of intercity scheduled passenger traffic. If we knew the postwar national income, the amount of passenger-miles of intercity transport could be estimated.

All the estimates of the postwar national income thus far observed have been based either on full employment or on a small amount of unemployment. Indeed, the purpose of many of these studies has been to figure out the amount of national income with full employment at expected rates of production. Thus, they are not so much making predictions as setting goals to be attained. But since these goals are supposed to be reasonable and attainable, it may be possible to view them as predictions.

Some of these estimates are shown in Table 2, expressed in 1943 dollars per capita.

TABLE 2. NATIONAL INCOME PER CAPITA IN 1947 AT 1943 PRICES
WITH ANNUAL RATES OF INCREASE OVER 1939 *

	1947 Income per capita at 1943 prices	Increase per year of 1947 over 1939
Interstate Commerce Commission †	939	.042
Goldenweiser and Hagen, Federal Reserve Board ‡	1001	.050
Mayer, Brookings Institution §	886	.034
Woytinsky, Social Security Board **	1050	.057
Sonne, National Planning Association ††	1175 (1950)	.057
Tucker, General Motors ‡‡	880	.032

* The contributors of these estimates are usually careful not to claim them as predictions, but rather the incomes that will result from a minimum of "frictional" unemployment and a small military force, at what they consider to be the productivity per worker. Their estimates have been changed to 1943 prices by using the cost-of-living index number. The prices of 1943 are considered to be approximately the same as 1929. In obtaining the per capita figures, the population figures are those in the U.S. *Statistical Abstract*, supplied by Thompson and Whelpton.

† Interstate Commerce Commission, Bur. of Transport Economics and Statistics, *Post-War Traffic Levels*, Washington, D. C., October, 1944.

‡ E. A. Goldenweiser and E. E. Hagen, "Jobs After the War," *Federal Reserve Bulletin*, May, 1944, p. 424.

§ Joseph Mayer, *Postwar National Income*, Pamphlet 55, The Brookings Institution, 1944.

** W. S. Woytinsky, unpublished report.

†† H. C. Sonne, *A Preview of National Budgets for Full Employment "Model T,"* National Planning Association, June, 1944.

‡‡ R. S. Tucker, in *Measuring and Projecting National Income*, National Industrial Conference Board, Inc., Studies in Business Policy, no. 5, 1945.

These estimates show extraordinary yearly rates of increase varying from 3.2 per cent a year to 5.7 per cent. Previous peacetime experience shows much lower increases. From 1884 to 1939, the increase was around 1.6 per cent a year. Even the very exceptional increase from 1919 to 1929 was only 2.9 per cent a year, the largest increase yet observed from recorded data for a period of a decade. A more comparable experience was the growth from the prewar to the postwar years of World War I. The rate of increase from 1915 to 1929 was 1.9 per cent. This rate, applied to a similar period around World War II, from 1939 to 1953, gives a result of about $125,000,000,000 in 1943 prices.

Another way of approaching the subject is to estimate the future productive labor supply and the future productivity per unit of labor and multiply the two together. This is the method generally used. There is not a great divergence in the estimates of the labor supply. Two or three million are placed in the military forces or in military training and a minimum "frictional" unemployment of 1,500,000 to 3,000,000 is recognized. It should be observed, however, that the unemployment in the prosperous decade following World War I was estimated to be 11 per cent of the labor supply, which would mean after this war some 6,000,000 to 6,500,000 unemployed.[9] In 1953, then, with a labor force of 60,500,000 or 61,500,000, the employed at civilian jobs would be around 52,000,000.

The predictions of the productivity per unit of labor show more divergence among the estimators, the figures ranging from around 1.3 to 2.4 per cent per year.[10] If the increase is figured for the years 1919 to 1939 on the basis of a trend line for income per employed person,[11] it is found to be .85 per cent a year, but the actual increase for the first postwar decade after World War I was 3.2 per cent a year. It is more reliable to predict from a trend and make an adjustment afterward for the swing of the business cycle. Taking the average income per employed person for 1938-40 or $2000 in 1943 prices, and increasing it at a rate of .85 per cent a year, the projected figure for 1953 is $2254. But it seems very probable that business conditions during the first postwar decade will be well above the trend. Taking the actual production at 15 per cent above the trend, the income per employed person would be $2592, an increase of 2.8 per cent a year. With 52,000,000 employed, this would mean an income for 1953 of $135,000,000,000 at 1943 prices. It is recalled that the projection on the trend of per capita income was $125,000,000,000.

The opinion that the 1947 projections by the various estimators are too high was based on the evidence of past experience, particularly with unemployment. But the future may be very different from the past experience, especially in governmental spending to create more civilian jobs and hence a larger national income.

[9] Even in March of the prosperous year of 1940, there were 7,600,000 unemployed (including those in emergency work or on relief), or 14 per cent of the labor force. If only those seeking work (4,300,000) are counted as unemployed, then the percentage of the labor force was 8.

The estimate of 11 per cent is computed from annual estimates published by Simon Kuznets, of the National Bureau of Economic Research.

[10] Many investigators think 2 per cent a year is about right. Livingston, of the U.S. Department of Commerce, found the increase in national income per worker to be 1.7 per cent a year. Woytinsky gets a much larger figure (gross product) of 2.4 per cent a year. Tucker considers 1.9 much too high.

[11] Calculated from Simon Kuznets, *National Income, 1919-1938*, Occasional Paper no. 2, National Board of Economic Research, April, 1941, p. 25, column 3.

In the past, the revenues of the federal government have generally balanced expenditures except in war years and during the depressions of the 1930's. During the war, governmental expenditures far exceeded revenues, and deficit spending by the government raised the national income enormously. During peacetime, deficit spending could also increase the national income to large amounts. Loans abroad to purchase American exports have a similar effect on national income, as was the case after World War I until 1927. Deficit spending may actually occur, presumably on the expectation that, when the desired income is attained, part of it may be recovered in taxes to pay for the previous deficits in spending. In such a case, the projected trends on the basis of past experience, which give an income of $125,000,000,000 to $135,000,000,000 in 1943 prices, will not be a good indication of what will actually happen, but will be underestimates. The various estimates of income based on full employment may be better predictions. The goals set by the estimators may be nearer what will happen. How much deficit spending may increase national income we do not know. But suppose we allow for some such effort toward creating jobs for all the labor force except those in the military forces and in training and the "frictionally" unemployed and set the income for 1953 in 1943 prices at $140,000,-000,000 or $145,000,000,000.

If, then, the national income is around $145,000,000,000 in 1953, what will the intercity passenger traffic be? The fluctuations of intercity passenger traffic around its trend conform to the fluctuations of national income around its trend. Thus, during the swings of the national income in the 1930's, the intercity passenger-miles per dollar of national income were around .37, slightly higher for the better years and slightly lower for the more depressed years.[12] With passenger-miles of .37 for every dollar of

12 Intercity passenger traffic trends, however, have not always paralleled national income trends. With the coming of the automobile, the trend of scheduled passenger traffic decreased, while the trend of national income was upward. During this war, with gasoline restricted for use in private automobiles, scheduled passenger traffic increased faster than the national income. But in the postwar years, with the restrictions on gasoline for private automobiles removed, the trends of passenger traffic as compared with trends in income should be perhaps

national income in 1953, a national income of $145,000,000,000 would mean 54,000,000,000 passenger-miles of scheduled intercity transportation, as contrasted with 33,000,000,000 in 1940, an increase of 64 per cent in thirteen years. This increase seems very large, yet in 1944 the increase over 1940 was about 300 per cent. It is assumed that there will be a high degree of business prosperity in the postwar years.

With an intercity passenger traffic of 54,000,000,000 passenger-miles, how much will go to scheduled aviation? In 1940, air passenger-miles were 3.5 per cent of total intercity scheduled passenger-miles and, of course, much less in earlier years. The curve of growth of these percentages is a slightly concave curve, which, if extended by a second-degree parabola, yields an estimate of 15 per cent in 1953. This extension, based on so small a segment of a new curve of growth, does not give us a feeling of much certainty. But assuming that the percentage is of the order of 15 per cent, then for 54,000,000,000 passenger-miles, the amount going to aviation will be 8,000,000,000. It is recalled that the direct method of projecting air passenger-mile growth, when the second-degree parabola was used for projection, pointed to a magnitude of around 6,000,000,000.

A very uncertain factor in determining the number of passengers in the future and one of great importance is the fare charged. Hence, we turn to considerations of fares in the succeeding paragraphs. But without especially considering the rates except as they are factors affecting the trends in past passenger growth, the indications point to passenger-miles in 1953 of the order of 6,000,000,000 or 8,000,000,000.

Passenger Air Rates and Number of Passengers

It is generally true that, as the price is lowered, the number of sales increases. Yet it is also true that with the price remaining the same, the sales may increase. The rate of fares for air travel has remained at about five cents a mile since 1939, but the

much the same as in the 1930's. The airplane brings the possibility of increased intercity passenger traffic; but it may be offset by the increased competition of private intercity transportation.

passenger-miles have increased from 750,000,000 to 2,200,000,000 in 1944. A stationary price may be accompanied by increased sales because there are influences other than price on volume of sales, such as the state of business prosperity and variations in the quality of the product sold. It is well understood among the airline companies that an improvement in service will increase the number of passengers.

But it is also true that, other things being equal, a lowering of rates will increase the number of passengers. This relation of price to demand has received much study in regard to many industrial and agricultural products. The curve showing this relationship is generally a concave one, not a straight line. Thus, when the price of cotton is high, the sales are few. As the price of cotton is lowered, the sales increase gradually, but, as the price falls very low, the sales increase much more and out of proportion to the fall in price. For air transportation, the nature of the demand curve means that, if the rate of fare is dropped from 3 cents a mile to 2.5 cents, the increase in the number of passengers will be very much greater than will be the increase when the rate is lowered from 5 cents to 4.5 cents. Any estimate of the number of passenger-miles in the future is contingent upon the fare charged per mile.

This relation between the number of passengers and the rate of fare charged has been used by Mr. Edward Warner in making some estimates of future traffic.[13] He makes his estimates by comparing the rates by air with those of the railroads. If, for instance, the air rates could be made equal to those of railroad coach fare, figured at 1.89 cents per air-mile, then he estimates the passenger-miles of air traffic would be 24,000,000,000, of which some 8,000,000,000 would be taken from private automobile intercity traffic and from new travel created by airplanes. Presumably, some 14,000,000,000 passenger-miles would be taken from railroad coaches and Pullmans at that low rate. Warner estimates that this amount of traffic might occur soon after the war, assuming virtually full employment for normal working hours, approximately as in the best years of the 1920's.

[13] Edward Warner, "Where Next?" *Air Transport*, September, 1944, pp. 32-37.

At the other extreme, if the air fares should remain at the present rate of slightly more than five cents a mile, Warner thinks the air passenger-miles would eventually increase to 5,500,000,-000. In between, if the air rate could be lowered to that of the Pullman rate plus berth, figured at 3.31 cents per air-mile, then the air passenger-miles would increase to 11,000,000,000. Warner's figures give three points on a demand curve. By interpolating for other rates on the curve, we find the relationship shown in Table 3. From this table, it is seen that the more the rate is lowered, the greater is the increase in passenger-miles.

A similar demand curve has been constructed in a competent study made by a large industrial company not engaged in the manufacture of airplanes (which wishes to remain anonymous), later referred to here as the industrial company study. The shape of the demand curve is about the same as that based on the Warner estimates, but the passenger-miles are lower for the different rates, as is shown in Table 3. This demand curve was constructed by first locating two extremes — one at a rate of 5 cents in 1960 and the other at 2.5 cents for the same year. These two extremes were averages of estimates made by heads of airlines as to the percentages of intercity passenger traffic that would go to the airlines at the rates and times stated. For the 2.5-cent rate, the opinion was that 35 per cent of total intercity traffic would go by air, and for the 5-cent rate the percentage was 10. By estimating the total intercity passenger traffic, the number of air passenger-miles for these two extremes was determined. From these figures, estimates can be made for years earlier or later than 1960. An examination of Table 3 shows what a powerful factor the rate of fare is in determining the number of passengers. These figures are, of course, averages; that is, they consider other factors as held constant, such as general price level and the stage of the business cycle.

It is difficult to make a critical appraisal of the estimates in Table 3. The industrial company estimates may be too low as the growth of intercity passenger traffic may have been underestimated. Also, we do not know how reliable are the extreme points in their demand curve based upon estimates of the per-

TABLE 3. AIR PASSENGER-MILES FOR VARYING RATES
OF FARE PER MILE

Fare per mile	Passenger-miles (in billions)		
	Based on Warner's estimates, no year stated	Based on the industrial company study	
		1953	1960
1.89	24.0		
2.00	21.5		
2.50	15.4	11.3	14.5
3.00	12.0	8.6	10.4
3.50	9.8	6.6	8.0
4.00	8.0	5.2	6.4
4.50	6.5	4.2	5.2
5.00	5.5	3.4	4.2

centages of intercity traffic going to airlines in 1960 at rates of
2.5 cents a mile and 5 cents a mile. Warner's estimates are based
upon an expectation that, with air fares equal to coach rates,
7,000,000,000 passenger-miles will come from Pullman traffic (the
total Pullman passenger-miles in 1941 were 7,900,000,000 in air-
miles), 7,000,000,000 passenger-miles will come from railroad
coaches, and 8,000,000,000 from private automobiles and from
new traffic. These items are necessarily difficult to estimate exactly. But, in view of railroad plans to compete to hold their
passengers by improved services, it may be that Warner's estimates are too high. Warner was apparently basing his assumptions on not much change in rates or services of the railroads.

Another estimate of total passenger-miles for air travel at a fare
of 2.5 cents has been made by A. E. Raymond, Vice President,
Engineering, Douglas Aircraft Company.[14] His figure of 14,000,-
000,000 passenger-miles, though considered a maximum, is quite
close to those of Warner and of the industrial study shown in
Table 3. Raymond, however, says that this low rate of 2.5 cents
per passenger-mile in 1950 "appears possible of attainment with
new equipment." [15] But to state that the figure of 14,000,000,000
passenger-miles "appears possible" in 1950 is different from pre-

[14] Raymond, op. cit., pp. 50-53.   [15] Ibid., p. 53.

dicting that it will occur. Perhaps, then, not too much reliance should be put on the date 1950, since the number of passenger-miles predicted would mean a phenomenal increase of 11,700,-000,000 passenger-miles in the five years before 1950, whereas it took twenty-five years to build up 2,300,000,000 passenger-miles by 1945. However, a forecast of 14,000,000,000 passenger-miles when the fare is 2.5 cents is not out of line.[16]

Still another and different calculation on future passenger-miles may be noted. In 1944, L. C. Sorrell and H. A. Wheeler [17] projected the trend line of passenger-miles in air travel to 1949 with a result of 4,100,000,000 passenger-miles, a result lower than that of the forecasts quoted previously. In 1945, Sorrell used a somewhat different method of forecasting with somewhat larger results.[18] It was noted that from 1935 to 1940, air passenger-miles increased 25 per cent a year. Assuming that the rate of increase will probably be less in postwar years, calculations at 20 per cent a year from 1945 to 1950 indicate 6,500,000,000 passenger-miles; at 25 per cent, 9,700,000,000; and at 22 per cent, 7,500,000,000 passenger-miles. The reader can make his choice of these estimates.

But, whatever may be the number of passenger-miles for the different fares charged, it is desirable to make some inquiries as to what rates are likely to be set in postwar years.

Passenger Fares on Airlines

The fares charged on airlines, although set by executives in

---

[16] This estimate by Raymond of 14,000,000,000 is interesting because he uses a different method of forecasting from that of the other studies quoted. The procedure was to find out for what lengths of trips it would be better to take a plane than a Pullman, railroad coach, or bus, counting the traveler's time as worth $1 an hour with air fares at 2.5 cents and the charges on other media remaining as they are, and on the basis of appropriate speeds. These breaking points beyond which it is better to travel by air will be 60 miles on Pullmans, 150 miles on railroad coaches, and 165 miles on buses. "It seems reasonable that (as a maximum) the airplane may attract travel equivalent to the amount above these breaking points." (Raymond, *op. cit.*, p. 55.) In 1941, 14,000,000,000 passenger-miles were traveled on distances beyond these breaking points.

[17] L. C. Sorrell and Harry A. Wheeler, *Passenger Transport in the United States, 1920-1950*, Railway Business Association, 1944, p. 64.

[18] L. C. Sorrell, "Prospective Passenger Traffic, Volume, Rates and Service," in Lyon and Sorrell, *op. cit.*, p. 72.

offices, are not determined with freedom of choice. If they were, predictions would be extremely difficult to make. In setting the fares, executives are responding to such forces as costs, governmental policies, competition, various company policies, and national interests. Some of these forces may now be considered.

First, we may note the general course of air passenger fares in past years. In 1926, the fare was 12 cents a mile; in 1930, 8.3 cents; in 1931, 6.7 cents; in 1932 and 1933, 6.1 cents; in 1935 and 1936, 5.7 cents; in 1939, 5.1 cents, and since 1939, the fare has been slightly above 5 cents. In 1945, it is 5.1 cents a mile.[19] The curve of fares shows a drop of 50 per cent in the decade from 1926 to 1936, but only a 9-per-cent decrease in the eight years since 1936. It seems reasonable to think that, as fares decline, the rate of decrease will be less and less; that is, as the fares decrease, it will be increasingly difficult to push them lower. Large decreases in the future would, in general, not be expected.

One school of thought holds that, if the airline companies can increase their passenger traffic by holding the fares at the same level, then lowered fares are not to be expected until the available traffic at the higher fares has been fully developed. Thus, John Frederick, writing in 1943, says, "Rate reductions of any consequence will probably not come soon or to the extent popularly supposed, although over the next five years they may prove a factor mildly stimulating to air travel."[20] The argument is that the airline companies were not self-supporting until the war without very high mail payments from the government, and that they ought not to risk being thrown back on governmental support by unwisely lowering rates.

On the other hand, there is the policy, often followed in the past, of trying to reach a larger market by lowering prices, with the expectation that low rates of profit on a large number of sales will gross a larger profit than a higher rate of profit on a small number of sales. Then, too, in the United States there is always the possibility that competition may force prices down.

The limit below which prices cannot go for long is costs. Hence, in discussing rates, it is important to consider costs.

19 Civil Aeronautics Board.
20 John H. Frederick, *Commercial Air Transportation*, p. 303.

The Costs of Air Passenger Travel

A careful study of the costs of air passenger travel has been made by the Curtiss-Wright Corporation,[21] and this may be used as a basis for estimating rates of fare to passengers. This study is based on a comprehensive list of cost items and apparently none are omitted. Included are: (1) direct flying expenses, including salaries, fuel, airplane prices, depreciation, maintenance, insurance, passenger supplies, route utilization, and a load factor of 65 per cent; (2) indirect flying expenses, including costs of ground facilities, communications, meteorological expense, miscellaneous station equipment, and a portion of traffic expenses; (3) traffic and advertising costs; (4) general and administrative expenses. Finally, a fair return on the investment, set at 8 per cent of the above total costs, is included.

The procedure was to obtain the present costs of the various sub-items that make up all these costs, such as salaries and price of fuel, and carry them forward into the postwar period. The estimated costs are for an operation of 40,000,000 ton-miles annually, at which level the ratio of indirect flying expense to direct is found to be 47 per cent.

The Curtiss-Wright study assumed that the war would be over in 1946, but the authors state that, "Whether or not these events (the closing of the war) transpire in the years mentioned would not necessarily alter the size of the estimates made in this analysis, although the dates would be changed." [22] The postwar years were viewed as having two periods. One is the transition period, which is characterized by use, in the main, of the old equipment in planes. This period gradually shades off until about four years after the war, when the new equipment in planes of more economical design will have become available in sufficiently large numbers to be in general use. Thus, the second period was thought of as beginning some four to six years after the close of the war, or in the second half of the first postwar decade.

The authors figure that during the transition period the revenue

[21] Curtiss-Wright Corporation, *Air Transportation in the Immediate Post-War Period,* 1944, Sec. IV, pp. 56-60.
[22] Curtiss-Wright, *op. cit.,* p. 3.

required to cover cost plus return on investment will be from 3.5 cents to 4.5 cents per passenger-mile, and they are inclined to think the rate charged will be about 4.5 cents a mile. For the latter half of the postwar decade, when the improved planes will be in wide use, the authors estimate that the revenue required will be from 3 to 4 cents a mile. A rate of 3.5 cents a mile would mean, based on the demand curves in Table 3, from 7,000,000,-000 to 10,000,000,000 passenger-miles, while a rate of 4 cents would result in from 5,000,000,000 to 8,000,000,000 passenger-miles.

It would seem that direct flying costs could be projected somewhat more reliably than indirect costs, particularly overhead. To the outside observer, it appears that some of these costs might be cut a good deal more than Curtiss-Wright cuts them, particularly for a second-class of travel which would be similar to coach travel on railroad trains. It also seems possible that the indirect costs of flying could be reduced below the Curtiss-Wright estimates. The costs around an airport per unit of transportation are subject to reduction with increased traffic. The desire for mass markets is always great for American industries, and business enterprise may work successfully toward a lower cost in order to induce more travel. Under the impetus to develop mass air travel, there is some talk of trying to lower the cost to around 3 cents a passenger-mile or slightly less. The time at which such low costs may be obtained is not stated, but presumably it would be only after the first postwar decade.

The Lower Limits of Costs

Further light on the costs of passenger transportation may be had by inquiring how low aviation costs can go. At the present time, air passenger fares are somewhat comparable to those of railroad Pullmans, and it is commonly thought that the airplane will take away much of the railroad Pullman traffic that travels over three hundred miles, provided the railroads do not improve their service and lower rates. Railroad Pullman traffic is sometimes viewed as a limit beyond which aviation is not likely to go. But with the possibilities of lowered rates on airplanes, it seems probable that all railroad passenger traffic going over a hundred miles will be vulnerable.

But when we pass from railroads to buses, we may ask whether the course of air passenger traffic will not certainly find a limit at the bus level of costs. This question has been considered by Edward Warner.[23] He has compared the bus and the present DC-3 airplane (Table 4). The bus and the DC-3 are very nearly equal in gross weight and in payload capacity. But the costs for the bus are about 20 cents a mile as compared with 68 cents for the DC-3. The air costs are about three and one-half times as much as the bus costs, and the rates are in approximately the same ratio. A comparison between air and bus costs on several of the items suggests strongly that the airline companies, though able to reduce many of the costs of the different items, will never in the foreseeable future be able to bring them down to the costs of the bus lines. It is difficult to see how the airplane costs could be brought down to those of the bus in fuel and oil, in wages, in station expense, in maintenance, and in depreciation. The bus travels 5 miles on a gallon of gasoline, the airplane but 1.6 miles.

TABLE 4. COSTS OF BUS AND AIRPLANE TRAVEL *

Items	Costs per mile	
	Airplane DC-3	Bus
Fuel and oil	8.56	2.58
Pay of crew	9.63	3.58
Maintenance, equipment and overhead	9.30	3.60
Station expense	13.19	2.38
Insurance and accidents	2.29	1.05
Advertising and solicitation	8.39	0.96
Depreciation of equipment	5.04	2.03
Office force pay	1.79	1.00
Taxation and licenses	1.41	1.40
Passenger service cost	3.42	

* Edward Warner, "Air Transportation Prospects," address before Engineering Society of Detroit, December 15, 1943 (mimeo.), p. 11.

[23] Edward Warner, "Air Transportation Prospects," address before Engineering Society of Detroit, Dec. 15, 1943 (mimeo.).

The original cost of the airplane itself is ten times that of the bus. The airplane requires a larger crew than the bus, and it must also have a meteorological service and a landing service.

On the basis of this analysis of costs, it would appear that the airplane will never be as cheap a system of travel as the bus, although it might become as cheap as the railroads. Furthermore, the airplane may not capture much of the very-short-distance traffic, but it is possible that the helicopter may take passengers on trips of thirty to fifty miles.

Though bus traffic and short-distance travel under thirty miles may define the limits of airplane passenger traffic, we do not foresee that aviation will necessarily approach these limits very closely — at least not within the second decade after the war. But it will carry a good-sized share of the total intercity passenger traffic.

Future Passengers and Fares

It seems within the realm of possibility that fares of 3 cents a mile are attainable at some future date. Such a rate would be a reduction of about 40 per cent over present levels. From the demand curves in Table 3, a rate of 3 cents would bring from 9,000,000,000 to 12,000,000,000 passenger-miles. The year in which the rate of passenger fares might reach 3 cents a mile is not certain. It is, of course, possible to set rates below costs with the help of the government. Such a policy is more probable in international than in domestic travel, except for local air transportation with stops at less than a hundred miles.

Perhaps more probable rates for domestic air passenger travel for the early 1950's would be around 3.5 cents, or somewhat higher. A factor in the costs is the volume of passengers. In the early 1950's, by various methods of projection and from studies of rates and costs, passenger-miles should be at least 6,000,000,-000, with perhaps 2,000,000,000 or 3,000,000,000 more, as judged from calculations on previous pages. These estimates are based upon many assumptions, an important one being a high level of business activity during the first postwar decade. All indications point in that direction. However, a short business recession and a marked reduction in productivity of possibly short duration would not be unexpected. Such a depression might very well postpone the date of these forecasts and would also reduce the estimate of the number of passenger-miles.

Non-Scheduled Operations

While passengers in general depend upon scheduled services and like them because of their convenience, economy, and certainty, they sometimes want special services for emergencies and unusual occasions, as, for instance, for sport events, taxi services, ambulances, etc. In 1940, the aviation companies doing a non-scheduled business flew over 9,000,000 miles in their charter operations alone, which was about 8 per cent of the revenue-miles flown that year by the scheduled operators. These companies do business other than transporting passengers, such as dusting crops, advertising, taking photographs, and conducting sight-seeing trips. While the scheduled airlines may do a non-scheduled business also, there are many non-scheduled companies, a large number of whom operate from a single airfield and are called "fixed-base operators."

It does not seem probable that these non-scheduled airline companies, except a few rendering taxi services, will restrict their business to the transportation of passengers. Their service in transporting goods is discussed in a later chapter. The economic survival and success of these companies depend on their total operations, one of which may be the transportation of passengers.

Looking toward the future, one possible type of service of the fixed-base operators is the extension of the range of air travel where the scheduled service ends; that is, the air traveler going to a small place not scheduled for regular air service may hire a special plane to take him to his final destination. An illustration is air service for persons who wish to spend a week-end in a small resort on a lake or in the mountains. There will likewise be some emergency services demanded by business agents, salesmen, and travelers to small places not having scheduled feeder services. The amount of use of such a service depends upon the prices charged, which in turn rest upon the joint costs of the passenger transportation with other services. Not enough is known to make a prediction, but a possibility of such extension of service by fixed-base operators exists, especially in those areas where local scheduled air service is not in operation.

With this business may be combined a "fly-it-yourself" rental service, which may appeal to fliers who have neither the money nor the time to own and fly their own aircraft, but who will want to fly occasionally or make trips where there are no scheduled airlines. The non-scheduled passenger operations are not large for the railroads and buses, but there is some renting of automobiles, and there are auto taxicabs. The proportion of non-scheduled to scheduled flying may well be large as compared to that of railroads and buses.

After the Postwar Decade

In attempting to foresee the volumes of passenger travel beyond the postwar decade, it might be well to consider the growth curves of other inventions in transportation and communication in recent times. If these curves show common characteristics, they may be useful in predicting the growth of aviation. They are probably most useful for prediction over long periods of time. It is not known, of course, that the growth of aviation will follow the curves of other inventions, but they may give some suggestions as to the probabilities.

The automobile is a recent transportation invention which has been used for scheduled intercity passenger travel in the form of the bus. Unfortunately, the statistics of intercity passenger-miles by bus do not go back to the origin of bus transportation, but cover only the years since 1926, and the coverage of the figures in the first part of this period is probably not complete. The trend of bus passenger-miles for this fourteen-year period from 1926 to the beginning of the war is approximately a straight line increasing at an average of about a half-billion passenger-miles a year. Bus passenger-miles, after some twenty to twenty-five years of growth, were still increasing.

Statistics of automobile registrations are more accurate and go back to the early origins of automobile transportation. These

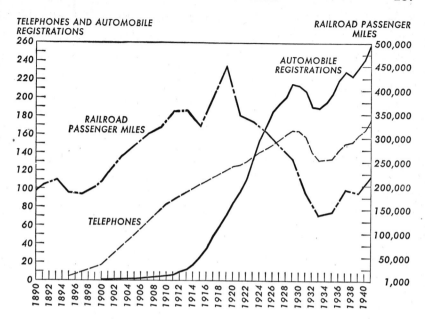

Figure 13. THE GROWTH CURVES OF DIFFERENT COMMUNICATION
AND TRANSPORTATION INVENTIONS, AS MEASURED BY THEIR USE

The automobile registrations per 1000 population for the early years were
quite few. Then the number mounted rapidly, but since the 1930's has
shown a tendency to level off. The curve of growth resembles an elongated
S curve. The growth in the number of telephones per 1000 population resembles somewhat less the S curve and is more elongated. If the data were
available for years before 1895, the early growth would be, like automobile
registrations, very slow for many years. The railroad passenger-miles per
1000 population represent the later growth of the use of the older invention and do not, in this chart, include the figures for the early years of the
use of railroads. The downward curve of the railroad passenger-miles
during the 1920's is due to the competition of the automobile, private and
public.

are data largely on non-scheduled transportation. The curve of
growth of automobile registrations is shown in Figure 13. In
order to eliminate the influence of population growth, the curve
shows the number of automobiles per one thousand persons. The
curve of the growth of automobile registrations is concave until
the early 1920's, and then, rising very steeply, becomes convex
within the same decade. During the 1930's, there were fluctuations due to business variations, but the curve was upward in a

more or less straight line of gentle slope. With the cessation of automobile production during the war, there was a leveling-off, but an upward growth is expected after the war. The number of automobile registrations has been increasing for over forty years and will probably continue to do so in the postwar decade.

The airplane comes to the traveling public of the United States a quarter of a century after the arrival of the automobile. The airplane, unlike the automobile, has been used first not so much by private owners as for commercial purposes — the carrying of mail and passengers. The curve of growth of the number of air passengers per one thousand population for the first fifteen years of air passenger traffic is shown in Figure 14. It is somewhat like

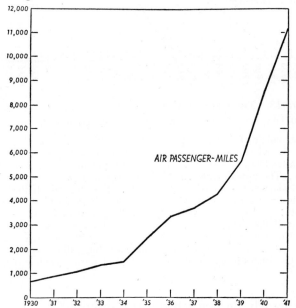

Figure 14. THE GROWTH CURVE OF AN INVENTION, THE AIRPLANE, IN AIR PASSENGER-MILES PER YEAR IN THE UNITED STATES, 1930-1941

The curve of passenger-miles flown by the air transport lines in the United States resembles the form of the curve of the production of automobiles. The plane was not adopted for extensive use as soon after its invention as was the automobile, but, during the 1930's, the shape of its growth curve was much like that of the automobile from 1910 to 1920. The curve is not carried beyond 1941 because of the disturbing influence of the war.

the curve of the growth of automobile registrations in its early beginnings. It is a concave curve; but we cannot say for certain by any extrapolation when it will become convex and level off. Automobile registrations are still growing forty years after their origin. Forty years of air passenger growth would take us to 1965, or to the end of the second postwar decade.

The railroad is a transportation invention with a longer history, dating back to 1830, a time so early that there are no records of the number of passengers or of passenger-miles. There are, however, a few statistics, and they show that the miles of track per 100,000 population continued to increase from 1830 for sixty years. The territory, as well as the population, was increasing during this period. But in the New England States, with the same area during this period, the railroad mileage of track per 100,000 population increased for forty-five years from its beginning in 1835. Recent data show that travel by railroad continued to expand until the coming of the private automobile and auto bus, which became very effective competitors in the 1920's. One may speculate as to whether air passenger traffic at some time in the future may not decrease if private flying becomes very widespread.

Still another invention with a longer history than the automobile is the telephone, a communication rather than a transportation invention. The telephone was invented at the beginning of the last quarter of the nineteenth century, and the curve of the number of telephones per one thousand population (shown in Figure 13) appears to have been moderately concave until the middle of the first decade of the twentieth century. Since then, the curve has been increasing in approximately a straight line of gentle slope until World War II, though with marked fluctuations in the 1930's. The number of telephones per one thousand population has been growing for sixty years, and its growth may continue into the postwar years. Sixty years of growth of air passenger traffic would reach into the 1980's.

Does the observation of the nature of growth of the steam railroad, the telephone, and the automobile give any suggestions which will aid in forecasting the future increase of air passenger-miles? In regard to the automobile and the telephone, there are no indications from the statistics that their growth has stopped after forty and sixty years, respectively. The growth of passenger traffic on the railroads continued for over three-quarters of a century, until about the end of World War I, when the appearance of the automobile brought a decrease in the number of railroad passengers.

These long periods of growth are thought to be due to the fact that these inventions reached a larger market by extending into the lower-income groups. Certainly this is the case in the number of telephones and the number of registered automobiles. For railroad passengers, it might be assumed that the higher-income classes traveled more, but it is more reasonable to think that the lower-income classes traveled increasingly by rail until the coming of the bus. American business, through mass production, has been developing larger domestic markets by reaching down into the lower-income groups. In an industry such as motion pictures, where the product involves units of small expenditures by the public, the acquisition of a market among the lower-income groups comes quickly. For automobiles, railroads, and airplanes, the penetration downward is slower. At the same time that the market is developing among low-income groups, the wages and earnings of these groups are rising over long periods of time because of the increased productivity which has occurred largely through technological progress.

These observations may be applied to aviation in the second postwar decade and afterward. At the present time, it is the businessman and the well-to-do classes that travel by air. But the aviation companies may be expected to try to enlarge their markets by penetrating into the lower-income groups. At the same time, it is quite possible that the earnings of these groups will slowly increase. The operation of these two factors, then, tends to prolong the period of expansion of aviation far beyond the first postwar decade.

One other observation of value in estimating future aviation growth is that, even when the growth has a slackening rate of slope, the actual annual increments may be large. Thus, after the curve of the number of automobile registrations had become convex and was tending to flatten out, there were some 700,000 registrations added per year — a much larger number than in the 1900's when the curve was concave and growing at an increasing rate. So also, fifty years after the appearance of the telephone, the rate of growth was lessening but there were some 750,000 new telephones added each year. We may expect that, even after the curve of growth of air passengers has become convex, the annual number of new passengers may be large.

There are various factors which will influence the growth of passenger travel after the first postwar decade. These factors are the growth of population, the volume of production, and the level of business conditions and technological developments.

Influence of Population Growth

The increase of population in the United States since its origin has favored the expansion of all types of activity. Some 35,000,000 immigrants have come to this country since 1820, in addition to the natural increase of births over deaths. From 1900 to 1930, our population increased by about 16,000,000 each decade. These recent increases meant rapidly developing markets for the then new transportation invention, the automobile, just as a rapidly growing population in the nineteenth century accompanied an enormous expansion of the railroads. The airplane will have no such favorable conditions. The population of the United States for the decade from 1950 to 1960 is expected to increase by about 6,000,000,[24] and less each decade thereafter. The increase will be greater if immigration is permitted, but if there is difficulty in furnishing employment to the labor force already here, there will be resistance to allowing much immigration. There will be some stimulus to transportation because of increases in population, but less than in former decades.

Income in the Second Postwar Decade

In the preceding discussion of national income for the first

[24] *Statistical Abstract*, Bureau of the Census, U.S. Department of Commerce, 1943, p. 9.

decade after the war, it was thought that there would be a much larger than normal increase during much of this period. This expected increase in productivity over normal peacetime will be the result of previous wartime shortages in goods, the great accumulation of purchasing power, and a possible large postwar volume of exports. At the end of World War I, in 1918, there was an increase in the national income far beyond the normal rate of increase.

Eventually, however, the exceptional demand for goods will be satisfied and the accumulated purchasing power spent. There will then occur a great slackening in the growth of national income or a depression of greater length and magnitude than usual. This was the experience after World War I. The large growth of income in the 1920's was succeeded by the depression years of the 1930's. During the first decade after World War I, from 1919 to 1929, the per capita national income (in stable prices) increased at a rate of 2.9 per cent per year. But for the two decades from 1919 to 1939, the per capita national income (in constant dollars), measured by a straight trend line fitted by the method of least squares, did not increase at all. There was a great loss of income in the second postwar decade.

We do not know, of course, that the experience after World War I will be repeated in the two decades after World War II. The two periods are similar as to shortages of goods, accumulated purchasing power, and the probable loans abroad and large volumes of exports. These stimulating influences lasted about a decade after World War I. The length of this period may not be the same after this war, and short depressions may occur. An uncertain factor is the extent to which governmental controls may be operative in holding back inflationary tendencies following the war. Most important of all is the extent to which governmental planning and spending may avoid a prolonged and severe depression after the above-mentioned stimulating influences are exhausted.

It seems reasonable to believe that eventually we shall be able to control the extreme fluctuations of business conditions and be successful in providing full employment. But it may be questioned whether we shall have attained such ability during the immediate postwar decades. Probably, the anticipated exceptional growth of income following the war will be succeeded by a period of a marked decrease in the growth of national income.

The discussion in the immediately preceding paragraphs of possible business conditions during the second postwar decade was for the purpose of considering their influence on air passenger transportation. We know that the fluctuations of intercity passenger transportation, of which air transportation is a part, follows the fluctuations of business and of national income, though the trends of intercity transportation and of national income may differ, even with one going up and the other down. So, in the second postwar decade, if there are, for considerable periods, strong recessions in national income, the effect on air transportation will be adverse. But with the trend of air transportation markedly upward, more so than that of railroads or buses, the recessions in income may not affect it as much as it will other types of intercity travel. In so far as air travel is luxury or business travel, the effect will be greater than if it were less elastic. In general, the rate of growth of air transportation in the second postwar decade may not be so great as in the first.

The Influence of Technological Improvements

Much of the increase in the number of air passenger-miles predicted for the first decade after the war will be due to technological improvements which will operate to lower costs. Some of these technological improvements will be found in the planes used about four or five years after the war. Technological advances may be expected in the second postwar decade and the years following. In Chapter 5, there is an extended discussion of the probable technical developments in aviation. It is there indicated that much is to be expected in the improvement and use of the turbo-jet power plant and reciprocating engine. Important economies are expected from lessened drag, and from the new large planes.

There are social conditions that will affect the rate of utilization of improvements on the airplane. Competition is said to hasten the use of improvements, and there is likely to be competition, especially between nations in the field of international transport. The prospects of reduced costs, increased numbers of passengers, and more profits will have a stimulating effect. Patent applications appear to be positively correlated to some degree with the business cycle.

There is a lapse of time between the idea of an improvement and its appearance in actual use. The more radical the change, the greater the lapse of time. At the present time, the airline companies think of a great change in size or design in terms of from five to seven years from the beginning of the designing to full utilization. Even after a new and improved plane is flown, one or two years may be needed to work out the faults and fit it for rugged service. Most of the new planes of the second postwar decade will be planned in the first decade after the war. The life of a transport plane is usually spoken of in terms of six or eight years, though very likely many of the present DC-3's will be flying more than six or eight years hence.

The improvements in an invention are made generally to increase its efficiency, or else to add to its consumer appeal in the form of comfort, ease, or beauty. In so far as these improvements increase efficiency, the cost per unit of function tends to be reduced, though the total cost may increase. The new large planes seating a hundred or more passengers cost a great deal more than the small planes, but the direct flying costs per seat-mile are reported to be less for the larger planes. The improvements in planes and in aviation in general, which seem sure to occur for several decades to come, even though we do not know what they will be, will have the effect of reducing the costs of transporting a passenger. Hence, it is not unreasonable to look for further reductions in costs beyond those indicated for the first postwar decade, say, toward a cost of three cents a passenger-mile, or perhaps even lower. These lower costs will increase the number of passengers greatly, subject, of course, to possible competition of lower rates on railroads and buses.

Conclusion

For the first postwar decade, the number of passenger-miles for air traffic is expected to be around 6,000,000,000 or 8,000,000,000 for the middle of the period, though there may be a few more or less. This forecast is based on an assumption of extraordinarily high production for most of the decade, and on a fare around three and a half cents to four cents a mile. If the fare should be three cents a mile, considerable increase in passenger-miles will follow. After the first decade, the trend of income expansion may slacken very greatly, and there are many indications that the rate of air passenger traffic growth will decrease. Even though the population becomes stationary, air passenger traffic is likely to increase slowly, but to a fairly large amount during the latter quarter of the century.

7

Carrying the Mail

AIR MAIL has been important, not only because of the advantages of speedier mail delivery, but also because the federal government has fostered the development of American civil aviation through the payment of air mail revenues. Air mail revenue was the backbone of the air transport industry up until a few years before World War II. Without air mail payments, practically all airline companies would have reported losses before the war.

Air Mail Rates

The federal government determines the size of air mail payments to the airline companies and fixes the cost of air mail postage for the public. An act of Congress could transfer all of the first-class, non-local mail to the air. Air mail rates differ from passenger and express rates in that they are determined by a governmental regulatory body for the benefit of the public.

The air mail rates set by the federal government have fluctuated widely over the period that air mail has been in existence. In 1918, the postage rate was set at twenty-four cents an ounce. When the amount of air mail was not so large as expected, the rate was reduced to sixteen cents an ounce in the same year. The volume of air mail increased but not sufficiently, so the rate was further reduced to six cents an ounce. However, plane loads were so light that air mail was supplemented by regular first-class mail. Since this seemed to be discriminatory, the surcharge for air mail was eliminated in 1919 and ordinary first-class mail was sent by plane. This practice was continued until 1924, when a through transcontinental air mail service was established with the inauguration of night flying.[1] Night flying made possible overnight delivery between Chicago and New York and freed air mail from dependence on surface transportation. Air mail became of real postal value and the Post Office Department felt the public would be willing to pay a surcharge to receive its benefits. (From 1924 to 1927, a zone system was in effect in which the rate varied according to the distance. In 1926, the charge was 10 cents per ounce up to 1000 miles and 20 cents over 1500 miles. In 1927, a flat rate of 10 cents was fixed, regardless of the distance, but the unit of weight was changed to a half-ounce instead of an ounce. In 1928, the rate was lowered to 5 cents for the first ounce and 10 cents for each additional ounce. In 1932, the rate became 8 cents for the first ounce and 13 cents for each additional ounce. From 1934 to 1944, a rate of 6 cents for each ounce was in force. In 1944, the rate was changed to 8 cents per ounce.)

Subsidy

The determination of air mail payment rates has been complicated by the problem of "subsidy." The costs of carrying passengers and mail are so intricately interconnected that it is practically impossible to separate them in order to allocate costs. The allocation of these joint costs, therefore, depends upon public policy rather than upon accounting practices, and the determination of public policy has hinged on the issue of "subsidy." The word "subsidy" has many meanings, but in general it is conceived of as some kind of public aid. American public thinking has construed subsidies to be antithetical to a free, competitive economic system. However, public aid of various kinds has been given to other forms of transportation. These are taken for granted and the controversial issue of subsidy has not been raised. For example, public highways have been built at federal expense for the use of the automobile, harbors and canals have been dredged for ships, and land has been purchased by federal funds for the laying of railroad tracks. In the field of aviation the issue has mainly concerned the covering of passenger traffic losses by air mail payments.

[1] Francis A. Spencer, *Air Mail Payment and the Government.* Washington, D.C.: The Brookings Institution, 1941, p. 26.

In 1925, when the air mail was turned over to private operators, Congress was anxious to avoid giving any subsidies to the industry. Subsidy was interpreted to mean payments to companies in excess of postal revenues. Therefore, they set forth the rule that no route was to be established unless the carrier agreed to receive air mail payments which were less than the postal revenues returned to the government from air mail on the route.[2] Under this rule the government could incur no loss from air mail transportation. On the other hand, the aviation industry maintained that subsidy existed only when the payments to contractors exceeded the actual costs of carrying the mail.

The administration of the rates under this law was difficult and expensive, and the airlines did not receive sufficient revenue. In the hope of making the airlines self-supporting on the basis of their passenger traffic, the government attempted to adjust the air mail payments in order to cover some of the costs of passenger service.[3] The mail payments were set so that equipment and services could be added in order to attract passengers from other means of transportation. Eventually, this meant partial governmental regulation of passenger rates and services.

Under the administration of the Interstate Commerce Commission from 1935 to 1938, there was considerable confusion as to the basis on which the mail payments should be set, but in general the rates were fixed by a method under which mail pay was expected to make up the difference between the total costs of operating the service required by the government and the non-mail revenues on that service.[4] In other words, it was a deficit-covering payment. By varying the amount of pay applicable to passenger service, the Commission could encourage a rapid expansion of passenger service with low fares, or it could encourage exclusive mail plane service.[5]

This practice has continued under the Civil Aeronautics Act. Mail rates have been set principally on the basis of the need of

[2] *Ibid.*, p. 30.
[3] Oliver J. Lissitzyn, *International Air Transport and National Policy* (Studies in American Foreign Relations, no. 3). New York: Council on Foreign Relations, 1942, p. 141.
[4] Spencer, *op. cit.*, p. 134.   [5] *Ibid.*, p. 144.

the carrier. In determining the rates, the Civil Aeronautics Board was instructed to take into consideration the needs of the carriers in order to maintain and develop air transportation for commercial, mail, and national defense purposes. However, the Board has attempted to vary the rates in order to encourage managerial efficiency and to discourage inefficiency and extravagance. Conditions in the air transportation system have changed so rapidly that rates have needed to be changed frequently. The setting of rates on the basis of predicted revenues and volume of business has been difficult because the predictions are often incorrect.

In 1943, for the first time, the total non-mail revenues of all airlines exceeded the total operating expenses.[6] In other words, the carriers as a whole would have made an operating profit even if they had received no air mail revenue. Of course, the individual airlines differed; the smaller airline carriers were still dependent on air mail revenues for a profit. The question arises as to how low air mail payments should go when the airlines are·able to operate at a profit without them. The Board has interpreted the minimum constitutional rate for air mail to be "one which will yield a reasonable return upon that part of the air carrier's total investment which is properly apportioned to such service." In order to do this effectively, it is necessary to allocate costs between passenger, express, and mail service, an extremely difficult task because so many of the costs are joint costs.

However, if the government transfers all first-class, non-local mail to the air, the deficit-covering nature of air mail payments may continue. The expansion of routes, planes, and services in order to carry all first-class mail by air would require increased expenditures by the airline companies. These new routes would undoubtedly be less profitable, at least until passenger and express business had been built up. For some companies this would result in deficits. Larger companies could finance the new routes out of passenger and express profits on the major trunk lines if this were the accepted policy. Much depends on the types of new routes that are required. If they are of the nature of local feeder

---

[6] From *Annual Report of the Civil Aeronautics Board*. Washington, D.C.: Government Printing Office, 1943, p. 29.

lines, federal aid will undoubtedly be needed, similar to that given when the present domestic air routes were being established. The operating costs of these feeder routes will be high in the first few years of establishment and the traffic potential comparatively small. Air mail traffic would provide the major source of revenue at first on these routes, but the government would probably adopt measures to encourage passenger and express traffic in order to make the air carriers self-supporting. Air mail payments to cover these costs might be justified on the basis of public benefit.

All First-Class Mail by Air

The idea that the government transport all first-class, non-local mail by air without surcharge has become increasingly widespread. It is in the public interest that mail be transported by the fastest service available. There are many political factors favorable to the transportation of first-class mail by air. Various recommendations have been made to Congress favoring the carriage of all non-local letter mail by air. In 1937, Senator Copeland, for the Senate Committee on Commerce, submitted Senate Report 185, Seventy-Fifth Congress, in which he pointed out: [7]

> The United States Post Office from the earliest days of our Republic has been a persistent pioneer in the encouragement of transport. Contracts for the transportation of mail by stagecoach, canal boat, pony express, railroads, ocean steamships, and finally, airplanes were designed, not merely to pay the cost of transportation of the mail but to share the cost of the construction and to encourage the operation of better vehicles to give faster service for the convenience of travelers and trade. This policy has been well sustained by successive Congresses for eighty years and should be continued. It imposes no great burden, because the revenue derived by the Government returns a substantial part of the cost. . . .
>
> It is the guiding principle behind all the operations of our post-office system that every community is entitled to the fastest

[7] Quoted by Colonel Edgar S. Gorrell, president of Air Transport Association of America, 78th Congress, 1st session, "A Bill to Amend the Civil Aeronautics Act of 1938," *Hearings,* February, 1943, pp. 108-109.

available means for the transportation of first-class letter mail. To give frequent, punctual, and quick communication and transportation of first-class mail, without the imposition of a surcharge, is regarded as one of the essential means Government has at its disposal to promote the common welfare. . . .

The transportation of mail without a surcharge by the fastest available mode of transport should benefit all classes. To the rich corporation, as to the less wealthy one and the small businessman, it will be pleasing, because of the vastly improved facilities it will offer for correspondence. To everybody it affords a rapid means of communication with distant friends and relatives, a privilege from which many are at present debarred by reason of the surcharge. Lower-cost air postage will give increased energy to trade and will confer many advantages which are in the public interest. . . .

The transportation of all first-class mail by air would be a very large undertaking, and would mean an enormous extension of airlines. For the immediate postwar years, this does not appear to be feasible. A more practical proposal is to transport by air all first-class mail going more than four hundred miles, since the saving in time is greater for the longer distances. Even this proposal would mean a very great extension of routes to small places, almost to the same extent as carrying all first-class mail by air. A still more practical proposal would be to carry by air all first-class mail going over four hundred miles where time would be saved by doing so. These different proposals will be examined.

The argument for transporting by air all first-class, non-local mail traveling over four hundred miles is supported by the fact that first-class mail returns a profit to the Post Office Department on the basis of their method of accounting. In 1940, the excess of revenues over expenditures for first-class mail was $137,000,000, and it was used mainly to subsidize other classes of mail which do not provide sufficient revenue to cover the expense of their handling and transportation.[8] Since the public is paying the highest postal rates for first-class mail, it would seem reasonable

[8] Curtiss-Wright Corporation, *Air Transportation in the Immediate Post-War Period*, Report no. BR-69, 1944, p. 102.

to expect that it should receive the fastest delivery service available. If this air service required larger expenditures of money, the rates of other classes of mail could be raised in order to make them more nearly self-supporting. Furthermore, for the last few years, air mail has also been returning a profit to the Post Office Department. In 1940, air mail resulted in a deficit to the Post Office of $9,000,000, which declined to $3,000,000 for the year ending June 30, 1942. In the fiscal year of 1943, for the first time in air mail history, the trend changed to a profit of nearly $18,000,000 and the estimated profit for the fiscal year of 1944 was $31,000,000.[9]

The Lea Bill to amend the Civil Aeronautics Act of 1938, introduced into Congress in January, 1943, provided for a report to Congress "concerning the feasibility and advantages of transporting by air all classes of mail wherever delivery thereof would be speeded by the use of air transportation, and there shall be included in such reports a plan for accomplishing such transportation and the recommendations concerning the time when such plan should be put into effect." [10]

In the hearings on this bill before the House Committee on Interstate and Foreign Commerce, Colonel Edgar S. Gorrell, president of the Air Transport Association of America, pointed out that the surcharge on air mail favors the rich corporation over the poor corporation in the solicitation of business. Furthermore, he felt that air mail would decrease geographic inequalities and put all business on the same basis in economic competition. With overnight delivery in the United States, all business houses would have equal opportunity to bid on business offers in New York City, for instance.

William A. Burden, Special Aviation Assistant to the Secretary of Commerce, predicted in 1943 that within a few years after the war "all of our long distance mail traffic will go by air." [11]

Charles I. Stanton, former Administrator of the Civil Aeronautics Administration, states: [12] "It seems to me that it is sound

9 Charles I. Stanton, "Air Mail Comes of Age," *Flying*, August, 1944, p. 25.
10 78th Congress, 1st session, *Hearings, op. cit.*, p. 1.
11 *Aviation News*, September 13, 1943, p. 9.
12 Stanton, *op. cit.*, p. 150.

to carry all first-class mail by air whenever its ultimate delivery will be advanced thereby, with other forms of transport used whenever they may accomplish the same result at less cost."

All-up air mail has already had a precedent in European countries. Before World War II, there was a trend in Europe to transport first-class mail by air without surcharge whenever time was saved by so doing. Almost every country in Europe carried letter mail by air without surcharge whenever air service assured earlier delivery. In 1937, England instituted the "all-up" British Empire air mail service, principally to cement empire relationships. It was found to stimulate correspondence to an unusual degree, although it was in effect only until 1939, when it had to be suspended because of the war. These European countries had larger elements of state subsidy in their total revenues than there were in American domestic revenues.

The carrying by air, then, of all first-class mail going four hundred miles and more over present air routes is supported by a good deal of opinion, is feasible technically, and, as will be shown later, will add very little to the costs of postal service. It therefore is to be expected. But may we not expect that the social pressure for more extensive air mail carriage will force the creation of new routes?

Extension of Mail Routes

The air transportation of all first-class mail traveling over four hundred miles would require an extension of mail routes and services and a development of feeder lines. For an efficient all-up mail system it would be necessary to provide next-day delivery to every important community in the country. At the present time, passenger and air mail plane services are identical except in the case of All American Aviation, Inc., which operates a pick-up service for mail only. There were only two certificates in 1944 which did not include air mail service, both of which were not in operation.[13]

There are about 1200 first-class post offices in the United States

[13] William J. Madden and Albert E. Beitel, Examiners, *Investigation of Local-Feeder Pick-up Air Service*, Docket no. 857, 1944, p. 17.

and 3600 second-class post offices. In comparison, there were only 288 points certificated for air service in 1943, and many of these were suspended because of wartime conditions or had never received service. But, in 1939, the 1200 first-class post offices produced 78 per cent of the non-local first-class mail pound-mileage and the second-class post offices, only 12 per cent.[14] Since the points certificated for air service were mainly in the larger cities with first-class post offices, the mail coverage was perhaps more adequate than might appear from the comparison of total post offices and certificated air points, if a large proportion of the mail is between urban centers rather than from urban to rural areas.

The Post Office Department has had very little experience with air mail service to small communities. The feeder-line mail service of All American Aviation, Inc., was instituted in 1939 as an experiment. This mail route was located in Pennsylvania and West Virginia and served 56 communities with two routes 1040 miles long. The mail was picked up and delivered while the plane was in flight. By 1945, the system had been expanded to five routes 1568 miles long, serving 118 communities. The air mail carried on these routes in 1944 was estimated to have produced postal revenues of $1,915,000 as compared with $534,000 mail pay received by the company.[15]

Several estimates have been made of the number of routes necessary in order to have complete air service for the United States. According to Warner, 284 stations in 1944 served 64 per cent of the population, counting the population within a twenty-five-mile radius of the airport. To serve the remaining 36 per cent of the population, 2100 more stations would be required. As the number of stations increases, the smaller the additional proportion of population served.[16]

J. Parker Van Zandt estimates that two hundred feeder routes of the type of All American Aviation, each contacting an average

14 J. Parker Van Zandt, "Air Transport," *Transportation and National Policy,* Part II, Section I, p. 347.

15 News Release from All American Aviation, Inc., Wilmington, Delaware, May 12, 1945.

16 Edward Warner, "Requirements of Local Air Transport Service," *Aeronautical Engineering Review,* vol. 3, no. 2, February, 1944, p. 27.

of twenty points, would service 90 per cent or more of the non-local first-class mail.[17] This would require a thousand additional smaller planes. The per-mile cost of these routes might be small, but yet considerably more than the primary routes.

One report relating to proposed air service in the Rocky Mountain States set up a prospective feeder line in which the expected costs were compared to the present costs of air mail.[18] The mail payment to the airline per route-mile of the proposed feeder route was only $347, as compared with $981 per route-mile for scheduled air carriers in 1930 and $512 in 1940. But the comparison of mail payment per route-mile per million urban population was to the disadvantage of the feeder service. For the feeder route, $806 was the annual mail payment per route-mile per million urban population, compared with $29 in 1930 for scheduled air carriers and $13 in 1940. Although feeder lines may be expected to have higher costs on the basis of population served, it will not be as high in general as on this proposed route. The mail payment per route-mile to All American Aviation, in 1944, was $341, and the mail payment per route-mile per million population was $74. This $74 is higher than the $13 for scheduled air lines, but it is less than the $806 expected in the Rocky Mountain feeder route.

Although the feeder lines are expected to have higher per-mile costs than the ordinary air mail service of today, yet there are several items which are cheaper for the feeder airlines. The air pick-up system can operate efficiently and safely without the airway and navigation facilities which the primary air routes require. The pick-up equipment which the city to be serviced must purchase at present for All American Aviation pick-up costs only approximately $150. An airport is not necessary.

The experience of All American Aviation shows that one pick-up station can serve a number of post offices. In 1940, 805 post offices dispatched mail through 66 pick-up stations, an average of 12 post offices per station.[19] In 1944, three routes had one round

---

[17] Van Zandt, *op. cit.*, p. 347.

[18] United Air Lines, Inc., Exhibit U-75 before Civil Aeronautics Board, Docket no. 152, July 31, 1944.

[19] Madden and Beitel, *op. cit.*, p. 18.

trip daily and the other two routes had two trips daily. Six planes
were in daily use and two were held in reserve. All American
Aviation believed that night service and planes of larger capacity
than those being used would result in better service. In 1944,
the average monthly mail loads were approximately 80,000
pounds, and express, 14,000 pounds. The development of express
traffic was not expected to reduce the mail rate to a large extent,
since air mail yields a considerably greater revenue per pound
to the Post Office than does express.

If passengers were carried on the air mail feeder routes, mail
costs would be reduced. Up to the present time, the All American
Aviation feeder line has carried no passengers. But the examiners
for the Civil Aeronautics Board, in the investigation of local-
feeder pick-up air service, concluded from the experience of this
company that there is probably no element of risk or danger in
carrying passengers in planes using a pick-up device, although
a considerable amount of experimentation is still necessary.[20]
Estimates of future costs of feeder-line mail service are often
based on an assumed average load of two passengers at a rate of
five cents per passenger-mile. Passenger services on the feeder
lines are expected to be without many of the features which
trunk lines have today — meals, hostesses, stewards, heavy and
expensive cabin furnishings, etc. The cost will also be lower if
the second crew member is not required to be a pilot, but only
to take care of the mail sorting and the pick-up device.

The Airline Traffic Survey of Originations and Destinations for
November, 1939, and September, 1940, showed that there was
not a great potential passenger traffic from small cities. This
might indicate a similar conclusion as to the potential mail from
small cities. A letter from the Postmaster General,[21] dated
November 5, 1943, to the Chairman of the Civil Aeronautics
Board stated that he expected the increases in air mail volume to
follow the normal trade channels which have been covered for
some time by air transportation. However, he further stated that
there were some areas where traffic potentials for feeder routes
suggested early self-sufficiency or where the public benefit to be

20 *Ibid.*, p. 66.   21 *Ibid.*, pp. 23-24.

derived overshadowed the factor of cost. Such an expansion would have the support of the Post Office Department.

There is not much actual evidence on which to base a prediction of the potential mail traffic from small places if air transportation service were available. Plane loads from small cities and towns, even with all first-class mail going by plane, would undoubtedly remain smaller than on the present major air routes, since small towns originate less mail than large urban centers. However, air mail volumes might be increased on present routes to small communities if there were more advertising of the air mail services available. The experience of All American Aviation showed that the number of pieces of mail dispatched from pickup points increased at a greater rate than the amount received at such points. The number of pieces received increased approximately five and one-half times from January, 1941, to July, 1943, while the number of pieces dispatched increased about sixteen times for the same months.[22] This might indicate that senders of mail to these cities were not aware of the fact that there was air mail service to these cities and air mail volumes might increase if the fact were known. Although the Post Office at present does not feel that there is a great need for air-feeder services to small cities, a demand might be created if a few more such feeder lines were established. A city which saw other cities receiving such services would want to get similar services

Some of the prospects for extending air services to smaller places have been reviewed. They will be discussed further in the chapter on local air service. It is shown there that the costs of local air service will be so large and the traffic potential in the immediate future so small that, omitting consideration of mail transportation, the extension of air routes to these smaller places without subsidy will proceed slowly. But this process may be speeded by public pressure. There are many who will feel that the great value of air transportation is being received by only the larger cities and that the smaller places should not be discriminated against and denied the benefits of air mail. It is, therefore, likely that public opinion will force a more rapid ex-

[22] Calculated from figures from Madden and Beitel, *op. cit.*, p. 20.

tension by means of mail subsidies. How far this extension will go in the first postwar decade is a question that cannot be answered in terms of measurement. However, a limit can be seen, the limit of time saved. For many places near a city with an airport, the more frequent schedules of trains and other means of transportation will bring mail sooner than the infrequent schedules by air.

Air Service on Rural Mail Routes

In June, 1942, there were 32,292 rural mail service routes, totaling 1,420,971 miles. The average length of a rural mail service route was 44 miles. The cost for this service to the Post Office Department was 20.48 cents per mile, including carriers' salaries and equipment. The number of star routes in June, 1942, was 11,400. The one-way length of these routes was 303,524 miles, with an average length of 26.6 miles. The average cost per scheduled mile was 6.04 cents.[23] In 1939, a contract was awarded for an air star route (the only one that has been awarded) to be located totally within the State of Ohio, with a one-way distance of 23 miles. The rate was set at 62 cents per airplane-mile for a base load of 250 pounds a trip and one cent per airplane-mile for each 20 pounds in excess. The rate for future rural mail routes and star line routes might be expected to approach that of feeder lines if passengers were allowed. It would appear that the helicopter would be suited to rural mail routes, although the helicopter rates are expected to be higher than airplane rates.

Estimates of the Future Volume of Domestic Air Mail Traffic

If all first-class letter mail traveling over four hundred miles is transferred to the air, what will be the future volume of air mail?

The Curtiss-Wright Corporation has made a study predicting the future volume of air mail, basing its estimates on an expected increase in the gross national product.[24] In the past, the report shows, there has been a fairly close correspondence between the total volume of first-class mail and the gross national product.

[23] *Ibid.*, p. 22.   [24] Curtiss-Wright Corporation, *op. cit.*, pp. 100-103.

Assuming that all first-class mail traveling over four hundred miles will be transferred to the air at the regular first-class rate by government action, and that there is approximately a 50-percent increase in the gross national product five years after the end of the war, taken as 1950, 86,800,000 ton-miles of air mail are predicted.

The effect on postal costs of eliminating the air mail surcharge and sending all first-class mail traveling over four hundred miles by air was shown to be negligible by the Curtiss-Wright report. In 1940, the Post Office paid $39,500,000 for the transportation of all first-class mail. If the airlines had carried all mail going over four hundred miles at an average payment of sixty cents per ton-mile, the airlines would have received $35,200,000 instead of the $19,100,000 they did receive. The actual railroad revenue on the first-class mail of $20,400,000 would have been reduced to $6,700,000. Thus, carrying the first-class mail moving over four hundred miles by air would have cost the Post Office $41,900,000 ($35,200,000 plus $6,700,000), an increase of only $2,400,000 in 1940. However, the Post Office would have lost $9,500,000 in revenues by dropping the air mail surcharge. Thus, the total increase in expenditures would have been $11,900,000. But this figure is only 4 per cent of the total 1940 expenditures of $296,000,000 for first-class mail, and but 8.7 per cent of the excess of revenues over apportioned expenditures on first-class mail. The first-class mail produces an excess of revenue to the Post Office over expenditures because of the greater number of pieces per pound than in other classes of mail. This excess amounted to $137,000,000 in 1940 and was used mainly to subsidize other classes of mail. If transferring all mail to the air increased total first-class postal expenditures, a part of this excess revenue could be used, and other classes of mail could become more nearly self-supporting.

An estimate of the future amount of air mail from another source [25] gives a somewhat lower figure than that of Curtiss-Wright. The difference appears to arise from the fact that the increase in the total volume of letter mail is not expected to be

[25] The corporation making this study in 1943 wishes to remain anonymous.

as large as that estimated by Curtiss-Wright. A graph of the
total number of pieces of mail handled by the Post Office shows
a rapid growth between 1896 and 1912, after which the number
of pieces increased at a slower rate and the curve began to level
off, decreasing in the depression years of 1930-1935 and coming
back to the pre-depression point just before the war. The prediction assumes that the growth of all classes of mail after the war
will be relatively small, since domestic mail is no longer in a
period of rapid expansion. Letter mail has remained at a fairly
constant percentage of total mail for a period of years, so its rate
of growth is expected to be slow also. Assuming all letter mail to
be sent by air at a three-cent rate, 53,000,000 ton-miles are expected in 1950, and at a six-cent rate, 24,500,000 ton-miles. At a
rate of sixty cents per ton-mile for mail payments to the airlines
after the war, which was the rate paid to the larger airlines during the war, both of these predicted estimates would return a
profit to the Post Office in 1950, the six-cent rate showing a considerably larger profit than the three-cent rate.

J. Parker Van Zandt makes no predictions as to the future air
mail potential, but he has analyzed the figures to show what the
results would have been of transporting by air all non-local, first-
class domestic mail traveling over four hundred miles in 1939.[26]
The non-local first-class mail in that year totaled about 70,000,000
ton-miles of which about 75 per cent traveled four hundred miles
or more. If this were transferred to the air, over 50,000,000 ton-
miles would be added to air mail figures. If the weight of con-
tainers were included, the total would be increased to 70,000,000
ton-miles, or seven times the 1940 quantity. Mr. Van Zandt attempts to discover how this would affect the total postal revenues
and comes to the conclusion that first-class mail would still yield
the same amount of revenue to the Post Office. The mail payments to railroads for first-class mail would be decreased 75 per
cent, but this would be only 15 per cent of the total railroad
receipts from the Post Office, since the railroads carry also
second-, third-, and fourth-class mail. It is suggested that this reduction might be made up by an increased amount of these

26 Van Zandt, *op. cit.*, pp. 345-348.

classes of mail. This was found to be the result in England's all-up Empire mail service, and the revenue to steamships was not adversely affected. Mr. Van Zandt does not provide for second-, third-, and fourth-class mail going by air. The Post Office in 1939 received 2.3 mills gross revenue per net pound-mile of non-local first-class mail. Although in 1939 air mail rates were twice those of ordinary letter mail, the Post Office received only 1.2 mills gross revenue per net pound-mile of air mail. At the 52-cents-per-ton-mile rate, the first-class mail would still yield a profit of $1.40 per ton-mile, or more than $100,000,000 a year. This was due to the fact that the average haul of air mail was almost three times that of ordinary letter mail (average haul of domestic air mail in 1939 was 1397 miles, as compared with 478 miles for non-local domestic first-class mail), and also because letter mail has a greater number of pieces per pound.

Mr. Van Zandt points out that in 1939 the average aggregate cost to the Post Office for transporting non-local letter mail and air mail was 49 cents per ton-mile. If one-fourth of the mail were continued at this rate and the remainder by air at an average compensation of 52 cents per ton-mile (to the air carriers), then the total Post Office excess revenues would remain the same.[27] If compensations above 52 cents per ton-mile were required, then this could be taken out of the profits of first-class mail. Whether or not the air carriers can transport 70,000,000 ton-miles of additional mail at a payment of 52 cents per ton-mile depends on the number of additional routes and schedules required and on the average size of mail loads.

Foreign Air Mail

The first foreign air mail line was established in 1920. It connected Seattle, Washington, and Victoria, British Columbia, a distance of approximately seventy-four miles; [28] thus it was very similar in character to domestic air mail routes. Another foreign air service, between Key West, Florida, and Havana, Cuba, was

[27] Van Zandt, op. cit., p. 347.
[28] Post Office Department, A Brief History of the Air Mail Service, Division of Air Mail Service, p. 5.

also inaugurated in 1920. In 1928, a contract to Pan American included service to Cuba, Mexico, British Honduras, Republic of Honduras, Nicaragua, Costa Rica, and the Canal Zone. The additional foreign air mail routes which followed in the 1930's to the east and west coasts of South America and across the Pacific and Atlantic Oceans have been described in previous chapters.

Legislation providing for foreign air mail contracts and payment was passed in 1928 and 1929 in the Foreign Air Mail Act. The rates were based upon the amount of space reserved for mail. In reality, it provided a guarantee of minimum income to the contractors.[29] This legislation remained in effect until 1938. Under the Civil Aeronautics Act, the need of the carrier became one of the basic standards for determining air mail payments. Mail rates have been determined so as to enable the carrier to meet its expenses. For example, the rates for the trans-Pacific services were first set at $2 per plane-mile for the first 1000 pounds. Since this resulted in annual losses to the company, the base rate was raised from $2 to $3.35.[30] In terms of excess of mail payments over postal revenues, the aid given to foreign air mail is greater than to domestic air mail. In 1935, the excess of mail payments to the carriers over postal revenues was 58.1 per cent of the carriers' revenues; in 1940, it was 24.5 per cent.[31] As these figures show, foreign airlines are progressing toward being self-supporting, but have not gone as far as have domestic air carriers. On only one international route have the postal revenues exceeded the payments to airlines. That one is the trans-Atlantic route of Pan American Airways. Due to war conditions, the Post Office revenues from December, 1939, to November, 1940, exceeded payments to the company by a half million dollars.[32] By 1941, the mail volume was so large in comparison with the base load that payments to carriers averaged about $10 per pound.

Governmental aid has probably been the greatest on the trans-Pacific lines. The carriers had to bear the cost of establishing the facilities for stops at the Pacific islands between California and

[29] Lissitzyn, *op. cit.*, p. 143.   [30] *Ibid.*, p. 148.
[31] *Ibid.*, p. 153.   [32] *Ibid.*, p. 154.

the Orient. Furthermore, mail and passenger traffic has been lightest on the Pacific routes. Public aid has been decreasing in importance in airline revenues on Latin American routes. Mail routes to Canada and Mexico are similar to domestic lines in the United States and have been the farthest advanced toward self-support of the United States foreign air mail lines.

The advantages of transferring all first-class mail to the air are even more obvious in the case of foreign than in that of domestic mail. Greater speed would be provided in almost every instance, since the foreign distances are long and the competing means of transportation — water travel — is much slower. Railroads and trucks provide competitive means for land mail that is sometimes as fast as by air, but in foreign air mail there are no effectively competitive methods of transport.

Foreign air mail is particularly in the public interest, since it involves the factor of national prestige. The operation of efficient and extensive airlines to foreign countries is good advertising for a nation's industry. Absence of an airline permits the prestige to fall to other countries.

Air mail service promotes intercourse and co-operation between the United States and foreign countries. This will be particularly important if international co-operation is to be successful. The United States Department of State has already used air mail to some extent to receive reports and send instructions to representatives in foreign countries. There is a political advantage in having one's own air mail lines to foreign countries, since the mail sent by such lines cannot be delayed or censored by outside interests. Air mail provided by one's own airline carriers is an asset in diplomatic competition.

Air mail is also an instrument of colonial policy. The purpose of England's "all-up" Empire Air Mail Scheme was to promote administrative cohesion, provide cultural contacts, and in general to promote Empire allegiance and loyalty.

Foreign air mail is of economic advantage because it speeds up business correspondence. Sending orders, quotations, credit information, bills of lading, drafts, checks, etc., by air mail may prevent business from going to competitors who do have the advantages of air mail. It is reasonable to expect that American businessmen will desire to have these advantages in their competition with businesses of foreign countries.

American airlines to South America have been particularly important, both for political and economic reasons. The South American continent is almost an equal distance from Europe and from the United States. The penetration of German and French airlines in South America would have put the United States at a disadvantage if comparable American airlines had not been set up before the war. The success of the program for Pan-American co-operation would have been impossible without rapid air transportation between North and South America. American business is increasingly using air mail to South America. The percentage of letter mail carried by air from the United States to Latin America (excluding Cuba and Mexico) increased from 3 per cent in 1930 to 16.5 per cent in 1939.[33]

Curtiss-Wright Corporation has made a prediction of the future volume of foreign air mail similar to that made for domestic air mail. In an average year (1930-39) approximately 5,000,000 pounds of first-class mail are sent from the United States to foreign countries. Since the figures are not available, incoming mail is not considered. As with domestic mail, the volume of foreign mail tends to correspond to the business cycle with a lag of about a year. On the basis of this relationship and adding a factor for new mail business to be created by air mail, at the projected levels of gross national product, Curtiss-Wright estimates that the total first-class mail by sea and air will be 7,400,000 pounds in the first postwar year and 9,700,000 in the tenth.[34]

The proportion of the total first-class mail traveling by air would depend on the comparative rates of surface and air transportation unless the government transferred all first-class mail to the air. Prewar air mail rates were high in comparison to surface rates, yet air mail volume was rapidly growing. Air mail rates are expected to be substantially reduced in the postwar decade. Competition from foreign countries with low air mail rates will be a factor in forcing American air mail rates down.

[33] *Ibid.*, p. 341.   [34] Curtiss-Wright, *op. cit.*, p. 141.

Curtiss-Wright predicts a decline from the prewar average rate of sixty cents an ounce to five cents an ounce ten years after the war (unless the government transfers all first-class mail to the air).

The United Air Lines similarly made a prediction of total overseas letter mail.[35] The prediction, based upon a projection of the national income, was for 11,000,000 pounds of overseas letter mail in 1950 and 12,200,000 in 1955.[36]

First-class overseas mail is divided between the Atlantic, Latin American, and Pacific areas in a ratio of about 50:23:30 respectively.[37] Curtiss-Wright breaks down the future air mail volumes geographically on the basis of the pattern of traffic which has existed in the past. However, in the *Survey of United States Overseas Mail*, the Economic Bureau of the Civil Aeronautics Board demonstrated that the total volumes of United States letter mail to certain areas were more mature in development than others. The total volume of trans-Atlantic letter mail has been relatively stable since 1923, decreasing, beginning in 1939, due to war conditions. Trans-Pacific air mail increased considerably in volume from 1923 to 1930. Since 1930, the volume has decreased. Letter mail to Central and South America and the West Indies has shown the greatest rate of growth. The rate was rather rapid between 1923 and 1930, decreasing during the years of depression, and then steadily increasing from 1933 to 1940.

Thus, we may expect absolute increases in the volume of air mail to all areas, but the percentage of trans-Atlantic air mail to the total will be decreasing. Air mail to the Pacific and South and Latin American areas will increase in proportion to the total foreign mail leaving the United States because these areas are increasing in population and in economic development.

Conclusion

There is a strong possibility that all first-class domestic mail

[35] Exhibits of United Air Lines, Inc., before the Civil Aeronautics Board, Docket no. 1345, Exhibit no. U-30.

[36] Both this and the Curtiss-Wright estimate were based on figures from the *Survey of United States Overseas Mail*, Civil Aeronautics Board, Economic Bureau, September, 1943.

[37] Curtiss-Wright, *op. cit.*, p. 141.

traveling over four hundred miles and all foreign first-class mail will be transferred to the air on existing routes by government action in the postwar decade. This is supported by both political and economic factors. Carrying all domestic letter mail traveling over four hundred miles will require an extension of the present trunk lines and a network of local feeder lines, and these same political and economic pressures are likely to speed the construction of such feeder lines during the first postwar decade. Air mail potentials from small towns are lighter than those from large urban centers. Mail payments will be higher on feeder routes unless passenger and express traffic bear some of the cost. Although air carriers are now self-supporting on the basis of passenger and express revenues alone, the importance of air mail payments in the development of civil aviation may continue in the establishment of local feeder routes.

Foreign air mail at present is more dependent on mail payments than is domestic mail, but it is progressing toward becoming self-supporting. Volumes of mail to Latin America and the Pacific countries are expected to increase substantially, while the volume of trans-Atlantic letter mail has shown a mature trend.

The postal rates for air mail service are so much a subject of policy and choice, rather than of discernible and inevitable trends, that they are difficult to predict. But the pressure for low rates, comparable to those of railroads and steamships, is very real and likely to be effective.

8

The Transportation of Goods

THE CARRYING OF CARGO has been one of the later developments of airline business. Air transportation began with the carriage of mail; operations were then extended to include passengers. But even up to the present time air cargo has not been developed to any great extent. In 1928, the weight of passengers carried on domestic airlines was forty-five times the weight of the cargo; while, in 1939, the weight of the passengers was forty times that of cargo.[1] Although the amount of air cargo has been small compared to air passenger traffic or railroad shipments, yet its percentage increases have been great. The number of ton-miles of air cargo increased more than 300 per cent from 1935 to 1940, reaching 3,500,000 ton-miles in the latter year. When this is compared to the 584,000,000,000 ton-miles of freight carried by other methods of transportation in 1940, it can be seen that air cargo transportation is still in its infancy. Our problem in this chapter is whether air cargo will "grow up," so to speak, in the future and take cargo from other means of transportation or whether it will be restricted to small volumes of particular kinds of goods.

Air Cargo in World War II

Prior to the war, the goods carried by airplanes, in addition to passengers and mail, were thought of as express rather than as cargo. In 1939, three-quarters of the goods carried by planes were in packages weighing less than five pounds.[2] Sometimes a

[1] Calculated from John H. Frederick, *Commercial Air Transportation*, Chicago: Richard D. Irwin, Inc., 1943, pp. 297, 397, on the basis of 200 pounds for a passenger and his baggage.
[2] Illinois Central System, *Air-Freight*, Research and Development Bureau, 1942, p. 16.

shipment weighed over one hundred pounds, but not often. The war first called wide attention to the fact that planes can carry heavy loads. Bombs weighing many tons, trucks, heavy machinery, and other weighty articles were carried by military planes.

The new big cargo planes of 3000 cubic feet capacity were accurately described as "flying box cars," since the standard railroad box car contains about 2700 cubic feet. The seaplane *Mars*, which weighs 148,500 pounds, has a cubic capacity of a fifteen-room house. And much larger planes are being designed.

The question, then, is no longer whether the airplane can carry heavy cargoes, since this has already been demonstrated during the war, but "Will airplanes carry these great loads of freight in peacetime?"

The Problem of Costs

In wartime, costs are secondary to the major objective of winning the war. Military operations are carried on more or less irrespective of economic costs. But such is not the case in peacetime in our capitalistic system of private enterprise. The airplane has to compete with the railroad and the steamship on the basis of cargo rates.

At the present time, the rates are all in favor of railroads and ships. In 1942, the average charge for railway express was 9.1 cents per ton-mile, while air cargo was 77 cents per ton-mile. The air cargo rate was reduced in July, 1943, to about 70 cents per ton-mile. Rail charges for freight in less-than-carload lots was only 3.8 cents per ton-mile in 1942,[3] while the charge for carload lots was slightly over 1 cent per ton-mile. The rate for ocean-going freight was slightly over 2 mills (1939) per ton-mile.

However, the kinds of goods that go by air more nearly approximate railway express or parcel post than the above categories. The parcel post rate is about 20 cents per ton-mile, which is approximately one-fourth the air rate in 1943. The railway express rate is about one-ninth the air rate. Perhaps an even better comparison with air rates is the average rate for first-class railway

[3] Association of American Railroads, *Initial Study of Air Transportation*, January, 1944, pp. 40, 42.

express, which was about 14 cents per ton-mile in 1940. Air rates were, then, five times the rate for first-class railway express.

One might think from these figures that little cargo would go by air because it is so much cheaper to ship by other methods of transportation. Yet at these high rates the volume of air cargo increased almost forty times in the prewar decade.[4] This rapid growth is apparently due to the demand for speed, since it is said that the airline companies have not made any great effort to develop cargo or express traffic. It is possible that there might be a continued growth of air cargo in the future even at these rates, for there is an unknown amount of goods that might be attracted by speed to air transportation even at high rates. But it is obvious that even more goods would be transported by air if the rates were lowered. The airline companies have just recently begun to see the great possibilities in air cargo and to be interested in obtaining cargo business. It is probable, therefore, that the airline companies will make an effort to increase the volume of air cargo by lowering rates if that is possible.

An Estimate of Cargo Costs in the Near Future

Attempts to estimate with precision future costs and rates for cargo are naturally hazardous in such uncertain times and in a phase of the industry which is so little developed and changing so rapidly. However, such an attempt has been made by the Curtiss-Wright Corporation.[5] Certain factors which are quantitatively measurable are selected for study and the future estimates are called "economic rate bases." In addition to the measurable factors in these economic rate bases, many intangible factors, such as governmental subsidies, public pressure, competitive factors, etc., will come into operation. However, it may be assumed that rates will approximate the predicted economic rate bases. For this reason and to simplify the exposition, these economic rate bases will be referred to as estimated cargo rates.

Curtiss-Wright takes into consideration two periods. One is a

---

[4] Frederick, op. cit., p. 397.
[5] Curtiss-Wright Corporation, *Air Transportation in the Immediate Post-War Period*, Report no. BR-69, 1944.

transitional period after the war, lasting about two years, when the stock of planes will be present types plus the heritage of the military troop and cargo carriers modified to suit peacetime needs. The second period is around 1950, estimated to be about five years after the war, when the new postwar planes incorporating the design improvements of the war come into use. These new planes are expected to appear earlier than four or five years after the war, but perhaps not in large enough numbers to have significant effects on traffic. The rates for carrying cargo are also estimated for two types of planes — one carrying both passengers and cargo, the other, all cargo.

The method employed in the Curtiss-Wright study is to carry forward the measurable costs for passenger transportation with such modifications,[6] usually downward, as appear possible and likely in the first few years after the war. Certain adjustments were then made to change these costs to cargo costs. In figuring the costs for cargo carried in passenger planes, the costs were estimated to be about the same for cargo as for passengers except that the traffic and advertising expense was placed at less for cargo than for passengers. For a small trunk-line combination passenger-cargo plane of 20,000 to 30,000 pounds gross weight and seating twenty to twenty-five passengers, with stops

---

[6] The projection was on the basis of the Mentzer-Nourse method, slightly adjusted. For direct flying expenses, crew salaries and insurance were held constant, 100-octane fuel was estimated at 16 cents, 12.5 cents for 87-octane, 45 cents a gallon for oil. Airplane prices were generally set at a manufacturers' cost of $10.50 a pound. Depreciation time for airplanes was six years. Maintenance cost was 20 per cent less than the Mentzer-Nourse formula. Passenger supplies were placed at 2.35 mills per passenger-mile; flying time per plane per year on trunk lines, from 3100 to 3450 hours per year, with a load factor of 65 per cent.

The ratio of direct flying expenses to indirect flying expenses was 47 per cent, assuming that the average airline company operates approximately 40,000,000 plane-miles annually. Indirect flying expenses include costs of ground facilities, communications, meteorological and other miscellaneous station expenses not directly related to the operation of the plane.

The traffic and advertising expenses were held at the 1941 figure of 8 cents per revenue passenger ton-mile.

The general and administrative expense was estimated to be 6.7 per cent of all other expenses for the average company operating 40,000,000 plane-miles annually. At the same time the return on the investment was to be 8 per cent of all the above costs. (Curtiss-Wright, *op. cit.*, pp. 57-61.)

100 miles apart, these calculations yielded a cost of 37.5 cents per ton-mile, not counting ground-handling charges.[7] For a larger combination passenger-cargo plane, of 40,000 to 75,000 tons, with stops of 500 to 1500 miles, the costs are about 27.5 cents per ton-mile for this postwar transition period. For still larger planes of 100,000 to 150,000 pounds, the rates are 22 cents. These costs of under 40 cents a ton-mile are for large companies with equipment improved over the present, expected several years after the war. The average revenue for air express, omitting revenues for collection going to the American Railway Express, for all airline companies in August, 1943, was about 47 cents a ton-mile.[8]

An important part of air cargo transportation is getting shipments to and from the airport. This service is rendered at present by the Railway Express Agency. The ground handling and pick-up costs amounted, in 1941, to 26 cents a ton-mile for an eight-pound package transported 1000 miles by air.[9] The Curtiss-Wright study attempted to estimate how much ground-handling costs could be reduced by changes in the present service. The great bulk of hauling to and from the airport occurs at certain peak times, one of which is the late afternoon. By regularizing this service at the peak time and fitting it to a market that will be satisfied with an overnight, door-to-door service, the study indicated that the charges of hauling to and from the airport could be cut almost in half, assuming also a considerable increase in the volume of cargo by air.

But getting cargo to and from the airport is only about half the ground-handling costs. There are, in addition, platform expense, clerical costs, losses, insurance, rents, and so on. Adding these in, the average ground costs per ton-mile are estimated to be about 8 cents for a package of 25 pounds going by air a distance of 750 miles, which is about one-third of the 1941 ground costs. A prin-

[7] These costs are broken down as follows: direct flying expense (65 per cent load factor) per revenue ton-mile, $.3055, traffic and advertising expense, $.02; general and administrative expense, $.0218; and profit and income tax, $.0278. (Curtiss-Wright, *op. cit.*, p. 64.)

[8] Association of American Railroads, *op. cit.*, p. 38.

[9] Curtiss-Wright, *op. cit.*, p. 65.

cipal reason for this further drop in costs is an assumed increased weight per package to 25 pounds, which reduces the cost per ton-mile more than it is increased by a probable shortening of the average distance transported from 1000 to 750 miles. When this ground-handling charge of 8 cents is added to the estimated cost of haul by airplane of 37.5 cents, the resulting costs are 45.5 cents per ton-mile. While this is much less than a prewar charge of 80 cents a ton-mile, it is still about three times the cost of first-class railway express. It is possible that competition may bring the air rates down to around 40 cents a ton-mile in the early postwar years.

Rates for all-cargo planes can be lower than in a combination passenger-cargo plane because the empty weight of the plane is reduced, passenger expenses are eliminated, and indirect flying expenses are lowered to a considerable extent. Indeed, the sum of the direct and indirect flying costs for an all-cargo plane is figured to be a little over half of what it is in the combination passenger-cargo plane. The estimated rate, without ground handling charges, is set for the second year after the war at 21.6 cents per ton-mile for all-cargo planes, which is about 16 cents per ton-mile less than for planes carrying both passengers and cargo.[10] If the shipments in all-cargo planes average heavier than those in passenger-cargo planes, the ground-handling costs will be less than 8 cents a ton-mile. If they are 5 or 6 cents per ton-mile, the total costs will come down to 27 or 28 cents per ton-mile in all-cargo planes, a charge about double first-class railway express.

The all-cargo planes being operated commercially, at the time of this writing, can be counted on the fingers, so there is not a great deal of experience on which to base prediction. Since there are so few all-cargo planes, schedules are less frequent than for the combination planes, and it is more difficult to balance loads between two points. But, in the postwar years, when much more cargo will be carried, the situation will be ripe for more all-cargo planes.

10 Curtiss-Wright, op. cit., p. 64.

Cost Estimates Beyond the Transition Period

These estimates, it is recalled, are for the first two or three years after the war. But the Curtiss-Wright study includes a second period around 1950, when more efficient planes, constructed according to the improved specifications of the airlines, will be available in quantity. Under these conditions, the Curtiss-Wright study estimates a reduction in air transportation charges from 37.5 cents per ton-mile to 30.1 cents in combination passenger and cargo planes; from 21.6 cents to 17.4 cents in the all-cargo planes for a small trunk-line plane of about 25,000 pounds with stops every one hundred miles. However, many of the new planes that will be used five or six years after the end of the war may very well be larger planes, affording a saving in costs per unit of payload. For a plane weighing 40,000 to 75,000 pounds, making stops every 500 to 1500 miles, the airport-to-airport costs will be about 22 cents per ton-mile for the combination passenger-cargo plane and some 11 to 13 cents a ton-mile in all-cargo planes. If to these costs are added the ground-handling charges of perhaps 6 to 8 cents a ton-mile, then the total costs become 29 cents and 19 cents for the two types of planes, as compared with an average charge of about 9 cents for rail express and 14 cents for first-class rail express. The Curtiss-Wright study, then, foresees a possible cargo rate some five years after the war of from one and a third to two times the present rate for first-class rail express.

Another Cost Estimate

Before discussing the significance of these estimated cargo rates, another report on estimated rates will be cited. It is that of Edward P. Warner, which was presented in a talk before the Engineering Society of Detroit in December, 1943. Warner approaches the subject by trying to figure the percentage of savings that may come from possible improvements over present practices in the use of the Douglas DC-3. Warner figures 10 per cent can be saved by using planes of 50,000 pounds instead of the 25,000 of the DC-3. He also counts on a saving of approximately 6 per cent from improvement in aerodynamic efficiency through flush riveting, better wing forms, and other refinements. There are other aerodynamic improvements not yet certain, although probable (but not including the flying wing), which would save another 5 or 6 per cent. Other changes, such as less stacking at the landing fields, smaller fuel loads, new types of fuels, and improvements in structural design will cut costs another 6 or 8 per cent. Finally, an unnamed percentage of reduction is possible in overhead costs. These reductions made by Warner led to an estimate of about 16 cents cost per ton-mile,[11] exclusive of pickup and delivery charges in combination passenger and cargo planes, at some time during the postwar years. Warner's estimate is lower than the Curtiss-Wright figure of 22 cents for the year 1950. Like the Curtiss-Wright, Warner's estimate for the all-cargo plane is about 40 per cent less than for the combination plane.

The estimates of these authorities are possibilities rather than definite predictions. Business depressions may reduce the volume and prevent the rates from being greatly reduced. Also, we do not know what competition or regulation may do in forcing rates down. Rates will also be affected by the proportion of business that goes by all-cargo planes; and there are other intangibles.

These studies do indicate, however, that well within a decade after the war the costs of carrying cargo by air can be brought down to a figure around one-third of present rates but still around twice as much as present first-class railway express rates.

In the More Distant Future

As to a further distance into the future, say ten to twenty years, it is not possible to do much with the quantitative estimates of costs. Some speculation is possible as to the aerodynamic developments. If the flying wing, which must be very large, is used, the total cost reduction due to aerodynamic improvement may be raised to 20 per cent, but it will have to be limited to routes offering heavy traffic.[12] There are also possibilities in turbine

---

[11] Edward Warner, "Air Transportation Prospects," a talk before the Engineering Society of Detroit, December 15, 1943, p. 10.

[12] Warner, *op. cit.*, p. 7.

engines, reduction in fuel consumption, and lighter body materials.

Savings in the cost of fuels may also be made. The Germans are said to have made considerable use of the diesel engine, whose fuel is much cheaper and safer and especially suited to long trips. Then, too, we do not know the future of the jet-propulsion plane, which consumes cheap fuel, but must carry large quantities of it. Another economy will come from the decreasing rate of obsolescence as the rate of plane evolution becomes less rapid.

There are two other possibilities which have been given little attention. One of these is the use of the glider. Most authorities of the air industry see little future for the towed glider, believing that the additional space provided by the glider can be built more economically into a big plane. But the subject needs more study, especially in regard to the glider's great flexibility in serving many small towns without loss of speed, and in regard to the possible types of glider construction. There are a few engineers who are quite enthusiastic about the possibilities of the use of the glider. The second possibility which has not received much attention thus far is the pick-up and delivery of packages by planes without stopping. This type of service may be well adapted to smaller towns, although at the present time very few packages other than mail are handled in this way.

The use of the glider and the non-stop pick-up device is dependent to a considerable extent on how the system is organized. Modern pick-up planes drop a hook on a line while in flight which catches another line tied to a package or a glider, and the package may then be drawn into the plane or the glider adjusted to its proper distance from the tow-plane. A shipper could have a glider loaded with goods picked up at the factory by a tow-plane and flown to the shipping destination. But the problem arises as to how a towing service could be organized so that the gliders could be picked up at factories just at the time when the shipment is ready to go. Presumably, such a towing service could be more easily organized in or near a large city where there would be a good deal of air cargo and by a commercial service not following a regular schedule. Also, such a system would seem to be better suited to a business such as that of florists who ship by air often and over long distances. As long as the glider requires a pilot, the towing service can furnish the pilot or the shipper can have in his employ a man who can pilot a glider when needed. In estimating the possibilities of such a pick-up system, it should be remembered that there are other competing services in the United States that meet the needs of the shipper very well.

In estimating the costs of air cargo in the more distant future, the factor of volume is of the greatest significance, as it is in all economic processes. As volume of business increases, the overhead expense does not increase proportionately to the increase of direct flying expenses, and hence its allocation to the ton-mile expenses becomes proportionately less. Volume has the same effect on a transportation business that mass production has in manufacturing. Since costs and volume are so closely interwoven, we should look into the probable volume of cargo.

Kinds of Air Cargo

The kinds of goods shipped by air in the past have been those which demanded great speed and/or which could bear the high air rates. Luxury goods, such as flowers, furs, or fashion goods, have been able to bear the expense, as have some goods having a high value per pound, such as movie films, jewelry, and financial documents. Some perishable goods needing speed in transportation, such as orchids, have been able to bear the air charges, while others — berries, for instance — have not. Some newspapers and publications, or materials that go into their making, have a high time-utility and have at times gone by air. Another kind of air cargo is emergency goods, such as replacement parts for machinery. The saving of time by air is greatest for goods traveling long distances as, for instance, between our eastern cities and the Pacific Coast.

The types of goods sent by air in April, 1934, are shown in Table 5.

By 1941, the volume of air cargo had increased, and rates had

TABLE 5. TYPES OF GOODS SHIPPED BY AIR IN 1934 *

Items	Percentage of Total Shipments
Valuable papers	28.3
Advertising and printed matter	20.8
News photos	14.3
Parts — auto, plane, machine, tools	6.5
Newspapers	4.8
Films	4.6
Clothing and textiles	3.2
Miscellaneous	17.5
Total	100.0

* Frederick, *op. cit.*, p. 412.

been reduced. Some new types of goods had been attracted to air transportation, and the ranking of other goods had been changed. Table 6 shows the breakdown by types of shipments for April, 1941.

The most noticeable change in the percentages of shipments for 1941 and 1934 is the increase in the shipments of machinery and parts from 6.5 per cent in 1934 to 23.3 per cent in 1941. This may be accounted for by the fact that there was a great deal of preparation for war in 1941. Whether in peacetime so high a

TABLE 6. TYPES OF GOODS SHIPPED BY AIR IN 1941 †

Items	Percentage of Total Shipments
Machinery — Hardware	23.3
Printed matter	15.1
Store merchandise	13.4
Valuables	8.3
Electros-matrices	6.1
Transcription records — radio parts	4.5
Freight manifests	4.4
News photos	4.4
Motion picture film	4.3
Cut flowers	3.6
Jewelry	2.6
Personal baggage	2.2
Optical — camera	1.8
Food and raw samples	1.8
Drugs	1.5
Liquor	.3
Miscellaneous	2.4
Total	100.0

† Association of American Railroads, *op. cit.*, p. 42.

percentage of air cargo will be machinery parts may be questioned. However, in periods of business prosperity the pressure for orders is often such as to increase the demand for quick delivery of machine parts. Another change is the increase in air shipment of store merchandise from a negligible percentage in 1934 to 13.4 per cent in 1941. Food begins to appear as an item in 1941.

Future Kinds of Air Cargo

What we seek to know is the types of goods that will be shipped by air when rates are substantially lowered. Several airline companies have made traffic surveys to find out what types of goods are potential air cargo for the future.

In the early part of 1941, a survey of the West Coast and Chicago was made for United Air Lines. Personal interviews were conducted with 1137 industrial executives, representing 585 companies in 100 different industries, to find out how much would be shipped if the air rate were two and three times first-class rail express rates. The types of materials which the survey showed would be shipped in large volumes at the estimated lowered rates are listed below. The companies covered in the survey estimated the numbers of pounds of these goods which they would probably ship but, in view of the fact that the study was a sample and included only two markets, it does not seem feasible to work out the percentages. The types of goods are the following:

Advertising matter	Knit goods
Aircraft parts	Machinery and machine tools
Automotive products and parts	Merchandise, retail and wholesale
Coffins and bodies	Plastics and chemicals
Communication equipment	Printing and publishing materials
Electrical apparatus	Petroleum and refining materials
Financial papers and material	Scientific instruments
Flowers	Women's clothing and apparel

While the survey showed a great variety in the types of goods expected to go by air, there was a marked concentration on a few that would seek shipment at the proposed rates. Nearly 90 per cent of the Chicago tonnage came from nineteen industries and commercial types of business, and on the West Coast about the same percentage came from twenty-two types of business. While some increase was expected in merchandise, the estimate shows expectation to be along the lines of producers' goods, too.

A more extensive study of the goods likely to be shipped by air was made by Air Cargo, Inc., based on the estimated shipments by railway express in 1939, for a group of thirty-three industries which produced 54 per cent of the total air express tonnage. Newspapers and perishable agricultural products were not included. The procedure was to gather the opinions of the companies as to how much of each type of goods would be shipped by air at seven different rates, varying from 15 cents a ton-mile to 62 cents. From these opinions, demand curves were constructed for different segments based upon distance and weight of shipment. On the basis of these demand curves, it was possible to compute the diversion from rail express for each type of goods and to estimate the percentage of the total production of each type of goods in the United States that would go by air. Thirteen classes of industries are ranked in their importance of estimated air cargo shipments in Table 7.

One outstanding indication of Table 7 is the large volume of wearing apparel, especially women's apparel, that is expected to be shipped by air. At all rates, the tonnage of women's and misses' outer clothing is expected to be at least 40 per cent greater than the tonnage shipped in any other group, and at some rates it will be five times as great. The second largest user will be the machinery industry, and third, the motor vehicle industry. At high rates, the motion-picture industry will be the third largest user. In general, for the lower rate, which is near that charged by first-class rail express, the ranking of these industries is much like that for rail express. Any new business that will be created by air cargo is not represented in the foregoing classifications, since they are based on the volumes of rail express in 1939.

TABLE 7. RANK OF VARIOUS INDUSTRIES IN TONNAGE EXPECTED
TO GO BY AIR ON BASIS OF DIVERSION FROM RAIL EXPRESS AT
DIFFERENT ESTIMATED RATES *

Railway Express Tonnage Shipped	Industry	Average Rate per Ton-Mile						
		62¢	47¢	21¢	15¢	32¢	22¢	19¢
		Rank						
199,750	Apparel	1	1	1	1	1	1	1
67,400	Machinery	2	2	2	2	3	2	2
40,400	Chemicals and drugs	8	6	4	3	6	5	4
25,500	Motor vehicles	4	3	3	4	2	3	3
23,800	Leather and leather products	9	7	5	5	4	4	5
17,900	Textiles	11	11	8	6	11	11	11
9,500	Professional and scientific instruments	7	9	7	8	10	8	6
9,000	Rubber products	10	8	6	7	5	6	8
8,400	Non-ferrous metal products	6	10	9	10	9	7	7
6,000	Motion pictures	3	4	10	9	8	10	9
5,450	Printing and publishing	5	5	11	11	7	9	10
5,250	Cutlery, tools and hardware	13	12	12	12	12	12	12
360	Recordings and transcriptions	12	13	13	13	13	13	13
418,710								

* Air Cargo, Inc., *Air Cargo Potential in 33 Selected Industries,* 233 Broadway, New York 7, New York, March, 1945.

Projection of the Amount of Air Cargo

Air express has grown very rapidly in the past. For the decade preceding World War II, the pounds of air express increased at an average of 43 per cent a year. The ton-miles of express carried by the airlines in 1928 were about 65,000, while in 1942 there were 11,700,000 ton-miles.[13] This growth was accompanied by some lowering of rates. From 1935 to 1941, the rates were lowered about 10 per cent, and in 1943 they were further lowered 12.5 per cent. But, even at the present figure, they are between five and six times first-class railway express, so that, while this growth of cargo shipments was accompanied by rate reductions, air rates were never low enough to compete with the rates of other carriers.

[13] The 1928 figure is estimated from the pounds carried. In 1941, the ton-miles were only 5,200,000.

If the growth of air express after the war (beginning at 12,000,000 ton-miles) continues at the prewar rate (43 per cent a year increase), then six years after the war the ton-miles of express will be 105,000,000. Against this figure should be set the ton-miles of express carried by the railroads, which was, in 1940, 1,650,000,000 ton-miles. It is from railway express that the airlines will probably draw most of their business except for the new traffic created by the airplane's speed. But this 1,650,000,000 ton-miles of railway express business will not become very accessible to the airlines unless there is a closer approximation to its rates. It might be questioned whether one-sixteenth (1,650,-000,000 divided into 105,000,000), of the railway express business is susceptible to the attraction of the airplane's speed, more or less irrespective of equated costs. Or can more of the railway express business be captured by the airplane?

Potential Pool of Air Cargo

The Curtiss-Wright Corporation, in their studies, attempt to estimate the future volume of air cargo by considering railway express and parcel post as the potential pool of air cargo and then eliminating all the business from this pool that is not suited to air transportation.[14] First, they subtract all railway express that is not first-class, leaving 834,000,000 ton-miles of first-class railway express in 1939. From this is deducted 160,000,000 ton-miles moving less than 350 miles, 187,000,000 ton-miles of goods producing less than $1 in revenue, and 167,000,000 ton-miles which are sent to destinations not on airline routes (after making deductions for estimated overlapping). These deductions leave 320,000,000 ton-miles available to air cargo, which become 344,-000,000 in 1940 due to increases in business activity and may be expressed as 290,000,000 air-ton-miles, since air routes are shorter than rail routes. By similar calculations, 33,000,000 air-ton-miles of parcel post are available for air cargo, making a total of 323,-000,000 air-ton-miles, from which the airlines may draw business. But not all of this is susceptible to the appeal of speed unless the air rates are low.

[14] Curtiss-Wright, *op. cit.*, p. 94.

The types of goods in this pool are described as "an extensive variety of manufactured goods such as processed raw materials, machines, sub-assemblies, and such store merchandise as clothing, shoes, millinery, hats, dry goods, drugs, toilet articles, leather goods, household appliances, etc. Some high-priced perishable products were also included." [15]

How much of this reservoir of traffic the airlines will get depends upon the rates. The amounts of air cargo estimated by Curtiss-Wright at different rates are set forth in the next paragraph.

Curtiss-Wright Estimate of Future Volumes of Air Cargo

The estimated volumes of cargo at different rates are derived in the Curtiss-Wright study from a demand curve, one end of which is 3,500,000 ton-miles of air express (carried in 1940 at 80 cents per ton-mile). At the other end of the curve is 327,000,000 ton-miles, which was derived as indicated in a previous paragraph (moving by railway express and parcel post at a rate estimated to be 10 cents a ton-mile, a rate lower than the first-class and parcel-post rates). Between these two extremes will be intermediate rates, resulting in various volumes of cargo. The demand curve showing these various volumes is constructed so that there is greater elasticity at the lower rates — that is, a lowering of the rate by 2 cents at 25 cents will cause a correspondingly greater increase in volume than a reduction of 2 cents at 50 cents. The volumes of traffic will be larger in 1950 than in 1940, since it is assumed that production will increase about 50 per cent in the decade from 1940 to 1950. Another increase of 40 per cent by 1950 is expected because of an anticipated doubling of air route mileage, and an additional increase of 30 per cent is allowed for new business created by the airlines. The results of these computations are presented in Table 8, which shows estimated volumes of traffic in 1950 for different rates.

The authors of the Curtiss-Wright study believe that a rate of 40 cents a ton-mile is possible in the first year after the war, resulting in 38,000,000 ton-miles of cargo; for the third year after

[15] *Ibid.*, p. 94.

TABLE 8. ESTIMATED AIR CARGO TRAFFIC AT VARIOUS
TON-MILE RATES IN THE CURTISS-WRIGHT STUDY *

Rates per Ton-Mile	Cargo in 1950 in Millions of Ton-Miles
80¢	10.9
70	16.5
60	27.7
50	42.2
40	65.5
30	110.1
20	253.1

* Curtiss-Wright, *op. cit.*, p. 96.

the war, they expect a rate of 35 cents and 65,000,000 ton-miles, and in the fifth year after the war, a rate of 30 cents and a traffic volume of 110,000,000 ton-miles. This 110,000,000 ton-miles is about one-sixteenth of the total railway express in 1940, and about one-third of the pool of express and parcel-post traffic suitable for airline transportation. These rates and volumes do not take into consideration the variations which may occur in the business cycle.

Other Estimates of Future Air Cargo

In the spring of 1945, A. E. Raymond, of Douglas Aircraft Company, made an estimate of the ton-miles of cargo expected in 1950.[16] A rate of growth similar to that before the war is assumed and the volume adjusted to a rate of 35 cents a ton-mile (presumably this does not include cost of transportation to and from airport), which is the tariff of the newest all-cargo services in airline operation. The result is an estimate of 135,000,-000 ton-miles of cargo in 1950. This is a good deal higher than the expected volume (under 100,000,000 ton-miles) computed for a similar rate by Curtiss-Wright, as shown in Table 8. Raymond estimates that at a rate of 15 cents a ton-mile, 3,900,000,000 ton-miles of cargo will be carried by the airlines.

Another company, which wishes to remain anonymous, estimates a volume of air cargo very nearly the same at 35 cents

[16] A. E. Raymond, "An Adequate Air Transport System for the United States," *Prospects and Problems in Aviation*, edited by L. S. Lyon and L. C. Sorrell, The Chicago Association of Commerce, 1945, p. 62.

a ton-mile as that computed by Mr. Raymond, as shown in Table 9. This estimate was obtained by getting the opinions of various airline companies as to what will be the ratio of air express ton-miles to the total of air express and first-class rail express ton-miles when the air rates are 82 cents a ton-mile, and what the ratio will be if air rates are 17 cents a ton-mile, or nearly the same as first-class rail express. In 1960, the higher ratio turned out to be 25 times the lower — at 82 cents air cargo is 3 per cent of the total, and at 17 cents, 75 per cent. These ratios were applied to the projected curve of air plus first-class rail express ton-miles, the projection being determined by the correlation with the curve of industrial production which was extended to a point thought desirable for minimizing employment. This point in 1950 was about 50 per cent greater than the 1940 production, which happens to be the projection made by Curtiss-Wright. Between these maximum and minimum points for air express, a demand curve was worked out for intervening rates, and the results are shown in Table 9. The estimate of this study, at a rate of 30 cents a ton-mile in 1950, is 152,000,000 ton-miles, as compared with the 110,000,000 of Curtiss-Wright and 105,000,-000 by a direct projection of past air cargo growth.

Warner, in his 1943 Detroit speech previously referred to, says that, at a door-to-door rate of about one-third the present rate (or a little under 30 cents a ton-mile), the prewar volume of air express (about 5,000,000 ton-miles) would be ten to fifteen times greater (or 50,000,000 to 75,000,000 ton-miles).

The survey of Air Cargo, Inc., shows estimates of the amounts of air cargo at different rates for the industries included in their

TABLE 9. ESTIMATED AIR CARGO TRAFFIC AT VARIOUS TON-MILE RATES IN THE "INDUSTRIAL STUDY"

Rates per Ton-Mile	Cargo in 1950 in Millions of Ton-Miles
80	16
70	21
60	30
50	50
40	87
30	152
20	290

study as described in previous paragraphs. The results are shown in Table 10.

TABLE 10. DIVERSION OF GOODS FROM RAIL EXPRESS TO AIR, ESTIMATED FOR 33 INDUSTRIES

Average Rate per Ton-Mile in Cents	Cargo in Millions of Ton-Miles
62.1	3
46.8	8
21.3	66
14.8	189

Since these tonnages represent only a part of the total air cargo, they are not comparable with the other studies quoted. Nor does this study take into consideration possible increases in production. For a rate of 30 cents a ton-mile, Air Cargo, Inc., obtained an estimate of less than 65,000,000 ton-miles, while the other studies show an expected ton-mileage of from 110,000,000 to 152,000,000 at that rate. Since the Air Cargo survey included industries accounting for about half of the air express in 1939, and since that year had a lower production than is expected in the future, their findings are probably not out of line with the others.

Business Conditions and Air Cargo

These estimates of cargo volume at around 100,000,000 ton-miles five years after the war's end are all made without reference to business booms or depressions. The studies, which took into consideration the growth of production, used straight trend lines. Most such trend lines go through the middle of the curve of business with prosperity above and depressions below. After most recent wars there have occurred depressions of considerable magnitude, more or less attributable to forces generated by war. Depressions occurred after both the Napoleonic Wars and the American Civil War. After World War I, the first severe depression occurred about two years after the war's end and lasted about two years. The second depression did not occur until a dozen years after the Armistice of 1918. In view of the past, it is certainly not improbable that a severe business depression will occur within the first five years after World War II. Such a depression, if it lasts two years, might prevent the volume of air cargo from reaching the figures estimated.

The assumption was made in the Curtiss-Wright study that the gross national product would be 50 per cent greater in 1950 than in 1940. This is a rate of 4.1 per cent a year and is a high rate of increase, as compared with that of the decade beginning with 1916, when the increase in the national income in stable dollars was 2.6 per cent a year. From the end of World War I to 1929, the national income in 1929 dollars increased only about 50 per cent, or a little more than 4 per cent a year. Of course, we have a vastly larger industrial plant now than we had during World War I, but much of it cannot be used in peacetime without many alterations. Moreover, plant capacity does not determine volume of production. We have never produced up to our full national capacity in peacetime. On the other hand, there is much talk of making a great effort to maintain a very high level of income in the postwar decades, and there is a vast accumulated purchasing power and a great scarcity of various types of goods.

Other Retarding Factors

That the growth of air cargo may be somewhat slower than indicated by the preceding predictions is to be expected from a consideration of the fact that a lowering of air rates will not be instantaneously followed by complete adoption of air transportation. Businessmen will have to acquire the habit of using air express and air cargo. The period of time required may not be very long, but there is a lag between the announcement of a lowered price and the reaping of the business that will come from lowered rates, especially if the additional business comes from new customers.

Another possible retarding factor to the growth of the air express is the lowering of rates for express carried on the railroads. As the airlines cut into the express business of the railways, the latter may attempt to hold their business by cutting rates, especially if the pick-up and delivery of air express should not be done by Railway Express. Railroads may also improve their service by developing more speed, giving better delivery service, and so on. These possibilities are discussed in the chapter on railroads.

In view of these retarding factors, it would not seem probable that the volume of air cargo will reach 100,000,000 ton-miles by five years after the war. Perhaps 75,000,000 ton-miles would be a better estimate.

Air Cargo Farther in the Future

It is generally considered hardly worth the effort to carry quantitative estimates of the volume of cargo forward as far as a decade or two. However, the general expectation is that the amount of air cargo will continue to increase beyond the first decade after the war. Lowered rates will be made possible by the adoption of new and improved equipment and the use of all-cargo planes. The new equipment which will be adopted by the airlines during the first four or five years after the war will last for a half-dozen years or longer, but it will be supplemented by new types of planes which are being developed through technological advances. All-cargo planes can carry freight more cheaply than combination passenger-cargo planes and are expected to be increasingly adopted as the volume of freight becomes larger. The all-cargo planes are expected to be used mainly on the routes which have the greatest density of traffic. Greater volumes of air cargo will also enable rates to be further lowered. The first express business that will be taken from the railways will be goods going over three hundred and fifty miles, those requiring great speed in transportation, and those having high value per pound.

Since we cannot make quantitative estimates of the amount of air cargo after the first postwar decade, we might attempt to discover what limits there may be for the increase in volume of air cargo.

One limit not likely to be reached is the traffic carried by trucks at rates as low as four to six cents a mile. Nearly all the items of expense in the trucking business are lower than they are likely ever to be in aviation. Trucks have a crew of only one person, burn less gasoline per mile, have a lower original price, and have smaller ground-handling charges. It is likewise difficult to see how airplanes, in the visible future, will be able to compete with railroad freight. It is recalled that in 1940 only about 323,000,000 ton-miles of railway express and parcel post were potential air cargo. Within a decade, planes might carry one-quarter or one-third of this available traffic, and, in addition, the volume will be increased by good business conditions and the new business created by the airlines. Larger percentages of this railway express will be carried in the second decade after the war. However, it is difficult to see how the airlines are likely, in the visible future, to carry more than 500,000,000 ton-miles of domestic cargo. Of course, they may not carry this much; we are speaking of limits. This sum would be 140 times the amount carried in 1940, but still not much more than one-tenth of 1 per cent of the shipments carried by the railroads.

The Pattern of Air Cargo Transportation

In addition to volumes and rates of air cargo, there are various aspects of the territorial distribution of this transportation which are of interest. The first point to be observed is the special benefits of air cargo transportation over long distances because the savings in time by air are greater, the longer the distances traveled. For this reason, air cargo will especially stimulate trade between the east and west coasts and between the northern and southern states of the United States.

Furthermore, air cargo traffic will be greatest in areas where there is great population density, for it is there that the largest volumes of business are found. We have seen how large volumes of business make possible lower rates and the use of all-cargo planes. The extension of all-cargo plane service to the smaller cities and towns is likely to be slow in coming. Feeder lines to these smaller places or a system of dropping and picking up packages without stopping could be developed through governmental subsidies. In view of the probably slow development of air cargo service to the smaller places and less densely settled regions, it seems that the great air cargo routes will need to remain integrated with surface carriers.

The planes used will vary in size and construction to meet the various demands of runways, volumes, frequency of stops, and so on. A small plane with a seating capacity of thirty passengers which may be converted to all-or-part-cargo plane in about fifteen minutes is expected to be widely used. A large number of planes having a gross weight of 50,000 to 100,000 pounds will be used, especially for long hauls. The most common cruising speed for the next decade will probably be around 250 miles per hour.

Some air cargo is expected to be carried across the Atlantic to Europe, south to the Latin American countries, and across the Pacific and the Arctic to the Orient. But a discussion of international cargo is postponed to the chapter on ocean shipping.

In Other Countries

Nations vary widely in the manner of their probable use of the airplane. In the United States, there is already a well-developed system of cargo transportation on rails, highways, and waterways, so air cargo will meet severe competition. Few other countries have such a good system of ground transportation. Western Europe has an excellent rail and road network, but it is cut up by seas, national boundaries, and autarchic traditions, the last two stopping most surface as well as air traffic and often making transportation routes too short for aviation to be of much benefit. Countries in which it is difficult to construct highways and railroads because of geographic conditions, as in South and Central America, are very favorable for the development of air cargo transportation. Indeed, air cargo has already developed in Central America to a considerable extent, and the airlines there now carry, without subsidy, a great variety of freight, from live animals of all sizes to cheap, bulky agricultural products and mining machinery. Alaska has similarly found extensive use of the airplane for freight as well as passengers, as have northern Canada, Siberia, Africa, New Guinea, and other such countries.

Costs of air cargo transportation will also vary from country to country because of differences in wage scales, type of air-carrier organization, methods of advertising, and so on. Lowered costs might be thought to encourage air transportation, but, since countries with poor ground transportation usually have low incomes per capita, air transport development may be curtailed rather than encouraged, although this is more true of passenger operations than cargo.

In the United States, the favorable factors for the development of air cargo are the great distances, the magnitude of production, and the demand for speed. Air cargo is also likely to develop in countries such as China and the Soviet Union, where there are great distances to be covered and, in addition, a low development of surface methods of transportation.

Conclusion

The amount of air cargo in the United States in the first five or six years after the war will probably be between 75,000,000 and 100,000,000 ton-miles annually, carried largely in passenger-cargo planes, but to an increasing extent in all-cargo planes. This will be between fifteen and twenty times as much as was carried in prewar years. The types of goods carried by air will be valuables, perishables, luxury and emergency goods, and, principally, will be those goods traveling long distances. Air cargo to smaller places and areas of sparse population will be slow in developing if these areas already have good ground systems of transportation. Air cargo rates will be between 30 and 40 cents a ton-mile, including pick-up and delivery in combination passenger and cargo planes, or around two and three times present first-class railway express rates, and in all-cargo planes they may be around 40 per cent lower. During the second decade after the war, with many more cargo planes and increased volumes of business, rates may be 15 cents per ton-mile. The volume of cargo may be increased to around 300,000,000 ton-miles. The total amount of railway express that could be transferred to the air is probably not over 500,000,000 ton-miles. Air cargo is expected to have a more rapid development in countries with poorly developed surface transportation, with large areas, large populations, and natural resources. In such countries a much larger proportion of cargo will be carried by air than in the United States. Favorable factors for the development of air cargo in the United States are its large area, great volume of business, wealth, and demand for speed.

9

Landing Places

THE AIRPORT, or other landing place, is an important, integral part of an air transport system. An airplane must have an airport from which to take off and another airport at which to land at its destination. An airport system is as necessary for the airplane as the highway system is for the automobile. The airport will undoubtedly constitute a greater problem in the postwar decade than either air personnel or airplane supply or design. The majority of airports today are too small to meet the needs of the modern large plane, and they are in most cases not capable of orderly expansion. The runway system has not been laid out to accommodate the large volume of traffic that is expected in the postwar decade. Nor are there a sufficient number of airports. Large cities will each need a number of airports, whereas now many have only one. In 1944, there were 2942 airports in the United States, principally in the larger cities. Many of these cannot be enlarged because of their location. Cities with 25,000 population and less will want air services, and the airports that do exist in cities of this size are usually inadequate.

Furthermore, the airport problem is difficult because of the uncertainty of the future design of the airport. With the increasing size and wing-loading of planes, the trend of the airport has been toward more and larger runways, so placed that landings and take-offs can be made in any direction. This has required larger areas for the airport and ever greater cost of construction. The airplane design has dictated the requirements of the airport. Now a number of experts are advocating that the airport of the future be a single-strip runway and the airplane design be modified to meet the requirements of the airport.

Size of Airports

There are a number of factors which must be taken into account in determining the size of the airport, no matter what its design. If the airport is designed to fit the plane, the most important of these factors are the size of the planes using the runways, the wing-loadings, the landing speeds, and the means of landing. However, Edward P. Warner, Vice Chairman of the Civil Aeronautics Administration, says larger and larger airports will not be necessary because of the increase in the size of aircraft. "Given constant ratios among weight, power, and wing area, and the same number of engines in each case, a 100,000-pound airplane needs no more space for take-off than one of 20,000 pounds weight, and relatively little more for landing."[1]

Another factor in determining the total size of the airport is its location in relation to buildings, trees, wires, and other obstacles. Obstructions in the approaches make a larger airport necessary because obstructions reduce the effective length of landing area available. Presumably, airport location and zoning, to be discussed later, will regulate the approaches and enable airports to be as small as possible.

Still another factor is the elevation of the airport. The greater the elevation of the airport above sea level, the larger the landing area needed. Planes land and take off at higher speeds and climb at flatter angles as the altitude increases. High altitudes cause a decrease in the lifting effects of air on the wings and also in the horsepower in some types of engines. "Other factors being equal, a plane would need double the take-off run which is needed at sea level to rise from the ground at an altitude of about 7500 feet."[2] Thus, Denver, which has an altitude of 5200 feet, would need a larger airport than Chicago, at an altitude of 598 feet, for the same types of planes. Hot air in warm climates has the same effect as increased altitudes, since the density of the air decreases with an increase in temperature. At present, provision for instrument landings also increases the size of the runway necessary.

---

[1] Kurt Rand, "Do Runways Limit Plane Size?" *Flying*, January, 1945, p. 142.
[2] John Walter Wood, *Airports*. New York: Coward-McCann, Inc., 1940, p. 10.

Whether or not this factor continues to exist depends upon the technological development of instrument landing systems.

The increased volume of air traffic in the postwar decade will make it necessary to increase the size of airports to some extent. This is especially true in the large cities where traffic congestion has already become a problem. However, traffic control systems and airport design are continually being improved so that more planes can land per hour on a runway. This speeding-up of ground time is especially important for efficient air transportation.

In 1944, the Civil Aeronautics Board set tentative standards for airport size as shown in Table 11. These classifications take into account four general groups of planes: small private-owner type planes; large-size private-owner types and small transport feeder planes; present-day transport planes; and the largest planes in use and those planned for the immediate future. During World War II, airports became larger. At the end of 1944, there were about 1151 airports with paved runways of 3700 feet or more, as compared with less than sixty such airports in 1939.

The size of the airport has been one of the major factors in the rapid obsolescence of airports in the past. Airplanes were continually becoming larger and airports were not expanding. If the airport must change with the changing design of planes, then airport size cannot become stable until airplane design ceases to change so rapidly. On this basis, the best method of building an airport is to obtain sufficient area for future expansion. John W. Wood is an exponent of this school of thought and has suggested a traffic-control airport-expansion plan which has six runways, thus allowing for wind direction, and plans the development in various stages as the volume of traffic increases. A design for

TABLE 11. AIRPORT CLASSIFICATION STANDARDS BY LENGTH
OF LANDING STRIP AND GLIDE APPROACH

Planning Classification	Length of Landing Strip in Feet	Glide-Path Approach to End of Runways
1	1800 to 2700	20 to 1
2	2700 to 3700	30 to 1
3	3700 to 4700	30 to 1
4	4700 to 5700	30 to 1
5	5700 and over	30 to 1

New York's new airport at Idlewild, submitted by committees representing the mayor and the airline companies in the planning stage of the Idlewild Airport, was similar to Mr. Wood's in that it provided for various stages of development and had a system of runways that allowed for wind direction.

A differing view is held by Wolfgang Langewiesche who says that 95 per cent of the planes today can safely use a grassy landing strip, two thousand feet long. He states that the tricycle gear makes possible cross-wind landings so that strips perhaps only 200 by 1200 feet are necessary rather than landing fields. He emphasizes the need of more airports of this type rather than larger ones of the conventional type.

J. H. Geisse, of the Civil Aeronautics Administration, is another advocate of the single-runway airport, and he advises modifying plane design to meet the limitation of such an airport. He suggests a four-wheel landing gear which would enable cross-wind landings, necessary with a single-strip landing field. The additional landing gear would not interfere with the performance of the plane or increase its cost to any great extent. The airport which he proposes would be only 146 acres in area, as compared with the usual 640 acres of today, with a single runway 10,560 feet long, which could handle eight take-offs and landings per hour.[3]

Thus, the use of the single-runway design would decrease the size of the airport. Airports with a large volume of traffic could have a number of parallel landing strips. This type of runway layout would eliminate the unused space between intersections of runways built to take account of wind direction. In the amount of space necessary for an all-way airport, a number of parallel, single-strip runways could be built.

The size of the airport may determine to some extent how near the urban center the airport can be built. This problem is discussed in a later paragraph.

Surfacing of Runways

In the early days of aviation development, turf was the com-

[3] John H. Geisse, "A Landing Gear Yardstick for Postwar Airport Layouts," *Aviation,* January, 1944, p. 120.

mon surface of the airport. With the coming of large transport
planes and heavy use of the fields, hard-surfaced runways have
become common for large airfields. The turf surface has several
advantages in that it is easily resurfaced and, being resilient, can
adjust to minor settlings and movements. It provides friction
for the tail skid on the private airplane. In case of accidents, it
gives greater safety for the occupants of the plane. The turf surface is less expensive initially and it provides an all-way landing
area. The Civil Aeronautics Administration's plan for building
3050 new airports for postwar flying tentatively proposed that
2300 of these fields would be turf fields without any paving.[4] The
techniques of constructing turf surfaces have been so improved
that turf-surfaced fields can now withstand intensive use by all
but the heaviest planes.

The hard-surfaced runway has the advantage of a smooth, firm
surface which can be used under all weather conditions and
enables planes to take off at higher speeds. The hard-surfaced
type has a higher initial cost than the turf-surfaced, but the maintenance cost is much lower.

Other types of surface have been tried experimentally; for
example, gravel or cinder surfaces, a mixture of gravel, shell, or
crushed stone mixed with the soil, asphalt mixed with the soil,
and bituminous concrete and asphaltic-macadam pavement,
which are comparable to those used on highways. However, none
of the runway surfaces so far used are considered entirely satisfactory, and the aviation industry is still looking for an improved
type of runway surfacing.

Airport Drainage

Some provision must be made at airports for the removal of
surface water and water below grade but close to the surface,
especially if the soil is non-porous, such as clay, or hard-surfaced.
According to John W. Wood, the special problems of airport
drainage, as contrasted with other types of drainage, are the size
of the total area to be drained, the size of runway pavements and
aprons which are non-porous, the speed with which drainage

[4] Joan David, "Let Your Airport Go to Grass," *Flying*, February, 1945, p. 42.

must be accomplished in order to keep the airport in constant use, the heavy loads transmitted to drainage structures by the weight of plane wheels, and the added tax on existing municipal and state drainage systems by the sudden run-off of water from airport landing areas. The drainage system must be designed according to local conditions and with the future expansion of the airport in mind.

Runway Layout

Runway layout has been increasing in complexity. Laying out an airport in the 1940's is such a complex problem that it requires a specially trained airport architect if costly mistakes are to be avoided. The best layout provides for the most efficient use of the area available, is capable of expansion for future needs, and organizes and regulates the traffic of the airport.

In 1944, the Airport Section of the Civil Aeronautics Board did not specify the number of runways necessary, but stated that there should be runways to permit landings and take-offs within 22.5 degrees of the true wind direction above four miles an hour for 70 per cent of the time for Class I airports, 75 per cent of the time for Class II airports, 80 per cent of the time for Class III airports, and 90 per cent of the time for Class IV and Class V airports.[5] In order to allow for the possibility of the wind's blowing in any direction, at least four runways would be necessary. As has been stated, the tricycle landing gear has made the take-off less dependent on wind direction.

The most conventional runway layout today is some variation of those shown in Figure 15. One of the principal factors in determining the best runway layout is the facilitation of plane movements through the airport.

Traffic Circulation and Control

As air transportation has grown in the past, the number of plane movements through each airport has continually increased. At the average airport, there has been increasing difficulty and hazard because the paths of the planes cross each other in taxiing

[5] John C. Ross, "Airports for Everybody," *Flying*, March, 1945, p. 41.

Figure 15. ARRANGEMENTS OF LANDING STRIPS IN AIR FIELDS

to and from runways and plane-loading areas and to and from loading points and hangars. As traffic increases, the difficulties will be increased. Taxi distance from the hangar or loading point to the runway for take-off has been long, thus adding to the traffic congestion and detracting from the speed of airplane movements.

The traffic congestion in the air from planes arriving at the airport and waiting to be landed has been temporarily solved by stacking the planes vertically from the control tower rather than stringing them out horizontally. The necessity of planes having to wait to be landed, however, increases the total trip time of the plane and lessens one of its most important advantages over other modes of transportation. It also increases the total costs of the trip.

One solution for this problem of congestion in the air is to eliminate cross-circulation on the airport and use runways which will facilitate the rapid handling of traffic. Single-runway airports at which the wind direction can be ignored will help solve the traffic problem, particularly if the strip is long enough for the plane to land, discharge passengers or cargo at the airport station, and take off by continuing in the same direction on the single runway. The plane-loading stations are also a point at which congestion may occur.

Assisted Take-Offs and Landings

A factor of importance in determining airport design and size is the possibility of assisted take-offs and landings. Many types of assisted take-off are being worked on and increasingly perfected. The British and Germans used rockets to assist the take-off of heavy military planes during the war. The rockets were fastened under each wing and the empty cases dropped after the plane was in the air. Hydraulics, compressed air, and gunpowder are some of the other methods used. The Consolidated Vultee Aircraft Corporation of San Diego has experimented with a motor on a catapult car which runs on rails. F. R. Shanley and F. P. Cozzone have used a falling weight, which drops down a deep underground shaft built in the center of the airport. Mr. Irving Metcalf, of the Development Section of the Civil Aeronautics Board, has devised a method by which a large flywheel placed underground in the center of the airport revolves at a high speed by means of a small motor. The resulting energy is transmitted to a cradle resting on the airport runway on which the transport plane is placed. Landing by means of a cradle traveling at the same speed as the plane has been suggested in order to enable the plane to dispense with the landing gear, which is a very heavy weight to carry. Another method of getting increased range and payload has been refueling in the air.

Various methods of shortening the landing run of planes are also being worked on. Brakes on heavy-engined planes are unsatisfactory because they generate so much heat that they sometimes vulcanize the tires to the wheels. The use of reversible pitch propellers on multi-engined planes has been suggested. This method is viewed as especially hopeful. Wing flaps are in common use, and double edges on the front part of the wings and other types of air brakes have also been suggested.

Instrument Landing

Methods of instrument landing also affect the size and design of airports. Instrument landing enables a pilot to land at an airport when it is impossible to land with visual reference to the earth, because of atmospheric conditions or lack of landing lights at night. Early instrument flying and radio directional aids made it possible for the pilot to find the airport, but did not make a safe landing possible. The methods of landing were crude and unsafe and put an emotional strain both on the pilot and on the passengers. Furthermore, it took a considerable length of time to get a plane down, so that, if there was a large amount of traffic, it became congested and the hazard of collision was increased. The first successful instrument landing system was developed in 1930-31. However, instrument landing was greatly improved during World War II. The promise of radar leads to the expectation of landing in nearly all kinds of weather without delay.

At airports, certain runways are designated for instrument landings, and special equipment is required. At present, the number of plane movements per hour to be handled on such a runway has been increased to a maximum of twelve per hour. The Civil Aeronautics Administration has stated that today's record shows a possibility of twenty planes landing an hour by instrument through new techniques. It is expected that provisions for instrument landings at airports will be increased since dependability of air service requires flights in all kinds of weather with complete safety.

Airport Lighting

Airport lighting is necessary for twenty-four-hour transportation service unless in the future new and vastly improved methods of instrument flying become common. Some of the lights that are necessary are: airport beacon, illuminated wind-direction indicator, boundary lights, range lights, contact lights, approach lights, obstruction lights, roof marking, ceiling projector, landing-area flood lights, traffic lights, apron and exterior floodlighting, interior lighting, and temporary marking. Airport lighting must be distinctive from all other lighting in the area, especially for locating and identifying the airport. Governmental regulation is necessary to prevent installation of similar types of lights by anyone except the airport officials. The lights should be arranged so as to be as little obstruction to the planes as possible. Standards have been set up by the Civil Aeronautics Board in order to make airport lighting uniform and thus easily interpreted by the pilot so that he can land at airports with which he is not familiar. Since airport lighting is essential for the safety of the airplane, passengers, and cargo, there should be a supplementary source of electric power in case of failure of the main system.

There is increasing elaboration of lighting equipment at airports and a tendency to control the lighting system so as to get the greatest usefulness for each special purpose. The lights are used only when and where needed, and the type of light varies with the purpose for which it is used.

Airport Buildings

The early airport and the modern airport of today are in sharp contrast, especially as to type and number of buildings. The early airports usually had a very simple building or shed that was used primarily for shelter. Today the airport buildings are complex and must provide organization of traffic and multitudinous activities, including many services not directly attendant on air transportation. The buildings must be placed in relation to the runway layout, the size and the shape of the airport, and with respect to a possible expansion of the airport.

The airway station is a connecting link between air and surface facilities for passengers, freight, and mail. In order to get the maximum benefits from the speed of the airplane, the movements of traffic through the station must flow smoothly — streams of traffic in different directions must not conflict with each other.

The modern well-equipped airway station has passenger waiting rooms, announcements of air schedules, ticket and executive offices, telephone and telegraph services, news-stands, post office, restaurants, lunch counters, soda fountains, bars, rest rooms, hotels, pilots' and stewardesses' rest rooms, radio and weather bureau, traffic-control room, and many other services.

Location and Zoning

In the 1930's there was considerable agitation for the building of airports as close as possible to the metropolitan center. Plane passengers sometimes spent more time in getting to the airport than in flying to their destination. This decreased the advantage of speed that the airplane had over other means of transportation. In Chicago, for instance, there was talk of building an airport on the lake front adjacent to the Loop. In the planning for postwar airports in the early 1940's, however, the predominant idea was to build the airport some distance from the metropolitan center and connect the two by broad express highways with no stop lights. A successful helicopter will probably support this arrangement, since it would provide rapid, convenient travel from the urban city to the airport. Assisted take-offs may decrease the space necessary for an airport, but even then the airport could not be too close to the city center, since the high buildings of the city are obstructions to almost any type of aircraft except the helicopter.

Some of the types of airports suggested with the main idea of providing airports in the metropolitan area itself appear so extraordinary in comparison to present-day airports that they are considered radical. With the advent of the helicopter, these will undoubtedly be forgotten. However, some suggestions which have appeared radical in the past have come to be considered as fully possible. For instance, one architect suggested, some years ago, a circular airport with hangars and terminal buildings placed underground in the center of the field. The aircraft would enter the hangars immediately upon arrival by means of trapdoors. War conditions favored the construction of underground buildings as a protection from bombing, so such a plan may be within the realm of possibility. Single-strip airports were considered radical and impractical, but the tricycle gear and the four-wheel landing gear will probably make them feasible. Thus, we must be cautious in ruling out suggestions for airport design which seem somewhat fantastic today, but may come within the realm of the possible in the future.

It is difficult to predict exactly what will be the requirements of the airport of the future, but it is probable that airport design will become more standardized and change less rapidly than it does today. The railroads and automobiles and their necessary equipment were stabilized within certain limits after a period of experimentation and it seems probable that the same will occur with airplanes and their airports.

The location of the airport partially depends upon the size of the future airport. Advocates of the single-strip airport believe that this type of airport could be located nearer to the urban center because it requires less space than the all-runway type. A single-strip airport would require less land than the all-way airport and thus could be located on ground which costs more per acre and is more favorably located for the use of the public. Outlying areas provide more and cheaper land for construction and expansion and better flight conditions.

Some airports will be located for special use. Factories may build airports immediately adjacent for transporting raw materials and finished or semi-finished products. It has been suggested that the areas or cities with airports would attract factories and business that would use the air facilities. Since it is expected that all communities of any size in the United States will have air connections, it is not probable that the airport would relocate business from city to city to any great extent. There is more possibility that the airport situation might relocate factories in relation to the metropolitan area. It is said that certain industries have already included among their reasons for relocation a desire to obtain space near the factory for the landing of cargo planes.[6] If the factory wanted to build its own airport, it would need sufficient space, and thus could not be located in the metropolitan center. Businesses which were not large enough to build their own airports would be attracted to the vicinity of public airports. Any immediate effects on the location of business will be more probable in the case of new businesses or those opening branch offices rather than in already-established businesses. The railroads were an important factor in locating industry and business, but they were being built at the same time that industry was arising and expanding rapidly.

Zoning the area around the airport is necessary in order to prevent the erection of obstructions, such as telephone wires, power lines, tall buildings, etc. The trend has been toward longer runs and a flatter angle for take-offs. Thus, the space free from obstruction around the airport has been increased. In the early zoning laws, the flight path was 7:1 (7 feet of horizontal distance traveled for 1 foot of height). Now, in most cases this has been increased to 30:1.

[6] *American City,* May, 1942, p. 44.

Several Committees on Airport Zoning and Eminent Domain have been organized by the Civil Aeronautics Board in order to set up zoning standards and revise and standardize zoning ordinances. They found it difficult to set definite standards for zoning because of the differences of locality, altitude, meteorological conditions, and performances of aircraft — all of which affect the length and angle of take-off. However, it did recommend zoning standards for five tentative classifications: Class 1, 20 feet horizontal to 1 foot vertical; Classes 2, 3, 4, and 5, 30:1; runways for instrument landings, 40:1, with this ratio starting at a point 4500 feet from the beginning of the runway.

The effects of airports on the real-estate values of property surrounding the airport will be discussed in the chapter on real estate.

Specialization of Airports

In the early days of aviation, one airport served the needs of all kinds of aircraft. In the future, in the interests of efficiency and safety, some airports will be specified for particular types of uses. Cargo planes and passenger planes may land at different airports in the large cities on the main trunk lines. Such a separation depends on the existence of all-cargo and all-passenger planes. Freight and passengers are ordinarily carried on the same plane and thus necessarily land at the same airport. The postwar potentials of transcontinental or long-distance air cargo indicate that there will be sufficient air freight to justify the use of some all-cargo planes. Freight and passengers differ in the plane characteristics which they require. Passengers need comfortable chairs and surroundings, sound-proofing, pressurized cabins, personal attendants, etc., which add to the cost and are not required for cargo. On the other hand, floors need to be reinforced for cargo, and large doors and loading devices are necessary. Thus, cargo can be carried more efficiently and more economically if it is separated from passengers. Until cargo traffic has been sufficiently developed, passengers and cargo will continue to be carried on the same plane as they have been. On the feeder lines, they may be carried together, although we do not have much information on the feeder-line cargo potentials.

Just as cargo and passengers require different characteristics in the plane, they also require different types of services at the airport. Passenger stations need large ticket offices, rest rooms, restaurants, bars, magazine stands, personal-service shops, and recreational facilities, which are useless for cargo airway stations. If the freight airport were minus the automobile traffic of passengers and sight-seers coming and going, the transfer of freight from truck to plane could be accomplished much more efficiently. If passenger planes and cargo planes land at the same airport or are carried in the same planes, their unloading and servicing would have to be accomplished in different sections of the airport, thus making necessary considerable taxiing on the ground. An airplane operates at lowest efficiency on the ground, and efforts have been made to reduce the amount of taxiing that must be done. Furthermore, taxiing complicates the traffic-control problem at airports. If cross-circulation of planes can be reduced the traffic problem is simplified. A further argument for specialization as to cargo and passengers is found in the specialization of other forms of transportation. Bus transportation and trucking facilities are almost completely separated. Freight yards and passenger depots are separated as much as possible; they cannot be as completely separated in small towns as they are in the large railway terminals. In the same way, airport facilities will not be highly specialized in the smaller ports, where cargo and passenger traffic is not large. But for large cities, especially where many transcontinental planes land and take off, we may expect specialization of airports as to cargo and passengers, although the amount of cargo traffic must be large to justify the costs of another airport.

It has been recognized for some time that it is dangerous to have training planes at the regular commercial airport. The beginner should learn to fly at an airport where the traffic and its regulation are at a minimum. The presence of training planes at the commercial airport would slow up the flow of airplanes through the port. Planes for private sport may use the same airports as training planes, or aviation clubs may own their own. The airplane has been used as a source of recreation, and, if this continues, there will undoubtedly be airports built especially to serve planes used for this purpose. They may be owned by aviation clubs somewhat like the country clubs of today, and additional recreational facilities provided, such as tennis courts, parks, clubhouses, etc.

The size of the airport itself may place some restrictions upon the planes that may use it. An airport could be classified as to the size of the planes that could use it or according to the function of the planes using it. There may be some correlation between the two, but it would be better to classify airports according to the functions of the planes, since, as has been pointed out, the requirements of various functions are usually different and plane designs are increasingly fitted to the airport.

Flight Strips

The term "flight strip" was originally defined by Lieutenant Colonel Stedman S. Hanks and copyrighted by him in order to fix permanently the definition of the term. By strict definition, a flight strip "is an area not less than 200 feet in width and not less than 1800 feet in length (the area may be 1800 feet by 8000 feet), with clear approaches, located in a highway right-of-way or adjacent to a public highway, on public land, developed with state and/or county funds (including federal aid) appropriated to the State Highway Departments."[7]

The primary object of these strips is to provide great numbers of auxiliary landing areas conveniently located for various purposes. Their two major purposes are for use as emergency landing areas between airports and for the use of the private plane.

At the present time, flight strips fall within the domain of the State Highway Departments. Land adjacent to the highway is expected to be acquired for the flight strip by eminent domain, as is the land for highways. Engineering service and advice are to be provided by the federal government at the request of the individual states.

[7] Wood, *op. cit.*, p. 320.

The need for flight strips for private fliers is based upon several assumptions. The first assumption is that the private flier will fly in the private plane rather than in a helicopter. The helicopter needs a very small area in which to land, as compared to the area of a flight strip. The second assumption is that regular airports would not be available. John Wood says that, "although each year there is a greater number of airports, their use is increasingly restricted to some type of commercial operation, and the number of landing areas for private plane operation has decreased." [8] A third assumption is that, even if regular airports were available to private planes, the landing strip would frequently be more convenient, especially if the plane were roadable. Since flight strips would be more numerous than airports, there would be a greater chance that the strip rather than the airport would be located near the flier's destination or home, and, because it is adjacent to the highway, it would be easy for the private flier to reach it by auto or by roadable plane. Since flight strips are small in size (though the minimum will be 360,000 square feet), they might be located in areas which are too small for an airport.

It seems probable that, with the existence of the helicopter, the principal business uses for the small plane will be as taxis between cities, as company planes for executives, and for industrial uses, for example, by newspapers. They will also be used by wealthy sportsmen. These uses seem to be too limited to justify an intricate system of flight strips. In all probability, a limited number of flight strips will be built for the private plane and to serve as emergency landing fields.

Military aviation also has interest in flight strips. Such strips are one method of decentralization of air facilities in wartime. Military strips are somewhat larger in size than flight strips for civilian uses. According to army definition, the strip is normally 8000 feet long by 500 to 1000 feet wide, with a paved runway 150 feet wide, strong enough for static wheel loads of at least 12,500 pounds. The Director of the Flight Strip Division of the United States Public Roads Administration [9] says that their location is

[8] *Ibid.*, p. 320.
[9] F. Schnepfe, "The Design of Flight Strips, Standards Adopted by the United States," *Roads and Bridges*, February, 1943, p. 25 ff.

usually free within about a hundred square miles. For these military flight strips, an approach slope of 30:1 is asked and if possible 40:1. For ordinary flight strips, the government requires only 20:1. For military strips, an obstruction slope of better than 7:1 for at least 500 feet is required for approaches at the sides. Some of the considerations for choosing the location of the flight strip, for civil use as well as military use, are levelness of land, cheapness of land, solidity of soil, presence of woods for hiding planes, absence of fog and smoke, direction of prevailing winds, and efficiency of surface transportation.

The civilian flight strips, to be most useful, would be located not too far from cities or towns or settled farmlands; that is, not in isolated areas. This would increase the cost of the land to be used. However, public expenditures for highways have been high, and if flight strips were considered essential for civil aviation, they would undoubtedly be constructed.

At the present time, it is considered best that a flight strip should not be nearer than six miles to an airport in order to avoid congestion in air traffic. However, if all planes, including the private plane, had radar, this restriction might not be necessary.

The minimum equipment at a landing strip might be a wind indicator, means to tie a plane down, and a telephone. If private planes were parked or stored at the landing strip, a hangar would be necessary, although planes have often been left in the open despite wind risk, weather damage, and perhaps theft of parts of the plane. If private planes were prohibited from using major airports, it would be necessary to provide some means of fueling planes and also some repair service. These services at the landing strip could be combined with similar services for automobiles. It is uncertain as to how much lighting equipment landing strips would require. It would partially depend upon how much use was made of the landing strips. If there is widespread use of the private plane rather than of the helicopter, and if technological developments make the private plane safe for night flying, then the flight strips will undoubtedly be lighted. Automobile highways have been increasingly lighted, especially at bridges and junctions of major highways, and the costs of such lighting are being continually lowered.

Seaplane Bases

Seaplane bases differ, of course, with the type of craft which they are constructed to serve and the volume of traffic anticipated. Some of the types are those for private light-plane operation, those for feeder-line or short-distance operation, those for coastal operation and transoceanic service. The trend in size of seaplanes has been toward larger boats for long-distance travel, and this has necessitated increased area and depth of water of the seaplane base.

The number of seaplane bases in the future will depend upon the number of seaplanes that are in use. There were only 111 seaplane bases in the United States in 1939, 21 of which belonged to the Navy or Coast Guard and were closed to the public, while 63 of the remainder had no hangars, leaving only 27 first- or second-class bases. Only 42 of the civil seaplane bases were on rivers (15) or lakes (27) of the interior, including the Great Lakes, and only 5 of these had hangars.

Seaplane bases can be built in any harbor, protected sound, wide river, or lake or reservoir of one and one-half to perhaps five miles' diameter. For practical purposes it should have security against interference from surface vessels when planes are landing or taking off or lying at anchor, mooring buoys, sufficiently low banks in the approaches, freedom from ice, a landing float or dock, aviation gasoline supply, a ramp or marine railway for hauling planes to land, and, if possible, hangars and service facilities.

While a combination with a land airport is desirable, especially where transplaning is expected, it does not seem to be usual for either small or large plane bases because of topographic difficulties, though a partial integration is often achieved in the oceanic ports.

The seaplane base can be built at less expense than the land airport because there are no expensive runways to construct. This might appear to give some advantage to the seaplane, but at the same time the seaplane base is limited in its specific location, while the land airport has a much greater number of possible sites.

Helicopter Fields

Strictly speaking, a helicopter does not require an airport for its operation. The runway layout is incompatible with the helicopter, since it can cover short distances by hops through the air easier than by rolling along the ground. The accounts of the helicopter's arriving at airports in the early days when it was being perfected show the consternation of airport control operators and ground crew at the unconventional behavior of the craft. It could hover just outside the control tower and ask for permission to land and come down directly in front of the hangar instead of taxiing to it from the runway. In getting to the gasoline pump, it could jump a row of planes instead of taxiing around them.

The requirements of a space for the helicopter to land on are very simple and flexible as compared to those of the airport. The helicopter can land on any space that is large enough to accommodate the span of the rotors, and it will use landing spaces similar to the parking space for the automobile. The amount of space necessary for parking a helicopter may be relatively small if the rotors are capable of folding back. However, it can use many parking spaces which are not available to the automobile. For instance, it can use a rooftop for a landing space. This may result in the remodeling of roofs of skyscrapers, office buildings, department stores, etc., in order to accommodate helicopters of customers and employees. Some homes may be built with flat roofs so that the family helicopters can be parked on them.

Since the helicopter will undoubtedly be used to transport urban residents to the airport, some space will need to be set aside at the airport for the landing of helicopters so that they will not interfere with plane operations and yet land the passengers near enough to the airway station so that they will not have to walk a long distance.

Military Airports

Civil airports are important in a system of national defense against air attack since they can be converted to military purposes during wartime.

The important features of military airports are dispersion, concealment, and camouflage. A large number of civil and military airports, intermediate airports, and landing strips provides dispersion, preventing the wiping-out of an entire air force by the destruction of only one airport. Concealment is accomplished by placing buildings and planes in forests adjacent to the airport or landing strip. Hangars may also be built underground, perhaps as at Pantelleria, inside steep hills next to plains. Camouflage is achieved in a number of ways — fake airports, imitation roads or rivers across airports, prevention of hangars' casting identifying shadows, and runway construction that is not discernible from the air. Poland's air power was easily made ineffective by Germany's bombing because she lacked dispersed airports. Owing to the large geographical area of the United States, dispersed airports are naturally provided. However, before World War II, some of these civil airports were not available for military use because they were not large enough and did not have the facilities to accommodate military planes. Airports of the future will be more easily converted to military uses, since they will be built to accommodate the larger planes developed during the war. The plans for the civil airways will take into account their conversion to military uses. If the United States maintains an air force for defense purposes, some airports will be restricted to bases for military planes and for training military air personnel.

Government Regulation

Since the civil airway network is the basis for national air defense, the federal government has an interest in the civil airport. Its interest also arises from the facts that air transportation is a public utility and that planes quickly travel long distances and may pass many state borders in one flight. Only feeder lines will be intrastate. The federal government has provided money, land, advice, and other kinds of aid for the development of the railroad, automobile, steamboat, and other transportation facilities. It has also given aid to air routes through mail subsidies and through federal financing of a part of the cost of civil airports. There has been considerable agitation to make the airport pay for itself by the charging of various fees to visitors and to commercial firms which use the field as a flying base or test field, as well as to companies which seek the right to sell gasoline, oil, etc., at the field. However, the federal government has followed the practice of doing everything to encourage the airlines rather than taxing them for use of facilities. Airports, in general, are constructed by city governments or from their funds. Where the expenses are great, the charge to the airlines for use of the airport is large. The airport has about the same relation to the airplane as the highway does to the automobile. The highways are built and supported by public funds. Airports have been expensive to build and their operating expenses have usually brought a yearly deficit. World War II will probably be a stimulus to federal financing of airports, although city governments are expected to continue to bear the major part of the cost of construction.

In September, 1944, the Civil Aeronautics Administration presented to Congress, in answer to their request, its Airport Plan, which is the result of a comprehensive study of the airports now in existence, their deficiencies, and the probable needs in the next ten years if aviation develops as is now indicated. The numbers of airports in 1939 and 1944, by class, are shown in Table 12. The experts have recommended a program of $1,250,000,000, to be financed jointly by federal, state, and local governments, which emphasizes chiefly facilities for private flying and airports for cities of less than 25,000 population. The proposed 3050 new airports, which would more than double the number in existence in 1945, and the 1625 improvement projects must meet certain requirements set up by the Civil Aeronautics Administration which

TABLE 12

Number of Airports, 1939 and 1944.

Class	Number 1939	1944
1	1693	981
2	424	810
3	57	443
4	—	403
5	—	305

will allow for expansion in the future if larger planes and increased traffic should make it necessary. Population was used as a primary basis for the recommended distribution of the airports. The importance of the locality as a trading area and its importance to air routes determined the class of airport which was suggested. As now planned, the new total of 6305 airports would make air service available to 88 per cent of the counties in the United States, whereas it is now available to only 53 per cent.

Foreign Airports

The more distant future may see some type of international control and planning of airports. World War II has already created the basis for this. The United States government with American money has built airports in many of the Allied countries. At the time they were built, the airports were promised to the countries in which they were built, after the war. Later in the war, discussion arose about this arrangement, some people advocating the retention of these airports by the United States after the war. The existence of these American airports in foreign countries makes necessary some formulation of policy as to foreign airports.

In the postwar decade, it is expected that there will be scheduled air operations with most of the foreign countries of the world. Any scheduled airline is dependent upon having an airport at both ends of the route and at intermediate points if the plane must refuel. There has been much confusion heretofore as to the rights of a plane in a foreign country. Since each nation has made its own regulations, planes could be barred from landing, forced to pay high fees, etc. At the International Civil Aviation Conference, held in Chicago in November, 1944, fifty-four nations attempted to come to some agreement on these problems. Although the conference did not accomplish quite as much as was hoped, forty-six countries have signed the International Air Services Transit Agreement, which grants to contracting states (1) "the privilege to fly across its territory without landing, and (2) the privilege to land for non-traffic purposes." Also, by the International Air Transport Agreement, each of twenty-

eight contracting states grants to the others the privilege to fly
across its territory on designated routes without landing, of landing for non-traffic purposes, of carrying cargo, mail, and passengers to and from the homeland and between intermediate states
along the way.[10]

Integration with Other Transportation

The airport is the transition point for freight and passengers
from air to ground facilities or to other air facilities. Thus, it
would seem to be advantageous for the port to be integrated with
other means of transportation. Since aviation is new and the
railroads and highways already established, one might ask if they
would determine the location of the airport. Since airports require considerable space, both on the ground and in the surrounding air, and the ground to be used should preferably have
certain characteristics, they cannot be placed just anywhere. The
airport which can be built near to a main highway may have
certain advantages over others less favorably located. However,
the successful development of the helicopter will facilitate the
transition between the various forms of transportation.

Financing of Airports

It is expected by some authorities that, as the volume of airplane traffic at the airport grows in size, airports can become
more nearly self-supporting. However, the volume of airplane
traffic depends on a larger number of airports, thus increasing the
number of units to be supported.

Furthermore, one important method of increasing the volume
of air traffic is to reduce costs to airline companies by eliminating
airport charges. Providing airport facilities for the airline companies free of charge encourages civil aviation.

In order to finance airports without charging airlines for their
use, cities have obtained revenue from a number of auxiliary
sources. One such source is admittance fees charged to sight-
seers. Some European airports, with entertainment facilities, be-

10 International Civil Aviation Conference, Final Act, Part I, Doc. 488, GD/70
(mimeo.), Appendixes III and IV.

came most attractive spots for visitors as well as recreational centers for residents. Rotterdam had over 200,000 visitors a year before the war. Amsterdam's Schiphol Airport had over 350,000 visitors a year. La Guardia Field in New York has had 225,000 visitors in one month, or 7000 per day, and many more on some holidays. La Guardia Field charges 25 cents per car in its public parking area, receives 10 per cent of the gross receipts of a bus service to the airport, receives 50 cents a tour from four guided tours of hangars and station, and charges 10 cents per person to view flight operations from the upper deck of the loading platforms. It was estimated conservatively that the airport should receive $130,000 a year from this source. New York City also receives yearly amounts for the restaurant concession and the sale of oil and gasoline.

If recreational and entertainment facilities are added to airports, they will be another source of revenue. Air sight-seeing tours might provide a source of income. Commercial sight-seeing planes accounted for 9.8 per cent of the flights made at the Chicago airport in 1940.

According to the American Municipal Association,[11] only about 10 per cent of the 650 municipal airports which were in use in 1941 were self-supporting. The other 90 per cent regularly used tax funds to meet deficits. The survey showed that the typical airport terminal, one of about 200 listed as regular stops on scheduled airlines, gets about 86 cents of each dollar of income from landing fees, hangar and storage fees, rents, and income from oil and gasoline sales. Charges for rents, hangar fees, storage, etc., varied widely from city to city. For the 200 terminal airports, 53 cents out of every dollar of expenditure went for salaries, while the rest was spent for light, heat and power, hangar operations, insurance, and other operating and maintenance expenditures.

With the present type of airport, the expenses that are expected to increase as traffic increases are those incurred in maintenance of the field area, runways, field lighting, and air traffic control. Field lighting will probably increase no matter what the type of

[11] *American City*, August, 1941, p. 11.

airport, although with a single-strip airport duplication of lighting for many runways would be unnecessary. It is estimated by J. H. Geisse, of the Civil Aeronautics Administration,[12] that single-strip airports could be constructed for $7200 (not including the buildings). This type of airport would relieve municipalities of the heavy financial burden which they now bear with the present type of airport.

Conclusion

An extensive system of airports is important for the future development of scheduled air transportation and private flying. Commercial airports have been increasing in size, equipment, and complexity of layout. However, many of the airports of the future may be of the single-runway type, with smaller and simpler landing places for private planes. Smaller airports may also be possible through improved means of instrument landing, assisted take-offs, and better systems of traffic control. The decreasing size of some airports will enable them to be placed more conveniently near the center of the city, and the large airports will be connected by through express highways. As air traffic and private flying increase and as more all-cargo planes are used, there will be some specialization of the airports in the larger cities for particular types of uses. Flight strips will be constructed if there are large numbers of private planes in use, but it is expected that the helicopter will become the most extensively used private aircraft in the future, and its requirements for landing space are simpler and more flexible than those of the airplane. Governmental aid to airports will include financing, regulation, and zoning laws.

[12] Geisse, *op. cit.*, p. 353.

10

Flying Service to Small Places

UP TO THE PRESENT TIME, the residents of large cities have been the principal recipients of the benefits of air service. Every city in the United States with a population of 250,000 and over has an airport at which the airlines make scheduled stops, but only about one-third of the cities with less than 10,000 population are certificated for air service. The people living in small towns and villages want the advantages of air passenger transportation, air mail, and air cargo which the large cities now receive. The expansion of air facilities into the local field is considered by many authorities to be one of the most promising developments of aviation in the future. In this chapter we shall discuss the network of air routes necessary to provide adequate air service to small communities, the patterns that might be used in setting up these routes, the potential numbers of passengers from small places, and the costs of such service.

Character of Local Travel

In order to predict the future of local air travel, we must know the travel habits of the people who live in small towns and villages — the frequency with which they travel, the length of trips, and the means of transportation which they have been using in the past.

People living in small towns and villages take more trips per person than people living in large cities. This fact is demonstrated in Table 13, which shows that the inhabitants of villages take three times as many trips per year as the residents of a metropolis. These figures were collected in a survey made by Paul W. Stewart and Associates in 1943 for the Greyhound Corporation.

TABLE 13. OUT-OF-TOWN TRIPS PER PERSON, 1941 *

Size of City	Trips per Person
1,000,000 and over	3.7
500,000–1,000,000	5.6
250,000– 500,000	6.1
100,000– 250,000	5.3
50,000– 100,000	6.2
25,000– 50,000	8.1
10,000– 25,000	8.7
5,000– 10,000	8.8
2,500– 5,000	12.9
1,000– 2,500	11.5
Under 1,000	14.4

* Calculated by L. F. Hampel, of the Economic Research Section of United Air Lines, from the survey made by Paul Stewart and Associates (August, 1943), *Survey of Travel in 1941 and Potential Market for Helicopter Service*, prepared for Greyhound Corporation.

Individuals selected at random were asked how many out-of-town trips they made in 1941. The results, showing a larger amount of travel per capita from small communities, may be partially explained by the fact that small towns do not provide all the professional and commercial services required or desired by their residents, so that travel to adjacent larger towns is required. Another factor in explaining these results lies in the different character of an out-of-town trip for residents of large cities as compared with that for residents of small towns. A person who lives in a small town may travel a comparatively short distance and yet have made an out-of-town trip, while a resident of a large metropolis may travel a similar distance, but still be within the city and not be counted as having made an out-of-town trip.

Short-distance trips constitute a large proportion of the traveling done by residents of small towns and villages. Eighty-seven per cent of the trips made by persons living in towns with less than 5000 population were under 50 miles in length. In contrast, only 45 per cent of the out-of-town trips made by people living in places with over 250,000 inhabitants were 50 miles and under in length. Very few of the trips made from towns with 5000 inhabitants and less were for as long a distance as 250 miles.[1]

[1] Paul Stewart and Associates, *Survey of Travel in 1941 and Potential Market for Helicopter Service*, prepared for Greyhound Corporation, August, 1943, p. 19.

The townspeople make most of these short, frequent trips in private automobiles. Six out of seven of the out-of-town trips of inhabitants of small communities are made in this manner. People living in large cities use the private automobile only seven out of ten times in making trips. The automobile is particularly adapted to this frequent, short-distance travel. It is available to its owner for use at any time and independent of formal schedules. It is subject to the will of the individual driver, enabling him to make his own selection of routes, limited only by the established network of highways and roads. In addition, the automobile can take the traveler directly to the door of his destination. That the private automobile is used mostly for short-distance travel is shown in an analysis made by Professor Lewis C. Sorrell. The results of this analysis showed that, of some two million automobile trips, 85 per cent were for distances of less than twenty miles, while only 5 per cent were for distances of over forty miles.

The people living in small communities travel, of course, by bus and railroad, as well as by private automobile. In common-carrier travel, short trips made by people of small towns and villages again predominate, as is shown in Table 14.

In making these short-distance trips, the people of small towns use the bus more often than do the people of large cities. Data

TABLE 14. COMMON-CARRIER PASSENGER TRIPS PER CAPITA BY LENGTH OF TRIP AND BY SIZE OF COMMUNITY, 1941 *

Size	0–50 miles	50–100 miles	100–250 miles	over 250 miles
1,000,000 and over	.4	.4	.2	.3
500,000–1,000,000	.8	.3	.2	.2
250,000– 500,000	.5	.4	.4	.5
100,000– 250,000	.6	.3	.3	.3
50,000– 100,000	.9	.3	.2	.2
25,000– 50,000	1.2	.3	.3	.3
10,000– 25,000	1.2	.3	.2	.2
5,000– 10,000	1.2	.2	.1	.2
2,500– 5,000	1.7	.2	.1	.1
1,000– 2,500	1.3	.1	.1	.1
Under 1,000	1.8	.2	.1	.1

* Calculated by L. F. Hampel, United Air Lines, from Stewart Survey.

on bus travel have been broken down by size of community by the Greyhound Corporation, which kept a record of the tickets sold in a sample of six hundred communities in the last week of June, 1943. If this sample is taken as representative of the full month of June, Table 15 shows the number of bus trips per person for the month of June by size of community.

TABLE 15. BUS TRIPS PER PERSON FOR JUNE, 1943, BY
SIZE OF COMMUNITY *

Size of Community	Bus Trips per Person per Month
500,000 and over	.03
100,000–500,000	.07
50,000–100,000	.10
10,000– 50,000	.15
2,500– 10,000	.33
1,000– 2,500	.41
Under 1,000	1.43

* Calculated from Madden and Beitel, *Investigation of Local-Feeder Pick-up Air Service*, Docket no. 857, pp. 12 and 13.

A comparison of the figures in this table for 1943 and those of the Stewart Survey, collected in 1941, shows the wartime swing from automobile to bus travel because of restrictions on the use of gasoline. In 1941, persons living in cities of 50,000 to 100,000 made .18 trips per month by bus, rail, and air combined, while in June, 1943, each person made .10 trips per month by bus alone. In the villages of 1000 to 2500 population, there were .41 bus trips per person per month in 1943. This is more than twice as many bus trips in 1943 as the total of .18 trips by rail, bus, and airplane taken in 1941 per person, but only a third of the 1941 total if automobiles are included.

We are interested in knowing whether people living in small communities made trips by airplane before the war as well as by private automobile, bus, and railroad. The use of air service by people of small towns and villages depends upon the availability of these services. To what extent did airlines provide service to small communities before the war?

Distribution of Air Service

There has been some disagreement among authorities as to what constitutes air service to a community. Some declare a city to have air service when it has an adequate airport within or near its boundaries at which planes make regularly scheduled stops. Others define all communities as being served by air transportation whose residents can reach an airport within forty-five minutes of travel from their homes. This last definition is unsatisfactory if precise measurement is desired, because the distance that can be traveled in forty-five minutes varies with the community. Much less distance can be covered in this amount of time in the congested traffic of the city than on the open roads of the country. A more satisfactory definition of communities receiving air service is one which considers all communities located within a radius of twenty-five miles of an airport as receiving such service.

Using the first definition of air service — that is, that every city or town with an airport certificated for regular stops receives air service — we can tabulate the distribution of air service by city size. Table 16 shows the number of incorporated communities that were certificated by the Civil Aeronautics Board for air passenger service at the beginning of 1944. There were also nine unincorporated communities certificated for service.

TABLE 16. COMMUNITIES CERTIFICATED FOR
AIR PASSENGER SERVICE, 1944 *

Size of Incorporated Community	Total Number of Cities	Number Certificated	Percentage Certificated
1,000,000 and over	5	5	100.
500,000–1,000,000	9	9	100.
250,000– 500,000	23	22	96.
100,000– 250,000	55	40	73.
50,000– 100,000	107	48	45.
25,000– 50,000	213	56	26.
10,000– 25,000	665	61	9.
5,000– 10,000	965	23	2.
2,500– 5,000	1,422	12	1.
1,000– 2,500	3,205	3	.09
Under 1,000	10,083	0	0.
Total	16,752	279	

* Madden and Beitel, *op. cit.*, p. 4.

Before the war, most of the cities — four out of five — with 100,000 population and over were certificated for air service, but only about one out of two of the cities between 50,000 and 100,000 in size received such service. About 1 per cent of all the incorporated places in the United States were certificated for passenger air service. Of the total population of the United States, 32 per cent, or about one-third, lived in communities receiving passenger air service according to this definition of air service.[2] Of the population living in incorporated places, 51 per cent lived in places which had airports.

[2] Madden and Beitel, *op. cit.*, p. 4.

Using the third definition of air service — that which includes all people within a twenty-five-mile radius of the airport as being served by airline operations — we can make another estimate of the population of the United States which has the benefit of air service. Edward Warner has computed the population living within a twenty-five-mile radius of an air passenger stop to be 64 per cent of the total population of the United States.[3] On this basis, nearly two out of three persons in the United States have air service accessible to them. However, air service is most accessible to urban populations, since, as is shown in Table 16, almost all large cities have air service, while few towns and villages do.

There is no sharp line of demarcation between local and non-local service. In general, local air service might be said to be routes on which stops are made relatively close together and on which many of the intermediate points are small cities, towns, or villages. Large cities may be terminals or intermediate stops on these routes. Some of the present trunk routes have stops at small towns, but these are only auxiliary to the service of the large cities. On a few of these routes, the proportion of local travel is high even when the routes connect large metropolitan centers; for example, Galveston—Houston, Vancouver—Seattle, and Hartford—New York.[4]

Air Travel in Small Communities

To what extent do the people living in small communities make use of the air service available to them? Since the airplane is used principally for long-distance travel — 92 per cent of the air travelers going distances over a hundred miles [5] — and since few small places are certificated for air service, we should expect to find few people who live in towns and villages traveling by air. Table 17 shows the number of passengers per day traveling by air on trips over a hundred miles, tabulated by city size.

[3] Edward P. Warner, "Requirements of Local Air Transport Service," *Aeronautical Engineering Review,* February, 1944, p. 27. Based on the 1930 population.
[4] *Ibid.*, p. 13.
[5] Civil Aeronautics Board survey of 187 certificated stations in September, 1940. (Calculated.)

TABLE 17. PASSENGERS PER DAY, TRAVELING OVER 100 MILES BY AIR, SEPTEMBER, 1940 *

City Size	Estimated Passengers per Day
250,000–500,000	56
100,000–250,000	21
50,000–100,000	8
25,000– 50,000	5
10,000– 25,000	3
5,000– 10,000	2
2,500– 5,000	1

* Calculated from figures based on Stewart Survey.

It is clear from Table 17 that big cities furnish more air passengers per day than do the smaller towns. We have further data on the number of air passengers in small towns, collected by the Civil Aeronautics Board. Table 18 shows the total air passengers, including arrivals and departures, in the small cities and towns receiving air service in September, 1940.[6] In towns of 10,000 to 25,000 population, the median number of air passengers per day was 5.2; in towns of under 10,000 inhabitants, the median number was 2.

TABLE 18. AIR PASSENGERS ORIGINATING IN SMALL CITIES AND TOWNS IN SEPTEMBER, 1940, MEDIAN NUMBER PER DAY*

City Size	Number of Cities	Median Number of Passengers per Day
45,000–50,000	3	15.5
40,000–45,000	3	6.2
35,000–40,000	7	15.8
30,000–35,000	7	10.1
25,000–30,000	11	13.9
20,000–25,000	8	15.5
15,000–20,000	16	6.3
10,000–15,000	15	4.7
5,000–10,000	12	4.2
Under 5,000	6	3.8

* Calculated from Madden and Beitel, op. cit., Appendix.

In almost all the smaller cities and towns which received air service in 1940, there is some reason to expect a comparatively

[6] A considerable number of cities which were certificated for air service either had never received service or were suspended from service in 1940. Therefore, these figures do not agree with those in Table 16.

large amount of long-distance travel in relation to that of other towns of similar size. Included in this group of towns are Las Vegas, Nevada; Del Monte, California; Rochester, Minnesota; Daytona Beach, Florida; Battle Creek, Michigan; and Reno, Nevada. It might be concluded that the airlines had selected for air service small towns which were likely to yield more passengers than the average towns of this size. In these towns, the number of air passengers per 1000 population is greater than for the large cities. For towns between 5000 and 10,000, the estimated passengers traveling by air in 1940 were 82 per 1000 inhabitants, while, in cities from 250,000 to 500,000, the air passengers per 1000 inhabitants was 54. The number of air passengers per 1000 population for small towns would probably have been decreased if air service had been extended to a larger number of them. These small towns had a higher per capita rate of travel by air than the very large cities, but are probably not a fair sample. However, if a large number of small towns receive air service, the per capita air travel might be greater, for there would be more places available as destinations.

Complete Local Air Service

There has been considerable speculation as to what would be required to extend air service to all cities, towns, and villages in the United States. Edward Warner, of the Civil Aeronautics Board, has calculated what one-hundred-per-cent air service for the United States would mean in terms of planes, costs, number of stops, etc.[7] According to his conception of complete air service, plane stops on the average would be made in small places ten or twelve miles apart in densely populated areas and fifty to sixty miles apart in sparsely settled regions. He calculates that 3400 such air stops would be required to bring air service within a twenty-five-mile airline distance of about 99 per cent of the population and within a ten-mile distance of 75 per cent of the population. In 1943, there were only 288 points certificated for air service, excluding points certificated for pick-up service only, and, as of August 31, 1943, service was suspended at 112 points.

[7] Warner, *op. cit.*, pp. 45, 47.

One hundred and sixty thousand miles of new routes would be necessary for this extended coverage, as compared with the present route mileage of about 40,000 miles. Warner believes that an average of three round trips per day over these routes would be required to justify the addition of so large a number of stops. If an aircraft flew an average of 400 miles per day, or 150,000 miles a year, some 2000 new aircraft would be needed for these additional routes. The 200,000 air route-miles of this hypothetical plan compares with the prewar 1,350,000 route-miles of surfaced roads in the United States (excluding city streets), 250,000 route-miles of the railroads and 350,000 miles of the intercity buses. The vehicle-miles per year would be 750,-000,000 for aircraft as compared with the prewar vehicle-miles of 400,000,000 for steam railroads and 1,250,000,000 for intercity buses.

With an average passenger load of two or three passengers on the local routes, Warner thinks the average mail pay necessary to keep the services going at prewar costs would be 40 cents an aircraft-mile, or $150,000,000 a year, in addition to the $21,400,-000 mail compensation paid in 1941. Twenty-seven cents per plane-mile was paid for mail carriage in 1941. With an average load of six or more passengers on local routes and with lower costs, the estimate of air mail payments of 40 cents per plane-mile at prewar costs could be reduced to about half that rate. Warner presents this picture of a complete air service coverage of the small communities without prediction as to the probability of its establishment and without evaluation as to its desirability.

It should be noted that, as more and more stations are added to the air routes, smaller and smaller additional proportions of the population are served. For instance, 284 stations now serve 64 per cent of the population, counting those living within twenty-five miles of an airport as having air service. But, to serve the remaining 36 per cent of the population, approximately 2100 additional air stations would be required.[8]

The domestic air route-mileage (certificated) increased from 25,000 miles in 1929 to 48,000 in 1941. Fitting a second-degree

[8] *Ibid.*, p. 27.

parabola to these data and projecting it for a decade yields a total domestic route-mileage of 112,000 miles ten years after the war. But in January, 1944, there were 435 applications on file with the Civil Aeronautics Board for postwar routes totaling about 315,000 miles. A considerable amount of duplication of routes is included in this figure. The proposed routes would connect the largest of the cities not yet furnished with air service, but smaller places along the routes would also receive stops. In view of this large number of applications and of the essentially new nature of the routes into local areas and to smaller cities, the foregoing projection of 112,000 miles is probably a good deal below what the actual development will be.

As can be seen, the complete coverage of the United States with air service would be a large undertaking. Its development depends upon a number of factors: costs of service and the prospects of lowering them, the size of passenger potentials, technological developments, and government policies. We shall first discuss the costs of local air service.

Cost of Local Air Service

The cost of local air service will be higher than that for the trunk lines unless some new and unforseen economies are adopted for local service. There are several reasons to account for this. In the first place, the size of the planes used on these routes is likely to be small. Experience with the planes in use now shows that small planes cost more to operate per seat-mile than large planes. For example, a plane with twelve seats costs 35 per cent more to operate per seat than a plane with twenty seats, and a plane with eight seats, 68 per cent more.[9] (These costs include overhead and are based upon present airplane types.)

The use of small planes on these routes is linked up with the small volume of business in local air operations. If the number of air passengers from small communities increases, larger planes can be used, which would lower the costs per seat-mile. Large planes can be used on the routes with a large traffic volume, such as between Washington and New York City, where in 1940 there

[9] *Ibid.*, p. 45.

were an average of 25.5 non-stop trips daily, eight flights with one stop, and five with two stops.[10]

Another factor which increases the cost of local air service is the high cost of making frequent stops by airplane. If the small towns of the United States are to have air service, planes must make frequent stops, since small towns are often located close together, particularly east of the Mississippi River. If stops are made every 20 miles, the total costs of operation, based on present experience, are 45 per cent greater than for a plane stopping every 300 miles. At stops 40 miles apart, the cost is 20 per cent greater; 80 miles apart, 8 per cent greater; and for stops every 100 miles, 6 per cent larger. Thus, stops at intervals of less than 50 miles add between 15 and 60 per cent or more to the cost of operation, depending on the spacing of the stops. Stops at intervals greater than 100 miles do not increase the costs of operation to any great extent.

Frequent stops increase the costs of operation because of the time lost on the ground. Time spent on the ground decreases the service that can be secured from each airplane, increases fuel consumption, and increases the working time of the flight crew. Unnecessary taxiing and excessive circling of the field in landing and taking off also increase the costs of operation.

Costs in the Future

Since costs are very important in determining the extent of local air service development and the fares charged, we are interested in knowing what the prospects are for lowered costs in the future.

Improvements in the design of planes may lower costs of local air service. During the war, most of the advances in the aerodynamic design of planes were in connection with large planes. However, many of these improvements are applicable to small planes.

The use of the tricycle landing gear may aid in decreasing the amount of time spent on the ground at airport stops. The tricycle landing gear makes the plane partially independent of wind direc-

[10] *Ibid.*, p. 16.

tion in landing, and some authorities believe that single runways can be used most of the time if planes are equipped with tricycle landing gears. The layout of the single runway will decrease the time spent in taxiing, landing, and taking off. A cross-runway may be used in emergencies. If the runway is laid parallel with the direction of the route, the plane will not have to circle the field before landing and after taking off.

Other improvements can also be made at airports to reduce the time necessary for stops. The elimination of private planes and training planes will lessen the congestion at commercial airports. The time required to receive and discharge passengers and baggage can be reduced by more efficient planning and management.

Economies can be made in airport maintenance. In small towns, where the number of planes stopping per day is relatively small, the airport employees could be assigned to other duties or work part-time. This would constitute a considerable saving in airport costs.

Similarly, economies can also be made in the services on planes flying local air routes. The furnishings for the planes could be less luxurious and lighter in weight. The services of a stewardess could be omitted. If small planes flown by only one pilot were used, costs would be lowered. The elimination of a co-pilot would effect a 4- to 6-per-cent saving in total costs, depending on the size of the plane.[11] This type of reduced service would have to be tested for safety and approved by the Civil Aeronautics Board.

Let us take a specific plane as an example in order to appraise the results of reductions in costs. It might be assumed that for local air service the necessary fare for self-support and a reasonable profit on the DC-3 at the prewar price levels, with a 65-per-cent load factor, would be 4.8 cents per passenger-mile. For a ten-passenger plane of similar type, the seat-mile costs would be increased 50 per cent, raising the fare to 7.2 cents a mile. Making stops at intervals of thirty miles would increase the cost 20 per cent, bringing the fare to 8.6 cents. If the cost of making stops every thirty miles can be reduced one-third, and if the

[11] *Ibid.*, p. 47.

operating costs can come down 20 per cent, which Warner thinks possible,[12] the costs would be brought down to 6.4 cents per mile. With stops every fifty miles, the costs could be reduced to slightly over 6 cents a mile for a ten-passenger plane. With the possible savings mentioned above in ground operations expense, the cost for a ten-passenger plane might be reduced to 5.8 cents for stops every thirty miles and to 5.4 cents for fifty-mile stops.

Fares for Local Air Service

We have been interested in costs and their reduction in order to estimate the fares for local air service in the future. In 1942, the fare on trunk lines was five cents a passenger-mile. Since costs of local air service are greater than those of trunk-line service, fares of local air service would be expected to be higher. In view of probable economies, the fares on proposed local routes are usually set at around five cents a passenger-mile. This figure is high in comparison to the rates offered by buses and railroads.

In 1942, buses provided transportation at an over-all average fare of about 1.4 cents per passenger-mile and about two cents per mile for trips under 100 miles. The railroad fare, by coach, was about 2.2 cents per mile. Since costs by private automobile are about 1.8 cents a mile, entire families can be transported at a very low cost per person. Even if the fare per passenger-mile by airplane should fall as low as four cents, the air rates would still be nearly twice as much as competitive fares on other transportation systems.

Increase in Local Passenger Traffic

Fares on local air service routes can be reduced if the volume of passenger traffic increases. The reverse is also true. If the costs are lowered, more passengers from small communities will travel by air. These two factors interact on each other.

With fares of local air travel of five or six cents a passenger-mile and with bus and rail fares around two cents a passenger-mile, how many passengers may be expected to travel by air? In 1940, the most recent year for which there are published data,

12 *Ibid.*, p. 45.

the air passengers traveling to and from small places were very few. For 18 places under 10,000 in population, the median number of passengers at around five cents a mile was two passengers per day from each place, and for the 88 places under 50,000 the median number of air arrivals and departures was approximately six.[13] Bus travel was much greater. From 3012 places under 10,000 in June, 1943, when the limitation of gas for private use meant a good deal of bus travel, there were 29 departures alone, and from places with less than 50,000 there were 39 leaving by bus per day.[14] The railroads in 1941 did not carry as many passengers from these small places, according to the Stewart Survey [15] — 11 departures per day from places under 10,000 in population and 17 per day from places with fewer than 50,000 population.

The prospects of the much more expensive air service cutting into the low-priced bus and railroad trade, for most small places, would seem to rest largely upon the pressure of emergency, and at first perhaps upon novelty. Probably not many passengers would travel by air for distances under fifty or seventy-five miles in an emergency, because there would be little saving of time, and it is recalled that most travel to and from small places is for short distances. In addition, most small places will have infrequent air schedules, which limits the use of air service for emergencies. Small places near large cities may present a more favorable picture. On four short routes from small cities to big city terminals, the average passenger payload in 1939 was 2.84 persons per route.[16] In two years' time the payload had increased to 4.32, an increase of about 25 per cent a year. This limited evidence suggests that the present small number of daily passengers from the median small city or town may be expected to increase. But with price differentials as they are between the airplane and bus, we should not expect aviation to cut deeply into the business of the

---

13 Madden and Beitel, *op. cit.*, Appendix.

14 *Ibid.*, p. 58.

15 Stewart Survey, *op. cit.* The data from this survey are the best available. For these smaller places, they are few and erratic, but when smoothed give the figures quoted above. They should be considered as approximate estimates only.

16 Warner, *op. cit.*, p. 29.

buses. While this differential is around three cents a mile now and is not likely to be less during the postwar decade, the total difference for a short trip is not great, perhaps three dollars for one hundred miles. There are many different situations in which people will choose local airplane travel rather than the bus or railroad even at the higher air rates. The situation may also be favorably affected by the helicopter, if it is able to transport passengers as cheaply as the plane, because it can land as close to the center of a small place as a bus. Also, it should prove able to fly in cloudy or wintery weather better than the airplane. In addition, the use of aircraft may create new traffic, as did the automobile, but new habits of using air transportation for short distances are not likely to develop immediately after the war, except for selected areas or towns.

Subsidization Through Air Mail Payments

The cost of local air service to the consumer may be reduced by the government's paying part of the cost with subsidies. This can be done through the overpayment for mail services. In the early days of aviation the scheduled air passenger service between cities was supported largely by government payments for the carriage of mail. Deficits incurred from passenger operations were made up by large payments for mail service. It is only within the last few years that the passenger services on airlines have become self-supporting. Since air passenger service to large cities was subsidized through governmental mail payments until it became self-supporting, it might seem reasonable to expect that the same would be done for small communities. There may be a good deal of sentiment mobilized as political pressure to have the government help the small towns obtain the advantages of aviation through subsidization. The Civil Aeronautics Board determines the rate of compensation paid the air carrier for the transportation of mail. The Board is not confined to setting a rate that is a reasonable compensation for service, but is empowered to set a rate which will insure that the air carrier, operating under capable management, will be able to perform the service of carrying the mail. If Congress extends the coverage of air mail, the Civil Aeronautics Board, under this provision, could set high rates of mail payment which would enable passenger service to be extended to small communities.

The rates of air mail payment to air carriers have declined since the inauguration of air mail service as passenger traffic has increased and operating costs dropped. In 1929, the mail payment was $1.09 per plane-mile. By 1933, the rate had been reduced to 54 cents per plane-mile, by 1943, the payment was 26 cents, and further reductions are expected.

What rates of mail payment would be necessary to subsidize local air service? An experiment has been in progress since May, 1939, which yields some evidence on this point. All American Aviation, Inc., was authorized to collect and deliver mail from 117 places with an average population of about 17,000 (excluding Philadelphia and Pittsburgh, the terminal cities) over a route 1402 miles long. The mail is dropped and picked up while the plane is flying at full speed. The average distance between these 117 pick-up towns is about fifteen miles. No passengers are carried on this route, but there is some express. The compensation paid All American in 1943 was 50.26 cents per airplane-mile, which was about twice as much as the rates on trunk lines in that year. Since the loads on this route were light, the payment per ton-mile was high — $16.60, as compared with $1.50 on the trunk airlines in 1942, and $6.36 per ton-mile in 1932 on the trunk lines. The loads carried by All American averaged 60 pounds per plane-mile, while the average on the trunk lines was 350 pounds.

The pounds of first-class and air mail per 1000 population is greater in the cities than in the villages. For cities of 150,000 population and over, first-class and air mail is nearly three times as great in weight per 1000 inhabitants as in places under 2000. The carriage of mail might be supplemented by transporting cargo on these routes. However, in the years that All American Aviation has been in operation, very little cargo or express business has been developed.

A more probable source of revenue on these pick-up routes to small places would be the transportation of passengers. It has been suggested that the planes stop for passengers at fifty- or seventy-five-mile intervals, or when signaled, while mail would be picked up every ten or fifteen miles without stopping. If the number of passengers averaged five per trip at a fare of six cents a mile and twenty-five cents a mile were paid for mail, the revenues would probably equal the expenses. However, it is doubtful if the high average of five passengers per trip could be achieved at the present time. And twenty-five cents is a high cost for carrying a pound of mail a mile, although this is the rate now paid to air carriers on trunk lines. On the basis of the hearings of the Civil Aeronautics Board on "feeder" routes between small places, Madden and Beitel, examiners for the Board, proposed that a mail compensation of twenty-five cents a plane-mile be allowed the companies making applications if an average of two passengers per mile were developed at a fare of five cents a passenger-mile.

The public demand for air service to small places, particularly for air mail service, may support the payment of rates as high as twenty-five cents a plane-mile for mail or higher. Since there are several companies willing to undertake local air service at a prospective cost of thirty-five cents a plane-mile, it is quite probable that the penetration of aviation into the local market will proceed on some such basis. Larger towns or small cities will probably be the first to receive air service in this extension of air services downward to the small communities, since they will be most able to supply the passenger potential required.

Speed and Local Air Service

Speed is the most important asset of air transportation. Passengers choose a "through" service when it is available. In local air service, some balance must be achieved between the speed of the service and the number of points served. Frequent stops increase the amount of time spent on the ground and thus reduce the value of air service to the customer. It is difficult to set a limit on the size of town below which it is not advantageous for a plane to stop. Aviation is set up over routes rather than by particular places. If a plane is traveling a route between two large terminal cities, it is often advantageous to stop at places

of 5000 or 10,000 along the route in order to pick up more passengers.

The extent to which frequent stops decrease the average block
speed is shown by the fact that a plane with a cruising speed of
180 miles per hour would have its average speed from take-off to
take-off decreased to 150 miles an hour with one stop every 400
miles, to 118 miles an hour with stops at 100-mile intervals, and
further decreased to 65 miles an hour with stops every 20 miles.[17]

The air passenger finds his traveling time increased, not only
when frequent stops are made, but also when he must travel a
long distance from his home or place of business to the airport.
Airports are usually located farther from the center of a town than
is the bus or railroad station. In towns of between 15,000 and
25,000 population with scheduled air service, 24 airports are less
than 3 miles from the center of the city, 23 are between 3 and 6
miles away, and 4 are from 6 to 10 miles distant.[18] If the distances to be traveled on a trip are short, the time required to get
to and from the airport may be greater than the time spent in
the air.

For a trip of 40 miles with one stop, not much time is saved by
air travel if the distance to the airport is great. Let us take as
an example the case of a passenger making a trip of 40 miles,
with the plane traveling at an over-all speed of 65 miles an hour,
and making one stop along the route. The time spent in traveling
the 40 miles would be 37 minutes. If it took the passenger 20
minutes to travel to the airport and the same amount of time to
travel from the airport, the total trip-time would be 77 minutes.
If a bus, making the same trip, averaged 25 miles per hour, the
trip would require 113 minutes. If we count 5 minutes to go to
and from the bus station, then the total time by bus would be
123 minutes, or 46 minutes longer by bus than by airline. The
saving of time by airplane would not be great.

On a 100-mile trip by airplane, with stops every 20 miles, and
with 20 minutes between airport and city, the total time by air,
at the foregoing speeds, is 2 hours and 13 minutes. By bus, the

[17] *Ibid.*, p. 36.
[18] John H. Frederick, *Commercial Air Transportation*, p. 64.

traveling time for a 117-mile trip would be 4 hours and 40 minutes, or more than twice as much time as by air. On a railroad, averaging 38 miles an hour, the time required to make the same trip would be about 3 hours.

From the above examples it may be seen that there is not much saving of time by air travel for trips under fifty miles if the distance to the airport is great. For distances of a hundred miles and over there is an appreciable saving of time by air, even if the distance to the airport is considerable. Airports must be near the center of the city if the benefits of aviation's speed are to be received in local air service. It is probably easier to build airports near the center of a small town than of a metropolis.

Frequency of Schedule

Another important factor in the speed of air service is the frequency of the schedule. In 1940, the median number of flights per day from towns under 10,000 was four, or two departures and two arrivals. For places from 10,000 to 25,000 population, the median number of flights was eight.[19] The scheduling of plane flights in small towns is likely to be infrequent. This is in contrast to the frequent schedules of large cities. Between Washington, D.C., and New York City, for instance, there were 38.5 daily air flights in September, 1940.[20] Buses and railroads often have infrequent schedules in small towns also. On the basis of schedule frequency, none of the common carriers are able to meet the competition of the private automobile, which is available for use by its owner at any time.

Helicopter Air Service

The air services discussed in the previous paragraphs have been based on the airplane, but there is also in prospect a helicopter service. Within the decade following the war, a helicopter bus carrying twelve or fifteen passengers is expected to be developed successfully. There are many applications before the Civil Aeronautics Board, including that of the Greyhound Bus Corporation, for helicopter-bus lines.

[19] Madden and Beitel, *op. cit.*, Appendix.   [20] Warner, *op. cit.*, p. 16.

Very little is known about the economics of helicopter-bus operation, but the advantage of the helicopter bus apparently lies not so much in reducing costs as in developing the market for aviation. Its potentiality in this regard is due to the fact that it can land near the center of a town. Hence less time and money are expended in reaching the helicopter landing field than an airport for planes. This time factor between home or business and landing field is particularly important in small places where short trips predominate. If the helicopter can save fifteen minutes going to and from the airport, even though it has a lower cruising speed than the airplane, it would probably have an advantage in time over the plane on local journeys, that is, on trips of around a hundred and fifty miles. The helicopter also reduces the amount of time necessary for ground stops because it requires no time for taxiing and simplifies the process of landing and taking off at the airport. It is, therefore, quite possible that a considerable share of the air service to small communities in the postwar decade may fall to the helicopter.

Pattern of Local Air Service

There are several patterns of service which may be followed in setting up local air service. One type is a system of frequent stops at small places along the route of a main trunk line between large cities. This is similar to the present bus-line system. The disadvantage of this pattern is that the traveling time for "through" passengers on the trunk line is increased. However, since the passenger potential on the route would be increased, the schedule frequency could be increased.

A second pattern is designed primarily to serve small cities, but also to enter large cities. For instance, between Chicago and St. Louis, there may be a route, less direct than the "through" trunk line, which will connect a large number of small places. The bus lines have found this type of service attractive, since a large proportion of their passengers go from one small place to another. In February, 1943, the Greyhound Company made an analysis of a week's passenger traffic on eleven routes between big city terminals, all of which routes were more than 225 miles in length.[21] Of 130,000 passengers, 5 per cent were from terminal to terminal, 38 per cent were from an intermediate point to the terminal, and 57 per cent were intermediate-point to intermediate-point passengers.

The distribution of traffic is different at present on the airlines and also seems to be different on the railroads. Since the airplane is especially suited to long-distance journeys, it appeals particularly to passengers traveling to large cities which are far apart. On the Pittsburgh-Philadelphia route of Transcontinental and Western Air, Inc., 57 per cent of the passengers were found to have destinations at four cities of over 25,000, 23 per cent at places of between 5000 and 25,000, and 20 per cent were destined for small communities of under 5000 inhabitants.[22]

For the railroads, according to one report made by Transcontinental and Western Air, Inc., on twenty-seven smaller cities, there was a higher proportion of passengers from the small city to the adjacent metropolitan area than from one small city to another.[23]

Air service to many small communities not located on the direct trunk lines may follow this pattern. For these routes, with relatively small air traffic potentials, small planes and helicopter buses will be most suitable.

A third pattern which air service to small communities might follow is that of radial routes in which air routes from a large city center radiate outward to surrounding smaller places.

Radial Routes

The radial pattern of transportation appeared in the United States with the development of commuting. The streetcar, the electric suburban train, and the automobile enabled the metropolitan population to spread outward toward the suburbs, making it necessary for people to commute back and forth between their homes and the metropolitan center. Buses and trains run outward to the end of the line and back again carrying these passengers. Business is organized to a large extent on the basis of

---

[21] Madden and Beitel, *op. cit.*, p. 14.
[22] *Ibid.*, p. 14.　　　　[23] *Ibid.*, p. 15.

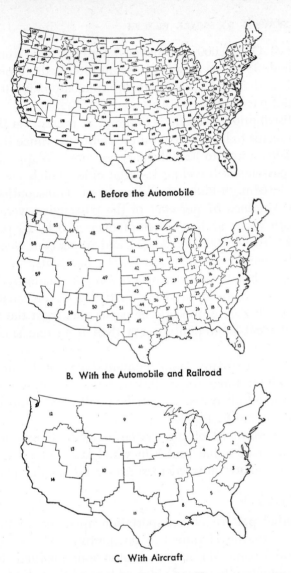

A. Before the Automobile

B. With the Automobile and Railroad

C. With Aircraft

Figure 16. TRADING AREAS AND TRANSPORTATION

In the pre-auto era, shown in Figure 16 A, there were 210 trading areas in the United States, each centering around a city; while in the auto-rail era of about 1935, the trading area was greatly enlarged over what it was in the days of the horse and buggy. There were then 60 (Figure 16 B). Rand McNally and Co. who constructed these maps, figures that, with the airplane, there will be only 14 trading areas (Figure 16 C). Certainly for those who use the airplane, the increased speed of travel will enable them to go much longer distances.

the trade area. There is a flow of trade toward a big city and a similar outward flow. Businesses organize their selling, distribution, and advertising systems on the basis of the trade area.

It has been suggested that aircraft will be used on radial trade area routes, thus distributing the urban population into a still larger metropolitan area and increasing the size of the trading area. Mail and cargo could be transported on these routes as well as passengers. The helicopter would be better than the airplane for this type of service, since it can be used in densely populated areas and can bring the passenger in close to the heart of the city. Helicopter transportation connecting the airport and the center of the city would save some time on an airplane trip, but would mean an additional transfer for the passenger.

However, there appear to be a number of disadvantages to the organization of local air transportation on the basis of radial routes. At the present time, with high fares, the traffic potential between small towns and cities is small as compared with the numbers of passengers carried by planes flying between large cities. Furthermore, the radial system does not permit good load factors on the aircraft. The plane is full, or nearly so, as it nears a city and almost empty as it approaches its other terminal, which may be a small place. For instance, on the air route between Caribou, Maine, and Boston, Massachusetts, the passenger load on the segment approaching Boston was 6.5 times as great as on the segment approaching Caribou. The average number of passengers per flight on successive sectors, starting from Boston, is as follows: 6.5–5.9–5.2–4.1–3.6–2.1–1.6–1.0.[24] The average load per sector is 3.75. A plane on this route must have considerably more than six seats to handle an average of 6.5 passengers on one segment, for on some days there will be more than seven passengers. A common carrier must plan to accommodate the variations in passenger loads rather than turn away passengers. As a result, it is difficult for such a system to operate at an average load factor of 50 per cent. To operate efficiently and economically, the aviation industry requires a payload of not less than 60 per cent. The buses and streetcars have the same load-factor

[24] Warner, *op. cit.*, p. 16.

problem, but it is more acute in aircraft, since passengers are not allowed to stand in transit. Railroads also face the same problem, but the railroad economics can be adjusted more easily to various load factors than can airline operations. Likewise, in railroads, passengers can be allowed to stand in the aisles if there is a particularly large amount of traffic.

Routes that move between two big terminals or that load and unload passengers from town to town appear to be better economic prospects for the airlines than radial routes. The bus companies found from experience that radial routes were not economical, and they changed from the market-area system of radial routes, with which they began, to longitudinal intercity routes.[25] Yet there may be particular areas in which radial routes would be economically feasible. The small towns and villages located near to great cities may generate more passengers than other small places. Unfortunately, the data of the Stewart Survey were not classified by the proximity of small towns to large cities. It is possible that there is a larger proportion of high-salaried and well-to-do citizens living in towns near to cities than in those places farther away from metropolitan areas. It is also possible that the travel habits of these citizens living near to trunk lines and express routes are different from those farther removed. There might be a sufficient passenger potential from this class of small towns to justify the organization of certain radial routes.

In general, it would seem that the best pattern with which to begin the penetration of air service into the small communities is that of longitudinal intercity routes. If these routes multiply, they will serve both large cities and many of the small communities that would have been included in the system of radial routes.

Conclusion

There are 288 certificated stops for airline service in the United States. Counting people living within twenty-five miles of an airport as being served by air, 64 per cent of the population receives air service. Of the 288 stops, 164 are in cities and towns

25 Madden and Beitel, *op. cit.*, p. 45.

of less than 50,000 population, while only 47 are in towns of under 10,000 population. There are 868 small cities of between 10,000 and 50,000 in the United States and 15,675 incorporated places with less than 10,000 inhabitants. The people of these small communities want the benefits of air service as well as the large cities. Public opinion is expected to be mobilized and to exert political pressure to extend air service — especially mail service — to small communities. It is estimated that a total of 2400 certificated stops would be required to serve the entire population of the United States.

The costs of air service to small communities will be higher than are costs on the main trunk lines because of the increased cost of frequent stops and the use of small planes. However, it is expected that costs can be brought down to around thirty-five cents a plane-mile. If the Post Office pays twenty-five or thirty cents a mile to local air carriers for mail service and a load factor of two passengers can be maintained at a fare of six cents a mile, it is believed that air service can be furnished to small places with one or two round trips per day. Air service in small communities will meet strong competition from the private automobile and the extensive railroad and bus systems, especially if the air traveler must go a long distance to the airport. The helicopter, with its ability to land near the center of a town or city, will help to solve the problem of time lost in traveling to the airport.

As air service is extended to more communities, the numbers of air passengers from small towns will increase. Even at high rates, passengers who want speed in emergencies or other situations will use air travel. There will undoubtedly be enough passengers to support a limited penetration of air service to small places, especially for towns of about ten thousand within a hundred or two hundred miles of large cities.

11

Private Flying

IN PRECEDING CHAPTERS we have discussed the transportation of passengers, mail, and cargo by air on scheduled and non-scheduled commercial flights. In this chapter we shall consider the use of private aircraft by individuals for personal or business reasons. By private flying is meant all flying except military and air transport service for hire, though reference will be made occasionally in this chapter to small planes used for hire.

The use of aircraft for private flying will have widespread social effects. It will produce a large potential market for the manufacturers of aircraft, a market that will be much larger than that for the sale of big transport planes. The use of private aircraft may redistribute urban population to some extent. Private aircraft may change the type and locale of vacations and recreational activities. Criminals may use aircraft in escaping from the scene of the crime. And the police may use the plane for the apprehension of criminals.

The social effects of private aircraft will be discussed in later chapters. Here we wish to discuss the types and necessary characteristics of aircraft that will be privately owned, the conditions required for an expansion of private flying in the United States, and the probable size of the postwar market for individual aircraft.

Private Flying Before World War II

Private flying in the United States had not developed to any great extent before the war. In 1941, the Civil Aeronautics Administration reported that there were about twenty-four thousand private planes in operation, a small percentage of which were used at times for commercial purposes. The development of private flying has been slow and somewhat erratic in the United States. At the end of World War I, there was great enthusiasm about private flying and much expectation. When Lindbergh made his famous flight in 1927, there was another burst of enthusiasm. But after each peak of interest and increased sales, the curve of the number of private planes in use flattened out and became a plateau. There was another wave of enthusiasm for the private plane during World War II, and greater anticipation than in any previous period. Will there be a new high peak of private plane ownership and then a cessation in the growth of private flying? Or will the long-expected family plane become a reality in American life?

The development of the private plane has been much slower than that of the automobile. In the thirty years after 1895, when the automobile was first sold to the public, the number of automobiles increased to such an extent that, in 1925, there was approximately one automobile for every two families. It has taken forty years (from the Wright brothers' plane) for the number of private planes to increase so that there is one plane for every 1450 families.

Private planes were used for a variety of purposes before the war. Some wealthy owners used them for recreation and sport. For others, the private plane was a hobby, much as the radio, in the first years after its invention, was a hobby. Other private planes were used for flying instruction. Some were used for special trips or for taking passengers up for short flights. Some of the private planes were owned by commercial organizations which used them for business purposes other than carrying passengers for hire. The percentages of the private flying time in each of these categories in the first six months of 1939, as reported by the Civil Aeronautics Administration, are shown in Table 19. There was no movement of any significance in the prewar years toward the family plane.

Reasons for Slow Development

We are interested in knowing the reasons for this lack of pop-

TABLE 19 *

Flying Hours by types in the United States from Jan. 1 to July 1, 1939

Instruction	43.2%
Pleasure	30.7
Commercial (for hire)	14.8
Business (not for hire)	11.3
	100.0

* John H. Geisse and Samuel C. Williams, *Postwar Outlook for Private Flying;* A Report to W. A. M. Burden, 1943, p. 85.

ularity of the private plane and its slow development. If we know these reasons, we shall have a basis for examining the future prospects of private flying.

The lack of popularity of private flying is shown by the fact that, in a survey of a sample of private plane-owners between 1931 and 1939, the mean period of ownership of planes for 83 per cent of the owners was less than 2.5 years.[1] Only 15 per cent of the flying students obtained pilot certificates.

In 1940, the Civil Aeronautics Authority made a survey of fliers of private planes to determine the reasons why students and owners of private planes gave up flying. Between 55 and 60 per cent said they gave up flying for financial reasons. A number said that the time spent in going to and from airports decreased the utility of the plane to too large an extent to make its use worth while. Other reasons given were that the airplane was not as useful as expected and that the pleasure was less than anticipated.[2]

These reasons are the ones reported for giving up flying; another survey has reported some of the reasons given for not planning to take up flying after the war.[3] Indifference ranked first in importance with 27.8 per cent, while fear was second, with 24 per cent stating either that they were afraid to fly or thought that aircraft were unsafe. Eighteen per cent gave as their reason for not taking up flying in the future the fact that they felt that there was no need for aircraft or that they were not practical.

[1] John H. Geisse and Samuel C. Williams, *Postwar Outlook for Private Flying;* A Report to W. A. M. Burden, 1943, p. 117.

[2] *Ibid.*, p. 111.

[3] John Foster, Jr., "The Personal Plane Sales Target," *Aviation*, January, 1944, p. 117. Survey by Edward G. Doody & Co. for Parks Air College.

Thirteen per cent lacked self-confidence because they felt that they were too old to fly or were physically unfit. The fifth most important reason for not planning to take up flying was the cost, both initial and operating and maintenance cost. Only 3.9 per cent based their negative answer on the absence of landing and service facilities, and 2.3 per cent on the lack of public acceptance. We may inquire as to how much of a deterrent some of these factors may be in the future.

Safety

The fear for personal safety in flying is decreasing rapidly because of the diminishing accident rate and also because of increased familiarity with flying through the vast amount of wartime aviation. The number of accidents per 1,000,000 miles of private flying decreased from 18.8 in 1930 to 13.1 in 1940, a 30-per-cent decrease. In 1940, 1,270,000 miles were flown per fatal accident, as compared with 359,700 miles per fatal accident in 1930. Yet the accident rate for private flying in 1940 was still higher than that in scheduled air operations; there were 13 accidents per 1,000,000 miles flown in private flying in 1940 as compared with .45 in scheduled operations.[4]

Of the accidents in private flying in the fiscal year of 1942, as reported by the Civil Aeronautics Board, 59 per cent occurred in taking off or landing, while taxiing added 13 per cent of the accidents. Landings can be made safer by radio control at the airport, by radar and other methods, although these will not be used extensively immediately after the war for private planes. Another improvement is the tricycle landing gear, which prevents the plane from tipping onto its nose and enables landings to be made in cross-winds. Research is also in progress on other types of landing gear.

Thirteen per cent of the accidents in private flying occurred in making forced landings. The development of the helicopter will reduce this type of accident because it can land more slowly and more safely in unprepared, small spaces.

Only 3 per cent of the accidents were due to stalls and spins.

[4] *Civil Aeronautics Journal,* January 15, 1944, p. 12.

This percentage may be even further reduced by the use of stall-proof, spinless planes which have been produced by plane designers.

Another 3 per cent of the accidents were due to collisions. The number of collisions might be expected to increase as the number of planes in the air increases. The wartime development of radar and improvement in traffic control give strong hope that many of these collisions may be avoided in the future.

Radar will also be helpful in conquering the present hazard of weather conditions in private flying. Improved visibility in fogs, storms, or darkness will reduce the possibility of flying into mountains and other obstacles.

The hazards of private flying are certain to be reduced in the future by the engineering achievements which will be incorporated in the postwar planes. However, if there are a larger number of less-skilled pilots flying planes, there may be a temporary rise in the accident rate. In general, though, an improvement of the safety record is expected in the postwar decade.

Costs of Private Flying

The major reason for discontinuing private flying, cited by the respondents in the survey previously mentioned, was the high costs of flying. If private flying is to be increased to any large extent, these costs must be reduced.

The costs of private flying are divided into the original price of the plane and the cost of maintenance. Prior to the war, the price of a small private plane varied from $1164 to $61,000. Sixty per cent of the sales of private planes in 1939 were of a two-place, single-engined cabin monoplane, with the prevailing value between $1200 and $1300. Cruising speeds range from 72 to 155 miles an hour,[5] with landing speeds ranging from 30 to 48 miles per hour. The cruising ranges of private planes varied from 216 to 675 miles. Their gross weight was from 1000 to 1800 pounds, with a useful load of 574 to 1140 pounds.

It is expected that these types of private planes will be marketed immediately after the war at a price somewhat above the

[5] *Aerosphere,* 1941.

prewar level because of the wartime rise in the price level. Automobile prices are expected to be about 20 per cent above prewar prices for the same models. New models of private planes will also be put on the market. Several manufacturers have announced planes to sell for $1000.[6] Some fliers will reduce the original cost of the plane for themselves by belonging to flying clubs or by renting their planes by the hour.

The cost of maintenance includes the direct cost of operation, rental space, depreciation, and insurance. The costs per hour of flying have been figured out by Geisse and Williams for a $2000 light plane at various numbers of flying hours per year. The cost varies from $8.50 to $11.50 an hour, depending on the number of hours flown.[7] The breakdown of these costs is shown in Table 20.

TABLE 20. OPERATING COSTS PER HOUR OF A $2000 LIGHT
PLANE FOR A YEAR OF 100 HOURS AND OF 200 HOURS

	100 Hours	200 Hours
Direct operating cost	$ 1.77	$1.77
Hangar rent	1.80	.90
Depreciation	2.00	1.00
Hull insurance	3.10	1.55
Liability and property damage	1.57	.78
Life insurance ($25,000)	1.25	2.50
	$11.49	$8.50

These costs can be lowered somewhat. In some cases, it will not be necessary to use a hangar, and hangar rents may be reduced. As the cost of the plane is reduced, the cost of depreciation decreases. As there are fewer changes in planes from year to year, the rate of depreciation is expected to decrease. The costs of insurance should be reduced by perhaps a half as the safety record improves and as actuaries have better data on which to base their rates. Engines of the future may operate at lower costs and need less frequent overhauling.

Regulations

One limitation on private flying has been the large number of regulations to which private fliers have had to conform. These

---

[6] Geisse and Williams, *op. cit.*, pp. 64-65.   [7] *Ibid.*, p. 17.

regulations were made in the interest of safety for the flier and for the public. The rules have been so numerous and detailed that many have felt that they were an unnecessary burden. The Safety Bureau of the Civil Aeronautics Board has taken some steps to improve the situation. A number of revisions were made effective July 1, 1945. Others will follow. It is difficult to work out a simple set of regulations and yet provide safety for the flier and the public. Relaxation of regulation may mean more deaths, but it is felt that the development of private flying should not be blocked by too much regulation. It may be assumed that a rational working set of rules will be worked out in time, but it is probable that there will still be more regulation of pilots of private aircraft than of drivers of automobiles.

Landing Places

The fact that there are relatively few landing fields in the United States means that the destinations to which a private flier may go are limited. There are about three thousand airports in the United States, which is, on the average, about one to a county. A great many new airports were built during the war, and it is expected that more will be built in the postwar decade, but some of these projected airports will be limited to scheduled or military transportation and not be open to private planes.

The provision of landing places convenient for all private fliers would necessitate a tremendous number of them. Even if enough were built so that the private flier could land within ten or fifteen miles of his destination, he would still require some form of transportation, probably the automobile, to get him to the final place he desired to go. This inability to land exactly at the point of ultimate destination would decrease to a large extent the plane's advantage of speed, especially since private aircraft will be used primarily for short-distance travel.

It has been suggested that the need for a large number of landing places might be partially solved by the use of vacant fields which could be cleared of obstructions and kept well-sodded. Improvements are being made in the techniques of sodding fields for the use of planes. In rural and sparsely settled areas there will be many areas which can be used for such purposes, but in congested, urban areas, sufficient space will not be available.

Another suggestion is the use of what is popularly called "landing strips." These strips are smaller than airports and cheaper to construct. Yet a one-way landing strip would require ten acres of land, and an additional area for parking. If two runways at right angles were provided in order to allow some adaptation to wind direction, a minimum of twenty acres would be required. In addition, the approaches to the strips must be free of tall buildings. In the open country, it is expected that these strips would be built alongside highways. They could be located closer to the city than airports, but they would still provide a limited service for the private plane as compared to the convenience of the automobile.

To provide the flexibility necessary for the successful development of the private plane, a very large number of landing places will be required. Just a few landing places will not be of much use except for recreational or sport flying. Shall we, then, build a large network of landing fields over the United States in anticipation of a great extension of private flying in the postwar decade? The proponents of the private plane are in favor of such a program. If private airplanes were sure to come in large volume, the building of such landing fields would obviously be good social planning. But there is the distinct possibility that private flying in airplanes will not be developed to a large extent because of the factors of lack of safety, lack of convenience, high cost, and, most of all, because of the factor of a competing and substitute invention, the helicopter. However, the private plane may be used for special purposes, by ranchers, for example, or by farmers with large farms, or by sportsmen, and for business and pleasure travel between aviation centers with adequate landing places.

Helicopters

Although the helicopter is older in conception than the airplane, it was only in 1939 that a successfully controlled helicopter was flown in the United States. The fundamental problems of helicopter design have been solved, and there was considerable use of helicopters during the war, but this does not mean that the helicopter will become the family aircraft immediately. There is quite a difference between solving the basic problems of the helicopter and turning out a comfortable, efficient, foolproof, and cheap machine for John Doe and his family. Great inventions, after their fundamental formulation, always require many improvements and refinements before they become suitable for a wide market. The first models of most important inventions are usually very crude as compared with their later stages of perfection. Before an invention can come into wide use, it must be simple to operate, not easily breakable, readily repaired, low in cost, and quickly serviced. It is often necessary to spend millions of dollars over many years to make an invention ready for widespread popular use. So it is expected that it will take some time for the helicopter to become widely used.

Sometimes, even though the fundamental problems of an invention are solved, the invention never becomes widely used. This was true, for instance, of the autogiro. In 1919, the fundamental problems of the autogiro were said to have been solved and the Pitcairns spent many millions of dollars on its later development. Yet the autogiro was never brought to a stage of development that enabled it to meet the requirements for popular use. The death rate of inventions is high. The question is, Will the helicopter prove to be like these other inventions which never came to be widely used?

When the demand for an invention is great, it is much more probable that the necessary improvements will be made than if the demand were small. Does the helicopter have any characteristics which other aircraft do not possess and for which there is a great demand?

Vertical Flight

An aircraft that is able to land and take off vertically can bring the flier close to his ultimate destination. If a large amount of time must be spent in getting to and from landing places, the time saved by air travel over surface travel is lost. Since a great number of the trips taken by individuals in privately owned conveyances are for short distances, the amount of travel necessary to reach the airport or landing place becomes proportionately more important in private flying.

An aircraft that can land and take off vertically can be used in cities, where space is very limited. Since the population of the United States is largely urban, it is very important that private aircraft be adaptable to city use. The helicopter's ability to fly vertically means that it can land on roofs of buildings if they are flat and free from obstruction. The flier can land very close to the place in which he works, even if the area has few or no open spaces, or he can land in the yard of his home if it is a good-sized yard. The ability to land in a small area, perhaps fifty by fifty feet, without prepared runways, means that the helicopter can land almost anywhere except on sloping hillsides or in areas with many trees or wires.

Speed

The basic asset of all types of air travel is speed, but in private aircraft the ability to fly slowly at times is very important. As a nation of automobile drivers, we are accustomed to slowing up in the face of danger or when we wish to stop. Some small airplanes are capable of relatively slow speeds, but the minimum speed of a plane is still high compared to that of the automobile or the helicopter, and the plane can never stop or hover in one place as the helicopter can. The ability to fly slowly makes it easier to fly in among trees or buildings, to land more accurately and safely, and to follow a given course more easily.

When vertical flight and slow flight are combined in one machine, the resulting advantages are many. The pilot can fly low and follow a course by easily observable landmarks, making instrument flying much less necessary. Beacons, beams, radar, radio, and lighted air lanes are not required. The combination of these two qualities helps to overcome the danger of bad weather. The helicopter can fly slowly in a fog, stopping if an obstruction is sighted suddenly. If overtaken by sudden fog, snow, windstorm, or darkness, the helicopter can land slowly in any small place that is convenient, even in zero visibility. The addition of slow flight to vertical ascent and descent also improves the adjustment of the helicopter to the congested urban areas.

The maximum speed of the helicopter is lower than that of planes of similar horsepower. Since the principal asset of any aircraft is speed, it might be questioned whether the helicopter's slow speed might be a liability. Helicopter models of today travel at ninety to one hundred miles an hour. Speeds of one hundred and twenty or one hundred and forty miles an hour are expected in the immediate postwar models. Some engineers think that ultimately speeds may go up to two hundred miles an hour and above. Yet the helicopter will probably always be slower than the airplane. If speed alone were the test of adoption, the airplane would win, but the helicopter has other advantages over the private plane.

Helicopters are two or three times faster than automobiles, buses, or local trains for all but very short distances between destinations. Air distances are generally about 17 per cent shorter than the routes followed by land vehicles. In urban areas, automobiles and buses are often delayed by the necessity of slowing down or stopping at street crossings. These facts give the helicopter an advantage over surface transportation.

Noise

Another factor which makes the helicopter adaptable to urban use is its quietness in flight and in landing, as compared with the noise of the airplane. Residents of cities, especially those living near airports, have already complained about the excessive noise of the airplane. The propellerless plane, if it should ever come into common use for private flying, would make less noise than the present plane. Helicopters are relatively free from propeller or rotor noises. The rotor has a definite beat that is noticeable to an observer, but it is not objectionable, even at close range. Rotor noise is most noticeable when the helicopter is in forward flight and the engine is throttled back to approximately 75 per cent of its maximum power. Engine noise is greatest when the machine is hovering. The noise twenty feet below a hovering XR-4, with the engine exhaust unmuffled and turned downward, was found to be 115 decibels; in the cabin it was 111 decibels. The over-all noise — of the propeller, rotor, and engine — is about like that of a farm tractor or large truck. No attempt had been made on this craft to silence exhaust noises, insulate mechanical noises, or otherwise reduce the noise level.

Needed Improvements in the Helicopter — Failure of Engines

Helicopter engines cannot stall as automobile engines sometimes do, but they do fail to operate at times. If the possibility of engine failure in helicopters is not reduced to a minimum, their use will not be as widespread as otherwise.

In the present helicopter, if the motor stops, the rotors revolve automatically, the helicopter becomes an autogiro, and the craft is landed much more gently than it would be in a straight fall. Experience with present machines indicates that, if the engine stops at a height of around twenty-five feet or less, the rotors retain enough speed to land the craft without appreciable damage. Also, if the engine stops at heights of four hundred or five hundred feet, autorotation will permit the helicopter to land without a serious bump, but the landing is achieved with greater success if the descent is not vertical but at an angle. The slower the whirling of the rotors, the more rapid is the drop. For this reason it is desirable, under circumstances of slow rotation, to translate some of the downward motion into forward motion. But if there is a forward motion in landing, the helicopter loses one of its most important characteristics, that of landing vertically in a very small space. If a householder uses his back yard or the roof of his house on which to land vertically, and if there is no other available space, a stoppage of the engine near his home may mean some damage. Obviously, the flier wants a helicopter that lands in a small space not nearly all the time, but every time, even if the physical danger to the flier is not great. Extensive use of the helicopter is dependent on a guaranteed landing in a small space, particularly in a city, in the yard of a home, or on the roof of a building. If a large landing place is needed for rare emergencies, the helicopter loses much of its advantage over the airplane.

The airplane engine is very reliable — with dual magneto and good filtering of gasoline — and engine failures are infrequent. The engines of planes used in scheduled airline operations are becoming safer, for, in 1942, 65,000,000 miles were flown per accident because of engine failure, as compared with 15,000,000 miles in 1938. In domestic private flying operations, in 1941, 93,000 miles were flown per accident, excluding instructional flying, with about 17 per cent of the accidents being due to engine failure.[8] At this rate, 530,700 miles were flown per engine failure, or an engine might fail once in 2653 journeys of 200 miles each, although the possibility of a helicopter engine's failing when hovering might be greater. Accidents due to engine failure or structural failures in other parts of the machine are beyond the control of the flier and usually cannot be avoided by improved flying technique. In private flying (excluding instructional), in 1941, about 400,000 miles were flown for every accident due to an engine or other structural failure. In the same year, accidents due to weather were only 3 per cent of all accidents in private flying, while those due to the personal factor, such as lack of judgment, carelessness, and bad technique, accounted for 65 per cent of the accidents in private flying (excluding instructional) and 56 per cent in scheduled passenger flying.

One solution of the problem of engine failure in the helicopter is to attach two engines to the rotors. If one engine stops, the other engine will bring the helicopter down vertically. But two engines and coupling arrangements will weigh more, and the useful load of helicopters is already small. Furthermore, a helicopter with two engines will be expensive, particularly for personal, non-business flying.

Even if there is delay in the satisfactory solution to the problem of engine failure in the helicopter for the purchaser of limited income who lives in a city, and who wants to land in his

---

[8] *Civil Aeronautics Journal,* January 15, 1944, p. 12; and *Civil Aeronautics Journal,* November 15, 1943, p. 155. Instructional flying is estimated to constitute about 40 per cent of private flying operations.

yard and on the roof of a building near where he works, the helicopter will have a considerable use. It can be used by businesses which are able to buy and maintain helicopters with two engines and to employ skilled pilots. It can also be used by persons who live in less congested areas than are found in a city block where the aircraft may land in the street or an adjoining space if engine failure prevents it from landing in the yard. Its use in agriculture, in rescue work, and in many other ways may also proceed quite successfully, irrespective of the slight probability of engine failure. This hazard appears to be more of an obstacle in flights over crowded population centers. It may be that helicopters will be prohibited over cities until this problem is more successfully solved. Approaches to cities may be made over waterways, since the helicopter can be equipped with rubber floats. Another possibility is the provision of emergency landing areas at intervals along the authorized approaches. Wide boulevards without trees would be very well suited to this purpose, with endings near landing places on the ground or on the tops of buildings. Provision of these boulevards would be costly and take time, despite the fact that they would be attractive additions to cities. Before such boulevards could be provided, the problem of engine failure may be solved. Many inventions, in their early development, have presented problems which were as formidable as that of engine failure in helicopters, and which were later successfully solved.

Rotor Breakage

Another possible hazard in the helicopter which, if not corrected, would appear to hinder its extensive use is the breaking of a rotor while the plane is in flight. The solution to this problem lies in the use of a rotor which can bear a great deal of stress. At the present time, rotors are made of wood, but a light metal rotor is a very likely achievement. With metal rotors, the breaking of rotors should be so infrequent as to cause no worry. The possibility of railroad wrecks is not a deterrent to train travel today, although hot-boxes and broken rails do sometimes cause wrecks and loss of life. The breaking of rotors will probably be so infrequent that it will not limit the use of the helicopter in peacetime.

Rotors may also break if they strike objects, such as wires, trees, and other aircraft. Some autogiro pilots have reported that rotors did not break when they struck birds, while others disagree. There is no conclusive evidence at present as to what would be the result if a helicopter rotor should strike birds or hailstones. The avoidance of this hazard is a problem for the helicopter pilot, rather than for the inventors or the manufacturers.

Controls

One important difficulty is the control of the helicopter by the pilot as to speed, direction, landing, etc. At present, the controls in the helicopter are more complicated and elaborate than those in an airplane and thus it is more difficult to fly in spite of its ability to fly very slowly. There are five such controls in present models, and the constant attention of the driver is necessary. The co-ordination of all these controls is said to require a considerable amount of skill. For widespread use, the operation of an invention should be relatively simple. The controls in an automobile, for instance, are quite simple for starting and stopping and for controlling the speed and direction. The gearshift has become automatic in some makes of cars.

Engineers believe that the controls of the helicopter will become much simpler in the future.[9] It may be possible that at some future date the pilot of a helicopter will merely push a few buttons to direct its flight, but a great deal of experimentation will be necessary before this simplification of controls will be achieved. As long as the controls of the helicopter remain complicated, its use will be restricted to professional and highly skilled helicopter pilots.

[9] Grover Loening, *The Helicopter's Limited Future,* lecture before the Brooklyn Institute of Arts and Sciences, Dec. 3, 1943; Col. H. F. Gregory, "What You Can Believe About the Helicopter," *Saturday Evening Post,* May 27, 1944, pp. 22-23.

Other Improvements

In northern climates, there is the problem of ice formation on the rotors and in the carburetor in the wintertime. If the formation of ice on the rotors makes it impossible for the helicopter to fly, the pilot can safely make an emergency landing when ice begins to form, but this decreases the reliability of the machine. If the helicopter is to be a form of transportation which does not have to be supplemented by other means of transportation, it must be able to fly, without fail, in all kinds of weather. The ability to fly in winter climates would give the helicopter an advantage over the automobile, since snow and ice often block roads to surface travel. The solution of the problem of ice formation on rotors is probably the passing of hot air from the exhaust into the hollow metal rotors. The problem of ice in the carburetor would seem to be less serious in helicopters than in planes, since helicopters fly closer to the earth and can land more readily.

Vibration of the helicopter is also a problem that needs improvement, although the amount of vibration has been considerably reduced over that of early models. At present, this vibration is not very noticeable, but modern travelers expect and demand great comfort. The vibration is due mainly to lack of balance of the rotors. The vibration would be less with two or four rotors than with three. There is such a high degree of precision in present-day manufacturing and there are so many recourses against vibration that there is reason to feel confident that vibration in helicopters will be conquered. It is a difficulty that is not concerned with safety or adaptation to congested areas, but one that will retard the number of purchasers or passengers.

In taking off or landing, the whirling rotors of the helicopter produce a strong current of air along the ground, as do the propellers of an airplane. This strong current of air scatters loose top soil or other light objects. If a helicopter lands on a busy street, this material will be blown about. However, the grass in a yard is said to hold the dust and dirt quite well. There appears to be no correction for this wind difficulty. It is probably not sufficiently serious to discourage purchasers, but it may limit the use of the helicopter in city areas to some extent.

Engineering problems

The foregoing improvements of the helicopter are those required by the user. A list of improvements from the engineering
standpoint would be quite different. The engineer views the helicopter as a very new invention, with a large number of possible
designs or patterns, but with few or none of them as yet completely tested. There may be one, two, or four rotors. The torque
of the helicopter in flight may be overcome in several different
ways. Many different suggestions have been made on the number
and placement of the rotors. In 1945, there are three different
types of helicopters with contra-rotating twin sets of rotors, thus
eliminating torque. In one, the two sets are on the same axis. In
the others, they are on different axes on each side of the fuselage
— in one case, intermeshing and very close together. There are
various ways of applying power to the rotor blades and several
different ways of getting both lift and forward motion from the
rotors. There is also the possibility of applying jet air force to
the rotors. A great deal of research is required to test all of these
many possibilities. When this is completed, the best-designed
helicopter will be forthcoming. Engineers expect this research to
take a number of years. Two or three years' time is required now
to design and build a single model at a cost of at least a hundred
thousand dollars, although the time may be shortened if the need
is pressing, as in wartime. Even after these more fundamental
aspects of helicopter design have been tested, and rejected or
approved, there will be hundreds, if not thousands, of lesser improvements which will help to make the helicopter cheaper, more
comfortable, simpler, sturdier, and more reliable. Every great invention goes through such a process of evolution.

The engineers, realizing the long period of time that will be
necessary to complete the experimental and research work on the
helicopter, attempt to discourage prospective owners who expect
to be able to buy a helicopter almost immediately. But it is quite
possible that the engineers may be too conservative. It will take
a long time to try out all the possibilities and make the suggested
improvements, but the difficulties of the helicopter from the
user's standpoint may be solved reasonably well before all the

various engineering alternatives are worked out. Automobiles were in use before many of their present improvements, such as the self-starter, were added. The same thing may occur in the case of the helicopter.

The helicopter arrives at a time when the airplane industry has reached a high stage of development and when two decades of experimentation on the autogiro are behind it. This was not the case with the plane of the Wright brothers or with the automobile, both of which developed at a time when there were no closely related, supporting industries. In addition, the government supported a great deal of research on the helicopter during the war for military purposes. It is not known how much of this research will be applicable to the peacetime helicopter. The aviation industry appears to be willing now, for the first time, to spend money and effort on small aircraft for private flying equal to that previously spent on commercial transport and military planes. The fact that the helicopter arrives at such a propitious time should make its development more rapid than it would otherwise have been.

Prospects for Helicopters

The foregoing discussion of the improvements needed in the helicopter does not reveal any impossible barrier to its successful development. In fact, the nature of the barriers is such that the solutions needed for the user should probably be forthcoming in from two to ten years. In 1943, Sikorsky testified before the Civil Aeronautics Board that he thought two and a half years' work after the war should produce a practical helicopter and that the interim would be even shorter if the war lasted several years. There were at least forty organizations working on the helicopter in the early part of 1944.[10] As additional evidence of expectations, there have been many applications before the Civil Aeronautics Board to set up helicopter transportation lines.

Even though the successful technical development of the helicopter is assumed, the extent of its use by private fliers depends

[10] C. B. F. Macauley, *The Helicopters Are Coming*. New York: McGraw-Hill Book Co., 1944, pp. 163-165.

upon its market price. The price of the first few small private helicopters sold is expected to be five thousand dollars or more. As the volume of production increases, the price will be lowered. Helicopters were produced by assembly-line methods during the war, so the techniques for mass production are already developed.

The materials that go into helicopters or small airplanes are not greatly different from those that go into an automobile, and hence the prices would be nearly the same if the volume of production were the same, except for the fact that the cost of aircraft engines in 1944 averaged about ten times as much per horsepower as that of automobile engines.[11] The price of a small helicopter with one engine should come down to twenty-two hundred dollars or fifteen hundred dollars at prewar price levels, and later the price may be reduced still further through the economies of mass production.

One very important factor in determining the future prospects of the helicopter is the existence or non-existence of competitive inventions. We have predicted in previous paragraphs that the development of the small private plane will be restricted by the competition of the helicopter. If the helicopter likewise has competitors, then its development may be limited. Do any other aircraft have the peculiar qualities of the helicopter which are in great demand, namely, vertical flight, slow speed, and little noise?

The autogiro is able to ascend vertically, perhaps thirty feet, before starting forward flight, and it can land in a much smaller place than an airplane. But it requires more space for landing than the helicopter. Since its ability to rise and ascend vertically is relatively limited, it cannot be adapted as easily to congested urban areas as the helicopter. For most purposes, the autogiro seems to be superseded by the helicopter.

The dirigible or airship is unsuitable for private flying. It is able to rise vertically, but it has many disadvantages, including slow speed, large size, and the difficult process of landing and mooring.

11 C. L. Morris, "What's Ahead for the Helicopter?" *Aviation*, November, 1944, p. 117.

If the small airplane is made roadable, it will offer more serious competition to the helicopter. The adaptability of the plane to urban areas and to individual needs would be considerably increased if it could travel along streets or roads from landing place to ultimate destination. The flier would not have to wait for a taxi or bus, and would be freed from the necessity of having his automobile waiting for him at the landing field.

A roadable plane was successfully constructed in 1939 by Waldo Waterman in California. Waterman's machine had removable wings, which were left at the airport, while the fuselage could be kept in the garage at home. Several roadable planes are reported to be under construction. They are expected to travel about forty miles an hour on the road.

There are many problems involved in building a roadable airplane. The wings are too wide for most streets and roads, and must be folded back over the fuselage as on planes aboard navy airplane carriers, or they may be detached and left at the airport. Another problem with the roadable plane is how to dispose of the propeller when driving along a street. If it remains unprotected on the nose of the plane, it is subject to damage and is a hazard to other vehicles. Announced designs have the propellers in the rear. Manufacturers have had a great deal of experience in producing both airplanes and automobiles, and the technological problems of the roadable airplane could undoubtedly be solved if there were a sufficient demand for it.

The roadable plane might make unnecessary the owning of both an automobile and an airplane, although the roadable plane would not be as efficient a machine on the ground as is the automobile. But if the roadable plane could travel on the road at forty or fifty miles an hour on not too much gas, there might be some people who would give up an automobile for such a plane. A reasonably good roadable plane that did not sacrifice too much load capacity as a plane and that proved moderately good on the roads would be expected to increase considerably the number of persons using planes, in case the helicopter failed to mature. But the roadable plane, like the ordinary airplane, must land at a regular airport or landing field, so that it, too, is restricted as to where it can fly by the number and location of landing places.

Roadable Helicopters

If a roadable airplane can be built, is it not possible also to build a roadable helicopter? The usefulness of the helicopter would be greatly increased if it were roadable. Landing places for helicopters would not need to be located so near to the place of work of the private flier. A man might land twenty blocks from his office building, in an area where there is more land available, and drive to a parking place near his office. A house-holder with a small yard could land near-by and drive to a garage or hangar attached to his house. Since many yards in urban areas are not large enough for helicopter landings, roadability would make the helicopter more adaptable to use in large cities.

The roadable helicopter would probably have some advantages over the roadable plane. The roadable helicopter might be smaller and thus more adapted to use on city streets. The rotors would be easier to fold back than the wings of a roadable plane, and there would be no problem of a propeller. The helicopter could land in closer to the city than the plane, thus reducing the amount of ground travel necessary. The roadable helicopter might eventually replace the automobile if it could be as cheap to operate, as reliable, as versatile, and as low in original price, but this is not probable in the near future or, indeed, later, as far as we can see.

At present, it appears that no work is being done on the road-able helicopter, and apparently aviation engineers have little interest in it at the moment. This is to be expected, since the problems of a non-roadable helicopter are not yet solved. Then, too, inventors, working on inventions that demand large expenditures for experimentation, generally get little encouragement from industry when the inventions are in their early stages of development. Business is often reluctant to spend large sums of money on an invention until the prospect of a financial return is in sight. The development of a roadable helicopter will require large sums of money even after the helicopter itself has been technologically perfected. Hence, the roadable helicopter, if it comes, is some time away. It would seem that the demand for it, because of its adaptability to urban regions and its flexibility for the owner, would be sufficient to insure its successful achievement and to make certain a low price through mass production at some time in the future.

Prospect of Private Flying

The above discussion indicates that there will be private flying in the future, either with the airplane, the helicopter, the roadable airplane, or the roadable helicopter. Probably there will be some use of each, since a complex culture such as ours needs a diversification of transportation vehicles. But it is more probable that one type will predominate in the future because of the fact that a low price cannot be obtained without a large volume of production. The most probable course of development seems to be a large sale of small private airplanes for a few years, to be succeeded by a rising curve of helicopter sales, and probably later by the roadable helicopter.

Whatever the medium, the probabilities strongly point toward a considerable development of private flying. Since the purpose of this study is to attempt to foresee the social effects of aviation, the fact that there will be much private flying is more important than what type of machine will be used.

It is likely that private flying, in the years immediately following the war, will be done by the professional and semi-professional pilot rather than by the average citizen. Skill will be required to fly small planes even with some simplification of controls. The early helicopters will not be easy to fly or to handle in emergencies. Early purchasers are likely to be businessmen, taxi and non-scheduled air firms, agricultural, mining, and fishery companies, and governments which will hire trained pilots. They will use helicopters or small airplanes for dusting or spraying insecticides, for patrolling forests, fighting fires, inspecting cattle ranges, transporting occasional passengers and sight-seers, Coast Guard work, emergency rescues, photographic mapping, ambulance work, deliveries by department stores, for gathering news, and for training pilots. Early fliers for other than business purposes will be well-to-do people who will use aircraft for recreation, sports, and week-end trips. Later, private aircraft will be flown by less skilled pilots. This will be particularly true when the helicopter controls have been simplified, the vibration reduced, and when emergency landings can be made with no great skill.

Amount of Private Flying

So far, we have made no definite prediction of the amount of private flying that is likely to occur in the postwar decade.

At the time of our entrance into World War II, there were less than 25,000 certified private planes. Figure 17 shows the numbers of private planes from 1927 to 1942. The large number in 1929 was the result of the stimulus of Lindbergh's non-stop flight from New York to Paris in 1927. The stationary condition during the 1930's was due to the depression and to the overstimulation in the late 1920's. The growth in number of planes from 1939 to 1941 was a result of the stimulation of the Civilian Pilot Training program. The fourteen-year period between 1929 and 1942 shows an average increase of 7 per cent a year. In comparison,

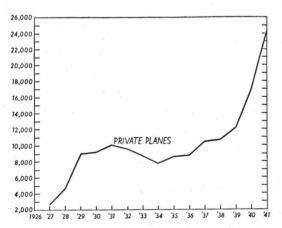

Figure 17. NUMBER OF PRIVATE NON-TRANSPORT PLANES IN OPERATION, BOTH CERTIFICATED AND UNCERTIFICATED, IN THE UNITED STATES BEFORE WORLD WAR II

the growth of the number of automobiles for the thirteen years after the number had reached 8000 was at a rate of 47 per cent a year.

If we project this rate of yearly growth into the postwar years, assuming 23,000 private planes at the end of the war, we get a figure of 45,000 private planes ten years after the war. With a high rate of obsolescence, there may not be 23,000 small civilian planes unless many small planes are released by the armed forces. Assuming 15,000 private planes at the end of the war and the prewar rate of growth, we reach a figure of 30,000 small planes in a decade after the war; but, if the rate of increase is doubled, the number of private planes would be 55,600. If we assume 23,000 planes after the war and a rate of growth of 14 per cent a year, there would be 85,000 planes at the end of a decade. On the basis of these assumptions, the number of private planes might vary between 30,000 and 85,000. In these projections a development of the helicopter is not taken into account. If a successful helicopter is developed, many who would otherwise buy planes will purchase helicopters.

In estimating future numbers of aircraft, we are not so concerned with an accurate estimate of the number of planes that manufacturers ought to produce as we are in some sort of useful picture of the extent of private flying to be used as a basis for figuring out the social effects of small aircraft. If there were 35,000 aircraft after the war, there would be about ten aircraft to 10,000 families. If there were 100,000 aircraft, there would be ten to every 3500 families. In comparison, there were ten automobiles to every eleven families at the beginning of the war.

Size of the Postwar Market

The problem may be approached by trying to estimate the size of the postwar market for private aircraft. There have been various marketing surveys which attempted to appraise the postwar market for small planes. These usually show the market to be quite large. The information is usually obtained from answers to such questions as, "Are you contemplating buying an airplane after the war?" or, "If the price of a plane is $2000, would you consider buying?" It is not clear how realistic the hopes expressed in these answers are. One such survey indicated that 78,000 people plan to pay at least $1500 for a postwar personal airplane as soon as it is available, 119,000 are ready to buy helicopters, and another 78,000 are potential customers but have not decided what type of aircraft to buy.[12]

We might assume that the buyers of private aircraft will come from the group of people who own two automobiles. Before the war, there were a million families with two or more automobiles.[13] No doubt, many of these automobiles were cheap or second-hand ones. Since a private plane or helicopter will cost more than an automobile, many of these million owners of two automobiles will not be able to afford an automobile and a small aircraft. Of the 475,000 families owning two automobiles or more, and having incomes over $10,000 a year, there will be perhaps only a small percentage who will want to own both an automobile and a private aircraft in the first decade after the war.

Another indication of the possible size of the private aircraft market is the number of automobile owners who, before the war, had cars retailing for more than $1350. There were probably from 180,000 to 330,000 such owners.[14] Of this number, not all would want a plane alone, or both a plane and an automobile.

A still wider conception of the potential market is the population with incomes over $10,000 a year, of whom there were 790,000 individuals and families before the war. Sixty per cent of these had two or more automobiles in 1941.[15] But there will be some individuals with incomes between $5000 a year and $10,000 who will want to own both an automobile and an airplane, even though it costs from $8 to $12 an hour to fly. As aircraft prices are lowered, the numbers of owners with low incomes will be increased.

In addition to individual or family owners, business concerns will own planes. Before the war, 13 per cent of the private planes were business-owned, 42 per cent were for commercial non-

---

[12] Foster, *op. cit.*, p. 116.
[13] Geisse and Williams, *op. cit.*, p. 166.
[14] *Ibid.*, p. 49.   [15] *Ibid.*, p. 169.

scheduled flying (for hire or instruction), and 45 per cent were for pleasure. Seventy per cent of private flying time was for purposes other than pleasure. In the years immediately following the war, we may expect an aircraft market for business and civil governmental purposes exceeding that for personal transportation and pleasure.

One factor affecting the market for small aircraft will be the number of pilots and student pilots in the United States. It has been estimated that about 250,000 pilots in the armed services will return. Of these, perhaps 15 per cent will be active in flying planes.[16] If the registered pilots at the beginning of the war are added to this number, there will be 93,000 pilots. If there are three pilots to a plane, and nine students to a training plane, a total of 52,000 planes will be required. If 13,000 are already in existence, 39,000 new planes will be needed.[17] The assumption that 2000 student planes will be needed and that there will be 37,500 service pilots wanting planes in a ratio of three pilots to one plane may be very wide of the mark.

In sharp contrast to these estimates, another report forecasts an actual sale of only 9500 private planes in the two years after the war, or not more than 5000 a year.[18] Although this is small in comparison with other estimates, it is still a greater yearly increase than occurred before the war.

Conclusion

It seems probable that the helicopter will be developed for general use and that it will curtail the use of private planes and the building of landing places on which the plane depends. With a low-priced helicopter, the amount of private flying will increase. This increase might occur near the end of the first postwar decade. The attempts to answer quantitatively how many private planes there will be several years after the war suggest one private plane to every three hundred or four hundred families. The psychological factor makes prediction very difficult in

[16] *Ibid.*, p. 194.   [17] *Ibid.*, p. 194.
[18] E. E. Lothrop, "Let's Be Practical About Postwar Plane Markets," *Aviation*, December, 1943, p. 114.

this case. There may be a very much larger sale than one airplane for every three or four hundred families in a period of boom psychology, probably followed by a marked regression. When helicopters are available, the total aircraft in use is likely to be considerably larger than the number of private airplanes. The amount of ownership by families will hardly compare with that of automobiles unless some extraordinarily successful, low-priced, roadable helicopter is developed. Probably most families with a choice between an automobile and a helicopter would choose the former. Only families with good-sized incomes will be able to own both. At some future date, a successful roadable helicopter may displace a good many automobiles. Helicopters will have much use by business concerns, governments, and various types of organizations.

12

Air Routes

SINCE THE AIRPLANE can fly equally well in any direction, constructing routes would seem to be no problem, at least so far as the atmosphere is concerned. But a plane must have a place to land and, in modern aviation, many flying aids along the route. Actually, routes must be constructed, but not in the same way in which a railroad or a highway is built. Their construction consists of lighting for night flying, markers, radio beams, emergency landing fields, weather-reporting stations, radio telephones, and electronic devices for landing. In this chapter, however, we are concerned with the choice of routes.

Factors Determining Air Routes

In military flying, shortness of distance is one of the principal factors in choosing a route, but in civilian flying, although distance is important, especially on long flights, it may be conditioned by other factors. The shortest route between two points is a line which, if extended around the globe, would divide it into hemispheres and is, for that reason, called a great-circle route. The great-circle route between New York and Chungking lies across the Arctic and is much shorter than the route across the Pacific Ocean. Ships and railroads have not followed the great-circle routes because of geographical barriers. Very long-distance travel has, in general, been from east to west or west to east, mainly because routes north and south have had obstacles to surface travel in the form of ice. But geographical barriers are of no importance to the airplane, and distance becomes a factor which must be considered afresh. If distance were the determining factor, then, in aviation, we should refer to China as our northern neighbor instead of a distant Oriental land, as we do with steamship travel.

It is the airplane's freedom from geographical barriers which makes air routes different from surface routes. For instance, the transition from land to water and vice versa in surface travel means unloading and loading again. The ease with which airplanes fly over both land and water leads to new international routes across water, with landings well into the interior. Such inland cities as Minneapolis-St. Paul, Chicago, and Detroit are closer to northern cities in Asia and Europe than either New York or Seattle. While the seacoast is no barrier to the airplane, and while most land obstacles are flown over with ease, mountains are still something of a hazard. Such was the case with the famous "Hump" of the Himalayas during World War II. In the future, mountains should cease to be a major concern.

An economic factor in the choice of routes is the distance between possible stops for refueling. This is important because the greater the distance between stops, the more fuel must be carried, which, in turn, restricts the weight of the load of passengers and cargo which can be carried. Hence the great-circle routes will not be flown if great distances must be flown without stopping. Rather, a longer one will be chosen, with possibilities of stops at from five hundred to fifteen hundred miles. This problem arises chiefly over oceans and in the cold regions of the North. It is also the reason for the sudden importance of very small islands in mid-ocean, such as Ascension or Midway, which were almost unknown before aviation.

Weather is also a factor in determining air routes. Fogs, storms, high winds, and ice create flying difficulties. The fogs around the Aleutian Islands and extending westward will be considered in using this route. Across the North Atlantic, the route via the Azores is often flown in preference to the northern routes because of more favorable weather conditions. Flying at higher altitudes and the use of electronic equipment are expected to lessen this barrier, though not to eliminate it.

The principal factor, however, in choice of routes for passengers, mail, and cargo transports is traffic potential. In general,

the traffic potential will be where there are the largest populations with the highest incomes. Since this has also been a de-
terminant in routes for surface transportation, there will be a
close similarity between surface and air routes. Political considerations in granting freedom of the air and freedom of trade
may delay the paralleling of surface and air routes, but probably
not for long. The search of the airlines for traffic is so compelling
that air routes will be where the commerce of the world now
flows as shown by the statistics of trade. The use of great-circle
lines for air routes, expected by many people, may be only a
myth. The air routes will connect the big cities from which exports go and to which imports come.

In the immediate future, the variations in air routes from
present trade routes will be because of factors of distance,
weather, obstacles such as mountains, etc. As the future unfolds,
there will be other variations due to the redistribution of population, trade, and income which aviation will bring. One of the
more immediate variations will be the opening-up of new places
for tourists to visit because of the shortening in the time of air
travel over surface methods. Then, too, there will be air routes
to lands now unsettled and undeveloped, which will be opened
up by aviation. Africa and South America hold possibilities of
such new routes. These various factors are discussed in more detail in the paragraphs which follow dealing with the international
routes of the United States. But, before discussing these routes,
a few remarks will be made concerning the routes within the
United States.

Domestic Routes

The two chief determining factors of American domestic routes
are traffic potential and governmental regulation in the interests
of efficiency. Traffic potential in the past has led mainly to
routes which connect the big cities. This was also true in the
early years of commercial aviation when the airlines were dependent primarily upon mail payments, for the volume of mail,
like that of passengers and cargo, is much greater to and from
the big cities. Governmental agencies of control have sometimes

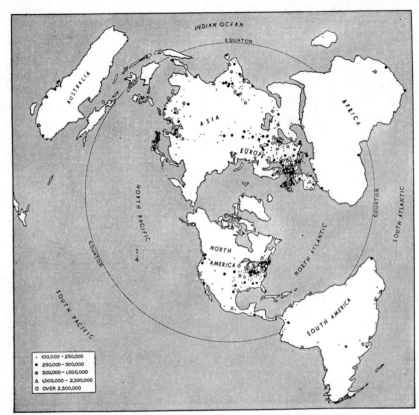

Figure 18. THE DISTRIBUTION OF CITIES OF DIFFERENT
SIZES ON A WORLD MAP

Except during wars, airplane travel is chiefly between large cities. Hence a
map of the location of the cities of the world shows the areas that will be
connected by most airlines and the airlines most frequently traveled. The
cities of the future may be located somewhat differently from those of the
present; but for the next few decades, the locations will not be greatly
different from the present ones.

granted routes in the interests of furthering competition, sometimes to encourage consolidation, often to avoid duplication,
nearly always to prevent overexpansion and consequent failure,
and occasionally to experiment with new plans.

In the future, the domestic routes will include smaller places
not now on the "trunk-line" routes. As air routes penetrate to

areas of less dense population, the choice of routes is, in the main, between two types, discussed in Chapter 10. As shown there, one type is the radial route which "feeds" into the "terminal" city and carries back trunk-line passengers whose destinations are near-by small cities or towns. The other pattern of routes is one joining the small towns like beads on a string. The former is probably somewhat less profitable than the latter because of the low traffic potential at one of its terminals, other things being equal. However, if the air-traveling public should more commonly reside around these big terminal cities, it may be that the radial pattern will be developed, although when air travel becomes more common, the pattern of long lines connecting towns may be more widely used.

International Routes to and from the United States

The possible routes between the United States and other countries have been the subject of a special study by the Civil Aeronautics Board, and an allotment of specific routes across the North Atlantic has been made. Arrangements must, of course, be made with the other countries for landing and taking on traffic. These routes are shown on the accompanying maps. They connect the United States with three large areas of the world, as discussed in the following paragraphs. There are, of course, various other routes, actual and proposed, to these different areas.

From the point of view of business the most important air route in the postwar decade for the United States is that across the North Atlantic to Europe. This route connects the wealthiest regions on the earth, which, in addition, are both populous and have historical connections. That air travel to Europe from the United States is of great economic consequence is shown by the fact that 26 per cent of the total air and first-class and cabin overseas passengers to and from the United States in 1937 was over the North Atlantic to Europe. In passenger-miles this traffic was even more significant — 40 per cent of the total overseas passenger-miles.[1] The travel over these routes will be subject to

[1] F. H. Crozier, *Overseas Air Service Patterns,* Travel Distribution and Composition, All Areas, Civil Aeronautics Board, December, 1944, p. 5.

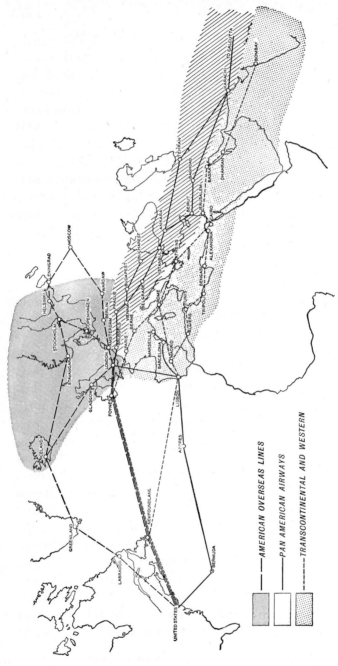

Figure 19. NORTH ATLANTIC AIR ROUTES FOR UNITED STATES AIRLINES

The Civil Aeronautics Board assigned air routes in 1945 across the North Atlantic to three United States companies. For Europe, the assignment was by areas rather than by definite routes between particular points. European companies will fly similar routes across the North Atlantic. There is some distortion in comparative length of routes on this map.

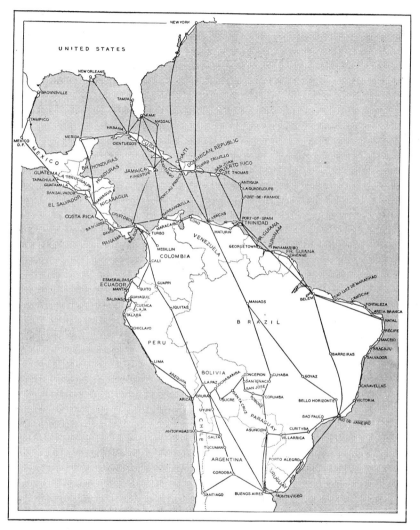

Figure 20. AIR ROUTES SOUTH FROM THE UNITED STATES

This map shows the air routes suggested by the Civil Aeronautics Board to cities to the South of the United States. Some of these routes will be flown in 1946; others are realistic possibilities.

275

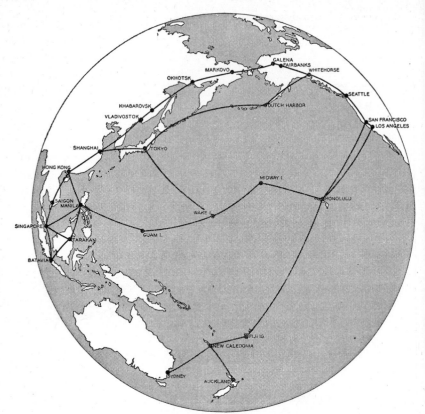

Figure 21. PACIFIC AIR ROUTES

Air routes suggested by the Civil Aeronautics Board across the Pacific
Ocean and along the land mass of Asia are shown in this map. The routes
along the mainland are shorter to the cities on the continent of Asia and
tap a larger population along the route than do the water routes farther
south.

competition from the airlines of several nations. However, the
United States furnishes a large part of the passengers over these
lanes.

The routes followed will be somewhat like those followed by
steamships, but with important variations. The routes will go
from eastern Canada and from the northeastern part of the
United States to Europe. There are three of these routes. The
middle one is from Newfoundland via Eire to the British Isles.

This route is characterized by a rather long non-stop flight. From Botwood, Newfoundland, to Foynes, Ireland is two thousand miles. For this long non-stop flight, the planes must have part of their passenger load displaced by a heavy load of fuel. This route goes on to London, a distance of thirty-five hundred miles from New York, and then spreads out to various European cities.

The long non-stop flight of this route to Europe could be avoided by the construction of floating islands along the way. The building of these seadromes has often been proposed, but no practical steps have been taken for their construction, the cost of which is estimated at $12,500,000 a drome.[2] The prospects for these seadromes become less bright as larger and speedier planes develop which are able to make long non-stop flights more efficiently.

To avoid the non-stop flight between Newfoundland and Ireland, planes can also fly farther north and land at Iceland. From Botwood to Reykjavik, Iceland, is fifteen hundred miles, but the detour by Iceland makes the total mileage between New York and London two hundred miles longer. Planes flying this more northerly route may land in Greenland in order to decrease the length of non-stop flight necessary. The take-off on this second route to Europe may also be made farther north, from Goosebay, Labrador. This northern route over Greenland and Iceland saves time and distance if the destinations are Norway, Sweden, the cities of the Baltic, Leningrad, or Moscow. The flight from Iceland to Oslo is only about eleven hundred miles — a shorter distance than from Iceland to London. From New York to Copenhagen over this northern route is thirty-nine hundred miles. By steamship, the Baltic cities were farther from the United States than the British and northwestern French ports. The saving in time and distance by air may encourage travel from the United States to these northern cities and also to Leningrad and Moscow. From Moscow, air connections take the traveler to southern Russia, Turkey, Iran, and Palestine. At the American end of this second route, take-offs could be made from Chicago or Detroit, and in Canada, from Toronto.

[2] *Scientific American,* September, 1943, pp. 118-120.

In the past a disadvantage of these routes over the North Atlantic to Europe has been the winter weather. This unpleasant
weather has even been a deterrent to the travel of passengers on
steamships. Perhaps it may be less for airplanes of the future.
The winds are generally from the west and often blow at fifty
miles an hour, and storms are frequent. Yet surprising weather
is sometimes encountered. Pilots have reported temperatures of
40° above zero in Iceland, dropping to 10° above zero at New
York. Landings in January have been made in the rain within
the Arctic Circle at 42° above zero.

To avoid the disturbance of winter weather, planes fly from
Newfoundland to the Azores. From Botwood, Newfoundland,
to Horta in the Azores is only fifteen hundred miles, about the
same as the distance to Iceland. From the Azores, the flight
usually proceeds to Lisbon, Portugal, or the planes may go
northwood to Foynes, Ireland. To London from New York via
Botwood, the Azores, and Foynes is forty-three hundred miles.
This third route, by way of the Azores, is a convenient one for
travelers wishing to visit the Mediterranean cities of Europe and
Africa. A variation is to avoid Newfoundland and to proceed
from the United States to Bermuda to the Azores.

Another possible way of avoiding the bad weather across the
North Atlantic is to fly by the shorter northern routes at high altitudes. By flying at high altitudes, clouds, rain, snow, and the
danger of icing can be avoided, and there may be a choice of
winds by varying the altitude. The winds are said to be very
strong at times. We have had very little experience with civilian
flying in the substratosphere, so it is not known exactly what the
difficulties may be. High-altitude flying is made possible by the
oxygen mask for military fighters and the pressurized cabin for
passenger planes. The large new planes with pressurized cabins,
which are especially designed for long, non-stop flights at an
altitude of 20,000 or 30,000 feet or higher, maintain a pressure in
the cabin equivalent to the pressure at an altitude of 8000 feet.
It is expected that, as soon as these planes are put into regular
scheduled passenger service, more flights will be made from
Botwood to Foynes, and even from New York to London, a dis-

tance of thirty-five hundred miles. This latter non-stop journey is expected to cost more, and its schedule frequency will depend on the number who are willing to pay the additional costs.

Thus, it may be seen that the most frequently traveled route is not only a function of the distance, the weather, the population, and potential intermediate traffic, but also a function of the type of plane developed. If these new large planes are as efficient over long distances — thus having low costs — as they are said to be, it is possible that non-stop flights will be made regularly and frequently from the mainland of the United States to the British Isles or to Continental Europe.

In studying possible air routes across the Atlantic, the Civil Aeronautics Board, of course, made extensive studies of possible traffic. It was found that the central route from the United States to London (via Nova Scotia and Eire) had the possibilities of the most travel. An important question was how many aviation companies should fly such a route. The action of the Civil Aeronautics Board, in granting certificates to three companies to fly this route, indicated its willingness to put the question to a test. In permitting three companies flying the flag of the United States to carry passengers and cargo over this central route, they also answered the much-discussed question as to whether there should be just one American company flying international lines, or several. The grant means that we do not have "one chosen instrument" handling international air traffic, but three companies who will compete, not only with foreign air services, but also among themselves. The northern route by way of Iceland was certificated to one company, as was the southern route going by the Azores. The Board went further in its award and indicated the various parts of Europe and Asia whose traffic would go to the three different companies. But flying passengers and cargo to and from these various European and Asiatic cities depends upon the consent of the countries concerned.

Routes to the South

The second great area of trade and travel with the United States is the one to the south of us, with routes to South America

and the Caribbean countries. Other routes lead to the near-by
lands bordering on the Gulf of Mexico, including the Bahamas.
Travel to and from these areas, including Bermuda, in 1937 constituted 55 per cent of the total air and first- and cabin-class
steamship passengers of the United States.[3] (There were relatively few tourist and third-class passengers.) Since much of this
was short-distance travel to the Gulf areas, the passenger-miles to
the south accounted for only 27 per cent of the total passenger-
miles. Of the total air travel between the countries to the
south and the United States in 1941, 77 per cent was to the
Gulf area, including overland travel to Mexico, 18 per cent to
the Caribbean areas, including Colombia and Venezuela; and
5 per cent to the other areas.[4] Thus, in these areas and at this
stage, the travel is largely for short distances, chiefly first-class
and cabin, with very much less travel to the more distant South
American ports.

These routes leave the United States from Miami and various
Gulf coast cities, such as New Orleans, Houston, and Brownsville. Planes to Mexico and areas beyond take off from California
and Texas cities, notably Los Angeles and El Paso. The planes
from these latter ports carry a large part of their traffic to the
interior of Mexico. Those from the Gulf and Florida cities carry
passengers to the cities bordering on the Gulf and to the cities
of the Caribbean, including the northwestern coast of South
America.

Much of the travel to the Gulf areas and near-by islands is for
pleasure. These lands are picturesque and have great possibilities
for vacation travel. Since they are not far distant, the cost of
travel to them is relatively low and within the economic reach
of many residents of the United States. Routes to the Caribbean
areas are about twice as long as to the Gulf areas, and the saving
of time by air travel is appreciable. For American residents there
are business opportunities in mineral and tropical products in

[3] F. H. Crozier, *Overseas Air Service Patterns,* Travel Distribution and Composition, All Areas, *op. cit.,* p. 5.
[4] F. H. Crozier, *Overseas Air Service Patterns,* Trans-Caribbean and Off-Shore
Island Areas, Civil Aeronautics Board, August, 1944, p. 8.

these areas. Then, too, there are historic and scenic attractions, as well as a good winter climate in parts of this area. Thus, considerable travel from the United States to Central and South America may be expected.

At present, relatively few routes cross the Caribbean lands and the Gulf areas to the other parts of South America. Below the Caribbean, South America is tropical until the great cities of Rio de Janeiro, Buenos Aires, and Santiago are reached. These cities are the foci of attraction for travelers from the United States.

These, then, are the most probable routes to the south in the decade after the war. Later, the air routes to the south will be determined by the volume of traffic and by the development of the interior of South America, which will be encouraged by aviation. The white population of South America is largely scattered along the coast line because of the transportation connections by ship. Up to the present time, there has been very little building of railroads in the mountains and jungles of the interior. The success of airlines in the interior of South America, in Colombia and Brazil in particular, argues for a development of the interior of South America. As a result, air routes from the United States may cross the lands of South America, in addition to skirting the coast.

The course of these routes will be affected by policies regarding cabotage and the ownership of domestic lines in countries of South America by airline companies of the United States. Some small countries may find it to their advantage to allow outside lines to carry domestic passengers between interior cities.

The amount of passenger traffic to the southern countries increased to a considerable extent between 1938 and 1942,[5] and is indicative of future possibilities. The first increases in air passenger travel to the south are expected to be for non-business purposes. Perhaps, later, business travel may build up to appreciable amounts. But whatever the interests of the passengers, the advantages of aviation over other means of transportation are

[5] *Ibid.*, p. 9.

so great in this region as to indicate a great extension of air routes over these areas to the south.

Routes to the West

The area to the west of the United States is a huge expanse of water many thousands of miles across. Between the distant shores of Asia and the United States went only 2.9 per cent of our total air, first- and cabin-class ocean passengers in 1937. About the same percentage went west to Australia and New Zealand.[6] Over these long distances, the saving of time by airplane is most impressive. Steamships require from sixteen to forty-eight days, whereas the military flying time from California to Australia is said to have been only two days.

The route of the steamships to the Orient is westward across the Pacific Ocean from the coastal cities of the United States. The air routes set up by Pan American Airways followed the general route of the ships. The first leg of the route is the longest non-stop flight of the trip — from San Francisco to the Hawaiian Islands, a distance of 2400 miles. At Honolulu the route divides. One route turns southward and proceeds over a series of island stops to Sydney, Australia, or Auckland, New Zealand, for a total distance from California of 7600 miles. The other route proceeds from Honolulu to Midway, to Wake, to Guam, to Manila, and thence to Shanghai, 9150 miles from San Francisco. Other areas can be reached by branches from this main route. The route to Tokyo would branch off at Wake. From Manila, the routes will fan out to various mainland ports.

Travel over the central route across the Pacific Ocean is greater in the summer months than in the winter. The peak travel in the summer is about twice what it is in the winter. This observation holds for most of the routes across the Pacific except the one to Australasia. The outbound traffic from the United States is heavier from August to November, but the inbound is greater from February to May.[7] Aviation may somewhat reduce the seasonality of travel on these routes.

[6] F. H. Crozier, *Overseas Air Service Patterns*: All Areas, *op. cit.*, p. 5.
[7] These data are based upon studies of the Maritime Commission.

The outstanding characteristic of this Pacific route is the great distance over water with no supporting population, after having passed Honolulu, until Asia or Australia is reached. There is a large amount of travel between Hawaii and the United States. The number of passengers, first-class, cabin, and air, between the Hawaiian Islands and the mainland of the United States, in 1937, was 6 per cent of our total overseas travel and larger than the number between the United States and Asia and Australasia. Hawaii is a very attractive recreational area, and by air the trip can be made from the Pacific Coast in an afternoon.

Beyond Honolulu, the absence of intervening population affects the economics of this transportation route. Obviously, it is desirable to leave Honolulu with as full a load of passengers as possible. The frequency of the schedules will depend upon the volume of traffic. The loads of fuel, which displace passengers, needed beyond Honolulu are, however, only for fifteen-hundred-mile hops. The future holds little promise of an increase in population in the areas over which this central route passes. The island stops between Hawaii and the Philippines are small and geographically isolated. However, these small islands are of great potential military value as air and naval bases.

In discussing these air routes, little has been said of great-circle routes. The air route to Asia which approximates a great-circle course goes over Alaska. The route from San Francisco to Calcutta via Nome, Alaska is 1200 miles shorter than westward across the Pacific Ocean. The trip from San Francisco to Shanghai is 2545 miles shorter by Alaska than across the Pacific. This northern route from San Francisco is shorter to all the mainland Asiatic cities than is the central route through Honolulu westward across the Pacific. However, because of the great speed of the airplane, the saving of a thousand miles does not reduce the total trip time as much as it would for a slow means of transportation, such as a steamship. For a forty-eight-hour trip, a saving of 15 per cent of the distance would reduce the total trip time by only seven hours. By boat, a saving of 15 per cent would be measured in days rather than hours. To a city like Manila, where the distance via Alaska is only 245 miles shorter, the time saved would be negligible. As to fares, a saving of a thousand miles at a rate of five cents a mile would reduce the total fare by fifty dollars, a considerable saving. For cities where the distance differential between the central and northern routes is not great, the saving in fares would be small, and there might be competition between the northern and central routes. The advantages of the northern route in saving time and distance are greater from Seattle than from San Francisco, and still greater from such inland cities as Chicago or Minneapolis.

The course of the northern route is by way of Fairbanks, Alaska, and thence to various stopping places in Siberia. These routes may then branch off to Tokyo and to Manila or continue along the coast of China or across the interior and on to Singapore, Batavia, or Calcutta. The northern route does not have as favorable weather conditions as the central route, but the weather is said to be no more difficult than that on some of the transcontinental airways flown in the United States. The northern route does have the advantage of shorter distances between stops, making possible smaller fuel loads. However, the greatest advantage of the northern route lies in the intermediate traffic potential. The population at the actual stops along the northern route between San Francisco and Batavia has been found to be seven or eight times as large as the population along the central trans-Pacific route, and twenty times as large if the population between stops is included.[8] The value to aviation of population and wealth along the route is apparent. The greater the industrialization of the country and the higher the per capita incomes, the greater the number of potential passengers.

The northern route, like the central one, has in prospect a large number of passengers for the first leg of the journey to the Orient. The number of passengers between the United States and Alaska by air, and first- and cabin-class in 1937 was almost as large as between the United States and Hawaii. Moreover, there is a good possibility of an expansion of air travel to Alaska. Alaska has many scenic wonders to attract vacation travel and

8 J. Parker Van Zandt, *The Geography of World Air Transport.* Washington, D.C.: The Brookings Institution, 1944, p. 28.

its economic development is expected to encourage people to settle there and to increase the business travel between it and the United States. In the more distant future, it is certain that industrialization will increase in China and also in Siberia. Hence the business interchange between the United States and these areas will increase. The inhabitants of China and Siberia will travel more by airplane in the future. This industrialization, however, will be achieved over several decades. For some time, at least, more travel between the United States and the Orient will originate in the United States than in the Orient. Although the distances are long and the costs of the journey will be large, China and Japan attract a number of visitors. The attractions for tourists in areas lying between Alaska and China on the northern route appear to be slight. However, the people along the upper part of the northern route do represent potential customers for international travel, although it is difficult to estimate their number.

The degree to which the potential passenger traffic in Alaska and in the countries beyond will be of advantage to American airlines depends on the nature of international agreements on air transportation. The northern route over Alaska has not been flown by scheduled planes in peacetime. The inauguration of scheduled flights over this route rests upon making arrangements with the various countries concerned. The land immediately west and southwest of Alaska is Russian. Negotiations must be made with the Union of Soviet Socialist Republics for permission for American planes to fly this route. Such permission may be granted. It may depend on a reciprocal agreement for Russian planes to fly along the coast of the United States. The right of cabotage must be granted by the Union of Soviet Socialist Republics to American airlines if the potential intermediate passenger traffic is to be realized. It will be much easier to arrange stops for refueling than for the right to take on and discharge native populations between cities in the same country. If the passenger potentials of the northern route are not utilized, the advantages of the northern route over the central route are somewhat decreased.

A factor of some economic importance for air transportation

between the United States and Alaska is the high degree of seasonality. Such travel is much greater during the summer months than during other seasons. The travel in July and August is five times that in February. This seasonality, however, is only for Alaskan travel and throws little light on what it may be over the northern route to China or Japan or the Philippines.

Other Routes

The discussion of air routes has thus far been from the point of view of the United States rather than from that of other countries. Britain is interested in airlines which will link the mother country with other members of the British Commonwealth of Nations. The routes that particularly interest her are to Canada, India, Australasia, and South Africa. England sees in aviation a means of transportation that makes possible faster travel between the various parts of her empire.

The Soviet Union will find aviation extraordinarily valuable for transportation across her own immense domestic area, which comprises one-sixth of the land area of the earth. Her international trade will point toward Europe, China, and India.

One way of getting a general picture of future air routes is to approach the problem from the point of view of industrialization as well as from that of geography. The combination of large populations and wealth, essential for the development of air travel, is a function of mechanical power. Industrialization, at the present stage of technological development, rests basically on coal and iron, although oil, electricity, and various metals are also important. Abundant mechanical power and machines to which this power may be applied are essential for a high degree of industrial development.

Areas possessing such natural resources and not highly industrialized at present are China, especially North China, Russia, and parts of Siberia and India, which may become industrialized before China. In addition to natural resources, these countries have the large populations necessary for industrialization. India has a population of 380,000,000; China, 450,000,000; and the Union of Soviet Republics, 190,000,000. There is much less assurance as

yet of a rapid and extensive industrialization of Africa and South
America. Europe and North America are the most highly industrialized areas. Therefore, the future air routes from North
America and from Europe to Siberia, China, and India will be
most important.

The shortest air routes from Europe to China cross the U.S.S.R.,
passing over populous and rich areas. Russian airlines are in
a favored position for developing these routes. Other countries are not so well situated for organizing them if it is necessary
to fly across the huge area of Russia without stopping. Even when
stops for fuel are allowed, if the planes of other nations are not
permitted to carry intermediate passenger and cargo traffic, they
are at a disadvantage as compared with the Russian lines.

Routes from India to Russia or from Russia to China present
few problems. Routes from India to Europe can run across
southern Europe and the Near East.

The routes we have been discussing are essentially broad belts
between regions economically able to support a good deal of air
travel in the near or distant future. There will be much less travel
in the Southern Hemisphere than in the Northern. Few well-
traveled routes will connect Africa, South America, and Australasia, as compared with the number connecting Europe, Asia, and
North America. Aviation makes it possible to reach Africa easily,
but it is difficult to predict what the future development of this
continent will be. Aviation will lead to some exploitation of
African natural resources and make possible the development of
its interior, but how important Africa will become in the world
community of nations is hard to tell. Such countries as Africa
and South America, which do not have adequate surface transportation, find air transportation a very great aid. Even though
South America may not become strongly industrialized unless
adequate coal is produced, air transportation may be highly developed because of the poor surface facilities.

Conclusion

The most important determining factor in present and future
air routes is traffic, actual or potential. Other factors are dis-

tance, space between stops, geographical barriers, weather, and political considerations. The determinants of traffic are population density and income. Indexes of these are the existence of large cities, the extent of manufacturing, and the flow of commerce, particularly manufactured articles. These are also the determinants of rail and steamship traffic. Hence air routes will lie close to present trade routes. There are, however, important variations, because of the factors listed above. Also in the future, new regions will be opened for settlement, other peoples will industrialize, and airplanes will have some effect over long periods of time in redistributing populations. Hence these traffic routes will be somewhat different in the future because of aviation.

13 | International Travel

IN THE PAGES OF THE BIBLE the great Psalmist sings, "If I take the wings of the morning and dwell in the uttermost parts of the sea . . ." International aviation makes this fantasy of the ancient poet a reality. And there are those today who gaze skyward at the planes flying to other lands and become transported into a world of imagination as truly as was the Psalmist. Freed from the practical considerations of everyday life, they contemplate breakfasting in Chicago, flying across the North Pole, and dining in Calcutta on the same day. The Arctic Circle, densely populated, becomes the Mediterranean of future world commerce and culture. They foresee "one world" where wars will be no more. Boundary lines mean nothing when we "take the wings of the morning"! Perhaps these things will come to be. Only a scant hundred generations of mankind separate the poet David, with his vision, from the Wright brothers.

Once having seen the vision of international aviation, it is difficult ever to become pedestrian again. But we want to know what will happen the day after tomorrow as well as a hundred generations hence; and costs, production problems, and statistics are very pedestrian.

The first international flight over water occurred in 1909, when Blériot crossed the English Channel from France to England.[1] Charles Lindbergh's flight from the United States to France in 1927 brought to popular attention the fact that international flying over the Atlantic was a possibility. Short-distance international routes between near-by countries had already developed widely, along with domestic flying. Longer-distance flights, as

[1] M. J. B. Davy, *Air Power and Civilization*, p. 73.

from London to Capetown or from Paris to Indo-China, waited upon the development of larger airplanes. By the beginning of World War II, international flying over long distances, across oceans, and over nations, was firmly established. The Dutch established, in 1930, the first world air route to the Far East, the Amsterdam-Batavia airline. Later, Dutch airlines established a service from Java to Australia and from Holland to French Indo-China. Other Dutch lines operated between the north coast of South America and the West Indies. British international lines mainly connected England with various parts of the British Empire and ran in general in the directions of Australia and South Africa. In 1939, a British air route to North America was established. The French developed airlines to Indo-China, to Central Africa, Madagascar, and to West Africa, and thence to South America. Germany had routes to the Far East and to South America. American airlines stretched across the Pacific, the North and South Atlantic, across Africa, to Central and South America, and to Canada and Alaska.

The coming of World War II, while it interrupted civilian flying, did not stop international aviation; rather it speeded its development. The Air Transport Command of the Army and the Naval Air Transport Service of the United States flew 208,000 miles of routes during the war, covering most of the world — a very spectacular achievement, made possible through the co-operation of the already-established commercial airlines of the United States.

Commercial aviation between nations, disrupted by the war, will now be resumed. Few opportunities have been so challenging. There is the economic reward which will come, after a short lapse of time, to a new business. New routes will be established, laying the basis for economic enterprises and new settlements. The new means of transportation will create a great deal of travel which would not have occurred otherwise. A more closely knit world will be built.

This chapter is concerned with the underlying structure of international aviation, rather than with its social implications. In it will be discussed the expected costs and fares of future international air travel. Estimates will be made of the number of passengers traveling by air between nations in the first postwar decade and beyond. In later chapters, we shall discuss the effects of aviation on international political relations, and governmental policies regarding international aviation. Let us look, first, into some of the characteristics of international passenger travel.

Characteristics of Overseas Passenger Traffic

There is no basic technical distinction between domestic and international aviation, since the plane flies above the earth and is not affected by geographical conditions. The only difference is that, in international flying, the plane starts from one country and lands in another and often crosses oceans in so doing.

The major part of the scheduled air operations is domestic rather than international. In 1938, three times as many miles were flown in domestic as in international operations. [2] Scheduled domestic mileage in the United States exceeded the total miles flown by all Greater European airlines in both domestic and foreign service.[3] Of the 216,000 persons engaged in aviation operations in 1941, only 3 per cent were employed in international services, and perhaps one-sixth of this number were foreigners employed abroad.[4] There were 4.5 aircraft in scheduled domestic service for every plane in international operation.

The overseas passenger traffic, including air and water travel, is relatively light. The best travel period between the two World Wars was the five years from 1926 through 1930, when an average of over half a million United States residents traveled overseas annually.[5] It is probable that not more than 5 to 7 per cent of the American population has traveled overseas on social or business tours.[6] According to passport applications, the great majority of American citizens — about 80 per cent — travel across the ocean for pleasure and in connection with family affairs,

---

[2] J. Parker Van Zandt, *Civil Aviation and Peace*. Washington, D.C.: The Brookings Institution, 1944, p. 16.
[3] *Ibid.*, p. 16.   [4] *Ibid.*, p. 20.   [5] *Ibid.*, p. 75.
[6] Lewis C. Sorrell, *Airline Passenger Prospects in the Overseas Trade of the United States*, Postwar Studies no. 1, Part I, Air Transport Association of America, 1943, p. 19.

while only 11 per cent go on business.[7] The greatest amount of travel between the United States and other countries is done by residents of this country. In most years, about 80 per cent of the arrivals and departures at our ports are made by American residents. The movement of this traffic is highly seasonal, with the peak in the summer. The distribution of travel by area shows a marked concentration in traffic to and from Europe.

Before World War II, American international travel by air consisted largely of traffic between the United States and Latin America. Pacific and Alaskan air routes had been established, but the traffic to these areas was extremely light. Air service across the Atlantic had just been established in 1939, when it was interrupted by the war.

With these general characteristics of overseas passenger travel in mind, we may inquire more specifically as to the character of international aviation in the postwar decade. Let us first consider the types of planes to be used in international flying.

Equipment

Much international flying is for only short distances, between nations with adjoining boundary lines. However, most people think of long, transoceanic flights when they speak of international aviation. These long-distance, non-stop flights require different types of planes from those used for short distances. Another factor which influences the type of planes to be used in international flying is that many of the international routes of the future will go over northern areas and near the Arctic Circle, where there are winds, snow, and ice in the winter season. Volumes of passenger travel, weather conditions, and other factors influence the type of equipment to be used in international flying.

The most extensive transoceanic flying before the war was done for our country by Pan American Airways in large flying boats, called "clippers," and seating approximately ninety persons. But during the war, most of the flying of the Air Transport Command and the Naval Air Transport Service was done in land planes. Of the very large new planes, only one, the *Mars*, is a

[7] *Ibid.*, p. 2.

seaplane. There was little construction of flying boats during the war, despite the fact that their landing places cannot be destroyed by bombs and that an air harbor can be quickly organized. On the other hand, seaplane bases cannot be hidden easily.

The advantages of the flying boat lie in its ability to make an emergency landing at sea, its roominess, and its freedom from the need of expensive air fields. All of these features were attractive in the early days of transoceanic flying. However, as transoceanic flights became routine during the war, the fear of forced landings decreased. Also, the advantage of the seaplane's being free from the need of airports has less importance since more adequate airports are being built and land planes can find airports at most destinations. Furthermore, land planes are much faster than seaplanes. Another advantage of the land plane is that it brings the passenger to his ultimate destination without changing to another form of transportation. Thus, there is a great probability of an extensive use of land planes in flying across great bodies of water.

The planes that will fly the long non-stop international routes will be large planes. There are several reasons for this. In the first place, any long flight requires a large amount of fuel, and it is the large plane that can carry the needed fuel. Secondly, the demands of the customers require a large plane. They want a smooth flight, free from unpleasant weather conditions, which usually means pressurized cabins which can fly "over the weather." The passengers want room to move around in the plane on a long journey. They prefer a non-stop journey, if possible. And they certainly demand speed. Another factor influencing the size of plane is the frequency of schedule. With smaller planes, take-offs can be made more often. The frequency of the schedule, in turn, depends on the volume of traffic; if there are a large number of passengers, then frequent take-offs can be made with large planes. There are also economic advantages in the large plane for long-distance flights. The direct flying costs per seat are said to be quite low in the new large planes.

The tendency at present is to plan planes that will carry around eighty to one hundred passengers. Such planes transport four or five times as many passengers as are carried in the present DC-3, which flies across the oceans as well as between American cities. At the present writing, the DC-7 of the Douglas Aircraft Company, a Consolidated Vultee plane, and the Stratocruiser of the Boeing Aircraft Company, known as the Boeing-377, have been announced. Others are being planned. Pan American has placed an order for twenty-six DC-7's.[8] They have top speeds around four hundred miles an hour and cruising speeds of about three hundred and twenty-five miles an hour. They will be able to fly from New York to London in eleven or twelve hours. These planes are to have pressurized cabins which maintain, at heights of 20,000 or 30,000 feet, a constant pressure equivalent to that at an altitude of 8000 feet. These planes will fly in the substratosphere, avoiding much of the bad weather on the routes across the Atlantic. The Consolidated Vultee plane, Model 37, is planned to carry 204 passengers at a cruising speed of 310 to 342 miles per hour. Pan American Airways has fifteen of these planes ordered. Costs of these large planes are in terms of a million or a million and a half dollars apiece. Larger planes are being discussed. One is now being planned able to carry three hundred or four hundred passengers.

These large planes are not expected to be used in large numbers until near 1950, since it takes some time to make flight tests, incorporate the improvements that are apparent into the design, and put the planes into production. Until that time, the planes used will be modifications of the transport planes being flown across the oceans by the military forces. Early in the war, the army largely used DC-3's, since they could be constructed quickly from the machinery already in existence. But later, new and larger transports were put into use. One of these is the Constellation, which carries about sixty passengers, can fly at great altitudes, and has a reported cruising speed of approximately three hundred miles per hour.

In the future, there will be many international flights of short distances. The planes and equipment for these short-distance flights call for no special discussion. The planes will be similar

[8] Release by Douglas Aircraft Co., Inc., for the newspapers of October 24, 1944.

to those used for short-distance flights over land. For some years there will be few scheduled non-stop flights from American cities directly to Europe. Rather, American planes will make stops *en route* in Newfoundland and then fly non-stop to Foynes, Ireland. In the winter, many trans-Atlantic flights may be made by way of the Azores.

The evolution of the airplane continues at breath-taking speed, and it is difficult to predict future technological developments with any degree of certainty. But gains are expected in speed, safety, and comfort.

Expected Costs

The costs of flying between nations are the same as for flying within the borders of a nation in that for equal distances the cost of fuel, the size of the crew, and the operating expenses of the plane are the same. There are many other factors, however, that affect the cost, such as load factors, volume of transportation, seasonal nature of travel, international competition, and policies of subsidy.

The prices charged in international flying are related more or less to costs, although national policies may cause these prices to depart widely from costs. Yet, in attempting to find the future passenger fares, the best approach is to consider the costs. The costs of domestic flying in the first postwar decade have been considered in earlier chapters dealing with passengers, mail, and cargo. The costs for the domestic transportation of passengers were expected to be, at first, 4 or 4.5 cents a passenger-mile and later 3.5 cents, or possibly as low as 3 cents a passenger-mile by the second decade.

It is thought that the costs of international travel will be higher than those of domestic travel, particularly in the first few years after the war. There are several reasons to account for this. In the first place, the total number of international travelers may be smaller than that of domestic passengers. Although the North Atlantic trade and passenger traffic is large in comparison with other international routes, yet it is small compared with the volume of domestic travel in the United States, say, between the Atlantic and Pacific Coasts. In 1937, there were only 169,000 first-class, cabin, and air passengers between the United States and Europe, or an average of 465 passengers a day. In comparison, the airline passengers on the domestic lines in the United States in 1937 numbered about 3000 a day. A small number of passengers means a higher cost per unit. As is the case with railroad transportation, a large part of the cost of air transportation is overhead cost. The unit costs decrease as the scale of operations expands. These overhead costs of maintaining an extensive and technical organization for air transportation continue, no matter how small the traffic.

A second reason for the increased cost of international flying is the seasonal nature of much of international travel. In the summer months of 1938, more than twice as many steamship passengers went to and from Europe as in the winter months. The monthly indexes for 1938 for first- and cabin-class passengers were as follows, beginning with January: 51, 53, 61, 90, 122, 136, 139, 151, 163, 111, 63, and 60.[9] The summer months had better conditions for steamship travel, and they were the months in which people took long vacations. The air travel to the south, except on the routes with heavy tourist travel, such as on the Miami-Nassau or Miami-Havana routes, have not had a marked seasonal distribution. This is partly explained by the fact that the traffic has been largely of a business nature. If tourist travel to Latin America increases after the war, seasonal characteristics may appear. Steamship travel to Latin America had peaks in the midwinter months and in July.[10] Air travel may decrease the seasonal nature of trans-Atlantic travel to some extent, since the travel of business executives in all seasons will be increased. Furthermore, high-altitude flying in pressurized cabins may prove so comfortable that the winter weather will be less of an obstacle to passengers on airplanes than it is to passengers on steamships.

[9] F. H. Crozier, *Overseas Air Service Patterns*, Trans-Atlantic Areas, Research and Analysis Division, C.A.B., September, 1943, p. 16. Monthly average equals 100.

[10] William A. M. Burden, *The Struggle for Airways in Latin America*, 1943, p. 104.

Hence, uneconomical, seasonal distribution may be less in air travel than in ocean travel.

A factor associated with the seasonality of travel is the tendency of international traffic to be unidirectional at certain periods. On steamships, the load has been unequal going and returning, especially in early summer and in the autumn. The unevenness of traffic means a low payload factor for the plane on a round trip. If cargo and mail can be substituted for passengers in these periods, the passenger routes can be operated more economically.

It is probable that, for a time, the promotional costs will be greater for transoceanic than for domestic travel, thus increasing the costs of foreign travel over those for domestic travel. Also, more personal service for passengers will be required on large transoceanic liners than on domestic planes.

The authors of the Curtiss-Wright study, previously discussed, think that the costs of international flying may range between 3.5 and 7.5 cents a passenger-mile in the first decade after the war, as compared with domestic costs of 3.5 to 4.5 cents a passenger-mile.[11]

Some of the planes planned for postwar international flying have low operating costs. The Boeing Stratocruiser, B-377, which carries around one hundred passengers, advertises a direct operating cost of 1 cent a passenger-mile,[12] but does not define direct costs or length of trip. The DC-7 is expected to transport 86 passengers at an operating cost of 3.8 cents per 200-pound-mile, with an average payload factor of 65 per cent, over a range of 2400 miles, and with overhead expenses running 85 per cent of direct operating costs.[13] The load factor in practice, however, is not likely to be so favorable, and the direct flying costs are likely to be smaller than all the other costs. Also, the non-stop distances flown across the Atlantic may be greater than 2400 miles in many cases. Thus, it is not clear that in practice the operating costs will average as low as 3.8 cents a passenger-mile.

[11] Curtiss-Wright Corporation, *Air Transportation in the Immediate Post-War Period*, Report no. BR-69, 1944, pp. 75, 121.
[12] November 15, 1944, release of Boeing News Bureau, Boeing Aircraft Co., Seattle 14, Washington (mimeo.).
[13] Gaither Littrell, "New Giant," *Flying*, June, 1944, p. 156.

Expected Rates

The rates charged may differ from the costs. We are interested to know what the future rates may be. Before the war, the rates across the North Atlantic between New York and London in summer were 11 cents a mile, and on the longer winter route, 8.6 cents a mile.[14] The steamship rates with which the airplane will compete were between 5 and 6 cents a mile for an average of the first- and second-class. Third-class rates were about 2.3 cents per passenger-mile, and, with such low rates, probably few third-class passengers will be attracted to air travel. Rates in what is known as steerage were as low as 1.5 cents a mile.[15] It is, therefore, the first-class and cabin trade which is vulnerable to air competition, though the air rates may, in less than a decade, approximate those of second-class and tourist. The newspapers have carried reports that Pan American Airways plans to sell tickets after the war at $100, or 2.9 cents a mile, from New York to London,[16] and to Honolulu from San Francisco for $96, which is 4 cents a mile.[17] Pan American Airways has also advertised a proposed passenger rate per mile on the route to Rio de Janeiro and Buenos Aires as low as 3.5 cents a mile.[18] These proposed fares of Pan American are much lower than those charged before the war. They are probably not based upon estimates of actual costs, but will depend either upon expected governmental payments for mail at high rates or upon a large and favorable volume of well-distributed business.

One English authority expects the price of a ticket from New York to London by air to be four hundred dollars immediately after the war and about two hundred dollars ten to fifteen years later.[19]

Mr. F. H. Crozier, Chief of the Research and Analysis Division

[14] J. Parker Van Zandt, *European Air Transport on the Eve of the War,* 1939, p. 13.

[15] The steamship rates include cost of food and sleeping quarters for the trip, but not the tips and extras.

[16] *Chicago Tribune,* June 18, 1943.

[17] *Chicago Sun,* September 14, 1944.

[18] *Ibid.,* August 4, 1944, p. 21.

[19] Peter Masefield, "The Future of Air Transport: A British View," *Atlantic Monthly,* January, 1944, p. 37.

of the Civil Aeronautics Board, in computing revenues from assumed volumes of traffic between Europe and North America after the war, uses a rate of six cents a passenger-mile, although he does not say that this rate is a forecast.[20]

Competition between American airlines and between American airlines and those of other countries will influence the rate of fares charged. Pan American's announcement of intended rates of 2.9, 3.5, and 4 cents a mile may have been influenced by the threat of competition from other American lines. British airlines, and possibly those of Sweden, Canada, France, and Holland, will be in competition with American airlines. A highly competitive system, based on national interests and subsidies, may force rates below costs, with the losses paid for by the different governments in one way or another.

Expected Number of Passengers

The rates for transoceanic air trips after the war will clearly be low enough to draw passengers away from the steamships. We want to know what the extent of this anticipated diversion will be.

In 1930, the peak year of overseas travel, there were 1,454,000 passengers to and from the United States, of whom 47 per cent were first-class and cabin-class, which are the classes most vulnerable to air competition. It is also possible that many of the passengers who formerly traveled second-class or tourist may travel by air if the air rates should be reduced to four or five cents a mile, as they may be during the first postwar decade. The second-class and tourist passengers were 25 per cent of all the steamship passengers. First-class, cabin, second-class, and tourist-class passengers, the potential air travel market, were 72 per cent of all the transoceanic, United States international surface travel in 1930. There is a possibility that a very small portion of those who travel third-class may be drawn to the air.[21]

[20] Crozier, *op. cit.*, p. 4.
[21] These estimates include the travel to the West Indies, Central America, and the Caribbean. About 90 per cent of these passengers travel first-class, and in number they constitute about twice as many as the passengers to South America and to the Orient combined. A very large proportion of these travelers go com-

The proportions of first- and cabin-class passengers were not the same on all routes or for all steamship companies. Of the European-United States travel in 1937, 18 per cent was first- and cabin-class. To and from South American ports, 85 per cent was first- and cabin-class, although the total numbers were not large. To the Canal Zone and to Alaska, the first- and cabin-class passengers were 80 and 75 per cent, respectively, while to China, Japan, and the Philippines, 31 per cent traveled in these classes.[22]

The proportions of first- and second-class passengers, plus cabin and tourist, may, of course, not remain the same after the war. There were some significant shifts during the 1930 years of depression, notably in the proportion of first-class passengers to Europe; but for all overseas United States international travel, there was not a great change in the percentages by classes of accommodation. Therefore, no sharp changes are expected in the first postwar decade.

Even though two-thirds or three-quarters of the ships' passengers are ultimately vulnerable to air, it is largely first-class passengers that are expected to be diverted to the air during the early postwar years, unless competition or governmental policy force a sudden and sharp reduction in rates, which is not expected.

Estimates of the diversion of passengers from steamships to airplanes in the United States, international, postwar passenger traffic have been made in studies of the Curtiss-Wright Corporation. A forecast is made of the postwar surface traffic, assuming no diversion to air transport. The volume of postwar overseas travel is projected on the basis of its observed positive correlation with the domestic business cycle in past years. Such factors as higher taxes, accumulated savings, deferred vacations, and possible restrictions in travel to certain areas are taken into consideration in the projection. The anticipated volume is 2,228,000

paratively short distances, such as from Miami to Havana or to Nassau. If these Gulf and Caribbean passengers are subtracted, the total in 1930 becomes 1100, of whom 34 per cent were first-class and cabin and 31 per cent second-class and tourist. Thus, omitting the West Indies and Central American travel, 65 per cent, or about two-thirds, were first- (and cabin) and second- (and tourist) class passengers.

[22] Lewis C. Sorrell, *Airline Passenger Prospects in the Overseas Trade of the United States*, p. 6.

passengers in 1955, an increase of 53 per cent over the 1930 volume. Using this volume as a basis, it is then estimated how much of this traffic might be diverted to air on a basis of competitive rates and service. The analysis is made separately for each major area of foreign travel, since the characteristics of travel in the different regions varied considerably before the war.

The prediction of the postwar travel in the Atlantic area takes into account an expected restriction in travel in the first few postwar years. Assuming air travel to be only slightly more expensive than first-class steamer, in these first few postwar years, 25 per cent of the high-class traffic that there would have been if there had been no air travel, 15 per cent of the tourist, and 5 per cent of third-class will be diverted to the air. As air routes are added, the amount of air diversion will increase. By the tenth postwar year, the percentages of diversion by classes should be 60, 40, and 10, respectively. These estimated losses amount to about 35 per cent of all passengers between Europe and the United States.

The Curtiss-Wright study estimates that almost three-quarters of the water-borne passenger travel between the United States and Middle America, including Central America and the West Indies, will be diverted to the airways by the end of the first postwar decade. Nearly all of the prewar travel to this area was first-class, cabin, and tourist, and represented almost altogether tourist and vacation travel. In number of passengers, this traffic was about 35 per cent of the United States-European travel, but in passenger-miles it was much less.

The total number of passengers to South America was small before the war — not quite 3 per cent of the number of North Atlantic passengers. Curtiss-Wright estimates that a large percentage of this traffic will be diverted to air. The proportion of business travel to South America was higher before the war than that to Europe and may be larger after the war because of the expected industrial development of South America. Furthermore, South American travel has been principally first- and cabin-class, which is most vulnerable to air competition. Over 62 per cent of the prospective steamship passengers are estimated as being diverted to the airlines by ten years after the war.

Of the Pacific travel, which is about 15 per cent of the number of passengers that cross the Atlantic, it is thought a smaller percentage of passengers will be lost. Pacific travel is expected to increase more slowly because the long distances involved make the trip expensive, and because travel to some sections of the Far East may be restricted for several years after the war. About 40 per cent is estimated to be diverted to air travel by the end of the first postwar decade.

As may be seen, the percentage of loss of steamship travel to the airlines varies from route to route. The greatest loss (75 per cent) is expected to occur in the traffic to Middle America, and the lowest loss (35 per cent) in the European travel.

For all routes combined, the loss of steamship passengers is expected to be almost 50 per cent. The steamships will still carry nearly all the third-class passengers, a fair proportion of the second-class, and a small percentage of the first-class. If business conditions are not so favorable in the postwar decade as the Curtiss-Wright study assumes, the percentage of air diversion may be somewhat less.

The postwar air travel might also be predicted by projecting the curve of international air passengers in prewar years. It is difficult to project this curve for two reasons. In the first place, international air travel may be said to have existed only since 1930 and the figures of passengers flying internationally are difficult to obtain. International air travel for civilians was abandoned in large part after 1940. Thus, the yearly data on international air passenger travel give a very short and uncertain series for extrapolation. Furthermore, conditions for international travel will not be the same in the postwar decade as in the prewar years. The experience gained by the military forces in transoceanic flying will be available. Also, the fares charged are likely to be much less than the prewar rates. On general considerations, then, an extrapolation of the prewar international air travel between the United States and other countries for more than a decade after 1940 is likely to be wide of the mark and possibly an underestimate, depending, of course, on what sort of curve is used.

If, however, the prewar curve of international air passengers, using the data from 1930 to 1940, is projected to 1953 by using a second-degree parabola, we get a figure of about 450,000 air passengers. This figure, it is thought, should not be interpreted as the total air passenger estimate for 1953, but as the total that might have occurred if the forces of the prewar period had remained in effect. But conditions will not be the same in the postwar period. Lower fares, more frequent schedules, more extensive promotional activities, better planes, and other factors will create a large number of new air passengers. The experience gained during the war in flying across the oceans will also stimulate international travel. Thus, the number of air passengers is likely to be greater than the projection estimate of 450,000.

The problem may be approached by projecting the curve of sea-borne international passengers, assuming no air transportation. A trend line through the total international travel (omitting immigrants and emigrants) from 1920 to 1938 gives a pre-World War II point of about one million international sea-borne passengers a year. This figure is hypothetical and, because of unusual postwar conditions, may be greatly in error; but it may be used in making future estimates. Beginning, then, after the war with an estimate of about one million passengers, it is desired to know how rapid the rate of increase will be to, say, 1953. After World War I, there was a period of prosperity; and the international travel, omitting immigrants and emigrants, increased about 48 per cent in six years. On such a basis, after World War II, there will be about 1,500,000 sea-borne passengers, of whom about 1,100,000 will be first-class, cabin, second-class, and tourist. If 50 per cent of these classes are lost to the airplanes in the postwar decade, perhaps 550,000 passengers will be taken by the airlines — a slightly higher figure than the 450,000 estimated by extrapolating the prewar passenger growth on international airlines. From the two projections above, the air-borne passengers might be expected to be of the general order of perhaps 450,000 to 550,000 passengers.

However, the expected number of air travelers across the oceans will be greater than the number diverted from steamship travel, since aviation will create new traffic. Many people will be able to travel abroad by air who would not go by boat, because of the great savings in time afforded by the airplane. Thus, the total international air passenger travel after the war will consist of two kinds — those who would travel by steamship if there were no air transportation and the new passengers who would not take the voyage if there were no airplanes.

New Passenger Traffic Created by Aviation

There is very little to guide us in making even a guess as to the amount of new international travel which aviation will develop. The potential market is made up of business travelers and those who will travel for pleasure, education, or family reasons. Quick trips to foreign countries are expected to be very attractive to business representatives. A round trip to Europe from the United States can be made in two days, less than the time required to make a one-way trip by train from east of the Mississippi River to the Pacific Coast. The journey from the central part of the United States to the Caribbean area or the northern seaboard of South America will be made in a fraction of a day, while the trip to Brazil and the Argentine is expected to take a little less than a day. In a period of business prosperity, the finances of a trip, say, six cents a mile, could be absorbed into the cost of production of many commercial firms.

The limiting factors in the amount of international travel for business purposes appear to be the extent of business enterprises in other countries and the number of proprietors, officials, managers, and other business representatives who might travel. In the Census of 1940 the number of businessmen in types of occupations are presented. A few of these types, some of whom are likely to travel abroad in business, are listed in Table 21.[23] In addition to these classified groups, there are various miscellaneous businesses whose representatives may travel. We do not know what proportion of the individuals represented in these statistics will travel in foreign countries for business purposes, or what individuals other than proprietors, officials, and managers in these industries might go abroad for business reasons.

[23] *U.S. Census*, 1940.

TABLE 21

Proprietors, managers and officials
Mining	32,000
Construction	125,700
Manufacturing	428,300
Wholesale trade	240,700
Finance and insurance	164,800

Special managers and officials
Advertising agents	35,700
Buyers and department store heads	72,400
Purchasing agents and buyers	33,300

Traveling salesmen and sales agents	632,700

Of those who might travel for pleasure, education, or family reasons, there is likewise little evidence on which to make estimates. In Table 22 there is listed the number of families and single individuals in 1935-36 who earned incomes that might permit them to travel in foreign countries. In this table are shown also the average annual outlay per family or single individual for savings, for transportation other than by private automobile, and for recreation. The costs of travel vary. A trip to the Bahamas from Florida costs little, while a trip to China or Europe would cut seriously into the annual income of many American families. Expenditures of American travelers in foreign countries averaged $479 apiece, not including steamship fares, in the late 1920's.[24] There were, in 1935-36, nearly 1,200,-000 families with incomes over $4000 a year and about 1,000,000 single individuals who earned over $2000 a year. However, these were depression years, and there may be twice as many earning these incomes in postwar years if the times are very prosperous. It cannot be known, however, how many of these people will travel in Europe, in the Caribbean area, or elsewhere.

The authors of the Curtiss-Wright study have ventured an estimate of the amount of new travel to all foreign countries that will be created by aviation. Of an estimated number of air passengers between the United States and other countries — not including Mexico and Canada — amounting to 1,250,000 in 1953, 42 per cent are newly created by aviation and 58 per cent are

[24] J. Parker Van Zandt, *op. cit.*, p. 76.

TABLE 22. AVERAGE EXPENDITURES FOR TRANSPORTATION,
RECREATION, AND SAVINGS OF FAMILIES AT DIFFERENT INCOME
LEVELS IN THE UNITED STATES, 1935–36 *

FAMILIES

Incomes	Per cent of Total Families	Expenditure for Savings	Transportation † Expenditures	Recreation Expenditures	Number of Families
2,000	79.1				23,242,858
2,000– 2,500	8.4	182	22	62	2,464,860
2,500– 3,000	4.5	315	24	81	1,314,199
3,000– 4,000	4.0	529	31	105	1,181,987
4,000– 5,000	1.4	904	35	136	402,595
5,000–10,000	1.7	2028	48	206	510,010
10,000+	.9				283,791
	100.0				

SINGLE INDIVIDUALS

Incomes	Per cent of Total Families	Expenditure for Savings	Transportation † Expenditures	Recreation Expenditures	Number of Families
2,000	89.8				9,036,440
2,000– 2,500	4.9	279	70	102	493,751
2,500– 3,000	1.6	422	78	128	161,275
3,000– 4,000	1.7	677	92	156	172,091
4,000– 5,000	.6	1126	116	184	61,596
5,000–10,000	.9	2141	153	270	85,898
10,000+	.5				46,949
	100.0				

* From *Consumer Expenditures in the United States*, National Resources Planning Board, 1939, pp. 20, 23, and 32, 34.
† Transportation other than automobile.

diverted from sea-borne vessels. Thus, these authors think that by the middle of the first postwar decade almost half of international air travel will be new traffic created by the airlines.

The amount of future international travel will depend partially on what the rates of fare will be. The Curtiss-Wright study assumes that the fares will be slightly below the rate for first-class steamship accommodations, or about 4.5 to 5 cents a passenger-mile by 1953. If these rates prevail, then the projected estimates previously submitted of something under a half-million air passengers is probably a good deal too low. It seems more probable that the number will be between two-thirds of a million and a million, which is almost what the total sea-borne international travel was in the middle 1930's.

Cruises

In the foregoing discussion, only regularly scheduled passenger transportation has been considered. There is the added possibility of chartering airplanes for cruises. In slack seasons, steamship companies have often used their ships to furnish passengers pleasure or educational cruises. At times, this type of business has reached a good-sized volume. Of the 365,000 passenger trips taken overseas by residents of the United States in 1939, 83,000, or about 23 per cent, were on cruises.[25] The possibility of air cruises is not likely to be overlooked by the air transport companies. Before such tours can be conducted, however, it will be necessary for the nations on the route to grant permission for planes to land at their airports. It seems that the monetary returns from tourist travel will probably be sufficient incentive for foreign nations to grant such rights.

A possible disadvantage of the air cruise is that it will not offer the leisurely ocean voyage which was afforded by the steamship cruise, and which many found especially attractive. On the other hand, the air cruise will enable travelers to spend more time in interesting places, some of which could not be reached by ship. By airplane, less time will be spent in traveling and more time at the points of interest.

A trip circling the globe would be interesting and spectacular and would appeal to the imagination of many people. The flying time for a journey around the world would be probably less than one hundred hours. Such a trip could be made within a short vacation period. Air cruises should be attractive to the airlines in case there is a marked seasonality in international aviation. In the dull season, inactive planes could be used on cruises to regions with a good climate, recreations, historic scenes, and other attractions.

[25] *Ibid.*, p. 135.

After the First Postwar Decade

In estimating the number of international air passengers, it was assumed that there would be a high degree of business prosperity during most of the first postwar decade, subject perhaps to some depressions of short duration. The justification for this assumption was discussed in the chapter on domestic air passengers. That this period of great productivity will continue throughout the second postwar decade seems improbable. Indeed, after World War I, the national income increased greatly during the first postwar decade, but very little over both decades, as measured by a trend line in terms of per capita dollars of equal purchasing power. Overseas travel fluctuates with business conditions, especially the travel for pleasure, vacation, or education. The estimates of international travel for the first postwar decade are based, not on the trend line of overseas travel, but on the fluctuations upward from that trend. It is unwise to assume that the trend of international air travel will increase over the two decades as it will in the first, but if the passenger rate should be lowered in the second postwar decade to 3.5 or 3 cents, then the growth in the number of passengers will be stimulated.

Any shift in passengers that is to take place from steamships to airplanes is likely to occur quickly if the air rates are low enough. Assuming an air rate of around five cents a mile, the number diverted from the higher classes of steamship travel will probably be largely determined by the end of the first postwar decade. If the air rates drop to 3 or 3.5 cents, then much of the less expensive classes of travel are expected to be diverted to the air also. But the new traffic originated by air travel may well continue to increase for an indefinite period in the future. Edward Warner, in his Wilbur Wright lecture in 1943, stated that it seemed reasonable to expect that the new passenger travel created by air transportation across the Atlantic might be twice as large as that diverted from steamships.[26]

In the long run, transportation inventions mean more and more

[26] Edward Warner, "Postwar Transport Aircraft," 31st Wilbur Wright Memorial Lecture. Reprinted in *Aeronautical Engineering Review*, October, 1943, pp. 14-15.

travel across long distances and political barriers. One expects as a result that, over long periods of time, the interconnections of business between nations will be furthered by these same inventions. Yet, there are limitations and barriers to such expansion. There are various political barriers, such as tariffs, trade restrictions, currency fluctuations, and autarchic policies. While such barriers do not destroy trade and travel, they do limit it. Also, there are difficulties due to language and cultural differences. For the United States, as well as for other Western nations, there is a limit in the size of their future populations, which will probably be stationary or decreasing before the century is over.

On the whole, a rather great expansion of overseas air travel is probable during the third quarter of the century.

Conclusion

Aviation brings to international travel, much of which is long-distance travel, a great saving in time, as compared with the much slower steamship. For this reason, a great increase in international travel is expected if the rates are sufficiently low. The costs of air travel in the first part of the postwar decade are expected to range between 3.5 cents and 7.5 cents a passenger-mile. Later, costs are expected to be reduced somewhat. The actual rates charged may be lower than costs because of national rivalries and competition, and the deficits may be made up by subsidies. Shortly after the war, it is thought the rates will be of the order of 4 to 6 cents a passenger-mile, unless national competition is unusually keen, in which case they may be as low as 3.5 cents. The downward course of rates points toward 3 or 3.5 cents a passenger-mile. For *de luxe* travel over long routes, the rates will be higher.

The number of passengers — vacationists and business travelers — traveling between the United States and other countries is expected, by the latter part of the first postwar decade, to be between 650,000 and 1,000,000, assuming very prosperous economic conditions. Of this travel, a very substantial portion will be newly created by the airlines.

★ ★ ★ ★ # III. SOCIAL EFFECTS

14

Population

CHANGES in the population of a country affect almost all the phenomena of social life, especially the economic institutions. Populations constitute the market for business enterprises, and they also supply the labor force.

It is customary to discuss population in terms of inflow and outflow. For any area, the inflow is birth and immigration; the outflow, death and emigration. Our inquiry, then, is to ascertain whether aviation will produce any changes in the inflow and outflow of population. There is also the question of the quality of population, which, at first sight, would seem to be unaffected by aviation, but which should be examined.

The Birth Rate

Aviation will probably have the effect of reducing the number of births slightly, particularly among the families with high incomes, who are the ones that will make most use of aircraft for a decade or so after the war. This probability is based upon the theory that the automobile, when it was being widely adopted in the 1920's, reduced the birth rate because families postponed the expense of bearing and rearing a child in order to own an automobile. In a similar manner, it is thought that some families will be smaller than they would otherwise be because of the expense of owning and operating aircraft. This point will be discussed more fully in the chapter on the family.

While some families may be smaller because of aviation, the birth rate is not likely to be affected appreciably. The number of families which are smaller because of aircraft must be very numerous to influence the birth rate. For instance, if around

2,000,000 babies were born a year, and with a population of about 130,000,000, there would have to be 10,000 fewer babies born in one year to drop the birth rate from 15.4 per 1000 population to 15.3. Of the few hundred thousand families that are likely to own private aircraft in the first decade after the war, not all will purchase aircraft in one year, and not all will limit the number of babies because of the ownership of a helicopter. Hence it does not appear that the reduction in birth rate due to the ownership of aircraft will be very large.

These remarks have concerned the United States. Quite a different situation exists in those countries or regions where methods of birth control are crude and relatively little practiced, such as China, Siberia, India, and Africa. It is undoubtedly true that most cities of the Orient or the tropics, which may be connected by plane with the Western world, already know something about birth control. It has been shown [1] that urban areas of various continents for which we have records have lower birth rates than do the surrounding rural areas. However, the birth rates may fall even lower where there is only a restricted use of the methods of birth control. In so far as the airplane increases the contacts between these regions and the Western countries, it will bring to some extent the ideas and customs of the Western world, which emphasize higher material standards of living. The desire to advance the standard of living is usually correlated with a falling fertility rate; [2] that is, when people begin to desire better homes and clothing or begin to want luxuries, they usually find it necessary to limit the number of children. This limitation of offspring will be facilitated by the diffusion of the techniques of birth control of the Western cultures. There are new discoveries from time to time regarding the limitation of offspring. A recent discovery of great importance is the determination of the date of ovulation in women. This knowledge will make possible a lowered birth rate among people with very low incomes, such as among the masses of India and China. Western attitudes

[1] A. J. Jaffe, "Urbanization and Fertility," *American Journal of Sociology,* vol. 48, July, 1942, p. 48.
[2] *Ibid.,* p. 60.

and methods of birth control will, of course, be disseminated in time to the peoples of the Orient, but the airplane may speed the process. The airplane will open up many regions now more or less closed to ship, railroad, and automobile, such as the interiors of Brazil and Africa. With the coming of the culture of the Western world to such isolated regions, a lowered birth rate will almost surely follow. The airplane is only one factor in this process.

As to raising the birth rate, there is little indication that aviation will be a force in that direction.

The Death Rate

The effect of the airplane on the death rate is more obvious than that on the birth rate, for the aerial bomber is an agency of great destruction in wartime, not only on the military forces, but also on the civilian population. The raids in England in 1940 killed 23,000 civilians.[3] In one month, September, 1940, 7000 were killed in air raids in England. In Germany the loss of life was much greater, since the air raids were more devastating than in England. At present, we have very little information as to the total number of deaths during the war, especially since civilian figures are lacking, on which to predict the influence on future population. We do know what effect World War I had on the death rate. In that war, the total death rate in Germany and France was raised by about 50 per cent, and for all combatants actively engaged, about 25 per cent. Air raids were not a cause of many deaths during that war.

The death rate in the first year and a half of World War II was not high, but after Germany invaded Russia in June, 1941, the rate of loss of life is thought to have been about what it was on the German and French forces in World War I. In the later years of the war, this death rate may have been raised somewhat. Since wars are of short duration, as compared with periods of peace, the total population of a country is not reduced in size very much by war deaths. The effect of war on the size of popula-

[3] *Statistical Bulletin of the Metropolitan Life Insurance Company,* March, 1943, p. 9.

tions is more noticeable a generation or two after the war is over; that is, if the young soldiers had not been killed in such numbers in war, they would have lived to marry and produce offspring. A loss of five hundred thousand killed in war means that the population of a large country like the United States will be smaller by several million in a generation or two. We do not know how much the war death rate is raised because of the airplane, but, in view of its use in bombing cities and the civilian population, it seems probable that there are more deaths in war because of the airplane than there would have been if there had been no bomber. The technique of bombing is still developing and its destruction in any future war may be greater.

In peacetime, the number of deaths is increased by aircraft accidents. The use of rapid transportation facilities has increased the number of accidents. The deaths from automobile accidents have averaged some thirty-five thousand a year over the past decade.[4] The airplane has likewise increased the number of deaths. However, aviation has been increasingly safer, and a passenger in a transport plane is about as safe as in a railroad train or in a bus. The number of passenger fatalities per 100,-000,000 passenger-miles on the scheduled airlines was 4.1[5] in 1942 as compared with .205 passenger fatalities on the railroads.[6]

The number of deaths in the United States in scheduled airline accidents was 71 in 1942 and 46 in 1941. The total number of deaths from all causes was 1,385,187 in 1942. Hence fatal accidents in air passenger transportation have had no appreciable effect on the death rate in the United States. In the future, with the number of passenger-miles ten times as great as at present, the total deaths may be of the magnitude of five hundred a year, though the progress of safety measures may make the number much less. The deaths from private flying operations in 1942 were 218, and in 1941, 325; and they were around the same numbers in the years immediately before the war. In 1940, the miles of private flying per accident were 1,200,000 as compared

4 *Statistical Abstract, 1943,* p. 447.

5 *Annual Report of the Civil Aeronautics Board,* Washington, 1943, p. 37.

6 Interstate Commerce Commission, *56th Annual Report on the Statistics of Railways in the United States,* Washington, 1944, p. 75.

with 40,000,000 in scheduled passenger operations. Thus, the fatality rate per million plane-miles flown in private flying is much greater than in scheduled passenger flying. If ten times as many private planes are flown after the war, the deaths might be of the order of several thousand per year. The total deaths from aviation accidents a decade after the war, then, might be 3000 or 4000 a year — and more in the second decade if private flying of helicopters becomes widespread. A death rate of 1200 per 100,000 would be raised, say, three or four points. Such figures are hardly estimates. They merely give an idea of the magnitude of the effect of aviation on the death rate a decade or more after the war.

On the other hand, aviation is of some aid in preserving lives, as will be shown in another section which deals with health and medicine. Already the airplane has been used to transport anti-toxins and medicines to places where they are scarce. The airplane was used during World War II to transport the wounded and ill to better hospitals than could be established near the front lines. The increased speed with which superior medical services were administered by the use of the plane may have been a sufficiently important factor to have affected the soldier death rate. Although the plane has been of great aid in peacetime in individual cases, it may be doubted whether its use as yet has been sufficiently extensive to affect the death rate appreciably. The service of aviation in the interest of health and of saving lives will be extended as aviation grows.

The airplane may, indirectly, be an influence on the death rate in the outlying and partly isolated regions which it helps to open up and develop. The first contact of an old culture with another has often markedly affected the death rate in one way or another. Some Indian tribes have disappeared through diseases resulting from contacts with white cultures, while others have had their numbers augmented. In more recent times, the contact between complex cultures and simpler civilizations has often resulted in the extensive diffusion of hospitals, modern medical science, and techniques of sanitation. The introduction of modern transportation methods and agricultural techniques has tended to stabilize the food supply, thus reducing famines. A very good illustration is the case of Java, where the population has doubled since 1900 under Dutch control, in large part through the reduction of the death rate.[7] Panama has now become the most healthful spot in the tropics because of the introduction of modern sanitation by the American health authorities of the Canal Zone. The use of the airplane to reach mines on Hudson Bay, in the Andes, or in the jungles of Brazil will open up these areas to the influence of modern civilizations. Thus, the airplane may have some effect in reducing the loss of life in remote places which would be less frequently reached without it.

The airplane may also bring to Western culture some influences harmful to human life from regions with less advanced cultures, particularly those in tropical regions. Insects and bacteria of the tropics may be carried by airplanes to areas in the temperate zones. However, this danger can be combated. At the present time, airliners leaving tropical centers for the United States and Europe are inspected before leaving and the interiors of the planes are disinfected before landing. A high degree of control will be exercised over this danger, which might affect the health and lives of whole nations. Short of some unknown epidemic, it does not seem likely that the death rate of a whole population will be affected.

Aviation, then, will increase the deaths due to accidents, but will save lives by virtue of its use in carrying medical aid and patients and by assisting in the introduction of health work in areas not using modern medical techniques. Quantitative estimates of its effects in the future are not possible.

The Distribution of Population

The use of aircraft has more effect in moving people about than on changing birth and death rates. Any important transportation agency moves populations. Ships brought people to America; the railroads built up cities; and the automobile dis-

[7] Warren Thompson, *Population Problems*. New York: McGraw-Hill Book Co., 1942, p. 258.

persed city people outward and drew rural inhabitants in toward the outskirts of cities.

The most obvious effect of aviation is to shuttle people back and forth between market and factory centers, and to increase the mobility of populations between customary or new points of travel. People may travel without changing their habitations, and hence without having the distribution of population affected. However, aircraft is expected to redistribute the residences, and possibly the places of work, for some city dwellers and inhabitants of smaller communities. The possible influence of aviation on the shifting of homes and businesses will be discussed in the chapter on cities. Undoubtedly some dispersal of homes outward from the city will occur, at first chiefly among those families who have large incomes. But the amount of dispersal outward from the city is not expected to be as great as that caused by the automobile, since neither the airplane nor the helicopter is as suitable for local transportation as is the automobile and the bus.

Instead of being a medium for short-distance transportation, the airplane's greatest utility is for covering long distances quickly. Since the plane requires no track or highway, but only a place to land, it has been particularly useful in penetrating remote regions, as is notably the case in the territory of Alaska. It might be expected, then, that aviation would distribute population to Alaska and various other areas as yet only sparsely settled.

The Increase of Population in Remote Areas

Of the 33,000,000,000 acres of the earth's land surface, only a small portion is densely populated — southern and southeastern Asia, Europe, eastern North America, and a few islands and strips of coast elsewhere. Thus, there is plenty of unpopulated land for settlement. Much of this land is not suitable for development. The climate is either too hot or too cold and the land arid, mountainous, or rocky. Only 8 per cent of the earth's surface is arable, and, of this small amount, nearly one-half is now under cultivation.[8] There are 2,700,000,000 acres that may

[8] O. E. Baker, *Geographic Review*, vol. 13, p. 25.

be brought under cultivation, three-quarters of which lie in the tropics. In addition to agricultural products, there are also minerals, wood, chemicals, and animal products. Of these latter products, those that are likely to bring great increases of population are coal, oil, and iron. The discovery of new sources of power and new inventions may change the distribution of population in the future as agriculture and manufacture by mechanical power did in earlier eras.

It is clear that transportation is not the sole factor in the settlement of land. Railroads go through the deserts and arid lands of Nevada and Wyoming, but the population is small. In fact, there are few places on the earth that have not been reached by some form of transportation. Even as long ago as fifteen thousands years, when man traveled on foot and by small boats, he had settled all the major areas of the earth. Clearly, there must be some economic basis of livelihood or some attraction in addition to transportation inventions to bring people to settle in an area.

Economic Incentives

It is certain that the airplane will open up many economic opportunities over the world. A large number of these opportunities will be in lands already populated. However, in this chapter our attention is directed toward economic incentives in unpopulated regions or those with small populations or regions where the population may be increased by this new means of transportation.

Perhaps the outstanding incentives in the unsettled areas of the world are mining prospects. The demand for minerals is very great, owing to the significant rôle they play in industry. Chromium, nickel, and cobalt command a good price. The sources of minerals are unrelated to the distribution of fertile agricultural lands. They are often found where there are few people, and often in places inaccessible because of natural barriers and the absence of means of transportation. The accessible sources of minerals have, in general, already been discovered and exploited. How aviation aids new mining enterprises will be set forth in another chapter. But here it is desirable to observe that the populations of mining centers are often quite small — a few thousand inhabitants to a mining community, consisting of the miners, their families, and the various individuals engaged in service occupations to support them. For instance, the populations are small in the new mining towns recently developed by aviation in northern Canada.

Mines vary in size, to be sure. If there are large quantities of coal or iron ore in a small area, the mining towns which grow up around them will be above the average in size. The effect on population of the exploitation of the natural resources, other than by agriculture, varies with the product. Thus, new ore fields, bauxite lands, and hardwood forests have varying capacities for sustaining populations. While populations may be maintained for many years, mining is essentially exploitive in nature and does not provide communities of people as stable as those provided by agriculture. Mines become exhausted or else are worked to the point where it does not pay to mine them further. Many mining towns, formerly prosperous, are now "ghost" towns. Such is Virginia City in Nevada, the home of the famous Comstock Lode. Further, isolated mining spots, while habitable with the aid of science, are not always attractive places in which to live. At the mines that have been aided by aviation in New Guinea, Australia, Honduras, Bolivia, and in other places, the effect on population has been to develop small, scattered communities, of a few thousand inhabitants. Aviation may dot the map of unsettled areas over various parts of the world with small population units of more or less uncertain duration of life.

With regard to the extension of agriculture into areas not now cultivated, the airplane would seem to play no great part. It is true that the amount of cultivated land can be doubled; but this would be made possible through irrigation and drainage and through the clearing-away of jungle growth, in which the airplane would not be used. Yet the airplane would provide a rapid means for keeping new and distant agricultural settlements in touch with established centers of population. Landing fields for planes are more easily constructed than are railroads or highways. Hence, in an indirect way, aviation may speed the development of agriculture in the tropics. If agriculture is developed in these regions and accompanied by increases in population, aviation will be a factor.

The Nature of Settlement of Population

The movement of population into unsettled areas, either for mining or agriculture, is likely to be a process of infiltration rather than a mass movement. The migration to the United States from Europe in the nineteenth century was a huge mass movement, but one of the few such instances in the history of migrations. Mass movements are relatively rare. Furthermore, people who migrate in the twentieth century must carry along many more of the "gadgets" of civilization than was the case in the eighteenth and early nineteenth centuries. Today, new communities require hospitals, drugstores, newspapers, merchandise, radios, electricity, and many more things. Modern migration must be organized.

The first encouragement to migration in an unsettled area is a communication and transportation linkage with outside civilization. In earlier centuries, the boat was important as a linkage between settled and unsettled areas. It required no construction of roadways, and, in combination with the magnetic compass, the large boat facilitated settlement along the rims of continents and islands. Like the boat, the airplane needs no expensive construction of roadways and it can take people into the interior of lands; and it can do this much more rapidly than the boat took people across bodies of water. However, conditions are different in the twentieth century from what they were in the sixteenth, seventeenth, and eighteenth centuries in that the acreage of land available for agricultural settlement in the temperate climates is less now than it was in the days of migration by ship.

The airplane is remarkable for the speed with which it can establish a settlement, bringing in not only the population but also supplies, mining equipment, and so on. It is also remarkable for its ability to explore and to survey a region for natural resources. Thus, the setting-up of new communities of population is facilitated by aviation.

New settlements are expected to develop along air routes. Earlier, such settlements developed along railroads. New communities were established along the routes connecting the Pacific Coast with the populations of the Mississippi Valley. The airplane is not likely to have such an effect in the United States, since the country is already settled; but the situation may be different in western Canada and Alaska. The shortest great-circle route to the eastern coast of China and Japan lies across Alaska; this route is also of strategic military value. If planes fly that route, then aviation favors settlements along it, especially where the planes stop to refuel. Though the route across Alaska or via the Aleutians is the shortest route to Japan and coastal China, yet the question may be raised as to whether planes will fly over it. In general, the route that will be flown will not be the shortest one, but the one that will produce the greatest amount of intermediate traffic along it. In the case of the Asiatic Pacific, one possible route is via Hawaii. But this route lies across vast stretches of water and there are not many sources of intermediate traffic. Since the route through Alaska is the shortest and there are no competitive routes over more populous territories, it is likely that that route will be flown.[9] Hence there is a good prospect of communities in Alaska being served by air, and for the population of Alaska to increase. At the present time, Alaska, with an area of 586,000 square miles, contains only 40,000 white people, or one white person per 9000 acres. The problem of increased population is one of economic opportunities, transportation, and climate. Economic opportunities in Alaska lie largely in lumber, mining — at present chiefly gold, silver, copper, and lead — fish, and animal products. Agriculture is limited, but can be developed to aid in the support of the Alaskan population. The air route will afford passenger connections with the outside world and air cargo will be important.

The extent of population increase depends upon air rates and economic opportunities. The white population of Alaska was stationary between 1920 and 1930, but increased 37 per cent be-

[9] J. Parker Van Zandt, *The Geography of World Air Transport*, Brookings Institution, 1944, pp. 24-32.

tween 1930 and 1940. This was the decade of aviation development, first from Ketchikan to Juneau along the length of the panhandle, from Juneau to Fairbanks in the interior and on the other side of the towering mountain range, and from Fairbanks to Nome at the Bering Straits. It was not until 1940, however, that regular flights from Seattle to Alaska were instituted. This expansion of aviation was more or less heroic in view of altitudes, fogs, icing, and soil conditions. Since there will be important transportation routes across Alaska, sufficient economic opportunity, and a good enough climate, there will probably be considerable increase in population in the decades immediately following the war.

The initial process of settlement and increase of population is promoted by aviation because of the plane's speed and lack of need of a constructed roadway. The process of settlement does not cease, however, with aviation's initiatory contribution. There is reason to think that, once started, the population growth will not continue to rest on aviation as the sole method of transportation. In the mining towns of Canada, established by means of air transportation, after the population was large enough to sustain them, roadways were built to provide cheaper transportation by truck and automobile. Boat service to Alaska is now infrequent and inadequate because the population is not large enough to justify frequent service. But, with a large population and a greater productivity, steamship service to Alaska may be improved and become very convenient. In the same way, as the population of Alaska grows, highways and railroads are likely to be constructed. These, in turn, increase population. The first contribution of aviation to population is not the measure of its total effect. The later population increases, due to other modes of transportation, are also the indirect effects of aviation.

Reduction of Population Density Differentials

The effect of aviation on the distribution of population is not confined to settling uninhabited or sparsely populated areas. It also has some effect in reducing density differentials in regions already settled. A pipe connecting two pails of water will equalize the levels of water in the pails. Human transportation may be viewed in the same manner. A transportation line connecting two unequally populated areas tends to reduce the differential of population density in the two areas. However, the population of an area of low population density may be increased also by immigration from other areas than those of high population density.

This principle may be illustrated by a consideration of the population in the states of the Pacific Coast and those east of the Great Plains. Population pressure is not as great on the Pacific Coast as in the eastern part of the United States, as may be shown by wage rates and income. Each decennial census shows the railroads and highways are still taking migrants from east to west. The pressure is in the process of being equalized.

Aviation is another transportation system which will help to carry the population westward, but it will have more effect than if just another railroad line had been added or a new highway built. As a transportation system, aviation makes a new contribution of speed. This speed will make possible the opening-up of new markets in distant areas. New markets are a stimulus to business activity and create a demand for an increased labor supply. This process is much like that which took place in Britain when her ships opened up markets all over the world. England's population in the seventeenth century was around four or five million, while in the twentieth century, the population of England had reached forty-one million. Other factors than shipping helped to make this increase, but if Britain's export markets were cut off or greatly reduced, her present population could not be sustained.

Aviation's speed has the effect of linking the Pacific Coast much closer to the Mississippi Valley and the Atlantic seaboard. It opens up new markets in the East for the products of the Pacific Coast that may be sent by air. Speed is of particular value in the shipment of such products as perishable fruits, flowers, fashion goods, machinery, parts of equipment, and for a great variety of emergency orders. Aviation also means that salesmen, buyers, and executives can make business contacts much more speedily and effectively. Thus, industries of the Pacific Coast are stimulated to new growth because of the opening-up of these new markets, and the population of the Pacific Coast grows because a larger labor force is needed — assuming no great increase in labor-saving machinery. The advance of technology in labor-saving machinery is constantly increasing the productivity of industry without increasing the labor force. It is hard to foresee how fast or how far this may proceed in the future. The extent to which the population of the Pacific Coast will be increased depends on the rates offered by aviation companies for passengers, and particularly for cargo. It also depends on the competition between the products of the Pacific Coast which can be shipped by air and those produced in the eastern states. The increase of population on the Pacific Coast may not be very great quantitatively, but the influence of aviation is in that direction.

The flow of population toward areas of low population density, like that toward the Pacific Coast in the United States, may also occur in other parts of the world. Population tends to migrate toward areas which are relatively sparsely settled and which have potentialities for industrial development. Historically, industrialization has meant an increase in population. We may expect this to occur in the future, unless it is counteracted by birth-control practices. Siberia is an example of an area where population increases may occur through industrialization. During World War II, considerable industrialization has taken place in Siberia, and it is generally thought that this trend will be continued in the postwar decades. Siberia has coal and iron deposits which are favorable to industrial development. Industrialization means a widening of markets, in which the airplane plays an important part. Thus, aviation is expected to be a factor in augmenting the population in Siberia.

In nations which are already industrialized, the airplane may open up new markets. It is said to bring any place on earth within less than two days' travel time of any other place. But its assets to business will be limited if the rates are high or the schedules inadequate. Expanding trade may bring increases in population in the areas already industrialized, as well as in the new areas being developed.

Quality of Population

It is customary to treat the subject of population in terms of quality as well as in terms of quantity. Will aviation affect the quality of peoples? The first thought that comes to mind in answer to this question is that superior physical qualities are demanded of aviators in wartime. Physical fitness is also a matter of importance to commercial pilots on airlines in peacetime. There is a premium on quick reaction time and on good eyesight, particularly. Obviously, the physical requirements in peacetime are not so great as they are for fighter pilots in wartime. The question arises as to whether, with the exception of private flying, there will be a selection in terms of physical fitness and whether, because of the popularity of aviation, there may not be a widespread cultivation of the art of keeping physically fit. If personal flying is largely in helicopters, which are capable of flying very slowly, no great asset is seen in athletic ability, perhaps little more than in driving an automobile.

The discussion, in the chapter on health, regarding the spread of new diseases and the plane's influence on the practice of medicine and hospitalization may be interpreted in terms of the quality of population. Aircraft, like automobiles, promote vacations in the out-of-doors, which may have something to do with health. The plane's influence will be greater, however, in promoting the spread of outdoor sports.

In general, it is thought that aviation will not have much influence on the physical quality of population.

Social Classes

Quality of population is sometimes discussed in terms of social classes. Social classes are usually thought of as groups of people who have differences in status and habits which set them off from each other. The distinctions of social class may have little to do with inherent qualities of population. One of the principal factors in determining class status in the United States today is economic success, and heredity is much less important in economic success than is usually thought. There is some mobility between social classes, but enough stability to develop these characteristic distinctions. In the United States, there has been great mobility between social classes in the past. The poor boy had a chance of becoming rich and politically powerful. With a relatively high standard of living in the United States, class differences have been less apparent than in other countries. Many inventions have had the effect of lessening class distinctions. Mass production of men's and women's clothing has decreased the visible differences between the rich and poor. Similarly, plastic jewelry and rayon stockings have enabled the girls who work in stores and factories to look more like the daughters of the rich. Will aviation also have the effect of decreasing class distinctions, or will it favor the rich?

Air travel today, with free dining service, the attendance of stewardesses, and fares over five cents a mile, is said to be luxury travel. With helicopters costing perhaps five thousand dollars and travel in private airplanes at five or ten dollars an hour, poor people cannot afford the pleasures and advantages of private flying. Aviation, then, in its early stages, is largely available only to the upper classes, as the term is popularly used. This was also true of the automobile in its early stages. The great significance of the Model T automobile of the Ford Motor Company was that it enabled the average man to have a possession that had hitherto belonged exclusively to the rich. The automobile no longer differentiated the rich from the rest of the population in the United States.

The aircraft industry looks to the time when there will be a large market for private aircraft. But a large market cannot be created unless prices are brought down. Leaders in the aviation industry want to bring prices down, but they cannot set them lower than costs without going bankrupt or receiving financial support from the government. Technological advances and mass-production methods will be most effective in lowering prices. How far prices may go downward is discussed in other chapters, but it is expected that the advantages of aviation will be less and less confined to the rich and will spread among the masses with lower incomes. If passenger air rates reach three cents a mile, people of all classes can travel by air, although the bus and rail-

road coach may draw proportionately more from the lower income groups. It is in the private ownership of aircraft that class
distinctions will remain longer and be sharper. The price of
planes and helicopters may remain above a thousand dollars for
a long time. If owners of aircraft require an automobile also,
then a large market among the masses with lower incomes is not
in sight either. The cost of the use of aircraft will remain high if
they are used largely for week-ends, vacations, or long-distance
travel. For some time in the future, then, the private ownership
of aircraft will be a mark of class distinction. But the drive for
mass production is a very powerful one in business, and ways and
means may be discovered in the more distant future to make it
possible for the average man to own a roadable helicopter.

Conclusion

The growth of population by births will be affected very little
by aviation, but the deaths in the United States may be increased
by several thousand a year. The influence of aviation on the distribution of the population of the world is expected to be more
significant than that on the birth and death rates of a locality.
This influence operates by furnishing a quick means of transportation to sparsely inhabited, out-of-the-way localities, where minerals, chemicals, and other natural resources may be exploited.
Some encouragement may be given to settlement in the tropics.
Sparsely populated regions lying on air routes between great
population centers will be especially favored. The increase in
population will be accompanied by a process of infiltration
rather than mass migration. Aviation, furthermore, will tend to
lessen the differential of density in population between widely
separated, populated areas with differing degrees of population
pressure. Thus, aviation is expected to have some influence in
increasing the population on the Pacific Coast in the United
States.

15

The Family

THE FAMILY is a universal social organization. There has never been a known people without some kind of family organization. However, the size and organization of families have varied from age to age and from area to area. For example, in China the family includes, besides the parents and children, grandparents, uncles, aunts, brothers and sisters, and other relatives. In the United States today the family often consists of only the mother and father and one or two children. The reproduction of children and the development of character and personality are usually considered to be the basic functions of the family. But the family has performed many other functions in various ages. In the pioneer days in the United States, the family was large in size and almost a small community in itself. It produced the food and clothing which it used, built the home and farm buildings, and was an independent economic unit. Children learned their vocational and household skills in the family and also received much of their formal education. Most of the recreational and social needs were satisfied within the home. Today in the United States, with its high standards of consumption based on factory production, the family is too small to perform these many functions, and most of them are now performed by outside institutions. Factories produce food, clothing, and shelter. Even a large amount of the cooking is done by the restaurant or delicatessen. The theater, dance hall, and social center take care of the recreational needs. The school performs the educational function; the church, the religious. Only the rearing of children and the satisfactions of the affectional needs of personality are left as functions of the family.

S. Dept. Interior

Servicing Isolated Areas. Where the population is sparse, the means of transportation are usually poor. In the North, rivers are often frozen for many months of the year and not navigable. The airplane has been used extensively in many isolated areas of the world for bringing contact with the outside world. Aircraft are also a very good means of exploring new territory. (*Chapter 14, Population.*)

Delivery Service by Helicopter. The prospective use of helicopters has been announced by a number of department stores. Delivery of mail by helicopter in rural regions is also a possibility. (*Chapter 23, Marketing.*)

Mining Town Dependent on Aviation. Bonanza, Nicaragua, shown below, and its gold mines were constructed from building materials and machinery flown in by airplanes. There are many mining towns in various isolated spots of the world whose only practical communication with the outside world is by aviation. Some of these towns have populations of four or five thousand. (*Chapter 24, Mining.*)

S. D. A.

Aerial Dusting of a Melon Crop with an Insecticide. At present, the most extensive use of aircraft in agriculture is for dusting. The use is particularly extensive in the cotton fields. Its use in this respect calls for cooperation and planning. This practice is more suitable for large areas. (*Chapter 29, Agriculture.*)

Checking Soil Erosion. The plane is excellent for making soil surveys, particularly with the use of aerial photography. Farmers have been taken up in planes to impress them with the need for terracing and contour plowing. (*Chapter 29, Agriculture.*)

Fire-Fighting Parachute Jumper. The forester is releasing himself from his chute preparatory to removing his protection suit and starting for the fire. The uses of aircraft in fighting fires are many and varied. The helicopter is expected to be of great value. The annual loss from forest fires is about $35,000,000 in normal times. (*Chapter 30, Forestry.*)

Means of transportation have been a factor, both directly and indirectly, in the changing rôle of the family. Transportation facilities have made possible the growth of the cities. The concentration of large numbers of people into a small area — that is, the city — depends on the transportation of food from the farms, fuel from the mines, wood from the forests, and products from various other cities. The railroad and the factory first made city life possible, and it is principally the complex nature of city life which has changed the functions of the family.

More recently, the appearance of the automobile has modified family living. Rapid personal transportation of the breadwinner to his place of business made it possible for the family to move to the suburbs, which provided more space for children to play, and more healthful surroundings. The automobile has increased mobility. Week-ends and vacations are spent in driving. Less time is spent in the home by the various members of the family. The automobile has even increased the mobility of the family home, since some families have lived in trailers and traveled from place to place. Educational opportunities for rural children have been improved by the automobile. The school bus has carried the children to the consolidated school with its improved educational facilities, and it has transported the older rural youth to the town high school.

These remarks are merely illustrative, rather than fully descriptive, of the changes in family function and organization that have occurred as a result of new methods of transportation. After World War II comes a new form of transportation, aviation. Will it have any effect on the family and, if so, what will be its nature?

The Influence of Passenger Transportation by Air

The steamship, railroad, and automobile have increased passenger travel, resulting in more frequent separations of the members of the family. Formerly, when transportation facilities were less well developed, travel was difficult. Travelers undertook a journey with reluctance because of the slow and uncomfortable travel, exposure to the elements, and the difficulty of obtaining food and shelter. The result was that the family was rarely separated because of traveling by its members.

Today the situation is quite different. Travel often separates family members. Employees of transportation media — sailors, railroad engineers, brakemen, firemen, porters, and so on — must necessarily travel. Then there are traveling salesmen and buyers, and inspectors who go from city to city. Businessmen attend conventions and association meetings. Farmers take their stock to market. Public speakers and theatrical productions go on tour. Large-scale farming depends on migrant laborers who move with the harvesting seasons. From these illustrations it is seen that occupations often result in the separation of family members through travel.

The extent of family separation is shown by the United States Census of 1940. A spouse was found to be not living at home in one out of twenty cases. Some may have been working in other cities, expecting to return later. However, not all of these absences were due to travel as such. Some of the absentees were in institutions, such as prisons or hospitals. But a large proportion were away, no doubt, because of the great facility of travel. It is difficult to imagine one out of twenty being away from home in the agricultural civilization before the railroad.

Passenger travel by airplane, with its great advantage of speed, is another invitation to travel. Although the transportation of passengers by air is already highly developed, its expansion is confidently predicted for the years after the war. In so far as aviation grows by taking passengers away from the railroad and the steamship, its influence on the family would not be changed. But aviation is expected to create new passenger traffic, especially for long-distance travel, such as from east of the Mississippi River in the United States to the Pacific Coast, and from the United States to foreign lands. Thus, aviation would increase the total volume of travel, and, as a result, the number of family separations. The railroad and steamship had the same effect in the days of their expansion. It may be argued that, since a traveler will reach his destination in less time by airplane, the time away from home may be reduced by that much. On the other hand, any time saved may be spent on the business duties or the vacation away from home. Passenger aviation is more likely to appeal to a single member of the family than to the family as a unit. Scheduled air passenger travel makes it easier for members of the family to be separated from each other, and family living is affected to this extent.

International air passenger transportation will make a strong appeal to people to travel in foreign countries because of the shorter time required for such travel. Before the war, a round trip to Europe by ship, plus the train trips between the home town and the port of embarkation, consumed an entire two-weeks' vacation. By plane, approximately ten or eleven days of a two-weeks' vacation can be spent in Europe. Similarly, the number of trips to the countries south of us will be greatly increased. Many families will travel together, but more families will be separated by the increased travel abroad.

The Influence of Private Flying

Members of a family will not only fly on scheduled passenger routes, but they will also fly in aircraft owned by the family. What effect will flying in small non-passenger planes have upon the family?

The effect of non-passenger flying will depend upon the extent to which members of the family fly in their own planes. This question has been discussed in the chapter on private flying. There it was indicated that, within the first decade after the war, it is probable that only families with incomes over $10,000 a year, which are capable of owning an automobile in addition to an airplane or helicopter, will make much use of the privately owned aircraft. Out of 32,000,000 families in the United States in 1941, the number of families with incomes of $10,000 a year or more was 710,000. The number with $5000 a year and over was 1,945,000. Not all of these families will own helicopters or airplanes. Hence, for a decade after the war, not very many families will be affected by flying in privately owned planes.

In the succeeding decades, it is expected that the helicopter will be much improved, and that there will be a considerable demand for it, enough to support some mass production, which will result in lowering the price to around that of a medium-priced automobile. It is also thought that later a helicopter will be developed whose rotors will fold back and which will travel on the ground at about forty miles an hour by having the power of its engine transferred to the wheels. If a roadable helicopter is developed and is sold for fifteen hundred dollars (at present dollar values), the influence on family life may be appreciable, although a roadable helicopter would still be a poor automobile and hence not a substitute. When helicopters become more common, their influence on family life will be more widespread. One of the first effects will be on family recreation.

Effect on Recreation

One of the earliest uses of family aircraft will be for vacations and pleasure trips. Seacoasts, lakes, and mountains will be accessible to more families, since aircraft is an especially good means for going long distances quickly. Northern families can go South for the winter months; and Southern families can find summer resorts. However, the greater the distance traveled, the more expensive the flight. Thus, the helicopter will first be used for vacations by families with large incomes.

Personal aircraft seating four to six persons will be more expensive than those seating two. The difference in price will be greater than between a two-seated and a five-seated automobile. As a result, it would seem that, for many families, the family aircraft may not be able to transport the whole family on a trip as readily as does the family car. Hence, privately owned aircraft may tend to separate the members of the family more than the private automobile does.

The automobile changed somewhat the nature of recreation of the family. In some ways, the automobile has held the family together as a unit. Often the whole family goes driving on Sundays in the automobile. On the other hand, the automobile has also produced separation and conflict. It has proved attractive to youth, and they have desired to get the use of the family car for activities and recreation which does not include other family members. Many family arguments have turned on the problem of the use of the family car by the younger members of the family. The airplane or helicopter should be just as attractive to youth as is the automobile, and disciplinary problems are likely to arise in families owning aircraft. Family aircraft are likely to increase the separation of families in recreation and to segregate the young from the old.

Private aircraft will make the owning of a second home for vacation purposes somewhat more attractive. With such aircraft, vacation homes can be located in areas of natural beauty, farther out from urban centers than would otherwise be feasible. Cheap, prefabricated houses may make it possible for more people to own vacation homes, which presumably are beneficial to the health of the family, especially to that of the children.

Effect on Family Expenditures

When the automobile was being widely adopted in the 1920's in the United States, it was a highly valued possession. At first, automobiles were quite expensive, but, as the price was gradually lowered, more and more families were able to buy them. The families who were able to acquire them displayed them with pride and were envied by families who could not afford them. There followed some competition among families, each family struggling "to keep up with the Joneses." This rivalry in conspicuous spending and display was said to have led to sacrifices in the traditional pattern of family spending. Money was obtained to purchase automobiles by doing without servants. Clothing stores reported that men and women were wearing their old clothes, instead of buying new ones, in order to use the money on automobiles. Less money was spent on furnishings for the home. The home came to be popularly described as a couple of rooms over a garage — a parking place for the night. Although the effect of the automobile on family expenditures has not been measured statistically, there is undoubtedly some truth in these statements.

Privately owned aircraft may have a similar effect on family expenditures, although it cannot be seen at this time that aircraft will be adopted and used by the family to the extent that the automobile has been. Nor are we assured that any "Model T" aircraft will be as cheap or as widely sold as was Henry Ford's famous automobile. Still, owning a plane or helicopter may raise a family on the social and economic scale in the eyes of the community. Some families may take out mortgages to purchase an airplane, or otherwise make sacrifices in some phase of their standard of living to secure one. The acquiring of family aircraft will require a readjustment of family expenditures.

Effect on Home Sites

The effect of aviation on the location of residences will be discussed in the chapter on cities. There it will be indicated that any such influence is not expected to be great, at least for a decade or more after the war, because of the high rates expected for local air transportation, the difficulty of securing adequate landing places near one's place of work in the center of the city, and the high prices likely to be charged for helicopters. For a long time, families living outward from the city are likely to depend on the bus, train, and private automobile for regular transportation into the city. The spreading of homes outward from the city has been made possible by the invention of fast local transportation; that is, buses and commutation railroads. The airplane is essentially a long-distance form of transportation rather than a local one, but the helicopter can be used for local transportation, although it is not ideal for this purpose because of the congestion of population in the cities. There may be some families who will depend on a roadable helicopter for transportation and who will buy home sites farther off the paved highways than they would otherwise do. Some wealthy families may use helicopter buses for commutation. But, at the present time, the scattering of many homes outward from the metropolis because of local air transportation is not foreseen for the postwar decade.

However, it is probable that many homes will acquire larger lots in order to provide landing places for helicopters, although these helicopters may not be used for daily transportation into the city. With favorable conditions, helicopters can land on a yard space, say, fifty by fifty feet, but a plot of ground one hundred by one hundred feet or larger would be more convenient in case of emergencies. Lots within the city, especially those close in, will, in general, for some time be too small or crowded for helicopters. Families able to own both a helicopter and an automobile will presumably be able to own large lots on the edges of suburbs for their residences. Some urban families will probably move outward in order to be able to land a helicopter on their own land, even though they remain dependent upon the conventional types of transportation into the city. The existence of larger lots will in itself tend to scatter families out somewhat, since more ground will be required for the same number of families. Larger home sites will mean more space and air for the members of the family.

Bombing During a War

The previous discussion has concerned family life in peacetime. However, there may be wars in the future, and the airplane has brought war to the civilian population. During a period of bombing raids, the effect of the airplane on family life is profound. Members of the family who remain in the city during a period of bombing often sleep in bomb shelters which are shared by large numbers of people. For those who have shelters in their homes, the noise and danger of the bombs upset the healthy routine of family life. When families must leave the cities which are being bombed, the family is often broken. Children in a family may be separated from each other, or even from their mothers. Thus, under the conditions of bombing raids on cities during a war, the impact of the airplane on family life is highly disruptive.

The Size of Family

The trend in the size of the family in the United States has been downward, at least since the first census in 1790. However, the rate of decrease has been much greater since 1920. Will aviation have any influence on this trend?

The size of the family is affected by various social conditions.

One of these is economic. For instance, the prohibition of child labor and the enactment of compulsory-education laws in England were followed by drops in the birth rate in regions affected by these regulations. Karl Pearson claims this connection to be causal on the basis of evidence he collected in correlation studies. The social and economic conditions of urban life are thought to be the cause of the difference in birth rates between urban and rural areas. The size of the family is smaller in cities partly because the expense of maintaining a large family is greater in the city than in the country. It is said that city children become self-supporting, or partially so, later in life than do farm children, and so are a charge on the family income for a longer period of time.

The economic factor is again evident in the situation where families choose between an expenditure of some size which they want to make and having a baby, which will add to their expenses. It is said that in the 1920's many families who could hardly afford to own an automobile chose to postpone having children until after they had bought a car. Although there is no proof of this statement, it seems quite probable. When parenthood is voluntary, such things as material goods, vacations, and travel compete with children for a place in the family budget. On this theory, it is possible that some families, desiring very much to own aircraft, may keep their families small for a time in order to finance the ownership of a helicopter. Such calculations are not always made in precise figures, nor is a sharp, clearcut decision made on a particular day. Rather, a family buys a plane and the family remains small. There is evidence to show that the losses in population because of postponement of marriage and having children, by large numbers of people, as occurs in periods of economic depression, are never fully made up later.

On the other hand, privately owned aircraft may stimulate the location of more families in the suburbs on larger plots of ground, where living conditions are more favorable to child life than city streets, but whether living in the suburbs is much of a factor in increasing the size of the family is a question.

After considering these possible influences of competitive expenditures and suburban living on the size of the families who will own aircraft, the guess may be hazarded that any influence of this nature will be small, but probably in the direction of strengthening somewhat the trend toward smaller families.

Conclusion

An exploration of the possible future influence of aviation on family living does not reveal any effects of great magnitude or of a revolutionary nature, as was the case with the railroad and automobile. The influence of air passenger transportation is in line with the general trend of increasing separation of the members of the family from one another, especially through travel of the husband. It will provide for more distant travel for family members on vacations. The influence of privately owned aircraft on family life is contingent on the development of the helicopter and the roadable type of rotor craft. This influence will probably not make itself felt until the second decade after the war and later. Whatever influence it may have will, in general, be felt first by the families with larger incomes, well above perhaps five thousand dollars. Privately owned aircraft are expected to provide more vacations and vacation homes, to become a means of conspicuous family display, to increase the yard space of family residences, to create problems of control of adolescents, to necessitate adjustments in family expenditures, to encourage the trend of living in the outlying suburbs, and perhaps to have a slight influence in favoring the trend toward smaller families.

16 | *Cities*

ONE OF THE OUTSTANDING DEVELOPMENTS of the last seventy years has been the growth of cities. In 1870, 25.7 per cent of the American population lived in cities, while today 56.5 per cent of the population is urban. The concentration of large aggregates into small geographical areas is dependent upon good transportation facilities. The manufactured goods produced in the city are exchanged for the agricultural products of the country by means of transportation facilities. Since the growth of urbanism has been dependent on transportation facilities, we would expect a new means of transportation such as aviation to exert some influence both on the development of urban growth and on the configuration of the city.

The various means of local transportation are correlated with different types of urban pattern. In ancient times, when humans and animals were the principal forms of transportation, a wall was often built around the city, constituting both a political and economic boundary. A tax was levied upon goods entering the city, and customs officers were stationed at the gates to collect the tariff. The people living within the city possessed certain political rights. In the early days of the railroad era, the means of local transportation were still poorly developed. The cities had no walls or customs collections on goods, but an economic boundary line could be drawn for the assessment of city taxes, and those inside the city lines received such economic services as water supply, and fire and police protection.

As local transportation facilities developed, the population began to live farther away from their places of work in the city center. The electric interurban train and the local steam rail-

Figure 22. THE DISTRIBUTION OF THE POPULATION OF A CITY,
BALTIMORE, AND LOCAL TRANSPORTATION

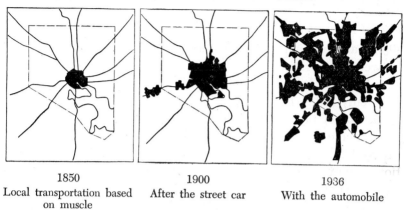

1850	1900	1936
Local transportation based on muscle	After the street car	With the automobile

road developed satellite towns. The bus and electric streetcar
built up the suburbs at the periphery of the old city. The automobile further scattered residences along the roads and highways and in the spaces between the suburbs. The resulting pattern was one of highways and railroad lines spreading outward
from the center of the city, with the population distributed along
these lines of transportation more or less in the form of a starfish
or perhaps an octopus with outstretched tentacles. The economic
boundary line of cities have become rather vague and ill-defined.
The political boundary lines have changed slowly or remained
fixed, while the economic limits have moved outward. As a result, the two are no longer coterminous.

Not only have the economic limits of the city moved outward,
but the increased speed and means of travel have extended the
influence of urban attitudes and ways of living over a much
larger area. As a result of the new means of transportation and
communication, the metropolitan community, which is much
larger than the central city, has come into existence. The population of the metropolitan community is highly congested in the
city center, decreasing gradually in concentration toward the
periphery. The sphere of influence of the metropolitan community covers a much larger geographical area.

Now comes a new form of transportation — aviation. What effect will it have on the city?

Use of Aircraft in the City

The airplane is primarily a form of transportation to be used between cities rather than within cities. It is expected that there may be some local air service, with stops perhaps every fifteen or twenty miles; but the terminals of such service, if a plane is used, cannot be within the congested city center itself because the airplane requires a relatively large amount of space for landing and taking off.

The most promising type of aircraft for urban use is the helicopter, which can land and take off vertically from a small space. As has been pointed out in other chapters, the helicopter is expected to be used first by business concerns who can afford the original and operating costs and hire professional pilots. Since the widespread use of the individually owned helicopter is not expected for some time, the effects of aviation on the configuration of the city are far in the future.

One of the first uses of helicopters in the city may be for air bus lines. These would undoubtedly be faster than surface transportation because of the greater speed of the helicopter and its freedom from traffic congestion. Commuters or traders, using helicopter lines, could live farther out from the city center than the present suburbs. However, the number moving out for this reason will be small compared with the number who would move out if they could depend on a privately owned helicopter for commuting.

Effect on Residence Areas of Helicopter Use

Since the private helicopter or the helicopter bus line provides a more rapid means of travel into the city, it might be expected to scatter the population farther outward around a city and into the areas between present suburbs. This effect of the use of the helicopter, if it occurs, will become apparent some time after the first postwar decade. The delay in the use of the private helicopter has been discussed in other chapters.

The helicopter requires a landing space of from fifty to one hundred feet square, depending on the size of the helicopter. This area is much greater than the parking space required for an automobile and acts to restrict the use of the helicopter in the city. There are many vacant lots in the outlying sections of American cities which could be used for landing fields for helicopters. The helicopters could be kept in garages on such vacant lots rather than in garages at the owners' residences. It would be desirable for such lots to be within short walking distances of the owners' homes. This would be feasible, since the helicopter's ability to fly vertically makes it possible for such landing fields to be near buildings. Since vacant spaces are found mainly in the areas between present suburban settlements where real-estate values are lower, there will be a tendency for these areas to be built up. One deterrent may be the lack of community facilities in these areas, such as schools, fire protection, sewer systems, and so on. However, these may be developed as the areas become more populous. In general, the effect will be to distribute urban homes over larger areas.

This tendency toward greater spacing would be decreased to some extent by the development of the roadable helicopter. Since the roadable helicopter can be landed at a common landing field and driven home, there would be little effect on the spacing of houses. It is expected that the rotors can be folded back so that the helicopter garage will not need to be very much larger than the garage for an automobile.

The tendency toward greater spacing of houses would also be decreased by the use of roofs for landing places for helicopters, since large yard space would not be necessary. The small private helicopter is expected to have a weight comparable to that of an automobile and a large one to that of a truck or bus. The majority of private homes at present either do not have flat roofs or roofs that are sufficiently strong for rooftop landings. However, the roofs of many apartment houses, with some remodeling, might be suitable.

If the roofs of houses are used to a considerable extent for helicopter landing places, the type of architecture of homes may be influenced. The flat roof is becoming more common and more fashionable. New insulation materials are making the gable roof less necessary. A cover could be constructed on one part of the roof for storing the helicopter.

Effect on City Center of Helicopter Use

The urban driver of a helicopter needs a landing space at his work or in the central business district, as well as near his home. Since business concerns will be the first users of helicopters, the landing space required at first will be only enough to accommodate commercial machines. The space required for such purposes will be small compared to that necessary when the helicopter comes into extensive use by individuals. Where will this space be found?

There are very few vacant areas in the center of a large city. The few small ones that do exist are often used as parking places for automobiles. In general, they are too small for both the landing and parking of helicopters. One solution might be to use these areas for landing places and to store the helicopters in an adjacent building. There are at present some downtown buildings in which automobiles are parked, often utilizing many floors. The same might be done with helicopters. Elevators or ramps would take the machines to the various floors. The folding-back of the rotors would make the space necessary to park the helicopter comparable to that used for the automobile. Since such structures for parking automobiles have been successful, presumably such buildings for helicopters would be possible from an economic standpoint.

More vacant areas could be created by removing old buildings or those which have only a few stories. This would be an expensive process, however, since real-estate values are high in the central business district and, in addition, there is a cost of razing buildings.

An area with lower real-estate costs and more vacant space is the so-called "blighted" area around the center of many cities. The encroachment of the business district into this area has caused the more prosperous residents to move to more attractive residential areas located farther from the city center. The real-estate value in these old areas declines, the houses fall into disrepair, and the area becomes a slum interspersed with small businesses, lodging places, and warehouses. Landing spaces for helicopters could be provided in this blighted area at much less cost than in the central business district. However, the distance from the blighted area to the city center may be fifteen or twenty blocks, more or less. This distance would be an obstacle to the use of landing places in these blighted areas unless the helicopter were roadable. If it were not roadable, auto-taxis could be used from the landing place to the central business district, entailing a small additional cost, or in some cases the distance will not be too great to be walked.

Another way of meeting the demand for landing space for helicopters in the center of the city would be the utilization of the roofs of buildings. Most buildings in the centers of cities are not suitable in their present form for rooftop landings. The roofs are not flat, not strong enough, or contain obstructions like chimneys, tanks, wires, and so on. Remodeling of a roof to make it suitable for helicopter landings will be rather expensive in some cases. If the resulting landing space is small and further decreased by the presence of parked helicopters, the number of helicopters accommodated may be so small as not to be worth the cost. The number of helicopters that could utilize the landing space on a small roof would be increased by parking the aircraft on the floors beneath the roof. In some cases, the whole building might be used for parking, or, in an office building, perhaps only the few top floors would be used for parking helicopters.

The use of roofs for landing places in the city center is somewhat complicated by the fact that the buildings are of unequal heights. The tallest buildings would be the easiest on which to land, since wind currents are sometimes strong in between tall buildings which are built close together. Also, there may be sudden and great changes in wind velocity around corners of buildings.

The use of roofs for helicopter landing places will be tried first by business concerns. A department store which delivers goods by helicopter might use its roof for landing, if the cost of reconditioning is not large. A helicopter bus line might land on the roof of its downtown terminal building, though a large building would be needed for such a purpose. A ground landing is more probable. The roofs of post offices might be the landing places for helicopters carrying mail to the airport. The roof of the post office in Philadelphia was used for a year for the landing of autogiros. As experience with rooftop landings grows, more roofs can be reconditioned to meet the increasing use of helicopters.

City centers which have already been developed change very slowly. Buildings are very costly to build or to raze, and investments are made for long periods of time and are not readily changed. Land values are very high in the central business district, and space is at a premium. Land must be income-producing in order to pay the taxes. The size of taxes is often a function of capitalized income. But, in the case of vacant lots, the value of the land is a result of the demand for it. This demand is related to the prospective income from structures built upon the land. A regimentation of zoning and building could readjust the economic structure to these tall, widely separated buildings, but it would require a good deal of time.

City architects have envisioned the city of the future as having a business area of tall buildings widely separated, with non-stop automobile highways. Such conceptions are in line with the adjustment to aircraft, but, if they are ever achieved, it will be far in the future. Chicago continues to have its huge stockyards near the center of the city, although if they were being constructed today they would be located elsewhere. Broad, non-stop, and conveniently located automobile highways from city centers have still not been constructed after forty years of extensive use of the automobile. Any radical change of the pattern of the downtown business section to make it better adjusted to the airplane will take a long time and will be in the direction of increasing the space between buildings.

Multiplication of Business Centers

The ecology of cities may be approached on the basis of the fact that the helicopter has increased freedom of movement as compared with surface means of transportation. Great freedom to move in any direction encourages decentralization, as is illustrated by Oriental and other cities which were built when walking was common and pack animals were used. These cities are said to have few specialized areas for specific functions. Legs, like helicopters, can go in any direction. The automobile must have roads, the locomotive a railroad track, and boats are restricted to water. All the helicopter needs is a small landing space, plus, of course, gasoline stations.

It is true, of course, that freedom of direction was not the only factor in the distribution of the buildings of these old cities. The low height of buildings was also a factor. The effect of low buildings is to spread out the area occupied, or to make more than one such area, especially if the population is large. Freedom of direction of movement coupled with a restriction on the height of buildings seems to have the effect of dispersing the business area into several different areas.

European cities were, for the most part, built before the railroads and fast means of local transportation, but these cities have been changed to some degree by the adoption of these facilities. American cities, in general, have been built up after the development of railroads and rapid-transit transportation and show less tendency than do the European cities to have many business centers dispersed over the urban area. The buildings in European cities also are low. On a continuum of urban configuration from dispersed to centralized business centers, European cities would fall between Oriental and American cities.

The effect of the automobile, which has greater freedom of direction than the streetcar or elevated rail line, is to disperse the business centers. This is illustrated in Los Angeles, one of the few American cities that has had its major period of growth after the introduction of the automobile. Its population grew from 320,000 in 1910 to 576,673 in 1920, when the automobile came into extensive use, and to 1,238,000 in 1930. In Los Angeles, the central business section does not occupy the dominant place it does in New York, Chicago, and other large cities which were built before the use of the automobile. There is more than one large business section in Los Angeles, despite the fact that the established pattern in other cities was one with a single large business center.

The effect of the increased freedom to move in any direction which is offered by the helicopter would apparently be to encourage more than one business area. This will be particularly true in cities which may be developed largely after the use of aircraft has begun and which have poor systems of surface transportation. Of course, in the United States this situation would be very rare, but some cities may arise in the interior of China or Siberia which will depend largely on air transportation.

The freedom of movement of the helicopter may be restricted, however, in several ways. At first, the freedom of movement may be limited by traffic regulations if there is danger of forced landings. Later, this hazard should be decreased. Also, like the automobile, helicopter traffic may become channelized. In the early days of the automobile, it had great freedom of direction, since it was adapted to any city street and able to travel on almost any road. In the latter phases of adjustment to the automobile, however, it does not in practice go equally in all directions, but follows certain channels of through-traffic routes. In the same way, the helicopter will have its "beaten path," so to speak.

If a new city were built on the basis of adjustment to the helicopter, it would need a good deal of space in the business section, and, if the city were large, several business sections would be expected in different parts of the city. As to whether these business sections would be specialized, one for financial institutions, another for office buildings, another for amusements, another for mercantile stores, and so on, the helicopter would make no special contribution. Other factors would determine such specialization.

Influences of Airports

The configuration of the urban area is more likely to be influenced, in the first decade after the war, by the need of airplane airports than by the use of the helicopter. Airplanes require large airports, free from building obstructions. Thus, large airports must be built out beyond the area of city homes, though not of suburban ones. For convenient use, the airport must be connected with the center of the city by a through, express highway, even though the helicopter may be used for much transportation.

Very large cities will require more than one airport to accommodate the volume of passenger and cargo traffic and the demands of private fliers. The air space can easily become congested, and there is a limit to the number of planes that can fly from a runway per unit of time.

What sort of distribution of population, economic establishments, residences, or amusement places may these airports and express highways bring about? Gasoline stations, restaurants, and garages are already growing up around airports. There are also buildings for the offices and various employees of the air companies. Since it is expected that most of the present airports will need to be expanded, there is a tendency not to locate many buildings very near to the airport. However, once the boundaries are pretty well determined on one or more sides, there may be many other types of buildings and businesses. Very likely these will deal with the business of the airlines, and with servicing the airport, the planes, and the workers around the airport.

In European cities, there has been a tendency for certain types of recreation to develop around the airports. The fact that transportation between the city and the airport is likely to be fast and convenient makes it more probable that recreational activities will grow up around airports, although the noise of the planes may be a deterrent to some forms of recreation. The environs of an airport are suitable for parks, golf courses, and playing space for various types of sports. There are possibilities of roadhouses, dance halls, and restaurants in the neighborhood.

Airports are transfer points for passengers. Some will transfer to other trunk lines, while others will transfer to lines to near-by towns. If the wait is very long, the passengers may go into the center of the city. Presumably, most of the waiting will not be long, otherwise the passengers would not travel by air. Passengers will need some services while waiting. Shops, newspaper stands, restaurants, bars, barber shops, and other such services will grow up around the airport, particularly since it will not be as close to already established shops as is a bus or railroad station.

If a hundred thousand small private planes are in use in the first decade after the war, commercial airports will not be able to accommodate them all, and separate airports for private planes will be constructed, perhaps nearer the city. If a roadable plane is developed, there will be a demand for small airports around the outskirts of the city. Good highways to these landing fields will be needed. It should not be difficult to build such roads, since these fields will not be in the sections of the city that are congested with houses and criss-crossed streets. Although the helicopter, which does not need a regular airport, is expected to be most commonly used as a private aircraft, a few airports will be needed.

Effect on Metropolitan and Trading Areas

Modern transportation and communication inventions have made possible the development of the metropolitan community, and we would expect aviation likewise to have some effect on it. Through the use of the automobile, particularly, the customs and attitudes of the large city have been extended to the people in the surrounding territory. Observers have noted that small towns located near large cities have characteristics different from those of the small towns located more distantly. For instance, small communities within a wide radius of large urban centers have lost a large part of their former isolation and provincialism. We may expect this radius to become even wider with the development of aviation, particularly private aircraft. Aviation makes it possible for people living farther out to come to the city to shop in the stores, use the recreational facilities, attend meetings, and for other activities. The sphere of influence of the large city will reach farther out with its newspapers, financial functions, department-store delivery service, advertising, police and fire services, and so on.

An important idea in developing the concept of the metropolitan area is that of the city as the center of a marketing area. Various criteria may be used to determine the boundary lines of this marketing area; for example, newspaper distribution, delivery zones, freight differentials, or commuting distances. The boundary lines vary with the type of criterion used. For instance, the market area is larger for women's fur coats than for men's suits. But, in actual practice, there is a sort of average boundary for a large number of goods. The boundaries are determined by the time and cost of travel into the city, as well as by the distance of other large trading centers.

What effect will aviation have upon the trading area of a city? The use of aircraft may be expected to affect many of the factors which determine the trade area; for example, commuting distances may be increased, retail shopping areas enlarged, and delivery services may cover larger areas. These effects, of course, are dependent on the provision of the facilities of air travel to smaller places by radial routes around the big city or by long interconnecting routes with frequent short stops or by the use of private aircraft. The general effect of the increased speed of air travel will be the enlarging of the trade area, unless the new boundaries run into the trading area of another city. The higher fares of air travel as compared with bus and railroad coach will limit the activity of new enlarged trading areas. With greater distances and high costs of travel, the trade with the outlying area is likely to be restricted to goods of high unit costs for the individual consumer, such as household equipment or luxury goods.

The trading area is based, not only on purchases by ultimate consumers, but also on trade by middlemen. Wholesalers and retail buyers will be factors in enlarging the trade area, as will be discussed in the chapter on marketing.

Differentials in Growth of Cities

Since railroads made possible the creation of cities other than those on water routes, it is sometimes thought that airplanes will bring new cities that have no rail or water advantages, but which will be advantageously located on great-circle or other air routes. In considering this question, it is necessary to take into account different kinds of countries. In the United States, which is well settled and highly urbanized, it is not likely that there will be many cities created by aviation. The expansion of railroads in America occurred at the time when this was a new country and many cities were being built. In Europe, railroads connected towns already in existence and led to their increased growth rather than developing new cities. It may be that in Siberia, China, and the interiors of Africa and South America aviation will help to build new cities. However, up to the present time, the new communities which have been created by aviation have usually been connected with the exploitation of natural resources and have been small in size. After these towns have been started by aviation, highways for trucks and automobiles have been added. That aviation may lead to the creation of towns along airline routes across undeveloped countries is a distinct probability, but it also seems probable that the further growth of such places will be aided by other means of transportation, notably the automobile, and possibly the railroad. Where the terrain in the undeveloped regions is very mountainous, the coming of highways and rail tracks will be slowed.

A more realistic question for the United States is whether aviation will not speed the growth of selected and particular cities which lie along air routes and which are convenient stopping places. Many inland cities have visions of future greatness via the air routes, which will give them the advantages which seaport cities have formerly had. For instance, by air Chicago is closer to some of the cities of northern Europe than is New York. This will give Chicago an advantage over other cities not so favorably located.

Cities throughout the United States are, in the 1940's, making great plans for building airports and providing inducements for the airlines to make stops at those particular cities. The first cities which develop extensive airport facilities may be able to offer some inducement to the airlines to plan stops at those particular cities rather than at others with more retarded plans. No doubt, there is some choice of stopping places in setting up air routes, but there are other economic forces that point strongly toward certain cities as stopping points, irrespective of the salesmanship of any particular city. Such forces are the suitable distance for refueling, the presence of transportation connections, and so on. If these more or less inevitable economic and technical forces dictate a particular city for frequent stops, that city is likely to be chosen by the airlines, even if there is little or no promotion by the city.

In promoting airport facilities, city planners realize that the result will not be the capturing of an industry, as the motion-picture industry was captured by Los Angeles, or as automobile manufacturing was concentrated in and around Detroit. The significance of an airport to a city lies in the encouragement which it is expected to give to trade and industry in general. For instance, air mail is a great aid to business. Fast transportation is important in the supplying of parts or the quick replenishing of inventories. For many industries, air cargo means the rapid meeting of demand, which is of great significance in a highly competitive economy. New industries may locate in a city serviced by many airlines, but such service will probably not be the determining factor.

Hence, air facilities may promote some communities more than others by supplying a stimulus to the industry and merchandising of these communities. The degree of this promotion is difficult to assess. In the United States, where large communities are already excellently serviced by truck, bus, and railroad, and often by boat, the principal contribution of the airplane is speed. If this speed is important to business, some differential in growth may occur. It does not seem probable that the airplane will change cities as much as did the development of the railroad or the big ship.

Another factor to be considered in the growth of cities is the possible increase of population from the junction of transportation routes. In the case of railroads, it is generally conceded that the joining of two or more lines has been a source of population growth. The new population has been made up of members of the train crew who lived at the junction city, local transport men, the force required to do the warehousing, repairmen, and service men. In addition, this population requires merchandise, living facilities, and all kinds of services.

In the case of the airplane, somewhat the same forces will operate, but not necessarily to the same degree as at railroad junctions. Air passengers are primarily interested in speed and would not be expected to remain long enough to patronize hotels or to buy great quantities of goods from local merchants. Similarly, individuals who come to a city to take an airplane are in a hurry, and the community represents a point to pass as quickly as possible. Since airports will be situated some distance from the business section of the city, air passengers will not have much opportunity to buy in downtown stores. Thus, the transference of passengers at an airline junction would add little to the development of a community. The same will be true of air cargo traffic, since the plane will carry products requiring great speed, and the demand for warehouses will not be so great as in the case of railroads.

Some of these junction points of air routes will be centers for repair, routine check-ups, servicing, and fueling. The men in these service occupations around the airport will live at the junction point, as they do at the railroad junctions. However, the airlines will require fewer such service centers than the railroads, since airplanes cover more distance in an hour than do the railroads.

The principal junction points of airlines will be the metropolitan areas which will be stops on the trunk lines and will be the centers of small feeder lines. As a result, the activities and population of these metropolitan centers will be augmented to some extent.

Aviation, then, in the United States is not expected to have much effect in creating new communities, except an occasional small one in an out-of-the-way area where there are natural resources of value. But aviation will favor the growth of some cities because of the stimulation of international trade or because they are favorably located for convenient stopping places for planes.

The larger cities will be aided more than the smaller ones which will not have as frequent service for mail, passengers, and goods.

The location of cities and also city planning may possibly be affected by another aspect of aviation, namely, the military threat of bombing from the air, which will next be considered.

The Threat of Bombing

World War II was the first war in which we had effective, systematic bombing of cities on a large scale. As the war went on, the bombing became more destructive. The bombing of English cities by the German rocket bomb was more destructive than the bombing of Dutch and French cities early in the war. Then huge fleets of B-29's with great bomb loads caused even more extensive and complete damage in Japanese cities. Finally, the two atomic bombs, dropped on Hiroshima and Nagasaki, killed 70,000 people, injured 120,000, and made 290,000 homeless. If the war had lasted five years longer, it is staggering to think how destructive bombing might have been.

In the United States, the fear of bombing of American cities was not great in the early stages of the war. Later, with the development of the long-range bomber of the B-29 type and projected plans for planes of even longer range, people began to feel that in another war the oceans would not protect the United States from bombing. Reports of German plans, discovered after Germany's surrender, to build rockets which would cross the Atlantic Ocean in seventeen minutes further increased this feeling. The prospect of a future combination of the atomic bomb and the rocket into one long-range projectile which could be directed by remote control to its target was a sobering thought. The question is, What effect will the threat of these future types of aerial destruction have upon urban communities during years of peace?

Possibilities of Escaping Bombing

The terrible destructiveness of the atomic bomb might be averted by agreements among nations not to use it in future wars. Or nations might not use it through fear of retaliation or because of a widespread revolt of sentiment against such a weapon.

Poison gas and bacterial warfare were not used in World War II, whatever the reason.

Another possibility is that war may be banished by an agreement of states or by a newly created world state, so that there would be no occasion for the use of the atomic bomb. In both this possibility and the first one, cities in peacetime would be unaffected, for the threat would be felt to have been removed.

A third possibility is that an effective means of defense against rockets may be found. In the history of warfare, methods of defense have been developed sooner or later for every new method of offense. These methods often do not provide perfect defense, but they yield a chance of some degree of safety. If some electronic device were able to deflect the rocket from its course, or to prevent the explosion of the atomic bomb, the pressure for changes in cities would be less. There apparently is not even a theory for such a defense at present.

Various Urban Adjustments

If, however, none of these possibilities develop — that is, of non-utilization of the atomic and rocket bombs, a world state, or an effective defensive weapon — then there are five courses of action that may be taken by cities.

Wider Spacing of a City's Population

One of these possibilities is the redistribution of the population and buildings of a large city over a much wider area, so that the density would be greatly reduced. For instance, a city of two million population might be distributed into one hundred cities of twenty thousand each. An undertaking of this kind for existing cities would be tremendous in view of the difficulty of moving buildings and large masses of people. The expense involved would be very great, and existing property values would be destroyed. More extensive systems of local transportation would be required, and many more units of public utilities would have to be built.

Such a program could be carried out only with a strong belief in the imminence of bomb destruction and under the guidance of a strong central government. Human beings have at times done very heroic tasks to escape destruction. The Pueblo Indians of the southwestern United States built whole towns in excavations high up in the sheer cliffs of canyons to escape the attacks of their enemies. It was perhaps as difficult an undertaking for them with their meager tools as to move our big cities would be for us with our marvelous wealth and technology.

The decentralization of our cities into smaller units could be planned over a series of years, since the world is too weary to fight another war soon. The effect of the railroad, the automobile, and the helicopter, as previously shown, is to disperse the buildings and people of cities, but the process is slow, and the normally expected result even over a long period of years will hardly be carried far enough to afford protection against modern bombing. A more concerted program, backed by a strong public desire to accomplish the task, would be necessary to carry out an effective wider spacing of a city's population.

Moving Underground

Another course of action is to move cities underground to some degree. Underground buildings afford perfect concealment and a considerable degree of protection if the excavations are deep enough. Modern science enables underground buildings to be well ventilated, lighted, and well constructed. That people would live underground for several decades between wars hardly seems probable, especially since it would be simpler to disperse the population while the war is being fought. However, there are some vital facilities, such as central electric stations, water supplies, railroad stations, and factories, which might be placed underground, or underground quarters could be set aside for use in case of war. The list of activities for which emergency underground provision may be needed will be found to be quite extensive, even if there is some degree of urban dispersion. Planning of this nature may occur.

New Types of Construction

A third possible means of protection of cities against bombing is the construction of stronger and more stable buildings in view of the fact that not all bombs will be atomic bombs, and incendiary bombs, gas bombs, chemical bombs, and other types will still be used. Steel-frame houses and buildings are much more resistant to shock than are brick buildings, and less susceptible to fire than wooden ones. A large amount of destruction from bombing in World War II has been caused by the collapse of a building of stone or bricks onto another building or into a street. It has been estimated that if a six-hundred-pound bomb of TNT landed on top of a structure such as the Empire State Building, it would destroy only the top four or five floors, while a four-thousand-pound bomb would destroy only eight or nine floors.[1] Dwelling houses can be built with stronger structures and with a room or basement of fire-resistant material.

New buildings, as they are constructed in the normal course of events, may be set somewhat farther from other buildings than has been the practice, even if there is not a planned and extensive dispersal of city buildings. Suburban buildings have been somewhat more widely spaced, but such spacing has not occurred in the center of cities where land is at a premium and where short distances are desirable for pedestrians. With increased means of local transportation stimulating suburban growth, some degree of increased spacing of buildings may result, in combination with the influence of prospective bombing.

Plans for a Wartime Evacuation

A fourth course of action for cities is the planning for a dispersal of buildings and people when a war comes, rather than in peacetime. This was mentioned in connection with planning for underground factories in wartime. Such plans need not be confined to underground constructions, but may include the dispersal of populations as to dwellings and places of work. Under this procedure, the people would continue to work and live in cities much as they do now, although the normal trend toward

[1] Willy Ley, *Bombs and Bombing*. New York: Modern Age Books, Inc., 1941, p. 114.

dispersal might be speeded. But during war, evacuation into new sites would be extensive, particularly for very essential war-time activities in vulnerable cities. Since all energies in wartime are directed toward prosecuting military activities, this evacuation would probably have to be selective rather than complete. Evacuation would not be possible in case of a sudden and extensive attack. It is, of course, necessary for a nation to be on guard against a surprise attack at all times. These rapid relocations would be facilitated by allocations well in advance and by assembly-line methods of building construction. Even during World War II, trailers were used for homes in many cases, and houses were fabricated which could be put up in two or three hours.

Location of Cities in the Interior

A fifth effect on cities of the threat of bombing is the relocation of entire cities and the building of new cities in the interior of a country. Such a movement of whole cities took place in Russia during World War II. As the Germans captured one city after another on the western border, factories and machinery were moved inland to the environs of the distant Urals. While this transfer of cities occurred during the war to avoid capture, it could not have been done successfully had not the Soviet Union, before the war, begun constructing cities and locating industries near the coal and iron ores of the Ural Mountains. This construction during the 1930's was in large part a military measure, since the new locations were rather far removed from the populous areas of the west.

The interior location of manufacturing is particularly desirable in case of invasion, but it is also desirable as a protection against bombing. Despite the fact that bombers of the future may fly distances of ten thousand miles or more without landing, it is still true that, the greater the distance, the less successful the bombing campaign. In the United States, the location of more factories in Tennessee, Iowa, Utah, and Colorado would not be a guarantee against bombing, but it would make the cities less readily bombed than if they were nearer the boundaries.

The Human Factor

The possible courses of action for protection against bombing have been reviewed. None of these courses is easy to undertake. They all involve profound changes in cities and their locations, either during peace or war. While an effort has been made to keep the discussion realistic, and to present courses of action that are possible, there still remains the question of what human beings are likely to do in view of these possibilities.

It is possible that, as a people, we may forget the atomic bomb and the rocket during years of peace, much as people who live near a volcano forget about its possible destructive eruption. These terrible tools of war will not, of course, be forgotten by particular leaders and individuals, nor wholly by the people, but they may be forgotten to such an extent that no action will be taken for protection against them. An analogous case is behavior during a business cycle. History shows that business moves through successive periods of prosperity and depression. To smooth out these fluctuations of business it is argued that the construction of buildings, private or public, should not be undertaken in boom times, but should be postponed to periods of depression, when the unemployed need work. Yet, when prosperity comes, we seem to forget these plans. People seem to react to existing conditions rather than to plan for the future. It is as though a mist or fog limits their vision to the immediate environment. So the threat of bombing may seem so remote that nothing, or very little, will be done to prepare urban populations for its possible coming. We may rationalize by saying that war will be prevented or that an international organization will be effective.

The effect on cities of the threat of bombing, then, cannot be predicted on the basis of a trend, as has been done in other aspects of aviation. The influence of the threat depends a good deal on human choice and decision. Possibly there will actually be inadequate preparation of cities for bombing, though some plans for evacuation and transfer of production may be made. The impetus for a city to space itself outward may be accentuated, and the drift of industry in the United States westward and southward from the eastern and northern boundaries may be speeded a little.

For a more adequate and large-scale adjustment of cities to expected bombings, a greater sense of urgency, arising perhaps from more experience in bombing, would be needed. The trend of government toward greater power and more functions will aid in programs of adjustments of cities to the threat of bombing.

Conclusion

The development of aviation, both scheduled air service and private flying, is expected to influence the configuration of the city. However, the change will be very slow, because buildings last over a long period of years. In the first few years after the war, the major changes will occur from the need of airports for planes in scheduled air service and from the initially small number of helicopter owners who will locate farther out from the city center in order to get sufficient space to make helicopter landings near their homes. As the use of private helicopters increases, the problem of finding space for landing and parking areas in the center of the city will be intensified. Roofs of downtown buildings and vacant lots, perhaps in the blighted areas around city centers, will be used. The greater freedom of movement of the helicopter could help to increase the number of business centers in a city, but at first helicopter travel will likely be channelized along routes, as is the automobile traffic of today. Metropolitan and trading areas may be enlarged through the development of local air service. Inland cities will increase in importance if they become terminal points for international airlines. Aviation facilities may promote one city more than another by supplying a stimulus to industry and business, but this effect will not be as marked as that which occurred when railroads developed. The influence of the threat of aerial bombing in wartime on city planning and on the location of cities depends upon public attitudes, the degree of expectation of another war, and upon governmental policy. If some planning is undertaken in order to protect cities against future bombing, factories and industries may be decentralized, public utilities and transportation facilities may be dispersed somewhat over a larger area, and adequate space may be set aside for underground construction in wartime. Particularly does the threat of the rocket and of the atomic bomb indicate the need for a scattering of the buildings and the population of cities over larger areas and also the relocation of cities well into the interior.

17

Religion

IT IS GENERALLY ACCEPTED that religion has two aspects: the institutional and the personal. The institutional aspect of religion finds its embodiment for the most part in the church which organizes religious beliefs and practices into a formal structure, with officers, rituals, symbols, and a theology. The personal aspect consists of the subjective, unorganized, and informal phases of religion. Religion, both institutional and personal, has always been strongly conditioned by the society and culture from which it springs. It is to be expected that an invention as important as the airplane will have some effect upon the religious life of the future. It will be our purpose in this chapter to anticipate, if possible, the impact of aviation upon the church, religious ideologies, and personal religion. We will consider first the institutional aspect of religion, the church.

Urban Churches

The most direct effect on city churches is likely to come through the impact of aviation upon population redistribution. The probabilities of a changed distribution of urban population have been discussed in the chapter on cities. There it was indicated that a redistribution of city population toward outlying suburban districts is some distance in the future, since it is dependent on a widespread use of the family plane or helicopter. If and when the population of the city is redistributed toward more outlying areas than the present suburbs, the church will be affected.

Population shifts in the city in the last few decades have occurred through movements of nationality groups and through the development of the automobile and other local forms of transportation. There are a number of adjustments which churches have made to these population changes and which can be made in the future if the development of aviation causes further shifts in population.

One type of adjustment is for the church to remain in its original location and to draw its members back to it. The church members may use the automobile, or in the future, the family aircraft to reach the old church which they attended before they moved out. Downtown churches are an evidence of this type of adjustment. The downtown church does not minister to an immediate local neighborhood, but draws its members from a large area through outstanding leaders and programs or through sentimental attachments of its members to the old church.[1] Some of the churches left behind in the movement of their members attempt to adjust to the new type of neighborhood by institutionalizing, by becoming neighborhood houses, or by federating, while other churches make little or no attempt to adapt to the new conditions, and die.[2] The death rate of Protestant churches is very high because the incoming groups are often European foreign-speaking people who cannot be integrated into the British-American traditions of the Protestant church.[3] In the Catholic church, the death rate is low because the incoming groups are often of Catholic tradition, and the old church is easily adapted to the new group. The outgoing groups move into new parishes and become integrated into the Catholic churches located in those parishes.

Another type of adjustment is for the church to move in an attempt to follow its members in their new locations and to escape from communities which are unfavorable to them. Some churches, in following this type of adjustment, have been forced to move several times because of continuous population shifts, thus necessitating a series of church buildings and causing continuous losses in membership. Even when the church moves with its congrega-

---

[1] Samuel C. Kincheloe, *The American City and Its Church.* New York: Friendship Press, 1938, pp. 100-101.
[2] *Ibid.*, pp. 22, 106.   [3] *Ibid.*, p. 22.

tion, the church may die because of lack of recruitment in the new area and among the younger generation, or because of disagreements and divisions among the membership over problems of moving.[4]

New churches may be built in the new centers of population outside the central city. This has occurred in past decades with the increase of suburban population. Where new churches were not established, the existing ones expanded greatly with the growth of population in these areas.

In general, suburban churches are stronger community institutions than metropolitan churches,[5] but the movement of families to the suburbs from the inner metropolitan regions may cause some former church members to cease attending church. After moving, there may be a period of hesitation before joining a church, or members may decide to take a vacation from church activities, and the non-attendance at church may become a permanent habit.[6] Or, in some cases, the citified newcomer may not feel at home in the more village-like churches and object to any restrictions that they might put on his manner of life. Furthermore, the redistribution of population may be of such a nature as to locate families long distances from local suburban churches which they might attend. Studies have indicated that distance from churches, even though the members own good transportation facilities, is not conducive to church attendance.[7] Therefore, the development of family aircraft and population redistribution may make the administration and organization of local church life more difficult than it is today. If, on the other hand, the nature of the population decentralization were such as to locate people in small villages and towns in the hinterlands of the large cities and to cause a reduction of exceedingly large cities, we might expect, on the basis of the analysis of church activities in smaller cities as compared with larger ones at present, that church work and attendance might increase. The small town or village provides an atmosphere which is congenial to the traditional type of church organization.

[4] *Ibid.*, pp. 103-04.   [5] *Ibid.*, p. 116.   [6] *Ibid.*, p. 92.
[7] Letter from Samuel C. Kincheloe, Chicago Theological Seminary.

Since the first families to move from the inner city toward the periphery are those of higher-than-average economic status, the financial conditions of the churches they leave will be affected adversely, even though only a small percentage of the church members may move. Some of the leadership of the church may also be lost in this way.

The airplane, particularly the family aircraft, may tend to exert a negative influence upon church attendance among groups where the tendency to attend churches is already slight. In general, the automobile decreased church attendance because the attraction of pleasure driving or week-end trips was too strong a competitor of church services.

Rural Churches

The rural church differs in many ways from the urban church. Its rôle in the community is more important. For many rural church members, the church is still the most important social institution in the community. As a result, the competition of week-end flying or pleasure trips will have less effect in decreasing church attendance in rural areas. But, as rural communities increasingly take on urban and secular characteristics, the church begins to lose its importance. The airplane and the family aircraft will aid in this process of secularization and urbanization of the rural community, along with the radio, the movies, the automobile, and other modern inventions.

There are a number of ways in which private aircraft might strengthen the rural church. At present, in sparsely settled rural areas, ministers often serve more than one church. They may conduct services on Sunday morning in two churches if they are not more than twenty miles apart or conduct a morning service in one church and an afternoon service in another if the churches are a greater distance apart. In other cases, the minister alternates Sundays between churches. The use of a private aircraft would facilitate the necessary travel of the minister and enable him to minister to churches located farther apart and yet visit them more frequently. Although small aircraft are expected to be affected by weather conditions in their early development, they will probably still be about as dependable as automobiles, which are often blocked by snow, mud, impassable bridges, or other difficulties. A rural minister either of one church or a combination of two or more churches would also find a small plane or a helicopter very helpful in making calls on his parishioners. This would be particularly true in ranching and farming areas, such as Montana and Wyoming, where people live many miles apart. The helicopter would perhaps have an advantage over the private plane for pastoral calling, since the helicopter could land very near the house itself. In western areas where the distances are particularly long, the airplane's speed might be an advantage over the helicopter.

Whether the rural minister will use the small plane or helicopter in his work will depend to a large extent on the cost. Since it is often difficult for rural churches to finance the minister's living expenses, it would seem that the cost of aircraft would prohibit its use until it becomes as cheap to buy and operate as the automobile. However, state and national denominational organizations often aid rural or small churches in meeting their expenses, and, if the advantages of aviation appear to be great enough, financial aid may be forthcoming. One such advantage might be that if the rural minister can serve several churches, his financial support can come from a larger membership. Even so, finances will be a limiting factor in the use of aircraft in rural churches.

The automobile is said to have led to the abandonment of many small country churches and to their amalgamation with larger churches or with village churches, much as it led to the consolidation of single-teacher schools. Private aircraft would make possible attendance at churches a greater distance from the members' homes, perhaps leading to the consolidation of rural churches. But it will probably be some time before private aircraft will be cheap enough for rural people to own them.

The Missionary Movement

A religious activity that might be considerably affected by the development of aviation in the postwar years is the missionary movement. Missionary work is usually done in areas which are relatively isolated from the rest of the world, both socially and geographically. Transportation to these areas and within them is often limited. Aircraft will bring many of these places into routine travel areas. This increase of travel will facilitate the work of missionaries in that more frequent contacts can be made with the homeland by mail and by visits. The home church can supervise the missionary work more closely and better under-stand the needs and problems of the missionary. With the air-plane, perhaps larger numbers of travelers will visit these areas on business or pleasure trips.

More frequent contacts between divergent cultures, however, may decrease both the desire and the need to do missionary work. Greater familiarity on the part of the homeland with other cul-tures may bring greater tolerance and understanding of differ-ences. When strange ideas and foreign customs become familiar, people often lose their fear or hatred of them and sometimes even adopt some aspects of them. Yet there is also the possibility that increased contacts may accentuate differences and create more conflict. Eventually, however, increased contacts will lessen dif-ferences and bring some assimilation.

Aviation will probably first bring material conveniences to backward and isolated areas. Missionaries have been increasingly concerned with improving agricultural methods, promoting better medical care, and creating better living conditions in general. Aviation will make it easier to supply these isolated areas with machinery, medical goods, and other materials for this work.

When higher material standards of living have been achieved in these regions and cultural differences diminish, a large part of the present work done by missionaries will have been accom-plished, and missionary work may decline in importance. Avia-tion, however, will be only a minor force affecting missionary work, for many other factors will promote or slow up missionary activity, such as the financial or organizational strength of the parent religion, the extent of secularization, and so on.

Administration

It is expected that aviation will facilitate the organization and administration of churches on a larger scale just as it is expected to do the same thing in business organization. Most religious denominations have national, regional, or international organizations. At present, some denominations have a relatively strong centralized administration, while others have a high degree of local church autonomy. With scheduled air travel and personal aircraft, the number and frequency of contacts between the local church and the state or national administrators may be expected to increase. The state, national, and international organizations of churches will become increasingly significant in influencing local church control and ideological beliefs, even where local control has been important. Contacts between church members at national and international conventions will be increased, since people will be able to travel long distances much more readily.

It may be that the development of aviation will contribute to the growing movement for unity, both national and international, among Protestant denominations across creedal lines. Such organizations as the Federal Council of Churches of Christ in America, the World Council of Churches, and similar groups are now developing co-operation and interchange of ideas between religious denominations. It is believed by many that these groups represent preliminary stages in the integration of denominations into federations or unions. Aviation would promote this movement in that it would increase interdenominational contacts through various conferences and meetings and facilitate the overhead administrative work necessary for federations or unions by greatly reducing the time spent in transportation.

Religious Ideas

It has often been said that present-day American life is characterized by an emphasis upon materialism. It may be that aviation will further promote this characteristic, which has been opposed by the church. A philosophy of materialism measures personal success by the possession of things and encourages worldly pleasures, while religion emphasizes the spiritual life and love for mankind. The ownership of private aircraft, like other material objects, will be greatly desired, not only for its usefulness, but also as a mark of social status. It might be concluded that aviation will further promote materialism. At least, it does not appear to be likely to counteract it.

Aviation may also increase the tempo of social change. When daily life changes rapidly from decade to decade or from year to year, it is difficult to make and enforce detailed and specific codes for conduct as was customary in eras of comparative social stability. Religious codes which set forth specific types of behavior to be followed become inapplicable in a relatively short time if the rate of social change is rapid. But codes must have persistence and duration if they are to be learned and enforced. In society today, it is extremely difficult for a minister to inculcate in his congregation rigid codes of conduct. More emphasis is being put and will be put on tenets of behavior which take into account the occurrence of rapid social change or which are phrased in general terms or principles which are divorced from specific content; for example, "Love thy neighbor as thyself."

The trend toward secularization has been in progress in urban areas for a number of decades. Thus far, it has appeared to be an expanding and irreversible process. The development of aviation will promote secularization rather than reduce it. This will be most apparent in rural areas where radio, movies, and other modern inventions, including aviation, are bringing to country people the manners, wishes, aspirations, and beliefs of the city.

As has already been mentioned, aviation may promote the interchange of religious ideas and standards of conduct between different cultures through increased cultural contacts. Religions may become less parochial and ethnocentric. Since it is the universal elements in religion which are receiving greater stress at present, it may be that the airplane will help to bring about the understanding of one of the principles of Christianity, namely, the brotherhood of man.

Personal Forms of Religious Belief

There is a type of religious experience which is principally emotional, if not purely so. In character, it is non-ritualistic, informal, and subjective. It is personal, often springing from a deep and total absorption in an object of interest. Testimonies that religious experiences of this personal sort have come to those who fly planes are many. Some are more articulate about these experiences than others. Such writers as Anne Morrow Lindbergh and Antoine de Saint-Exupéry have given deep expression to these sensations that come with contacts with the elements. The eternal longing of men to become a part of a great whole, to be set free from the petty cares of everyday life, to ascend exultant with the stars, the wind, the moon, has constantly been obscured by the great materialization in life. It is often easy to forget in cities that there are elements that are not man-made. Yet this mystical communion with the world outside oneself is given voice through the newest of material inventions — the airplane.

Conclusion

Aviation will affect religion in both its institutional and personal aspects. The urban church will be affected by shifts of population because of aviation in much the same way as it was affected by the automobile. Church attendance may be decreased somewhat by the competition of private aircraft. The rural church may be strengthened to some extent by ministers' use of aircraft to serve more than one church and to make more frequent pastoral calls, or by church members using it to travel longer distances to federated churches. The work of the missionary movement and its administration will be facilitated and speeded by the airplane, eventually perhaps making missionary work less necessary through decreasing cultural differences and promoting the material development of backward areas. Also, aviation may promote the movement toward national and international organizations of Protestant denominations. On the other hand, aviation will contribute to the trend toward secularization, which is antithetical to religious organization. While the airplane promotes materialism, it provides a means for the expression and encouragement of the emotional, personal aspects of religion.

18

Health

AVIATION will affect our health in several quite different ways. First, flying creates certain health problems, leading to a new branch of specialization, aviation medicine. Secondly, the health of the nation will be affected by the possible introduction by plane of new diseases from all parts of the world. On the constructive side, the airplane may be used as an ambulance, and also for transporting urgent medical aid and supplies in emergencies or disasters. The airplane may also have some effect on the organization of medical service. These aspects of aviation and health will be dealt with in this chapter.

AVIATION MEDICINE

Aviation medicine is a relatively new field, but one of growing importance. More attention has been given to it since the beginning of World War II; first, because the mechanical performance of the airplane has now outstripped the human factors in flying, and, secondly, because, with the growth of commercial air transportation, an increasing proportion of the population flies in the airplanes of today.

Aviation medicine is concerned with the effects on the human body of traveling several miles above the surface of the earth at high speeds. When human travel was confined to the earth and sea, there were no practical reasons to study the effect on human beings of the rarefied atmosphere miles above the earth. Yet two hundred and forty-one years before the first successful airplane flight — that is, in 1662 — Robert Boyle made some experiments which later had a direct application to aviation. He studied the weight of the air, the relationship between its volume and its pressure, and the effect of a vacuum on the blood. Later, experiments were made in balloons; experience with high altitudes in mountain climbing also contributed to aviation medicine. It took the invention of the airplane, however, to give a real stimulus to aviation medical research.

World War I

In 1916, the airplane as a war weapon began to be fully appreciated and government-sponsored research on the medical aspects of flight was begun. At the beginning of the war, the principles of pilot selection had not been worked out except in Germany, where research on this problem had begun in 1910. At first England took men for pilots who were unfit for regular army service on the theory that it was easy to ride around in an airplane.[1] The results were disastrous in terms of air casualties. At the end of the first year of the war, statistics showed that out of every hundred fliers killed, two met their death at the hands of the enemy, eight from some defect in their planes, and ninety on account of some individual deficiency, such as physical unfitness, recklessness, carelessness, etc. Of these ninety fatalities, sixty were found due to some physical defect.[2] As a result of research, standards for pilot selection were set up which increased the efficiency of the English air force to such an extent that, at the end of the second year, the fatalities due to physical defects were reduced from 60 per cent to 20 per cent, and, at the end of the third year, to 12 per cent.[3] By the end of 1917, all of the principal countries in the war had medical departments which were integral parts of their air services.

However, the problems of high-altitude flight were little studied and only vaguely understood during World War I because there was no real need for solving them, since the major part of the flying was done at relatively low altitudes.

[1] See *Fortune*, February, 1942, p. 95.
[2] Brig. Gen. W. H. Wilmer, "The Early Development of Aviation Medicine in the United States," *The Military Surgeon*, September, 1935, p. 115.
[3] *Ibid.*

Post-World-War-I Aviation Medicine

Between World Wars I and II, Germany again was more active than other nations in high-altitude research. By 1939, some two dozen high-altitude laboratories had been established in Germany, each equipped with pressure tanks. The psychological and physiological effects of altitude on men were studied. Extensive research had also been done on oxygen masks.

In the United States, for a number of years following World War I, there was not much interest in aviation medicine and there were relatively few advancements in the field. The Army School of Aviation Medicine, established in 1919, was maintained through these years, moving in 1931 to Randolph Field, Texas, where it remains today. The school has continuously carried on aviation research on the effects of altitude, problems of blind flying, psychological examinations, color vision, pilot selection, etc. A number of other schools and laboratories were working on various problems during these years, and slow but steady progress was being made in aviation medicine. Writing in April, 1941, F. E. McDonough, of the Mayo Clinic, surveyed the situation as follows:

> After twenty years aviation medicine numbers among its workers several hundred physicians, prominent universities have engaged in research in its various aspects; medical schools are beginning to give courses of instruction in it and the armed forces recognize it as a specialty and designate its practitioners as "flight surgeons." It has an extensive literature, a number of textbooks, an organization formed in 1929 called the "Aero Medical Association of the United States" and a publication, the *Journal of Aviation Medicine*.[4]

World War II

Intense aviation medical research came only during World War II, mainly because there was an important military necessity for such research. The airplane that could fly at higher altitudes than the planes of the enemy had a military advantage, and anti-

---

[4] F. E. McDonough, "Aviation Medicine: A Survey," *Proceedings of Mayo Clinic*, April 2, 1941, p. 217.

aircraft defense weapons constantly pushed up the altitudes at which planes could fly safely. The nations engaged in the war were in a race to reach the high altitudes first. Pressurized cabins and pressure suits were not considered suitable for military combat, since their protection could be lost through enemy gunfire. The human body, therefore, had to bear the effects of high altitude, and the crucial factor became aviation medicine. Since the results of aviation medical research have military value, they were not published to any extent during the war. In the postwar years a vast amount of literature may be expected to appear on this subject, revealing the great advances made during World War II.

Anoxia

One of the new hazards to health from flight at high altitudes is anoxia. Anoxia, or altitude sickness as it is sometimes called, is due to lack of oxygen in the body tissues. The air at high altitudes contains approximately the same mixture of elements as at ground level, but, since there is less air pressure, smaller amounts of oxygen get into the blood stream. In order to supply the flier with the oxygen he needs to live, oxygen tanks and masks have been devised. Ordinarily, at between eight thousand and ten thousand feet above sea level, the flier begins to use his oxygen mask. A person flying at ten thousand feet can live without additional oxygen, but he begins to breathe faster in order to get more oxygen, and there are other minor changes in his body. At higher altitudes, effects of lack of oxygen may appear which are not unpleasant to the flier, but may be dangerous to his ability to fly his plane. The person who lacks oxygen shows characteristics which are similar to those of a person who is intoxicated. He loses his good judgment; his visual and hearing facilities and his motor control are impaired. But, like an intoxicated person, he may have an increased feeling of well-being and not realize the danger of the situation. Many of the accidents in the past which were thought to be due to pilot error are now believed to have been due to his lack of oxygen. At twenty thousand feet, if the oxygen supply is cut off, the symptoms of oxygen lack may appear in an interval of from three to thirty minutes. At twenty-five thousand feet, the interval varies from fifteen seconds to fifteen minutes. At higher altitudes, the flier will lose consciousness in less than a minute after his oxygen supply has been cut off.[5] However, there are limits to the ability of oxygen tanks and masks to enable people to live at higher altitudes. Because of the low atmospheric pressure at forty thousand feet, even though the person may be breathing pure oxygen, sufficient oxygen will not be getting into the blood stream.

The use of the oxygen mask to prevent anoxia on commercial airlines has many difficulties, besides the technical problem of creating an efficient oxygen mask. The mask must be sufficiently variable to fit many types of faces. It is not particularly comfortable to wear and hampers ordinary movement through the plane except with special arrangements. Since lack of oxygen is not accompanied by pain or distress, it is difficult to impress on the public its danger. The use of oxygen masks on sleeper planes involves the risk of misplacement of the mask during sleep, with harmful, even fatal, results. The solution of the problem will be the pressurized cabin which will involve none of the difficulties of the oxygen mask.

Aeroembolism

Another result of low atmospheric pressure is aeroembolism. At sea level, the lungs contain a certain percentage of carbon dioxide, oxygen, and nitrogen. These gases are also dissolved in the blood and the spinal fluid. The dissolved oxygen is used by the body tissues, but the nitrogen, being inert physiologically, remains in the blood. As the atmospheric pressure is reduced, the gases in the blood and spinal fluid expand. If the pressure is reduced quickly, the expansion of the nitrogen produces bubbles, which hinder the circulation of blood and cause aches and pains, particularly in the joints. If one of these bubbles occurs at some vital spot, the result may be paralysis or even death. In military flying, aeroembolism is prevented by breathing pure oxygen for

[5] Herbert S. Zim, *Man in the Air: The Effects of Flying on the Human Body.* New York: Harcourt, Brace & Co., 1943, p. 78.

from thirty to forty-five minutes before going up. This takes the nitrogen out of the blood. Aeroembolism may also be prevented by ascending slowly so that the nitrogen is gradually eliminated from the body rather than coming out of solution and forming bubbles. The use of the pressure cabin will prevent aeroembolism in the commercial airplane of the future.

Other Effects of Reduced Atmospheric Pressure

There are various other effects of the reduction of atmospheric pressure. The gas in the stomach and intestines expands, and the results may be quite painful. Military pilots are kept on diets which exclude foods such as beans, cauliflower, carbonated beverages, etc.

Pressure changes also produce painful effects in the ear if the inner and outer pressures on the eardrum are not equalized. The Eustachian tube is the mechanism which allows air to enter and equalize this pressure. Yawning or swallowing ordinarily opens this tube. If the tube is clogged, abnormally constructed, or swollen shut by an ordinary cold, the pressure will not be equalized, and painful effects result. Abnormal sinus conditions will produce the same effects in the air spaces of the sinuses.

The effects of reduced atmospheric pressure will be avoided in scheduled civilian flying by pressurized cabins, which maintain the pressure in the plane at levels to which the human body is accustomed. Private planes are not expected to fly at heights over ten thousand feet, but owners of private planes without pressurized cabins should understand the dangers of flying at high altitudes without proper precautions.

Airsickness

Airsickness is one of the hazards of flying, however, which pressure cabins will not reduce. It is similar to the sickness which is experienced in automobiles or ships or other means of transportation. Its symptoms are nausea, vomiting, fear, pallor, sweating, vertigo, and prostration. Airsickness may cause partial or total disability for several hours or days after its occurrence.

There is considerable controversy in the field of aviation medicine as to its exact nature and causes.

Airsickness may be prevented to a large degree by avoiding rough or turbulent air in flying. Flight in the calmer air of the stratosphere will be helpful in avoiding it. The pressure-cabin plane will further contribute to its prevention, since it can ascend and descend rapidly and thus avoid the roughness of air at the lower altitudes. Airsickness needs to be further studied in order to prevent it as far as possible in air passengers. During World War II, some progress was reported in preventing seasickness by medication. A full report is awaited on the subject. Science has solved difficult physiological problems; but the impetus given by aviation may not be enough to solve the problem of airsickness. The solution of this problem is of importance to the airlines, since the possibility of airsickness may be the determining factor in the choice between air and land travel or air and water travel.

Speed

Speed itself has no harmful effects on man, and there seems to be no limit physiologically to the speed at which man can travel. A person travels more than eighteen miles per second on the earth normally anyhow because of the earth's revolution and its course around the sun. Aeronautical engineers claim that speeds of seven hundred miles per hour are possible with present plane designs. Planes have already traveled over seven hundred and fifty miles an hour in power dives in military flying. Speeds of three thousand miles per hour or faster are expected if rocket flight becomes a reality, since the V-2 bombs of World War II are said to have traveled at that speed. Experts in aviation medicine do not expect such speeds to cause any physiological difficulty.

"Blackouts"

Although there are no harmful effects of speed itself, changes in direction of travel or changes in acceleration at high speeds may cause physiological difficulties. Pilots in aerial acrobatics or military dive-bombing are subject to "blackouts" when coming out of a dive. Gravity forces the blood to the lower part of the body, and unconsciousness and internal injuries may result if the change in direction and speed are great enough. "Redouts" occur when the blood is forced in the opposite direction. Military pilots have prevented "blackouts" and "redouts" to some extent by changes in posture. This hazard will not be serious in scheduled airline travel, since these planes will not be making sudden changes in direction or speed. However, when the beginner is learning to fly, if he makes errors which cause a sudden change in direction or speed, he may become unconscious and lose control of the plane, perhaps causing an accident.

Aeroneurosis

One of the new occupational diseases of aviation is "aeroneurosis." It is a very complex disease in that it is caused by many factors, most of which are hard to define or to predict in the individual pilot. Doctor Harry G. Armstrong, of the United States Army Medical Corps,[6] recognized and defined it as the result of the continual emotional stress from the fear of falling, fear of accidents, the fear of being grounded because of a physical defect, the fear of loss of status and salary at an early age from grounding, and the general tension of flying. The pilot who develops aeroneurosis has gastric distress, nervous irritability, fatigue, insomnia, and emotional instability. In selecting military pilots during World War II, the Air Corps attempted to eliminate the pilots who would develop aeroneurosis too easily. These standards and tests which have been evolved through military experience and experimentation will undoubtedly be used to some extent by the commercial airlines in their selection of pilots.

Flying Fatigue

All pilots are subject to "flying fatigue," which is one aspect of aeroneurosis. It results from the stress of flying. These individuals do not recover their forces in the course of the average rest periods, and they are tired on awakening. When detected in

---

[6] H. G. Armstrong, "A Special Form of Functional Psychoneuroses Appearing in Airplane Pilots," *Journal of American Medical Association*, 1936, pp. 1347-54.

time, these cases respond to physical rest and a change of environment from flying. If neglected, the condition may develop into aeroneurosis. Individual pilots differ in length of time in which they can fly without developing flying fatigue. It will probably be more economical for commercial airlines to set up schedules providing frequent rests for pilots rather than to discover symptoms in the pilot and then provide for a vacation period.

Effects on the Ear

In the past, pilots have suffered frequently from conditions of the ear caused by atmospheric changes or harsh, monotonous propeller and exhaust noises. Noises of all frequencies are present in the plane and these create a very unpleasant effect on the ear. High-frequency deafness often occurs, but lasts only temporarily. In some persons, however, repeated exposure to these plane noises may produce permanent deafness. Such sounds may be reduced and controlled by acoustic treatment of the cabin.

Influence on Airplane Design

As airplanes become more complex, and as more and more people fly in them, it becomes increasingly necessary to design the airplane in accordance with the physiological and psychological needs of pilots and passengers. In the early days of flying, emphasis was put on the selection of the proper kind of personnel and it was assumed that they could withstand the effects of flying. Today, the instrument board of the plane is so complex that even the best-selected pilots are taxed to co-ordinate all the instruments. Since the airplane has become a common carrier, the public flies on planes, and there can be no passenger selection as there is pilot selection. Thus, we have seen cabins become closed, heated, and sound-proofed. There are other aspects in which we can expect the design of planes to conform to the physiological and psychological needs of passengers and pilots.

The problems of the pressurized cabin have virtually been solved, and they may be expected to become standard for planes which fly above ten thousand feet. As has been pointed out, this will solve the problems of low atmospheric pressure at high altitudes, which produces such harmful effects on the human body. Wind, ventilation, cold, heat, glare and illumination, and vibration are all problems which must be solved as far as possible by plane design.

Aviation medicine is also concerned with plane design in its relation to the prevention of accidents. The statistics on accidents in aviation, collected by the Civil Aeronautics Authority, are classified according to the cause of the accident. It has been found that the majority of accidents are caused by pilot error. Aviation medical experts raise the question as to whether these accidents should not be attributed to technical factors in the plane rather than to the error of the pilot. The aircraft manufacturing industry has been working on the problem of a simplified arrangement of the instrument board and a decrease in the number of instruments which the pilot must manipulate. Medical experts claim that there are physiological and psychological limits to the number of operations which one person can do, and suggest that the operations involved in piloting a plane must be simplified. Such a simplification would undoubtedly decrease the number of accidents now considered caused by pilot error.

The Future in Aviation Medicine

Aviation, then, creates a new branch of medicine. That we do not yet know all that needs to be known in this field is a certain indication of a further development of aviation medicine. New problems will arise as we travel at greater altitudes and greater speeds, and research will be carried out to solve these problems.

DISEASES CARRIED ON AIRCRAFT

Because the airplane has tremendously shortened the time of travel between countries and continents, the people of the United States are within a short time distance of the plague spots of the world. Infectious diseases may be carried back and forth from infected areas by insects which lodge in the plane, or by the passengers.

Transmission by Passengers

Airplane travel intensifies the problem of the transmission of diseases between countries because the airplane's speed enables a person to go from one country to another in a time which is shorter than the incubation period of most diseases. By boat, the length of time taken by the journey was usually longer than the incubation period, and a person who displayed symptoms suggestive of any infectious disease could be quarantined before landing. Most diseases have incubation periods of several days; for cholera and bubonic plague it is from two to five days.[7] During this period, the disease may not be recognized because the individual feels normal. After the incubation period, the symptoms appear, but they may appear slowly, and it may not be until several days later that the disease is recognized. Yellow fever has an incubation period of from three to six days; typhus fever, from five to twelve days; smallpox, from ten to fourteen days. With airplane travel, it is possible for an individual to contract a disease in a distant country and not know that he has it until his return to the United States.

Transmission by Insects

A number of studies have been made showing that airplanes do transport insects and that insects are capable of surviving high altitudes and long-distance flights. In 1931, a survey of the planes entering Miami from the Caribbean Islands showed that live mosquitoes of several varieties were present.[8] As a further experiment on the problem, a hundred mosquitoes were purposely set free in a plane in the Caribbean islands. On the twelve-hundred-mile trip to Miami, the ordinary procedures of opening doors, loading the plane, etc., were used at the three stops. At Miami, twenty-two out of the hundred mosquitoes were found to be alive.[9]

In 1938, another survey at Miami showed that 187 out of 398 planes coming from Central and South America carried dead and live insects of various kinds. Even after the planes were sprayed a half-hour before landing, 166 out of 651 insects were found to

[7] Zim, *op. cit.*, pp. 309-310.   [8] *Ibid.*, p. 314.   [9] *Ibid.*

be alive. Fewer live mosquitoes were found in 1938 than in the preceding year, which might indicate that disinfection is becoming more efficient.[10]

In 1930, a mosquito, the *Anopheles gambiae*, of the African variety which carried the African strain of yellow fever, was discovered in Natal, Brazil. Over 90 per cent of the population of Natal came down with yellow fever, and the death rate was high. It is not known exactly how the mosquitoes got from Africa to Brazil. At that time there were some experimental flights across from Natal to Africa, but the mosquitoes could have come from some French destroyers who came to Natal at the same time.[11]

So far as is known, no infectious diseases have been transported to the United States by plane. However, in 1943, at a military airport near California's southern border a number of persons developed symptoms of an unusual disease after a flight of planes had come in from South America via Panama. Each of the victims had been bitten by a blood-sucking insect (*Paratriatoma*) which transmits disease. The insect had never been seen in California before, but was known to be present in South America. The resulting disease in this case was not serious.[12]

The most probable disease which may be carried into the United States by aircraft is yellow fever, since the mosquito which carries the infection is prevalent in Central and South America. The population of the United States is said to be highly susceptible to this disease, and a human case or infected mosquitoes might start an epidemic.

Malaria also offers a potential danger. India, with a total population of 353,000,000, has annually 100,000,000 cases of malaria, with about 1,130,000 people dying of this disease every year. In the entire world, approximately 800,000,000 live in regions where there is malaria. In the United States alone, 3,000,000 cases of malaria already occur each year.[13]

[10] E. V. Welch, "Insects Found on Aircraft at Miami, Florida in 1938," United States Public Health Service, *Public Health Reports*, vol. 54, no. 14, April 7, 1939, pp. 561-566.
[11] Zim, *op. cit.*, pp. 315-316.   [12] *Ibid.*, p. 315.
[13] Malcolm C. Grow and Harry G. Armstrong, *Fit to Fly*. New York: D. Appleton-Century Company, 1941, p. 349.

Some of the possible diseases that may spread by insects are the following: by the mosquito — malaria, yellow fever, dengue fever, and filiariasis; by flies — African sleeping sickness, typhoid fever, and yaws; by lice — relapsing fever and typhus fever; by ticks — an American form of typhus fever; by fleas — bubonic plague; by sandflies — sandfly fever and Oriental sore. Other tropical diseases are spread by water, milk, and other beverages, and by all kinds of food. Such diseases are typhoid fever, amoebic dysentery, amoebic liver abscess, undulant fever, cholera, and dysentery.[14]

Control up to the Present

As early as in 1933, the problem of diseases carried on planes was recognized, and international control was instituted by the International Sanitary Convention for Aerial Navigation at The Hague in April of that year. Although the problems were discussed in common, the actual applications of the measures adopted were left up to the individual countries. The aim was to make the regulations uniform and to prevent inconveniences and loss of time as far as possible, yet with a maximum of protection.

In England, measures for the control of diseases carried on planes were already highly developed before World War II because Imperial Airways flew to and from countries where there was cholera, smallpox, typhus, yellow fever, and malaria. These measures were as follows.[15] An airplane departing from areas known to have such diseases was required to have the crew and passengers physically examined if there were any suspicious circumstances. Any person known or suspected of having an infectious disease was not permitted to leave by plane. Also, people known to have been exposed to such diseases were not permitted to fly unless they had been vaccinated or inoculated against the particular disease to which they had been exposed. The medical officer at the airport was responsible for seeing that no infected

[14] Ibid.
[15] H. E. Whittingham, "Preventive Medicine in Relation to Aviation," Proceedings of the Royal Society of Medicine (United Services Section), vol. 32, pp. 455-472.

articles were taken on board and that there were no infected insects, rats, etc., on the plane itself.

In the United States, Pan American airliners from South and Central America are sprayed with an insecticide shortly before arrival in this country. The crew and passengers are inspected upon landing and the airplane is searched for insects. The Pan American sanitary code requires a "certificate of origin" for all air passengers from Central and South America north of 30° South latitude. This certificate lists all stops and places visited during the flight and during the six days before embarking. If the health inspector at the port of debarkation finds a passenger has come from a yellow-fever area, he can advise the health authorities at the traveler's destination to watch him for the next few days. If there is a major epidemic at the point of the traveler's origin, he and any other passengers may be examined and held under quarantine.

Future International Control

It would seem that health conditions will become an international problem and that the freedom of the nations will be curbed in the interest of world health. In the United States, when a person contracts a contagious disease, his freedom of movement is restricted in the interests of public health. In a similar manner, one might suggest quarantining the continent of Africa, in which a major portion of the people suffer chronically from malaria. However, it is difficult and unprofitable to quarantine a continent or a nation.

The more probable solution to the problem is an increase in health work in all parts of the world. The international organization of nations will be an agent for co-operation between nations in controlling disease. Through it, medical information and aid can be exchanged. The countries which most need medical services and disease control are often the nations which can least afford it. In large, thinly populated areas, the eradication of insect pests is costly and inefficient. However, it may be to the interests of the urban, densely populated areas to finance such eradication. Where people live under crowded conditions, diseases are more difficult to control, once they get started. Because of the airplane, all nations are confronted with the same health problems, and the solution of the problem for one nation is dependent on the solution of the problem for all nations. The diseases of the European continent are now the diseases of the American continent. These diseases of so-called "white civilization," tuberculosis, syphilis, etc., were transmitted to the less developed nations in many cases by traders, missionaries, or other contacts. At the introduction of a new disease into a country, the results are more disastrous because no physiological resistance has been built up to combat the disease. Such resistance can be built up only over a relatively long period of time. In the future, the airplane may further spread the diseases of America and Europe to Africa and Asia. Likewise, the diseases of Africa and Asia may be spread to the European and American continents. Stringent measures must be taken if we are not to have the same diseases prevalent in every part of the world. The standards of health in Africa and South America will be as important to the United States as the maintenance of standards of health in one of our states is to its neighboring state. It is a safe prediction that international aviation will stimulate, throughout the world, programs for the eradication of many contagious and infectious diseases. Success in this program will increase the growth of world population.

AIR AMBULANCES

The function of an ambulance is to transport the sick and wounded to a hospital or other place where medical aid can be given. The two qualities most necessary in an ambulance are speed and comfort. The earliest ambulances were animal-drawn vehicles. These were supplanted by the truck or automobile when the motor vehicle was invented. Today the airplane combines advantages of both speed and comfort. At first it was believed to be dangerous to transport many types of patients by air, but during World War II the air transportation of sick and wounded has been continually extended to more types of injuries and illnesses.

Early Development of the Air Ambulance

The first attempt to construct an air ambulance in the United States was in January, 1910, when Captain George H. R. Gosman and Lieutenant H. L. Rhoades flew an airplane of their own construction as an air ambulance. Their attempts to obtain funds from the War Department for further development of the air ambulance were unsuccessful. It was in 1915, during the retreat of the Serbian army into Albania, that the airplane was first used to any extent to transport sick and wounded. Two French aviators carried twelve wounded men from Prizren to Scutari, a distance of fifty miles.[16] The air ambulance was not used in World War I except in one or two isolated instances by the French. In the United States, after that war, successful airplane ambulances were built by army personnel, but an accident in 1921 discouraged work on the air ambulance for the following ten years.[17]

In the decade preceding World War II, the airplane was used in aerial relief for disaster victims or to provide medical aid in isolated, sparsely settled regions with poor transportation. In disasters, doctors, medical supplies, food, and other items were transported to the scene and patients carried back. When it was impossible to land airplanes, food and supplies were dropped by parachute.

Great Britain used the air ambulance in transporting patients from areas where transportation might have been slowed by congested roads or from distant regions, such as the outlying islands of Scotland or the Channel Islands.[18] Before 1937, Poland had divided her territory into sectors of one-hundred-mile radius, each served by an airplane ambulance with specially trained nurses.[19] In Sweden, the airplane ambulance was used in the transportation of sick and injured from isolated sections of the country, notably Lapland.[20]

[16] Lt. Col. T. E. Darby, "Airplane Ambulance Evacuation," *The Military Surgeon*, August, 1932, p. 163.

[17] Lt. Col. David N. W. Grant, "Airplane Ambulance Evacuation," *The Military Surgeon*, March, 1941, p. 238.

[18] Harry G. Armstrong, *Principles and Practice of Aviation Medicine*. Baltimore: Williams and Wilkins, 1939, p. 494.

[19] *Ibid.*, p. 495.

[20] Lt. Col. L. H. Bauer, "The Development of Commercial Aeronautics and

Before World War II, Australia had an extended system of medical aid traveling by air for her outlying, isolated areas.[21] In 1928, the first "flying doctor" service was inaugurated, with its base in Northwest Queensland. The work was supported by a number of co-operating organizations and received state and federal governmental aid. Each of the bases served an area having a radius of about three hundred and thirty miles. The bases were tied together by a wireless communication system, with the "mother station" located in a town with good hospital facilities, as many cases needed hospitalization. The service attempted to give the very best in medical care. Not only were emergency calls answered, but regular visits were made by airplane in towns which had no doctor.

It is reported that an important result of this aerial medical service in Australia has been the feeling of medical and surgical security felt by the isolated people of the continent. Sheep and cattle men, miners, telegraph operators, and patrol officers of isolated stations have taken their wives and children to isolated areas where they would not have felt safe before. In some districts the people regard a good landing ground as being of as great importance as a roof over their heads.[22]

In the United States, a considerable amount of peacetime aerial relief was carried on in the years between the two World Wars. In the earlier years, this work was carried on almost exclusively by the army and navy. Army air ambulances were used both in attending plane crashes and for the transfer of emergency cases from remote posts to army hospital centers. The Coast Guard, beginning in the late 1930's, did extensive work with the air ambulance, especially in transferring emergency cases from ship to shore and in rescue efforts at sea.[23] Commercial airplanes were

of the Airplane Ambulance," *The Military Surgeon*, February, 1930, vol. 66, no. 2, p. 165.

[21] Dr. J. McF. Rossell, Councillor of the Australian Aerial Medical Services, N.S.W. Section, "Flying Doctors in Australia," *Canadian Hospital*, March, 1939, p. 36.

[22] *Ibid.*, p. 86.

[23] See S. R. Winters, "Hospitals on Wings," *Hygeia*, February, 1939, p. 113, for an account of some of the rescues.

also used in disasters and carried huge cargoes of supplies and relief personnel into stricken areas and carried refugees out.

Air Ambulances in World War II

However, the extended use of the airplane as an ambulance came during World War II. The air ambulance has a great advantage over the motor ambulance in military use in that it is free from the congestion of roads. In war, the greatest number of casualties occur at a time when traffic of men and supplies toward the front is at its height. Evacuation of the wounded by truck is thus always slowed down by the congestion.[24] Early in the war, transport planes delivered supplies to the front and on their return trips were converted into temporary flying hospitals to bring the wounded back to base hospitals. Later, however, specially designed flying hospitals were used to some extent.

During the campaigns in Guadalcanal and New Guinea, evacuation of the wounded was accomplished entirely by air. In cases where transportation by mule train through mosquito-infected jungles would have meant fourteen to twenty-one days of difficult travel, it was accomplished in less than an hour by plane.[25] This rapid transportation improved the chances of recovery, since general hospitals have specialized facilities which cannot be maintained in the field. In March, 1944, the War Department announced that, during 1943, 173,527 wounded men [26] were evacuated by American military aircraft. In the North African theater as many as six hundred patients were moved in one day by air. This is three times the number that could have been carried by a hospital train on a single trip. The planes had specially trained air nurses and doctors and were equipped for the administration of plasma and oxygen.[27]

[24] Grant, *op. cit.*, p. 239.
[25] *New York Times*, September 8, 1943, p. 5.
[26] The figures on total evacuations refer to patients admitted to a medical service and therefore include not only non-battle casualties, but also patients air-evacuated more than once from one hospital to another. Thus, the figures cannot be compared with figures of battle casualties. (*New York Times*, March 27, 1944, p. 6.)
[27] *New York Times*, August 15, 1943, section 6, p. 14.

Helicopters

The first use of helicopters as air ambulances occurred during World War II. Most of them carried two or four litters, plus medical personnel and pilot. Helicopters were found to be more easily maneuvered than any military plane that would attack them, but not so speedy. They were of great advantage in evacuating the wounded in areas with no landing fields or in thick jungles where an airplane could not land. They were capable of picking up the wounded almost at the spot at which they had fallen, since helicopters require very little space in which to land and take off. The helicopter's ability to fly smoothly even in rough air gives added comfort as an ambulance plane. It seems reasonable to expect that in any future wars helicopters will be extensively used to transport the wounded from the field to stations back of the lines for medical treatment. They are expected to be much improved, and models specially constructed for ambulance use will be available, carrying perhaps a dozen or more wounded.

Air Transportation of Hospitals

One development during World War II was the transportation of fully equipped hospitals by air. During the early part of the war, an Alaskan hospital was destroyed by fire. A fully equipped twenty-five-bed hospital was flown from St. Louis to Nome, Alaska, and was in operation thirty-six hours after the Air Transport Command took off with it. In Africa, they flew a complete two-hundred-fifty-bed hospital from one front to another.[28]

In August, 1943, a complete provisional hospital was moved by air from one side of Sicily to the other during the conquest of the island. Within two and a half hours from the time the move was started, the hospital was set up to receive fifty patients. Ten big transport planes were used to carry the hospital forty-four miles from Agrigento on the southern coast to Termini on the north coast.[29]

[28] *Ibid.*
[29] *New York Times,* August 25, 1943, p. 2.

Peacetime Use of the Air Ambulance

The air ambulance was used successfully for military purposes during the war. On the basis of this experience, what can be predicted for its use in civilian life in the postwar decade? War conditions are different from those of peace. Wounded soldiers in foreign lands were long distances from American hospitals. During a war, the costs of using air ambulances are not taken into consideration. But in peacetime the air ambulance will have to be fitted into an organization of ambulance services already in existence. It will have to compete with the automobile ambulance on the basis of the best type of services to be rendered and on the basis of relative costs. Special facilities will be required for the use of the air ambulance. To make a prediction for its peacetime use, we must consider what kind of civilian ambulance service we have, how much the service costs, how it is organized, and how it is used.

City Ambulances

There are very few available statistics on ambulances in the United States. The best to be found are for city ambulances. New York City has one hundred and twenty ambulances in the city service, maintained and operated from hospitals of which seventeen are municipal and thirty-five voluntary. The ambulances of the municipal hospitals are owned and maintained by the City of New York. The voluntary hospitals own their own ambulances, and the city grants the hospital stated uniform sums for maintenance. The service is free to the public except when the case is compensable under the Workmen's Compensation Law or a liability case in which damages are recovered. During 1943, these ambulances responded to approximately three hundred thousand calls.[30]

In 1934, Milwaukee was reported as owning sixteen ambulances; Los Angeles, fourteen; Kansas City, eight; St. Louis, seven; Detroit, seven; Baltimore, five; and Oakland, three.[31]

[30] Letter of October 9, 1944, from Edward M. Bernecker, M.D., Commissioner, Department of Hospitals, City of New York.
[31] Joint Committee on Public Emergency Ambulance Service, "Outline of a Plan for Public Emergency Ambulance Service," *Hospital Council Bulletin,* November, 1938, p. 10.

City ambulances usually are not driven great distances. An ambulance may be used to carry a patient to a hospital or to a berth on the railroad if he is to travel any great distance, and one may be waiting to meet him at his destination. As was found in a Chicago survey,[32] the private automobile is a strong competitor of the ambulance, although medical authorities do not consider the former an adequate substitute for the latter.

The air ambulance will not be used for transporting patients within the city, since it is most suitable for traveling long distances and requires an airport to land. While the helicopter is capable of landing in very small areas and could be used within the city, its advantages over the automobile might be small. Most cities zone their ambulances so that the patient is taken to the nearest hospital which is not far way. Patients coming from the suburbs in ambulances might find the helicopter ambulance somewhat faster, since it would avoid any traffic delays. However, automobile ambulances have special right-of-way privileges.

Hospital Ambulances

The air ambulance is of greater advantage when there are longer distances to be covered. For instance, patients in small towns or rural areas which are without hospital facilities might be transported by ambulance to towns or cities with such facilities. Thus, it would be profitable to know what ambulance services are now available in small towns and rural areas. However, there are no figures available on the number of private ambulances in existence, or on the number of public ambulances owned by small cities or towns.

As to the hospitals owning ambulances, only one national survey has been made. This was made in 1935 by the American Medical Association.[33] It showed that 717 hospitals throughout the United States, out of a total of 6246, or 11 per cent, owned ambulances, and the majority of these were concentrated in a few Eastern states, 52 per cent of them being in the five states of Con-

[32] Ibid.
[33] Hospital Number, Journal of the American Medical Association, March 7, 1936, p. 795.

necticut, Massachusetts, New Jersey, New York, and Pennsylvania.

In the past hospitals have been loath to own and operate ambulances. They have felt that ambulances were a part of a transportation system and that hospitals were concerned with medicine. However, it has been suggested [34] that public ambulances should be housed in hospitals or adjacent to them, rather than in police stations, fire stations, or private undertakers' establishments. This arrangement is advantageous, since other locations are too remote from immediate medical service and control, and the ambulance staff can be occupied with hospital duties when not on ambulance call. The attitude of hospital authorities toward hospitals owning and operating ambulances may be in a period of change.

University of Iowa Ambulances

The University of Iowa Hospital in Iowa City developed a unique ambulance service in 1932. By 1939, this consisted of a fleet of twenty automobiles, each averaging eight thousand miles a month. The service was restricted to state patients and included both the trip to the hospital and return. Approximately twenty-four hundred patients were transported each month by this service. The service was free-of-charge to the patients and supported by an annual state appropriation. The cost per patient-mile averaged about one and one-half cents, which included driver's salary, garage rent, depreciation, and all operating expenses of the cars. On the average, each outgoing and incoming ambulance handled five well-attended passengers at a time. The trips were arranged geographically so as to avoid unnecessary mileage.[35] This is an unusual case, but it might become the pattern of ambulance service in the future for which aircraft would seem well suited.

Prewar Air Ambulances

As to the prewar ownership and operation of air ambulances,

---

[34] Joint Committee on Public Emergency Ambulance Service, *op. cit.*, p. 10.
[35] *Hospital Management*, July, 1939, p. 19.

there is likewise little information. In the early 1920's, O. J. Whitney, Inc., had charter ambulance services.[36] They achieved spectacular results in flying pneumonia serums, special supplies for a flooded area, and other unusual cases. Some private planes for charter were convertible into ambulance planes. One Chicago undertaking establishment, for instance, which had ambulance service, had a special arrangement with the owner of a private charter plane. The automobile ambulance of the funeral home transported the patient to the airport, where he was transferred to a cot which fitted into the plane after the removable seats were taken out.

Many patients traveling by air use the regular airlines, although only ambulatory patients are allowed on the scheduled airlines. In 1943, 13,257 persons traveled by air to and from Mayo's Clinic in Rochester, Minnesota. Almost all of these patients were ambulatory and used the regular methods of transportation to and from the airport, which is only ten minutes from the Mayo Clinic. In those instances in which an ambulance was necessary, the ambulances were furnished by the Mayo Clinic. Ambulance planes from different parts of the country have transported patients to and from Rochester in a number of instances.

Need for Ambulances

Ambulances are needed in an emergency when there is a hurry to get a patient to medical services. This implies that there is some distance between the patient and the medical services. In cities with hospital facilities this distance is not great, and the automobile ambulance is most suitable.

Is there a need in the United States for ambulances which travel long distances where the air ambulance would have an advantage because of its speed? Such a need might arise in the case of patients requiring unusual medical services. Specialized medical care is usually concentrated in large cities where it is available to the largest numbers of people. Some medical centers are unique in the type of services they offer. Patients travel from

---

[36] C. F. Greeves-Carpenter, "The Flying Ambulance," *Trained Nurse and Hospital Review*, March, 1938, p. 263.

all over the United States to the Mayo Clinic because it has a reputation of offering services which people may feel they cannot get elsewhere. There are also other types of specialists who have skills for rare and unusual operations. Patients will travel long distances to get this care. If the air ambulance enables people to get to specialized medical care more easily from longer distances, the specialists may become even more concentrated in the large urban centers.

There is also a need for ambulances which travel long distances when inadequate medical facilities exist where the patient lives. The extent of this need depends on the distribution of medical facilities in the United States, particularly hospitals and physicians The present distribution of hospitals follows rather closely the per capita wealth of areas. The poorer states, such as Mississippi, Kentucky, and Arkansas, have fewer hospital beds in proportion to population, and qualitatively poorer institutions. Taking Nevada and New York as examples, we can see something of the comparative adequacy of medical facilities in sparsely populated versus densely settled areas. Nevada has 6100 square miles per hospital, while New York has 86.6 square miles. The ratio of hospital beds to population was 1 bed to 72.9 people in Nevada and 1 to 58.3 in New York in 1943. There were, in 1942, 631 square miles per physician in Nevada and 633 people per physician; the corresponding figures for New York are 3.6 square miles per physician and 482.6 people per physician. Thus, it would seem that sparsely populated areas are not so adequately served as the more densely populated areas in amount of medical facilities. However, the figures for Nevada may be somewhat misleading, since both population and hospital facilities may be concentrated in certain areas. The population in agricultural states would be more evenly distributed than in a desert state such as Nevada. According to a study made in 1938, there were 1,828,735 people in the United States who lived more than thirty miles from a hospital.[37]

[37] Council on Medical Education and Hospitals, American Medical Association, *Growth and Distribution of Hospital Facilities in the United States,* July, 1938, p. 3.

It would be interesting to know whether the hospitals built during, say, the last twenty years have been built in areas of few medical facilities or whether they have been built in the larger cities which already have adequate medical facilities. In 1940, 64 per cent of the beds in general hospitals listed in the American Medical Association registry were in cities of over twenty-five thousand. This figure does not include the specialized hospitals, such as children's, maternity, eye, ear, nose and throat, etc., which would probably raise the total percentage. No studies have been made showing the trends in the location of hospitals.

The plans for the future made by the medical associations and hospital committees are to provide an integrated system of medi-- cal services. The villages and rural areas will have health centers; small hospitals will be designed and staffed for the towns. These institutions will co-operate with the larger hospitals. Selected patients will be sent to the large hospitals for diagnosis and treat- ment, while the smaller hospitals and health centers will be able to receive laboratory and consultative services from the large hospitals. At present such a setup is only in the planning stage. Experimental programs following this plan have been set up in parts of New England, in certain counties in Michigan by the Kellogg Foundation, and in a number of hospitals aided by the Commonwealth Fund.

The air ambulance might be useful, either in alleviating the present difficulties caused by uneven distribution or in promoting the proposed plans. If the plans of medical and hospital experts for integrated medical service materialize, the air ambulance could be used to send the patients needing special diagnosis and treatment to the larger hospitals, and the special consultants from the larger centers could travel by plane to the smaller hospitals. Laboratory and diagnostic samples could be sent by air. If the present distribution of hospitals remains unchanged, or if the new hospitals develop in the larger cities rather than in the areas without medical facilities, then those who live long distances from hospitals or medical centers could make good use of the air ambulance if it were available. The use of the air ambulance seems to turn upon the cost.

Cost of Ambulance Service

The automobile ambulance costs considerably more than the average private automobile — anywhere from $2400 to $7000. This high cost arises partly from the fact that the automobile ambulance cannot be produced by mass-production methods as is the private automobile. Furthermore, the ambulance contains special equipment.

The regular air ambulance likewise will cost more than the average private plane of the future, since it will not be produced on a broad mass-production scale. A considerable amount of experience has been gained in the transformation of ordinary planes into ambulance planes. During World War II, the majority of wounded transported by plane were carried in regular transport ships which came to the front for other purposes, were transformed into ambulance planes in a few minutes, and carried back the wounded. Small planes of the future could be built so that the seats were removable and a cot could be put in for its use as an ambulance. The cost would be reduced if helicopters or transport planes could be easily transformed into air ambulances. If the seats in the private plane can be made easily removable with little additional cost, the commercial air ambulance will find a strong competitor in the private plane, just as the automobile ambulance today finds strong competition in the private automobile.

The low cost of one and one-half cents per patient-mile of the ambulance service of the University of Iowa was attained because the service was well organized geographically and a number of patients were carried at the same time. In order to attain similar low rates in the air ambulance, several types of organization might be used. For instance, the airlines might maintain regular ambulance routes to cities where there is a heavy demand for ambulance service, such as Rochester, Minnesota, where the Mayo Clinic is located. Or the hospital might organize the ambulance service, as the University of Iowa did. Although there is considerable resistance against this type of organized hospital service at present, as has been noted, it might be modified later.

Another alternative is for governmental organization or sponsorship of ambulance services. Even if some other agency organizes the service, the government may support it, as in the case of the University of Iowa service and the public ambulance services in the large cities. The federal government has been increasingly active in providing medical services. In 1909, it owned only 71 federal hospitals; in 1943, 827. In 1942, there were 353 more federal hospitals than in 1941. At the same time, the number of proprietary hospitals decreased by 80.[38] Public health and health facilities are increasingly considered a responsibility of the federal government. Approximately eleven million veterans will now look to the government for medical care.

In view of this trend, it seems possible that the federal government may feel that provision for public health in rural, isolated, or economically poor areas is a federal responsibility, wholly or in part, and provide for airplane or helicopter ambulances. It has already used airplane ambulances to transport war patients within the United States. In May, 1944, 636 patients were moved from Halloran General Hospital on Staten Island to institutions in Cleveland, Indianapolis, Battle Creek, Boston, and Pittsburgh.[39] Although these patients were war veterans, a precedent may have been established for federal sponsorship and participation in the operation of airplane ambulances.

Miscellaneous Effects of the Airplane

While the airplane and the helicopter enable the patient to be transported more comfortably and more quickly to hospital and health facilities, they also enable the doctor to be transported to the patient at a high speed. This is the type of service which has been used in Australia. There, one physician who was equipped with a plane covered nearly twenty thousand miles in a six months' period and treated 326 patients in that time. In general, these Australian services are like those of a country physician.

Thus, if the patient cannot be moved, a doctor may come by

---

[38] Proprietary hospitals include individual and partnership hospitals and corporations unrestricted as to profit.
[39] *New York Times,* May 19, 1944, p. 6.

plane. Or, in sparsely populated areas where there are no physicians, or an inadequate number, a doctor may make regular calls throughout the area, traveling by plane. He may also make special emergency calls. A physician in a rural and isolated area can become more specialized if he can cover a larger territory. If the territories of doctors overlap, the doctors can divide the types of cases between them and each specialize in a given field. County or state organizations may provide physicians with helicopters in sparsely settled or economically poor areas.

Although operating rooms can be built in planes, and, indeed, were used in the war, it would be too expensive to transport operating rooms and surgical facilities for one patient. Hospitals and operating rooms will not be transported by air except in case of major disasters in which the number of casualties is high and the distance to hospitals is great.

The airplane will enable diagnostic samples to be sent to central laboratories much faster than was possible previously; thus, curative measures can be started earlier than formerly.

In the future, when hospitals are built, their designers may take into consideration the distance from the regular airport, and will undoubtedly allocate some space for the landing of helicopters close to them. Since helicopters are expected to be less noisy than the regular airplane, the problem of their noise near the hospital will probably not be important.

The average physician will have to know a great many more diseases than he did previously, since a person traveling by plane from a distant country may arrive with a tropical or sub-tropical disease.

The process of specialization and integration of medical facilities in urban and rural areas tends to break down the old pattern of the family physician who ministered to every health need of the family and had a close personal relationship with it.

Fast transportation will facilitate doctors' attendance of their state or national conventions. Those who formerly could not leave their patients long enough to travel long distances by rail or automobile will be able to attend a conference and return in a relatively short time. This should raise the standards of the medical profession because of the stimulation of such meetings. Doctors in outlying or isolated areas will be able to keep abreast of the latest medical discoveries and techniques.

The trend in medical service today toward preventive measures should be facilitated, in sparsely settled areas and those with inadequate medical personnel, by the airplane and helicopter. People living in these areas can more easily travel to medical centers for periodic health examinations, or physicians can come at regular intervals to towns which have none.

The use of the airplane and air ambulance will be very valuable in epidemics and emergencies, such as floods, earthquakes, etc. Medical personnel and supplies can be carried to the scenes of disasters. The helicopter will undoubtedly be important in rescue work of persons in places not easily accessible with other means of transportation. For instance, the helicopter could rescue persons from flooded areas and quickly transport them to safe areas. Special medical supplies can be flown to epidemic areas very quickly.

Conclusion

Aviation has brought to medicine many new problems concerned with the effects of flight on the human body. Since more people are traveling on planes as passengers, aviation medicine will be important in the development of aviation. A much greater development of this branch of medicine is expected in the future.

Another health problem which is created by the airplane is the importation of diseases from other countries through the air transportation of persons with contagious diseases in the incubation period and thus not discernible. Perfect control of this problem has not yet been found. The transportation of insect carriers of diseases, especially from the tropics, is a danger, but can be controlled through the use of disinfectants and careful inspection. The wide scope of this problem leads directly to a frontal attack on diseases everywhere. As a world-wide problem, international co-operation is needed and will be created. One of the results will be an increase in population.

The air ambulance will be a major service in any future war, and the helicopter will be especially flexible for the needs of the battle area. The use of air ambulances in peacetime is a matter of policy and is not inevitable. There is a peacetime need for air ambulances where long distances exist between the patient and the medical facilities. Sparsely settled areas and economically poor areas do not have adequate medical facilities today. The use of the air ambulance depends on the cost, which can be kept low by efficient geographical planning and hospital co-operation, by easily convertible planes, and by federal aid. Regular air ambulances will have competition from private planes and helicopters. The rural and isolated areas may have planes to transport a general physician through the area and to transport to medical centers patients who need hospital or special services. Hospitals already in existence will extend their areas of service through the transportation of patients by regular airline service, air ambulances, and private planes and helicopters.

19

Recreation [1]

THE MOVEMENT toward more recreational facilities and activities has been one of the outstanding social trends of our time. This movement is associated with the growth of urbanism and industrialism. Men have always had some kind of pleasurable activities, but in the past many of these were obtained in their regular work to secure food, shelter, and clothing. Hunting and fishing afforded pleasure even though the product provided daily food. The pioneer farmers of America combined social life with home-building and corn-husking. But modern city dwellers who work in factories and industrial establishments, doing monotonous, repetitive tasks, derive no such personal satisfaction or emotional outlets in their work life. The result has been a drive to reduce working hours in order to have leisure time for recreational activities. These play activities have become proliferated until they constitute a large business enterprise and involve huge expenditures of money on the part of the public. It has been estimated that, in the early 1930's, the total annual expenditure on recreation amounted to over ten billion dollars, or perhaps one-seventh of the total national income.[2]

This trend toward commercialization is one of the significant aspects of the modern recreation movement. Homemade entertainments and play involving no monetary expenditures have been giving way to the commercial sale of recreation and the payment of professionals to amuse us. Large-scale advertising is used to encourage people to utilize the recreational facilities

---

[1] Lami Gittler (Mrs. Joseph B.) contributed material for the preparation of this chapter.
[2] Jesse F. Steiner, *Americans at Play.* New York: McGraw-Hill Book Co., 1933, pp. 182-183.

available. Publicity is employed to build up outstanding personalities in sports and in the entertainment field to attract people to attend spectacular events. Family budgets allocate considerable sums to be spent for recreational purposes.

A second, more recent, trend in the recreational movement is the use of travel as recreation. At one time travel was quite uncomfortable and inconvenient. A voyage across the ocean was hazardous and required from four to six weeks on a small vessel in cramped quarters and with inadequate food. Stagecoaches were likewise slow and uncomfortable, and they were often attacked by bandits. People traveled only when it was necessary. Then came the modern railroad, with its many comforts, also the luxury ship, and travel became more pleasurable. However, it was the automobile that contributed most to the use of travel as a recreation. Indeed, in the early years of the adoption of the automobile, it is surprising how much it was viewed as a pleasure vehicle. It helped to develop Florida and the Southwest as winter resorts. The number of visitors to national parks increased from 919,504 in 1920 to 3,152,845 in 1931,[3] mainly through their easier accessibility by the automobile. The motor vehicle was particularly used for pleasure driving within the environs of towns and cities and for week-end and Sunday trips. Automobile travel enabled people to see new and different scenery and to visit friends and relatives over wider areas.

Travel

The trend toward the use of travel as recreation is furthered by aviation, for it brings a new method of travel that affords pleasure in itself, as well as providing transportation to various recreational activities. There is reason, therefore, to think that aircraft will make to recreation a contribution somewhat similar to that made by the automobile.

Traveling in an airplane is a pleasurable activity in itself. In the early planes, as in the first automobiles, the passengers were exposed to the elements; the whir of the propellers, the rush of air currents, and the sheer drop into space when one looked over

[3] *Ibid.*, p. 38.

the side of the cockpit made flying a completely new and, to some, terrifying experience. Today, however, with enclosed cabins which are sound-proofed against the noise of the motors, with comfortable chairs, and meal service, flight in an airplane is very similar to railroad or ship travel. Passengers on their first flight are often unaware of the fact that the plane has left the ground until after it has done so. However, with all these comforts, passengers sometimes are affected by airsickness — a malady similar to seasickness in water travel. But, in general, the journey is smooth and comfortable, with luxurious accommodations.

It is in the small private plane or the glider that one particularly experiences the thrills of flying. The thrills of gliding were described by the late Richard du Pont, at one time an outstanding figure in the sport of gliding, who said:

> When you're up in a glider, it's you and the elements. There's no noise and you can even hear people talking on the ground when you're thousands of feet up. The buzzards come snooping by to see what sort of foolishness is going on and you get the impression you're pretty much of a guy, flipping around with nothing to hold you up but the air.[4]

Flying brings at times an ecstasy, a sense of power, of achievement and mastery. It appeals to the imagination. There is a sense of rapid flight, of going to new places, and of being out in the open spaces. Thus, airplane travel may be a pleasure and a recreation in itself.

The novelty of flying through space in an airplane may wear off with repeated experience, as did the novelty of automobile driving. Indeed, some consider routine flying as rather monotonous. The view of the ground is sometimes hidden by clouds or high altitude, and flight in the stratosphere provides no scenery such as one finds along automobile highways. The relative pleasures of automobiling and flying may be debated for a long time. Certainly, the automobile presents a close view of varied scenes which is not present when flying high in the air. The heli-

[4] Kyle Crichton, "Birds Without Feathers," *Collier's*, October 5, 1935, p. 19. Reprinted by permission of *Collier's, the National Weekly*.

copter flies at lower altitudes and affords a better view of forests, fields, and farms. The types of response to automobiling and to flying will no doubt vary from individual to individual.

In addition to being a pleasure in itself, aviation is also a means of transportation to other forms of recreation, as, for instance, hunting and fishing, or visiting historical scenes. There are a great variety of recreations which are made accessible by aviation. Some of these may be classified, from the point of view of time, into vacations, week-ends, and the short periods of afternoons or evenings.

Vacations

The vacation type of recreation is affected by aviation in that the traveling time to distant places can be reduced greatly, especially where long-distance travel over water is involved. When the time spent in travel to and from the destination is reduced, more of the vacation period can be spent in other activities. Therefore, the ratio between vacation travel and other vacation activities is affected by aviation.

It may also be inferred that the effect of aviation will result in vacations being spent farther away than would otherwise be the case. When vacations are of two weeks' duration or less, travel time is an important factor. So far as time is concerned, one living in the eastern part of the United States could spend a short vacation in Europe, Mexico, northern Canada, or on the Pacific Coast. The radius of vacation possibilities for an individual is thus increased several times over.

However, time is not the only factor which determines where a vacation will be spent. Budgeting the finances of a vacation is as important as budgeting time. If one spends a vacation far away from home, the amount of money spent on travel as such will be greater, even though the time be less. The travel costs alone, of a vacation spent one thousand miles away, would be around one hundred dollars. Thus, it is likely to be the persons with large incomes who will use the airplane for vacations in distant places.

The Week-End

Another use of the airplane for pleasure travel is for a short trip on a week-end. The week-end as a period of leisure is a fairly recent phenomenon. Formerly, Sunday was the only day of rest. Now the week-end period may extend from Friday evening or Saturday noon to Monday morning. The week-end rest period is a product of the shorter working week. The movement toward a shorter working week has been a trend over many decades — a trend that has proceeded rather more slowly than is generally thought, but it appears to be one that will continue into the future, slowly for some time. The movement is affected by the cycle of business. During the depression of the 1930's, the working week was shortened rapidly. In wartime, the working week, including overtime, was appreciably lengthened.

The longer week-end has been used for recreation as well as for resting. The movement toward the longer period appeared at about the time that the automobile was coming into general use, which led to a good deal of short travel and brief visiting on Saturday and Sunday. Aviation will not decrease this correlation of pleasure travel with the long week-end. Where scheduled passenger planes are available and the schedules are frequent, the range of week-end vacationing will be extended. The influence of aviation on the week-end period will be even greater for those who own personal aircraft. The owner of a personal plane is independent of schedules. He can take off and return at any time. Since the helicopter is not so adaptable to congested urban conditions as the automobile, it is probable that the owner, at least for some time, will use the helicopter little during the working week, but mainly on week-ends and vacations. Thus, the week-end is likely to be a period for a good deal of personal flying for those who own machines. Flying enthusiasts who do not own a machine may rent one, fly with a pilot, or join a flying club where planes are available to the members.

As to the types of amusement which vacation and week-end air travel may stimulate, there are several.

Outdoor Recreation

First may be mentioned hunting, fishing, camping, picnicking, and visiting the scenic beauties of nature, which are abundant on the North American continent. The plane and the helicopter are both suited to reaching isolated spots of natural beauty or good hunting and fishing areas located far from regular means of transportation. The automobile, even though it is dependent on a road, fostered this type of recreational activity. The helicopter requires no road, only a landing space; but it is as tied to a gasoline station as is the automobile.

The demand for outdoor life is evidenced by the large numbers of licenses granted each year to hunters and fishermen. During the 1929-30 season, seven and a quarter million people were licensed to hunt or fish or both, and this number does not include those who required no license.[5] The growth in the numbers of hunters and fishermen before the war was so great that it was feared that wildlife would be destroyed. Aviation can be of great aid, however, in preserving wildlife. The plane has already been used to stock streams and lakes with fish. It can also be used to feed wild game. Furthermore, the amount of land for hunting is probably increasing. With the population of the United States approaching a stationary point, and with fewer farmers necessary to feed the population because of increasing mechanization, there will be some abandonment of farms. Already many thousands of acres have returned to brush, and perhaps will eventually return to forests. So there will be a good deal of opportunity for hunting and fishing. The airplane will make accessible choice hunting and fishing areas in the western United States, in Canada, and in Mexico.

These areas will be accessible with personal aircraft to those who possess them; or scheduled passenger lines may take the hunter to a regular stop in the region, from which he may proceed by renting air or other transportation.

Before the advent of the airplane, there were a few large hunting expeditions for so-called "big game" in remote areas, such as Central Africa. Aviation could revolutionize expeditionary

[5] Steiner, *op. cit.*, p. 47.

hunting. Such expeditions are costly, but they could be made with airplane and helicopter more easily and more frequently.

Parks

The enjoyment of nature far from the habitation of man is not solely the prerogative of hunters and fishermen. The attendance at our national and state parks is testimony to the general love of this kind of recreation. Attendance at national parks depends upon their accessibility. The automobile greatly increased this accessibility, and aviation should make them even more accessible and increase their popularity. Without aviation, it is not easy for a New Yorker to visit Yosemite or Yellowstone Park. With the airplane, it will be much simpler, although the costs of travel will still be an important factor. Indeed, it is possible that the accessibility of national parks with airplanes, automobiles, and railroads may lead to so great an increase in popularity that even more parks will be needed. In 1915, before the automobile came into extensive use, there were only ten national parks, but by 1930 their number had been increased to twenty-two.[6]

There has been some concern about the effect of the noise of aircraft on the solitude and quiet of Nature's secluded spots, for these are the assets most sought by visitors. There has also been some question as to the effect of the noise on wildlife. For these reasons, airplanes have been forbidden access to the national parks, and there is no disposition at the present time to change this ruling. Planes may be flown to a near-by landing field and the passengers taken into the park by other means. But, if this rule were changed and landing fields were provided in the parks, the effectiveness of aviation in increasing attendance and use of the parks would be greater. As to the noise of aircraft frightening game and destroying the quiet, it must be recalled that the forests and other lands for hunting and fishing measure many millions of square miles, although some spots will be frequented more than others.

[6] World Almanac, 1944, p. 495.

Vacation Lands

One influence of transportation has been to develop vacation areas in particular regions. The Riviera in France, protected from the northern winds by the high Alps, has been a favorite winter area in Western Europe. Italy is also such a vacation area for peoples living in Western Europe north of the Alps. In the United States, New England has become a vacation land for both summer and winter seasons. Florida and Southern California have become popular for winter visitors with other attractions than the climate, such as ocean bathing, horse-racing, etc. The automobile and the trailer have greatly increased the popularity of these regions. What effect will aviation have on this trend?

In general, aviation has the effect of increasing the radius of travel, although its effectiveness in this is restricted by the increased cost. The majority of people who use the plane now travel relatively short distances of around four hundred miles, although its advantages in time-saving are more noticeable on longer journeys. Therefore, aviation is expected to increase the travel to the existing vacation regions built up by the railroad and automobile. Western spots, such as Sun Valley in Idaho, should be even more popular for winter sports if air service can be provided to near-by main-line airports. So also, the Southeastern states, the Gulf area, and the Southwest should expect an increased number of pleasure-seekers because of aviation.

There is, however, the possibility that these vacation areas, built up in former years, may be passed by for more distant regions with different attractions. For instance, many winter resorts are not so warm as the visitors would like. The shores of North Africa are warmer in winter than the coast of southern France. On the North American continent, spots in Mexico, farther south than Louisiana, offer a surer guarantee of warmth and sun, and, in addition, the varied attractions of a foreign land. Locations in the Caribbean and Central America will be attractive to winter vacationists. For the summer season, there are possibilities in Alaska and northern Canada, which are farther north than Maine, Minnesota, or Washington. Airplane schedules are likely to be frequent to Mexico and the Caribbean, and very probably good service will be furnished to Alaska.

In considering vacation lands outside the boundaries of the United States, Europe should not be overlooked. Europe has always had a great appeal to Americans as a place to visit. Not only did the ancestors of a major part of the American people come from Europe, but there are also many European attractions of historical, artistic, and scenic interest, as well as different types of recreation. Many of the American people have never visited Europe. However, the expectation of greatly increased travel to Europe rests upon the tremendous reduction in the time required to go from New York to London or Paris by air. There is a possibility that the travel to Europe in the 1950's may be more than double what it was in the 1930's.

Thus there seems to be a considerable possibility that travel to vacation regions more distant than Florida, New England, and California will be increased by the airplane. It cannot be said, however, with much certainty that this increased vacation travel to other lands will take tourists away from popular areas within the United States, although that is a possibility. The total volume of vacation travel may increase. Its increase will be affected by the amount of income earned by the population and by the possible sacrifice of other expenditures in favor of travel. Over a long period, income levels have been rising, and there have been increasing expenditures for travel and for recreation.

Hotels

One result of the use of travel as recreation has been the increased number of hotels and resort hotels. Hotel accommodations are needed, whatever the recreation sought, except possibly that of camping. The automobile had considerable effect on the hotel business, especially in small towns and in resorts. Before the automobile, guests at resorts stayed for relatively long periods. With the automobile, these periods became much shorter. It is not clear that aviation will continue this trend. But there will be an extension of the hotel business into those areas developed by aviation. Hotel owners are already planning expansion to care for air travel.

The automobile brought the tourist camp, the tourist cottage, and the "motel." The airplane tourist needs such accommodations outside towns or cities more than does the automobile driver, since the airplane cannot enter the center of the town as easily as can the automobile. However, tourist cottages for private fliers on the outskirts of a city can be supported only with an abundance of customers. Such a tourist camp could hardly support its own private landing field, especially if the landing strips were paved. There would even be considerable cost to maintain an unpaved, sod-covered landing field. However, a camp could be located beside a landing strip built and maintained by the government. For helicopters, which may well prove to be the main aircraft for private flying, landing space could be provided without great difficulty. One obstacle to the creation of such cottages for private fliers is the noise of aircraft, but the helicopter is not so noisy as the plane. A combination automobile and helicopter camp is a possibility.

Correlated Recreations

The various types of recreation found in vacation regions are more or less independent of the means of transportation used in reaching them, and, when aviation comes into more general use, they will probably be much like those in existence now. However, with aircraft, the vacationist has a larger selection of climates from which to choose the one in which he wishes to spend his vacation. Aviation also makes it easier for him to see and enjoy the recreations of foreign countries. Likewise, it enables him to find recreations which are unlawful or not permitted in his own state, since some recreations are illegal in one country and not in another. For example, many citizens have enjoyed the Mexican gambling resorts not far from the border. With more rapid transportation available, the accessibility of these places may entice a larger number of people.

The Country Club

A special form of recreation that is likely to be linked to private flying is that provided by the country club. Already there are country clubs which have their own flying fields. The Miami Aviation Country Club on Biscayne Bay is one example. The club is planned to be an exclusive aviation club for persons owning and flying their own planes. The runways have already been completed and reported ready for limited service to fliers, but the building plans have been held up by wartime restrictions. A hangar clubhouse is planned which will provide lounges, recreation rooms, and hangar facilities for visiting planes. A twenty-two-unit apartment court adjoining the airport will provide accommodations for nonresident visiting members. A permanent residential area is planned for club members who wish to have their homes adjacent to the airport and have their own private hangars. Facilities for deep-sea fishing and other sports are provided, in addition. The club will make passport arrangements and handle other details for members who wish to fly to the Caribbean area. A seaplane base in the bay is planned.[7]

For aviation country clubs in which the members do not live on the grounds one problem is transportation from the city to the club. The Miami Aviation Club provides transportation from the club to the member's hotel or residence in the Miami area. Private helicopters would simplify this problem of transportation.

Aviation country clubs such as the one in Miami are obviously for the wealthy, and their development is likely to be quite limited.

The Sports Spectacle

Another type of recreation that may be affected by aviation is the sports spectacle. Athletic contests and games draw large paid attendances in the United States. Big grandstands and stadia have been built in many cities. Games are broadcast over nation-wide networks of radio stations. Newspapers feature the sports spectacles. Athletic games receive much more newspaper space than hunting and fishing, although the latter draw more participants. What will be the effect of aviation on sports contests which draw paid attendances?

[7] *Aviation News*, November 6, 1944, p. 18.

One effect would appear to be to increase the attendance. This increase in attendance is more likely to occur in the case of the exceptional spectacle rather than the regularly scheduled events; for instance, in a boxing match between two heavyweights of championship quality or an end-of-the-season, intersectional football game. Such outstanding contests receive a large amount of newspaper publicity and have become exceedingly popular. The communication inventions have the effect of magnifying the stars of any entertainment, whether it be the opera, theater, bands, boxing, or baseball. The two or three top players receive proportionally much larger salaries and more public attention than do the second-rate players. Thus, a winning team in a popular sport is ballyhooed to an extraordinary degree. Celebrities, politicians, and screen stars particularly, attend sports spectacles — thus raising both their own and the spectacles' prestige and thereby increasing the attendance. With the airplane, such featured games have the possibility of drawing attendance from a much larger area than when railroads and automobiles are the means of transportation.

Sports Attendance

Whether aviation will do much to increase the attendance at the usual run of scheduled games is a question. In the main, the attendance at these is local, and trains, buses, and automobiles serve the purpose. College and university football games on Saturday might attract alumni from greater distances if air transportation were available. Baseball attendance, except at postseason championships, is likely to be little affected by aviation as long as the status of the game remains as it is today.

It would seem, therefore, that the attendance at the regular scheduled games of most competitive sports, such as boxing, wrestling, baseball, football, basketball, and hockey, will be little affected by aviation, although for international, national, or regional sports spectacles, aviation provides the means for increased attendance. Actually in most sports there are not just two types of games — the routine, scheduled one and the great spectacle — but there are gradations in between. The effect of aviation should be to magnify the sports spectacle in contrast to the routine scheduled game, just as the communication inventions magnified the stars of the theater or sports over the lesser players. Television may play an even more important part than aviation in this process of exaggerating the importance of sports spectacles.

The Radius of Sports

Another possible effect of aviation on sports is that of widening the base of their operations, especially for those sports and games whose teams travel to different cities and areas. For example, professional baseball is organized on a regional basis. The two major baseball leagues play their games only in the northeastern quadrant of the United States. None of their games are played on the Pacific Coast or in the Southern states. No doubt this restriction in area is partially due to the extent of travel time required. It is certainly easier to play in a circuit of a small radius. The size of the radius is set in part by the speed of transportation. The question is, Will aviation have the effect of bringing Pacific Coast cities and cities of the Southern states into the major leagues, with a national rather than a regional basis? The speed of aviation will make it possible for one to travel from the Atlantic seaboard to the Pacific Coast in less time than it now takes to go from New York to Chicago by ground transportation — a distance now traveled by major league teams. But there are many other factors than speed that determine where games shall be played, such as the cost of traveling longer distances, the size of a city and its probability of furnishing spectators, the suitable number of cities in an organization, and, of course, the rigidity of the present league organization. The baseball pattern has been set for years and there is no trend to help in making a forecast. So it can hardly be said that aviation will lead soon to an organization of professional baseball on a nation-wide basis, though it is possible and may occur in time.

The scheduling of college football games is somewhat more fluid from year to year than is the pattern of organized baseball. It is possible and even probable that, if the trends in college football of the 1920's and 1930's continue, more intersectional games, involving considerable travel, will be scheduled. The financing of much college football seems adequate to pay the costs. Professional football has hardly evolved sufficiently to speculate very much on its organization on a national basis.

International Competition in Sports

A very interesting question, suggested by the idea of the widening base of operation of sports, is whether aviation will lead to increased international competition in sports. William James, the philosopher, proposed international competition in sports as a possible substitute for war. Although international sports would not solve any of the basic causes of war, it undoubtedly increases the knowledge and familiarity of the various national customs among nations. The Olympic games have been the outstanding competition of this kind. In tennis there are also representatives of nations all over the world engaged in competition. Boxing and wrestling fans are accustomed to seeing performers from other nations, although there is no organized national rivalry in these contests. Baseball teams from the United States have played teams from other nations, notably Japan. Between European states there is competition in soccer. Many sports are peculiar to only a limited number of countries. For instance, cricket is played very little in nations outside the British Empire. Widening the base of operation in sports may mean that other countries may become increasingly familiar with these games that have formerly been limited in scope.

In Europe, aviation would seem to make it easier to have more international competition in sports by virtue of the time-saving in travel. There are not many sports, outside of horse-racing, in which there will be competition between the United States and Mexico. Canada already has teams from her cities competing with American teams in ice hockey, and there is very likely to be more exchange of representatives in other sports, such as tennis. As to sports between the United States and European countries, a fifteen-hour trip between the two continents by air may mean considerable competition in games and sports. Golf, tennis, basketball, and soccer are possibilities, as well as boxing and wrestling. If the number of travelers between Europe and the United States is doubled or trebled by aviation, then the peoples of the two areas will become increasingly familiar with their outstanding athletic personalities; and interest in personalities is as important as interest in the game itself in developing followers of a sport.

The Arts

The possible international exchange of teams and leading athletes in different sports suggests also an interchange of celebrities from the theater, concert hall, and lecture platform, and entertainers in general. Except in the case of music, language is more of a barrier in the international exchange of arts than it is in sports. However, there has already been considerable international travel of artistic celebrities. Concert tours through many different countries have been a long-standing practice. English lecturers, novelists, and poets have very often appeared before American audiences. American entertainers, such as Buffalo Bill and Tom Thumb, have made international tours. This international exchange of celebrities would certainly seem to be furthered by a means of transportation which will take a pianist from the United States to Australia in two days or an opera singer from Buenos Aires to New York in less than a day. Already, American booking bureaus for concerts are planning expansion into Europe, and in England similar bureaus are developing an Empire musical plan in which artists will be sent to all the British Dominions by air.[8] This program is probably a part of the general plan to use aviation to tie the British Commonwealth of nations closer together. Through aviation, musical artists can easily be exchanged between the United States and South America.

Motion Pictures

The motion-picture industry has already felt the influence of aviation. The airplane has been used to expedite the distribution of film to different centers. It has also been used to trans-

[8] Letter from Grace Nylen, General Manager of the *Musical Courier*.

port parts, equipment, and material used in the production of pictures. Motion-picture executives have used the plane in scouting for locations on which to produce movies in distant areas of the United States and in Mexico and Canada.

Will aviation lead to the use of artistic talent from a wider area? In Hollywood there are already many actors and actresses from foreign lands for long-term contracts. However, fast air travel will facilitate the process of negotiating for contracts with these foreign stars and will enable contracts to be made for brief assignments covering a period of only a few days. By airplane, talent can be brought to Hollywood from New York, Europe, and South America for such short-term employment. The increased facility of transoceanic air travel should make the producers of Hollywood more familiar with the talent in the various cities of Europe. The reverse process is also possible; that is, European companies may draw on American talent. Already, various stars from the studios of Southern California have made pictures in England.

Language difficulties will probably hinder this exchange of talent. The interchange between American and British film talent will probably be greater because of a common language. Language difficulties will be an obstacle to the employment of American actors and actresses in Moscow, Paris, Berlin, and other foreign cities, even if the financial inducements were sufficient. In view of the wide distribution of the English language, it would appear that aviation would strengthen financially the Anglo-American motion-picture industry more than those of non-English countries.

It is possible that the locale for taking motion-picture scenes may be affected by aviation. At present, scenes of foreign countries are usually artificially reproduced in the studios by elaborate movie sets. However, there has been some necessary travel for making motion pictures of the desert, the ocean, or some famous places. This travel has been expensive and oftentimes inconvenient. With private planes, frequent passenger schedules, and with specially built, all-cargo planes, it seems quite possible that aviation will serve as an aid in taking shots at the authentic locale of a story.

Recreations Directly Associated with Flying

In addition to these various effects of aviation on recreation, there are several different kinds of amusements associated directly with flying and landing places.

In the chapter on landing places, it was pointed out that some amusements have already collected around airports, such as restaurants, observation buildings, swimming pools, etc. In the future, parks may also be found near the smaller airports, together with botanical gardens, arboretums, and possibly playgrounds and golf links. The through highways connecting the airports with the city center will make these amusements easily accessible to urban residents. Those cities which have zoological gardens and arboretums already in existence will naturally be loath to change their location. The movement toward recreation grounds near airports may thus be a slow one and may not occur in all cities.

Other types of amusement based directly on planes are air races and stunt flying. Air races were held with considerable success in a number of cities for a half-dozen years or more before the war. Still earlier, particularly after World War I, stunt flying exhibitions were given in many towns and cities. Returned aviators from the battlefields of Europe did a certain amount of barnstorming from town to town and were thus able to amuse the populace as well as to gather in some income that they would not otherwise have earned. Aviators compete for speed records at air races, and various types of planes are shown. The National Air Races, held in Cleveland, Ohio, in 1939, offered prizes totaling $85,000 with three trophies being awarded — the Bendix, the Greve, and the Thompson. Each trophy had a different speed qualification and each was limited to a certain type of plane. Huge grandstands have been built, and, in 1938, there was an attendance of 270,000 persons.[9]

The St. Louis Air Race Association, prior to the war, sponsored an "Aerobatic Competition," in which eighty-four different stunts were performed by competing pilots. This contest also drew great crowds.[10]

9 *Newsweek*, September 4, 1939, p. 47.
10 *Scientific American*, July, 1937, p. 54.

It is difficult to see what the future of air racing and air stunting may be. The novelty of flying may have been a factor in the
popularity of this type of recreation in the prewar years. There
is often a factor of fashion in amusements. Certain games become extremely popular for a time and then are abandoned.
Such was the case, for instance, with mah-jongg and miniature
golf. However, in certain types of transportation adapted to individual use, racing and stunting have maintained popularity
over the years. This is eminently true with the horse and also
with the automobile and the boat. It seems probable that some
form of air racing and record-making with different types of aircraft will continue. It is possible also that the public will be interested for some time in stunt flying and exhibitions.

Another type of flying that has proved very attractive as a sport
is gliding. Flying in motorless planes reached a very high degree
of development in Germany after World War I, when restrictions were placed on aviation in general, but not on the use of
gliders. German pilots acquired great skill in flying gliders and
were able to travel hundreds of miles to a given destination and
then, without landing, return to their starting-points. In the
United States, gliding became popular in the early 1930's and
pilots developed skills similar to those found in Germany and
other countries. Glider clubs and associations were formed and
national meets were held annually. Gliding became a sport
greatly enjoyed by a limited number of enthusiasts.

As to the future of gliding, again it is difficult to forecast with
any assurance. Gliding may be promoted and enthusiastically
supported by its fans. On the other hand, the private plane and
rotary aircraft may be so popular that gliding will be eclipsed.
The number of gliders in the United States declined from a peak
of 1360 in 1932 to approximately 150 in 1940. However, gliding
affords a sense of thrill and adventure which is attractive to some
sportsmen. Although gliding has never been as popular in the
United States as in Europe, and has declined since the 1930's in
its number of adherents, it could become a fad or fashion in the
future and have considerable popularity. On the other hand, it
might continue to decline further as a sport.

The flying club is another form of recreation of the general type discussed in the earlier paragraphs of this chapter. People with limited incomes who cannot own their own aircraft will be able, through the flying club, to engage in the sport of flying, since the planes will be owned co-operatively and the club will also make provisions for the servicing of the planes. In general, the members will use the planes for sports rather than for utilitarian or practical purposes. In the distant future, if aircraft are very cheap and owned by many people, there would appear to be no occasion for flying clubs. However, planes will be expensive to own and operate for some years in the future and far beyond the means of the average citizen. On the other hand, voluntary types of co-operation in the use of common instruments, such as tractors, harvesters, laundering facilities, etc., have had only a limited success in the United States. Then, too, there is a substitute for the flying club in the private owner with his own airfield who rents his machines for sports purposes as well as for practical use. In either case, whether a co-operative association or a private enterprise for profit, the recreation of private flying is provided.

Finally, among the recreational activities associated with the airplane may be mentioned the construction of small model planes. This practice began as a hobby, largely for children. Similarly, toys and model-making have occurred in other fields of transportation, such as the railroad train, boat, and automobile. Many amateur radio sets were made at home in the early days of radio. The construction of model planes is also a hobby with some adults, as well as with children. In 1938, Air Youth of America, Inc., was founded for the purpose of offering a clearing-house for these hobbyists, with Winthrop Rockefeller as the chairman. A non-profit organization, its membership consisted of some two million boys and girls. It published a monthly journal called *Air Youth Bulletin* and sponsored a radio program over the Mutual Network.[11]

Model airplane building is both recreational and educational. This latter aspect is one of the reasons for its being sponsored by

[11] *Christian Science Monitor,* July 6, 1940, Magazine Section, p. 14.

a large number of public and private schools over the United States. With the approach of the war and the growing realization of its national importance, instruction in various aspects of aviation began to be included in the curricula of the school systems, as will be discussed in the chapter on education. For the younger children, the making of models became a method of instruction in the elementary principles of aerodynamics. This type of instruction was extremely popular with school-children because of the recreational aspects of model-building.

The hobby of making model planes is an extensive activity at the present and it is probable that it will continue for some time. It is an important effect of aviation on recreation, since it has had an influence on the recreational life of many millions of young people. As aviation matures and flying becomes more commonplace, the keen interest in this hobby may decline, but some construction of models will probably always occur. Toy planes will undoubtedly be sold for an indefinite time and model-building may become a permanent feature of our educational system.

Impact on Other Recreations

In the preceding paragraphs, a number of possible effects of aviation in increasing and developing various types of recreations have been discussed. In the main, these have been additions to the existing stock of recreations, but aviation may also cause a diminution of activity in other lines. Various amusements compete for our time and money, and in this competition some may give way to those fostered by aviation.

Very little can be said with much assurance on this point. One might speculate in regard to yachting and motor-boating. No doubt there are enthusiasts of these sports who would never give them up for flying. On the other hand, there are some persons who own an automobile and a yacht who would not give up an automobile and would hesitate to take on a plane in addition, but who might consider substituting a plane for a yacht. Motor-boating and sailing are enjoyed, too, at much the same non-working hours as the recreational use of aircraft. Therefore, it may be questioned whether the recreation of boating may not either diminish or else have a slower rate of growth than it would if private flying did not exist.

The impact of aviation on recreation may also operate to reduce somewhat the amount of time spent in pleasure driving in automobiles, especially for those who have large incomes. The effect may not be so much on the number of automobiles owned as on the amount of their use.

It is doubtful whether aviation will reduce to any great extent the recreational hours spent at home. It is quite probable that television receiving sets will be marketed at about the same time as private aircraft. Television is expected to prove to be a home attraction of strong appeal. Then, too, there are other inventions that will add to the pleasures in the home. But certainly the use of aviation for week-ends and vacations will reduce to a certain extent the time spent at home.

The expenditure for the purchase and maintenance of aircraft will not all come from surplus income. Many of these expenditures for planes and rotary aircraft will be made possible by economies in regular types of expenditures. These sacrifices may not all be made from expenditures for other recreations. They may also be made, for instance, from savings or from expenditures for adornment; but many will undoubtedly come from economies in expenditures on other types of recreation.

In some cases, other recreations will be stimulated rather than reduced by aviation. Such will be the case of those recreations that are correlated with aviation. Outstanding among these will be tourism. Aviation is expected to increase the expenditures for sightseeing; for visiting historical sites, locations of scenic beauty, art galleries and museums; for participating in the night life of other countries, and games of chance; attending horse-races, etc. Also, it seems probable that it will have a stimulating effect on the following of outdoor sports, such as camping, horseback riding, hiking, hunting, fishing, etc., which require forests, streams, or other favored spots of nature.

Conclusion

The most important influence of aviation on recreation is that it will increase the amount of travel for pleasure, as did the auto-mobile. This travel is expected to occur on week-ends and in vacation periods. Tourist travel in foreign lands and in distant parts of the United States will be stimulated. Vacation lands in Canada, Mexico, and in and around the Caribbean Sea are likely to be attractive to Americans on vacation, in addition to the popular vacation spots in the United States. Attendance at our national parks will be increased. In the field of competitive sports, the big-spectacle events will be favored by aviation; the attendance at most regular, routine contests will probably be little affected. Over a long period of time, sports may come to have a wider base of operation; teams will travel longer distances to compete. International competition in sports is expected to increase. In the arts, more frequent interchange of artists between nations is clearly indicated, especially in the field of music, where language is less of a barrier. Motion-picture talent may be drawn more readily from larger areas, and it is possible that taking shots on distant locations will be facilitated by aviation. Recreations are likely to be developed around airports, such as restaurants, observation rooms, parks, zoological gardens, aboretums, and possibly swimming pools, tennis courts, and golf links. For a time, at least, there will be air racing and stunting. The construction of model planes will bring amusement to millions of youths and to many adults. Flying clubs may have only a brief extension into the future. The impact of aviation on other types of recreation may depress the growth of sailing, yachting, and motor-boating. There is likely to be some sacrifice in time given to automobiling in favor of flying. On the other hand, some sports will be accelerated, especially those associated with tourism and outdoor sports.

20

Crime [1]

ALL SOCIETIES of peoples have values or norms by which they define certain types of nonconforming behavior as antisocial or criminal. Some types of behavior are considered right and proper; others are prohibited. Any major changes in the pattern of living, such as a new transportation system, may change the existing definitions of right and wrong and bring new ways of accomplishing antisocial or criminal acts. Both the railroad and the automobile made an imprint on the structure of crime. Railroad trains, during the early settlement of the United States, were the object of attack by criminals who robbed passengers and cars carrying mail, freight, and express. On the other hand, the railroads helped to break up outlawry in the Western territory of the United States by decreasing its isolation from established government in the East. Both express and freight trains have been used by criminals as means of escape. Railroad transportation has affected the problems of jurisdiction and extradition. A special class of police was created by the federal government to deal with mail robberies. Finally, coming under the concept of "white-collar crime," [2] there were exploiters and promoters of railroads who broke the laws.

The automobile has had an effect on crime in that it has provided a quick means of escape for criminals and has also been a means of their capture. It has been an object of theft on a large scale, and an increase in judicial machinery has been necessary to

---

[1] George B. Vold, Professor of Sociology of the University of Minnesota, aided in the preparation of this chapter.

[2] A form of crime involving the manipulation of business in such ways that profit will ensue from "sharp" practices, such as fee-splitting, rebates and concealed dividends, protective associations, misrepresentation in advertising, etc.

deal with it. Automobiles have created traffic problems and special courts have been set up to handle the violations of automobile regulations. The truck was a tool of rum-runners in the days of national prohibition; and the private automobile is said to have been a factor in encouraging lawlessness in youth.

Like the automobile and the railroad, it seems probable that aircraft will have an influence on crime and law enforcement. In general, much of the influence is not expected to be felt, in so far as it involves the personal plane or helicopter, until aviation has become rather fully developed. Therefore, its influence during the first postwar decade may be little. However, scheduled air passenger traffic may soon affect some types of criminal behavior, although there is a lag between the direct use of an invention and its indirect effect upon a type of behavior.

. Some types of crime will not be affected at all by aviation, or only very slightly. We shall proceed by considering the direct uses of aircraft in transporting illegal goods or criminals, and then some of aviation's indirect effects on crime, concluding with a discussion of its uses by the agents of law enforcement.

Smuggling

The smuggling of goods or persons across national boundaries without payment of customs duties or contrary to immigration laws is closely related to the means of transportation available. The airplane is an additional means for avoiding inspection or the payment of charges. In so far as aviation increases the volume of international travel, the probability of illegal entries is increased. The increased speed of air travel, in comparison to that of ships and railroads, will probably be a factor in reducing the amount of time required for inspection at points of entry. The traveling public which uses air transportation will dislike long delays with customs officials and will exert pressure to reduce the time consumed in inspection and payment of duties. This increased hurry in customs inspection will aid in the successful concealment of articles.

On the other hand, airline travel may deter smuggling to some extent because of the differences in personnel on planes as compared with ships. The better-trained, higher-paid personnel of a plane will be less susceptible to bribery, it is argued, than is the case with those performing more menial tasks on ships at lower wages. Whether a cabin boy would be more likely to aid in smuggling than a pilot, is, of course, a question.

A greater opportunity for smuggling appears to lie with the use of the private small plane or helicopter. The airplane will be less useful for smugglers than the helicopter, since the plane will have to land at an air strip, park, or port where it could be rather easily detected. Planes can, of course, land and take off from open fields and, in the future, perhaps from short, one-way landing strips, but the helicopter is more versatile than the plane.

Across the borders to the north and south of us, more petty smuggling will occur over regularly traveled routes and between cities and towns rather than in unpopulated areas. Such crossings of boundaries are more likely to occur between Toronto and Detroit than they are across the long northern border of sparsely settled Montana. Patrols at those air highways would be most effective. But if the smuggled goods are very valuable, then a long and costly détour may be worth the price. Such might be the case in smuggling in aliens or such light-weight goods of high value as opium. The cargo could be delivered quickly at an appointed place and time from an aircraft which could return immediately across the border.

In the 1920's, when the sale and manufacture of liquor was illegal, there was much smuggling across the border. The most common source of entry was by water route, with small boats landing cargoes of liquor at isolated points. Airplanes were used to a very limited extent. Liquor and beer are bulky products which are better suited to trucks or large airplanes than to small private aircraft. Also, costs by air are higher than by truck transportation. Still, private aircraft could be adapted to such purposes and with less chance of highjacking.

Smuggling is largely a problem between nations, and in the United States chiefly between ourselves and Canada, Mexico, and the Caribbean countries. But, on other continents, the nations involved are more numerous. The question of patrolling borders will be discussed in the chapter on aviation's effect on the administration of government. The northern and southern boundaries of the United States total about fifty-eight hundred miles. Obviously, it is difficult to patrol such long borders, and private aircraft, because of their greater range of freedom than the automobile, do present some new opportunities for illegal entries. It might be thought that one solution would be the repeal of tariffs which make the smuggling of goods profitable. But, because of economic and political considerations, it is not likely that tariffs will be lowered. Even if there were no tariffs, inspections are necessary, and a watch must be kept for stolen goods.

Disposal of Stolen Goods

Detection of stolen goods is of the same general nature as the detection of illegal, smuggled goods, except that most stolen goods do not cross national boundary lines. The problem of selling such goods is a serious one for criminals. It has been solved in the past by the creation of an illegal occupation, the operator of which is known in criminal language as a "fence." The truck and the automobile have been useful in the transportation of stolen goods. Aircraft will have some superiority over the automobile in the disposal of such goods because it can move "hot" goods to distant markets with greater speed. Jewelry, bonds, and other goods of high value per pound will probably be the most common illegal goods sent by aircraft. When helicopters become sufficiently common, so that the movements of any particular one are not conspicuous, they will probably escape detection more easily than the automobile does today. Thus, aviation aids criminals in the disposal of stolen goods and creates new needs for their detection and apprehension.

Location of Illegal Activities

Certain illegal businesses continue to operate to a limited degree despite the law. The outstanding activities of this kind in the United States are certain types of gambling, prostitution, and the sale of liquor in communities and states where it is illegal. These activities are often not thought of as criminal, since they are permitted by law in many countries. Furthermore, some of them are permitted at one time and declared illegal at another. How will these activities be affected by aviation?

Gambling is illegal in many cities and communities. In cities where the police are effective in prohibiting gambling, citizens who like to gamble may seek opportunities to play games of chance outside the area. Gambling rooms have been located on ships outside the country's jurisdiction or across the border in Mexico. Sometimes, suburbs adjacent to a city prohibiting gambling may permit gambling and attract customers from the large city. These gambling establishments depend on transportation to bring their customers. Aircraft will extend the range of this business except in the cases where the gambling is done in or quite near the city. Consider the case of Las Vegas, Nevada, which has a very large number of gambling places and various other attractions. Aircraft may enable Las Vegas to draw more customers from California cities, and from other areas as well. Reno, Nevada, is a similar case. There are some Mexican towns that specialize in gambling. Aviation will enable such places to intensify their specialization.

The question might be asked whether this concentration of gambling in a few centers will encourage its prohibition elsewhere. This is not necessarily the result. The large gambling centers will be patronized by the wealthy classes who gamble large sums of money and can afford to travel long distances to find opportunities to play. Many who gamble have neither the money nor the time to go so far. Some gambling rings operate on the basis of two-dollar or smaller bets by the individual customer. Thus, specialization may not mean its prohibition elsewhere. Indeed, there is the possibility that the stimulation of a recreation in one place may lead to its stimulation in other areas. Other cities may desire to have the same benefits from gambling and lax laws that Las Vegas receives.

Prostitution appears to be somewhat different from gambling in its future relation to aviation. No towns specialize in prostitution, although during the war cities near army camps and industrial boom towns had extra large numbers of prostitutes. Prostitution exists in all large cities, and the vigilance of the police varies from one city to another. At one time, the vice was segregated in certain districts. This pattern of segregated districts has been broken up in almost every city. The scattering of prostitutes from one center occurred about the time that the automobile was coming into use and suburbs were beginning to develop. It is not known that the automobile was a contributing factor, but it did make the prostitutes in more outlying areas accessible to city customers. Tourist camps and roadhouses have been connected with prostitution. Automobile trailers, sometimes used for prostitution, have increased the mobility of the prostitutes.

It does not appear that the distribution of prostitution would be affected very much by aircraft. For the individual customer, there is no particular advantage in seeking a large-scale organization of prostitution as there is in gambling. In cities specializing in gambling and other amusements, there are probably more than the usual quota of prostitutes. If aviation helps to increase the number of customers in these places, the number of prostitutes may be expected to increase also. On the whole, however, the future influence of aviation on prostitution appears to be slight.

If the sale of liquor were prohibited for the whole United States or for large parts of it, then it seems probable that aircraft would be used either to bring in liquor illegally or to take customers to a place where liquor could legally be purchased. The automobile served such purposes during the prohibition era. But with the sale of liquor permitted in most of our large cities, the question becomes, Will those in areas where the sale of liquor is banned use aviation in going to cities where liquor can be bought? This would hardly seem to be the case in view of the ease with which bootleggers can bring liquor into areas where its sale is prohibited, and in view of the costs to the individual of an air journey. However, the prospects of obtaining liquor may be an added incentive to travel to a particular place, but perhaps this will seldom be the determining factor.

The airplane, then, makes the dweller in an area where gambling, prostitution, and taverns are prohibited a little less confined by the restrictions. Aviation is expected to encourage the growth of those cities and towns that specialize in these activities, which are restricted in many communities in the United States.

The Transportation of Criminals

The criminal is usually in haste to get away from the city in which he has committed a crime. He has found the automobile and all forms of transportation useful to this end. Since airplanes provide the fastest type of long-distance transportation, they should be useful to the fleeing criminal. They have already been used to some extent to transport criminals from one point to another for the purpose of committing offenses. Sampsell and McNab, two notorious Western bank bandits, by operating in one state on a certain day and then repeating the operation in another state on the following day, fooled the officials for several months.[3]

The scheduled airlines probably have little advantage over other common carriers, unless the criminal is traveling a long distance. Private aircraft, if available, would be more suitable, since the scheduled airlines can be easily checked by the police. However, private aircraft will be rather conspicuous and easily observable until the time when they become quite common. They will probably be more useful to the criminal world than the scheduled airlines, just as the private automobile has more advantages than the bus lines. The automobile can be parked close to the place of the crime ready for escape. Aircraft are not quite so convenient in this regard, except possibly the helicopter. They have an advantage over automobiles in that they are not confined to a highway and enable the criminal to escape in any direction, thus making it more difficult for the police to pursue them, although the police will also have planes for pursuit.

Criminals often attempt to escape into a foreign country because co-operation between law-enforcement agencies is more difficult between two countries than between states within a nation, especially if different languages are spoken. Since aviation draws all countries of the world closer together, there may be an increase in the number of criminals escaping to foreign countries.

Aviation as a means of escape will not be open to the petty

[3] Letter from August Vollmer, Berkeley, California, February 1, 1945.

criminal because of the high costs. It is rather for those who participate in crimes involving large amounts of money. The activities of these criminals are often not confined to one city. Thus, to a gangster who operates in several cities, a quick means of transportation between cities will be an advantage. If aviation favors the travel of business executives, it should also encourage the travel of the executives of the criminal underworld.

The discussion so far has concerned aviation as a means of transporting illegal goods and criminals. A resulting influence of this use of aviation is the increasing development of organized crime.

Organized Crime

There are few lone criminals. Juvenile delinquency often develops from gang activities, and adult criminals usually maintain some kind of group organization. The planning and execution of crime, the disposition of the goods, and the protection from the police and the courts are all better accomplished if there is an organization. One of the outstanding characteristics of professional crime is the magnitude of its field of operation, frequently including many cities and sometimes being on a national or international scale. A criminal syndicate controlling slot machines, for instance, is often a carefully organized business concern with corresponding subdivisions of duties and personnel. Just as any large business has its district managers, office workers, salesmen, and collectors, so the slot-machine "rackets" have organized territories with a hierarchy of personnel, each dependent upon the other and all loyal to the syndicate. The organizations of such criminal activities as gambling, prostitution, or the sale of liquor often approach the size and complexity of a legitimate corporation. The procurement of young girls for prostitution has frequently covered several cities. Indeed, it has been an international problem, and, through the League of Nations, an agreement was made in an attempt to control the international white-slave traffic. Bootleggers in the prohibition era tended to operate in only one city because the business was rather exacting in the attention it required for protection against the police and other bootleggers, but there were instances of operation in two or more cities at the same time. The operation of burglars in more than one city is common and means an organization of at least a rudimentary sort in each city. The unloading of "hot" goods in another city favors intercity organization; also the successful escape of a criminal from one city to another encourages intercity operations.

In the big business of crime, aviation may be expected to extend the area of operations as it will do in many legitimate businesses. With aircraft, a professional criminal can keep in touch better and more often with whatever organization he may have in the different cities. Again, what little effect aviation may have in strengthening the organization of crime is largely for the bigger operations.

Theft of Aircraft

Aircraft may not only aid criminals by transporting them and their stolen goods, but aircraft may come to be the objects of theft. Such was the situation with regard to automobiles. In fact, now there are few objects stolen as often as are automobiles. We may expect some theft of aircraft in the future. The extent of such theft depends on how many aircraft there are. At present, there are some thirty-three million private automobiles, while the number of private helicopters and planes may be only in the hundred thousands during the first postwar decade. Even if a roadable helicopter becomes practical, it hardly seems probable that the number of private aircraft will approach, in the visible future, the number of automobiles. Then, too, the ability to fly private aircraft will not be as common as the ability to drive automobiles, and hence the opportunity to steal them will be limited. However, planes and helicopters will both become simpler to fly and thus the possible pilots will become more numerous. It may be expected that aircraft will become objects of theft to a limited extent in the first or second decade after the war.

Traffic Violations

With the expected growth of air transportation in the postwar period, there will be a wholly new type of traffic violations; that is, violations of the rules and regulations relating to aircraft. Automobile regulations regarding parking, speed, etc., are broken in great numbers every day. There are now many regulations regarding private planes and their flight. Indeed, one of the reforms needed in aviation is a reduction in the large number of regulations which govern flying. But even with an extensive simplification of the rules, there must necessarily be many regulations of air traffic. There must be regulations concerning flight altitudes, traffic lanes, flights in the vicinity of landing areas, fog signals, aircraft lights, crossing of range approach channels, air space restrictions, etc. There are likely to be many violations of these extensive regulations and hence aviation will add to the already large number of laws that are broken. The violations of such regulations will be subject to court action even though the violators are not criminals.

There are various units of police attempting to prevent the occurrence of traffic violations and accidents. Cars must be kept within the law as to speeds, and congestion must be prevented at crossings, near industrial plants, and on narrow roads near cities. Will aviation present a need for further police regulation? Perhaps in the immediate postwar years there will be little need for such extra duties of the police. Soon, however, the flight of personal planes over cities will require active supervision. Already, the police of New York City have been needed to prevent low flying over the tall buildings of that city. The flying of private helicopters over cities will surely present problems of regulation. The amount of danger of their crashing or of forced landings where there is no adequate landing space will be factors in determining the laws. The possibility of the engine's stopping in a helicopter is expected to be decreased as its evolution continues. However, the helicopter may be required to enter cities over rivers, lakes and other bodies of water, and it may be required to fly over boulevards or wide streets where there are landing possibilities along the route. Police will be needed to enforce such regulations. There are also problems of congestion around landing places, problems of flying at various altitudes, and "stacking up" over a landing field. Regulation of these problems will require supervision and enforcement. Since not all private aircraft will be equipped with radio receivers, various types of signals and markers will be developed. Police patrols in aircraft may be necessary to insure that these regulations are observed.

Regulations in the open country will be less exacting. The traffic problems of the airplane in the open-country sky are not analogous to the traffic problems of the automobile on the highway. Landing places for cross-country flights will be numerous, especially for helicopters. There will also be many refueling stations. Problems of congestion around such places will not be serious for some years, and whatever problems may arise can be handled by existing authorities.

Aircraft are well suited to traffic observation of automobiles. Patrol planes, equipped with two-way radio equipment, flying over cities and over congested road crossings on days of celebrations or parades may be very useful. The problem of facilitating automobile transportation in cities necessitates surveys from time to time to aid in laying out through highways or in eliminating crossings or in the routing and rerouting of traffic. The airplane has already been used for such purposes and undoubtedly will be in the future.

Use of Aircraft in Law Enforcement

Criminal behavior is also affected indirectly by aviation through its aid to law-enforcing agencies. Aircraft can be used by police departments as well as by lawbreakers. This subject has been discussed in part in the chapter on public administration, but there are several additional observations which may be made here. Some use of airplanes in routine police duties has already been made by a few police departments, notably those of Nassau County (Long Island) and New York City. The Nassau County police first used an airplane for apprehending and transporting a criminal in 1927. Between 1927 and 1934, planes were rented from Roosevelt Field and flown by commercial pilots. In 1934, the Air Division of the Nassau County Police Department was established and their own planes were used, piloted by members of the police force. The use of the airplane for practical police activity was considered to have been extremely satisfactory and the cost of maintenance was not felt to be prohibitive, considering the convenience and time saved.[4] New York City has operated its own planes for the last fifteen years by police fliers who have flown on a great number of varied missions. These included the rescue of persons in danger of drowning, enforcement of Civil Aeronautics Authority regulations, control of automobile traffic by two-way radio, escort protection for visiting notables, recovery of lost and stolen property, and photographic missions, which included taking pictures of proposed sites for public improvements and of areas under investigation in connection with the commission of crimes.[5]

One of the trends in police administration has been the rapid development of equipment to aid in dealing with crime. Aircraft and the special equipment used in connection with them will be a considerable addition to the equipment of police departments. The air "squad car" of the police will have special two-way radio equipment to facilitate air direction of police activities on the ground. It is also very likely that some of the police aircraft will be equipped with aerial cameras, which will be useful in making records and gathering evidence to be presented at court trials. These photographs can also be used for reconnaissance purposes.

Another trend in police work has been specialization — detectives, homicide squads, automobile patrols, fingerprint experts, traffic divisions, etc. To these will be added aircraft pilots, air police, and correlated specialists.

The use of aircraft by the city and state police for the pursuit and capture of criminals is expected to increase. Speed is, of course, of the very greatest value in apprehending criminals.

[4] Letter from Harold King, Commanding Officer, Detective Division, Police Department, County of Nassau, Mineola, Long Island, New York, July 26, 1944.
[5] Letter from Fiorella La Guardia, Mayor, City of New York, July 6, 1944.

Both police-owned planes and the scheduled airlines will be available for use in this work. The plane will also be used for the transportation of prisoners, or other persons wanted, especially where long distances are involved and speed is required. Already the airplane has been of value in the search for large articles, such as stolen automobiles. Some police departments have hired, on occasion, commercial planes with regular commercial pilots for special work, such as the search for dead human bodies in lakes or along shores. An observer in a plane flying over a body of water can see into the water and locate bodies which are under the surface and cannot be seen from boats. One of the likely uses of aircraft is for the patrol of harbors to help in cases of distress and to prevent illegal activities.

The use of aircraft in fighting crime in cities may be limited because of the relatively short distances and the infrequency of landing locations in a city. The helicopter will be somewhat better adapted than the airplane for use in law enforcement in cities. If the city of the future has many landing places for helicopters, and if the helicopter is safe enough to fly with little danger over cities, then the police may make use of it in large cities where automobile speeds are slowed up by traffic on the streets. However, aircraft will be used more readily by the police covering the large areas outside the cities.

State and National Police

There was a time when law-enforcement officers were local; there were sheriffs in the counties and police in the cities. About the time of World War I, the various states of the United States began to develop state police, and, by 1931, thirty-eight states had police systems.[6] The appearance of state police was simultaneous with the growth of automobile traffic. In fact, one of their major duties is the patrol of highways, to which other police functions have been added. The special need of state police arises from the ease with which a criminal flees from the jurisdiction of the police of a particular locality. There has been a movement in

6 Edwin H. Sutherland and Charles E. Gehlke, "Crime and Punishment," *Recent Social Trends,* p. 1140.

the states to extend the jurisdiction of local enforcement officers when in "hot pursuit." [7] Under the enabling provisions of the Interstate Compact Act, Congress has permitted interstate compacts recognizing the authority of police officials in territory outside their own jurisdictions when in the direct pursuit of criminals wanted in their own territory.

Aviation is expected to strengthen definitely the trend in the growth of state police. Private aircraft will be used more for long-distance travel than the automobile has been and thus will call for supervision from enforcement agencies covering larger units of area. Then, too, if criminals use private aircraft for escape, it is appropriate that their pursuit should be by other than local community peace officers. There are also certain types of offenses occurring in rural areas for which state police aircraft would be most practical. For instance, stealing of cattle, though less common now than formerly, would be better policed by aircraft than by other means. One can imagine that, if aircraft had existed in the days of outlawry and cattle rustling in the West, it would have proved to be a most effective weapon in tracing the stolen bands of cattle and in scouting for outlaws in their hideouts. Aircraft should also be valuable in tracking down poachers and illegal hunters in outlying sections of the country. The Royal Canadian Mounted Police, whose exploits on horseback across the wilds of northern and western Canada are familiar, will find aviation a great aid in law enforcement.

The same conditions which led to the creation of state police systems have also led to the development of national police, although at a somewhat later date. It was in the early 1930's that the national "police" of the Federal Bureau of Investigation grew into prominence, although the agency had been established in 1908. In the small country of England, with its Scotland Yard, national police or quasi-police existed long before the automobile. Nevertheless, it may be argued that transportation inventions led to greater centralization of law-enforcing authorities. As trans-

---

[7] This term refers to the legal definition under which the police officials of one jurisdiction may pursue and legally arrest a suspect in an adjoining jurisdiction, provided there has been no interruption of the pursuit.

portation inventions increased the opportunities for travel, they created the need for police whose area of jurisdiction was larger than the area that can be covered on foot or on horseback. Many of the crimes which have come under federal jurisdiction were affected in some way by automobile transportation. In 1919, the National Motor Vehicle Theft Act was passed, making interstate transportation of stolen automobiles a federal offense. In 1932, passage of the Federal Kidnapping Statute and the Federal Extortion Act, and, in 1934 and 1935, the passage of acts making the robberies of certain types of banks federal offenses, greatly extended the jurisdiction of federal police. The increased use of private aircraft which can cover long distances more easily than the automobile implies that aviation will lead to an even greater need for national police.

The evidence of the need for greater centralization of police administration is seen in the present problem of conflicting jurisdictions between law-enforcement authorities of very limited areas.

Jurisdictional Conflicts

With the growth of transportation inventions, police found the boundaries of cities and counties a hindrance to the capture of criminals. Before the beginning of the twentieth century, nearly half of the states in the United States had enacted legislation authorizing a police officer to go beyond the limits of their usual operation when in "hot pursuit." [8] In some states, the jurisdictions of city police were extended several miles beyond the city limits and in other states municipal police were given jurisdiction between towns and cities. This extension of areas of jurisdiction of local police will probably not be furthered by the airplane, except possibly in the case of states, since aircraft means longdistance travel, far beyond city limits. It hardly seems practical to extend urban limits that far. A better solution would be to increase the number of state and, especially, of national police.

Special problems of jurisdiction may arise in the probably rare cases of crimes committed in airplanes. Because of their unique-

[8] Sutherland and Gehlke, *op. cit.*, p. 1140.

ness, we may consider these cases further. Under present law, a criminal is subject to trial by the authorities of the area in which the crime was committed. But in the case of a theft occurring on an airplane, the administrative area over which the crime occurred will not be known. All that the police are likely to know is that at some point in the course of the flight a crime was committed. The plane may have crossed the borders of many counties or several states between take-off and landing. It will be very difficult under present definitions to determine what governmental unit should claim jurisdiction. This problem has been met for crimes on the high seas by special courts. Similarly, special courts might be set up with jurisdiction over crimes committed in the air. If the number of crimes committed in aircraft is not large enough to create special courts, then the function could be assigned to some existing tribunal.

These jurisdictional differences in cases where there is travel of criminals has led to extradition machinery whereby a civil unit, such as a state, may permit or refuse the removal of a criminal to the area where the crime was committed. Aviation will probably increase the number of extradition cases. Extradition practices could be made more uniform if the procedure were turned over to the federal courts, but it is questionable whether the influence of aviation will be sufficient to bring about such a change.

Co-operation of Administrative Units

The flight of a criminal from the jurisdiction area of his crime to another is handled by the co-operation of the different administrative units, except in the cases where the problem is dealt with by an over-all unit such as the federal or the state police. Even in cases involving state or federal police, co-operation with local authorities is often essential. Aircraft, like other transportation inventions, are expected to increase the amount of such co-operation between states, cities, and countries. This co-operation consists of furnishing information about the presence of criminals, giving permission to examine records, supplying data about suspected criminals, effecting captures, permitting extradition, etc. Such co-operation is inevitable in an age when criminals have a high degree of mobility because of transportation facilities, while police officers are confined by local boundaries of jurisdiction.

Similar administrative co-operation between nations may become much more necessary under the influence of aviation. International travel of citizens is expected to increase, and also the escape of criminals to other nations. An international police force which would deal with ordinary crime is not foreseen in the near future because the feeling of national sovereignty is very strong. However, there may be such a force to deal with disturbances which might lead to war. The functions of such international police may penetrate into various types of civilian activities which may be thought to be conducive to the outbreak of war.

International co-operation in dealing with crime is likely to be concerned with a variety of situations, such as harboring criminals, disposal of stolen goods, smuggling of goods, and the entrance of forbidden goods and aliens. Co-operation between nations in dealing with these problems is one of the many types of international co-operation being evolved. Aviation also encourages international weather forecasting and health inspection. These activities are often unobserved by the general public, who think of international co-operation as essentially political and military. They will help lay a basis for co-operative activities between nations in the prevention of civil crime.

Administration of Prisons and Parole Boards

Criminals are sentenced to prisons for punishment, safety, or correction. Aviation has little connection with such a system. However, replies of law-enforcement officers to letters of inquiry suggest that prison systems of certain states could be administered better if there were adequate air transportation. Periodic inspections of various kinds are made at frequent intervals in the prisons and penal institutions. It is felt in some cases that these inspections are not sufficiently frequent and not adequately staffed. The use of aircraft would be helpful in getting a limited force of inspectors around to many institutions in a short time.

Some criminals are placed on parole after serving only a part of their prison term. Other criminals are placed on probation and are never sent to prison. Persons on probation and on parole need supervision. Critics have often pointed out that the supervision is almost never adequate. This problem is made more difficult by the increasing mobility of the population, although persons on probation or parole are usually required to stay within a certain state or specified area unless permission is granted to leave. Aviation will have an effect on the behavior of persons on parole and probation only in so far as it increases their mobility within the specified area. If a parolee is working in a city that is distant from the headquarters of his parole officers or is permitted to move to another state, it becomes more difficult for the officer to supervise his behavior. But it is doubtful whether the use of aviation by the police will have any influence on increasing the efficiency of the parole system. The weaknesses of the system lie in the lack of financial support, the lack of the right kind of personnel, and the intrusion of politics and corruption into the system. Officials can make trips to other cities more quickly by airplane than by other means of transportation, but, in general, the care and custody of criminals will be very little influenced by aviation.

Conclusion

The nature of crime in the air age will probably not be much different from what it has been in the automobile era. In general, the effect of the airplane will be mainly on large-scale operations of professional criminals. The impact of aviation on crime will be more widespread when private flying develops to a greater degree. New opportunities for smuggling across long national boundaries will be opened up with private flying. The disposal of stolen goods will be somewhat facilitated. Aircraft will also be used in the transportation of criminals who are dependent upon speed for successful escape. Large-scale organization of crime will be encouraged by aviation, for the leaders can extend their operations more easily over a wider area by the use of aircraft as a means of transportation and communication. Prostitution and the illegal sale of liquor would appear to be little affected, unless, in the case of liquor, national prohibition were again put into effect. The growth of large gambling centers and their affiliated activities is expected to be stimulated as a result of aviation. There will, of course, be punishable offenses associated directly with the operation of planes, such as thefts and the violation of traffic regulations. Aircraft will be used by police officers as well as by criminals. The spatial organization of law-enforcement agencies is particularly expected to be modified. The trends toward state and national police organization and toward the co-operation of peace authorities of local and national jurisdictions will be encouraged. The problems of international co-operation in the control of crime and in extradition processes will be accentuated. The treatment of offenders will be little influenced by aviation, but the administration and inspection of prisons and parole boards may be facilitated.

21

Education

DEFINITIONS OF EDUCATION range from the broad concept of total human experiences to the precise work of special agencies, such as the school or the tutor. In the former, all of man's contact with other men and with nature is implied; in the latter, the formal, institutionalized induction of the individual into the life and culture of the group is the goal.

Although the introduction of any new idea, tool, or natural event adds to man's total experience, our main purpose in this chapter will be to examine the possible effects, in the future, of the airplane on educational institutions, and their ramification. The fundamental function of educational institutions is to adjust the individual to society through the stimulation of interest and subsequent instruction in the nature of phenomena, both natural and social, surrounding him. Since our culture will include aviation, it will be necessary for educators to reformulate educational programs in the light of this new development.

The Educational Program

A great deal of literature has been published in the last few years pointing out the need of subject matter in school programs pertinent to the multiple phases of aviation. Attempts have also been made to furnish schools with materials along these lines. Most of the material emphasizes the importance of aviation in the future, its effects upon our society, and the need of understanding how society will be changed because of the widespread use of aviation.[1] Educators have developed both immediate and

[1] See *Air-Age Education Series*, prepared by members of the Aviation Education Research Group, Teachers College, Columbia University. New York: The

future programs for acquainting children with the new invention
and stimulating their interest in its many mechanical, as well as
social, aspects. Essentially, it is an attempt to inculcate air-mindedness in American youth — a recognition of and an interest in
making the airplane a living tool in their lives.

The need for fostering an "air-mindedness" was recognized by
Robert Hinckley, Assistant Secretary of Commerce for Air, when
he described the educational problem in this manner:

> The main handicap to mass flying, all along, has been that travel
> in three dimensions is an awesome thing to two-dimensional
> people. I can remember that solid geometry seemed much more
> difficult than plane geometry. The air is a strange new element
> to man. And it will be taken in stride, as a matter of course, only
> by people who have learned the principles of flying in their
> youth and have applied those principles in actual practice. After
> that the fearful mystery is gone. Flight is then a matter of some
> principles in physics, like a change in the temperature.
>
> I call this process the "air-conditioning" of people. . . . We must
> have whole generations of people who are air-conditioned.[2]

Curricula

What are some of the changes that may occur in the curricula
of the schools in so far as they can now be seen? Several definite
trends are clearly discernible. Let us deal first with the elementary and secondary schools.

In March, 1945, it was reported that at least nine state departments had already issued courses of study in aviation education
extending from kindergarten through junior college.[3] The Department of Public Instruction in Nebraska, for instance, instituted an aviation education program designed to start in the
second grade of the elementary schools. This program, running
through the secondary schools with increasing degrees of inten-

Macmillan Company, 1942. Of special significance in this connection, see the
following books in the series: N. L. Engelhardt, Jr., *Education for the Air Age*,
and Hall Bartlett, *Social Studies for the Air Age*.

[2] Quoted in Lyle W. Ashby, "Education for the Air Age," *The Journal of the
National Education Association*, vol. 32, no. 3, March, 1943, p. 74.

[3] Ray Evans, Jr., and Eleanor M. Johnson, "Aviation: Its Place in Tomorrow's
Curriculum," *Education*, March, 1945, p. 442.

siveness, is carried on into the University of Nebraska in preparation for the teaching of pre-flight aeronautics.

Many plans of study for general science courses in the elementary and secondary schools have been presented which use the airplane as the focal point. One suggested course outline includes nineteen units, beginning with a study of materials used in airplane construction, and including such topics as fuselage, airports, level flight, engines, and navigation.[4] Units of the traditional general science course are incorporated or fused with these topics. For example, when materials used in airplane construction, such as aluminum, wood, and glue, are discussed, the author suggests tying in such concepts as adhesion, cohesion, density, and melting point.

Biology

Biology courses in high schools and colleges will undoubtedly be amended to include the study of animals and plants living in the air. Aerobiology, or the study of organisms that live in the air, is likely to have greater interest for students. The problems of altitude sickness, the relation of the human mechanism to acceleration, and the effect of flight on the sense organs will increase interest in the biology of flight.

Physics

New information on the physics of flight will be necessary in high-school texts. In one physical-science text which has been recently published, old physical principles are studied in their application to aviation.[5] Aerodynamics will become an increasingly important branch of knowledge in technological and vocational high schools and colleges. How much will be taught in the average high school remains an open question, but it seems highly probable that an appreciable portion of the physics course will deal with the principles of flight.

[4] Standish Deake, "Streamlining General Science for an Air-Minded Generation," *School Science and Mathematics*, vol. 43, 1943, pp. 567-71.

[5] J. G. Manzer, M. M. Peake, J. M. Leps, *Physical Science in the Air Age.* New York: The Macmillan Co., 1942.

Mathematics

It is to be expected that mathematics problems in the elementary and secondary schools will encompass problems of aviation. It is interesting to see that several mathematical texts have already introduced the new concepts and problems characteristic of the Air Age. Terms such as *aileron, airfoil, aspect ratio, camber, dope, gap, nacelle,* and *stalling speed* are supplementing the terminology in older arithmetic texts. Indeed, it may be necessary for an older generation to become orientated in this form of language usage.[6]

In the introduction to his book, *Mathematics in Aviation,* George Osteyee remarks that "older arithmetical books have problems dealing with railway express. This book has a chapter devoted entirely to air express." In the chapter on air mail he presents this type of problem: [7]

> The air-mail rate to Egypt from the United States is 70 cents per half ounce or fraction thereof. If letters to Egypt have the following weights, find the cost of the postage: ⅜ oz., ⅝ oz., 2½ oz., ⅞ oz., and ¼ oz.

Thus, to old arithmetical processes new substance is added. The child will be taught to multiply, add, divide, and subtract in terms of flight rather than in, or in addition to, the terms of the boat and horse of the past, or the railroad and automobile of today.

Social Science

Social studies, and social science in general, will in all probability assume the responsibility of pointing out the significance of the social impact of the airplane. Such topics as air power in World Wars I and II, the history of aircraft, the changes in local communities due to the widespread use of the plane, the international aspects of aviation, new geographical relationships and the airplane, and many other topics, will undoubtedly find their

[6] George Osteyee, *Mathematics in Aviation.* New York: The Macmillan Co., 1942.

[7] *Ibid.,* p. 15.

way into the social studies curriculum. There is a reasonable expectation of the introduction of this type of material, since the expressed purpose of these social studies courses is the incorporation of useful information regarding social problems as well as social science data which appear frequently in newspapers and magazines.[8] If the curriculum tends to be formulated in this manner, there can be little question that future social studies texts will bear the imprint of aviation.

Geography

It is plausible to assume that a greater interest in geography will emerge because of the impact of aviation and that more time will be devoted to the teaching of geography in the future than has hitherto been the case. Educational leaders are strongly in favor of this greater diffusion of geographical knowledge even at the present time. The United States Commissioner of Education has said:

> Now is the time to teach American people geography. I think . . . we are more illiterate in geography than any other civilized nation.
> . . . The reason is that we have never taught geography. Young people have stopped studying geography beyond the seventh and eighth grades of the schools.
> I recommend that in some way throughout the secondary schools and colleges and universities a real effort be made to acquaint American citizens with the realities of the world situation.[9]

Aviation will alter man's ideas of geography. Geography is the study of the physical characteristics of the earth and their relations to man. Its content at any given time depends upon the experience man has had with these physical characteristics, and geography has changed as man's ideas of the world have been transformed. Homer's world included a part of Europe, parts of

[8] National Education Association, Department of Superintendence, *The Social Studies Curriculum*, Fourteenth Year Book, 1936.
[9] John W. Studebaker, in George T. Renner, *Human Geography in the Air Age*. New York: The Macmillan Co., 1942, pp. 3-4.

Asia, and a part of Africa and was conceived of as a flat disk with an impassable river around the edge. Columbus created a new concept when he described the world as a cylinder. With the advent of the airplane, new conceptions of physical relationships have arisen.

The unique ability of the airplane to overcome the obstacles and barriers of other modes of travel, such as deserts, water, mountains, extremes of heat and cold, has created new routes of travel. Travel distances in the air age are better measured in terms of time than surface miles. The shortest routes for the airplane are the great-circle routes. For example, the air route from Chicago to the tropical Philippines is via Alaska. Similarly, Seattle and Charleston, two American seaports on the west and east coasts respectively, become roughly equidistant from Moscow. These shortened paths of travel, which ignore the obstacles of ice and jungle, are somewhat amazing to most of us who are familiar only with surface water and land routes.

Maps are an important aid in teaching geography. A readjustment and reorganization becomes necessary for geography teachers in the use of maps. Flat Mercator maps were fairly satisfactory for the water and land travel of limited distances and are still indispensable for surface navigation. However, Mercator maps, which divide the earth generally into eastern and western hemispheres, are not suitable for the representation of the great-circle routes, especially across the Arctic. To meet the needs of aviation, several types of map-making, using a flat surface to represent a monospheric world, have come into use. Instead of placing the North Pole at the top of the map and the South Pole at the bottom, as has been customary in past years, aviation maps give importance to the center of the flat map, through which great-circle routes are shown as straight lines. On azimuthal maps, the great-circle routes are straight lines and all distances from the center are uniform in scale. On gnomonic maps, the great circles are also straight lines, but area, scale, and shape are distorted even at moderate distances from the center. Any point on the earth may be chosen as the center of these maps. Other maps are drawn to show the greatest land mass on one half of the earth.

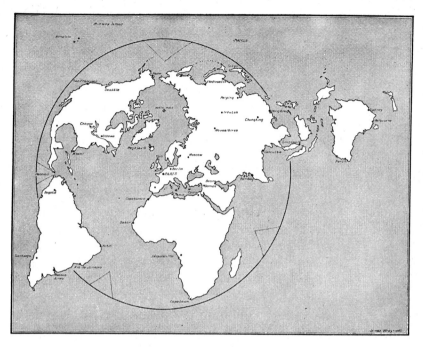

Figure 23. THE "MATTER-MOST" MAP

The hemisphere shown within the circle in the map above is drawn, centered at Paris, in such a way as to include 94 per cent of the population and most of the land area of the world, as can be seen from the map. Hemisphere maps have traditionally showed the "old world" and the "new," but in the Air Age with great-circle routes it is advantageous to draw a variety of hemispherical maps. This map, an equidistant projection, was constructed by S. C. Gilfillan and James Wray and is further described in "World Projections for the Air Age," *Surveying and Mapping,* Jan.-March, 1946, pp. 12-18.

The globe itself is really the only satisfactory map for the Air Age.

Aviation also brings other new emphases in geography. Areas of limited interest in the past assume new importance with the coming of air transportation. The regions and localities usually studied in school geographies are those which the student might either have the occasion to visit or about which he is likely to read or deal with in some way. Aviation will bring new regions into his scope, such as those which have formerly been relatively isolated because of barriers of ice, desert, mountains, or jungle. If there are economic attractions in these regions, such as mineral resources, or if they are *en route* between densely populated regions, they will become increasingly important. There will also be new curiosity in other cities, since the airplane, by virtue of its speed, will increase transportation to places that are now too far away for ready communication. With no place on the earth's surface farther away than perhaps forty to fifty hours of flying time, all the countries of the world will become neighbors. Children will be expected to know about places that seemed remote and inaccessible before the advent of the plane.

It is not feasible to develop the synopses of the chapters in the new geographies here, but one other emphasis of importance should be indicated. That part of physical geography which deals with weather will be increasingly stressed. Even to pupils in elementary and secondary schools, weather in an age of aviation will become significant. Instruction in wind currents, barometric changes, and air levels will probably be required in the basic training of all children.

The discussion of geography up to this point has been on the influence of aviation upon its teaching in the elementary and secondary schools. Teachers' colleges will be expected to train teachers in geography, as will other colleges and universities. In the universities, there will be many aspects of geography that will need to be studied a good deal more intensively; for example, air trade routes and new fields in economic geography. Meteorology should also be an expanding field for research. In fact, every aspect of geography needed for the public-school system should have a corresponding research activity in the university.

History

It is thought that a derivative effect of the new emphases in geography will be an increased desire for knowledge of the history and culture of the geographical areas formerly less well known. Aviation will particularly increase interest in the Orient. A trip from the United States to China, which requires three weeks at the present time, can be made by air in less than three days. The histories of Japan, China, and other Oriental countries have never been given much attention in the curricula of secondary schools, or, to any great extent, in colleges and universities. Such a movement toward more world history will develop slowly, and will not, of course, receive the emphasis that the history of the Western World receives. Anthropology will also probably receive increased emphasis in the colleges, and perhaps more anthropological information will be included in elementary and secondary courses. Population studies will cover a greater range of countries. Courses in trade and commerce, as well as those in economic resources, will have to be reworked and additional material placed in texts.

Languages

The field of language arts in the elementary and secondary schools, as well as in the colleges, will be influenced by the impact of aviation. Literature is now being published for courses in English which stress the adventure and travel of the airplane. One anthology of aviation literature for junior-high-school students includes such stories as Daedalus and his son Icarus, the magic carpet, the flying stool, the real-life stories of aviation pioneers, and so on.[10] In addition, similar readers for high-school students have made their appearance.[11] It has often been suggested that, for children's creative writing, flying is an excellent subject. Many teachers have reported on the amazingly vivid and imaginative work that has been written by both boys and girls in prose and poetry on some aspects of flying.

We can expect the airplane to exert its influence upon foreign-language study. Air vocabularies, including key words or phrases in different languages, have already been devised by teachers of foreign languages.[12] Increasing contacts with foreign-speaking people at airports and in international travel will bring greater interest in the study of foreign languages. Before the war, it was

[10] Rose N. Cohen, *Flying High.* New York: The Macmillan Co., 1942.
[11] E. A. Cross, *Wings for You.* New York: The Macmillan Co., 1942.
[12] Theodore Huebener, "An Air Vocabulary of 100 Words," *The Modern Language Journal,* May, 1943, pp. 353-355.

reported that the German aviation industry sought great numbers of young men who had foreign-language training as salesmen and engineers.

> For the personnel of the airports a wide knowledge of foreign languages is of great importance. A large number of air officials at home and abroad come in daily contact with passengers from all parts of the world. Participation in the councils of the International Air Traffic Association, of which the Lufthansa is a member, makes a knowledge of foreign languages on the part of the air officials highly desirable.[13]

Whether the aviation industry in the United States will experience the same need for foreign-language experts as did the Germans depends primarily on the international air commerce established in postwar years. If we have direct contact with non-English-speaking countries, it would appear that a need for foreign-language-speaking personnel in the industry would be necessary. The preparation of such personnel would naturally fall to the schools and colleges of the country.

Research

Many educators consider research a part of education at the university or college level, although a great deal of research is done in governmental bureaus, in industry, and in other organizations. It has been inferred in the discussion on curricula changes that aviation will have an influence on research, but we may make some brief comments about a few of these effects.

Aviation may have a particular effect on research which is carried on through expeditions. The airplane has already been used in Iran and Yucatan by archeologists. It has proved of value in locating sites of ancient cities, temples, and burial places. Without the plane, this work is slow and tedious. The helicopter should prove to be especially valuable in locating these sites. Aerial photography is a useful adjunct in this work. Air trans-

---

[13] Theodore Huebener, "What Our Enemies Think of the Value of Foreign Languages in the Air Age," *Hispania*, May, 1943, p. 193, condensed from *Luftfahrt und Schule*, November, 1938, Berlin.

portation will also facilitate the bringing-in of supplies to the areas where these expeditions are working.

Air transportation should accelerate the study of preliterate cultures by anthropologists. Primitive peoples are located in out-of-the way places, which are sometimes very difficult to reach. Air travel may enable the area of operation of a university or museum to be enlarged. American anthropologists have done their field work largely on the North American continent. Aviation may help to extend their work to South America or Oceania. Perhaps aviation will be disadvantageous to anthropology in that the penetration of air travel to all parts of the world and the consequent greater diffusion of cultures may speed up the disappearance of primitive cultures.

Aviation will also affect geological expeditions in their search for minerals and in studying variations in the earth's surface, particularly in otherwise inaccessible mountain regions. Aerial color photography will be especially useful in identifying soils and rocks.

It has been indicated in previous paragraphs that the influence of aviation on geography will be very far-reaching. The various emphases which aviation brings to geography call for a corresponding research on each. The effect of aviation on mapping is particularly important.

Research on weather has already been given great impetus by aviation. The study of the effects of conditions in the upper atmosphere on the earth's weather has been particularly stimulated. It is expected that this kind of research will be even more fruitful in the future.

The use of cameras on planes has already led to the development of new lenses and new types of cameras. There is need for new printing papers, for developments in color, and for three-dimensional views. It seems very probable that aviation will stimulate scientific inquiry in these directions.

In medicine, a good deal of research has already been instigated by aviation on the causes of air-sickness, the effect of altitude on different kinds of illness and injury, the effects of bacteria and insects in the upper air, and many allied subjects.

The greatest influence on research is, of course, on aeronautics itself. A whole new field of research has been created, branching out into physics, engineering, metallurgy, and many other different sciences.

Popularization of Flying

As was mentioned previously, the first step of the educational program with regard to aviation is to interest and to acquaint the pupil with the uses which society will make of this new invention. This part of the school program has already been highly developed. The schools have been exceedingly alert and have done much to prepare young people to accept the airplane. Often, inventions are resisted at the outset, but the schools have not only reduced resistance to the airplane, but have created a great enthusiasm for it on the part of the children. No doubt, their knowledge and enthusiasm has been partially imparted to their parents.

This achievement has been aided by congressional appropriations and the administrative leadership of the Department of Commerce. Through the United States Office of Education and in co-operation with the Bureau of Aeronautics of the Navy, a Model Aircraft Project was established in the schools in the forty-eight states, Hawaii, Alaska, Puerto Rico, the Virgin Islands, and the Canal Zone. The project called for the construction of eight hundred thousand solid models — covering eighty different types of Axis and Allied planes — for the use of army and navy personnel in plane spotting, estimating gun range, and so on. Civilian airplane spotters also used these models in learning to identify planes. The Bureau of Aeronautics supplied specifications and outlines. The project was discontinued on December 31, 1943, because its purpose had been accomplished. It is believed by those making out the final report that approximately eight hundred thousand models were made in the school shops in the country. About eight hundred thousand youths in over six thousand schools participated in this program. The military services have highly praised the schools' accomplishments. Educators report that the project stimulated interest in aviation as well as enthusiasm for the industrial arts program.

In December, 1944, the Army Air Forces were preparing a nation-wide program to disseminate information to educators as to what material was available to schools for educational purposes in connection with aviation, how it could be secured, and how the equipment could be most effectively used, in an effort to make available to civilian education the training experience of the Army Air Forces. The program was approved by the United States Office of Education and the Pre-Induction Training Division of the Army Service Forces. Nine area teams were set up which gave demonstrations to educators of the training aids and teaching techniques of the Army Air Forces.[14]

The introduction of aviation to school children is not peculiar to the United States. Various other countries, particularly Germany, have used the school to encourage its development. Before the outbreak of war, German schoolboys were given the materials and the time to build model planes. They were also allowed to fly their models in large fields. Young boys were taught glider flying, and by the time they reached military age they were experienced fliers, understanding aerodynamics and thoroughly at home in the skies. This considerably shortened their training as army pilots.

It has been indicated that industrial arts activities can be related to aeronautics from the first grade through senior high school. These activities include model plane building, model glider construction, building of a model airport as a sand-table project, the construction of model runways, hangars, and signal towers, the study of the operation, care, and maintenance of airports, etc.[15] Some teachers' colleges offer such preparation for industrial arts teachers.

Some phases of this program of acquainting students with aviation may be temporary, since airplanes will soon cease to be a novelty and education will not be needed to stimulate interest in them. However, the schools will undoubtedly use their manual-training shops for making models of airplanes, and will

---

[14] *Education for Victory*, December 20, 1944, pp. 13-14.
[15] Gordon O. Wilber, "Adapting Wood and Metal Shop Facilities to Air-Age Education," *The American School and University*, 1943 Yearbook, p. 321.

give aviation instruction in physics and mechanics for many years
to come.

The Utilitarian Trend in Education

For many years there has been a trend in education in the
direction of the practical and the vocational. Technical, vocational, and trade schools have been established in our cities. The
interest of the schools in aviation will probably encourage the
further growth of these institutions.

Occupational preparation for the aviation industry will probably be offered to a large extent by commercial schools, technical
schools supported by public funds, and by plant schools, and
only secondarily by the standard high schools. Already, the Los
Angeles city board of education maintains what are known as
vocational trade preparatory classes in aircraft sheet-metal work
in the regular high schools. The Frank Wiggins Trade School,
which is also municipally supported, offers a series of specialized
courses that provide training for employment in the aircraft industry.[16]

It has been reported that, even before the war, close to 50 per
cent of the workers in modern industry required extensive training.[17] Unless the armed forces and war industry have sufficiently
provided trained personnel for the aircraft industry for a long
time to come, the schools will in all probability be called upon to
supply workers trained in general machine fundamentals.[18] Walter J. Brooking has written, "Industry expects high schools to
train their machine-shop students in the fundamentals which are
the tools in the hands and minds of machinists and mechanics." [19]

For a short time, colleges and high schools, under the supervision of the United States Department of Commerce, provided
training for pilots. Between 1938 and 1941, elementary flight

[16] Vierling Kersey, "Trained Men for the Aircraft Industry," *The Nation's
Schools*, February, 1941, pp. 38, 39.

[17] Verne C. Fryklund, "Trends in Trade Education," *The Nation's Schools*,
1941, pp. 25, 38; Verne C. Fryklund, *The Selection and Training of Modern
Factory Workers*, University of Minnesota Employment Stabilization Research
Institute, 1934; *Review of Educational Research*, 1941, pp. 398-407.

[18] Director of Plant Education, R. G. LeTourneau, Inc., Peoria, Illinois.

[19] Walter J. Brooking, "What Industry Asks from High School Machine Shops,"
Industrial Arts and Vocational Education, May, 1944, p. 179.

and ground training was given to more than seventy thousand young men. With the advent of the war, this program was abandoned. It did result, however, in a large nucleus of fliers who were used in speeding up the training for army and navy pilots.

It is highly probable that the United States will build a military training program of fairly large dimensions, whether or not military training for all youths is required. This program will include the maintenance of an air force. The training of personnel for this air force reserve will probably be done by the military arm of the government at its own training fields, rather than in the colleges and high schools. This is not to say that there may not be some preparatory schools and some colleges that will provide instruction in flying, just as there are military schools today. But buying and maintaining flying equipment will be too expensive for most schools. It seems reasonable to think that the training of civilian fliers will take place in private air schools or in other schools strengthened by governmental aid. In case of sudden emergency, the program of training fliers can be enlarged by bringing in other schools and colleges, as was done at the beginning of World War II.

However, at present there are a number of high schools which are providing flight experience as "laboratory work" in aeronautics courses. The Civil Aeronautics Administration reported that more than six hundred high-school students in Wisconsin had such experience in the term ending in the spring of 1945.[20] It is estimated that a complete tabulation would treble that number. Wisconsin, Pennsylvania, Tennessee, and New York are outstanding in this work. The laboratory work introduces some difficult administrative problems, such as liability of the school district as the result of accidents, nature of the contract between aviation firms and school district, and the high costs per flight hour. There has been some criticism of this laboratory work as being too much influenced by the program originally formulated for the training of commercial pilots, but it is considered to be an expanding program.[21]

[20] Release of the Civil Aeronautics Administration, Information and Statistics Service, February 14, 1945.
[21] *School Review*, April, 1945, p. 195.

An interesting question arises in regard to the influence aviation may have on the physical-training education given in the schools and colleges. Rather rigid tests of a physical nature are given to aviators, not only in wartime, but also in peacetime. These tests deal in part with traits that are hereditary, such as eyesight and reaction time; but they also are applied to physical traits readily affected by experience, such as weight. Of course, nearly all hereditary traits are affected to some extent by training. As flying becomes more common in private planes, less insistence will be placed upon physical fitness, especially if aircraft controls are simplified. In flying, the premium may be not so much upon muscular fitness or speed of movement as upon physical qualities such as eyesight or good heart action. The emphasis would therefore be as much on eugenics as on physical education. However, flying may accentuate somewhat the development of physical testing in the schools and encourage physical education.

The Organization of Schools

Will the plane have any effect on the organization of the school system? Aside from local community schools, the predominant unit for the organization of the school system in the United States is the state rather than the federal government. The state gives some support to rural and county schools, trains teachers, prescribes courses of study, and sets standards of performance. The evidence seems to show that there is a trend toward greater emphasis upon the duties and responsibilities of the state department of education.[22] In 1938-39, there were three hundred and eighty-one supervisors of instruction in the non-vocational staffs of state departments of education, whose chief concern was with the improvement of instruction in the schools. These supervisors spent a large part of their time visiting schools.[23] Many states were definitely restricted in this field work because of the ex-

---

[22] Arthur B. Moehlman, *School Administration*. Boston: Houghton Mifflin Company, 1940; S. M. Brownell, "The Organization and Administration of the State School System," *Review of Educational Research*, October, 1943, p. 381.

[23] United States Office of Education, Studies of State Departments of Education, Monograph no. 6, 1940, p. 14.

pense and time involved. This was especially true in the central and western states where distances are great. In Colorado, for example, a large portion of the state is a full day's journey from the capital city. The widespread use of either the plane or helicopter would enable divisions of the state education department to do their work much more easily. The scheduled air transport services may be used, or the state office of education may have its own helicopter or small plane.

Another possibility of change in school organization because of aviation may be a greater development of junior colleges. The high schools in small towns were given impetus by the use of the automobile which gave rural youth access to high schools near to their homes. Will aircraft have a similar effect upon the junior college? The students of junior colleges, like those of high schools, tend to come from the surrounding neighborhood. The use of aircraft, either individually owned machines or some type of air bus service, might increase the area from which students will come to the junior college. Such a development will not come in the immediate postwar years, since it will depend on the extensive use of the helicopter or air bus. Such a possible effect upon junior colleges is to be expected only a decade or more after the war.

Centralization

The effect of new and better means of transportation, in general, has been in the direction of centralization of power and administration in state or national centers. In education, the American tradition is one of local administration, which is championed fervently by educators. Nevertheless, the educational functions of state bureaus have increased considerably over the years. Even the federal government has become more concerned with educational policy, if not administration. The intrusion of state and federal centers into local education has often begun with grants-in-aid, to which later there has been added some prescription as to policy. Aviation is likely to add its part toward this centralizing tendency, unless it is consciously resisted by educational policy-makers.

Rural Schools

Another question is, What effect will aviation have upon the rural school other than increasing its tie to the state and federal government? The use of air bus lines to transport children may be considered. This prospect is not immediate, if it occurs at all. The problem of safety will likely delay the use of the helicopter in transporting children to school, despite the advantage of aircraft in avoiding the problem of bad roads, especially in snowy climates. The motor bus made the consolidated school possible; it does not seem probable that the helicopter will do much more in this direction in the near future because of the costs, which are higher than those of the bus.

The effect of aviation in breaking down rural isolation and increasing contacts between the local school and the state administrators may indirectly influence the curriculum of the rural school. The rural-school curriculum is likely to be brought a little more in line with the educational changes taking place in urban schools. The decrease in rural isolation may also encourage better-trained teachers to come to rural schools.

The Location of Schools

Aviation may have some effect upon the location of schools, since schools are placed where there are children. If, at some time in the future, children are moved from the city center to far, outlying suburbs, schools will surely follow. Such has been the effect of the automobile, the electric train, and suburban steam railroad. The airplane will contribute its influence in the same direction.

If homes are spread over wider distances because of the helicopter, the problem of getting children to and from school is augmented. In some areas, there has been the difficulty of getting enough children together to support an adequate school. The motor bus solved this problem for many communities through the consolidation of schools. If the birth rate should fall much more in rural areas, and if homes should be more widely separated, the problem of furnishing adequate schools in many communities will again arise. This may not be very serious, since parents often choose a neighborhood in relation to its proximity to schools. The school situation, therefore, might prevent the helicopter from scattering homes too widely, or the helicopter might be used for some transportation to schools.

A newly created suburb sometimes offers fewer obstacles to good schools than do large city systems. There is less overcrowding, less politics in the school system, less red tape of bureaucracy, and fewer obstacles of all sorts. Suburbs have at times refused to be incorporated in a city because the residents wished to retain some control of the schools to which they sent their children. Families often move to the suburbs in order to obtain better conditions for their children, and they put a great deal of effort into the building of a good educational system. If aviation encourages dispersal into the suburbs, many children may be able to attend better schools.

A kindred question would be whether the development of air transportation will have any effect upon the location or development of colleges and universities. It is often argued that a large faculty promotes the exchange of ideas, the cross-fertilization of knowledge, as well as greater economy in maintaining good equipment, laboratories, libraries, and so on. Transportation, and to some extent aviation, may favor this centralization of great learning centers, though there may be other and opposing factors. Our universities began as colleges long ago when transportation was primarily local in character. Once they were established, they continued their separate existence, even though they are now quite close together in terms of modern transportation. Yale and Columbia, for example, are within three hours of each other by train. Even when a large city has several colleges or universities, it might be noted that they were founded when local transportation was inadequate. In recent years there has been an effort to get co-operation, if not a federation, between colleges in the same city. There have been efforts toward such co-operation, for example, in Atlanta, Nashville, and Chicago. However, the persistence of college and university tradition and the slow rate of obsolescence of school buildings are usually effective resistant forces to the centralizing tendencies of modern transportation. The effect of a highly developed air transportation system would seem to give support, though perhaps quite slight, to the strengthening of these co-operative university centers already established and to the centralization of research and learning in large universities.

The large university centers have their international aspects. For many decades in the nineteenth and early twentieth centuries, American students sought the advantages of the great centers of learning in Germany, France, and Britain. Now an increasingly large number of foreign students are attending the well-staffed and excellently equipped universities in the United States. With the increase in intercontinental travel by air after the war, and the great saving in time, there should be a considerable impetus for advanced students to travel to other lands for special instruction. Universities in the United States are expected to receive many of these students. In this way, aviation will increase the size of university centers.

At the same time, transportation may favor the dispersion of small colleges and junior colleges. There are advantages in colleges of small size, because they can give more personal attention to the student and can be more widely distributed geographically. If the attendance at colleges and junior colleges becomes larger and larger, tapping the lower economic levels of population, then the economy of the proximity of the college to the student will be more appreciated.

Some commuting to schools by air will probably occur, so it is likely that there will be landing places for helicopters near schools, whether they be small rural schools or urban universities.

Education Outside Schools

There is a good deal of education that takes place outside the schoolroom, such as through governmental agencies. Many industrial plants offer various educational programs. Adult education has become more widespread through public lectures, forums, discussion groups, clubs, churches, conferences, conventions, libraries, newspapers, magazines, books, and radio. Will the airplane exert any influence upon this type of education? There appear to be several ways in which it will.

One such effect will be the faster delivery of mail, which will mean more rapid dissemination of information. Books and newspapers may also be transported by plane to a limited extent. Modern inventions, especially the telephone and the radio, are bringing rural and isolated areas into ever-increasing contact with urban areas and are speeding up the diffusion of ideas. The airplane and helicopter will act as reinforcing agents in this process.

Libraries have used automobiles to carry books into areas where the population is too widely scattered to maintain a library. The helicopter or plane might be used in this type of activity.

A highly developed institution in the United States is the conference, convention, or association meeting. In many cases, individuals have been prevented from participating in these meetings because of the time required for traveling. Aircraft may increase attendance at such meetings by facilitating the travel necessary to reach them.

It has been said that education is all of life's experiences. In this large, over-all sense, the influence of aircraft on education is synonymous with its influence upon our civilization and culture. No human, cognizant of his surroundings, can remain untouched by the airplane. Even the most apathetic will respond to the changes the airplane has brought and is destined to bring.

Conclusion

Education may be considered as what takes place in schools, classes, and laboratories, or as all the learning an individual receives in adjusting to civilization. Using the latter concept, the impact of aviation on education requires this whole book to give the answer. As to the impact of aviation on the organized education of the schools, the most important changes will be those in the curricula, with scarcely a subject being untouched in some way. Significant changes are expected in geography, physics, and engineering, with lesser modifications in mathematics, biology, geology, and the social sciences. There will be special schools for training pilots, as well as the training programs of the War and Navy Departments of the federal government. In educational administration, aviation's effect will be in the direction of strengthening the influence of larger administrative units. The influence on rural education will probably be slight. Later on, there may be some influence on the location and specialization of schools. The great universities should be somewhat increased in size, with their influences reaching out to students in other lands.

22

Railroads [1]

AVIATION has come to the United States in a period when there are already great transportation systems in existence. Railroads, buses, and trucks have vast networks of routes over this country, carrying many millions of passengers and large amounts of freight and mail each year. Likewise, there are steamship lines from the United States to almost every country in the world. In addition, there are submarines, pipelines, bicycles, horses, and other kinds of transportation. Now a new form of transportation, aviation, has come into existence, and we want to inquire as to its relationship with the present systems of transportation.

In some historical instances, a new method of transportation has almost wholly replaced an existing form of transport. Horses largely replaced dogs and men as means of carrying goods, although both are still used in some parts of the world. The canal boat, used in the early 1800's, became obsolete with the development of the railroad. The railroad likewise replaced the horse for long-distance travel.

At other times, a new method of transportation has been merely added to the existing system, producing very little, if any, modification of the current means of transportation. A highly specialized form of transportation, such as the submarine, was adopted, without change in other types of transportation. The bicycle also caused very little change. Pipelines did reduce a certain type of

[1] The author is indebted to Julius H. Parmelee, Director of the Bureau of Railway Economics, Association of American Railroads, for assistance in supplying certain basic statistics of railway operations which have been used in the preparation of this chapter.

haul for railroads and boats, but, in general, it made few modifications.

The automobile was added to the existing systems of transportation without modifying some parts, but at the same time replacing the horse and, to some extent, the railroad for short-distance hauls.

From these illustrations, it may be observed that when the process is accumulative — that is, when a new invention is added to those already in existence — the new invention has some special functions which preceding forms do not have. The automobile is more flexible for personal use than a railroad, which is confined to a track and is costly to build and to maintain. The automobile is also more convenient and faster than the horse. By virtue of specialization of functions, a transportation system has been built up which is composed of heterogeneous special types. Some types specialize in underwater travel, in snow travel, in surface travel, water travel, or underground travel. Some types carry small numbers, others large numbers. The special characteristics of aircraft are long-distance travel, great speed, and above-the-ground transportation. At first glance, it is not clear whether aviation will replace some existing modes of travel or bring various modifications.

The results of the adoption of the airplane will vary, depending on the part of the world in which it is used. The airplane will have different effects in a country which has no railways and paved highways from those it will have in a country with a highly developed system of transportation. In this chapter, we shall be concerned with the United States, which has the most highly developed transportation system of any country in the world.

Railroads have played a very important part in the development of our modern civilization. Before their extension, America had a rural household economy with relatively little manufacturing and trade. In the post-Civil-War period, it was the railroads that made possible the continuous expansion of the western frontiers. They were often determining factors in the location of population. Cities which were bypassed by them declined in size, while those located on their routes prospered and increased in population. The railroads also furthered the industrial development after the Civil War. For almost a century they were very nearly our sole method of transporting passengers, mail, express, and freight over any but very short distances. Even in 1940, just before World War II, they were responsible for almost two-thirds of the total intercity passenger-miles and about the same proportion of ton-miles of intercity freight traffic. The railroads are still basic to our economic and social system, although their freight and passenger business was seriously affected in the 1930's by the economic distress of the depression and by the inroads of competition from the automobile.

In the postwar decade, air transportation is expected to expand in amount of passenger and cargo traffic and to increase in importance as a method of transportation. We want to know what effect this will have on railroads. How will the revenues of the railroad companies be affected? What classes of railroad travel are most likely to be diverted to the air? What effort will railroad companies make to maintain their passenger traffic? What improvements can be made in railroad travel in order to compete more successfully with airline service? These are the subjects to be discussed in this chapter.

Sources of Competition to the Railroads

The automobile proved to be a strong competitor of the railroads, especially for short-distance travel. Before the automobile came into widespread use, the railroads were carrying a billion passengers annually.[2] This number was equaled or exceeded in virtually every year from 1911 to 1923 and then declined as the production of automobiles increased rapidly. In the prosperous year of 1929, when the automobile had become well established, the number of railroad passengers had dropped 22 per cent, to 785,000,000. During the depression years, the number fell to a low of 435,000,000. Even as late as 1940, the number carried by the railroads was only 456,000,000, or not quite half of the number carried twenty years previously.[3]

[2] All figures in this section, unless otherwise specifically stated, apply to railroads of all classes, including Class I, Class II, and Class III.
[3] The 1940 figure includes 229,266,000 commuters, as compared with 224,627,-

The freight traffic of the railroads has likewise declined. The peak of freight tonnage originated was reached in 1926, at 1,440,-000,000 tons, a level which was maintained during the 1920's. The amount of freight traffic was cut a third in the 1930's from the volume of the 1920's, but this reduction may have been due in large part to the depression rather than to competition from the truck. However, in 1940, when business conditions were good, railroad freight tonnage originated was 1,069,000,000 tons, or about one-quarter short of the 1926 record.

As a result of the competition of the private automobile, bus, and truck, the railroads have abandoned many miles of track, usually short branch lines. From 1926 to 1940, almost twenty thousand miles of tracks were abandoned, or an average of 1325 miles per year. Since only about five thousand miles of trackage were constructed in these years, there was a net loss of 990 miles per year.[4] In addition to the abandoning of tracks, many railroad companies were reorganized because of financial difficulties.

This loss of freight and greater loss of passengers did not strike all roads equally. Short-haul freight, merchandise or package freight, and coach service suffered the most. It was the marginal roads which felt most keenly the competition from the private automobile, bus, and truck.

Another source of loss of traffic on the railroads is the pipeline system. It is true that for many years the railroads have carried only a small percentage of the crude petroleum produced, but recently the pipelines have begun to carry various petroleum products which were formerly transported by rail. Further, the widespread use of fuel oil in place of coal has reduced the rail coal traffic.

The railroads have experienced, in the last two or three decades, very serious competition from other means of transportation, but they still remain in their position of first place in our domestic transportation system. The railroads are the life-blood on which our cities depend, and our whole industrial struc-

000 other than commuters. The commutation traffic did not decline as rapidly or as much as coach and Pullman traffic.

[4] Calculated from I.C.C. *Statistics of Railways*, 1942, p. 13, Table 13.

ture relies upon them as carriers of finished products and suppliers of raw materials. During the war the railroads did not suffer from the combined competition of other transportation agencies, since there was a general shortage of all types of transportation because of war conditions. But in the postwar decade the railroad industry is likely to encounter stronger competition than ever before from highway transport, water transport, pipelines, and, in addition, a new competitor — the airplane. The effect of the combined competition of these agencies on the railroads may be expected to be great. However, our task is to attempt to assess the effect on the railroads of only one of these competitors, that of air transport. We shall first attempt to make some estimate of the effect air transport expansion may have on rail traffic and earnings.

Effect of Air Competition on Railroad Revenue

Although not all of the traffic of the airlines in the postwar decade will be taken from the railroads, the increase in air passenger and cargo traffic is expected to have considerable effect on the size of the annual net incomes of the railroads. In other chapters, predictions have been made of the probable airline revenues from passengers, cargo, and mail. These predictions are shown in Table 23. From this table it may be seen that the range of total probable revenues of the airlines is from $266,500,000 to $384,000,000.

The operating revenues of the railroads are much larger than those of the airlines, averaging for the decade ending in the last entire peace year, 1940, preceding the entrance of the United

TABLE 23.   AIR REVENUE, 1953

	Predicted Volume	Rate	Revenue
Passengers	6,000,000,000 to 8,000,000,000 passenger-miles	3.5 to 4¢	$210,000,000 to 320,000,000
Cargo	75,000,000 to 100,000,000 ton-miles	30¢	22,500,000 to 30,000,000
Mail	85,000,000 ton-miles	40¢	34,000,000
Total			$266,500,000 to 384,000,000

States into the war, $3,772,000,000. A possible railroad loss to the airlines of $200,000,000 would be a loss of only 5 per cent. However, the loss in net income of the railroads would be much higher.

As has been stated, not all of the increases in airline revenue in the postwar decade will be taken from the railroads. Some of it will come from new business created by the airplane, but undoubtedly a large proportion of the increase will represent a corresponding loss to the railroads. Since it is difficult to estimate this loss, we may make several assumptions as to possible amounts and see what the resulting effects will be on railroad net incomes. Table 24 shows the railroad revenues that might be expected with no loss of revenue and then, with reductions of $100,000,000, $200,000,000, and $300,000,000 losses to the airlines. Estimates are made for both high and low levels of traffic and earnings of the railroads. In this table, the various deductions and additions necessary to compute the net income in accordance with the accounting regulations of the Interstate Commerce Commission have been applied to the primary revenue data shown as the first entry of the first column. The several items shown are based upon the past experience of railways of Class I. While the results obtained are necessarily general and somewhat speculative in character, they serve to illustrate the points which we are considering.

We have assumed that business conditions will be prosperous in the immediate postwar years, and the revenues of the railroads are expected to be high, as well as those of the airlines. If there were no competition from airlines, the revenues of the railroads might be $6,000,000,000 or more, which was the average annual operating revenue of the railroads during the prosperous 1920's. If the loss of the railroads to the airlines were only $100,-000,000 a year, the operating revenues of the railroads would be reduced from $6,000,000,000 to $5,900,000,000. The loss in net income would be only $12,000,000, or 2.4 per cent. A more probable loss to the airlines from the railroads would be $200,-000,000. The percentage loss in operating revenues would then be only a little more than 3 per cent, but the loss in net income would be 7 per cent, or a loss of $35,000,000. But if the airlines increased to a large extent and took away from the $6,000,000,-000 revenues of the railroads $300,000,000, then the loss in net income to the railroads would be $60,000,000, or 12 per cent.

From the foregoing computations, it is seen that losses of railroad revenues to the airlines of from $100,000,000 to $300,000,000, when the railroads are doing a $6,000,000,000 business, would produce a reduction in railroad net income of from 2.4 to 12 per cent.

But the railroads may not have revenues of $6,000,000,000 after the war. A business depression may occur, in which case the business of the railroads will be reduced according to the intensity and duration of the depression. In the 1930's, for the four years from 1932 to 1935, the average annual railroad revenue was $3,281,000,000, and, in 1933, $3,138,000,000. Total operating revenues, then, of $3,000,000,000 are taken as a low level of earnings, and the effect on the net income of various amounts of losses to the airlines is computed.

If depression conditions exist, the revenues of the airlines will probably not increase to as much as $300,000,000. Both airlines and railroads suffer when business conditions are depressed. If the railroads have operating revenues of only $3,000,000,000 and no losses to the airlines, they would derive no net income at all, but have a deficit of $291,000,000. With a loss of $100,000,000 of operating revenues to the airlines, the deficit would be $320,-000,000, or an increase of $29,000,000 of loss. If the airlines took away $200,000,000 of operating revenues from the railroads, the deficit would be $353,000,000, and for a $300,000,000 loss in revenues, the deficit would be $378,000,000. Thus, if the airlines took $300,000,000 from a business of $3,000,000,000 of revenues, the decrease would be only 10 per cent, but the deficit would be increased by 30 per cent. It is obvious that the loss of traffic to the airlines would be much less serious to rail carriers when business is good and earnings satisfactory than when rail operations are at a low level, with net income small or nonexistent. Although the losses of railroads to airlines, indicated above, might not, by themselves, seriously jeopardize the financial posi-

TABLE 24. RAILROAD NET INCOME COMPUTED UNDER VARIOUS ASSUMPTIONS AS TO LOSS OF REVENUE TO AIR CARRIERS

I. At High Level of Earnings
(Millions of Dollars)

Item	Without Loss	Loss of $300	Loss of $200	Loss of $100
Total operating revenues	$6000	$5700 (5% loss)	$5800 (3% loss)	$5900 (1.7% loss)
Total operating expenses	4200	4020	4080	4140
Net operating revenue	$1800	$1680	$1720	$1760
Deduct				
Taxes				
Payroll	150	145	146	148
Federal income	350	295	310	325
Other	235	235	235	235
	$735	$675	$691	$708
Operating rentals	130	130	130	130
Net railway operating income	935	875	899	922
Add				
Other income	200	190	194	197
Income before fixed charges	$1135	$1065	$1093	$1119
Deduct				
Fixed charges	550	550	550	550
Contingent interest	85	75	78	81
	$635	$625	$628	$631
Net income	$500	$440 (12% loss)	$465 (7% loss)	$488 (2.4% loss)

II. At Low Level of Earnings
(Millions of Dollars)

Item	Without Loss	Loss of $300	Loss of $200	Loss of $100
Total operating revenues	$3000	$2700 (10% loss)	$2800 (6.6% loss)	$2900 (3.3% loss)
Total operating expenses	2360	2160	2230	2295
Net operating revenue	$640	$540	$570	$605
Deduct				
Taxes				
Payroll	86	78	81	83
Federal income	50	45	47	49
Other	225	225	225	225
	$361	$348	$353	$357
Operating rentals	120	120	120	120
Net railway operating income	159	72	97	128
Add				
Other income	125	115	120	122
Income before fixed charges	$284	$187	$217	$250
Deduct				
Fixed charges	550	550	550	550
Contingent interest	25	15	20	20
	$575	$565	$570	$570
Net Income	Def. $291	Def. $378 (30% loss)	Def. $353 (21% loss)	Def. $320 (10% loss)

tion of the rail industry, when coupled with additional losses from other competing types of transportation, they constitute important losses.

The discussion has concerned what will happen to railroad finances under conditions of competition from the airlines in good years and in bad. Nothing has been said as to when these good and bad years will come. Elsewhere in this study it has been argued that there are probabilities of a rather long period of prosperity in the first postwar decade, even though it may be broken by some months or years of severe depression. If this is the case, the situation will be favorable for the railroads, for it will give them an opportunity to prepare for less favorable periods in the second postwar decade.

Differentiation of Air Competition by Classes of Service

The revenues which the airlines take from the railroads do not come equally from all branches of the business. Air traffic is made up almost entirely of passengers, mail, and express, and traffic diverted from the railroads comes from these fields. Since the main source of revenue for the railroads is freight traffic, the diversion of passengers to the air will strike at types of rail traffic which, taken as a whole, are operating more often "in the red." Further depression of income in these categories would, of course, seriously aggravate an already acute situation. The year 1940 may be taken to illustrate this point. In 1940, the total net railway operating income (before fixed charges) of railways of Class I was $682,000,000, yet for passenger or allied services, which include mail and express, there was a net operating deficit of $262,000,000, calculated according to the cost-separation formula of the Interstate Commerce Commission.

Specific application of data pertaining to these matters will demonstrate more clearly the threat of air competition to these classes of rail traffic. Based upon past experience, railroad operating revenues at a level of $6,000,000,000 can be broken down into the percentages shown in Table 25.

Using estimates made in other chapters for volumes of airline passenger, express, and mail traffic, the apportionment of the ex-

TABLE 25. RAILROAD REVENUES APPORTIONED BY TYPES OF
SERVICE IN PERCENTAGE FOR A TOTAL OF $6,000,000,000 REVENUE

Freight	82.5
Passenger	10.0
Mail	2.5
Express	1.3
All other	3.7
	100.0

pected revenue of the domestic airlines, six years after the war,
is shown in Table 26. It is evident that business of the airlines
and of the railroads is quite differently distributed among passengers, mail, and express. If we assume that the business taken
away from the railroads is $200,000,000 or $300,000,000, distributed among passengers, mail, and cargo in the percentages
shown in the tables, the railroads (operating at a level of $6,000,-
000,000 operating revenues) would lose the amounts shown in
Table 27. Under these assumptions, the airlines would cut down
the passenger revenue of the railroads from 27 to 40 per cent, the

TABLE 26. AIRLINE REVENUES APPORTIONED BY TYPES OF
SERVICE IN PERCENTAGE AS EXPECTED SIX YEARS AFTER THE
CLOSE OF THE WAR

Passengers	80.0
Air mail	11.0
Cargo	9.0
	100.0

TABLE 27. LOSS OF RAILROAD REVENUES BY TYPE OF SERVICE,
ASSUMING $6,000,000,000 REVENUES AND A LOSS OF $200,000,000
OR $300,000,000 TO THE AIRLINES

Type of Service	Expected Revenue Without Loss to Airlines (in millions of dollars)	Amount Lost to Airlines		Percentage of Loss	
		$200,000,000	$300,000,000	$200,000,000	$300,000,000
Passenger	600	160	240	27	40
Mail	150	22	33	15	22
Express	78	18	27	*	*
	828	200	300		

* The loss to the railroads would be partly in express revenue and partly in freight revenue.

mail revenue from 15 to 22 per cent, and the express revenue perhaps around 20 per cent.[5]

As has been pointed out, the revenues to the railroads from passengers, mail, and express were running a deficit of over $200,000,000 a year before the war. The railroads would suffer if their revenues from these sources were cut 25 per cent, still further increasing an already existing heavy deficit in the passenger and allied classes of service. If the operating expenses of the railroads are not decreased in the postwar period, the competition of airlines will be felt even more keenly by the railroads. The operating expenses in 1940, restated in terms of 1944 operating conditions, show an increase of about 24 per cent.[6] If operating expenses are maintained at this level after the war, the net income from $6,000,000,000 of operating revenue will be reduced to a much lower level than the net income was in 1929, when the railroads were operating at a similarly high level of earnings.

The foregoing analysis shows that the expected growth of passenger traffic in aviation is likely to make it difficult for the railroads, even with increased traffic in the postwar years, to make any net income on their passenger service unless some particular effort is put forth by the railroads to meet aviation's competition. However, the railroad revenues from freight, which constitute four-fifths of their total revenues, appear to be secure from air competition in the immediate postwar years.

Differentiation of Air Competition by Length of Haul

The effect of aviation's competition on railroads is not only differentiated by class of service, but also by length of haul. Air competition is expected to be greatest for long runs of twenty-four hours by rail or longer, since the saving in time by air is proportionately greater the longer the distance to be traveled. Again air competition will strike at a weak point in railroad rev-

[5] Express revenues are collected from the public by the Railway Express Agency, which retains about 60 per cent of the total for its own collection, delivery, and other services, and distributes the remaining 40 per cent to the railroads and other transportation agencies that participate in handling the traffic.

[6] "Monthly Comment on Transportation Statistics," I.C.C., Bureau of Transport Economics and Statistics, May 5, 1944.

enue, since there is less movement of people and of goods over long than over short distances. The proportional decrease in revenue to railroads will be particularly great on the routes between the East and West Coasts and on the long routes between the Northern cities and Texas and Florida. These are the routes on which there is a high proportion of higher-priced Pullman services. These railroad services are particularly vulnerable to air competition.

Rail transportation for distances under three hundred miles are not so likely to suffer from air competition during the early postwar years. The automobile took away much short-distance travel from the railroads, but the amount of local traffic carried by the airplane is expected to be small in the immediate postwar years.

Reaction of the Railroads to Air Competition

The foregoing discussion has been concerned with the effect on net incomes of the railroads of various degrees of air transport expansion in the postwar decade. Indicated losses in passenger, mail, and express revenues, as well as some freight losses, would weigh heavily on all railroads. Some roads might be forced to reduce their passenger service; eliminate trains; cut Pullman, express, and mail cars off other trains; and increase the relative cost — or cost per unit — of rendering passenger service. Some companies might, in fact, find it necessary to discontinue passenger train operations entirely, rather than to operate them at a growing deficit.

It is improbable that the railroads would discontinue these deficit-producing passenger services in their entirety or that the public regulatory authorities would permit them to do so, even if they so desired. We still rely mainly on the railroads in our American transportation system, as was demonstrated during the war.

The railroad industry is peculiarly handicapped in protecting itself against competition, because it is expected, as a common carrier and a vitally needed agency of transport, to provide a required minimum of service whether business is good or bad. Yet there are several different policies which may be pursued by the railroads in order to limit or diminish the effects of air competition. No industry willingly faces the possibility of losing business without making an effort to meet the situation. For some time, railroad committees have been busy making studies and developing plans for the postwar decade. Of the various proposals being considered for maintaining rail passenger traffic, improvement of service and reduction of costs are being given the most attention.

Improvement in Railroad Service

There are various improvements that may be made in both coach and Pullman services. Improvements in coach service consist mainly in more comfortable seats and the construction of reclining seats for all-night sleeping. Also, improvements may be made in the form of air conditioning, better lighting, greater cleanliness, smoother tracks, and cheaper meal service. In addition to these greater comforts and conveniences, there may be, in many cases, faster schedules. Experiments are also being conducted with new types of trucks and improved braking equipment in order to assure smoother, more comfortable travel.

As early as 1934, the first "streamlined" passenger train was put into operation. Approval of this improved type of transport by the traveling public was instantaneous and emphatic. By December, 1939, at the end of five years of streamlined operation, there were 53 streamliners in operation on 16 different railways. By the end of 1941, this fleet had been increased by 66 more trains, bringing the total to 119, operated by 21 railways. With our entrance into the war in the closing days of 1941, the ordering of new trains of this kind ceased, although 14 more trains then on order were completed and put into operation, bringing the total to 133. These streamlined coach trains have usually grossed more per seat-mile than the added costs involved, including overhead. However, the passenger traffic on these streamliners may not have been entirely new traffic, for some of the passengers may have merely transferred from passenger trains of the older type. Yet streamliner train operations have made money for the railroads, and the companies plan further extensions for the postwar years.

The proportion of railroad passengers traveling in coaches was increasing in the late 1930's. In 1929, the coach passenger-miles constituted 46 per cent of the total rail passenger-miles, while in 1941, the percentage was 64. The increasing percentage of coach passengers has been favorable to the railroads, as a whole, even with coach fares lower than those for Pullmans, since coaches carry many more passengers than Pullman cars.

Prior to the war, Pullman service had not been as much improved as had coach service. The "roomette," an entirely new and novel small room unit, was first introduced in 1937. They were so successsful that approximately three thousand units of this type of accommodation were constructed and placed in regular service on important trains. Pullman has also developed and placed in experimental operation one "duplex-roomette" car, containing twenty-four small rooms, each room with all the conveniences of the larger rooms. It is hoped that this accommodation can be furnished at little, if any, more than the present charge for a lower berth. Four experimental "coach-sleepers" have also been constructed and placed in experimental operation on important coach trains. This car is designed to provide sleeping-car facilities at reduced cost, with daytime seating arrangements comparable to the modern *de luxe* coach. A traveler, by making his journey overnight, instead of going by day and stopping at a hotel at night, will save both money and time. With the coach-sleeper, the reclining-chair coach, and the *de luxe* duplex-roomette car, the railroads can make a strong appeal for the long-distance passenger traffic.

Another possible type of improvement in railroad service is in speed. It is the airplane's speed which gives it a competitive advantage over the railroad. Hence the railroads are thinking in terms of increased speed. In so far as greater speed involves smoothing out the curves of the tracks, the change will be slow and costly. But gains can be made with new equipment, especially lighter-weight cars and Diesel electric locomotives. The latter can take curves much faster than the steam engine. Better scheduling will shorten the time between stations. Improvement in train connections and schedules might enable the train time between New York and the Pacific Coast to be reduced to a total of fifty hours, a considerable saving in time over present coast-to-coast schedules. Yet fifty hours is at least four or five times as long as it will take a plane to make the same trip. Perhaps saving of time on short trips would yield more passengers for the railroads.

Improvements have already been made in other types of railroad traffic. Fast freight service has been established between important trade centers, thus expediting the movement of goods from producers to the shelves of trade outlets. Indications are that this type of service will be expanded in postwar years to meet the current marketing requirements for quicker turnover of stocks and reduced inventories. Pick-up and delivery service by rail carriers is continually increasing, both as to area of coverage and frequency of schedules. Improved facilities are being provided for loading and unloading at freight terminals. Such developments may improve the competitive position of the railroads.

These improvements will involve large capital expenditures. A 2,000-horsepower Diesel electric engine, for instance, costs about $175,000, and a modern coach about $60,000. A streamlined passenger train means an investment of $1,000,000. In addition to the original cost, streamliners have required modification or extension of many miles of signaling, extension of centralized traffic control (CTC) at many points, reduction of curves and grades, strengthening of many miles of track with heavier and better rail, new track fastenings, new ballast and ties, and better drainage. Streamliner fueling and general servicing facilities have been provided, along with shop layouts for inspection and repair of the newer types of power. This indicates the extensiveness of a program to improve rail service.

Expenditures for improved service can no doubt be financed by the rail industry. A large portion of the total costs will be for equipment. For this type of financing, equipment trust certificates will be utilized to a great extent. This class of rail security has always been readily salable at low interest rates. With respect to improvements to fixed plant, a substantial part of current large earnings will eventually find its way into improvement channels. Companies now undergoing drastic financial reorganization should occupy an improved credit position after the reorganizations have been completed. Even at the depth of the depression, from 1932 to 1938, Class I rail carriers made annual capital expenditures ranging from $104,000,000 to $510,000,000, and averaging $244,000,000 per year over that seven-year period. Thus, it is probable that the railroads will be able to finance these improvements.

Reduction of Railroad Rates

A second policy in meeting the competition of aviation might be to reduce railroad rates so as to promote full use of facilities. Although the rates of the airlines are higher than those of the railroad at the present time, they will be reduced in the future. To meet this increased competition, low rates would be an effective weapon of the railroads.

One difficulty in setting rates for railroad services is that so many of the costs are joint that there is no method of determining exactly the costs of one particular type of service. Using the Interstate Commerce Commission's formula of apportioning overhead on the basis of train-hours, costs of transporting passengers can be definitely determined. But this determination is difficult to make in advance of a rate reduction, since it is not known how large an increase in the volume of traffic the lowered rate will produce. Hypothetical results may be figured, but the best test is experiment.

It might seem unreasonable to some observers to discuss a policy of lowered passenger rates when the costs of transporting passengers have been in excess of passenger revenues from the middle 1920's to the boom war years. Yet many businesses have gained in amount of net income by lowering rates.

In view of the railroad deficits in passenger traffic, some might ask why the railroads should not willingly yield this traffic to airplanes and buses. Then the railroads could prosper on the profitable end of their business — that is, freight. The answer is found in the fact that the capital investment and fixed charges of the railroads are large. Even though they should discontinue the operating expenses in connection with passengers, they could not discontinue the passenger traffic's share of the cost of the investment in roadbed, rails, general plant equipment, etc. Then, too, public policy would not permit them to abandon their passenger service unless other means of transportation were sufficient. At present, at least, not all communities have their passenger transportation requirements met by buses, private automobiles, and airplanes.

It appears likely that the railroads will first try to obtain more traffic by improving their service and perhaps experimenting with lowered rates. If the lowering of rates is effective, it may lead to increased lowering of rates in an attempt to build up traffic.

Lowered Railroad Costs

The policies thus far discussed have been directed toward increasing the volume of business, but the railroads may also attempt to lower costs. Their freedom to lower costs is restricted because they are a public utility and must furnish services to communities dependent on them, even though the volume of traffic is low. They are not free to curtail their services in years of depression in the way a manufacturer of automobiles, for instance, may do. Large items in these costs are wages of employees and interest paid to the holders of railroad bonds. Some of the costs of railroads are fixed by law, such as taxes, retirement funds, social security payments, etc. Of course, there may be other ways of reducing costs, such as improvements in the production of power, reduction in the weight of trains, and increased operating efficiency in general. The policy of reducing costs need not wait until experiments in increasing traffic have been completed. In any alert business, there is always a policy of keeping costs low. But the intensity of efforts to reduce costs is often determined by circumstances and competitive pressure.

The need to reduce railroad costs will be particularly acute in the postwar years. The railroads experienced increased costs of operation during the war, but the freight rates remained the same as in the prewar years, while railroad passenger fares increased only 10 per cent. The railroads were able to meet the increased costs because of the greater wartime volume of business. The volume of business of the railroads will drop considerably from its wartime high, but will the costs go down proportionately? Reductions in wages and salaries will probably be subject to public disapproval, since efforts are being made to maintain a large volume of purchasing power in order to secure a high level of business prosperity. The prospect of reducing railroad costs to any large extent in the postwar decade is not bright.

After the First Postwar Decade

The railroads can bear a temporary depression, severe though it might be, for they can look forward to a period of general business prosperity when their revenues will increase greatly. But the permanent curtailment of revenues by virtue of competition from the airlines is different from the effect of depression. Aviation will continue to grow for at least several decades after the war, and air competition to railroads will increase. As we look farther ahead, it is not possible to determine very definitely the degree of attainment by aviation far into the future and the specific effects on the railroads.

The possible development of short-distance air travel in the second decade after the war is a matter of concern to the railroads because a large proportion of their passengers travel short distances. In July, 1939, only 23 per cent of the passengers of Eastern railroads traveled more than one hundred miles, and only 6 per cent over two hundred and fifty miles.[7] A large southeastern railway reports only 20 per cent of their passengers traveling over one hundred miles, and 45 per cent traveling less than twenty-five miles.[8] The Western railroads would show a larger percentage traveling over one hundred miles. Since the railroads carry some five hundred million passengers a year, there is a very large short-distance passenger potential for which the airlines might compete if they can bring the rates down low

---

[7] I.C.C. Exhibit in Passenger Fare Case, *Ex parte* 123.
[8] Federal Coordinator of Transportation, *Passenger Traffic Report,* p. 172.

enough. In addition, there are about five hundred million passengers a year on intercity buses. But since bus rates are lower than those of the railroads, bus traffic is less subject to invasion by aircraft.

As has been pointed out in other chapters, any penetration of the airlines into the field of short-distance service is likely to come slowly. At present, it does not appear that airlines could offer local service at rates as low as those of railroads and buses unless they receive government subsidies. However, there is probably a certain percentage of passengers traveling short distances who would be willing to pay the higher air rates for the speed which they can get in emergencies or in other situations. So it is possible that the railroads may lose a small percentage of their passengers traveling less than one hundred miles to the airplane in the second postwar decade.

Private Flying

Private flying should be considered as a possible threat to the railroads in the same way that the private automobile has become an important competitor. The volume of intercity traffic in private automobiles is not known but has been variously estimated as 187,000,000,000 [9] and 246,000,000,000 [10] passenger-miles in 1940, or many times the total intercity passenger traffic by bus, railroad, and airplane. One naturally speculates, therefore, as to the possible development of intercity travel by private airplanes.

Private flying will probably not expand into a very large volume until ten years or more after the war. The earliest use of private aircraft is likely to be for business purposes, and the craft are likely to be operated by professional pilots. There will be more private owners of small aircraft if a good roadable helicopter is developed. Such a development would increase the threat to the railroads. However, the advent of large numbers of these aircraft at low prices seems to be a decade or more distant.

If private intercity flying develops to a large extent, not all

[9] From evidence submitted by the Greyhound Corporation at the *Feeder Hearings,* before the Civil Aeronautics Board in October, 1943.
[10] Pullman Company, *Annual Report.*

the traffic thus transported will be taken from the railroads. Some of it will come from the private automobile. A certain percentage will be new traffic which would not have developed without private aircraft. Nevertheless, the railroads should not rule out the prospects of competition from private flying at some time in the future.

Freight and Express

From the evidence at hand at the present time, the railroads seem to have a rather secure position in the transportation of freight during the second decade after the war. The average revenue per ton-mile by rail has been running less than one cent for quite a number of years. It was 0.973 cent in 1939 and is slightly below that figure today. Comparably low rates for air cargo do not now seem to be attainable by airplanes. The price for cargo haulage by airplanes may come down a good deal in a decade or two, if flying wings, all-cargo planes, better power plants and more efficient fuel are forthcoming. But rates lower than fifteen cents a ton-mile do not seem to be probable within ten years after the war.

The outstanding contribution of the airplane in carrying either passengers or freight is speed. In general, the railroad freight that calls for speed is designated as express and travels much faster than freight. It is the railway express business, rather than heavy freight, that would be attracted by air transportation in the United States. If the airline companies can get rates down to fifteen cents a ton-mile in the second postwar decade and can furnish door-to-door overnight service, the railroads may lose a good deal of their express business.

At present, the express business of the railroads is very large in comparison with that of the airlines. The railway express ton-mileage in 1940 was 1,600,000,000 ton-miles as compared with 3,500,000 ton-miles of air express. In 1943, the air express increased to 15,000,000 ton-miles, but the railway express increased even more — 2,462,000,000 ton-miles.[11]

[11] Figures quoted by K. N. Merritt, Railway Express Agency, in letter of October 20, 1944. They do not include carloads.

Perhaps one-half of railway express will be available for air competition within a decade after the war if the airlines are able to extend their routes to smaller places and to make short hauls of one hundred miles or less. The first-class railway express, with present rates of about ten or eleven cents a ton-mile for the longer hauls, will suffer more than other railway express, which goes at somewhat lower rates. All express going over three hundred and fifty miles will be particularly vulnerable. As the volume of air express grows, rates can be lowered through economies in ground handling and the use of all-cargo planes. It is possible that rates may be lowered sufficiently to attract some of the non-first-class express.

The railroads may attempt to retain their express business by rate competition. This would be done through the Railway Express Company, which handles the express for all roads, as well as, at present, the ground handling for the airlines. In addition to rate reduction by the railroads, some improvements may be made in express service. The increased speed which is expected to be achieved in passenger trains will help retain some of the express. One advantage to the railroad is the fact that the express business is largely in the eastern part of the United States, where there are large concentrations of population. In this region, the railroads can furnish a two-day, door-to-door service as against an overnight, door-to-door air service. If the railroads maintain lower rates for express and take only a day longer in the eastern part of the United States, they will be able to hold a good deal of their business at the end of the postwar decade.

Conclusion

Much of the growth of aviation, as well as a favorable volume of traffic for the railroads, depends upon national business prosperity. If business conditions are good in the first postwar decade, the airlines are expected to take around $200,000,000 to $300,-000,000 of revenue from the railroads in the latter years of the decade unless the railroads adopt policies which successfully reduce aviation's competition. If the railroads are operating at a high level of income, the loss of $200,000,000 or $300,000,000 of operating revenue to the airlines would mean a reduction in railroad operating revenues of from 3 to 5 per cent and a reduction of net income of from 7 to 12 per cent. The loss in revenues from passenger service would be around 30 to 40 per cent, and from express around 25 per cent. The loss in passenger revenues will come principally from long-distance, higher-priced passenger service. If there is a depression during this period, with the railroads operating on a low level of earnings, they will feel very keenly the competition from the airlines.

In the years following the first postwar decade, the railroads are expected to continue to lose passengers to the airlines, but they will still carry nearly all the freight. If air cargo rates are as low as fifteen cents a ton-mile, which is possible, the railroads may lose around one-half of their first-class express, unless they develop very successful policies of rate reductions and increased speed of service. Air competition in local service is not expected to any significant extent until the end of the first postwar decade. Airlines may eventually carry a considerable amount of short-haul traffic, but it will be only a small percentage of the vast amount carried by bus, railroad, and truck. Private flying will decrease railroad passenger traffic to a large extent only if a cheap and sturdy roadable helicopter is developed. Airlines are expected eventually to handle nearly all first-class mail and some parcel post.

The railroads are planning to wage an aggressive campaign to hold their traffic, particularly by rendering improved service, such as more speed and faster schedules, by introducing new conveniences at low prices, and perhaps by making some reductions in rates.

How effective these plans will prove to be, when actually translated into practice, will depend upon many factors: the alertness and efficiency of the railroads themselves, the effectiveness of the rate and service competition offered by other agencies of transport, the degree of co-operation and co-ordination that can be developed in the transport field, and, finally, the national policy that may be adopted toward promotion and regulation of the several forms of transportation.

23

Ocean Shipping

THE MAJOR PART of both domestic and international traffic was once carried by water-borne vessels on canals, rivers, and oceans. The importance of domestic water-borne transportation declined with the advent of the railroad and the automobile. In international travel, ships remained the principal means of transport up to World War II. In the immediate prewar years and during the war, aviation became important in international transportation, challenging the supremacy of steamships. We are interested in knowing the extent to which water-borne international transportation will be affected by this new means of transport — the airplane.

Characteristics of Overseas Shipping

The water-borne international traffic of the United States is made up largely of freight; almost 80 per cent of the total revenues of shipping companies is obtained from this source. The cargoes are generally bulky, with low unit value, such as ores, coal and coke, iron and steel, lumber, grain, and cotton. In the late 1930's, approximately 35 per cent of the freight was wet cargo and carried in tankers. About one-third of the exports and imports of the United States was carried in vessels flying the flag of the United States.

The merchant marines of the various nations are not only economic organizations, but they are also instruments of national policy. They are used to promote the national prestige and business of the respective owner nations in different parts of the world. It follows, therefore, that there is keen competition between the shipping companies of the various nations.

The financial conditions of the steamship companies of the world have been in a depressed condition since World War I. It is impossible to state their profits and losses, since the financial records of these companies are not made public because national policy is concerned. However, it is known that there has been an excess shipping capacity since World War I, and governments have paid subsidies to shipping companies. The size of the combined merchant marines of the various countries, as measured in tonnage capacity, increased from the beginning of World War I to the beginning of World War II by about 41 per cent, whereas the world trade in the late 1920's decreased by 15 per cent, and, in the 1930's, exports and imports were sometimes less than before World War I. Many nations, including the United States and Great Britain, had to come to the aid of their shipping companies by the payment of subsidies. From 1928 to 1936 the United States concealed its aid in the overpayment for mail transportation, but after 1936 turned to direct subsidization of the operator.

With this summary of the organizational and financial aspects of the shipping industry, we may inquire more specifically as to the effect of aviation.

Expected Losses in Traffic

In preceding chapters, estimates have been made of the expected losses in ocean-borne passengers, mail, and cargo. Fifty per cent of steamship passengers are expected to travel by air rather than steamship in the postwar decade. First- and second-class ocean passenger traffic will be most vulnerable to air competition. Ocean freight is much less susceptible to air competition than passenger traffic because of the low value per pound of most of the freight. Some high-value goods will go by air express or parcel post at high rates. In general, a very small amount of ocean freight will be transferred to the airlines. As to international air mail, there is a strong probability that all transoceanic first-class mail from the United States that can be taken by airplane will eventually be so transported, but not immediately.

Expected Losses in Passenger Revenues

The estimated ship earnings from passenger services, including cruise travel, to and from American ports, were $172,000,000 in 1937, while the aggregate earnings from freight, including wet cargoes in tankers, were $730,000,000.[1] About $2,500,000 was paid to shipping companies for carrying mail. The total revenues to water-borne shipping to and from the United States mainland ports amounted on the average to about $900,000,000 a year in the latter years of the 1930's. How much of these revenues may be lost to the airlines?

Seventy-two per cent of passenger revenues ($124,000,000) was derived from first- and cabin- and second-class passengers.[2] If 50 per cent of first- and second-class and tourist passengers are diverted to the airlines, as was estimated by the Curtiss-Wright study, then the steamship companies are likely to lose about 40 per cent of their annual passenger revenues. If business conditions are prosperous in the postwar decade, the number of steamship passengers might be expected to increase by 50 to 75 per cent (assuming no air competition and no change from the 1930's in the distribution of passengers by classes); then the annual passenger revenues would be $250,000,000 or $300,000,000. If 40 per cent of first- and second-class revenues were lost to the airlines at this level of earnings, the steamship companies would still have as much revenue from passengers as they received in 1937, but the effect on net income is not known. In other words, if the numbers of passengers traveling on steamships increase sufficiently, they will make up the losses of revenues occurring in the first-, cabin- and second-classes from air competition.

Expected Losses in Cargo Revenues

It is difficult to estimate the possible losses of steamship cargo revenues to the airlines. Professor Sorrell has designated as vulnerable to air competition the ocean traffic of the United States which has a value of more than fifty cents a pound. The revenues

[1] From unpublished manuscript written for this report by Professor Lewis Sorrell.

[2] *Ibid.*

accruing to the shipping companies in 1937 from this class of
high-value goods were $20,000,000. The total revenues from
cargo transportation, including the revenues from tankers, were
about $700,000,000. Thus, about 3 per cent of the total cargo
revenues are considered as vulnerable to air transportation diversion at some time.

The shipping rate for these goods worth more than fifty cents
a pound, or more than a thousand dollars a ton, is about two cents
a ton-mile. This low rate will keep much of this class of goods
from going by air for a very long time. Since this whole class of
goods provides only 3 per cent of cargo revenues, the percentage
lost to airlines (at competitive rates of twenty to thirty cents a
ton-mile) will be considerably less than 3 per cent. The shipping
companies will find their cargo revenues reduced very little by
air competition.

Mail Revenue Losses

In the late 1930's the United States Post Office Department
paid annually about $17,000,000 for the transportation of all
foreign mail, of which about 7 per cent by weight was first-class.[3]
The million or so dollars paid the shipping companies for carrying
first-class mail was only a small fraction of the total revenues
which, in prewar years, were around $900,000,000 a year. Al-
though prewar air mail rates to foreign countries were very high,
they are expected to be reduced and to divert some of the steamship first-class mail. The prospects of the airlines' competing, for
parcel post and printed matter on the basis of costs, with present
steamship rates are not good for at least a decade or more. The
loss of steamship mail revenues in the first decade after the war
is likely to be a few million dollars at the most, unless public
policy forces the lowering of air mail rates through the payment
of subsidies.

Total Expected Losses in Revenues

The impact of aviation on the revenues of companies handling
water-borne ocean transportation may be summarized. If the

3 *Statistical Abstract*, 1942, p. 444.

revenues of the shipping companies are $900,000,000 a year at the end of the first decade after the war, the expected losses would be, from passenger revenue, $52,000,000 (or about half the first- and second-class passenger revenues); from mail, $3,-000,000; and from cargo, $2,000,000. On this basis the total losses of steamship companies to the airlines would be $57,000,000, or about 6 per cent of the total revenues. These calculations include the tanker trade in wet cargoes. If it is not included, the percentage of expected loss would be 7 per cent.

After World War I, the number of water-borne passengers and the tons of ocean freight both increased about 42 per cent (1921 to 1926). If, after this war, the $900,000,000 revenues of the shipping companies, assuming no air competition, were increased 50 per cent, the revenues would be $1,350,000,000. With aviation cutting into this business at the end of the postwar decade to the extent of $80,000,000 or $85,000,000, or 6 per cent of the total revenue, the revenues remaining would be much larger than in the closing years of the 1930 decade. It is obvious that the ability of ocean transportation to withstand the rivalry of aviation is tremendously affected by the course of the business cycle.

The variation in revenues of the shipping companies tells us little about what happens to net income, since the financial accounts of shipping companies are not made public. However, it might be assumed that the amount of net income would increase after the war with improvement in trade and travel and be adversely affected by increasing air competition.

Competition on Various Routes

The size of the potential air market varies on the different steamship routes. Hence the averages of the preceding paragraph do not reveal what the effect of air competition may be on the revenues of a particular shipping company. A steamship company engaged in a heavy cargo trade is much less sensitive to air competition than a company which gets a large percentage of its revenues from passengers traveling between New York and the United Kingdom. Professor Sorrell has worked out the percentages of revenues of shipping companies for different routes that are vulnerable to air attack. It is recalled that Sorrell defines as vulnerable all first-, cabin- and second-class passenger travel, all first-class mail, prints, and parcel post, and all cargo worth over a thousand dollars a ton. This does not mean that the airlines will take these revenues from the steamship companies immediately. Even if only a part of them are diverted to the air, the ranking of the routes would not be greatly changed. Table 28 shows the rating of the different routes as to vulnerability to air competition. On the basis of this definition of vulnerability, the steamship lines on the route between northern Europe (except the Baltic countries) and the northeastern United States are more vulnerable to air competition than other companies. The several steamship lines operating from southern ports in the United States carry cargo almost wholly, and their revenues will not be affected by air competition.

TABLE 28. VULNERABILITY OF SHIPPING REVENUES IN 1937 (PASSENGERS) AND 1939 (FREIGHT) TO AIR COMPETITION ON DIFFERENT TRADE ROUTES OF THE UNITED STATES

Route	Percentage of Total Steamship Revenues Regarded as Vulnerable to Air Competition
1. North Atlantic United States and Europe	
United Kingdom	57
Baltic	11
Continent — Bayonne Hamburg Range	53
Mediterranean: Spain, Portugal, and Azores	32
2. North Atlantic United States and South America	
East coast South America	19
West coast South America	16
3. Pacific United States — Asia, China, Japan, India	
Persian Gulf, Straits Settlement	19
Australasia	16
4. United States and Caribbean, West Indies, Central America, and Canal Zone	31
5. United States and Hawaii	23
6. United States and Alaska	38
7. United States and Puerto Rico	20
8. South Atlantic United States and other regions	2
9. Gulf United States and Europe, Mediterranean	0
10. Pacific United States and Europe, Mediterranean	0
11. North Atlantic United States and Orient	0
12. North Atlantic United States and Australasia	0
13. Gulf United States and Orient	0
14. United States and Africa	8
15. United States and Canada water-borne	13

If it is assumed that one-half of the first- and second-class passenger travel is lost to the steamship lines and that there is no loss of freight, Table 29 shows the percentages of revenue lost on the various routes at the 1937 level of earnings.

TABLE 29. EFFECT ON TOTAL REVENUE OF DIVERTING ONE-HALF THE FIRST AND SECOND-CLASS PASSENGER TRAFFIC OF 1937 UPON UNITED STATES AND FOREIGN-FLAG OVERSEAS SHIPPING

Route	Per cent Lost on U.S. Ships	Per cent Lost on Foreign Ships
1. North Atlantic United States and European	12	27
2. United States and Caribbean, West Indies, Canal Zone	17	15
3. North Atlantic United States and South America	11	4
4. United States and Hawaii, Alaska, and Puerto Rico	13	0
5. United States Pacific and South China, Philippines	24	2
6. United States Pacific and North China, Japan	11	12
7. United States Pacific and Australasia	37	2
8. Miscellaneous South Atlantic, Gulf United States and various areas Pacific United States and Europe, North Atlantic United States and Orient	1	.5

For all the routes considered in Table 29 (not including tanker cargoes), the expected losses in total revenues are 11 per cent for all American ships and 12 per cent for foreign-owned vessels.[4] After the war, the distribution of passengers and cargo by routes may be different.

Although not international routes, the intercoastal lines of the United States are also important. The shipping business along the coasts of the United States consists largely of cargo, with no mail. Only 7 per cent of the revenues comes from passenger traffic. These lines are not likely to suffer much from air competition.

Reaction of Shipping Companies

As previously stated, the steamship lines are not in a favorable position to meet new competition, since they have been operating under somewhat depressed conditions for the past fifteen or twenty years. These depressed conditions of steamship lines have

[4] Sorrell, unpublished manuscript.

existed in most countries, but we are concerned mainly with American-owned lines. In the closing years of the 1930's, American-owned lines received subsidies to the extent of $20,000,000 a year from the United States government.[5] With a prewar financial condition requiring subsidies, further steamship revenue losses will hit an industry already in depressed financial condition.

The competitive position of water-borne transportation has been affected by the wartime destruction of ships. The United States lost many ships, but an enormous tonnage of ships was built at the same time. Before the war, the United States had a total of 12,000,000 deadweight tons in overseas operations. About 27,000,000 deadweight tons were constructed by the United States from December 7, 1941, to December 31, 1943.[6] Because of the large amount of wartime construction of ships, the United States Merchant Marine may be not only the largest merchant marine of any country in the world, but may actually exceed the rest of the world. No doubt some of this tonnage of ships will be transferred to other nations, but for a while much of the world's trade will be carried in American-owned ships. Other nations will need the products of our farms and factories. It is not certain what the volumes of traffic will be thereafter.

Another result of the war has been the destruction of a large number of luxury liner passenger ships, particularly those owned by foreign countries. The *Coolidge*, the *Hoover*, and the *Manhattan* are among the American-owned luxury ships that have been lost.

Since the luxury liners operate largely a passenger service, with very little space provided for cargo, they are likely to be affected by air competition more than other lines. There has been some debate as to whether these luxury liners should be built again in view of the possibility of overseas travel going by air. It is argued that, if the surface ships are to hold their passenger trade, the appeal of these luxury superliners will be needed. But the issue

[5] *Ibid.*

[6] *United States Maritime Commission Report to Congress,* June 30, 1943, p. 6, and *1944 Proceedings, American Merchant Marine Conference,* vol. 9, October 14 and 15, 1943, p. 19.

narrows down to whether or not these ships can be operated for a profit. The superliners are estimated to have an annual net operating revenue of about $1,600,000 a year, which is not enough to pay for the cost of their construction, assuming a life of twenty to twenty-five years.[7] It is impossible to get official figures of the profits and losses of these luxury liners because, like shipping in general, they are instruments of national policy.

The fact that luxury liners are carriers of national prestige may influence the decision as to whether these ships will be built in the postwar years. It is possible, although not probable, that national rivalries between the United States, Britain, France, Germany, Italy, and Russia may lead to the construction of more superliners supported by government subsidy. However, it would appear more probable that national rivalries will find expression in the airliners. The great nations are likely to divert their subsidies from ships to airplanes.

If improvement in passenger service is difficult to obtain without uneconomical costs, can the ships lower their costs? Lowering costs on the large liners appears to be hardly possible without cutting the quality of the service and the conveniences. It would seem more economically sound to operate ships of smaller size, slower speed, and which would carry more high-rate cargo and fewer passengers. These ships might be around twenty-five thousand gross tons in weight, travel at a speed of twenty knots per hour, carry a substantial volume of high-value cargo, and provide accommodations for two hundred passengers. The passenger fares on these smaller ships could probably be lower than those on the luxury liners. The question then arises as to whether these ships would attract passengers. They would not have the customer appeal of the luxury liners, but they would be attractive to those who especially enjoy sea voyages, those who dislike air travel, and those who could not afford to pay air rates. They could compete with airplanes in comfort and conveniences, but not in speed, which is of increasing importance in present-day travel.

Although the costs of shipping could be lowered by abandon-

[7] *Marine Engineering and Shipping Review,* August, 1936, p. 340.

ing the large luxury liners and providing passenger service on smaller, joint-cargo-and-passenger ships, there are other items of high costs. One of these is labor. The level of wages is higher in the United States than in Europe and most other countries of the world, and this puts the United States lines at a disadvantage in competition with those of other countries. The cost of labor is higher, not only in the production of ships and their fittings, but also in the operation of the ships; that is, the wages paid to the crew and service personnel of the ships are higher. Reductions in the cost of labor are not very probable in the postwar years. The wage level was raised considerably during the war, and its fall to prewar levels is likely to be resisted.

It has been suggested that the steamship companies, in order to avoid the shock of overseas air competition, own the airlines operating between nations. This suggestion does not seem practical in view of the current policy in the United States of opposing anything that decreases competition. Furthermore, this arrangement would necessarily mean considerable reorganization of companies, which seems improbable. Such combinations would be advantageous to the investors only if the airlines made a profit. It may very well be that for some time after the war both the steamship companies and the airlines will need government aid. It is hoped, of course, that the international airlines will make adequate profits without subsidies. Airline profits will be affected by the balance between the volume of air traffic and the amount of equipment of the competing airlines of this and other nations. The shipping companies also have this problem of balance. In view of all these factors, it hardly seems probable that there will be a merging of steamship and airline companies.

So far, no very effective, constructive program of holding ship passengers against air competition seems to be forthcoming. With regard to mail, it seems hardly worth while for the steamship companies to try to hold the first-class mail by reducing charges, since such a small amount of revenue is involved. The mail and cargo that will be lost to the airlines cannot be held by lowered rates, since it is the traffic that demands speed that will go to the airlines.

Beyond the First Postwar Decade

The discussion up to this point has dealt largely with the first postwar decade. The trends apparent in the first postwar decade are expected to continue in the following decades. It seems reasonable to expect a slow but progressive reduction of the costs of operation of transoceanic airlines. There is little evidence that the steamship companies are likely to increase the speed of passenger ships; but rather that slower and more economically operated boats will be used. The lowered rates on these smaller and slower ships may hold some of the water-borne passenger traffic. Some passengers will always prefer an ocean voyage to air travel. It is probable that the steamship companies will face an increased loss of passengers in the second decade after the war.

With regard to mail, it is likely that more printed matter and a good deal of package mail will be going by air in the second decade after the war as well as the major part of first-class mail.

It is difficult to predict the future of air cargo, since it has had such a short history. However, the difference between ship cargo rates and the air cargo rates predicted for the first postwar decade is so great that it does not seem probable that air cargo will offer much competition to water-borne shipping in the second decade after the war. Yet a considerable amount of high-value cargo may be diverted from ships to the airlines. The domestic airlines took some express from the railroads in the prewar years, even though there was a great difference in rates. This may occur in foreign cargo operations, since the increased speed of the airplanes may attract an increasing amount — but still a very small percentage of the total — of high-priced cargo from the surface ships.

Conclusion

The effect of air competition on transoceanic surface shipping is likely to be very slight during the first year or two after the war. In the latter part of the first postwar decade, the steamships are expected to lose about fifty per cent of their first- and second-class passengers to the airlines, most of their first-class mail, and a small percentage of their freight traffic. The loss in passenger revenues will probably amount to forty per cent. In the second postwar decade, a large proportion of the remaining passengers are expected to be diverted to the airlines and an increasing amount of cargo of high-unit value. The amount of cargo diverted to the air will increase, but it will still be a small proportion of the total water-borne freight traffic. The percentage of loss in revenues from the diversion of first-class mail will be very small. The steamship routes across the North Atlantic between the United States and Europe will be most affected by air competition, since these routes carry the largest proportion of passengers per ship. The American shipping companies which operate routes to the south carry large proportions of cargo and will be little bothered by the growth of aviation. The impact of air competition will fall almost equally on American and foreign-owned shipping companies.

The surface vessels will probably have their annual total revenues reduced by about 6 per cent at the end of the first postwar decade, including tanker cargo, and 7 per cent, omitting tanker cargo. It is impossible to estimate the effect of air competition on the net income of shipping companies, since these net income figures are not made public. If the volume of international travel is large, the shipping companies will be better able to withstand air competition than in depression years. The American shipping industry has been depressed for fifteen or twenty years and has been the recipient of government subsidies. The shipping companies will have a surplus of tonnage after the war and will not be in a favorable condition for meeting air competition. Steamship companies are likely to make some effort to maintain their passenger traffic, but it is not certain what course will be followed. It is difficult for companies to offer improved services because of the high costs. Passengers may be carried along with freight on ships which are slower and smaller than the luxury liners. The shipping companies will adjust their operations to a larger proportion of freight in the postwar period. If they were to operate profitable airlines, they could use the profits, if there were some, to pay shipping losses, but it is not likely that American steamship companies will own airlines.

24

Manufacturing

MANUFACTURING is dependent upon the transportation system which brings to its doors the raw materials to be processed and then distributes the finished product. Boats, railroads, and trucks, the principal means of transportation in the past, have all affected the location and organization of manufacturing. The purpose of this chapter is to inquire in what ways, if any, manufacturing will be modified by the new system of transportation, the airplane.

General Observations

Aviation can render three services to manufacturers: the transportation of persons, the transportation of goods, and the transportation of mail. Since the major influence of the railroad and the automobile on manufacturing has resulted from the transportation of goods, this might be expected to be true also in the case of the airplane. The key to the influence of air cargo upon manufacturing is transportation rates. Rates determine the kinds and volume of goods that will be transported by air. As reported in Chapter 22, air cargo is likely for some time to be restricted largely to the class of goods that now go by railway express. Rates are likely to be around thirty and forty cents a ton-mile during the first part of the postwar decade, except for special contracts. Only a small percentage of manufactured goods can be sent by air at these rates. The impact of aviation on manufacturing will, in general, be slight until the time when air rates are reduced, but even slight reductions in rates will increase considerably the number of manufacturers that will be affected by aviation. It is possible that air cargo rates may be around fifteen or twenty cents per ton-mile by the close of the first postwar decade or during the second postwar decade.

The rates cited above are in terms of the general shipper whose packages are picked up by a commercial agency for delivery to the airport. If the manufacturer can organize his own means of conveyance of goods to the airport and ships quantities large enough to utilize considerable space on the plane, he may lower his own rates below those of the ordinary user of air express. Thus, air express may have more influence on certain manufacturing plants than on manufacturing in general.

Aviation is not expected to have as much influence on manufacturing as did the railroads or trucks. Yet there will be a variety of influences on selected types of manufacture. We shall examine now some of these effects.

Principle of High Unit Value

In most cases, objects with a high monetary value per unit of weight will be the first to be shipped by air, since the transportation charges are a small percentage of their value. The weight of goods to be shipped is important in air transportation, since, in addition to being propelled forward, their weight must also be sustained. However, objects with a high monetary value per unit of weight have not always been the first to be shipped. Men's suits have an average cost of four or five dollars per pound, yet there has been little transportation of them by air. High value per pound is not a dynamic factor that forces these products to go by air. It is rather that this characteristic makes it possible for these objects to go by air, and other factors enter into the determination. However, in general, manufacturers of expensive articles are expected to make first use of air transportation. In this class would be luxury goods, and such high-priced goods as drugs and scientific instruments.

Principle of Emergency

Since the principal contribution of the airplane as a means of transportation is speed, it is to be expected that manufacturers would turn to air transportation in case of an emergency. Canvasses have been made of many types of business which express goods by air to find the reasons for using air transportation. In almost all businesses consulted, an emergency has arisen some time during the year whereby they have had recourse to air transportation. Not very much appears to have been sent by air in any particular instance by most of those interviewed, but when the emergency shipments from all industries are added, the total probably constitutes an appreciable proportion of the total air cargo. The frequency of emergencies, or what is considered an emergency, in business is surprisingly great.

There are some products which have time characteristics more or less permanently or regularly. Christmas goods and gifts for other special occasions are often rush orders. Very perishable edibles, such as fruits, appear by seasons and need to be transported quickly. Products of the press and news reels have a value which quickly diminishes as time passes. There is also a premium on the quick acquisition by retailers of new articles of fashion, such as women's dresses, shoes, and hats. Styles may come in quickly and skyrocket to an unanticipated demand. A popular moving-picture actress may wear a new type of dress, gloves, or hat in a very successful picture, with the result that a great demand is created "overnight" for this particular style. Many of these orders for shipment need to be delivered in time for Saturday's trade. If these orders cannot be finished in time for the week-end trade, the shipment might as well not be finished until some time the next week. The speed of air transportation is helpful in meeting such emergencies.

The sporting-goods industries may have rush orders for equipment carrying special designs, letters, or awards. For instance, a Chicago company received a special order from a Salt Lake City football team for shoes for use in the mud caused by unusually heavy rains. Manufacturers of gloves have also experienced an unusual number of rush orders and have found air transportation helpful. The manufacturers of cellulose sausage casings have a perishable product and use air transportation.

Such time-utility commodities will not travel by air, however, unless the unit value is also high. The value per pound of most fruits and of newspapers is too low to pay present air cargo rates. On the other hand, many furs, hats, and dresses have a high unit value and have already been shipped to a considerable extent by air transportation.

In cases where manufacturers do make use of air transportation, are manufacturing methods otherwise affected? Since emergency goods are greatly needed at a specific time, they do not accumulate on the shelves of the retailer. Products such as newspapers and fruits cannot stay long in the hands of either the retailer or the producer. In the case of women's fashion goods, there is also a quick movement, but the tendency would seem to be for the manufacturer, rather than the retailer, to hold the accumulation of stock. If the retailer can get quick delivery of fashion goods by air, he will maintain a skeleton stock, passing any risk back to the manufacturer. But the manufacturer of women's fashion goods does not want to be stuck with out-of-date goods any more than does the retailer. In this case, air transportation may have a tendency to accentuate the peak or seasonal nature of production in these manufacturing plants. A manufacturer of goods for celebrations or special occasions, such as Christmas, can, however, distribute his production over the year somewhat if the goods are not perishable. If the orders for time-utility goods are geared to the speed of air express, the purchasing and supply problems of these manufacturing plants are likely to feel the reflex action of these rush orders.

An emergency of a somewhat different nature which often arises in industry is the need for spare parts of machinery or the necessity of repairs involving materials or skilled services which may not be available in the locality of the plant. Where these breakages will occur or what spare parts will be needed cannot be accurately foreseen, so that it is not possible to stock an abundant supply of parts without some waste.

Delays because of breakages or missing parts can seriously disrupt the manufacturing process. One begins to appreciate how elaborate is the production process when it is realized what an enormous number of parts such products as airplanes, automobiles, telephones, and refrigerators have. Since these parts are often supplied by various factories, many manufacturing establishments are essentially places of assembly of various parts made elsewhere. In such an assembly process, if an important part is missing because the subcontractor is behind schedule, the whole process breaks down. Air service in such an emergency can save a day or two over ground methods of transportation for plants east of the Mississippi and much more time for plants on the Pacific Coast if the parts come from the East. Some of these parts have a high value per pound, and they occupy strategic positions in the assembly process. The types of articles in this category are quite varied and include such things as plastic panels, aluminum trimmings, lubricating equipment, automotive parts, and so on. Precision tools, which average around thirty dollars a pound, have the same character as essential parts. During the industrial expansion of wartime production, when there was much need for parts of machinery, there was a rapid growth in this aspect of air cargo. This service is likely to be significant in the future in increasing the efficiency of manufacturing companies.

Principle of Weight

Since airplanes favor objects of light weight, the design and the packaging of many articles that are transported by air will be affected. For instance, luggage is being made of lighter material and advertised as "airplane luggage." The design features of goods are usually set by their functions and not by their transportability. However, their functions may be performed equally well when a light-weight material is used. A light-weight chair may be made as strong and comfortable as a heavy, bulky chair. Though not much furniture is likely to be shipped by air, still it is quite possible for the idea of light weight to permeate our whole manufacturing system, whether or not the products go by air. Such diffusion of an idea is observed in the instance of streamlining, which is of great efficiency in airplanes; somewhat less so in automobiles. Yet we have streamlined houses and streamlined furniture. A fad for light-weight objects could not be attributed solely to the development of aviation; the quality of light weight is also encouraged by railroads and automobiles. Yet the airplane is a significant factor in developing such a style.

Objects in light-weight metals can now be produced in large quantities, since we have great productive capacity for light metals and their alloys as a heritage from the war. Magnesium and aluminum alloys are particularly important in an age of emphasis on light-weight materials. There are also several plastics that are much lighter than wood; and plastics lend themselves more readily than metals to the fabrication of a multiplicity of objects.

Packaging for transportation by airplane is quite different from packaging for trucks or trains because the type of motion is different. Not so much padding is needed in airplanes as in railroads or trucks, where the riding is often rough. The packaging of flowers for air transportation has meant the discarding of the old, heavy boxing for a light-weight, strong, fiber material. The firmness in some of the material is attained by using a fluted surface. Packaging is also affected by the method of placing the cargo in the plane, which must be done carefully to insure the proper distribution of weight. Whatever the development in the various devices for packaging goods sent by air, a principal aim is lightness.

A change in the practices of crating is of economic importance to many industries in that the price of the boxing, the nails, and the labor involved often adds up to a sizable element in the cost of transportation. Crating for air transportation costs much less than for surface. Transportation by air may mean that more attention will be given to reducing the costs of boxing and packaging for shipping. Perhaps the tendency toward light packaging will also spread to some goods that go by truck and railroad. Certainly, the manufacturing plants producing boxing and packaging goods will be affected.

Principle of Distance

The airplane travels long distances much more quickly than other transportation media. If it can do this at a reasonable cost, aviation will have an effect on those manufacturing plants whose markets or sources of supply are long distances from the plant. Exporting industries, for example, are located long distances from their markets. However, in the first postwar decade, the rates for overseas air cargo are likely to be too high for all but a few selected industries which sell products with a high value per pound. Aviation will influence industries doing business in foreign countries in several ways other than the transportation of their products. Salesmen, buyers, and executives can easily travel by airplane to distant areas with which their companies have business connections without losing much time. This aspect of aviation's service favors the location of business enterprises and branch establishments in other countries, especially in South America and Europe. Equipment and machinery sold in foreign countries can be speedily serviced by American companies.

The problem of distance is also an important one for domestic manufacturing in the United States, for ours is a large country with great distances, especially eastward and westward. The necessity for traveling long distances in the United States is further increased by the great stretches of semi-arid, thinly populated territory which lie between the Pacific Coast and the Middle West. There is close interdependence between the Pacific Coast and the eastern part of the United States. The two areas provide markets and sources of supply for each other. However, the amount of manufacturing is relatively small on the West Coast as compared with that in the eastern part of the United States.

A low air cargo rate will be advantageous to both these areas. It will prove particularly attractive to producers and manufacturers on the Pacific Coast who are desirous of obtaining a large market, such as exists in the East. Many of the Western products seeking outlets in the East are agricultural products, such as fruits, flowers, and wine. In addition, there are motion pictures, airplane parts, aluminum, magnesium, and other products of great importance. The Pacific Coast area is new and rapidly developing, and the industries there now are not an index of those that may develop in the future. The airplane will be influential in the development of new industries in this area. Even if the amount of air cargo is not large, the use of planes by the personnel of industry and the use of planes in supplying parts will be of value to the Western manufacturing establishments.

The tempo of daily life has been increased as transportation has become more rapid. Business in general is likely to become more sensitive to speed as an indirect result of aviation. Speed as a characteristic of manufacturing may spread from industries that use airplanes to those that do not. This will particularly result from a wider distribution of air mail and also a greater use of aviation by businessmen generally. The fast pace of life in the United States may spread to other lands.

The Location of Industry

Both the railroad and the automobile affected the location of manufacturing plants. In the case of the railroad, factories necessarily had to be near a railroad station since the track was fixed. The factories adjusted their locations accordingly. With the development of trucking facilities, the light industries were freed from their close dependence upon the railroad. The truck brought more freedom to locate farther out on cheaper land. In addition, the bus and other means of local transportation made it possible to recruit labor in areas farther removed from the city.

The means of transportation is only one of a number of factors affecting the location of industry. These factors are: labor supply, wage rates, labor organization, sources of mechanical power, raw materials, and markets. The influence of any or all these factors on location is different for new industries from that on the relocation of older plants. New industries are free to locate according to choice, while there is an inertia about moving older plants. Many factories, built during the railroad construction era and before the coming of the truck, are still at their original locations. If the meat-packing industry of the Chicago area were to locate anew, it would hardly choose a location so near the center of Chicago as it now has. But to relocate farther out would be a very large undertaking. In general, light industry moves more readily than heavy. Also some industries, such as blast furnaces and steel mills, have many particularistic determinants as well as a huge plant to move. Yet heavy industry can be moved if the need is great enough. Under the necessity of war, the Russians moved much of their heavy industry farther east before the oncoming Germans.

Air transportation may enable the development of large industries in new regions, although it should be remembered that there are many factors other than the means of transportation which determine the location of industry. For instance, the apparel industry may develop to large proportions on the Pacific Coast. There has already been a considerable growth in the production of clothing, especially sport clothes for both men and women, in Southern California. Also, Hollywood, because the moving-picture stars often set the fashions, has become a center for style merchandise. But the growth of this industry has been handicapped by the fact that there was only a relatively small market near-by. If the airplane can open up the markets of the East for these sports styles and other clothing, the clothing industries in the West Coast regions will be greatly facilitated. A large proportion of women's clothing is expected to go by air after the war as was shown in Chapter 8, but low rates will be necessary to enable a large development. In general, it is thought that cargo rates in the postwar decade will be sufficiently low to stimulate the development of the clothing industry on the Pacific Coast.

There is a popular belief in many cities that the provision of air connections for the city will be helpful to business and encourage new industries and businesses to locate in these communities. This attitude is no doubt sound in that air mail service and fast transportation for executives and for the emergency needs of plants will be helpful to business and manufacturing. Perhaps it is true that, if these communities did not have airports, new industries might be reluctant to locate there. But that new industries will locate in a community because there are good airports does not seem probable, since all cities in the United States will have adequate facilities.

A more significant question is whether the location of a plant will be affected by the distance from an airport. An industry already established in a particular location will not move to be near an airport unless it ships a large proportion of its goods by air. In locating a new plant, however, an owner might very well take into consideration the distance from an airport, but how much weight would be given to such a factor is a question. Other things being equal, it would be desirable to locate near an airport, particularly if the industry plans to transport its products to and from the airport. The location of some stores, markets, and establishments near airports is more probable than that of manufacturing plants.

A variant of this question is whether plants may seek locations sufficiently far out from the city to provide their own landing fields. It is thought that not many manufacturing plants will have need of a plane of their own, at least not in the next ten or twelve years. The regular scheduled airlines can be used, and large airports are very expensive to build and operate. If small planes were used by industry, the landing field could be smaller and less costly. Sod landing strips are satisfactory a major part of the time and are cheaper than paved. Henry Ford, in the 1920's, had his own airplanes and airports, but he was a manufacturer of airplanes at the time. He used the planes for transporting his own materials and parts from one plant to another. It is quite possible that some other large concerns may have their own airfields.

The helicopter has considerable possibilities for use by industry, particularly in transporting cargo or executives and other travelers to the airport. Helicopters capable of carrying fairly large loads may be in operation by the middle or end of the first postwar decade. Such helicopters, traveling at one hundred or one hundred twenty-five miles an hour, would bring a factory in the city very close in time to the airport. Ordinarily, a landing field for a helicopter will need to be only fifty or a hundred feet square, depending on the size of the helicopter, although a larger field would be required if space for emergency landings were provided. Many factories are so located that they have sufficient space for a landing field for helicopters, and the relocation of factories to accommodate helicopters is not envisaged. If sufficient space did not exist, it would be cheaper to purchase adjoining land and clear an adequate space than to relocate the factory. If the plant is large and sends a good deal by air, it will provide its own transportation to and from the airport for manufactured products and raw materials instead of using an outside delivery service. Either the truck or the helicopter will be used for this purpose. With the helicopter, the plant could be located some distance from the airport.

Projecting our imagination farther into the future, there is some possibility of a few factories using gliders. There are several features of glider transportation which appear to be advantageous, but which have not been tested with practical economic experience. Gliders were successfully used by the Army Air Forces during World War II, but economic factors are not taken into consideration in military operations. Military gliders were used principally to transport men and materials to and from places which had no regular airports. A glider loaded with cargo can be picked up by a plane in full flight. It does not require a large and costly airfield either for landing or taking off; and carrying cargo it could be picked up at the factory airfield by a tow-plane and dropped off at its destination. The technological features of this maneuver are feasible.

On the economic side, the original cost of a glider is much less than that of an airplane because cheaper materials can be used and no engine is required. Airline companies could provide towing service for a series of plants, particularly if glider and tow-plane characteristics were standardized so that they would match each other. Many items of cost for regular transport planes, such as airport expense, overhead, promotion, and advertising, will be lower for gliders. Not enough is known to speak of rates and cost, but many aviation experts are of the opinion that the additional space of the glider can be built more economically into the transport plane itself.

In order to provide a reliable and suitable towing service, it would be necessary for the airline companies to set up an efficient tow-plane schedule. The advantages of air service in saving time would be lost if there were delays or poor schedules. It may be difficult to set up such schedules.

In spite of these difficulties, there are some types of production that might use gliders. A newspaper might use gliders to drop off loads of papers in various communities. A flower-growers' association might find glider transportation of use between two or three cities. Gliders might also be used in taking goods and materials to different branch plants in a big company.

For most purposes, the regular airline transport system is undoubtedly the most suitable. Gliders will be used only if the costs should prove to be very low and if the flexibility of the glider is sufficiently advantageous.

Having surveyed the various possible influences of aviation on the location of manufacturing plants, one might say in conclusion that the effect of aviation would seem to be very slight.

Size of Manufacturing Companies

One of the trends in industry is the increasing size of corporations and the concentration of ownership. There has been considerable resistance to this trend on the part of the public, the businessman, and the economist, who generally admire free enterprise and the competitive system. Will aviation favor this trend, or will it strengthen to a greater degree the small manufacturer?

The air express system as it is organized today is equally accessible to small and large manufacturers. The services of the Railway Express Agency in transporting goods from factory door to airport are likewise equally accessible. However, if the manufacturer does his own transporting to the airport, presumably at less expense than the charges of the Railway Express Agency or a similar service, it will be the large manufacturer who will be able to own his own helicopter or truck, rather than the smaller manufacturer. Also it will be the large manufacturing companies that will have their own landing fields or use planes as a shuttle between different branches. If cheaper air cargo rates are offered for contract services in handling plane-load lots of goods, this economy will accrue only to the large producer unless many small producers band together.

On the other hand, some of the goods that are most likely to go by air are produced by small manufacturers. The makers of luxury goods, which have a relatively small buying public, are often the smaller producers. So, too, the firms catering to rush-order business or existing for emergency trade may tend to be somewhat smaller. This may not be the case with perishable goods, such as newspapers or women's fashion goods. Probably those companies with foreign markets, especially branch offices in foreign lands, will be the larger houses.

Establishments of any size could use the scheduled airline services for travel of business executives, salesmen, and buyers. However, the large companies are more likely to maintain their own buying and distributing branches, and may, for this reason, have more occasion to use the speed of air transport for personnel. In this way, aviation may give an advantage to the large over the small manufacturer. Air mail does not appear to be a discriminating factor, except possibly for the large mail-order houses.

In conclusion, it might be said that what little influence aviation has on the size of establishments will be toward strengthening the larger producer.

Local Industries

Aviation will increase the size of the market areas of certain industries. The development of faster surface methods of transportation has increased the number of industries which have nation-wide markets, since fast transportation makes delivery over a wider area possible. One may visit cities in any part of the country today and see the same kinds of goods sold in the stores and the same types of advertising signs. Aviation will encourage this trend.

This development is oddly but effectively illustrated by industries manufacturing coffins. With present railroad transportation, state laws requiring that bodies be placed in caskets within twenty-fours after death restrict the market for coffin manufacturers, particularly since dealers do not wish to stock up with expensive caskets. Fast air transportation at reasonable rates is expected to extend the market area for coffins. Another illustration would be a national or regional newspaper, although it is controversial whether either will develop. Also, as has been mentioned previously, air cargo is expected to extend the market for some Pacific Coast products to the eastern part of the United States if low cargo rates are in force.

An indirect effect of these larger market areas is increased competition for local industries. Local manufacturers of coffins may suffer as a result of the use of the airplane to transport coffins. As for newspapers, there will always be local newspapers even if city dailies do cover larger areas in the future, but the local papers may have their subscriptions and advertising reduced somewhat. The effect of faster air transportation of commodities is to increase the competition of the nation-wide manufacturers as opposed to those serving a smaller local market.

It is easy to exaggerate this influence. For instance, at the time that rural free mail delivery was being considered in Congress, predictions were made freely by opponents of the measure that the bill proposed would mean the disappearance of villages. This prediction was based on the assumption that local merchants would be put out of business by big mail-order houses and that villages could not survive without local merchants. However, there are many thousands of local merchants still in business, and the village has not disappeared.

The actual extent of the airplane's influence in favoring the nation-wide producer will depend upon the differential between the costs of production of the large producer and of the local one. This differential should be sufficiently large to compensate for the probable higher rate of air transportation as compared with rail rates. The quality of the service must be considered too, for example in dispatching style goods. The peculiarities in the demands of consumers are also a factor, as, for instance, in freshness of the product. In all probability, the influence of air transportation in weakening local industry in competition with region-wide concerns will be slight in the near future. But, whatever the amount of its influence, it will be in line with trends initiated by other means of modern transportation.

Air transportation tends to operate slightly against some local manufacturers, but in other cases it may work out to their advantage in quite a different manner. It may do this by favoring decentralization of plants into smaller communities, whoever may own the plants. It is recalled that the process of much manufacture is essentially one of assembly of parts made elsewhere. Air transportation promotes this assembly method by reducing delays because of the lack of some of the parts. Of course, the most important determinants of the decentralization of plants are such factors as labor costs, rental values, and the most efficient size of plants. Yet transportation is a factor, and air cargo makes somewhat more practical small local plants making parts of producers' goods.

The Manufacture of Aircraft

Aviation has created a new manufacturing industry, the production of aircraft, which has been added to the ever-growing list of manufacturing industries. The aircraft industry expanded enormously during the war. In 1939, the aviation industry ranked forty-fourth among American businesses; during the war, it became the world's largest industry.[1] In 1943, it was more than five times the size of the prewar automobile industry.[2] In 1939, about 64,000 people were employed in plane production, and the value of the product was about $280,000,000. In the latter part of 1943, when the peak was attained, approximately 2,100,000 people, or thirty times the prewar level, were working in the aircraft industry.[3] The value of the product in the same year was approximately $20,000,000,000, or more than seventy times greater than the output in 1939.[4] In 1937, 3100 planes were produced, including both civil and military aircraft. Early in 1941, 1000 planes were being produced per month. This increased to between 8000 and 9000 per month in 1944. When the weight of output per month is taken, the increase is even greater because of the fact that production changed from lighter planes to heavy bombers. The total weight produced per month in 1941 was 4,000,000 pounds. In

[1] William A. Burden, *Reconversion and Air Power*, address to National Industrial Conference Board, September 21, 1944, mimeo., p. 2.
[2] Crowell-Collier Publishing Company, New York City, *Tomorrow's Customers for Aviation*, August, 1944, p. 2.
[3] "Wartime Development of the Aircraft Industry," Bulletin no. 800 of the United States Bureau of Labor Statistics, reprint from the *Monthly Labor Review*, November, 1944, p. 1.
[4] Crowell-Collier, *op. cit.*, p. 2.

May, 1944, over 102,000,000 pounds were produced, more than in
any previous month and thirty times the number in January,
1941.[5]

It is obvious that this industry will shrink greatly in size. The
amount of shrinkage is an important question, since it affects the
amount of employment and the welfare of communities, and
raises problems as to what to do with these plants. These questions are of very great moment to such communities as Los
Angeles, Buffalo, Baltimore, and other cities which are great
centers of aircraft production. It is also important to the laboring
man and to the returning soldier. Great exactitude in answering
these questions is not needed for the purposes of this study. We
want to know only the approximate size of the industries making
aircraft. The best approach to this question is to consider the
number of planes needed to carry the passengers, mail, and goods
and to maintain the military establishments that will be needed
both here and by purchasers in other countries.

The size of our army and navy air forces will be determined by
the government, based upon agreements as to policing and the
needs of national defense. Public opinion at present seems to
support a relatively large air force in peacetime, although, as
war conditions recede and taxes remain high, there may be shifts
in this opinion. The estimates made most often center around
some 20,000 to 25,000 military planes.[6] Since these planes are
already in existence, the important point for production is their
rate of replacement, which averages about 25 per cent a year.
This means an annual replacement of some 6000 planes.[7]

For domestic planes, passenger-cargo and cargo, if the ton-
miles of traffic in 1951 are 700,000,000, then some 2000 planes
will be needed if the type and performance are similar to those
used in 1940, when 358 planes carried 117,000,000 ton-miles of
traffic. But the planes in 1951 will be larger, on the average, than

[5] Bureau of Labor Statistics, *op. cit.*, p. 21.

[6] E. E. Lothrop, "Let's Be Practical About Postwar Plane Markets," *Aviation*,
December, 1943, p. 114; Col. J. Jouett, "Jouett Predicts Trends in Aviation's
Future," *American Aviation*, November 1, 1941, p. 16; E. R. Breech, "After the
War — What?" *Tenth Fortune Round Table*, November, 1941, p. 4.

[7] Jouett, *op. cit.*, p. 16.

the planes in use in 1940, although some local feeder lines may have smaller planes. If we assume that the carrying capacity of the planes will be two and a half times larger, then only 800 planes will be needed. The new postwar planes will also be faster. If the block speed is 60 per cent greater, then around 500 planes, with good scheduling, could take care of the business. The Curtiss-Wright study, previously cited, estimates that 571 passenger planes will be needed four years after the close of the war to transport passengers on scheduled flights. With a replacement rate of one in six years, some eighty to a hundred new planes a year would be needed, and fewer at a slower replacement rate. An estimate by T. P. Wright in the Wilbur Wright Lecture of 1945 is for an annual productive labor force of twenty-five thousand on transport planes in from eight to twelve years after the war. But from these figures we cannot deduce the number of planes produced, since we do not know how many employees are needed to produce a transport plane, and since "employment in airplane production" is not defined.[8]

In international aviation, the number of passengers traveling by air to and from the United States at the end of the first postwar decade is expected to be between 600,000 and 1,000,000. In the peak month, taking the mid-figure of the foregoing estimate, the daily number of passengers in one direction would be around 2500 or 3000, unequally distributed in the different travel zones. The planes would be medium and large-sized except in the Caribbean, where there will be a good many small planes. The number of planes required to carry the United States portion of their traffic would seem to be of the order of one hundred or less.

In addition to these domestic and American-owned planes in international service, there will be a foreign demand which will probably not be large. Other nations will compete with the United States for this market, and the funds of other countries

[8] Since writing the above, a prediction of the Civil Aeronautics Administration and the U.S. Department of Commerce, entitled *Civil Aviation and the National Economy,* has appeared, which estimates 11,500,000,000 air passenger-miles in domestic air travel in the United States in 1955 (as against our prediction of 6,000-000,000 or 8,000,000,000 by 1953) and for this and international service, 1200 planes will be required, of which 200 will be cargo planes.

for purchasing planes will be limited. There is also a foreign market for military planes built in the United States.

There will also be a market for private non-passenger planes. This market may be supplied in part by sales of United States Army and Navy trainer planes and other small planes in the first few years after the war. There were 24,000 private planes before the war, many of which have become obsolete or have passed out of private hands. Within five years after the war, assuming the same number of private planes at the close of the war as at the beginning and a rate of expansion as in prewar years, there will be about 35,000 private planes. With a doubled rate of expansion, there will be 46,000 private planes. Perhaps an even greater expansion may occur.[9]

The helicopter is an uncertain element. It does not appear probable that the annual production of helicopters will get into the thousands before the middle of the first postwar decade. There is a strong probability that either the helicopter, the roadable airplane, or the roadable helicopter may come into considerable use during the second postwar decade and be the basis for a large amount of manufacturing. With such competition, the increase in sales of private planes is not expected to be great.

For the immediate postwar years, it looks as though from 500 to 700 passenger and transport planes will be in domestic use and flying across the oceans. There are expected to be from 30,000 to 85,000 private airplanes. These estimates of private airplane product and military replacements have a very large error. To these totals must be added the planes manufactured in the United States after the war and sold to private purchasers in other countries. Presumably they will be a small ratio to the number manufactured for the domestic market. But even if 15,000 planes should be the annual production around the middle of the first postwar decade, this number could be manufactured in less than two months at the wartime rate of production, taking into con-

[9] In *Civil Aviation and the National Economy*, previously cited, 400,000 private aircraft (presumably including helicopters) are predicted for 1955, on the basis of a 30 per cent annual increase for a decade, starting with a base of 30,000 private aircraft and assuming that the United States Government spends $100,-000,000 a year on airports and other aids.

sideration that many of these aircraft will be small. These figures give some idea of the possible size of the manufacturing industry about the middle of the postwar decade.[10]

The size of the aircraft industry in the second decade after the war depends to a great extent on the market for private aircraft. If there should be several hundred thousand of these in use, the annual production would support an important manufacturing industry, but not nearly so large as the automobile industry.

Industries Related to the Manufacture of Aircraft

The establishment of plants manufacturing airplanes necessarily affects many other closely related industries. Some of these are competitive. If the competition of airplanes forces the railroads to construct new sleeping cars and new coaches, it will affect the industries making railroad equipment. Manufacturers of automobiles will be affected by the competition of private aircraft and by the development of airplane engines which are tending to reach a weight of one pound per horsepower as compared with much heavier automobile engines.

Other influences spread outward to closely related industries, such as the production of fuels. Airplanes use a fuel of high octane value. This stimulates a search for higher energy fuels, and new plants making these fuels are set up. The turbine engine may soon come to be widely used in aircraft. Its successful development may lead to its use in automobiles and railroad locomotives. If these engines are used, the production of kerosene will be increased unless new fuels are discovered. The manufacture of airplanes means that many airports will be constructed, utilizing the products of other industries. One such product is cement, which will be used for the runways of the airports and in the construction of new superhighways connecting airports with the centers of cities. Airports also increase the importance of electronics in the form of radio and radar for traffic control.

The construction of aircraft depends upon a great range of in-

[10] In *Civil Aviation and the National Economy*, an aircraft industry employing 759,000 more persons than in 1939 is predicted, provided the government aids aviation by an expenditure of $100,000,000 a year.

dustries supplying the materials for various parts of the airplane. Noteworthy among these are the industries producing the light metal alloys, especially those of aluminum and magnesium. There are many others, such as plastics, scientific instruments, and plywood. The effect on many of these supporting industries will merely be to increase the output to meet the increased demand because of the manufacture of airplanes. This increase will occur particularly in the basic industries, such as steel or paint. But in many cases, special products are called for. This type of demand affects the plants which process the basic materials to make a special transparent plastic for better visibility, a new type of fuel, a supercharger for high-altitude flying, or special alloys for turbine engines.

The nature of these special industries is indicated by the fact that the making of airplanes is largely a job of assembling parts made in various other plants. For instance, engines and fuselages are made by different companies. During the war, especially, sub-assembly plants were used. A new industry is at the center of a complex of many industries. The manufacture of aircraft affects a closely related cluster of manufacturing plants by increasing their output and by stimulating them to create new products.

Special Manufacturing Industries

Manufacturing is incredibly varied in the United States in the twentieth century. The different manufacturing establishments will use or make adjustments to aviation in many different ways. A description of these many varieties is not feasible, but some cases may be cited as illustrations.

For instance, several manufacturers of mining machinery have found that aviation is a stimulus to their production. This fact may appear surprising, since mining machinery is very heavy, and one thinks of airplanes as carrying objects of light weight. But planes can quickly reach otherwise inaccessible parts of the world where new mines are likely to be discovered. Instead of waiting for roadways to be built, mining companies get equipment in by airplane. Aviation has been particularly important in handling repairs and supplying parts to out-of-the-way mining places. One company, for instance, supplied twenty-eight thousand parts by air for repairs on mining machinery. Aviation and mining are discussed more fully in a later chapter.

Jewelry is a product that has a very high value per pound, and some companies have found that fast transportation by air has made necessary an enlargement of their repair departments to handle the jewelry sent in by plane. One jewelry manufacturer has a number of branch offices, but, because of fast air services, the company plans to eliminate about half of its branches, thus reducing the capital tied up in these branches.

Concerns handling film and motion-picture products have found air transportation very useful. Some of the larger houses have made plans to use airplanes for all interbranch shipments over three hundred and fifty miles in distance. Houses renting film use the overnight air services, with the result that fewer copies of the films are needed, and increased service is rendered by present inventories.

A correlated function of manufacturing is the distribution of the manufactured products. Many companies assume this function, even though their primary function is fabrication. Distribution requires advertising, sales promotion, the sending-out of samples, and so on. This phase of manufacturing is one of the first to be affected by aviation. Even manufacturers of bulky objects such as furniture will send out displays and samples by air.

Each manufacturing plant has its own peculiarities and will be affected in its own particular way by aviation. As air cargo increases, the number and varieties of uses of aviation by manufacturing industries will increase.

Conclusion

The airplane will not have as much influence on manufacturing as did the railroad, and probably not as much influence as the truck, especially in the first postwar decade or two. The manufacturing industries which will experience the earliest influences of aviation are those producing products of high value per unit of weight for which emergency needs often arise. In very many industries, a few emergencies arise every year which occasion the use of air transport. Industries with distant markets, actual or potential, will build on aviation. Some of these industries are on the Pacific Coast and others have business connections in foreign lands. Also, large companies with widely dispersed branches will make use of aviation. The location of industry will not be greatly affected, for there will not be, except in a few cases, sufficient advantages for an established plant to change. If an industry needs a landing field, additional land can be purchased. This will probably be done for the industries which will use helicopters to take cargo from the factory to the airport. New plants may be located with some attention to the accessibility of an airport. The efficiency of the manufacturing process will be increased by the reduction of delays for those industries employing assembly methods and using parts manufactured elsewhere. Aviation will, in general, favor the large rather than the small company. It leads also toward the increase in the number and size of manufacturing companies doing a nation-wide business and probably encourages somewhat the decentralization of the manufacturing process and, thus, local production. Aviation creates a new industry, the manufacture of aircraft, which will probably produce around fifteen thousand planes a year at the middle of the first postwar decade. It will be an expanding industry, especially if private flying increases, but it is not expected to reach the magnitude of the automobile industry unless in the distant future a very effective and cheap roadable helicopter is produced.

25

Marketing [1]

MARKETING HAS BEEN DEFINED as consisting of "those business activities involved in the flow of goods and services from the point of production to the point of consumption." [2] The activities included in this process of distribution are buying, selling, advertising, transportation, and warehousing. In carrying out these activities of marketing, a number of institutions and a variety of practices have been built up which constitute an important segment of our economic life. Just how important the process of distribution is may be seen from the fact that more than 50 per cent of the cost of articles to the consumer goes to cover the cost of marketing goods and less than 50 per cent to cover the cost of producing the goods. [3]

The ultimate objective of the marketing process is to place goods in the hands of consumers. In the marketing pattern, the goods may leave the producer for the wholesaler and go on to the retailer, or they may be sent from the manufacturer to the retailer, or, in some instances, they move from the manufacturer directly to the consumer. The manufacturer is likewise a consumer of goods, and, through similar steps, goods may move from the producer to the manufacturer. These various transfers of ownership of goods are facilitated by salesmen at various levels, or by buyers who travel to special markets. Knowledge about the goods is persuasively spread by advertising, which is itself

---

[1] Mr. Ralph H. Oakes, Professor of Marketing, College of Commerce, De Paul University, Chicago, contributed material for this chapter.

[2] H. E. Agnew, R. B. Jenkins, and J. C. Drury, *Outlines of Marketing.* New York: McGraw-Hill Book Co., 1936, p. 1.

[3] Paul D. Converse, *Essentials of Distribution.* New York: Prentice-Hall, Inc., 1936, p. 6.

organized into various institutions. Finally, the goods are sold through different channels to the consumer. Among these organizations there are a variety of customs concerning pricing, inventories, brands, fill-in ordering, packaging, and so on. This structure has evolved over the years as the character of modern industry and consumption has become more specialized and increasingly complex. In this chapter, we are interested in the ways in which the pattern of marketing will be changed by the development of aviation.

Transportation

Present-day marketing is dependent principally upon railroads and motor trucks for the transportation of goods. The main effect of substituting aircraft for surface means of transportation will be increased speed in the marketing process. The goods will move faster from manufacturer or producer to the retailer. The effects of increased speed will be particularly noticeable where goods are transported over long distances and may encourage manufacture and distribution for a national market rather than a regional or sectional market. As air service is extended to more and more towns through local feeder and trunk-line service, it will be possible to reach all the wholesalers and a large part of the retailers and consumers by direct air transportation.

Aviation will affect marketing, not only through the transportation of goods, but also through the transportation of marketing personnel, through the use of air mail, and through the use of business-owned aircraft.

The degree of influence of aviation's speed on the marketing process depends upon the rates that may be set for air service. If the rates are high, the influence of aviation on marketing will be greatly restricted. However, rates have been going down, and, as a larger market is secured, they will continue to go down. Thus, the effect of aviation on marketing will be progressively greater.

Wholesalers

Our system of distributing merchandise has given an important position to wholesalers, who buy from factories and farmers and sell to retailers or to manufacturers. Salesmen for wholesalers cover the retail stores in the area around the wholesale house. With this decentralized system, the salesmen can save more time and travel expense than if they covered the many retailers over the whole country. The wholesale system distributes the cost of selling over a wider variety of products than is manufactured by any one firm. Wholesalers are important in that they help to create a market demand for the manufacturer through their efforts to sell goods. They play an important part in financing, in the assumption of risks, and in physical distribution. The wholesaler can give faster service in the delivery of goods than the distant producer and can take advantage of bulk shipments and avoid minimum charges. The wholesaler can buy in quantities and can specialize in buying from various competing manufacturers better than can the less well-informed retailer who carries hundreds of items. But the essential point for this analysis is that the wholesaler is a center of distribution for an area and is affected by transportation systems.

In the days of the horse and buggy, when there were few railroads, the range of operations of a wholesaler was shorter than it would be today for the same population with the automobile and the railroad. The tendency of fast and extensive transportation systems to extend the range of activity has been observed in many institutions — government, industry, and war. In the case of wholesale operations, this tendency may be offset by the increasing density of population. The size of the field covered by wholesalers varies greatly according to the type of goods. The inexpensive, standardized household goods and food staples are distributed in smaller wholesale areas than are the more expensive articles, such as women's fur coats. There are so many other factors affecting the amount of territory covered by the average wholesaler that actual statistical evidence is not available, but the tendency of increased transportation facilities over long periods of time seems to be to increase the range of territory. The influence of aviation should be in this direction, although it may be counteracted to some extent by other forces.

Similarly, the effect of fast transportation would appear to limit the number of wholesale salesmen. If the same ground is covered in less time by virtue of better schedules and faster movement, fewer salesmen will be needed to make the same number of contacts. From 1929 to 1939, when the automobile was extensively used, the number of employees in the wholesale trade increased at only half the rate of those engaged in retailing. But aircraft will not be used unless the rates are low. For many salesmen, the automobile, the bus, and the day coach will be satisfactory and more economical than air travel.

The question might be raised as to whether aviation might reduce the number of wholesale houses. For many decades there has been much discussion and effort directed toward the elimination of middlemen, such as wholesalers or commission men. One method of achieving this elimination is through direct sales from the manufacturer to the retailer. Such direct selling has been the most marked trend in marketing in recent years. Important factors in this development have been the desire of large retailers or groups of small retailers to receive the savings from quantity buying and the desire of certain manufacturers to push the sale of their own goods more than did the wholesalers. The trend has been furthered by the advertising of particular goods and of special brands.

Aviation may decrease the need for wholesale distribution in that it will enable manufacturers to make quick deliveries to retailers. One of the principal functions of the wholesaler has been to provide the retailer with goods on short notice. He can do this because he has a store of goods located much closer to the retailer than does the manufacturer. But, with shipment by air, the retailer may be able to get the goods from the manufacturer as quickly as from the wholesaler. This might be especially true on the Pacific Coast. For instance, Western retailers could get automobile parts from Detroit by air almost as quickly as they could from Los Angeles or San Francisco by surface transportation. Retailers who deal with limited varieties of standard goods and parts may find that aviation frees them from the service of the wholesaler.

Style merchandise may be sold directly from the factory to the retailer because of the time factor.[4] The faster service will reduce the risk of fashions' changing before the goods have been received and sold, since goods will not have to be ordered so far in advance. Air transportation may enable small quantities to be shipped speedily from factories to retailers as economically as the larger quantities are shipped to wholesalers and then passed on to retailers.

A trend of interest in the wholesale marketing situation has been the development of manufacturers' branch offices. Such manufacturers' selling organizations, without stocks, have developed in the main with three types of goods,[5] which are noted here because of their relation to aviation. First are goods having high value per unit of weight, such as optical goods, which is a type of goods well suited to air transportation. The branch houses without stock rooms are adapted to this type of goods because there is little to be saved by shipping in bulk. The second type consists of those goods having great bulk in relation to value, such as machinery supplies. These goods are usually purchased in carload lots; hence there is no saving in storing them in branch warehouses. While not normally suitable for air shipment, such goods are very often expressed by air in cases of emergency, as when production is being held up because of the breakage of one part or the lack of one attachment. The third type includes the made-to-order goods, such as style merchandise, which are very likely to go by airplane.

In these cases, the services of many independent wholesalers have been taken over by the branch houses of manufacturers. At least two types of these goods are suited to air transportation, and, as a result, aviation may favor these manufacturers' selling organizations as against the independent wholesalers. On the other hand, the airplane may encourage the selling of these products directly by the manufacturer to the retailer without the ex-

[4] John H. Frederick, "How Air Transportation May Affect Marketing and Product Development," *Journal of Marketing*, January, 1944, p. 275.
[5] R. S. Alexander, F. M. Surface, R. F. Elder, and W. Alderson, *Marketing*, 1940, pp. 273-274.

pense of maintaining branch houses. This development will be a part of the widening area of selling which the airplane encourages.

In general, no sudden change in wholesalers' practices and functions is expected, but, in the long run, there will be some influence of aviation toward enlarging the areas of wholesalers. The saving of time by air shipment for distant areas in such items as those of high value per unit cost, of spare parts, special style orders, emergency parts, and so on, means that the retailer is less dependent on the stocks of wholesalers. The development of manufacturer sales to retailers will be furthered somewhat by aviation, as will be discussed more fully in later paragraphs on inventories and retail buying.

Retailers

Retail stores may be classified according to size into two types: the small independent unit, such as the country store or the neighborhood store, and the large retailer, such as the department store, the chain store, or the mail-order house.

It is difficult to see how the small merchants in villages and towns will have their business affected by aviation except in a very general way. Air passenger and cargo service to small towns will be slow in development, and the rates will be considerably higher than those of buses and trucks. It is possible that a pickup service, such as that of All American Aviation, Inc., will be developed for small towns, providing more rapid express and mail service. It is not certain that this service will be provided in the near future, but, even if it should develop, its use by small merchants would probably be only for emergency orders or to fill in gaps in the stock. Mail could be used much more by merchants than is done, but buyers like to see the goods they purchase.

In regard to the larger retailers, one of their chief developments has been their buying service. Previously, wholesalers generally performed this function of buying but, with the development of the chain store and co-operative retail organizations, the retail store has increasingly taken it over. In a survey of

Chicago retailers,[6] it was found that many expected that buyers would use air service, since buying costs are only a small part of the total costs of retailing. The time of buyers will be saved by aviation and, if the travel is from distant outlying regions, the expense will be less, even if air passenger rates are not lowered. If air rates fall nearer to present rail rates, either more travel by buyers may result or fewer buyers may be needed.

Few Chicago retail merchants interviewed expected very much use of the airplane for the transportation of goods to them from the wholesaler or the manufacturer, at air rates twice as high as present rail express rates, except in special situations. One such situation might be re-orders at Christmas time. Also it is often necessary to make special orders of merchandise because of emergencies, unexpected shortages, or the demand for quick displays of fashion goods. At present air rates or at the projected rates for the immediate future, few chain stores see much use of the airplane for the transportation of merchandise, since costs are figured very closely in these stores, and the margin is small.

However, there may be more shipment of goods to retailers by air than is now expected, especially in the more distant future when cargo rates will be considerably reduced. A result of such shipment would be a faster turnover of goods.[7] The rate of business turnover varies with the particular kinds of goods. The shorter the time required for goods to be distributed to retailers and sold to consumers, the greater the volume of business that either a manufacturer or a retailer will be able to do without expanding his facilities. The faster goods can move from producer to consumer, the less will be the expenditure per unit of product for cost of capital, rental of buildings, salaries of administrative executives, and general overhead.[8] Faster turnover would enable better utilization of existing facilities and the hand-

---

[6] Mr. Ralph H. Oakes interviewed 127 marketing executives in Chicago by personal and telephone calls as to how they thought air transportation will affect postwar marketing if air cargo rates average about 27 cents per ton-mile.

[7] George F. Bauer, "How Air Cargo Will Affect Four Basic Factors in Distribution; No. 1 — Effect of Time Savings on Turnover," *D and W,* October, 1943, p. 45.

[8] *Ibid.*

ling of larger volumes of business. This effect would be most evident in those cases in which the producer is located long distances from the market.

Chicago mail-order houses at present do not anticipate much use of air mail. They report little demand from customers for this type of delivery. On the other hand, mail rates are a determining factor in the use of air mail service by mail-order houses. With lower air mail rates and rural air delivery, air mail would be used by mail-order houses, but it is not clear that any changes in their practices or organization would result. Rapid air mail may favor certain types of goods, such as those which have first gone by air express and are discussed elsewhere.

All of the officials of large retailing establishments who were interviewed expect some use of air transportation on the part of executives. Other effects of aviation on retailing will be discussed under separate subheads in the paragraphs which follow.

Inventories

Merchants carried larger stocks of each particular line of goods before the coming of the railroad and the truck than afterward because these transportation facilities reduced the time required for restocking.[9] It might be expected that aviation would further reduce the inventories of retailers.

Of the Chicago retailers interviewed, nearly all were reluctant to say that aviation would have any effect on their inventory policy. They felt that they had already reduced their stocks to almost the lowest limit, which was a sufficient supply for customers to inspect. They did state, however, that, if their stock became depleted in certain lines, air express would be used to fill in the gaps quickly. Since their stocks could be more quickly replaced, they thought they might sell more goods. The airplane would be of use in keeping up their stock of goods in certain lines, even though it did not permit a decrease.

On the other hand, in a survey of prospective users of air service on the Pacific Coast,[10] many merchants reported that air

[9] Alexander, Surface, Elder, and Alderson, *op. cit.*, p. 483; Fred E. Clark, *Principles of Marketing*. New York: The Macmillan Co., p. 208.

[10] Booz, Frey, Allen, and Hamilton, *Chicago and West Coast Freight Markets,* 1941, privately issued.

cargo developments would enable them to modify their inventory policy and carry a smaller stock of goods. It might be questioned why more reductions of stocks of goods carried are expected on the Pacific Coast than in Chicago. Probably the distance of West Coast merchants from the Eastern sources of supply is the answer. At such long distances, the Pacific Coast merchants have needed to carry a larger supply than have those closer to the source of supply. The airplane will, in effect, bring the West Coast closer to the source of supply of those goods which are suitable for air transportation. It may also be that merchants in the South and Southwest may have their inventory policies modified by aviation, although no studies for these regions are available.

Aviation may enable retailers better to co-ordinate their supply with the demand. This is particularly true in times when prices are unstable and economic conditions uncertain. In these periods, inventories are kept as low as possible, since large amounts of money can be lost through the fluctuations of prices which occur between the time that the retailer orders the products and the time when he is ready to sell them. It may be that, in future times of uncertainty, such as the next depression or before an election or at the time of another war, when aviation will be more highly developed than now, merchants will rely to a great extent on overnight orders by airplane rather than keeping the goods in stock.

Retailers will continue to follow different inventory policies according to the nature of their goods, but there are particular types of merchants who are most likely to reduce their stocks through the use of air transportation. The Chicago merchants who deal in silverware and jewelry agree that some change in stock policy might result from aviation. Merchants dealing in fashion goods and in women's apparel think that quick fill-in possibilities because of aviation will mean that smaller supplies will be carried. These goods have a high value per pound or fashion characteristics which make their transportation by air feasible. As air rates are lowered, many other goods will become available for air transportation, and the reductions in inventories will become progressively greater.

Salesmen

The average salesman, whose territory is usually relatively small, is not expected to be much affected by aviation. The distances involved are too short, and, for some time, other methods of travel will be more economical. But, if a helicopter bus service with stops around every thirty to fifty miles is developed, it may be used occasionally as a supplement to other means of travel to schedule more conveniently the various calls over a given territory.

It is expected that air travel will be used to a considerable extent by sales executives and higher-salaried salesmen, especially those covering large territories. Air travel will also be used by salesmen who travel between widely separated centers of large populations, where customers give large orders at one time or where the unit value of goods or services is high. Salesmen who sell goods with seasonal or style considerations also need to make a very rapid coverage of their customers. With air travel, salesmen will be able to go to foreign countries to sell their products as easily as in the past they have used their automobiles and driven to their territories. Weekly or monthly routine visits by salesmen can be made to Latin-American markets.

Air travel, properly planned, may enable a smaller sales staff to cover a territory more economically than it could be covered by a larger staff using other means of transportation. Such a change is most probable where a large force of salesmen is employed.

Salesmanship often involves highly organized promotional work, such as launching a new product, special coaching, inaugurating a new campaign, or pepping up a lagging sales force. Aircraft are very useful in facilitating this type of sales management.

There is also the possibility that the influence of the airplane will be to slow up the growth in the total number of salesmen by reason of its possible encouragement of an increase in the number of buyers, which will be discussed in the following section.

Buyers

The small retailer relies on the wholesaler to do his buying for him — to assemble many hundreds of items of goods from perhaps as many sources and to grade, divide, and arrange the goods into quantities and qualities that the retailer may desire. But large merchandise organizations may find it more profitable to perform this specialized function of buying for themselves. As retail organizations increase in size, as the chain system develops, and as manufacturers become larger, the number of retail organizations with specialized buyers increases. There has also been a recent development of voluntary chain systems by which independent small stores co-operate to get the advantages of large-scale buying.

It is more convenient for buyers if markets are concentrated in one area, where they may find a wide choice in quality and price. Not all producers can locate in Chicago, New York, or San Francisco, but many can maintain large display rooms in these centers of trade. Merchandise marts, marketing centers, specialized buyers, and large-scale merchants and manufacturers are correlated. Fast airline transportation makes it easier for retail buyers and manufacturers, with their displays of goods, to meet in great marketing centers. Buyers will be likely to use air transportation because they are highly skilled persons who are of economic importance to their organizations. If the retail stores are located long distances from the great market centers, there is greater likelihood of buyers traveling by plane. The Chicago business executives who were interviewed felt that buyers will do a good deal of their traveling by air. Indeed, in one or two cases, the suggestion was made that the merchandise marts might pay the traveling expenses of buyers.

Aviation will reinforce the present trend toward an increase of buyer specialists.

Advertising

It seems probable that advertising agencies, both large and medium-sized, will make considerable use of aviation. Certainly, the executives of advertising agencies were among the first to make extensive use of airplanes. Advertising executives have used air service in order to keep in close touch with their customers. Their accounts are often large and their efficiency is increased by frequent contacts with their clients. The plane was thought of by these executives as an agent in competition for accounts. The novelty of plane travel is said to have had some sales effect, which may not be so effective when travel by air becomes commonplace.

Air service will also be used in the future for the transportation of copy, layouts, art work, and final copy for client approval. Some advertising men, when interviewed, were conservative about anticipating the use of aircraft for transporting advertising material. But it might be noted that much of this type of material used in connection with magazine printing already goes by plane. There is a considerable time factor in handling mats, plates, and most kinds of finished advertising which makes the plane of considerable service. The time factor is particularly important in "remembrance advertising," which is either dated — for instance, calendars — or which must be imprinted at the last minute, as at Christmas, with recipients' and/or donors' names; this type of advertising will be likely to go by air. It would also appear that special catalogues, *de luxe* booklets and brochures, special materials for sales meetings, and so on, may go by air.

The tendency of aviation to develop national, rather than regional or sectional, markets will have a corresponding effect of increasing national advertising. The development of other forms of communication has also influenced this trend.

Advertisers, then, will use the plane for purposes of speed, and no particular change in the structure of advertising is foreseen unless it is an extension into foreign markets. Several American magazines and newspapers are already distributed in foreign countries, and advertising material is, of course, used in these publications. As is discussed elsewhere, fast air transportation to foreign countries, particularly to the countries south of the United States, will enable business executives, including advertising men, to make business contacts without too much loss of time. Advertising copy for American corporations in Latin America is generally prepared in the United States; hence aviation is expected to expedite the use of this area of advertising.

Packaging

The importance of weight in air transportation has brought efforts to reduce the weight of air cargo by changes in methods of packing and packaging. Since air cargo is not subjected to the rough handling and sometimes violent motions of railroads and trucks, goods sent by air can be packaged in much lighter materials. Cargo is secured in the plane to prevent any shifting in flight, and thus goods moved by air require very little packing protection. Many light-weight but strong packaging materials are coming into use in air shipping. During the war, the Naval Air Transport Service repacked shipments for air transportation and were able to effect an average reduction of 15 per cent in shipping weights.[11] The reduction in weight of packaging not only affords reductions in shipping charges, but also in the costs of packing materials. The reduction in weight and cost of air packaging will be particularly evident in international air express and cargo if it develops to any great extent. The large number of junction points at which ocean cargo has to be handled makes strong packing-boxes necessary. Since air cargo can be landed directly at its final destination, it can be shipped with much lighter packaging.[12]

Shipment by air has some problems that are unique. One problem arises from the present practice of carrying cargo and passengers on the same plane. There will be an increasing number of all-cargo planes in the future, but for some time considerable amounts of goods will be carried in the planes which carry passengers. Some products, such as fish, have very strong odors, unpleasant to passengers. For products of this type, packages must be designed to confine the odors to the package. Already, synthetic rubber and also plastic "bags" and other wrappers have been designed for this purpose. One of these new wrapping sub-

[11] Frederick, *op. cit.*, p. 278.
[12] George F. Bauer, "How Air Cargo Will Affect Four Basic Factors in Distribution; No. 3 — Weight in Post-War Shipping," *D and W*, December, 1943, p. 27.

stances, called "Cryovac," is said to be quite effective in solving the odor problem in the transportation of fish.

Many planes will fly at high altitudes, where the temperatures are very low. For some goods, such as perishable fruits and vegetables, this makes refrigeration facilities unnecessary. For other goods, such as flowers, baby chicks, and so on, the temperatures are too low for the goods being shipped, unless the plane is heated or pressurized.

Markets

Modifications in the marketing process occasioned by aviation have been reviewed. There remains to be considered the question of whether the location of marketing centers may be changed, both internationally and within the nation, because of aviation.

Improved and more extensive transportation facilities have, in general, the effect of increasing specialization by localities. With a system of free trade and good transportation systems, goods can be exchanged freely between nations, enabling each nation to specialize in various types of goods. England, for example, with free trade, could specialize in manufacturing and neglect the production of foods, which she could obtain from other countries in exchange for manufactured goods. If, however, transportation facilities are poor or high-tariff policies are in effect, each country must be more nearly self-supporting. In the domestic market, railroad transportation has also led to geographical specialization. New York is a clothing market, Cleveland is a steel center, Detroit has automobiles, and Chicago the meat-packing industry. Will aviation, as a new agency of transportation, increase this trend toward specialized centers?

It may be argued that the railroads have carried this process as far as it will go, and airplanes, with their relatively limited use as carriers of cargo as compared with the railroads, will have slight influence. This may be true for a given area, but, for a very large area, aviation may further geographical specialization. In the United States, this influence will be chiefly noticeable with reference to the Pacific Coast and the saving of time by air between the Atlantic and Pacific seaboards. For example, instead of having centers of women's clothing or for furs in both the western area and in the region east of the Mississippi, the same center may serve both regions. The airplane tends to make marketing centers serve larger areas, as did the railroad.

As was discussed previously, the trend toward the concentration of retail buyers' markets in large centers is facilitated by air transportation.

This tendency toward specialization would probably spread outward to include more than one nation were it not for the barriers of tariffs, nationalism, and language differences. The plane makes it possible for new markets to be created in foreign countries. For instance, the ability of the plane to transport perishables in a short time makes possible the marketing in the United States of tropical fruits never before sold here. In some cases, foreign centers might gain at the expense of American cities. For instance, if buyers of women's clothing and hats can go quickly by air to a large style center such as New York, such centers as Hollywood, Houston, and Chicago may yield to New York City, but buyers may pass by all American cities for Paris, since a flight to Paris can be made in a day. In the same way, air transportation may bring South American buyers to American cities. It is interesting to speculate whether aviation will increase the buying of Canadian merchants in the United States, since there are great similarities of language and customs between the two nations. The British have hopes that aviation will tie the units of the Empire closer to the mother country.

Two or three minor possibilities might be mentioned in the distribution of domestic markets. A number of shops and services similar to those found around large railroad stations will grow up around airports. The number of these establishments, however, in ratio to the number of passengers, may be larger than has been the case with railroad stations, since airports are farther removed from the trading centers of cities than are railroad stations.

Small urban stores may be somewhat more widely scattered if the effect of air transportation in the distant future is to scatter, to some extent, the homes outward from the center. If helicopter service brings buyers in from fifty miles or more to a great marketing metropolis, the retail stores will serve a larger market.

With regard to the markets in small localities, there has been some speculation as to whether the air pick-up and non-stop delivery system might not bring a better special order service to villagers and hence reduce trips to larger stores. If there is any weight in this argument, it is probably quite slight and for some distance in the future.

Conclusion

No sudden and extensive changes are to be anticipated in the marketing organization in general in the years immediately following the war. All marketing activities will be speeded up by air transportation, and the marketing practices of certain industries may be considerably changed. Marketing in the past has been greatly influenced by the railroad, and the automobile has also left its impress. Aviation continues the influences of the railroad and the automobile. The trends in marketing have been toward an increase in direct selling from the producer to the retailer with a consequent increase in the number of retail buyers and a freeing of the retailer to some extent from the need of the wholesaler, toward a reduction in inventories, a reliance upon fast transportation for special orders, an increase in the areas covered by many wholesalers, toward bringing outlying regions into closer contact with market centers, toward creating national markets, and toward specialization of great marketing centers. The influence of aviation is to extend further all these trends. This influence is contingent on a considerable use of passenger, mail, and cargo planes and is expected to require a long time to be very effective.

26

Mining

MINING is one of the major occupations today, al-. though its great significance may not be apparent if comparisons are made on the basis of numbers employed. In an era of mechanical power, speed, and rapidly revolving tools, metals are basic to industry. Since there has been a great demand for metals for over a century, the ores and metallic substances in settled areas are already known and used to a large extent. Thus, we may expect that the new mines in the future will be in relatively unsettled and isolated regions. It is likely that there will be no modern transportation systems to these undeveloped regions, especially if they are located in the interior of a country. Airplanes, which require only a landing place, will be peculiarly useful in developing these mines. In fact, one of the earliest uses of aviation, like the early use of steam, was in connection with mining.

Early Uses of the Airplane in Mining

The influence of the airplane on mining was felt as early as the 1920's.[1] In fact, in 1919, the Granby Mining Company of Canada used four planes to carry ore from their mines to tidewater at Stewart, British Columbia. In the same year an experimental service was established in the region of Grass Valley, California, to fly light supplies and mail to a circuit of mines. Airplanes were used to save time in transporting mine rescue apparatus in 1923. The following year mining equipment was transported to a company operating in the Rouyn district of western Quebec.

[1] *The Engineering and Mining Journal*, November, 1935, p. 553.

Thus, before 1925, airplanes were used for a variety of services in different parts of the world — for inspecting property, prospecting, transporting ore, bringing in equipment, transporting workers between mining camps, and for effecting rescue work.

Mining companies made early use of the airplane chiefly because of the inadequate transportation in mining areas. Mines must be located according to the geographical distribution of minerals and not according to transportation facilities. A mining town is small, and its life is often short. The construction of highways or railroads is very costly. The local governmental bodies in these out-of-the-way places often do not have a sufficiently large tax base to build transportation lines. Since air facilities require a much smaller capital outlay, it is natural that planes should be used for emergency shipments of equipment and products and for servicing the small mining communities.

Water and land transportation to some mines is slow, and the methods are primitive. In South America, planes flew across the Andes at an altitude of fifteen thousand feet in thirty minutes.[2] With mules over jungle and ravine, this journey required four or five weeks. Time saved in mining is money made. In the famous gold fields of New Guinea, Bulolo Gold Dredging, Ltd., saved almost a year's time by supplying by air the whole equipment for four dredges and a power plant.[3] The yearly profit was $20,-000,000. The saving in interest, at 5 per cent, by the earlier winning of this profit more than offset the cost of the planes and their service.

By the 1930's, the experimental period was over, and the use of planes for a variety of mining purposes had been firmly established. During the decade of the 1930's, the airplane was very extensively used in mining operations in Canada, New Guinea, Australia, and Africa. To a smaller degree, it was also used in Alaska, Mexico, Nicaragua, Honduras, Peru, Bolivia, Brazil, and the United States. Its most outstanding use was in gold mining, but it was also used in transporting quartz, mica, pitchblende,

[2] William Van Dusen, "Mine Freight by Air in South America," *The Engineering and Mining Journal*, November, 1935, p. 569.
[3] *The Engineering and Mining Journal, op. cit.*, p. 554.

diamonds, radium, and various rare metals. The airplane was used only to a limited degree in mining products with a low value per unit of weight.

The Influence of the War

During the war and the period of preparation preceding it, there was a great demand for metals, particularly those used in alloys. The increase in mining activities in Canada and Mexico was quite impressive. The American purchase of mining products from Mexico created a wartime prosperity in that country which was reflected in its national budget. Wartime demand for mining products led to increased prospecting of territory, area mapping, and the opening of new mines. Canada's reliance on aerial prospecting for minerals was shown by the fact that twenty-seven geological parties and nine topographic parties were sent out during the 1941 season in Canada to search for deposits of tungsten, mercury, chromite, gold, copper, and oil.[4] In Peru and Brazil, there was a considerable increase in aviation for mining purposes during the war period. Such essential war materials as vanadium, tungsten, molybdenum, and others were transported by air, not only in Peru itself, but also from Peru to the United States.[5]

War conditions led to the air transportation of rare and precious metals to the United States, especially those that are found in extremely small quantities. The dangers that ships might be sunk forced these rare metals to the air, especially during the early part of the war. Quartz, mica, tantalite, and beryl were carried by plane from Brazil to the United States; and from India, mica and beryl. Tantalite was also flown to the United States from Australia and West and Central Africa, and tin and tungsten from China into India. The wartime emphasis on speed favored the use of the airplane, but the shortage of planes did not permit the increase that would otherwise have occurred.

[4] W. E. D. Stokes, Jr., "Many Aerial Survey Parties Active in 1941, Locating Mineral Areas and Laying Out Pipe Lines," *Mining and Metallurgy,* February, 1942, p. 65.

[5] Letter from Federico Elguera, Consul General, Consulate General of Peru, Chicago, Illinois.

The war not only created a great demand for metals, but it also led to much transportation of bulky cargo. Before the war regular airlines largely carried mail and small packages. However, in mining large pieces of heavy cargo were carried. The mining equipment had to be sectioned to be accommodated to the planes. Mining companies and the manufacturers of mining machinery were accustomed to this, since transportation by mule-back had set a limit of two hundred pounds for one mule. Experience in carrying heavy cargo was increased during the war through the transportation of war material, but not many new cargo planes were available to the mining companies.

Aids to Mining

The aid of aircraft to mining is of three kinds: discovery, servicing the mine, and maintaining the mining population.

Prospecting today, with its use of photography, the airplane, and the aid of geology, is far different from what it was in the days of the forty-niners or the Klondike gold rush. A low-flying airplane, equipped with an aerial camera using color film, is of great value in locating sources of metals. The helicopter will be especially suitable for flying close to the earth at low speeds to look for outcroppings of ore or to hover over a given spot. Equally important is its ability to land almost anywhere in order to inspect ground conditions or make preliminary tests. The experience gained from the extensive development of aerial photography during the war will be helpful in mapping areas of mineral resources. Color photography, if its cost is reduced, will be very useful, since the color of rocks, earth, and ore indicates the types of minerals to be found. The color contrasts enhance depth perception, bring out the detail, and facilitate interpretation.

Once the site of the mine is determined, the airplane brings in the mining machinery and various types of equipment. In case the equipment is very bulky, it is dismantled into parts, or the airplane may be modified to suit the load. Similarly, the plane is used to transport the products of the mine to points of transfer to surface means of transportation or to processing plants. Although the bulky nature of the cargo would seem to make it unsuitable to air transportation, such transportation often proves more economical than that by primitive methods over mountains, jungle, swamps, or snow. The bringing-in of the machinery is done but once; afterward only occasional parts are needed. But the shipping-out of the mineral products is a continuous operation. Hence the mines which yield a product of high value per pound are better suited to air transportation service.

The miners and their families must be maintained by supplies brought in from places outside the mining area. With a population as large as several thousand, much transportation is needed. In the beginning, dwelling houses, like machinery, are hauled in by air.

However, mining communities established by air transportation often become less dependent upon the plane after a time because of the construction of other means of transportation. If the mine is large and of long life and not located too far from existing lines of transportation, a roadway for trucks may be built, providing a less expensive form of freight transportation. Such has been the case, for instance, in Central America and Canada. Thus, a mining town set up by air transportation becomes somewhat less dependent on this method of travel.

Aviation Requirements in Mining

In many cases, the early planes used for mining purposes had to be adapted to meet the peculiar conditions of mining country, and special types of planes were required for different services. Pontoons or skis were needed in the lake country of the Far North. A special balance of the plane was required when equipment of considerable length was to be transported. Since much progress was made during the war in the designing of cargo planes, the specifications of cargo planes for mining hauls can now be achieved with greater efficiency. Prospecting by air calls for planes capable of flying near the ground at low cruising speeds. Landing speeds under sixty miles an hour are desirable, and the high-winged monoplane is preferred. Supplying mining camps and transporting freight do not require high speeds. Frequently, the distances to be flown are short — fifty to one hundred miles

— although some of the Canadian mines require flights of nearly one thousand miles.

Costs

The costs of mapping in prospecting for ore vary greatly, since they depend upon the type of terrain and the distance from the operating base, the weather conditions, and the scale and precision required in the map. Maps have been made in the past which varied in cost from two dollars to fifty thousand dollars a square mile.[6] Each specific project costs various amounts, depending on the conditions. However, in general, the same factors which reduce costs in transporting freight will also operate to reduce costs of aerial surveying and mapping.

Freight costs, when they are reported, also vary widely. For instance, in 1932, twenty tons of freight were transported at two dollars a ton-mile, including insurance, from Waterways to Great Bear Lake in Canada, an air distance of eight hundred miles. The water transportation was forty cents a ton-mile, but the water route was open only two and a half months a year and required from four to six weeks for the trip as compared to twelve hours at any time by plane.[7] In 1936, the cost of transporting freight by air to the Agua Fria mine in eastern Honduras was reported as seventy-two cents a ton-mile in tri-motored Ford planes purchased by the company.[8] Undoubtedly, economic conditions are quite different in the various parts of the world. Reports in the more recent years indicate a lowering of costs, although what is included in costs is not always stated. There are many ways in which costs can be lowered in the future. In general, the performance of single units is never as efficient as multiple operation. For this reason, many mining companies prefer to hire the services of an aviation company which has a large fleet of planes

[6] Leon T. Eliel, "Aerial Reconnaissance and Contour Mapping in Mining," *Transactions of the American Institute of Mining and Metallurgical Engineers,* vol. 126, Metal Mining and Mining Geology, 1937, p. 567.

[7] United States Bureau of Mines, "Use of Airplanes in Mining and Petroleum Operations," Information Circular 6767, February, 1934, p. 18.

[8] Felix B. Shay, "Air Transport at Agua Fria," Technical Publication 1156 of the American Institute of Mining and Metallurgical Engineers, published in *Mining Technology,* January, 1940.

rather than purchase their own planes and use their own pilots. Often the planes of the mining company do the pioneering and then competing aviation companies are organized.

For domestic transportation of cargo in the United States, the airport-to-airport rates for all-cargo planes may be as low as fifteen cents a ton-mile within a decade or so after the war. Even with these reductions, however, the truck will be a cheaper method of transportation than the airplane for a long time. The truck can be used where the terrain is somewhat level and not too wet or snowy. But many of the new mines will be in mountainous areas where surface hauling is expensive and slow and the airplane has a great advantage over the truck. In areas such as Brazil and the Andean mining regions, where the cost of constructing roads or highways is almost prohibitive because of the great distances and the natural obstacles, air transportation will undoubtedly continue to be used.

Postwar Demand for Metals

The immediate postwar demand for metals will probably be decreased to some extent. However, in the long run, an increasing demand is expected in view of the importance of metals today. Furthermore, metals will be of even greater importance, since they can now be combined in many ways to produce alloys which have superior qualities over the pure metals. The kinds of alloys are very numerous. Metals can be tailored to any specifications of weight, hardness, or elasticity by the proper additions of small quantities of certain rare metals. There are vast new potentialities in the alloys which the airplane will aid in making possible. However, while population and mechanization are increasing, yet the mineral resources of the world are limited, and Nature cannot replenish those already used by our civilization. Some metals can be used again by conserving scrap, but in general the supply of minerals is decreasing and the demand increasing.

As a result, we may expect the search for new mineral deposits to continue. Africa, South America, and Central Asia are possible new sources of minerals, and the airplane is especially suitable for reaching these unexplored areas. Engineers from America and Europe can reach any part of the earth in two days by plane. Already the plane has been used in the discovery and successful development of radium deposits on the northern shore of Great Bear Lake near the Arctic Circle, in the establishment of the Yellowknife gold mining camp in Canada, and in the discovery of iron ore in northern Quebec.

Oil is another natural resource on which our civilization, and especially aviation, is increasingly dependent. The airplane was principally responsible in locating the Agua Caliente oil field in central Peru in 1939 and the Rancherias and La Presa discoveries in Mexico, and was a supplementary aid in many other instances. It is to be expected that it will continue to play an important part in the future in locating oil deposits. It has also been used to make aerial surveys in the laying of oil pipelines. In the case of the 1530-mile main line of the National Defense Pipe Line in the United States, for example, all the aerial mapping was completed within three weeks.[9]

There are vast possibilities for the future use of radioactive elements, such as radium and uranium, if sufficient quantities of them can be found. Aircraft will be of value in this search.

The airplane is of importance in prospecting because, by providing an over-all view, it makes possible the discovery of mineral sources not visible from the ground. It shortens the time needed for surveying and making plans preparatory to mining. In areas of poor transportation facilities and short prospecting seasons owing to the climatic conditions, it lengthens the prospecting season, since the prospector can allocate less of his time to transportation to the prospecting area. With lengthening of the season, the chances of discovering minerals are increased. The airplane is also important in mining in selecting the most suitable transport routes for land travel, in locating adequate water supplies, solving drainage problems, and in moving men and materials.

[9] W. E. D. Stokes, Jr., *op. cit.*, p. 66.

Conclusion

In the past, the airplane has been of great value to the mining industry in prospecting, exploration, mapping, and transportation, and it will be even more important to mining in the future. At the same time, its use in mining has advanced aviation in that it has brought about the designing of planes for the transportation of heavy materials and has provided new metals and alloys for airplane construction. The use of the plane in mining had become commonplace before the war. Valuable time and money were saved, labor was lightened, unexplored areas were opened up, unknown terrain was surveyed and mapped by aerial photography. The rapid expansion of the use of the airplane in the mining industry in the postwar decades can be predicted.

27 | *Real Estate*

REAL ESTATE [1] will be influenced by aviation through two channels: first, through the nature and location of airports and landing places; and, secondly, through the redistribution of population. Other forms of transportation have affected land values through the location of transportation facilities and the resulting redistribution of population. The railroads were a causal factor in creating many towns and cities. Land was in great demand where these cities and towns sprang up along the railroads. Another form of transportation, the automobile, made it possible for cities to spread outward, causing an increase in land values on the outskirts of the city. Land values declined where the business section of the city center impinged upon the residential areas surrounding it. Also, land values increased along the automobile highways, particularly near intersections, which became advantageous business sites. Streetcars, subways, and elevateds have the effect of raising and maintaining the values of property in the central business districts. Water transportation affects land values at the stopping-points of boats. Canals and ocean vessels cause ports to increase in population and hence raise the price of land.

Airports

The location of the various types and sizes of airports will have important effects upon land values. The main airport for handling scheduled passenger and express traffic is usually situated some distance from the center of the city. Such an airport

---

[1] Basic materials and analyses for the conclusions on real estate are found in the chapters on population, family, and cities.

must be large, sometimes several square miles in area. Since there cannot be any tall buildings near the approaches to the runway, the influence of the airport is felt over a much larger area than the actual space which it occupies. The regulation of the approach is often measured by the slope of a line with a tangent of one-fortieth. At a distance of a mile from the entrance to a runway, there must be no buildings higher than one-fortieth of 5280 feet, or 132 feet. At one quarter of a mile away, the height of the buildings can be only 33 feet. (These regulations do not apply except to the approaches to runways.) In order to find sufficient open space and cheap land, these airports have been located on the outskirts of the city. The question arises as to what will be the effects on the land values of residences and businesses in the vicinity of these large airports.

Residential Property Near Airports

Since airports have usually been on the outskirts of the city, they have been in areas where residential buildings were few. During the war, in a few cases the expansion in the activity and number of airports impinged on residential districts. For example, on the south side of Minneapolis, the enlargement of Wold-Chamberlain Field into a major airport and its use as a base for much military aviation affected to real disadvantage a large residential section which was formerly considered highly desirable.

The tax assessors in nineteen large cities in the United States were asked in 1942 what effect the location of the airport had had on real estate.[2] The assessors in ten of these cities reported that there had been no discernible effect on the residential real-estate values because of the airport. The airports in all of these ten cities were outside the city limits. Seven assessors said that residential values had decreased, while two said that they had increased. It is not definite, however, in these two cases that the increase in values was due to the influence of the airport. From

[2] *The American City*, February, 1942, p. 101. The cities were Atlanta, Baltimore, Boston, Buffalo, Cincinnati, Cleveland, Dallas, Denver, Detroit, Los Angeles, Louisville, Miami, Milwaukee, Minneapolis, Portland, St. Louis, St. Paul, Spokane, and Washington, D.C.

this report it may be judged that by 1942 the effect of the airport
on the value of the sites of residences was slight, but that the
tendency was to depress values. The disadvantages to residential
property were the noise of take-offs and landings, especially during sleeping hours, increased dust, and accident hazards.

The noise of the planes is one of the principal disadvantages of
living near a large, busy airport. If there are many planes coming and going frequently, the amount of noise is quite appreciable, particularly for those people who are out-of-doors or in
buildings in which the windows are open. At the airport, the
noise is greatest from the planes as they take off, but the noise
of planes several hundred feet in the air can be heard far beyond the immediate proximity of the airport. It has been suggested that the noise of the engine may be reduced by the use of
mufflers, which, however, add weight and decrease efficiency.
But the principal source of noise in planes is the propeller, and as
yet no evidence has been reported that there is any likelihood of
significantly reducing the noise of propellers. The propellerless
jet plane is noiseless in the cabin, and only a brief screech is
audible to people below. Although the jet-propelled plane is
more quiet than the airplane, it is not expected that these planes
will be used domestically to any great extent in the first postwar
decade, or at least during the early part of it. The helicopter
also makes much less noise than the airplane, but widespread
private use of the helicopter will not affect the influence of the
large airport on real estate, since the helicopter will not supplant
the airliner in air passenger service between large cities.

The noise of airplanes has not yet been recognized by the public as a problem. At least, public opinion, if there is any, is
quiescent on the subject. But when the number of planes in the
air increases, the demand for a reduction of noise will become
greater, and some method may be found to accomplish it. If the
noise can be substantially decreased, the great open space of an
airport might be attractive for residence owners.

In smaller cities, where the number of landings per day has
been few, the neighborhood of the airport has been said to be
attractive for residences. This is understandable where an at-

tractive addition has been promoted by a real-estate company and where there is a pride and enthusiasm for this new system of transportation. But if, later, the landings become numerous and there is no solution to the noise problem, it is difficult to see how the real estate in the neighborhood would be desirable for residences. In many large cities, residents have often entered a vigorous protest against the location of an airport in the neighborhood of their homes.

In addition to large airports for the trunk lines, there will be some small airports or landing strips located closer in to the center of the city. If the traffic at these landing places is not large, the depressing influence on real estate for residences will exist to a lesser extent. Indeed, it is possible that the open space near these landing fields, if the landings are very few, may prove to be attractive to home-owners. The term "air park" is sometimes used in connection with this type of landing field. The term has propaganda value, for it suggests scenic beauty and spaciousness. If grass, flowers, and shrubbery are planted around these air parks, the neighborhood would be even more attractive for residences.

Landing places designed exclusively for private non-passenger aircraft will be located as conveniently as possible, and hence near residential sections of the city. It will not be feasible to locate them close to the central business section. These fields may be of sod and be spacious enough to permit landing into the wind, no matter in which direction it is blowing. The effect of these landing fields for private planes on real-estate values depends upon the extent of their use. In general, their influence is expected to be somewhat like that of the large airport; namely, to depress residential values if the landing fields are used extensively, and to provide some demand for a few stores dispensing food, drink, fuel, etc. However, the helicopter and the roadable helicopter, rather than the plane, are expected to be used as private aircraft, and so the activity at these private landing fields will not be great.

The undesirability of an airport in a residential section depends upon the amount of use it is given. At the present time, the airports in the smaller towns are not so busy as those in large cities. There are fewer airplanes landing and taking off, and the amount of noise and the degree of hazard are less. Therefore, residences are more likely to be built in the vicinity of airports in the smaller places. For example, in Cheyenne, Wyoming, with twenty-five thousand population, new homes have been built up to and beyond the airport. But if aviation develops as expected, even the airports in small places are likely to have many planes coming and going.

Business Property Near Airports

Business property values are not so likely to be affected by noise as are residential values. People do not sleep at night at their places of business, and they generally work indoors, in buildings which may be insulated somewhat against noise. Business locations are determined by whether the site is a suitable place to sell or to produce goods. The question, therefore, is whether the area adjacent to a large airport provides a suitable place to produce or sell. If so, the values of real estate in the vicinity for business purposes will be increased.

Since large airports at present are located where there are few buildings and almost no businesses, any businesses that are established near an airport will have a tendency to raise the value of the land. The evidence collected from the tax assessors' survey of nineteen large cities showed a tendency in that direction. An increase in the value of business property was noted by seven assessors, while three said that there was a decrease. The influence is evidently not strong, however, as nine reported no influence of the airport on the value of surrounding business property.

Large airports provide a great amount of space for store frontages. Studies of retail business frontage in various cities show that approximately fifty to eighty-five feet of business frontage will support retail stores required by one hundred persons.[3] A large airport, a mile square in size, will have a frontage for stores enough to support around thirty thousand people. It appears that

---

[3] Max Loeb, realtor of Chicago, who has been helpful in studying the influence of aviation on real estate.

not nearly this number of people will be clustered closely around a large airport.

Large retail and department stores will probably not be located near a big airport. Department stores are usually concentrated in an area accessible to many people and require buildings too large to be located near airports. While airports will be easily accessible to many people by through highways from the city center, they will be used mainly by people departing, arriving, or waiting between planes. The types of shops expected to be located at airports are restaurants, drugstores, gift shops, bookstores, magazine stands, etc. There will also be businesses having to do with the servicing and repairing of aircraft. Some machine parts and tools are likely to be sold in the neighborhood. The employees will also need food and refreshments. The effect of these activities and the demands of passengers on business real-estate values will probably be confined to the area immediately adjacent to the airport and not extend to areas adjoining the airport.

Landing strips for small passenger planes may be located between two near-by towns in order to serve both. Legislation has been provided in several states to facilitate such joint municipal ownership. In these cases, some new businesses and residences are likely to grow up near such a landing field, similar to those now found at cross-sections of busy highways.

Recreation Near Airports

It is probable that various kinds of recreation will be centered near airports, and this will have some effect upon real-estate values. The first recreational use of airport terminals was by sightseers who drove out to the airport to see the airliners take off and land. Observation towers for the public were built at La Guardia Field in New York City, and considerable sums are collected annually in admission fees. While watching the planes, visitors often wanted food and drink, and numerous concessions were granted. Many of the German airports had large restaurants located at a vantage-point for viewing the operations on the field.

Airports provide sufficient space for those recreational facilities which require large areas, such as parks, zoological gardens, arboretums, etc. The public can easily reach these recreational facilities by the fast transportation systems connecting the airport and the metropolitan center. Such facilities have already been installed at the airports of several cities. A swimming pool has been built near the Washington-Hoover Airport in the District of Columbia, and in Camden, New Jersey, a dog racetrack has been built across the road from the airport.

It is easy to see possibilities for other forms of recreations, such as picnicking and boating. The installation of skating rinks and dance halls will depend upon the number of visitors. Since outdoor games, such as baseball, football, tennis, and golf, call for a relatively high degree of concentration which would be disturbed by the noise overhead, locations near airports would not be ideal, but the convenience afforded by the plentiful space and good transportation facilities may outweigh this difficulty.

The location of recreational activities, particularly parks, near airports, makes the region attractive for homes near-by, if not quite close to, the airport.

Airport Districts

The discussion so far has concerned land near the airport. What about values of property not close to the airport, but outward from the city in the general direction of the airport? The movement of city populations and of businesses often shows a trend toward particular areas or districts. Will there be a demand for land outward on the side of the city on which the airport is located? The city of Cleveland has made plans for a development of this nature in the direction of the airport. There may be some demand for land in the district of the airport by businesses which find such a location advantageous. If there is recreational development in the district of the airport, and if through highways connect the district with the city, the area may be favorable for residence and perhaps for some expansion of local trade centers. On the other hand, as the planes converge on the airport, flying low, there is considerable overhead noise for miles away from the airport, though the ground noises at the airport cannot be heard. However, there are many factors which affect the location of homes and businesses other than the location of an airport. In addition, real estate changes hands slowly except in rapidly growing communities or districts.

Landing Places for Helicopters

A helicopter can land in a very small place, not much wider than twice the length of its rotor blades, if the engine does not stop. If the engine stops, a larger space is required for the craft, which then comes down with some forward speed. Helicopters can land in or near the center of the city, either on vacant lots or on the roofs of buildings. It is possible that, at first, cities may prohibit the flying of helicopters over the city, except along definite airlanes, because of the danger of accidents. No doubt there will be some accidents, but general use of helicopters and their employment as common carriers presumes a high degree of safety.

Helicopters are expected, therefore, to create a demand for vacant lots near the city center, somewhat comparable to the demand for parking places for automobiles. The demand in the first postwar decade will come principally from commercial concerns, such as taxi services, department-store delivery services, and other similar services, but there will also be some private owners of helicopters who will use them, rather than automobiles or buses, to come to the city.

Since there are at the present time no landing places in cities for helicopters, there is no direct evidence on which to base predictions. However, observations of downtown real estate in different cities reveal few vacant lots and high prices for land. Lower land prices are found in the so-called "blighted" area around the central business district, where the business section impinges on the residential district. Such areas seem the most probable for landing places for helicopters. They have an additional advantage in that there are few tall buildings to accentuate wind currents.

In general, it is not expected that the demand for landing

places for helicopters will have much effect on land values in the city center as a whole.

The roofs of buildings may also be used as landing places for helicopters. At present, roofs are not always flat or strong and often have encumbrances, but they could be made suitable. The problem of the size of the roof is a concern in emergencies when the engine stops and larger areas are required for landing. The roof of a large department store would usually be more suitable than that of a tall office building. The use of roofs as landing places would have no effect on the values of real estate.

The storing of parked helicopters is also a problem. With rotor blades folded back, they can be rolled into spaces not much larger than those required for automobiles. If they become numerous, they may be parked on floors of buildings specially planned for their parking. In this case, they simply create a demand for another building.

The effect of helicopters on downtown real estate, in general, would seem to be negligible. Subways, elevated lines, and through highways increase downtown values, but these media of transportation carry tens of thousands of passengers — many more than are likely to be carried by helicopters.

However, the downtown area is only one end of a helicopter trip. The other end will often be near a residential district. These residences, if they are to accommodate helicopters, should occupy lots somewhat larger than those of present suburban residences. Not many private owners will have helicopters in the first postwar decade, but in subsequent decades the size of dwelling lots may be affected somewhat. On the other hand, there is the possibility that vacant lots scattered here and there in a residential area may be used for landing places for helicopters. From these, an owner may drive his helicopter along the ground to the garage on his residential lot.

Residential dwellers who own helicopters will live out from the city some distance in the suburbs, where a large lot can be obtained. Since the helicopter will increase the demand for large residential lots, it would seem to have some influence on the dispersal of homes.

Population Dispersion and Real Estate

What real-estate dealers want to know particularly is whether aircraft will make it possible for people to live farther out from the city center than the automobile has done and thus precipitate land booms on the outskirts of the present suburbs. A land boom implies a considerable demand. It seems more probable that a few wealthy persons will locate on more spacious grounds on the edges of suburbs, rather than that there will be a mass demand, sufficient for a real-estate boom. Furthermore, a movement of this nature, however small, is not likely to arise until after the first few postwar years, because of the undeveloped state of the helicopter and the probable high price. Residents who live out beyond the suburbs and own both an automobile and a helicopter will be in the upper income levels.

Those who use helicopter service into the city will probably rely more on a helicopter bus than on individual machines. Not enough is known about the economics of helicopter passenger transportation to make possible a very definite statement about the cost of helicopter bus service, but the rates are expected to be quite high. At present, it appears that the rich will be able to afford such service much better than the average salaried person or wage-earner.

The helicopter may be used to transport a person from his residence to the station of a fast commutation railroad train rather than to take him all the way into the city. If this were done, owners could live much farther away from the suburban railway station than if they depended upon an automobile. A helicopter owner might live in a secluded mountain site some distance from the railroad station if it were not for the fact that he is dependent upon various community services, such as telephone lines, electricity, sewage systems, and water mains. He is especially dependent on the community for schools for his children. Helicopter passenger transportation seems more likely to be used by people who live in the trade area and come into the city occasionally rather than by those who live in the suburbs and commute to the city each day to work. Such helicopter transportation facilities would have no effect upon the real-estate values in the trade area outside the city limits.

As far as we can see at present, the helicopter will create a demand, some years after the war, for a few homes beyond the range of present suburbs or between the highways and railroads now joining suburbs to the city. These will be owned by wealthy people who work in the city. The prospects are not encouraging for any great burst of activity on the part of realtors.

Vacation Residences

Many persons have cabins, cottages, lodges, or summer homes at the beaches or in the mountains to which they go in summer, on vacations, or over week-ends. Helicopters may very well affect the location of these vacation residences, which are not particularly dependent on the social services of an incorporated community. The automobile has permitted the scattering of such vacation homes, but the automobile is tied to a highway or good road, whereas the helicopter is not. The helicopter would also make it possible to travel more quickly to the city when occasion demanded.

If prefabricated portable houses are developed, the possible areas for spending vacations will be increased, and a demand may be created for certain favored spots. Demands for these locations of vacation houses may not be wholly a demand for additional summer places, but in part a transfer from existing locations. If these new vacation developments come about slowly and not *en masse*, the real-estate business will not be affected very much.

Conclusion

The effect of aircraft on the business of buying and selling real estate will make itself felt on land values near landing places and on new sites demanded by the redistribution of population. For most airports, particularly large ones, the effect is expected to be, in general, to decrease values of lots for residences unless the noise of planes is reduced. For smaller airports or air parks, little used and surrounded by parks or recreational facilities, residence land values may not decrease, unless a great increase of noisy traffic is anticipated. The general area of the airport may be somewhat desirable for the location of businesses, though the presence of an airport would be a minor factor in determining the location of a factory. Through highways, with few street crossings, between the air port and the city center may lead to a rise in values of adjoining or near-by land. With the development of a successful helicopter, some wealthy persons may buy homes farther out than their present ones and use a private helicopter to take them to a near-by railroad station whence they may go to the city by train, or by helicopter bus. The helicopter is expected to affect the distribution of vacation homes. These influences are not looked for in the immediate postwar years, but should be noted probably around the latter part of the first postwar decade. The influence of the helicopter on the real-estate business, it is thought, will be very slight because of the fact that its development will be gradual and its use restricted for some time to persons with fairly large incomes.

28

Newspapers [1]

THE NEWSPAPER has repeatedly adjusted to the new inventions of communication and transportation which have come through the years. The influence of fast printing inventions, telegraphy, and the local telephone has, of course, been profound. The railroad and the truck extended the range of circulation of the urban newspapers so that the country dailies have lost some of their political power and circulation. The teletype, the telephoto, and radio have all been incorporated into the newspaper organization and have changed its functions and its structure. The airplane is another invention which will make changes in the newspaper world. It will not only make changes in the means of distribution, but also in the kind of advertising, the methods of newsgathering, and perhaps even the appearance of the papers.

To help discover the effect of aviation on newspapers a survey [2] of representatives of newspapers, wire services, press associations, magazines, advertising agencies, and government services was made in New York in 1943. In general, it showed that, because of the pressing problems growing out of wartime restrictions and limitations, journalists had little time to plan for the future. The executives interviewed were concerned primarily

[1] Professor Ralph O. Nafziger, of the School of Journalism, University of Minnesota, Minneapolis, Minnesota, contributed material to this chapter. Also, a survey was made by students in the Graduate School of Journalism, Columbia University, supervised by Eleanor Carroll, Associate Professor of Journalism, Columbia University.

[2] Of the fifty-one men and women interviewed in this project, eleven represented newspapers; two spoke for wire services; six, for magazines; six, for advertising agencies; six, for airline companies; the rest, for government services, foreign countries and agencies. Thirty-eight organizations were represented.

with ways to meet newsprint reduction quotas and to deliver papers promptly in the face of wartime transportation difficulties, and they had little time for studying how the newspaper will adjust to aviation in the future when rates will be lower.

Distribution

Newspapers were making use of planes to some extent before 1940. A few had their own private planes, others chartered or rented planes for specific occasions, and all, especially daily newspapers, made use of commercial airlines to send copy, pictures, and mats by air mail or air express. There was very little attempt to use air transport as a means for distributing the daily newspaper itself up to the time of America's entrance into the war. Some ten or twelve years ago, a small newspaper in McCook, Nebraska, delivered its afternoon paper outside of McCook by plane. A couple of thousand newspapers were distributed in this way.[3] The Chicago *Daily News*, some years ago during the summer holiday season, sent by plane a limited number of its papers to certain sections of Wisconsin and Michigan. This was an excellent means of promoting the *Daily News* to a desired clientèle, and deliveries could be made regularly during the summer holiday season when flying was favored by the best weather conditions of the year. However, while it was looked upon favorably as a means of promotion, the high costs involved could not be justified on the basis of circulation. There are no available records on the number of papers distributed by the *News* in this way.[4]

The Salt Lake *Tribune* made similar use of planes during the tourist season in sending about a hundred copies of its regular edition into the Yellowstone National Park. The practice was continued from 1938 through 1941. Since then, planes have not been available for that purpose. The *Tribune* also made a practice of delivering by air special election editions as far north as Idaho.

[3] Letter from J. M. Harding, assistant publisher of the Omaha *World-Herald*, November 8, 1943.

[4] Letter from John F. O'Keefe, of the Chicago *Daily News*, January, 1944.

During the war, the Salt Lake *Telegram,* an evening paper under the same management as the *Tribune,* sent about a hundred copies to Wendover, Utah, by plane. The distance was one hundred and twenty-five miles, and no other means was available to supply the men at the Army Air Base at Wendover with a newspaper. Arrangements were, therefore, made with the Civil Air Patrol to pick up and deliver the papers.[5] However, this is a special case.

Some years ago special air newspapers were flown from England to Central Africa, India, and Australia. This was expensive service, but readers were willing to pay for it. Papers were also carried between Paris and London before the war, but this was not considered practical. It was felt that either a matrix or microfilm should be flown across and the paper printed at the destination.[6]

Papers were flown to San Francisco for the Golden Gate International Exposition in 1939, to the national political conventions, to summer resorts, and to other points for special reasons. Airplane distribution of newspapers has been used in the past primarily for stunt purposes. At the average rate per ton-mile of eighty cents, air distribution of newspapers had not yet been made profitable before the war.

This use of the airplane depends upon developments in newspaper techniques, the progress of aviation technology, and, most important, upon other inventions producing equivalent effects. By the facsimile transmission of whole pages of newspapers a page of print can be sent from New York to a Chicago office in a period of minutes. Thousands of copies could be reprinted there within an hour after the paper had come off the press in New York. The success of this method has already been established, although it has not been used commercially. Teletype setting and telephoto engraving are other possibilities which will accomplish the same end — that of rapid communication of news to the reader. Which of these inventions will be used first is hard

[5] Letter from E. F. Baldwin, circulation manager of the Salt Lake City *Tribune* and the Salt Lake *Telegram,* November, 1943.
[6] Interview with a representative of the British Overseas Airways, October, 1943.

to foresee. The faster method will always supersede the slower, other things being equal, if the economic differential is not too great. If facsimile printing is commercially developed, the airplane will not be used (except in areas without such facilities), since transmission by facsimile is a matter of minutes, and, by airplane, of hours. If, however, the utilization of facsimile printing, teletype setting, etc., lags behind the expansion of the air services, then the airplane may be used for a period of time until a more rapid method is developed. Assuming, then, that facsimile printing, teletype setting, telephoto engraving, or any similar invention is not adopted, what will be the rôle of the airplane in the distribution of newspapers?

National Newspapers

It has been suggested that the use of airplanes to build up the circulation of big metropolitan newspapers might start a trend toward the growth of national papers. While nearly every metropolitan newspaper, especially in the East, has had aspirations of having at least a nearly complete edition of its paper distributed from coast to coast, newspapermen can see many reasons why such an ambition is impractical. Some of these reasons mentioned in interviews with newspapermen are:

1. A national paper could not handle all the advertising that now sustains small papers. Local advertisers in most cases are not interested in circulation beyond their business area. It was pointed out that the advertisers really pay for the papers, and it will be hard to convince them that they should pay higher rates in order to send papers to an area which they do not serve.

2. A national paper would be without local color. Local news will always be of great importance to the readers because small towns want their own coverage of local politics, crimes, meetings, parties, weddings, and so on.

3. A national newspaper would be at a disadvantage in point of time schedule against papers situated nearer the scene of big news events.

Regarding this question of whether there is a demand for a

newspaper outside its local area, Arthur Robb, *Editor and Publisher,* said: [7]

> There has always been a market for a New York morning paper of the same date in any city which it could reach. It is not a big or a profitable market. It could not be used today as a base for setting a new advertising rate, and unless and until it can be, I do not believe that publishers will gladly increase production costs to supply the distant areas to full capacity.
>
> With few exceptions, the overwhelming majority of newspapers are local institutions. They have no field that they can reach by air that they cannot reach now, and later, by land. By the same token, they can cover their local fields so thoroughly by land that there is not possibility that a metropolitan newspaper, with air transportation, can hope to supplant them.
>
> For instance, the *New York Times* might hope with an air delivery to multiply its present circulation in Chicago by 100. I don't believe that's at all out of the picture. The same goes for the New York *Herald Tribune.* There are people in Chicago who are not satisfied with the morning paper presented by either the Chicago *Tribune* or the *Chicago Sun,* but I doubt that their number tops 50,000 out of a population of, say, 7,000,000 for the present circulation area. No Boston paper now published could hope for any like result; nor could any Philadelphia, Baltimore, or Washington paper. . . .

However, Mr. Robb went on to give his views on how newspapers might make use of the airplane to their own advantage. He said: [8]

> . . . If the Chicago *Tribune,* the *New York Times,* the Chicago *Herald and Examiner,* the San Francisco *Chronicle,* the New Orleans *Times-Picayune* and others wish to increase their sphere of prestige and national influence without regard to the proceeds from advertising, they may want to use the airplane. All these papers could circulate far beyond their home areas and might gain advertising recognition comparable to that given the London and Edinburgh newspapers or the Sydney and Melbourne papers. The effort and expense might well be worth while. The United

---

[7] Correspondence with Mr. Arthur T. Robb, former editor of *Editor and Publisher,* September 7, 1943.

[8] *Ibid.*

States has no newspaper recognized as "national" in the British or Australian sense, with the possible exception of the *New York Times,* and that still dubious from an advertising standpoint. The airplane might well develop several in this country.

Mr. Robb does not believe, with our system of news gathering, especially through our press associations, that any community will feel the need for a metropolitan newspaper strongly enough to warrant added transportation costs for an air edition. He said:

> If local newspapers, in cities of 50,000 to 100,000 population, do their jobs, they have nothing to fear from metropolitan air competition. The air editions will go to the bankers, teachers, lawyers, realtors, etc., who must have up-to-date world news, but the core of circulation will remain untouched. The small city daily and weekly newspapers, therefore, will have to concentrate more and more on doing a thorough and accurate community job. That is entirely apart from the reporting of club and social and merely municipal events. They will have to become vibrant political and social forces. . . .

The general manager of the New York office for one of the major wire services said that the only two newspapers in the United States that could be called national — the *New York Times* and the *Christian Science Monitor* — were distributed widely for purposes of prestige and not as a practical money-making project. Neither carries much national advertising, he said.

A business manager of a New York newspaper mentioned in an interview that timeliness and promptness of delivery of a metropolitan paper are not nearly so important to out-of-town subscribers as to home-town readers. Most readers buy out-of-town papers for their features — book reviews, columns, etc. — and they would buy them if they were a week late. As illustration, he pointed out the fact that two thousand copies of *PM* were flown daily to California when the paper began publication in 1940. Because it was not profitable, the project was dropped, but the California circulation remained steady. Neither was there any effect on the Washington, D.C., circulation when air service was discontinued there. It should be noted, however, that *PM* is an unusual newspaper with some of the characteristics of a magazine. It can also be shown that local papers can hold their readers despite competition from metropolitan papers. Local newspapers in the villages on Long Island and in New Jersey have a good circulation, even though New York City papers are available.

One newspaper official saw the airplane as benefiting the small papers more than the larger ones. The Associated Press, United Press, and International News Service will be able to send mats and other features by plane instead of by rail, thus enabling small papers to have access to this material almost as soon as have the larger papers. In this way the advantages of both the metropolitan and local newspaper can be combined into one paper.

In conclusion, it might be said that, although the opinions of those interviewed were pessimistic as to a national newspaper, these opinions were more concerned with the immediate than with the distant future, and there are very strong probabilities that newspapers will circulate over a wider area than a city and its suburbs. Regional newspapers are more of a possibility than a single national newspaper for a country as large as the United States. London newspapers, which have a national distribution, cover an area that would be called regional in the United States. But whether there are national or regional newspapers, aviation furthers the effects of a national newspaper. Already we have common publication in different newspapers of stock-market quotations, editorials, syndicated columns, comic strips and pictures, and aviation will further promote this trend. So the effects of a national newspaper occur in part, whether or not the full newspaper is distributed nationally. And it is the social effects of a national newspaper or its equivalent in which we are interested, as it creates uniformity in our thinking, information, and tastes.

National Advertising

If a newspaper has nation-wide readers, then it becomes competitive with the magazines for national advertising. This additional national advertising revenue would be expected to pay for the increased circulation costs. One magazine editor who was interviewed believes that the newspaper advertising business is not built up on a national basis in this country to an extent where advertisers are willing to pay additional costs to support a national daily newspaper distributed by air. A representative of a New York advertising agency said that advertising men will continue to prefer magazines for advertising, because (1) they prefer color display to black and white; (2) magazines are read at leisure and their advertisements are studied longer; (3) magazines are kept longer so that the entire family has an opportunity to look through them; and (4) magazine advertisements are more effective because newspaper advertisements are merely reminders.

The development of rapid air travel may expand the trading area of cities, as has been discussed in another chapter. Newspaper advertising would be expected to expand in some scope to keep step with the trading area. Thus, newspaper advertising might become regional in character.

One advertising agent declared that regional or state-wide distribution of metropolitan papers would affect some national advertising adversely by creating a consumer market for some products that are available only locally, for example, jewelry. Retail stores would find it waste circulation to advertise in a nationally circulated paper.

This problem might be solved in two ways. One solution would be the publication of a city edition and an airborne edition. For example, a contemplated Philadelphia edition of the *New York Times* would run local advertising in the supplements containing local news, to be inserted in the general edition of the *Times* air mailed from New York. The airborne edition would carry the national advertising.

Or, depending on technical developments in this field and on economic advantage, the type could be set up in New York and plastic or stereotype mat plates or microfilm could be run off and air-expressed to such cities as Buffalo, Pittsburgh, Chicago, or others not too far away. There the paper would be printed and distributed. Such technique is now being used internationally with good results. The advertising aspect of decentralizing printing is that regional advertisements can be inserted and handled "regionally" rather than having to be sent to one central point. Thus, a newspaper could be both "regional" and "national" at the same time as far as its advertising revenue is concerned.

In general, the representatives of advertising agencies, as well as newspaper and magazine publishers and editors who were interviewed, agree that advertising will be changed only slightly if the use of the airplane in news gathering and newspaper distribution is increased, even if newspapers should assume a more national character. However, it is agreed that the new market created by air travel will make possible many new types of advertisements and will open new fields for advertising.

International Advertising

International advertising in newspapers will not develop to any great extent until fast airline schedules provide a connection between the foreign market and the American buying public, or between an American market and foreign buyers. In the first postwar years, only the well-to-do classes will be able to afford such trips. In the United States there is a class of people who make a yearly, or perhaps more frequent, trip to Chicago or New York to buy clothes. When a trip to London or Paris can be made by airplane in a similar amount of time and at a cost not much greater, then these people may travel to London or Paris.

A representative of a British newspaper who was interviewed said that many American products already are advertised in London and believed that advertising would not be materially affected by the internationalization of newspapers.

Some progress has been made in the field of international advertising in the case of *Time* magazine. A discussion of this will be included in the section describing the experience of *Time* magazine with the airplane.

Lower Rates

Since past experience and prospects for the future do not seem to indicate that newspapers will be willing to pay the added costs of air transport, what are the prospects for lowered air-express rates? As has been indicated in previous chapters, the trend of air-transport rates has been downward.

Because of the high air-express rates in the United States, only the most valuable cargoes can now be shipped by air express, or transportation charges will exceed the value of the product, and only those which of necessity have a great time demand will find air express of worth-while service. Newspapers and news magazines come into such a picture, for they have a very great time demand. It is still true that there is nothing as old as yesterday's news. But, at the same time, newspapers must be relatively inexpensive to the buying public.

There are several ways in which the rates may be lowered. Increased air traffic will lower air rates, but it is doubtful if even these lowered rates will be competitive on a rate basis with other forms of transportation. Many newspapers indicate that they will use air transport in some form should the air-express rate ever drop to eighteen cents. Probably this would be bulk distribution.[9] The second possibility, and the more probable, is that the airlines will be willing later on to make a special rate for newspapers and news magazines, just as special rates are provided now by various wire services for use of their facilities in the transmission of news. Pan American Airways provides special rates to magazines and newspapers at one-half the regular rate for scheduled shipments of eleven pounds or more. Pan American operates only internationally, however. As yet, there are no indications of any such move being under way among our national airlines.

The opinion is almost unanimous among circulation men that it is not economical for a newspaper to own its own plane for distribution purposes, but rather should make use of the scheduled airlines. The airlines will offer a more complete and effective service in the postwar decade to users of air express and

[9] The term "bulk distribution" means wrapping individual copies of a newspaper or magazine for one destination into one bundle. These bundles are broken apart and distributed through the mails, or go to local news dealers, or both.

freight. Feeder lines will enable newspaper distribution to small communities. The helicopter will make possible rapid distribution within a two-hundred-mile radius of the city, thus expanding the suburban area and its newspaper distribution correspondingly.

Distribution within a Nation

If the airplane is used for newspaper distribution, it is very probable that newspapers in the mountain states will be among the first to use it. Other means of transportation are not so well developed in that region, where newspaper circulations covers a wide expanse of territory. Airplanes bridging the present gaps in the transportation system and covering the wider distances at a great saving in time will logically fill a need.

Use of the plane or helicopter within the metropolitan city is improbable. Delivery is already speedy and efficient. As one newspaper representative said, "Why would any New York paper have use for a plane when they get their papers all over the city with a truck in ten minutes?" However, helicopters may be used to shorten the hauling between airports and "in-town" areas or to speed up air deliveries to the suburbs.

The airplane will probably not be used for the distribution of newspapers in small countries. British spokesmen in this country are generally of the opinion that England is so small that the airplane would offer no advantages over the present method of distribution. Papers printed in London by 2 A.M. are all over the country by breakfast time, so there is little need for plane distribution. It was suggested that the airplane might be used for overseas distribution to British dominions and possessions, and to other countries, either by microfilm or in bulk, but the teletype, television, facsimile, and other methods were viewed as being perhaps more feasible. During the war, many English newspapers were printed in several cities rather than at a central location and transported to other areas.

International Distribution

Since the chief advantage of the airplane is its speed, it would seem logical that it should play an important rôle in the distribution of newspapers and publications which are international in scope if other substitute methods of rapid transmission do not materialize.

During the war, the London *Daily Mail* [10] inaugurated a weekly trans-Atlantic edition printed in New York which contained a digest of a week's issues of the British edition. The trans-Atlantic paper was really a new idea in journalism, making use of microfilm. The paper was prepared in London, photographed, and the film, which was about the size of a dollar bill, was sent across by plane. The paper was printed in the United States, reaching the American reading public seventy-two hours after press time in London. The plan was entirely experimental. The *Daily Mail* stated that the American edition was a "spontaneous messenger of good will from one newspaper in England to the people who shape opinion in America." Distribution was free to business leaders, newspapers, radio commentators, etc. If the paper received a favorable reception in this country, it expected to increase its circulation after the wartime paper shortage was alleviated.

The London *Daily Mail* may be the forerunner of a trend which will follow the war. The war produced any number of publications in the United States and other countries which were designed to present the views of other nations fighting the war, particularly the governments-in-exile. They extended all the way from a few weekly mimeographed sheets to regular weekly and monthly publications running into a hundred or more pages. The attempts of one nation to influence another nation have been phenomena throughout history. For instance, in England during Queen Elizabeth's time, Spain was active in spreading Spanish propaganda to influential groups. In modern times, the attempts to spread propaganda have been greatly facilitated by transportation and communication inventions. The airplane, which can be used for transporting publications of the press between nations or in transporting film negatives or printing-press plates and stereotype mats for printing in the country of distri-

[10] *Editor and Publisher*, December 25, 1943, p. 20.

bution, will further facilitate the process of spreading propaganda and will reduce isolation. Should the world become even more nationalistic, we may see many nations presenting their points of view in the United States, and other countries as well, by having their news publications distributed here. With many nations trying to put across their individual points of view, international publishing may reach new heights.

The Chicago *Tribune* developed an overseas edition during the war, known as *Chicago Overseas Tribune*. In doing this, the *Tribune* was following its own precedent, for it had an army edition of its paper published in Paris during World War I.

The World War II edition was printed in Honolulu and consisted of twelve pages, each twelve and a half by nine inches. Distribution was in the central and southwest Pacific through army post exchanges and private agencies. The first run of the Pacific edition was fifteen thousand copies. Later on, Mediterranean and European editions were printed.

The paper was a weekly, and each week the overseas edition was made up in the *Tribune* office in Chicago on Wednesday night, plastic plates were made and shipped by air under a priority to Honolulu, where they arrived on Sunday. Printing was begun on Monday, with distribution of the papers starting that afternoon. The paper carried two pages of general news, with emphasis on Chicago and the Midwest, two pages of sports, an editorial page and a page of features, a back page of pictures and five pages of comics.

The format of the paper varied with the requirements of each war theater. To the Mediterranean area, where army printing shops were equipped to handle stereotype plates, the *Tribune* flew plastic mats, or ordinary dry mats instead of plastic plates. It was also prepared to send negatives for offset printing, when required.[11]

Time, the weekly news-magazine, is the only publication which has experimented widely with foreign air-service circulation, though *Newsweek*, another weekly, launched a Pan-American edition early in 1944. Both are seeking to reach the large poten-

11 *Editor and Publisher,* January 8, 1944, p. 64.

tial market overseas among English-speaking people of influence. *Time's* first venture was started in May of 1941, when shipments of an air-express edition began to Latin America and the Caribbean areas. Since then, the tonnage of its regular weekly shipments through Mexico, Central and South America, and the West Indies has made *Time* one of the larger regular users of air cargo facilities in the world. Its air-express edition had a circulation of 39,500 in 1944, more than twice what it was in June, 1941. The circulation would have been larger at that time had there not been wartime paper and transportation limitations. Copies of the air-express edition which were printed in Jersey City, New Jersey, and flown south from Miami, Florida, weighed approximately two and a half ounces; those printed in Mexico, Colombia, Brazil, and Argentina weighed somewhat more because of paper conditions there.

Time's air operation throughout Latin America is strictly commercial and essentially civilian, though the growth in certain areas, such as the Canal Zone and the West Indies, has been stimulated by military and naval population. All air delivery is via Pan American Airways, including Panagra and its other subsidiaries, except for a portion of Mexico served by LANSA, connections in Central America and Barbados via TACA, and into Aruba from Curaçao via the Dutch KLM line. The experience of almost three years, mostly under conditions of war, showed that for *Time* a satisfactory means of serving the entire Western Hemisphere existed. In 1944, *Time* circulation men believed peace would mean development of delivery that would compare very favorably with the customary weekly services within the United States. Problems arising during the war were temporary rather than fundamental and decreased with experience. There was a noteworthy achievement of regularity in flying schedules, and there was but one minor cargo loss up to 1944.

The shipments to Latin America combined bulk forwarding of the magazine, along with local mailing through the principal airports in the republics and colonies from Bermuda to Argentina and from Mexico to Chile. Originally, all copies were printed by photo-offset in Jersey City, bundled with copies for sub-

scribers individually addressed and stamped, and expressed to
Miami, Florida, and Brownsville, Texas, for forwarding by Pan
American Airways under its special commodity rates for magazines and newspapers. The magazines were thus air-shipped to
airports, where they were delivered to local post offices for final
delivery or, in the case of bulk newsstand shipments, turned over
to dealers.

The specific commodity rate provided for one-half the regular
air-express rate for newspapers and magazines shipped via Pan
American Airways if shipments had a minimum weight of eleven
pounds.[12] Insurance rates were not affected by the specific commodity rate, and each shipper had to make a declaration of value
and insure each shipment. The specific commodity rate meant
that magazines and newspapers could be sent via Pan American
Airways from Miami, Florida, for example, at the following rates
per pound, plus insurance, in 1944: [13]

To Asuncion, Paraguay	87	cents per pound
To Barcelona, Venezuela	43	
To Buenos Aires, Argentina	78	
To Havana, Cuba	10	
To Lima, Peru	59	
To Rio de Janeiro, Brazil	75	
To Mexico City, Mexico	32	

However, the rate varied from the shipping point. For example, the specific commodity rate to Mexico City, Mexico, was
only thirteen cents from Brownsville, Texas. Plane schedules influenced the route over which *Time* shipped to South America, or,
for that matter, any other country or continent, depending upon
how such schedules best tied in with one another to save time.

With the war, *Time* developed decentralized printing set-ups
in Mexico City (December, 1942) to cover Mexico and Central
America; Bogota (May, 1943), covering Colombia, Ecuador, and
northern Peru; Buenos Aires (July, 1943), covering Argentina;

[12] Pan American Airways rate data from their tariff schedules: "Pan American
International Air Express Service," no. 22, Effective November 1, 1943.
[13] Insurance rates do not exceed fifty cents per one hundred dollar valuation to
any point in South or Central America from Miami, Florida.

and São Paulo (March, 1944), covering southern Brazil and Uruguay. The prime reason for this was to reduce the weight being shipped over long air hauls, as planes were heavily loaded as the result of war demands. *Time* found there was no advantage economically from decentralized operation, as increased printing costs of smaller runs more than offset saving in transportation. It may be said that the economy of scale of centralized printing will, in international air-express editions of newspapers and magazines, be decreased by the added distribution costs of air shipping. Other factors abroad, such as legal restrictions, labor supply and costs, availability of necessary equipment and materials, will also enter into the international picture.

If newspapers and magazines are afforded a special rate in international air transport, as available over Pan American Airways since 1941 and used by *Time,* with American modern printing methods considered, prospects are that most American publications with limited international circulation will be printed in this country. However, in viewing such a future, a counter-consideration must be remembered: the present special air-express rate is granted by an American-owned-and-operated international airline. Such special rates may not be granted by foreign airlines operating internationally. Therefore, American publications may be afforded special rates only where American-owned international airlines go.

Time's so-called "Pacific Edition" resembled that distributed in Latin America. It was printed in Honolulu from film flown out from New York and had a paid circulation of about forty thousand, the greater portion of it among army and navy personnel. If press facilities had been available, a similar operation probably would have been duplicated in Alaska. Another edition was launched in Sweden with a similar set-up except for a lack of any military segment of circulation there and for some irregularity of publishing schedule because of delays in flying schedules under conditions of war and weather. The Swedish operation was different from *Time's* other operations in that distribution, as well as printing details, were handled by outsiders under contract.

From its inception, *Time's* air-express edition carried advertising especially directed to the countries in which it was sold. The Pacific and Swedish editions were part of *Time's* overseas edition, which went to all countries outside the Americas and carried advertising addressed to the general export market. The Canadian edition, distributed by regular means through the Dominion of Canada and Newfoundland, had its own particularly addressed advertising. Space in the three foreign editions could be bought separately or as a unit through *Time International.* Just as some newspapers in the world have come to be national in their advertising scope, so *Time* is directing some of its efforts toward becoming international. Since the air editions of *Time* reach businessmen, political leaders, and men of substantial means for the most part, it is able to offer a market to advertisers interested in reaching the people who influence others. Unquestionably, this has been an important factor in its Latin-American success from an advertising point of view.

There were also special air editions of *Time* printed in Australia, India, and Iran for United States Army units stationed there. These were like the other air copies except that they carried no advertising and were entirely bulk-delivered within their areas so that officers and soldiers could buy copies at Army Exchanges but could not subscribe. The issues were printed from plastic plates or films flown out from this country on official planes. As a result, the War Department issued a memorandum in 1943 to all commanding generals of overseas areas authorizing the establishment of reprinting of publications wherever possible and desired.

The "pony edition" was another *Time* product brought out during the war. It was a photo-offset miniature without advertising, weighing only an ounce. Originally it was devised in November, 1942, to fulfill certain subscriptions in the British Isles which had been entered on an air-service basis. It was designed to meet with wartime cargo restrictions. The services themselves also took over certain bulk air shipments to far corners of the world. Servicemen subscriptions to *Time* outside the United States were filled from the "pony edition." Other publications began to follow *Time's* lead and brought out miniature editions. As for the future, *Time* circulation men in 1944 said:

> . . . seemingly only miniature copies can be sent by air mail due to costs, and even an ounce is expensive at today's mail rates. After the war there will not be the present demand for, nor willingness of publishers to print, the smaller-size edition. Full-page copies with advertising, printed on light-weight paper, and bulk air-forwarded, as *Time* is now doing in Latin America, or printed from air-carried films or plates, as *Time* is now doing in Honolulu, Stockholm, and elsewhere, seem to be the answer for any magazine which seeks and commands a world news audience. The actual set-up will depend on air-rate structures and development of techniques for handling printing, distribution, and routine publishing details.[14]

The market for American newspapers and magazines distributed in foreign countries will be enlarged through the greater number of international travelers expected after the war, partially due to the stimulation of aviation. The foreign market for American publications will also be larger if Basic English comes into widespread use.

News Gathering

Up to World War II there was very little use of airplanes, privately or in scheduled air transport, for the distribution of newspapers. However, a number of daily papers in the country did make use of airplanes by having their own planes and using them for gathering pictures of special events of interest in their circulation areas, for promotion and good will, and for experimental purposes. The five main cases were the Detroit *News*, the Chicago *Daily News*, the Des Moines *Register* and *Tribune*, and the New York *Daily News*. All five had varied results and experiences, and all were forced during the war, either by other factors or by the war itself, to abandon their planes. All five found operating costs high, even prohibitive in some cases, while others charged off most of their expense to promotion and good will.

[14] Authority for information on *Time*: Walter K. Belknap, assistant circulation manager, Time, Inc., New York City.

W. W. Waymack, editor of the Des Moines *Register* and *Tribune*, in relating his experiences with planes, points to several aspects.

> Our first plane was procured in the spring of 1928 and was an experiment. We didn't know exactly what values we would get out of it, but obviously we thought we'd get enough to justify the experiment. From the beginning we thought in terms of news photography, both from the air and on the ground, using our own photographers. We thought in terms of service to the news department in covering particularly the state of Iowa, but also, to some extent, our region. In addition, we had in mind the promotional aspect. As a public service, we wanted to promote interest in commercial aviation — the development of airports and so on. We thought also that there would be an advertising and prestige instrument for our papers.[15]

In the period of a dozen years, up to 1940, the *Register* and *Tribune* owned together and successively a half-dozen planes, including one autogiro, which was primarily a "stunt" and was not able to carry much of a load. In the earlier years a considerable amount of "guest-hopping" was done. Aviation was very new and had captured the imagination, and those who had been up in an airplane were local heroes in many communities. When possible, the *Register* and *Tribune* plane operated for a day from fields near Iowa cities other than Des Moines, taking selected people for rides. Such methods could be of special use to certain departments of the papers because "hop" lists sometimes included persons in whom those departments were particularly interested.

Something was accomplished for efficiency and morale of the organization of the *Register* and *Tribune*. Thousands of rides were given to carrier salesmen throughout Iowa, as well as to others functioning in the circulation department. On a number of occasions, the plane and pilot were also made available for emergency public service, which generated appreciation and prestige.

But the main use of the airplane was made in the news depart-

[15] W. W. Waymack, editor of the Des Moines *Register* and *Tribune*.

ment of the papers. Pictures were emphasized in the two papers; the Sunday rotogravure section was localized to the area. Aerial photographs were tried, and, because aviation was then new and novel, they attracted a great deal of attention. It was commonplace to send out photographers and reporters by plane to any point in Iowa where dramatic news suddenly developed. The practice made for speed in news coverage and had a continuous prestige value. During the football season, especially, with an airplane (and sometimes additional planes were chartered), the Des Moines *Register* and *Tribune* were able to cover special games of major Iowa interest, both as to a personalized news report and as to pictures. It enabled the *Register* to get print as well as picture coverage into even the early editions of its Sunday paper. Both the *Register* and *Tribune* have been interested in boosting their circulation, and their circulation departments say that the airplane helped them in doing so.

World War II changed the picture, since all planes, with but very few exceptions, were put under government regulation to be incorporated in the war effort; all kinds of non-war flying were severely restricted, and pilots were drawn into the war training program in one way or another. As a result, the *Register* and *Tribune* had to give up both their plane and pilot. However, after the war they plan to use planes again in much the same manner as in the past.

The experience of the Detroit *News* is somewhat in contrast with that of the Des Moines *Register* and *Tribune*. When Wirephoto and Wirephoto portables came into use, the *News* found little need for its own plane for covering events in its area or for transporting pictures. The *News* felt that it no longer could justify the expense of maintaining a $25,000-plane, pilot, mechanic, and specially trained aerial photographer.[16]

Before the *News* used Wirephoto, the plane it owned was used to transport pictures from as far east as Boston and New York; as far south as Louisville, Kentucky (for the Derby), and Lakeland, Florida (spring training camp for the Detroit Tigers); and as far west as Minneapolis, Minnesota (the Michigan-Minnesota football game).

[16] Fred Gaertner, Jr., managing editor of the Detroit *News*.

In 1944, spokesmen for the *News* felt that the initial cost of a plane and its maintenance would have to be considerably less after the war than in the decade preceding 1940 to justify this paper in again owning a plane. The *News* felt that, inasmuch as it had Wirephoto and Acme telephoto services, and the prospects for putting portable AP and Acme transmitters into every newspaper office were good after the war, any need for planes for news and picture transport would be eliminated.

In the 1944 New York survey conducted by students in journalism at Columbia University, it was found that most of those questioned agreed with a magazine official who said that planes would not be used extensively for gathering news because faster methods, such as the telephone and telegraph, were available. As an OWI official expressed it, "Planes will be used to fall back on when you can't use other facilities, that's all." This same official further pointed out some of the instances where such air services had been used during the war under such circumstances. Pictures were flown rather than radioed during the war when there were no facilities for receiving radio photos. Such was the case in Naples during the Italian campaign. Planes were also used by the OWI during the war to bring news from the fronts where transmission by radio was impossible.

Similarly, in South America, negatives from abroad had to be flown to South American newspapers, since they had no equipment for developing radio news photos from abroad.

Thus the conclusion is reached that the airplane might have been important as a medium for assisting in the quick gathering of news had it not been for the communication facilities of radio, telephone, and telegraph, which are many times faster than any plane and much cheaper. The plane, though, may be used in areas that do not have adequate communication facilities.

However, the scheduled airlines have been used and will be used extensively to carry reporters and correspondents to cover their assignments. This use of airlines began in 1930, when Webb Miller flew to India to cover Gandhi's salt march. Miller traveled sixteen thousand miles in fifteen days. Planes are expected to play an important part in transporting reporters to distant and otherwise inaccessible places. The AP owned no planes before the war, but it used the regular airlines when a big story broke some distance away and had to be covered quickly. But the reporter will not fly from Europe or other places to report when he can put his story on the wire and have it in the office of his newspaper in the United States in a few minutes. All news-gathering agencies have bureaus in strategically located centers. The location of these agencies may be changed as the airplane reshifts the geographic areas of interest and importance.

One possibility that a representative of a news-gathering agency thought might be developed was a walkie-talkie set that could be used to give eye-witness accounts from airplanes directly to rewrite men in the newspaper office. This would cause a speed-up in news coverage and give a more personal touch to stories, perhaps resulting in more by-line stories.

Air developments may have a great influence on news photography if the predictions of some newsmen are correct. It has been suggested that some newspapers might have portable darkrooms which could be carried in a plane, and pictures of floods, etc., could be developed while returning to the newspaper office. One New York newspaper has used the airplane to carry a forty-four-pound picture transmitter to various parts of the country. It has also been suggested that planes could be used to transport photographers to far places and thereby increase the scope of photography.

One might come to the conclusion that airplanes will be used to some extent for the gathering of news in postwar America, but they will be used in addition to, and not in place of, present news-gathering methods.

Change in Contents and Appearance

In view of the fact that the airplane will favor a trend toward lightness in material, the question of whether the airplane will bring changes in the size and weight of newspapers after the war has often been discussed. In an interview, the aviation editor of a large chain of newspapers expressed an opinion that changes in the format, print, kind of paper, and the number of pages are quite likely. A new, thin paper of great strength and new presses to print this paper must be developed, he believes. In case large papers should try to compete with small locals, a special tabloid edition might be used. The Spanish language edition of *Time* magazine, distributed in South America by airplane in 1944, was printed on lighter paper, thus saving space and weight and reducing freight charges. Such changes in weight and appearance are dependent on the use of the airplane for distribution.

One airline official predicted in an interview that in the future we will read magazines of news summary and comment rather than four or five newspapers a day, as is now necessary in New York City. He pointed out that magazines can be more easily transported by air than newspapers because they are less bulky.

According to a New York advertising executive, newspapers cannot be made much lighter because they must carry a certain amount of advertising which must have a fairly good display.

The possibility of publishing a special edition of papers for airplane distribution was termed impractical by the publisher of one of New York's largest newspapers. Changing the papers for plane transportation would be too difficult and too costly.

Thus, the consensus of opinion of the magazine and newspaper officials, as well as of the advertising agents, interviewed in this survey was that there would be little, if any, change in the size and weight of newspapers after the war, whether or not airplane distribution were used extensively.

Conclusion

In the postwar national picture, then, some trends may be extrapolated from what we know of air transport now and what can be foreseen of the future. A most important factor is the equivalent inventions which may be developed, thus nullifying the effects of aviation on the newspaper.

Many circulation-minded newspapers will make use of airplanes, as need arises, to gather news and pictures when existing news facilities do not satisfy their demands. Newspapers which have large circulations and are interested in giving the best possible news coverage may find a private plane to their advantage in covering special events and for promotional merits. Similarly, large national press associations may make use of planes for sending specially trained men to cover events calling for special reporting and picture coverage. It does not appear that the large metropolitan daily will find it practical to own its own planes to distribute newspapers to other cities in bulk for either local mailing or delivery. However, the helicopter may supplant the truck for suburban delivery.

The use of air mail in speeding news copy to newspapers is already a reality. Prepared mats and syndicated material are at present handled in this way.

From the standpoint of newspaper distribution, the papers will find it best to make use of existing commercial airline facilities if they want air transport. Airline schedules are constantly being enlarged, covering a greater number of cities with a greater number of flights per day. Lowered air-transport costs within the United States will come about as air traffic increases. The airlines may grant special rates to news publications. Pan American Airways, operating internationally, grants such rates now. The use of air transport by newspapers is also contingent on the development of feeder lines with rapid schedules and the provision for better pick-up and delivery services between airports and metropolitan centers.

The extent to which newspapers will feel a demand for air transport will depend, in part, upon whether advertising will help support a national newspaper and whether readers are willing to pay an added price for an air edition of a New York newspaper.

Decisions as to centralized or decentralized printing of news publications to be shipped by air, both nationally and internationally, will reflect both the relative costs and advantages of each type of operation and the availability of facilities in the case of decentralized printing.

Commercial news publications on the international market will use air transport for the shipping of plates and films for decentralized printing, or for shipping the publications themselves, or use some other method of rapid transmission. Should an intense wave of nationalism sweep the world following the war, many countries may develop international publications shipped by air, some of them supported by subsidy.

29

Agriculture [1]

AGRICULTURE and agricultural life will be influenced by the use of the airplane in a number of ways. In the first place, the airplane is potentially an additional piece of farm machinery for use in spraying and dusting, in spreading seed and fertilizer, and in controlling insects and pests. Its use in these ways may change the structure of farm organization to some extent. Secondly, the airplane may affect agriculture by its use as a means of transportation of agricultural supplies and products. Thirdly, its use in other fields, such as by the Department of Agriculture in administering crop-control programs or for aerial mapping and surveying, will have indirect effects on agriculture.

Dusting and Spraying

One use of the airplane as a piece of agricultural machinery is in spraying and dusting to destroy fungi and insect pests on crops and orchards. The earliest known experiment in dusting with an airplane was in 1921, in Ohio, when a grove of catalpa trees were dusted by plane to kill catalpa sphinx. The results were satisfactory, and experimental work followed elsewhere, especially on cotton in Louisiana for control of army leaf worm and the boll weevil. In 1925, a commercial company was established in the cotton belt with eighteen planes and nine centers of operation. Similar work in dusting was going on at this time in foreign countries, such as France and Czechoslovakia. Between 1925 and

---

[1] Dr. Mary Jean Bowman, Department of Economics and Sociology, Iowa State College, Ames, Iowa, contributed material for the preparation of this chapter.

1928, over forty thousand acres of forest in Germany were dusted by plane for control of defoliators. In Russia, extensive experimentation was successfully carried out on airplane dusting for control of the Asiatic migratory locust.

The dusting of fruit and vegetables followed the work that had been done in forestry, cotton, and mosquito control. The persisting success in these latter fields provided the background of practice on which agriculturalists have since drawn in their work on vegetables and fruit.

Cotton

Airplane dusting of cotton for control of the boll weevil and army leaf worm has become an established practice, especially in the western cotton states of Louisiana, Arkansas, Texas, and Mississippi. In the Mississippi Delta, 10 to 15 per cent of the cotton acreage was dusted in the years just prior to the war. In Texas, only about 1 per cent is reported to be dusted in this manner. The large holdings are those most often dusted, although the small ones which are close together may also be treated. Airplane dusting of cotton has been used every year since 1927 in the Brazos River bottoms in Texas. The extent of the use depends on the nature and severity of occurrence of the injurious insects.

It was estimated [2] that, in 1943, approximately 330,000 acres of cotton were dusted by airplane out of about 22,000,000 acres harvested, or only about 1.5 per cent of the total crop. All of this dusting was done by individual growers or by commercial dusters with privately owned equipment. Much of the acreage not covered was made up of small farms in hilly sections and with a tenure set-up, which is not conducive to the spread of mechanized farming.

Fruits and Vegetables

In the dusting of fruit and vegetables, California has been the

[2] Estimate by the United States Department of Agriculture, Bureau of Entomology and Plant Quarantine.

major area for such activity. The total acreage of fruits and vegetables dusted by airplane in California has been as follows: [3]

1934	65,479	1939	73,094
1935	103,306	1940	69,521
1936	94,205	1941	176,596
1937	75,929	1942	132,701 [4]
1938	68,453		

Crops which have received extensive aerial dusting are tomatoes,
peas, beans, and peaches. Grapes, prunes, and potatoes have also
been so treated in most years since 1937, but much less extensively.

Florida ranks next to California in the extent of fruit and vegetable dusting and the lower Rio Grande Valley of Texas has recently become an important area for airplane dusting of vegetables. In the Middle Atlantic truck-garden area, there has been
a growing use of planes in recent years for dusting vegetables on
large truck farms. The Seabrook Farms in New Jersey carry on
extensive dusting operations on their vegetables, especially beans.
Some experimental work has been done in New Jersey, Massachusetts, and Maine on the dusting of cranberries and blueberries.

Grasshoppers and Mormon Crickets

Airplane dusting for control of the grasshopper and Mormon
cricket [5] has been used increasingly in recent years in the United
States since the United States Bureau of Entomology and Plant
Quarantine has undertaken widespread operations. In 1943, Bureau-owned and contract planes baited approximately 340,000
acres for control of these two insects. In 1939, 150,000 acres were
treated in California alone to stamp out a grasshopper infection.

[3] The figures are from the California Department of Agriculture.
[4] Reduction in acreage in 1942 is explained on the basis of shortage of planes
due to war. Dusting and spraying were considered of such importance, however,
that planes were allocated to dust the largest acreage in any year except 1941.
[5] See *Journal of Economic Entomology,* vol. 25, pp. 189-196, article by C. J.
Drake and G. C. Decker, for discussion of early work in aerial baiting of grasshoppers.

Distribution of Dusting Activity

The locations of commercial concerns engaged in dusting may give some idea of the distribution of dusting activity. The following list shows the number of commercial concerns engaged in dusting in March, 1942: [6]

California	9	Illinois	1
Mississippi	7	Kansas	1
Texas	6	Michigan	1
Arkansas	5	Missouri	1
Florida	5	Nebraska	1
Louisiana	5	Pennsylvania	1
Alabama	1	Utah	1
Arizona	1	Washington	1

California is shown to have the largest number of companies, and it also has the largest amount of dusting. The listing of one concern each in the Midwestern states indicates that some dusting is going on in these areas, but it is quantitatively unimportant at the present time. The dusting companies are small and the planes are used for other purposes as well. This list fails to show the extent of dusting done by farmer-owned planes, as on the Seabrook farms in New Jersey, or the dusting done under government auspices, particularly the United States Bureau of Entomology and Plant Quarantine.

Advantages of the Airplane for Dusting

One of the principal advantages of the airplane in dusting and spraying is its speed of application. One commercial company, in 1925, claimed that it could dust cotton one hundred times as rapidly as the best ground machines.[7] In combating fast-working pests, such as the army leaf worm in cotton, or in meeting emergency invasions of migratory pests, such as grasshoppers or the white-fringed beetle, the airplane offers the only effective method of protection.

[6] From list made up by the United States Bureau of Entomology and Plant Quarantine. Approximately two hundred planes, built and equipped for airplane dusting in the United States, were reported in 1943.

[7] Huff Daland & Co., Bulletin 2, 1925.

The equipment for dusting by plane can be moved rapidly from one area to another, enabling a small amount of machinery to give protection against emergency invasions of pests over a wide area. With the proper organization of services, a considerable saving can be made in the diminished amount of equipment necessary to insure protection at any one place. The high mobility of the equipment enables the planes to be in continual use by seasonal dovetailing of services. Planes used for dusting cotton in Texas may be used at a different season for dusting vegetables in Florida. One American commercial dusting company has sent planes to Peru during off-seasons in the United States.

The fact that the airplane is independent of ground conditions enables it to dust fields that would be difficult for ground machinery. Irrigation does not interfere with plane application of fungicides and insecticides. This is especially important in the case of the California vegetable crops. Muddy fields, after heavy rains, do not prevent planes from spraying to protect the fields again. Intertwining or tall-growing crops do not interfere with plane application as they do with that of ground machinery.

When flying close to the ground, airplane dusting results in good adhesion of dust. This has been especially noted in the dusting of cotton. It is believed that an electric charge is set up by the interaction between plane and ground when the plane flies low over the cotton. The dust covers the bottom as well as the tops of the leaves. The plants do not have to be wet with dew in plane dusting, thereby eliminating the necessity of night work.

For some crops a considerable saving in amount of dust required has been made possible by airplane application. This has been true of calcium arsenate, especially when applied to low-growing crops. However, larger amounts of dust are necessary in applications of insecticides and fungicides when ground machines apply dust to particular plants rather than covering an entire acreage evenly. The airplane is not accurate in dusting small sections of crops or in selecting any particular plant. The helicopter will be more accurate in spraying or dusting small areas. Technical improvements in the mechanism for distribut-ing the insecticides and in their composition will further decrease the amount of dust required by plane dusting.

The use of the plane relieves the farmer of the necessity of teaching labor how to dust and of supervising the dusting opera-tion. Dusting by airplane, of course, requires specialized labor, more highly skilled than for running ground machinery. Instead of a large number of men working with ground machinery part time, there will be a small number of skilled men dusting by plane full time. This will facilitate control and advice from expert entomologists in spraying and dusting work.

Disadvantages of the Airplane for Dusting

The drift of dust has been one of the major handicaps to airplane dusting in diversified farming areas. Where the acreages to be dusted have been relatively small and not contiguous, there has been considerable waste of dust because of drifting. Damage to bees may be considerable, and also to livestock. Liquid sprays have been and are being developed to meet this problem. How-ever, the liquid sprays are heavier, their application more costly, and in some cases, such as in treating tomatoes, the sprays have proved less efficient than the dust. The development of a heli-copter with a large load capacity will diminish this problem, since the slow speed and hovering power of the helicopter will increase the accuracy of aerial dusting.

The difficulties and costs of turning at the ends of the field have made dusting by airplane practicable only on large acreages. There is considerable danger in dusting by plane over rough terrain, such as exists in New England. The helicopter will be a solution to both problems. The helicopter can make short turns at the ends of fields, or it can hover over a small plot of ground. It can also avoid obstructions, such as tall trees or power lines. An uneven terrain necessitates flying, in airplanes, at heights which increase the drift and interfere with the adhesion of dust particles falling initially on the areas being treated. The heli-copter can avoid the obstructions of rough terrain without much loss of efficiency.

Inventional Development

The successful use of the airplane in dusting and spraying has depended upon three independent lines of research. First, there has been the development of the airplane and the mechanisms for spraying and dusting. Secondly, there has been research in the control of insect pests and fungi. This has involved both the study of their nature and habits and their reactions to various types of poisons. Thirdly, there are social inventions in organization, which include commercial organization and forms of salesmanship, the development of public institutions of education and research, especially those directed toward the serving of agriculture, and the organization for collective public action.

Mechanisms for Spraying and Dusting

The improvement of the mechanism used in airplanes for spraying and dusting is important for the successful future of aerial dusting and spraying. Most of the work done up to this time has been by commercial laboratories. Improvements are to be expected which will increase the efficiency and evenness of distribution of the liquids and dusts. An obstacle in the past has been the high initial cost of this equipment and the time and effort required to develop highly specialized equipment. As developments proceed, the resulting improvements are expected to reduce the cost.

Airplane Invention

Invention in adapting the airplane to the requirements of dusting and spraying is inseparable from the research to increase maneuverability in general. Spraying and dusting require planes which can turn sharply at the ends of fields, change altitude in a short distance when operating over uneven terrain, carry a heavy load of dust or liquid spray, and operate at a slow speed to minimize dust drift. The autogiro, although little used for this work, had some of these characteristics. The helicopter promises to have most of them, and its adaptation for dusting and spraying would be a matter of perfecting the details.

Oil Sprays

The problems of adhesion in dusting from greater height above crops and orchards to get adequate coverage and to prevent drifting led to the development of liquid sprays for use from planes. Most of this work has been done in connection with the spraying of woodlands and with mosquito control. With liquid-oil insecticides and fungicides, distribution has been found to be quick and even. The oil creeps and adequately covers the undersides of leaves and twigs. Spraying is now important for orchards and is expected to be developed for truck crops, especially tomatoes.

Oil sprays are expected to be important, since they reduce the dust drift. Dust applications of arsenate of lead or calcium arsenate have given good control of many insects, but are objectionable in that the dust drifts when there is any appreciable wind and cannot be used in areas where food crops are grown or near heavily inhabited areas. In California, the use of airplane dusting has resulted in heavy losses to beekeepers. In some cases stands of bees have been almost completely destroyed when located adjacent to sites where dusting operations have been carried on with arsenicals to control leaf-chewing insects. The losses of bees have been particularly heavy when adjacent to tomatoes which have been dusted with calcium arsenate.

> The drift of calcium arsenate from a field over which it was applied by airplane has been found to travel a distance of three miles in quantities that would remind one of a ground fog. Any pastures, fruit-drying yards, lettuce fields, homes and home gardens in the area would obviously receive a deposit of this poisonous material. When liquid sprays are used, the drift to adjacent areas is of little significance.[8]

Thus, liquid sprays are expected to cause less damage to the beekeeping industry, food crops, livestock, and human health.

Social Invention

Invention in social organization for aerial dusting, other than adaptation within commercial companies, has not been very

[8] Quoted from a letter from Dr. J. E. Eckert, apiculturist, Division of Entomology and Parasitology, University of California, January 12, 1944.

great. With increased governmental responsibility for control of air commerce and the use of airplanes in general in the postwar decade, social invention is likely to progress.

There are a number of possibilities for types of social organization for the spraying and dusting for insect control. The government may conduct the research; it may co-operate in research, demonstration, and actual dusting and spraying with commercial concerns; or it may carry on all these activities itself, independently of commercial concerns; or all of these activities could be left wholly to private commercial concerns.

Large-Scale Operation

There are advantages in large-scale operation. One advantage is that such operation encourages the use of professional entomological advice. The large commercial dusting companies which have many local headquarters and scores of planes have consistently made use of professional entomological advice. For the most economical results, it is necessary to know the nature and degree of insect infestation. It is important to use airplane dusting at the proper times and not to use it when natural control will be effective. When the work is done without professional entomological advice, it is largely a matter of guesswork. Since the service is relatively expensive and covers large areas in a short time, a large amount of waste can occur. Another advantage is that large companies are able to shift equipment from one region to another and from one kind of crop and pest to another over a wide area and thus effect economies by seasonal operation. They have the facilities for securing insurance against insect damage for contracting farmers. Large-scale services provide an adequate financial base for experimental work in improving services and in extending them to new kinds of crops and orchards and to new sections of the country.

Large farms or plantations are favorable to airplane dusting. It is easy to plan and co-ordinate the dusting within one big farm. In Mississippi, the large cotton-growers were the first to co-operate with the companies in large-scale cotton insect control. The large-scale, industrialized types of agriculture in California have contributed to that state's leadership in applications of insecticides by plane to both fruit and vegetable crops. South Africa has large-scale farming and the owners co-operate on insect control, largely through agricultural schools, which provide guidance and advice.

Co-operation

Since airplane dusting requires many acres of fields to be dusted at one time, the question arises as to how to obtain such a layout among a number of small farmers in order to make airplane dusting technically and economically feasible. Some of the possible agencies of co-ordination are commercial companies, farm managers, the state extension services, agricultural co-operatives, or the United States government. Up to the present time, the principal co-ordinators have been the commercial dusting companies, except in cases where plantations or estates were so large that they could conduct their own dusting operations. Contracts of farmers for commercial dusting, made out in advance, make possible a planning of operations by the dusting companies that gives the most satisfactory results possible within the existing framework of farming. Although the farms are rarely contiguous, yet, to the extent to which there is some co-ordination, airplane dusting is facilitated. State extension services operate similarly in farm-management advisory capacities in some areas. Although these services do not often give detailed individual guidance today, there is a possibility that they might act as a co-ordinating agent in airplane dusting programs.

Group action among farmers is a possible form of organization. In 1924, several large planters in the Mississippi Delta formed a corporation and obtained a plane to do their work. However, in the main there has been very little organization of this kind up to the present. Reports from the various states uniformly say that the agricultural co-operatives have played no part in the development of airplane dusting of the crops in which they are concerned. A partial exception occurred in New Jersey a few years ago when the Blueberry Co-operative Association arranged for the dusting of small, adjacent fields in order to conserve time, but even in this case most of the members made their own arrangements.

Governmental Aid to Commercial Firms

The organization of dusting facilities by an outstanding commercial dusting company in the 1920's was an example of a form of co-operation between the private concern and the government. The private company obtained contracts for from five thousand to seven thousand acres of cotton within a ten-mile radius in a number of districts. The Secretary of War released an army pilot to the company to do the work. The county agents co-operated in giving information as to the services available. The work was supervised and governed by a board, made up of members of the federal and state agricultural authorities.

The government has continuously given aid since the 1920's through special experimental laboratories and the United States Bureau of Entomology and Plant Quarantine in research work on the problems of aerial dusting. The dusting of the catalpa grove in Ohio, which served as a starter for much experimentation in the early stages, was undertaken under the auspices of the State Experiment Station at the request of the owner of the grove. The government organized two experimental stations in 1922, one the Gypsy Moth Laboratory in Massachusetts, and the other the Delta Laboratory in Tallulah, Louisiana. Co-operation between experiment stations and commercial concerns has recurred from time to time.

Government Operation

The United States government, which has already become an agricultural entrepreneur to a considerable extent, could plan and execute aerial dusting programs. Acreage allotments for soil conservation and for production and marketing quotas involve a degree of intervention in the decisions of the American farmer that is but a short step from such government intervention as would be involved in the planning of planting to facilitate airplane dusting in areas where it is technically feasible and economical. Insect and fungi control is usually a public, rather than an individual, problem. Treatment of a plague, such as a grass-hopper invasion, cannot be left to individual action if the public interest is to be protected. The individual farmer will not use control measures unless they appear to be profitable to him individually. Furthermore, the dusting of crops by airplane may cause damage to other property in the vicinity. Public regulation of airplane dusting to protect bees, livestock, and even human beings against drifting of poisonous dust is essential with the spread of aerial dusting, especially in diversified farming areas. California has already taken steps in this direction.

The government has long conducted research and experimentation, but only in recent years has it taken any active part in actual operations. In 1943, the Bureau of Entomology and Plant Quarantine maintained and operated, for pest-control purposes, two autogiros and six planes. Bureau-owned planes were used to treat twenty-two hundred acres of forest land for control of the gypsy moth in outlying infestations in New York and Pennsylvania, and approximately two thousand acres of crop lands were dusted for white-fringed beetle control in Alabama. Thus, the precedent for government participation in fighting pests through airplane spraying and dusting in the United States is already established. In postwar years, there is every reason to anticipate an increase in such activities, possibly through co-operative action on the part of the military branches of the government and the Bureau of Entomology and Plant Quarantine. Governmental participation would provide a means of maintaining a skeleton force of trained pilots, kept in practice by maneuvering planes under difficult conditions. It is more than likely that we shall have new pest invasions in the coming years, brought in by the airplane from the Orient, from South America, and from Africa. Government responsibility will be regarded as extending, not merely to quarantine to prevent the introduction of such pests, but also to stamp them out quickly if they make an appearance.

Future Expansion of Aerial Dusting

The future expansion of dusting and spraying by aircraft for the control of pests and fungi depends upon a number of factors:

organizational factors, that is, whether dusting is done by the individual, by the federal government, or by agricultural co-operatives or state extension services; the extent of infestations and the damage therefrom; cost of service; prices of the crops; and the supply of labor. In general, it can be noted that the costs of plane dusting will be lowered through technological improvements. Seasonal dovetailing with other types of plane use and co-operation enabling large areas to be dusted by one operation will further reduce the costs. The supply of pilots and mechanics from the armed services is expected to provide a large labor supply for plane dusting.

If dusting is left to the individual initiative of the farmer, the labor supply may be an important factor in the amount of dusting by airplane. If the supply of labor sufficiently skilled to operate ground machines is small and expensive, dusting by plane will be encouraged, and vice versa. The price of the crops to be dusted will also be an important factor in determining how much aerial dusting there will be.

Increased use of aerial spraying and dusting for fruits and vegetables is expected primarily in Texas and some other truck-gardening areas of that region, and in the truck-gardening areas of the Middle Atlantic area. The future success and expansion of fruit and vegetable dusting by plane depend upon the perfecting of dust and spray mixtures and the mechanisms for their distribution. The trend of prices for fruits and vegetables is more likely to be upward than is that for cotton. Consumption of fresh fruits and vegetables has steadily increased. The spread of nutrition education and the increasing use of air transportation for fresh fruits and vegetables will probably further increase this consumption. Therefore, the value of these crops will probably be an incentive to individual dusting, even if the government does not take over this function.

The aerial control of pests and fungi in field crops may be limited in the future because preventive measures are preferable to eradication. Damage by grasshoppers and crickets is best prevented by public measures to meet the invasions of these pests over areas where private investment in the spreading of dust would be uneconomical. However, there are a few cases in which private operation might prove economical, as in the case of alfalfa weevil, wheat rust, the sugar-cane moth borer, and for pests among sugar beets. The incidence of wheat rust has been reduced by the development of rust-resistant types of wheat. Development of resistant strains in other field crops is similarly diminishing the likelihood of airplane dusting of crops in the future. Airplane dusting of cane sugar has not been successful because of the type of spray used rather than because of the method of application. Successful airplane dusting or spraying must wait until further entomological work has been done. This method of dusting sugar beets has only recently become successful. Because of the tall, rank growth in the seed stage of sugar beets, dusting by air is the only practical possibility and its use will probably spread.

Dusting in Other Countries

Very little has been done thus far to fight agricultural pests by airplane in South America. There are a number of reasons why this practice may be expected to increase markedly in the coming years and have the active co-operation of both private and public interests in the United States. A growth of agricultural enterprise is to be expected in the South American countries, and in many cases the structure of agriculture may involve large management units, which are favorable to use of the airplane in pest control. Cotton, vegetables, and fruits are expected to be grown in greater quantities. More capital will be made available to South American countries in the years to come. South America is already air-minded and attitudes will favor further experimentation with the airplane. A part of the increased capitalization is likely to go into protection by air against agricultural pests. Continuance of our "Good Neighbor" policy is likely to lead to public sponsorship of co-operation with South American countries in dusting by airplane. Seasonal dovetailing of crops between the United States and South America can be arranged to the benefit of both.

Publicly sponsored dusting by airplane in the control of the pests in other countries is likely to become increasingly important in future decades wherever such methods are technically feasible. Many of the breeding grounds of the Asiatic migratory locust are along rivers and on poorly drained soil almost inaccessible except by air. Russia has demonstrated some of the possibilities of aerial warfare against locusts. The need for similar action in Asia and Africa is very great.

Sowing Seed

Grass, rice, and grain crops have all been successfully sown by airplane. The use of the airplane in seeding rice started as an emergency measure in California in 1929, and now almost all large rice acreages in California are sown by plane. The plane provides a tremendous saving in labor because the rice fields are flooded before sowing. The rice seeding has been on a commercial basis in California and has been dovetailed seasonally with crop dusting in order to reduce the costs of operation.

Winter cover-crop seeds have been, and currently are, scattered by plane in Mississippi. However, the most extensive use of the plane in seeding of grain crops has been in Russia, where the extensive fields and the deep mud give the greatest advantage to airplane sowing. The first important large-scale sowings in Russia took place in 1930-31 and there has been a steady development since. In 1932, 169,936 acres were planted by plane; in 1933, 331,721; in 1934, 370,500. This method of sowing is admirably suited to the large collective farm fields of the Soviet Union. Three thousand working hours are required to plant 2500 acres of grain by hand, 1000 hours are necessary with horse or ox-drawn machine, 200 hours with a tractor, and but 60 hours with an airplane.[9] The yield per acre can be increased by plane sowing because it is possible to sow directly after the snow is melted. To "sow in the mud" may mean an increase in the yield by as much as 50 per cent in a dry year. The sowing of grain by aircraft in the United States will probably be promoted to a greater extent by the helicopter than the airplane, since the average size of field is much smaller than that in Russia.

[9] *Jamaica Agricultural Society Journal*, May, 1936, pp. 294-295.

One of the problems of aerial sowing is to get the seed to penetrate the soil rather than to rest on top of it. One possible solution is the treatment of seeds to give them weight and penetrating capacity. The downward drive of the air from the rotor blades of the helicopter flown near the ground may have some effect in forcing the seeds into the soil. Since the sowing of seed is one of the principal agricultural processes, its problems warrant further research. If aerial sowing of seed is successful, the effect on agricultural practices would be great, particularly in reducing the labor supply necessary and in encouraging large-scale farming.

Spreading of Fertilizer

The broadcasting of fertilizer by airplane is a more recent development than the sowing of seeds. The airplane reduces the time required to spread fertilizer. It has been reported that as much commercial fertilizer can be broadcast in one seven-hour day by airplane as can be spread in a 55-hour work week by ground-operated equipment.[10] The use of airplanes for this purpose has been found to be an effective and comparatively inexpensive way to save labor and machinery and to prevent injury to fields which often results from the use of ground-operated spreaders. Superphosphate was applied to fields of lespedeza at one dollar per acre in the rich rice-growing section of Arkansas in 1943. Broadcasting by plane prevented injury to the oat crop interplanted with the lespedeza. Airplanes have been used to fertilize soils for crops requiring broadcast treatment rather than applications in the row. Just before the war, some range land in Florida was fertilized with "Uramon" fertilizer compound released by plane. Top-dressing of oat crops with nitrogen applied by plane has been increasing in Mississippi and other states.

The future importance of helicopter broadcasting of commercial fertilizers appears to be very great. Even though the efficiency of spreading fertilizer is not so great with the helicopter as by other methods, the economy in labor and time may overbal-

[10] "Airplane Reduces the Time Needed to Broadcast Fertilizer," *Agricultural News Letter*, July-August, 1943, p. 59.

ance the waste in fertilizer. If the practice of spreading fertilizer by helicopter should become widespread, technological unemployment, already caused by mechanized agriculture, may be further increased. There is a good possibility of the use of planes and helicopters in broadcasting of fertilizers in Europe in the postwar decade in order to hasten agricultural rehabilitation.

Mosquito Control

Mosquitoes cause damage to agriculture both directly and indirectly. The importance of mosquito eradication to human beings who live in rural areas where there is much marshy territory is obvious, especially when the Anopheles mosquito is prevalent and is infected with malaria. Mosquitoes also do considerable damage to livestock, especially to dairy cattle. They may bring serious loss in dairying through reduced milk production. Large numbers of mosquitoes also have bad effects on the efficiency of labor.

The first airplane application of poisons to control mosquitoes was the distribution of dusts to kill the Anopheles larvae in Louisiana in 1924. It was highly successful and has since become an established practice. Experiments were made in 1931 in aerial application of oil for mosquito control. The results were the destruction of almost 100 per cent of the larvae and pupae and the method was cheaper than hand-oiling when an entire area had to be covered. The cost is high by any method, aerial or otherwise. Aerial treatment may remain in the field of emergency activity in areas where continuous mosquito-control work is necessary. It is considered better practice to adopt the permanent methods of mosquito control; that is, drainage, filling, impoundment, etc.

Aerial application for mosquito control in the future will be encouraged by improved techniques for distributing liquid sprays by plane and the perfecting of the helicopter with a large load capacity. The helicopter will be especially useful, since it will permit spot treatment in places where trees, electric wires, buildings, etc., now limit the application by airplane. It is in the field of inspection and observation, however, that the helicopter is expected to achieve its greatest importance in mosquito-control work. In this regard, Mr. Thomas D. Mulhern, Associate in Mosquito Control of the New Jersey Agricultural Experiment Station, writes in a letter:

> We now have extensive areas which cannot be inspected with sufficient frequency because of the time and labor load involved. For example, there extends an almost unbroken line of salt marshes along the eastern and southern margins of the State of New Jersey. To satisfactorily inspect these marshes by present means of transportation would require travel partly by automobile and partly by boat and would involve the services of a very large inspection crew. With available resources it is now possible only to inspect sample sections. With safe, inexpensive helicopters that were easily operated it would be possible to fly over these areas at comparatively low altitudes, say 50 to 500 feet, readily locating the water accumulations, alighting on the marsh wherever it was considered advisable to take water samples. One man could cover probably as much area in a day as would now require the services of 50 men or more. Considering the utility of the helicopter, it is necessary to bear in mind that we have some areas where the presence of bays and rivers require a long trip to get from one point to another. For example, in one county there are two marsh areas less than five miles apart. To get from one to the other requires an automobile trip of more than 50 miles. We have utilized airplanes for this type of inspection but they are not satisfactory for they cannot alight on the salt marsh and they travel so rapidly that sufficient study cannot be conveniently made of the individual areas.

The opening-up of some mosquito-plague areas in South America after the war is likely to lead to considerable airplane dusting to kill Anopheles mosquitoes and clean up areas for human habitation. If mosquitoes can be brought under control, the agricultural development of these South American countries will be greatly encouraged. This is also true of some sections of the United States, Canada, Africa, and Asia.

Large-Scale Farming

Aerial methods may be an inducement to increase the scale of operations in farming. This would operate only where physical conditions are favorable to aerial methods; that is, level areas adapted to cultivation in large acreages, requiring the same kind of treatment at the same time. Large-scale farming would be encouraged where the prices for the crops involved, and the saving of crops through airplane dusting or their increase by aerial spreading of seed or fertilizer, are such as to make this clearly economical. The advantage of aerial methods combined with large-scale farming vary with different vegetable and fruit crops, in different parts of the country, with different degrees of infestation, at different stages in the general business cycle, and with the varying demands for agricultural products.

On the whole, airplane spraying and spreading of fertilizer have been undertaken primarily where the scale of enterprise in farming was already large for other reasons. Thus far, it has not constituted a sufficient inducement to change farming practices even in areas most suited to aerial application of insecticides, fungicides, and fertilizer. There is considerable likelihood that the future will see a growth of large units in vegetable production and hence there will be increased opportunity for airplane applications in that field. Other influences, such as the use of the tractor, are working toward large-scale farming and the airplane may be expected to add its influence.

Influence on Labor Needs

Aerial methods may change the nature of the labor demand. Airplane dusting, for example, relieves the farmer of the necessity of procuring and training labor to dust crops by hand methods and supervising the work. This shift to a larger power and equipment unit might mean a smaller resident farm population. The amount of skilled farm labor required to take care of a given acreage may be reduced. The new methods of dusting, seeding, and fertilizing, however, will not change the seasonal nature of cotton and fruit crops, since harvesting is still the most important part of the process of production. Aerial methods might actually emphasize this seasonality of labor, since they reduce the labor demand at otherwise less busy times. Farmers who dust their cotton may find it easier to hire labor to pick cotton under the present piece-rate system, since dusted cotton produces a larger, more uniform crop which can be picked faster, resulting in larger hourly earnings to the laborer.

Reduced Risk in Agriculture

Farming is notable for the uncertainties of nature as well as for the general business uncertainties which affect other groups in our economic life. One of the greatest factors in producing uncertainty for some types of farming is the ever-present danger of destruction of crops by pests and fungi. Aerial dusting is a kind of crop insurance against damage by pests. Where infestation varies among acreages and in moderate degree from year to year so that the number of treatments needed and the extent of damage, despite treatment, changes somewhat, insurance of this kind is practicable. Such insurance can also cover the risk of rain immediately after application of dust, which makes re-dusting necessary. Airplane dusting reduces the amount of damage in cases of emergency infestations, because it permits more rapid application than is possible by ground machinery.

The Airplane as a Carrier of Pests

The airplane, though helpful in combating pests, is also a carrier of pests. Insects are caught on the outside surfaces of the plane or in the cabins or storage spaces and are transported so quickly by plane that they arrive while still in good condition. Few insects could survive the slow journey by steamer and sailing vessels, though Hawaiian sugar planters suffered from invasions of pests from the Orient even by this slow means. Rapid transport by plane threatens to bring pests into areas previously free of these particular species or varieties. For example, there is danger of introducing the fruit fly from Hawaii into the United States, and there is danger of the importation into Africa of infected ticks which will threaten the animals produced there. Invasions of these pests are particularly serious because of the absence in the new areas of parasites which fight such pests. However, the plane's speed also enables the rapid importation of parasites to combat the pests introduced by plane. Such parasites have already been imported in some cases, and will probably be brought in more frequently in the future.

Elaborate systems of quarantine and control are being set up. Some of these were already established prior to the war, but increased air travel will augment the need for control. Control methods include inspection of planes, inspection of plant materials and animals carried by planes, and spraying and other treatment of planes traveling certain routes to kill injurious insects that may have lodged in them. There is some likelihood that these control measures were not carefully observed under conditions of wartime emergency and there may be a spread of pests in the postwar years, with resulting tightening of control methods.

Emergency Shipments of Farm Supplies

Emergency shipment of agricultural equipment has already proved helpful to individual farmers in areas not readily accessible by other forms of transportation or to those in areas located at some distance from sources of supply, even when other transportation facilities were good. Machine parts were high on the list of commodities carried by air express before and during the war. While much of this express was for industrial areas, rural areas were also covered. Such service is especially important for small but vital machine parts or other necessary agricultural materials, such as insecticides. If a harvesting machine, such as the threshing machine, breaks down, fast servicing of machine parts may be necessary to save the crops and save the farmer's time and labor supply. With lower costs of airplane express and with increased mechanization of agriculture in the future, services of this kind are likely to increase sharply. Improved techniques of depositing and picking up articles in flight will also encourage greater use of airplane transportation for products of this kind.

Crop Migration

Prior to the war, air express was used with increasing frequency in the shipment of propagative plant materials. This was becoming of considerable importance in the late 1930's in trans-Pacific shipments. Outbound shipments of hybrid corn seed, rust-resistant wheat, high-yielding queen bees, long-staple cotton seed, and other planting stocks were made from the United States to most of Latin America, much of Africa, and some parts of the Far East.

A major impetus was given to airplane transportation of seed during the war.[11] Much of this activity was because of wartime conditions and would not have been economical otherwise; however, there are tremendous implications for postwar agriculture. The planting stock of crops grown in Japanese-held countries, such as those of hemp and rubber, were flown to Central and South American countries. High-yielding hybrid corn, seed of long-staple cottons and disease-resistant wheat and rye were flown from the United States to Madagascar, South China, Burma, and Egypt. Acorns of corn oak were carried by plane from Spain to Southern California. Seeds of staple drug crops were flown from southern Europe to the Carolinas and Tennessee. Teak seeds were brought from Siam and Burma for planting in experimental farms in Central America. Many other crops have been exchanged between countries by air transportation. The result is an increase in plant-breeding and cross-breeding of different varieties from different parts of the world. Diversification of agriculture in many areas is encouraged. It facilitates the adaptation of the crops to the soil and to the local economy, and the planning of a world economy. It disrupts crop monopolies of one country or one region. When the means of transportation is no longer an obstacle, crop monopolies and cartels can be maintained only if the export of seed and planting stock can be prohibited.

11 Charles Morrow Wilson, "The Great Crops Move," *Harpers Magazine,* June, 1943, pp. 42-49.

Animal Migration and Breeding

Pan American-Grace Airways have carried on a traffic in breeding animals to and from isolated ranches in northern South America. TACA airlines have done the same in remote areas of Central America. Breeding animals have been hauled by plane in many instances in Canada. Russia, however, has done the most in this line, having hauled thousands of tons of breeding animals to remote Soviet republics. It is estimated that about twenty-five thousand tons or more were flown yearly during 1937, 1938, and 1939, principally sheep and cattle.[12]

Russia has also taken the lead in airplane transport of semen of highly valuable sires. It is expected that this practice will expand in South America, Asia, Africa, and the United States after the war.

Baby Chicks and Eggs

Prior to Pearl Harbor, certain California hatcheries were regularly shipping baby chicks by plane to Hawaii, and some hatchery eggs were shipped to Mexico, Central America, and South America.[13] In the case of the baby-chick shipments, chicks hatched in the afternoon were placed on a plane that afternoon or the following morning, and shipments were very successful. Chicks do not require feed for at least seventy-two hours and therefore hatcheries are asked to crate and load chicks within twelve hours of hatching time.

The American tropics, like most other hot countries, lack poultry. Eggs do not incubate well in the tropics and hence imported chicks are in great demand. Pan American Airways began to carry live chicks from hatcheries in Florida and Texas to poultry-growers in Caribbean countries in the late 1930's and the traffic increased rapidly.[14]

Turkey eggs are a prospective product for air shipment, since they are valuable in relation to weight and would probably do

[12] *Ibid.*, p. 43.
[13] Letter from Professor H. E. Erdman, agricultural economist, University of California.
[14] Wilson, *op. cit.*, p. 43.

better if the period of time in transit were shortened. It has been suggested by some of the poultry and egg specialists that airplane transportation of turkey eggs from California and Texas to Iowa and adjacent states might be economically practical.

Bees

Bees have been shipped to a limited extent by airplane. Queens and package bees can be confined only for a limited length of time and speed is of distinct advantage in assuring safe delivery. Shipment by plane would greatly extend the present limits to which bees can be shipped, as three days in confinement is generally considered to be a controlling safety factor.

California ships package bees — two or three pounds of bees with a queen in screened cages — to the western provinces of Canada and to the western states of the United States. Approximately seventy-five thousand to one hundred thousand packages of bees, with a gross weight of eight pounds per package were shipped in 1944. The shipments are made during late March, April, and early May. The bees have to be provided with adequate ventilation at all times and the temperature controlled so that it does not fall much below 45° F.

> Colonies of bees are also moved from one state to another in the production of honey and in long hops, transport planes would be a very desirable means of transporting them. With proper facilities, migratory beekeeping methods could be expanded over the present limited field. There are places in northwestern Canada, for instance, where several thousand colonies could be set down to advantage during the summer honey flow and then both colonies and honey transported out by plane in the fall. Due to the lack of suitable roads and train facilities, this practice is not possible at present.[15]

Fresh Fruits and Vegetables

Progress in the field of air freight has opened the possibility of air transportation of fresh fruits and vegetables in the postwar period. Because of their perishable nature, these products will

[15] Quoted from letter from J. E. Eckert.

benefit to an unusual degree from the speed of air carriers. The quality of certain fruits and vegetables can be greatly improved if the time between market and producer is decreased. Before the war, it required seven days for fruits and vegetables to move from California to Detroit. Traveling only one hundred and seventy-five miles an hour, an airplane can reduce this to twelve hours. This speedy delivery would enable fruits and vegetables to be ripened on the tree or vine, and the appearance, flavor, and nutritive and vitamin content would all be improved.

The cost of air transportation is one of the most important factors in determining the amount of fruits and vegetables shipped by air in the future. Wayne University, under a special grant for air-cargo research, made a study of the air-cargo potential in fresh fruits and vegetables.[16] Estimates were made of the ton-miles that would be shipped at various ton-mile rates. At a rate of fifteen cents per ton-mile, 24,000,000 ton-miles of fresh fruits and vegetables are expected to be shipped by air; at ten cents per ton-mile, 64,000,000 ton-miles; at seven cents, 333,000,000; at five cents, almost 1,000,000,000; and at three cents, the volume would be 4,000,000,000 ton-miles. Thus the freight expected at ton-mile rates of fifteen cents is six times the total air express in 1941. The five-cent rate is 233 times larger.

The lowering of air express rates to fifteen cents per ton-mile or lower depends upon technological developments in aviation and the organization of the flow of traffic. California, Texas, and Florida produce 65 per cent of the total ton-mile volume of traffic in fresh fruits and vegetables in the United States for all shipments over two hundred and fifty air-miles. The greatest consuming centers of these products are the large urban cities of the New England, Middle Atlantic, and the North Central states. Thus, traffic would flow from the West to the East and from the South to the North. If these urban centers ship products to the West and South on the returning planes, then the ton-mile rates can be lower. The fact that these fruit- and vegetable-producing

[16] Spencer A. Larsen, *Air Cargo Potential in Fresh Fruits and Vegetables.* Wayne University, Studies in Air Transport, no. 1. Detroit, Michigan: Wayne University Press, 1944.

states are long distances from the markets is an incentive to air shipment. A complicating factor is the fact that the fresh fruits and vegetables which move at the higher ton-mile rates are highly seasonal in character. However, this seasonality of products is decreased as the rates are lowered and a greater variety of fruits and vegetables are shipped by air.

The Wayne University study reached certain conclusions as to the products most likely to be shipped by plane. These conclusions were the composite judgments of a jury of ten produce merchants, chosen on the basis of their experience and knowledge of the trade. Their appraisals were made independently. Results showed that berries, particularly strawberries, are the most likely of all fruits to be shipped by air. At the fifteen-cent rate, strawberries make up the bulk of the potential traffic. At the five-cent rate, grapes, plums, peaches, and other fruits are expected to be shipped. At the three-cent rate, bananas are an important potential.

Of the fresh vegetables, only tomatoes are a potential at the fifteen-cent rate. Asparagus, beans, lettuce, peas, and celery are vegetables which become important as the ton-mile rates decrease. Table 30 shows the relative importance of the different fruits and vegetables at different ton-mile rates. The products are listed in the order of their importance in each group as potential air cargo. Only products yielding over one million ton-miles of potential traffic are included.

The more durable products are less likely to be moved by air. Even at three cents per ton-mile, apples, turnips, or potatoes are not expected to be thus shipped. Rates must be three cents per ton-mile or lower to make profitable the shipment by air of carrots, onions, sweet potatoes, bananas, cranberries, grapefruit, lemons, oranges, and certain other fruits.

Essentially, the demand for air transportation of fruits and vegetables is a luxury demand for tree-ripened fruit, out-of-season berries, and the like. Some demand may arise for tropical and semi-tropical fruits and vegetables that heretofore have not been produced for anything except the local market because it has not been possible to get them to the major consuming centers

---

TABLE 30. RELATIVE AIR CARGO IMPORTANCE AT VARIOUS TON-MILE RATES *

15 cents	10 cents	7 cents	5 cents	3 cents
Strawberries	Strawberries	Strawberries	Strawberries	Bananas
	Peaches	Grapes	Grapes	Grapes
		Peaches	Plums, prunes	Cantaloupes
		Cantaloupes	Peaches	Plums, prunes
		Cherries	Cantaloupes	Peaches
		Pineapples	Pineapples	Pineapples
		Plums, prunes	Cherries	Strawberries
		Raspberries	Pears	Cherries
		Avocados	Avocados	Oranges
			Honeydews	Grapefruit
			Tangerines	Honeydews
			Apricots	Pears
			Raspberries	Avocados
				Lemons
				Apricots
				Tangerines
				Raspberries
				Fresh figs
Tomatoes	Tomatoes	Tomatoes	Tomatoes	Lettuce
	Beans	Lettuce	Lettuce	Tomatoes
		Asparagus	Beans	Celery
		Beans	Peas	Peas
		Cabbage	Celery	Beans
		Peas	Asparagus	Cabbage
		Spinach	Cabbage	Cauliflower
		Corn	Spinach	Asparagus
		Cucumbers	Peppers	Spinach
		Endive	Cauliflower	Peppers
			Cucumbers	Cucumbers
			Corn	Broccoli
			Endive	Carrots
			Beets	Endive
			Broccoli	Corn
			Brussels sprouts	Beets
			Radishes	Onions
			Shallots	Turnips
				Radishes
				Brussels sprouts
				Shallots
				Sweet potatoes

* Spencer A. Larsen, *Air Cargo Potential in Fresh Fruits and Vegetables.* Wayne University, Studies in Air Transport, No. 1. Detroit, Michigan: Wayne University Press, 1944, p. 3.

in good condition. Some of the products of South America, heretofore little known in the United States and never consumed here, may develop a market here through air transportation.

The actual shipment of fresh fruits and vegetables depends

upon the rates charged by the air transportation companies. In the chapter on the transportation of goods, it was indicated that the rates likely to be attained during the first postwar decade will not be low enough to attract many agricultural products. Still, shippers and the airlines are proceeding with experimental shipments of a few commodities, such as fresh lettuce. Low rates — below fifteen cents a ton-mile — depend upon contract arrangements, with no ground-handling or pick-up charges, and also upon the ability to obtain a full load of goods for the return trip. It may be that factors, unknown to us now, will bring about rates sufficiently below fifteen cents a ton-mile to transport some fresh fruits and vegetables, but at present the evidence hardly justifies a prediction that there will be much shipment of fruits and vegetables by air in the first postwar decade.

Cut Flowers

Flowers were the most important horticultural product shipped by plane in the United States prior to the war, and shipments of cut flowers were increasing rapidly. Shipments of flowers by air in April, 1941, were 88 per cent greater than in April, 1939.[17] In the three years immediately preceding the war, shipments of cut flowers from California averaged nearly thirty thousand pounds annually.[18] Of these, 16,800 pounds were wholesale shipments and 12,600 were retail. Wholesale orders were almost entirely orchids and gardenias. Retail shipments consisted primarily of mixed lots of cut flowers shipped to areas within 600 to 750 miles from Los Angeles.

In the postwar years, extensive use of this service is expected for the shipment of flowers to and from the West Coast, South America, and possibly European countries. More exotic flowers from foreign countries will be imported into the United States, increasing the competition for flowers now grown on the home market. In particular, Mexico, Central America, and possibly Holland might offer the producers of this country new competi-

[17] John H. Frederick, *Commercial Air Transportation.* Chicago: Richard D. Irwin, Inc., 1943, p. 425.
[18] Letter from Professor R. W. Hodgson, Assistant Dean of the Agricultural Experiment Station at the University of California, Los Angeles.

tion because of the differential in labor costs plus definite climatic advantages.

The cost of transportation is, of course, important in determining the quantity of flowers that will be flown to market by plane. Most flowers are quite bulky and require a size of package out of proportion to their value. One of the major aspects of the retail florist business is the transmittal of orders by wire through members of an association. There are two such organizations in the United States, one of which cleared $13,000,000 worth of orders between members in 1943. Since a large part of this telegraph business is for funeral flowers, which are heavy and bulky, it is not expected that the parcel post by air will cut very heavily into the telegraph business, at least until rates go down considerably more.

Aerial Surveys in Soil Conservation

One of the most extensive uses of the plane in agriculture thus far has been for aerial surveys. Soil surveys are now based almost entirely on aerial photographs.[19] The United States Soil Conservation Service uses aerial photographs to make accurate planimetric maps and to record on them the facts of erosion, land use, slope, and soil. This procedure provides the basis for detailed soil-conservation plans of the Soil Conservation Service and of other land utilization and land-planning agencies and as a base on which to lay out farm plans. In addition, the aerial photographs have been used for compiling the printed conservation survey maps issued by the Soil Conservation Service. The advantages of aerial maps, as listed by Marshall S. Wright, for the Soil Conservation Service, are summarized below.[20]

1. Large areas rapidly covered, critical areas established, and groundwork begun within a short period of time.

2. Much recognizable detail can be supplied at much less cost than a map prepared by ground methods.

[19] See Ray Bourne, "Aerial Photography of Rural Areas," *Journal of the Ministry of Agriculture*, January, 1937, pp. 929-931, for discussion of soil survey by aerial photography.

[20] Marshall S. Wright, "The Application of Aerial Photography to Land Use Problems," *Soil Science Society of America Proceedings, 1936*, vol. 1, pp. 357-360.

3. When used as field sheets, the large amount of detail makes it possible for the surveyor to locate himself within a few feet on the photos, merely by visual inspection without the use of plane-table intersection. This speeds up the rate at which field recording can be accomplished.

These maps enable the soil conservationist to become familiar with the size of the farm, its wooded areas, slopes, soils, erosion conditions, arrangement of fields, and the location of farm buildings and roads before he makes his first visit to the farm. Tracings from the photographs can be used to map out special items of interest in soil conservation. In some areas of the West, the aerial photographs reveal erosion conditions difficult to observe from the ground. Aerial photography for use in soil surveys will be greatly improved as color photography becomes more practicable.

Crop Control

The agency making most extensive use of aerial photographs during past years has been the Agricultural Adjustment Agency, which used them to measure acreages in checking compliance with crop-allotment and acreage-adjustment programs and compliance with conservation practices. Whether large use will be made of pictures for these purposes after the war will depend on whether programs of similar character are carried on.

Land Use

The United States Department of Agriculture also used aerial photographs in the county planning programs to aid in the delineation of land-use adjustment areas, in the flood-control program in determining land uses and cover conditions in watersheds being surveyed; in the soil-survey program as field base on which soil types are mapped; and for a variety of other uses. The Department has aerial photographs covering some 2,160,000 square miles of the continental United States.

Sampling

Aerial photographs are an indispensable part of the Master

Sample of American farms, which the Bureau of the Census and the Bureau of Agricultural Economics are developing at the present time. The sample includes one-eighteenth of the agricultural and rural population in each county of the United States. The plan calls for the defining of small sample areas (one-fourth of a square mile to two or three square miles), and in many cases photographs are necessary in defining the boundaries. Recency of the photographs is important. Changes taking place within these defined sample areas are to be observed so that current estimates of numbers of farms, farmland, and other factors can be made. This technique is expected to make a great advancement in sampling and in methods for collecting data. There is no other known way of sampling a factor such as the number of farms.

Crop Estimates

The first estimates of crop acreage by aerial photography were undertaken in the early 1920's. It was not until the 1930's, however, that aerial photography became widely used in this country for crop estimates. A map of Vermillion County, Indiana, issued in 1934, was the first published map of a county completely mapped with the use of aerial photographs. In the same year an aerial survey of every farm in three counties in the state of Washington was made at less cost than a ground survey. It was used for land classification, valuation, utilization, taxation, road-building, erosion, weed control, and other agricultural projects and studies. Aerial photography for crop estimates has the greatest advantages when farms are laid off in irregular areas, as in the state of Washington, rather than in regular rectangles. Such photography for crop estimates will undoubtedly increase after the war if national agricultural programs require such information and the cost of re-photography decreases. Various sample studies may be undertaken by local initiative; for instance, state colleges or state extension services, using the helicopter rather than the airplane. Many new uses of aerial photography not previously regarded as practical or not yet even imagined may well appear. Annual photographic sampling of crops is in line with trends in agricultural research and program planning.

Surveying Breeding Grounds

Besides crop estimates, aerial photography may be used for surveying breeding places of insect pests and fungi. The survey may show the topography of the country and the location of streams and vegetation most likely to serve as such breeding grounds. With more detailed maps, some of the egg beds can be detected from the air. For this more detailed photography, the helicopter shows promise. Aerial surveys of mosquito breeding places are numerous and were some of the earliest of such surveys. Surveying of breeding places, because of weather conditions and changes in water level, often demand great speed of which only the airplane is capable. The airplane has been used in the United States in various places to check up in detail on mosquito breeding places in marshy areas.

Insecticides

Photographs of crops are used in planning dusting operations and in executing them. Photographic maps are available in the Department of Agriculture to guide dusters. Aerial photographic records of damage by insects and fungi may be used in the study of plant diseases and provide a quantitative foundation for plans in fungus eradication and insect control. Closely related to this work is the use of the airplane in spotting infestations by observation from the air. This is especially important in forest work. Airplanes were used in spotting infested trees in the drive to eradicate Dutch elm disease in the vicinity of New York City, and there are many other examples of aerial survey in the control of forest pests. There are doubtless some possibilities in the use of the plane for spotting infestation in agricultural crops, though education of farmers and the perfecting of systems of reporting obviate the need for such surveys in most cases in which they might otherwise be technically useful.

Miscellaneous Uses

Aerial surveys have been used in discovering the amount of damage to crops in certain areas in order to determine insurance payments.[21] The counties in the state of Washington that conducted an aerial mapping of every farm in 1934 [22] had many calls for these maps — requests for measurements from farmers in regard to land sales, plowing and harvesting charges, grain fires, and litigations. In one county, a mosaic map was constructed for the use of the county engineer and assessor. Aerial surveys were used in discovering outlaw cotton fields in Texas in a cotton-free belt which was established to prevent the spread of the pink bollworm from Mexico to the United States.[23] The plane may be used in similar types of scouting work.

Opening of New Agricultural Areas

Aerial survey work has become a first and fundamental step in modern times in the opening-up of new areas to habitation and to interchange with the rest of the world. This is, of course, particularly important in areas over which ground transportation is extremely difficult — the remote forested regions of Russia, the jungles of Andean South America, and parts of Africa are examples. The importance of the airplane to agriculture in this sphere is limited only by the rôle these undeveloped areas, remote from other means of approach, can potentially play in the agriculture of the postwar world.

Aviation has already played an extremely important part in the development of agricultural areas in Alaska, Canada, South and Central America, and in Russian Siberia. The figures on airplane transportation of merchandise illustrate this point. The isolated areas where ground communications are underdeveloped and where the terrain is difficult, especially in tropical or arctic areas, are the highest ranking in the tons of goods carried by air. In 1938, the Soviet Union was first, with 48,000 tons carried by

[21] *American Photography*, April, 1935, pp. 248-251.
[22] W. D. Staats, "Aerial Survey of Wheat Acres," *Extension Service Review*, vol. 5, no. 12, pp. 181-182.
[23] United States Department of Agriculture, *Weekly Newsletter*, February 26, 1919.

air; New Guinea second, with 13,000; Canada, 10,000; Honduras, 7500; and Colombia, 6000. The United States is sixth on the list, with only 5000 tons.[24]

Air transport is destined for expanded future rôles in these areas and in Asia and Africa as well. There is a potentially great development of the Amazon areas in rubber production, vegetable oils, and quinine. Guatemala and Yucatan are important in the development of the chicle-growing industry. Air service to these communities will be two-directional. Production and consumption materials will be brought to these areas, and agricultural products will be taken out for sale in urban and general world markets.

Aerial photography and mapping may be used in the planning of rural roads and highways in these areas. In the far interior of Colombia, South America, aerial photography showed millions of acres of fertile arable land in a district formerly considered to be only impassable jungle.[25] Such dramatic incidents cannot often recur in a world with few regions left unexplored. However, South America has used the plane for survey work since 1935, and the practice will undoubtedly be resumed after the war and will play a major rôle in the agricultural development of that continent.

Conclusion

The most assured influence of aviation on agriculture, in economic terms, is the reduction in loss from insects by their elimination through aerial dusting. Spraying may become more widespread when the helicopter comes into use. Seeding by airplane, except for rice and a few ground-cover crops and in muddy fields, is not expected in the future to any large extent, though it is possible that inventions to make seeds penetrate the soil may lead to much more seeding from the air. The spreading of fertilizer by the helicopter is a definite possibility in the postwar years. These uses tend to change somewhat present farm organizations.

[24] Oliver J. Lissitzyn, *International Air Transport and National Policy*, 1942, p. 50.

[25] *American Photography*, March, 1935, p. 183.

They encourage large-scale farming, co-operation among farmers, and governmental sponsorship and aid. Extensive use of aircraft in agriculture brings more technological unemployment and may accentuate the seasonality of agricultural labor. The transportation by air of fresh fruits and vegetables is not expected on a large scale unless the air rates are brought well below fifteen cents a ton-mile. Exchange of seedlings and the shipment of selected stocks from domestic and foreign sources will greatly benefit agriculture. In addition, aviation, through aerial photographic maps and surveys, aids in soil conservation, settlement of new areas, and crop estimating and control.

30

Forestry

THE FORESTRY SERVICE of the United States Department of Agriculture began using aircraft in forestry after World War I, and it has become increasingly important in the work of protecting our forested areas. One of the outstanding uses has been the aerial delivery of supplies by parachute to fire-fighters in inaccessible areas and recently fire-fighters have been landed by parachute. The successful development of the helicopter is expected to add many new aerial services in forestry work.

The Forestry Service administers an area of two hundred million acres — one-tenth of the land surface of the United States. The major part of this area is wild land, located in the higher and more remote mountainous sections. Transportation and communication facilities are limited, and there are many large areas where foot or horseback is now the only method of travel and the pack mule is the only means of transportation of supplies, equipment, and tools.

These forested areas are used for many purposes: grazing of livestock; harvesting of saw timber and other wood products; extraction of minerals; public recreation, including hiking, hunting, fishing, sightseeing, etc. In addition to supervising these activities, the Forest Service must plan and regulate the resource activities in order to get full value from the forest areas and to protect the areas from fires.

Fire Protection

The first use of aircraft in forestry work was for aerial patrol in the detection of fires. In 1919, the Forest Service established five bases in California. Seven army pilots made regular flights

Spraying Hemlock with Lead Arsenic. Protecting the trees from destructive pests is only one of several uses of aircraft in forestry. The helicopter is expected to be especially useful in spraying orchards as well as forests. (*Chapter 30, Forestry.*)

Airplane on the Range. The flat plains of the West are naturally suited to the use of the airplane. It is expected to be used for finding lost animals, for observing the condition of the grass and the water supply, for transporting food and supplies to men at work far out from the camp. Perhaps it foreshadows a new type of cowboy. (*Chapter 31, Stock Raising.*)

Shooting Coyotes from Planes. The destruction of prairie wolves is said to run to thousands of dollars a year. Hence the airplane saves the range owners of the West large sums of money. The hunters, besides receiving a bounty for each coyote, find shooting them from the air a great sport. Requirements are a skilled pilot, slow speeds, and accurate shooting. (*Chapter 31, Stock Raising.*)

Rescue by Helicopter. One of the earliest uses of the helicopter was by the U.S. Coast Guard in effecting rescues at sea. This aircraft has the potentiality of remaining stationary in the air and it also takes the wind rather successfully. (*Chapter 33, Public Administration.*)

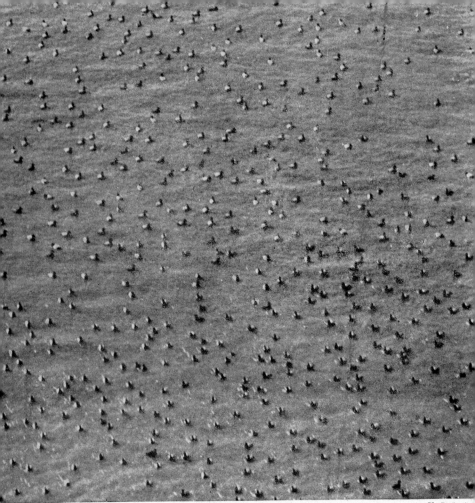

U. S. A. A.

Waterfowl Inventory. Aircraft are expected to be of great use in making a census of wild life and in conserving wild life. Photographs of duck enable a very accurate count to be made. The winter habitat of wild life may be observed from planes and, if necessary, food and protection may be provided during the hard winters. (*Chapter 33, Public Administration.*)

over national forest areas twice a day looking for forest fires. During the months from June to November these planes were flown over 202,000 miles and 422 forest fires were reported, 27 of which were discovered before they had been observed by the regular ground lookouts.[1] In 1919, the army carried most of the expense, but in 1920 Congress appropriated fifty thousand dollars for air patrol work. These funds were spent for observers, transportation, and other items, while the army furnished pilots and planes. During that year, thirty-seven planes were used, and, of the seven hundred and forty-one fires reported by the planes, twenty-six were first discoveries. A similar air-patrol program was carried on in 1921. In 1922, Congress made no appropriations, but the army made flights at its own expense during periods of greatest fire hazard. By 1925, sufficient experience had been gained to indicate that air-patrol methods were not as reliable as established lookouts for the initial detection of fires. Planes were used rather for observation of going fires, to plan and supervise fire-fighting activities, and to detect fires after a lightning storm. Thus, the scheduled fire-detection patrol work has declined in favor of the fixed ground-lookout system which was developed and enlarged between 1919 and 1928. The airplane has become an emergency aid to ground forces in scouting fires. However, air patrol is valuable on certain occasions; when there are smouldering fires in areas blind to stationary men, when smoke from widespread incendiary fires hinders observation from lookout stations, in newly acquired areas where the ground-lookout system has not been fully developed, following lightning storms when there has been a large number of strikes, during periods of low visibility caused by atmospheric or smoke conditions, when the fixed lookout system is partially blinded, and to observe spots, such as canyons or depressions, invisible to the lookouts.

Scouting Fires

Use of airplanes in scouting large, going fires is now an established practice of the Forest Service. A Forest Service observer

---

[1] *Use of Aircraft in Forestry*, pamphlet of the Forest Service, United States Department of Agriculture (mimeo.).

flies with the pilot. A reconnaissance of the burning area is made and the ground forces are supervised or directed through communication facilities. Aerial observation enables the observer to determine the intensity, location, extent, rate and direction of burning, and the type of material which is burning. He can discover what natural barriers to the fire exist and can plan a campaign of fire-fighting. Air observation enables the most efficient allocation of men and resources in fire areas.

The effectiveness of the airplane in picking routes of travel for fire-fighters was shown in 1939 in the Los Padres National Forest, California. Lightning had started a fire in an extremely rough area which had no trails. It was difficult to direct crews to the fire without knowing a safe route. An airplane, flying low over the fire, selected the shortest and easiest way in and the information was sent to headquarters.

Experimental work has been done in photographing fires from observation planes. Aerial photographs give information about the topography, fuel types, streams, roads, trails, and other ground features. Such photographs are much superior to maps or verbal description. Lack of the information which aerial photographs supply hampers effective fire-fighting methods, and no other method of obtaining this information is as effective or as fast. In Montana, a few years ago, operators in an airplane photographed the fire, developed and printed the negatives as eight by ten pictures, and dropped them to the ground, all within eighteen minutes. When planes did not have facilities for the developing process, the exposed films have been dropped at a base camp where they could be developed.

In such scouting of fires by plane, communication facilities are important. Before the war, the Forest Service had a two-way radio set between airplane and portable ground equipment. With such equipment, the air observer can report his findings to the ground forces at the fire, discuss the situation, and receive instructions. Direct contact between the fire line and headquarters is also possible with this equipment. Extended use was made of two-way communication systems during World War II, and undoubtedly this improved equipment will be adapted to use by the Forest Service in scouting fires.

The helicopter will also be very useful in this work. Its ability to fly slowly and to hover, if the altitude is not too great, give it advantages over the airplane in observation and photography.

Transportation of Men and Supplies

The transportation of men and supplies to forest fires is undoubtedly one of the most important uses of the airplane in forestry work, and the helicopter promises to be even more useful in such work.

The airplane has been important in fire control because of its speed.

> Speed is the essence of forest fire control. If one or two experienced and properly equipped men can reach a fire started by lightning or by man quickly enough after its start, control is relatively easy. The difficulty of control, number of men required for control, the costs and probabilities of loss and damage increase almost in geometric ratios with the passing of each hour. Over vast areas of the forests, firemen now proceed to fires on foot or on horseback. Average rates of travel run from one to four miles per hour.[2]

Thus, the value of the airplane or helicopter is obvious, if it can deliver men and supplies at the scene of the fire in a short time. In the past, such delivery was accomplished mainly by the plane landing the men and supplies at the landing field nearest to the scene of the fire. One factor which restricted its value in this procedure was the scarcity of landing fields for which, because of the rough terrain in most of the timbered areas, there were few sites available. Over a period of several years the Forest Service has established eighty landing fields, located mainly in the northern Rocky Mountain and Pacific Coast states. In many national forests, large lakes can serve as landing areas for seaplanes.

In order to alleviate the limitation or scarcity of landing fields, the parachute method of delivering supplies to fire crews was developed in 1936 in the Northwest. By this means, materials of

[2] Information from United States Department of Agriculture, Forest Service, November 13, 1943.

all kinds — pumps, hose, gasoline, canned goods, eggs and food of all kinds, radio sets, fire-fighting tools, water, etc. — are dropped to the scene of the fire. At first they were dropped with specially prepared wrappings. With careful packing, it was possible to drop some kinds of supplies, but there was too high a percentage of breakage. With parachutes of burlap, originally developed by the Forest Service, even fragile materials can now be dropped without damage. For several years before the war, more than one hundred tons of supplies were delivered by air each year by this method. In one instance, some ten thousand pounds of water and food supplies were dropped by parachute to fire-fighters on top of a bluff in the rocky, rough country of the 1939 Bald Mountain Fire in Los Padres National Forest in California. The plane delivered about fifteen hundred pounds per two hours, as against three hundred pounds per six and one-half hours by pack mule.

Before the war, parachute delivery of supplies by plane was merely an emergency adjunct to ground methods. Ground transportation was used if the fires were near roads. Since planes were of small carrying capacity and were not specially constructed for this work, the Forest Service had to do practically all of the pioneering itself. The war has developed a vast field of experience in delivery of supplies by air. However, the future use of airplane-parachute delivery of supplies will probably be superseded by helicopter delivery.

Parachuting of men to forest fires was being considered as far back as 1935, but it was not until 1939 that experiments were actually made. Dummies weighing one hundred and eighty pounds were attached to condemned army parachutes and dropped at various elevations, over different types of ground. After the tests proved successful, professional parachuters made the first jumps. Then regular fire-fighters made jumps successfully. The actual method developed was first to drop a burlap test chute in order to judge the wind drift. The pilot corrected his course and timing and the men jumped at his signal. A high degree of accuracy in landing on the desired spot was achieved. After the fire-fighters landed, the plane dropped supplies and tools by parachute. These men were ready to attack a fire in record time and to report results by short-wave portable radios. They were equipped with specially designed helmets, masks, and protective clothing. The parachutes also were especially developed for this work and were thirty feet in diameter, with a wide, scalloped periphery for a slow rate of descent and minimum oscillation and had two long flaps for steering. It was found that landing at the high altitudes of many of the forests caused no greater jolt than landing at sea level. Treetops proved to be safe and comfortable places to land. The parachutes were designed so that the man could easily detach himself from the chute and reach the ground by a rope which he carried. Furthermore, the chute would not catch in the trees and then slip and drop the parachuter to the ground. Either the jumper came straight through to the ground or was held securely suspended. It was expected that the jumping would cause some loss of energy, but fatigue was not noticeable in those men who were suited to this type of work.

Although the use of parachute fire crews up until the beginning of the war was limited, yet it had resulted in considerable saving, both in forest resources and in money spent on fire-fighting. For instance, on August 20, 1940, four parachutists controlled two fires in the Bitterroot National Forest, Montana, at a cost of only three hundred and twenty dollars. This was a saving of twenty thousand dollars over what it cost to control a previous fire under similar conditions in the same area with ground forces.

The similarity of the method of landing men and supplies to fight forest fires and that used in wartime to fight the enemy suggests the possibility of the use of gliders as well as parachutes. The method of picking up gliders while the plane is in motion has been successfully developed during the war. The glider can carry a bigger load than a parachute and would appear to be more suitable for that reason. It can also be used for several trips. It is more dependent, however, upon a suitable landing terrain than the parachute and, for that reason, cannot land as close to a fire or in as many varieties of topographical conditions. The adaptability of the glider to forestry work can be better judged after further experimentation. It may be found, though, that large helicopters can do all that gliders do, and hence there would be no need for them.

It is anticipated that the helicopter will make revolutionary changes in methods of fire-fighting. The Forest Service experimented with the use of autogiros before the war because they had some of the characteristics which the helicopter possesses. In 1932, an autogiro under contract was used extensively in the Pacific Northwest. At that time, its maneuverability and hovering characteristics were found to be very adaptable for observation and administrative use. The autogiro's principal drawback was found to be its lack of sufficient payload. The helicopter, because it can fly slowly and hover, enables the fire area to be observed more carefully and with greater detail. It can land men and materials with precision at the scene of the fire. The helicopter is expected to carry sufficient payload to make its use profitable in forestry work.

The helicopter is not dependent upon regular landing fields, but can land in small areas. The Forest Service could extend the number of flying fields, but there is a limit in the number of possible sites. Furthermore, the building of such landing fields is very expensive because of the physical characteristics of the areas involved. The helicopter could land on the flat ridgetops, small meadows or clearings, and canyon bottoms. In fact, there would be practically no limit to the number of places where it could land. Since it can hover a few feet off ground and load and unload supplies there, it would not need to land if the conditions were unfavorable. Helicopters, at their present stage of development, cannot climb vertically at altitudes over ten thousand feet. At that height they climb with a forward speed of forty miles per hour. Thus, if they were taking off from the ground in a mountainous region of that height, they would have to have some freedom from trees in order to gather forward speed. Forest fires occur in all altitudes, but the majority occur between one thousand and six thousand feet.

The use of the helicopter would elminate the necessity for

building roads. Road construction and maintenance in these areas is extremely difficult and expensive. For example, up to 1938, roads built purely for fire protection purposes in the state of Idaho alone totaled 1675 miles and cost $3,265,400. To complete the system, additional expenditures of $2,545,600 were required. In addition, 2854 miles of road, which was primarily for fire protection, but which had other uses as well, had also been built, at a cost of $9,860,302. This figure does not take into account the large annual maintenance costs. Instead of an intensive network of roads and trails, an extensive and much less costly system would be sufficient to give fire protection. The determining factor would be the comparison of the cost of construction plus maintenance of protection roads versus the cost of purchase and operation of helicopters.

Use of the helicopter would result in changed organization of fire-fighting equipment and men. Instead of locating at many points men who hike or ride to fires, fewer men could be stationed at central points from which they would be quickly flown to the fire area. Mobility of forces, which is an important factor in control, would be increased many times.

"Bombing" of Fires

The Forest Service, beginning in 1936, has experimented with the bombing or spraying of fires from the air with water or chemical extinguishers. To control a large fire in this manner would require great quantities of chemicals and materials. Thus far, airplanes have had a small carrying capacity, not sufficient to transport such large quantities. The objective of the Forest Service, instead, was to retard the spread of small fires in remote areas until the ground forces could arrive.

Up to the time of the war, these experiments had not been very successful. The bombing of fires was done in level flying at an altitude of three hundred to five hundred feet above the terrain. Flying close to small fires in mountainous country is difficult because of the uncertainty of wind currents, and the effectiveness of fire-bombing depends upon accuracy. Furthermore, the water and chemicals were found to scatter so widely when released from the planes that they were not successful in extinguishing the fire.

An effective development of this method depends upon a number of factors. Chemical research has been conducted by the Forest Service to determine the best combination of chemicals for extinguishing fires, and tests have been made with water, foams, liquid chemicals, dusts, and powders. Various types of bombs have been tested — bombs bursting on impact with the ground; bombs bursting in air; bombs with time fuses electrically ignited so as to burst at determined heights above the fire; and explosive bombs to throw dirt over small fires. A vast amount of knowledge and experience with bombing has grown out of the war. Bomb-sights have been perfected which make accurate marksmanship possible, and the lack of such marksmanship was one of the main drawbacks prior to the war. However, it seems probable that the real solution to fire-bombing difficulties lies in the use of the helicopter. Its ability to fly low over a spot and to hover would permit great accuracy of aim. In fire-fighting, the helicopter would not suffer from the disadvantages of its use in military bombing, since it would not be the target of enemy guns or planes.

So far, few positive results have been secured from the use of aircraft in fire-fighting, but it seems to give promise of a future effectiveness with the development of the helicopter, which would be capable of carrying several tons of payload and better fire-extinguishing substances.

Aerial Photography in the Forests

Aerial photography has been widely used by the Forest Service. Maps of large areas of the national forests have been made from aerial photographs. This type of photography is also useful for timber-type studies, range surveys, fire detection and suppression, transportation planning, and other activities.

During the 1920's, an aerial exploration of the Tongass National Forest in Alaska was made by the Navy in co-operation with the Forest Service, the Bureau of Public Roads, Geological Survey, and the Bureau of the Biological Survey. In 1926, the northern region of the Forest Service initiated an aerial mapping program. During 1938, more than 13,000,000 acres were aerially photographed; by the end of 1939, over 96,000,000 acres had been covered.

Aerial photographs have been utilized in planting surveys. These reveal the size, location, and distribution of open areas which need reforestation and aid in planning tree-planting programs.

Range survey work in the national forests is carried on with the aid of aerial photographs. This is similar to the use made of aerial photography in the livestock industry. Aerial photographs are also used in erosion, flood control, and watershed protection studies. Air photographs are used in engineering projects in the forest, in transportation planning, and bridge, road, and dam locations.

Management of Wildlife

Although still in the stage of experiment, the airplane promises to be useful in the general management of the wildlife resources in the forests. Annual estimates of the big-game population are necessary for good planning and management and to indicate range overcrowding or depletion of game by disease, predators, and starvation. Aerial survey has been very effective in game counts, especially in the winter when deep snows make ordinary travel difficult or impossible. Airplanes have also been used to distribute salt blocks to supplement the natural salt licks which elk, deer, bighorn sheep, and mountain goats often have to make long journeys to reach. In 1939, eighty-eight tons of salt were distributed throughout most of the big-game areas in Idaho where truck transportation was impossible. Large models of helicopters will be able to transport loads of food to places where neither trucks nor planes can go.

Aerial stocking of fish in mountain lakes has proved to be fairly successful. Fish have been dropped into isolated back-country waters. The stocking of mountain streams, as well as lakes, will undoubtedly prove successful. With the helicopter hovering or flying slowly close to the surface of lakes and streams, it will be easier to deposit the young fish in the exact location desired, with less chance of injury to them.

As on the range, the airplane, and especially the helicopter in the future, may be used for predator control. Other uses in wildlife management are in locating big-game herds, herding game, game patrols, and various kinds of surveys.

Tree-Planting

Airplanes have been used in the transportation of seedling trees to inaccessible areas. By this means, the small trees arrive in good condition at the planting site because of the fast transportation. Broadcast seeding of trees could be done by airplane if the method were a useful one. However, it has been found that the planting of nursery-grown stock is the best method and that, in most cases, broadcast seeding of trees by air is impractical.

Reseeding

Seeding of grasses by plane has been done in burned-over forest areas in order to obtain a quick cover crop to provide watershed protection. Areas have been reseeded in southwestern Oregon, California, Montana, Idaho, Arizona, and Texas. In 1932, mustard seed was sown by airplane on two thousand five hundred acres on the Matilija burn of Los Padres National Forest. By 1942, approximately twenty-two thousand acres had been sown to mustard seed by plane in California. The sowing of the mustard seed was successful in providing a quick cover of mustard plants over the burned area, in reducing soil erosion, increasing the infiltration of rainwater into the soil, and retarding the runoff of rainwater.[3] In 1943, approximately sixteen thousand acres of burned-over lands in the state of Utah were reseeded by plane. The costs were lower than those of ground methods and the results were considered as successful as those obtained by any other type of reseeding used in that area.[4]

[3] Letter of M. W. Talbot, Acting Director, California Forest and Range Experiment Station, Forest Service, Berkeley, California, April 27, 1942.
[4] Letter of Charles F. Moore, Regional Grazier, Grazing Service, United States Department of the Interior, Salt Lake City, Utah, August 3, 1943.

The plane can effectively cover a large area quickly, which is especially important on extensive burns where a good ashy seed bed is available. Where soil and climatic conditions are favorable, the costs of reseeding are usually lower in rough country by air than by ground methods. Optimum weather conditions are required in reseeding by airplane for the successful distribution of the seed, and waiting for favorable weather sometimes delays the operations for days. In order to achieve good distribution in windy weather, experiments have been made in the use of seed pellets. It is not known yet how effectively they will penetrate soils of different texture and moisture content.

A great deal more study is necessary on some of the other factors in the reseeding process. It is not known what species of seed should be sown in certain types of land and when and how it should be sown in order to assure a successful stand of forage. The Forest Service, through its Division of Range Research, is studying these problems. As in dusting and spraying, the helicopter may be found to be more effective than the airplane in reseeding activities.

Insect Control

The airplane can be used for the detection and control of forest insects in the same manner in which it is used in the control of insects in field crops, cotton, and fruits. In 1943, planes of the Bureau of Entomology and Plant Quarantine treated twenty-two hundred acres of forest land in New York and Pennsylvania for control of the gypsy moth. Control of forest insects, such as the spruce budworm, gypsy moth, and hemlock looper, by airplane have not been as successful as control of insects affecting cotton and other field crops. One of the chief difficulties has been the hazard of flying low enough over the treetops to place the insecticide where it is needed and to distribute it uniformly. Tests made with the autogiro before the war demonstrated its superiority for such work because of its maneuverability. The helicopter will undoubtedly be even more successful. With the development of concentrated liquid spray mixtures and oil-dust mixtures, the air control of forest insects is expected to grow to great importance.

Range Management

Vast areas of the national forest are used as range by ranch-owners who obtain permission to use the government-owned land. The Forest Service supervises and regulates the use of such ranges. In this work, the airplane and helicopter play a rôle similar to that discussed in the chapter on the livestock industry.

Rescue Work

Rescue work of persons lost in forest areas and in mountain-climbing is facilitated by use of aircraft. Fliers have dropped food and supplies to persons lost in the forest, for use until they can be rescued. Up to this time, rescued persons have had to be transported by ground to air fields and then flown out of the forests. In one case, an airplane was forced to land in a mountain forest because of a severe snowstorm. The passengers and pilot were found by a forest ranger, who took them on horses to a near-by ranch, where they were able to leave by another airplane. The helicopter will make possible immediate air evacuation of lost persons directly from the location where they are discovered.

Administrative Travel

Officials who have the responsibility for over-all administration of all forest activities will use aircraft to a great extent. The forest areas cover millions of acres in a number of states, and over such vast areas the airplane will be a cheap and rapid means of travel.

Stimulation of Conservation

It is thought that airplane passengers who get a panoramic view of the country will better appreciate some of the enormous losses caused by forest fires. This may stimulate more careful personal habits with fire in forested areas and also arouse interest in the conservation of the natural resources of the country.

Conclusion

The airplane has been successfully used in a variety of ways in forestry work. For most of the work done by planes, the helicopter appears to be even more suitable. The first use of aircraft in forestry work was in fire detection, but ground methods have proved to be more effective. However, in scouting going fires, planning routes, in photography, and in direction control, the airplane has proved to be very effective, especially in the early stages of the fire when time is most important. The plane is also valuable in transporting men and supplies for fighting fires. The use of parachutes may be supplemented by gliders or helicopters. The use of the latter may result in a saving in road-building. A special function of the plane is the "bombing" of fires. Other functions of aviation in regard to forestry are feeding and counting wildlife and studying their habitat. The helicopter will be especially useful in stocking mountain streams and lakes with fish. The transportation of nursery stock; reseeding burned-over land with ground covers; control of insects, pests, and predatory animals; photography; mapping; and the administration of recreation facilities are other uses of aircraft in forestry.

31

Stock Raising [1]

IN CERTAIN SECTIONS OF THE COUNTRY the livestock industry still employs the old horseback methods, with teams and wagons and prairie schooners, but, in the main, the mechanized versions of horses and wagons, namely, trucks of all kinds and descriptions, have supplanted them. Now a new mode of transportation, aircraft, has arisen, and the question is, To what extent will the airplane and helicopter be adapted to use in the livestock business?

Size of Unit

There are both large and small units in the cattle and sheep business and there are also farmers who have a few head of cattle and sheep on small farms. The latter are not considered in this discussion. A very large sheep unit might include as many as 10,000 sheep, and a very large cattle unit might include 2000 cattle. There are not many sheep units of this size in the country, for the running of such numbers calls for about 500,000 acres of land, depending on the quality of the range, while 2000 head of cattle requires 150,000 acres. Large herds of cattle run up to 750, or possibly 1000, head. Such large cattle and sheep units involve great distances and large areas of land, and these conditions are characteristic of the Western area, primarily in the states of Washington, Oregon, California, Montana, Idaho, Nevada, Wyoming, Utah, Colorado, New Mexico, Arizona, and Texas. On the coastal fringe of the Pacific Coast states, range conditions do not hold, nor do they east of the states mentioned, where farms are

[1] Margaret Coffin Holmes (Mrs. Hal Holmes), Ellensberg, Washington, supplied material which was used in the preparation of this chapter.

prevalent. This Western range covers 728,000,000 acres of forested and non-forested land. Because of rough terrain, small precipitation, and other adverse conditions, the range is suitable only for grazing. This area furnishes cheap feed for approximately 11,000,000 cattle and horses and 27,000,000 sheep and goats for a year's grazing. The range territory produces 75 per cent of the nation's wool and mohair, 55 per cent of the sheep and lambs (in pounds of live weight) and nearly 33 per cent of the cattle and calves.[2] In the range areas, operators should find the plane valuable in covering the long distances and vast areas.

Characteristics of the Livestock Industry

There are several different kinds of operations in the sheep and cattle business. Sheep and cattle may be run on a permanent year-in and year-out basis, with one operator raising his own breeding stock and keeping it year after year, or a rancher may buy several hundred or several thousand head of lambs or calves in the fall and sell the fattened animals in the spring. Both the sheep and cattle business call for a maximum of land and a minimum of labor. The labor is comparatively unskilled and poorly paid. Land is the all-important factor, for herds of cattle and bands of sheep must graze for a part of the year at least on natural grasses and feeds. Operations in the livestock industry are timed, essentially, by natural processes. Breeding, lambing, and calving, the weather and the changing seasons, the growth of grass, are all more important than going to and from places in a hurry. Thus, there is usually no great rush in the livestock industry. Yet one needs to keep informed as to the state and conditions of these processes and, when the area is large, it is difficult, without some means of rapid transportation, to keep informed about current conditions. For instance, with rapid transportation an operator can know exactly what, at the moment, is the condition of the grazing lands and be able to time the moving of herds or flocks from one area to another. On the other hand, meat-consumption habits, marketing procedures, and factors of supply

[2] United States Department of Agriculture, *Yearbook of Agriculture for 1939.* Washington: Government Printing Office, p. 944.

and demand are governed by other factors and do not run at the slow tempo of the natural processes. As a result, there has been some necessity to speed up marketing procedures, display of cattle to prospective buyers, and so on.

One of the characteristics of livestock raising is that there is a definite rotation of feeds and areas. The flocks and herds follow the grassy areas, either natural or cultivated. The location of the pasturage depends upon the season, the conditions of the grass, and the accessibility of the areas.

As is the case with all agricultural pursuits, the modern methods of financing have a great deal to do with the operation of both large and small units, and a budget must take into account such things as cost and depreciation of equipment, price of land or land leases, costs of animals, expenses of shearing (in the case of sheep), labor, gas and oil for transportation, marketing charges or freight, auto freight or trailing sheep to market, etc. These must be taken into consideration when adding a new type of transportation or machinery.

One might briefly characterize the sheep and cattle business as dependent upon the slow and natural processes and requiring comparatively large areas for operation.

Survey of Lands

The airplane provides a quick and easy means of inspecting livestock range. By knowing the conditions of the land, future movements of the bands may be planned. In trailing sheep from one weather level to high mountains or back out again, a quick preliminary inspection of the conditions ahead may be valuable. From the air, the shades of browns, yellows, greens, the trails and other signs, all indicate the condition of the range. One man in Montana,[3] unable to use a horse to survey his range, decided to use aerial inspection. His conclusions on range utilization checked very closely with those of the forest ranger who had made a ground inspection. Aerial inspection appears to be sufficiently accurate to make utilization surveys. Observation from

[3] *Use of Aircraft in Forestry*, pamphlet of the Forest Service, United States Department of Agriculture.

aircraft is especially effective in the detection of soil erosion, since it presents the picture as a whole. Washouts may also be noted. These may prove serious in dislocating trails and usual waterholes, and their quick detection may save extra days of trailing. In some large fenced areas, such as are found in Texas, feed is distributed on the ground. The owner or manager can tell by inspection whether it has been properly distributed. The surveying of lands may be accomplished both by first-hand observation from the plane and by aerial photography.

Hunting of Predatory Animals

Coyote hunting has always been a necessity among sheep men. One operator [4] of a very extensive ranch in Washington claims that coyotes cost him at least two hundred thousand dollars over a period of fifty years in the sheep business, or four thousand dollars a year. The coyotes had not actually killed lambs and sheep to that amount of value, but the payroll had to be increased from time to time to provide adequate hunters to help exterminate them. Coyotes remain a menace. Bears, cougars, and wolves also prey upon sheep and cattle, but by far the most active and cunning is the coyote. Newspaper accounts in the Western range country claim that losses from coyotes rose from 3 to 12 per cent during the war because of the scarcity of trappers and hunters. The airplane appears to be very efficient in hunting coyotes. In one instance, an experienced hunter, with a co-pilot who was also a good marksman, shot sixteen coyotes from the air near one band of sheep and bagged an average of five or six coyotes on each trip they made.[5] The helicopter is expected to be even more efficient than the plane in hunting coyotes because of its ability to slow down in the air and make quick turns close to the ground.[6]

[4] Personal letter.

[5] United States Department of Agriculture, Forest Service, op. cit., p. 9.

[6] George B. Sturm, Custer, South Dakota, writes in a letter: "Received your inquiry about hunting coyotes by plane. It surely is a great sport as well as being profitable in two ways. It gets rid of the coyotes and the bounty and fur more than pay the expense. Hunting coyotes is no job for green pilots. We fly low over the territory. Then, when the coyote is spotted, the pilot dives the plane down to about one hundred to a hundred and fifty feet. The shooter gets one snap shot each trip over. When the coyote is killed, we land, take off the

Transportation of Personnel

Planes may be used for the transportation of cowboys and herders. New hands may be brought to the ranch by plane; a sick herder or cowboy can be taken to the doctor in town; a skilled veterinarian may be brought to see ailing sheep or cattle; skilled mechanics can arrive by plane to fix a truck or other machinery which might otherwise hold up operations for some time.

An airplane can take buyers out to see a remote band in its natural location. This saves perhaps days of travel, and permits taking advantage of an immediate market, as well as saving the time, expense, and effort of bringing the band part way to meet the buyer.

The plane might reduce the number of employees required. For instance, the manager might add to his function the taking of supplies to the men, thus eliminating a packer.

One rancher has found that the plane enables him personally to supervise the shipping of animals from various points.[7] With ground transportation, this was impossible. Visiting markets in Chicago or Kansas City is possible when the owner can actually fly and see the condition of yards, feed lots, etc. Ranchers are often interested in legislation regarding sheep and cattle. Airplane travel, whether in personal planes or commercial airlines, makes possible quick attendance at hearings.

pelt, and take off to look for more game. One day we sighted four coyotes together, killed all four within a half-mile, so you see it is fast action and plenty of thrills. (The Piper Cub plane is well suited for this purpose, as it has a slow cruising speed when equipped with a special prop, lands and takes off in most any kind of reasonably smooth country, and doesn't consume much fuel. Can be used with skis when snow gets deep.) It is much easier to spot coyotes when there is snow on the ground. The shooter must be very careful not to shoot into the prop, struts, or ties. One miss shot and it might be the last.

"We carry a twenty-two pistol in case a coyote is crippled and finish him off with that. They are not nice to handle before they are absolutely dead. They don't hesitate to bite, and can do a lot of damage in a hurry with those teeth. If anyone wants to follow this sport, be sure of your plane, that it is in good condition. Be sure of your pilot, that he is cool and level-headed, and be sure that the gunner won't take chances and shoot something loose on the plane that will let you down.

"Well, I am a better hunter than I am a writer, but if you can use any of this, you are more than welcome."

[7] Personal letter.

Transportation of Supplies

Light-weight, vitally needed supplies could be carried by air, as, for instance, food for the men, sheep dogs, medicine, clothing, truck parts, etc. If costs permitted, heavier supplies could also be carried, and perhaps the time might come when camp moving and tending could all be done by air. The use of aircraft on livestock ranches would be facilitated by the use of the new point-to-point telephone, using radio waves of very short length, popularly known as the walkie-talkie. The men out with the cattle or sheep could telephone in their needs, or the foremen could phone out to the camp for information. This would not only make the trips by aircraft more timely, but in some instances it would make the air trip unnecessary.

Miscellaneous Uses

The condition of fences can be determined by air. This is especially important in Texas, where fences are used so extensively. Losses and litigation could be avoided by more frequent fence inspection.

Rustling of cattle and sheep might be detected by air, since it is often accomplished by truck at the present time. Airplane inspection would help to reduce this rustling. Planes can also be used to find lost animals. Animals are easily lost out of herds and bands through natural difficulties such as fog, by being dispersed by wild animals, or by simply wandering off in new country, unknown to the herder or cowboy. Windmills and waterholes can be inspected by plane. The uses of the airplane and the helicopter in forestry would also be valuable to a stockman who leased government forest reserves. Aerial transportation of fire-fighters, aerial photography of forests, scouting fires by airplanes, and aerial transportation of fire supplies, are all important in this respect.

Plane observation can be used in breeding operations with both cattle and sheep to discover whether the bulls or rams are bunching up too much or are fighting. Also airplanes are used for transporting, for scientific breeding, sires and semen, a matter of considerable economic significance in improving the quality of the stock. So far as can be ascertained, this use of aviation has been mainly over quite long distances to and in other lands, as shown in the chapter on agriculture.

Effects of Airplane on Ranch Organization

With air transportation, the owner or foreman will be able to spend much less time in travel and thus be able to attend to many other jobs that he would otherwise be unable to take care of. As one ranch operator states in a letter:

> Today, instead of starting out with the men on a week-end round-up at five o'clock in the morning, the owner or foreman will do many other jobs and attend to much business and leave in his pick-up at eleven o'clock, taking with him a hot lunch for the boys and arriving at a prearranged branding site about the time the boys are bringing in the cattle. The same thing goes for any movements or operations of cattle and sheep.[8]

The automobile has brought the vast ranges of the ranch closer to the livestock man, and the airplane or helicopter will continue this trend.

Costs

In determining the size of the aircraft market which the livestock business will provide, the costs are important. Costs include the original cost of the plane, depreciation, fuel, repairs, and overhead in general. Life insurance rates go up for the man who operates the plane, although this may not remain in effect in the future. There are also taxes, licenses, and other fees in connection with the ownership of aircraft. Frequent physical examinations and eye examinations are necessary to pass civil license laws, and these involve time and expense in travel. The rate of obsolescence of the plane and helicopter will probably be high until these inventions have been more completely developed.

If aircraft is to be economical, it should eliminate some of the overhead now existing, such as replacing horses, trucks, etc. The overhead on trucks as to tires, gas, and general wear and tear is

---

[8] Personal letter.

very great. If a helicopter or plane could take the place of two or three trucks, it would be worth its price and overhead because trucks wear out very rapidly in rough country and with rough handling. The service trucks might be eliminated, but it is doubtful if the hauling trucks could be eliminated for some years. To be economical, the plane or helicopter should be used to haul supplies, as well as to make surveys and to provide transportation for men. A packer can provide supplies for one herder in the mountains, or for two herders on the winter range. Helicopter delivery of supplies might do away with the packer altogether or limit the total number to one or two. This would reduce the present overhead and the money thus saved could be diverted to the maintenance of the helicopter or plane.

Reliability

If helicopters or planes are to replace present methods of transportation, they must be reliable at all times and in all kinds of weather. If they cannot be operated in fog, snowstorms, or blizzards, horses or trucks would have to be maintained for such emergencies. Thus, the plane would be an additional piece of machinery and would not reduce present overhead. The aircraft must also be readily serviceable so that standardized repair parts may be obtained easily and rapidly from a source not too distant. The plane or helicopter is expected to become as dependable as the truck, so fear of breakdown in isolated country or difficult terrain will not be a deterrent to its adoption. The helicopter's ability to hover is affected by high altitudes which characterize some of the Western grazing lands; but, in these altitudes, there will generally be sufficient landing space to permit a landing or take-off with some forward motion.

Government Regulations

Government regulation and licensing of private planes and helicopters must not be too extensive or complex or they may become prohibitive. Government aid in supplying airports and other facilities will do much to encourage use of air transportation among livestock owners.

One Texas rancher has summed up the situation in this way:

> After the war I should think there is a reasonable chance of
> there being at least 50 or 60 ranchers in Amarillo (Texas) who
> will find it profitable to own and operate a plane, providing first —
> good safe airplanes can be bought for not too much more than the
> price of a good automobile; providing, second — maintenance,
> upkeep and taxes are not too high on a plane to prevent it from
> being used economically; and providing, third — there are ade-
> quate facilities such as airports, storage and a minimum of CAA
> regulations governing civilian flying.[9]

Economy of Supplementary Uses

The advantages of the airplane or helicopter on ranches may
not be determined solely by its direct use in ranching. One
rancher says:

> I personally have used an airplane in looking after my cattle
> business for 13 years and have found it to be a very satisfactory
> means of getting from one ranch to another. The expense, of
> course, was far more than the use of the plane would justify, but
> inasmuch as I was using the plane in my other business, not con-
> nected with ranching, I could afford to use an airplane of suffi-
> cient horsepower that was safe, comfortable, and had a cruise
> speed of around 175 miles an hour.[10]

Thus, the uses of air transportation, supplementary to ranching
operations, may be important in stimulating the use of the plane
or helicopter by ranchers.

Size of Market

In making an estimate of the size of the market demand for
airplanes and helicopters after the war by ranchers, the size of
the financial base necessary to support the aircraft must be taken
into consideration. One large operator, who regards the livestock
man as a pioneer in all fields, says:

> A helicopter that could be handled by the manager or fore-
> man of a large ranch has considerable possibilities and possibly in
> a large outfit could be justified from the point of view of cost

---

[9] A letter from Lieutenant Colonel Jay A. Taylor, Amarillo, Texas, November
22, 1943.
[10] Ibid.

and economy. I don't think they would be of much value to anyone running an outfit of say, less than 2000 cattle or 10,000 sheep,
and it is very questionable if the original cost, upkeep, etc. would
be justified. However, the stockman is a pioneer and when such
machines become available, he will use them just as he used the
tractor when the reliability was very questionable and the cost
and maintenance could not possibly be justified from an economical point of view.[11]

If the figures cited in this letter — that is, ranches which run two
thousand cattle or ten thousand sheep, were accepted as the minimum size of ranch necessary to produce an effective demand
for an airplane or helicopter, then the total number of such
ranches would constitute the potential market. Although an accurate estimate of the number of sheep operators and the number
of cattle operators on the range is not available from the Census,
there are other possible approaches to the problem. The Forestry Service has listings of the ranchers to whom grazing permits have been issued on government-owned lands. These reports, made every five years, show the number of such permits
and are classified as to size of flocks and herds. The 1939 report
shows 1269 owners with over 200 head of cattle and 158 with
over 4000 head of sheep. A further breakdown of this class of owners for the year 1936 shows 8 owners with over 2000 cattle and
18 owners with over 10,000 sheep.
    These data, of course, do not give the total number of men in
the cattle and sheep business who might use air equipment, since
only the cattle and sheep grazed on government land are shown.
Furthermore, the number of livestock under permit is not necessarily the full number owned by the stockmen concerned. Nor
does the size of the band always indicate the wealth of the
owner. There are many dude ranchers, particularly in some of
the Wyoming areas, who have comparatively small numbers of
animals and yet could afford an airplane or helicopter.
    Another rancher estimates that only units which have from
$20,000 to $25,000 gross sales per year can afford a plane. These
figures seem too low. One might estimate roughly that the Grade

[11] Personal letter.

IV category of the grazing permits would represent a high enough bracket to be interested in airplane transportation; that is, those ranchers who have over two hundred head of cattle or four thousand sheep. In 1939, this would have included 1269 cattle-owners and 158 sheep-owners. To these numbers would be added the large owners who do not have grazing permits on government-owned lands. Perhaps only those owners who have as many as two thousand head of cattle or ten thousand sheep could actually justify the costs of the initial experimentation and upkeep of air transportation in the early years of its use on ranches. Regardless of the meager statistics on the subject, the cattle and sheep businesses are extensive enough to justify the belief that they would furnish a market for considerable numbers of aircraft if the usefulness of such is fairly certain.

Effects of Use of Aircraft

The airplane and helicopter, by bringing the vast distances of the range closer to the ranch-owner or manager, may make it possible to conduct ranching on a still larger scale. Small ranches will be less profitable, and the result might be further concentration of capital in the hands of the already powerful sheep and cattle men who have sufficient funds to adopt new devices. Capital would perhaps be attracted to these larger and more industrialized business units.

A whole new range of recreational facilities, linking up the dude ranches with the East by airplane service, might develop. Westerners themselves would have easier access to their park facilities. The increased contact of the West with other parts of the nation, both through visitors to the area and through greater travel by the Westerners, will break down the traditional isolation of the range. The free-and-easy manners of the West may be supplanted to some extent by the more individualistic and businesslike attitudes of the city. Other transportation and communication facilities have already started this trend.

The truck, the telephone, the radio, the private automobile all made changes in ranch life and ranch organization. The far ranges have been brought ever closer to the ranch management, and the ranchers themselves have been brought continually closer to urban life. The airplane will continue this trend.

Conclusion

The airplane and the helicopter are sure to prove very useful on livestock ranches, since the vast areas over which the animals graze are admirably suited to their use. Aircraft will also be useful to the livestock business which supervises and services the extensive and widely scattered activities of these large ranches. The uses to which aircraft may be put are many and varied. Among the more important are the inspection of the conditions of the grazing land as to grass and water; inspection of waterholes, trails, windmills, and the detection of washouts; the transportation, to the places where the animals are grazing, of food, supplies, foremen, cowboys, herders, veterinarians, skilled mechanics, or buyers. Aircraft have been used very successfully by hunters of the destructive coyote and other predatory animals, and are expected to be useful in catching cattle-thieves. The adoption of aircraft for these and other uses depends upon the cost. As prices come down, planes or helicopters, if large enough, may replace trucks and prove more durable; they may also dispense with some labor. Aircraft favors the large operators. Thus, it, like the barbed-wire fence, the telephone, and the truck, will change the cattle and sheep business of the West.

32

Government

THE FUNCTIONS AND PROBLEMS of government have been changing in the United States as this country has become highly industrialized and urbanized. Many new technological inventions have developed since American constitutional government was set up. The radio, the automobile, the railroad, and other major technological inventions have altered in one way or another some aspect of government. Aviation will likewise affect the operation of our system of government. In this chapter, we shall deal with the probable effects of aviation on government in general, including such topics as the effect on our federal system of government, on the functional divisions of government, on Congress, and on political parties. The next chapter will be concerned with the effect of aviation on the administrative activities of government.

Shifts in Power of Federal, State, and Local Governments

When the founding fathers of this country met at the Constitutional Convention in 1787, they provided for a federal system of government based upon the principle of a division of powers between the central government and the states. There were many reasons for their choice of this type of government, two of the most important being the variety of economic, religious, racial, and cultural differences existing in the country at that time and the strong feeling among many leaders against powerful centralized rule. Hence, the only powers of the federal government were those assigned to it in the Constitution, whereas the powers of the state governments included all others not delegated to the federal government.

However, there has been a marked trend toward the transfer

of power and responsibility from the local governments to the state government and from the states to the federal government. This trend has been especially strong since the middle of the last quarter of the nineteenth century.[1] The encroachment of the federal government upon the states may be illustrated by the greatly increased number of annual federal grants-in-aid to the states. Even prior to the last depression, between 1915 and 1930, the funds provided by the national government to the states increased more than tenfold.[2] During the 1930's, the federal aid to the states increased at an even greater rate, reaching a total of $622,501,569 in 1938.[3] These federal grants have been accompanied by federal regulations concerning the use of these funds. Supervision over the work or activity for which the money had been granted has increased greatly in recent years.[4]

Some students of government contend that the increase in federal activities and functions does not constitute an encroachment upon the domain of state functions. They point out that, rather than being transferred to the federal government, state activities have been extended by means of co-operative programs of federal and state governments. Thus, state and federal activities have taken on the character of co-operative relationships, enabling state governments to accomplish tasks to which they were previously unequal. However, the result has been greater state dependence on the federal government.

The strength of the national government lies in the degree to which it touches the daily lives of the citizens in their consumption practices, income, and daily habits. Today, the citizen comes in contact with the federal government in the payment of old-age pensions, unemployment pay checks, relief, personal taxation, regulation of wages and hours, policing, public health, and so on. Hitherto, most of these contacts were with the city, county, or state governments.

[1] Leonard D. White, "Public Administration," in *Recent Social Trends in the United States*; Report of the President's Committee on Social Trends. New York: McGraw-Hill Book Co., 1933, pp. 1393-1394.

[2] *Ibid.*, p. 1396.

[3] S. McKee Rosen and Laura Rosen, *Technology and Society*. New York: The Macmillan Company, 1941, p. 370.

[4] Leonard D. White, *op. cit.*, p. 1395.

Many factors have operated to produce the trend toward centralization. Technological factors, particularly the development of transportation and communication inventions, were very important, in conjunction, of course, with economic and social forces. Industry, commerce, transportation, and communication have become organized on a national scale, making their regulation by local or state units of government difficult. "Industrial and social relations overflowed the banks of the states and swept out over the nation in a flood too great to be controlled by any one state." [5] As a result, state boundary lines have been called into question. Professor W. Y. Elliott, for example, suggests the substitution of regional commonwealths for states.[6] The counties, too, are under pressure to merge and form larger units of political jurisdiction.[7] The organization of the divisions of government are very slow to change, however, and modifications have usually come through changes in function rather than in organization.[8]

If technology in general and transportation inventions in particular are partially responsible for the present trend of centralization, it appears reasonable to expect that aviation will further stimulate and reinforce this trend in government.

Fast air transportation will make possible more personal contacts over wider areas between political and governmental figures and the electorate. When Oregon was a territory, the time required for a trip to Washington, D.C., was about one hundred and fifty days. By airplane, this journey can be made in a day. One can now go from Oregon to the District of Columbia in less time than would be taken to go from one's farm to the county seat in those days. The airplane can make some of the government officials in Washington, D.C., much more familiar to the local electorate, although it is probably less effective in this regard than the radio and press. Often, the net result will be that the

[5] C. E. Merriam, "Government and Society," in *Recent Social Trends, op. cit.*, p. 1495.
[6] W. Y. Elliott, *The Need for Constitutional Reform*. New York: McGraw-Hill Book Co., 1935, chapter IX.
[7] C. E. Merriam, *op. cit.*, p. 1491.
[8] Carroll H. Wooddy, "The Growth of Governmental Functions," *Recent Social Trends, op. cit.*, p. 1274.

personalities of some Washington officials, such as the President or a cabinet member, will be more familiar to the people of a county or a city than are their own local officials. The fact that transportation is faster and communication more widespread does not *ipso facto* make the central government more powerful. However, the operation of these media often creates problems on a national scale and they facilitate governmental administration over large areas. Crises, such as wars or business depressions, increase the use of these media of contact between the central government and the people in local areas.

The tax base, which supports public services, is made larger by virtue of the transportation and communication inventions, which integrate the economic system over large areas, often over a whole nation, making taxation somewhat difficult on a narrower basis. Local tax areas have been increasingly unable to meet the demands of the community and have had to be aided by federal funds. In the depression of the 1930's, the needs were greater than could be cared for by the city, county, or state, with a few exceptions, and the national government assumed local functions, furnishing relief to the unemployed, paying for part of the education of children, and so on.

The county in the United States as a unit of governmental jurisdiction is of much less relative significance than it was in the days of the horse and buggy; that is, of the important business of all governments, national, state, and local, a larger portion was formerly handled by the county than is the case now. With the growth of governmental functions in general over the past century and with the frequent designation of the county as the agent to distribute federal or state public welfare funds, the county may have, from time to time, increased activities, but relative to other governmental units, the county has declined in governmental significance. This decline is due in part to the railroad and the automobile. The airplane does nothing to counteract these influences; rather, it supplements them.

The city will find its area of influence enlarged by virtue of the use of aircraft, particularly the helicopter. The economic and political boundary lines of cities have become differentiated through the rise of local transportation inventions. At one time, the political boundary of a city included the residences of all those who worked in the city. But local transportation enabled workers to live farther out and spread the economic city over a larger area. The political boundaries of cities have changed more slowly. There has been some agitation to extend the city limits — that is, the political boundary line — outward to take in the economic area, and create one large political unit instead of many villages, towns, and cities that now exist in the metropolitan area. Such a large boundary line for the metropolitan area would perhaps resemble that of a county or a small state, since it would probably include farms as well as urban communities. But there has been considerable inertia as well as active resistance on the part of suburbs and villages against amalgamation into one large metropolitan political unit.

Like other means of local transportation, aviation will enable workers and economic activities to be located over larger areas, although its effect may be slight for some time. It is difficult to predict the future political boundary lines of cities, but it seems probable that any change will be to include more area within the city. The increasing difference between the economic and political boundary lines which will be brought about through the influence of aviation may create greater problems of taxation, safety, and health, which will exert pressure to extend the political boundaries.

City governmental activities will be expanded through the measures taken to deal with the problems of aircraft, such as the provision of local airports and landing fields, zoning with reference to airplanes, regulation and control of personal planes, commuters' service, and local taxicab service, and the use of planes for policing, traffic control, and various other purposes.

States, likewise, will have their activities increased to some extent by the regulation and use of aircraft. For some time, states have had aviation boards and commissions engaged in promoting and aiding aviation. Like the railroads, the trunk lines will be interstate and subject to federal rather than state control, but there may be intrastate feeder lines which will come under state control. In addition, the state will make considerable use of the airplane in administration, forestry, agriculture, education, policing, and so on.

However, the great influence of the airplane, through the transportation of persons and goods over long distances, is to make widely separated regions interdependent. Regions within a country, and indeed nations, have already become a single business market so far as transportation is concerned. The increasing importance of regions is shown by the organization of many businesses on a regional basis. The Federal Reserve System of banks is set up on a regional basis. Many businesses have regional representatives and centers. The identification of a business with a particular state or locality is lessened by long-distance transportation systems, such as railroads and airplanes. It is this widening area of business that makes state and local governments less important relative to the national government, not only with respect to taxation and wealth, but also with respect to the feelings and loyalties of citizenship.

However, business organization is much more adaptable to change than governmental organization, and a regional governmental organization is much less likely to occur than a regional business organization. There has been some co-operation of states on a regional basis. For instance, the governors of New England have held conferences on regional issues, especially on problems having to do with waterways. The influence of the airplane is to encourage somewhat regional interests and to increase the number of regional governmental units.

The relative decline of local government is regretted by many people, partly because there exists a strong traditional and sentimental association of the early origins of democracy in this country with the distribution of powers and functions among local units. However, the same forces, namely, the transportation and communication inventions, which have helped to bring about the expansion and concentration of the federal government have also provided the agencies of democratic influence in the national government.

Increased Functions of Government

In addition to the trend toward centralization, there has been a trend in government toward increasing functions. For the past forty or fifty years, the increase in federal power has been mainly in the economic sphere.[9] Aviation is another industry which is added to the list which the federal government must regulate, and it is another public utility which necessitates governmental regulation of rates, service, and safety.

The governments of all countries, in their own interests, have been concerned with the development of aviation. In many countries, the airlines have been owned by the governments and operated by them; in others, governments have become large stockholders; while, in still others, the government has assisted in their management. In the United States, the federal government has encouraged aviation principally through the payment of subsidies for the carriage of mail. Since the beginning of World War II, the passenger and cargo operations of the main domestic trunk lines have become self-supporting and the period of mail subsidy may be at an end for these trunk lines. However, it may be necessary to provide subsidies for the development of local air service.

Large subsidies have also been paid to American international airlines. In view of the facts that costs of operation are higher for international airlines than for domestic and that the present volume of traffic is smaller, the federal government may find it necessary to continue to pay subsidies to international airlines until the traffic becomes much larger and until the possible competition with airlines of other nations becomes stabilized.

In addition to subsidies for the carriage of mail, the federal government in the United States has aided the development of aviation in many other ways. It has aided in the construction of airports, provided lighting facilities, radio directional aids, emergency landing fields, meteorological service, and so on. It has

[9] Note the Interstate Commerce Act of 1887, the Sherman Anti-Trust Act of 1890, the Elkins Act of 1903, the creation of the Federal Reserve System in 1913, the Clayton Act and the Federal Trade Commission Act of 1914, the Federal Radio Act of 1926, and the numerous enactments of the New Deal after 1933.

allocated large sums of money for research on designs of planes, new types of fuels and metals, and for the development of new kinds of aircraft.

The uses which governmental administrative units will make of the airplane will increase rather than lessen the activities of the government. For example, the Department of Agriculture may engage directly in aerial dusting and spraying for control of the boll weevil or the grasshopper. The airplane is a very effective instrument in the control of such pests, but, for its most effective use, large areas must be dusted at one time. It is difficult to organize the co-operation of many small farm units to obtain the advantages of large-area dusting. At all events, the control of pests is a public rather than an individual problem, and, through the use of the airplane, it may become an extensive governmental operation. The health departments of governments also are developing additional functions in the prevention of diseases brought in by airplanes through the importation of insects and bacteria. The next chapter will be devoted to a discussion of the many uses of aircraft by various administrative agencies.

Expanding Power of Government

As governments take on more functions, their influence and power are increased. But there are ways in which the airplane leads to an enhanced power of the state other than by the addition of functions.

The increase in nationalism through the influence of aviation, which will be discussed in another chapter, enhances the power of the federal government. More frequent contacts between the parts of a nation, particularly a nation which covers large territories, decreases separatist tendencies and distinctive localisms and unites a country into a more compact unit. The stronger the feelings of national patriotism, the greater is the power of government, as compared, for instance, with the power of industry, the power of the church, or the power of labor. In war, when nationalism is at a very high pitch, the actual power of government tends to overshadow that of any and all other institutions.

The power of governments is also increased through the

greater participation of nations in international affairs. More frequent contacts between the people of the various nations through air travel increase and intensify international problems, making it imperative that nations engage in various types of organization for international co-operation. These contacts will take place between industries, labor unions, cartels, and so on, as well as between governmental representatives, but the government, rather than other institutions, will have the responsibility for handling the international problems which arise. The increasing need to regulate, control, and promote commercial trade between nations will be particularly important in the augmentation of the power of governments.

It seems reasonable to predict, therefore, that aviation will accentuate the trends which are already enhancing the power of government.

Legislative Processes and Law

Although the power and functions of the executive and administrative branches of our government have been increased in recent times more than have those of the legislative and judicial branches, legislative activity may be increased to some extent through the influence of aviation. A great many laws have been passed concerning the use and regulation of aircraft since 1918, when the Post Office Department first received an appropriation from Congress for the setting-up of air mail service. After a number of acts dealing with specific aspects of aviation, Congress passed the Civil Aeronautics Act in 1938, which set up an agency with power to regulate all phases of aviation. Congress, however, outlined the broad policies which this agency was to promote. In addition to the body of federal laws governing aviation, state legislatures have passed legislation concerning the regulation and promotion of aviation within the states. Like the federal government, many states have created aviation boards or commissions to administer the policies laid down by the legislature.

The making of rules by bodies other than legislatures may increase faster than the passing of laws by Congress. Thus, it is expected that administrative agencies, rather than Congress, will deal with the problems arising from aviation. In recent years, there has been a tremendous growth in administrative rules and regulations formulated by committees, bureaus, authorities, and other administrative bodies not considered to have legislative power. These rules and regulations are often, in power and significance, the equivalent of enactments by legislative bodies. Such, for instance, were the decrees of the National Recovery Administration in 1933, affecting labor and industry. Rules which have the significance of laws are developed through such administrative bodies as the Federal Trade Commission, the Social Security Board, and similar agencies. While congressional legislation may in general deal with more fundamental policies, and while much administrative decision is in the nature of rules carried out under authority of Congress, still, if laws are thought of as rules regulating our behavior, the rulings of administrative bodies have the proportions of laws. As the administrative branches of government accumulate and expand, there are proportionately fewer of the rules regulating the behavior of citizens coming from congressional legislation and relatively more from administrative units.

It is, of course, theoretically possible that Congress will take over some of the decision-making functions of present administrative bodies. But it is difficult for Congress to handle the many details of administration and at the same time maintain the flexibility in laws which the complexity of modern society and the rapidity of change demand. Congress is not well organized for speed, since it is by definition a deliberative body, and deliberation is time-consuming. It is most probable that the complexity of society and the tempo of change will increase and that administrative bodies will legislate on matters that in a simpler age could have been dealt with by a representative legislative body. Aviation, itself, will increase the tempo of life.

On the other hand, aviation makes it possible for members of Congress to make more frequent personal contacts with their constituencies and to get quick responses of public opinion through air mail. Thus, aviation, while it increases the speed of social action, also provides means for a deliberative assembly to learn more quickly the conditions and opinions of their electorate. Transportation and communication inventions have in general been increasing the wide dissemination of information about public issues and the rapid formation and application of public opinion and aviation reinforces this trend.

Congress

How will aviation affect the structure and composition of Congress and other legislative bodies? The main basis of representation in the legislative bodies in the United States is geographical. Even in other countries, where occupation or industry are considered to be the basis for choosing representatives, some recognition is generally given to geographical differences.

At the time the Constitution of the United States was written and the government established, local differences were great because there were few contacts between the various localities. South Carolina was different from North Carolina, and North Carolina was different from Virginia. The home of Thomas Jefferson outside Charlottesville, Virginia, was in the West, much as Idaho is considered in the West today.

But as faster transportation linked the communities, they became less differentiated. The people from Maine to California and from Oregon to Florida began to wear the same sort of clothes, to use the same models of automobiles, eat the same types of canned food, and drink the same beverages. And so the patterns of consumption became much alike throughout the country. There still remain many problems peculiar to particular regions, especially as to industries, climate, tradition, and so on. Consequently, there still exist reasons for geographical representation, but, in general, geographical representation becomes less imperative with the growth of transportation facilities. Aviation will reinforce this trend and add its influence in the breaking-down of geographical differences.

At the same time that different localities have become more similar, there has been a correlative rise in national interests and welfare. The increased means of transportation have not only diminished the relative significance of local representation in

Congress, but has also increased the need for Congress to represent national interests. Voters have become increasingly conscious of national obligations in their selection of congressmen. Despite these shifts, there has been no change in the electoral basis of choosing members of Congress. Governmental forms are notably slow to change. This is particularly true of the Constitution of the United States, which requires, for any amendment, bicameral action in Congress and ratification by three-quarters of the states. Faster travel by air may sharpen the problem of this lag in governmental organization, one adjustment to which would be greater interest in national and industrial issues than in local or geographical matters by representatives elected on a geographical basis.

While transportation has been knitting together the different parts of nations, economic institutions have become more diversified. At the time of the writing of the Constitution, the United States was largely agricultural. Now, agriculture is the pursuit of only one-fifth of the population, while others find employment in many types of work which came into being with the Industrial Revolution. These include, besides various types of agriculture, financial organizations, transportation and communication systems, mining, special types of production such as chemical industries, manufacturing of electrical goods, food processing, iron and steel industries, and so on. The desire to get representation for the special interests and common problems of these economic groups — and also of ethnic groups and social classes, such as labor — has led to the organization of lobbies. Through lobbies these groups exert political pressure on Congress and thus secure indirect representation. As the nation becomes a more compact unit through the influence of aviation, these groups will be increasingly aware of their common problems and needs, and aviation will facilitate their organization into political pressure groups by promoting national conferences and enabling influential men to make quick trips to Washington or to state capitals.

The upward thrust of these organized social groupings and their intimate and often dominating relation to traditional government are one of the most striking of all governmental trends, and perhaps the most profoundly significant. We may safely forecast at this point prolonged discussion of the implications of the power of these groups, and the appearance of many proposals for modification of the traditional patterns of political organization. Economic councils and senates, scientific councils, mixed councils, political-industrial-scientific councils, of all sorts, are likely to be suggested for serious consideration, are in fact already before Congress for consideration.[10]

Political Parties

Political parties, though not recognized in the Constitution of the United States, are, realistically conceived, organized groups of persons having as their main objective that of securing and maintaining the control of the government and, through such control, obtaining various benefits and advantages for their members, as well as looking out for the welfare of their region and county. New technologies in the past have modified political party activity. For example, political party action was affected a good deal by the invention of the radio, which tended to reduce the number of speakers in a campaign, crowding out the smaller figures and emphasizing the more important ones. It is also said to have modified the style of campaign oratory and to have increased the importance of a good speaking voice in a political candidate. Television may emphasize personal appearance as radio has emphasized the voice.

One effect of aviation will be in the direction of giving political parties somewhat more of a national character. It is true that there are two large national parties in the United States, but, in reality, these national parties have the nature of a federation and perhaps are not as centralized or centrally controlled as the actual government. This federation is made up of local and state organizations. The lack of national character is shown by the absence of agreement on issues by these local and state machines. In New Jersey a local organization may be distinctly conservative, while in California the local organization is found to be strongly pro-

[10] C. E. Merriam, *op. cit.*, p. 1515.

gressive. The same variation is found in states. The strength of these local and state units has rested in large part on patronage. But as the administrative branches of national government expand, more jobs are given through civil service or national patronage, thus decreasing the importance of the local organization. Local party leaders look to Washington and to national party leaders for favors, advice, and direction. As stated before, aviation will tend to emphasize national, rather than local politics. However, these remarks should not be interpreted as minimizing the still very real strength of the local organizations in the political structure. Although the President, with his vast powers, has become a great nationalizing and centralizing influence in the party, yet he is usually unable to prevent the election of party candidates who are opposed to his policies, but who are strongly favored by their local communities.

The increased contacts between national representatives and their constituents will tend to enhance the prestige and power of national figures rather than that of local officials. The radio and the press have had this effect and the influence of aviation will lie in the same direction.

Another aspect of this influence on political parties lies in the general weakening of boundary lines. As business organization and transportation systems extend across state lines, state boundaries become less significant. The airplane, automobile, and railroad have had a great influence in weakening the issue of states' rights, one which, no doubt, has been quite comparable to the more dramatic influence of the Civil War of the 1860's. Politically, state boundaries remain and they are vital, yet state sentiment is probably much less important since business and transportation have become organized on a national scale and their products are sent readily and frequently across local boundary lines. The influence of this development on state political organizations is probably very slight. Yet the election of a majority of governors of one political party is perhaps less a guarantee than formerly that that political party will carry a national election. It is recalled that political parties thrive according to their ability to win elections.

Another line of speculation is based upon the influence of aviation on political parties in relatively isolated areas. These areas are usually thinly populated and of little party significance for that reason. Still, in many of the Southern states, these small rural counties have been the basis of political support for various state machines. The less well informed the electorate or any part of it, the greater the chance of its exploitation by party leaders. The airplane, like the radio and the moving picture, presents the possibility of reducing the isolation of these areas. However, this influence of the airplane may be greatly delayed or barred from penetrating to the common voters of these regions because of the high costs of local service and because there is little incentive to develop air transportation to these backward areas. These areas will probably change and develop more through the greater use of the radio and the extension of education than by the airplane.

Conclusion

Government is so closely tied up with social, economic, and technological forces that any change in any part of the culture tends to make changes in government. The development of aviation will reinforce the already existing trend to shift powers and functions from local to national centers, thus accentuating the movement toward centralization in government. In addition, government itself, as compared to other social institutions, will assume more responsibility and power. The executive and administrative branches of government, in particular, will have their authorities and duties expanded. Aviation will decrease the importance of geographical representation in Congress and strengthen lobbying to some extent. The effect of aviation on political parties will be to increase the power of the national organization of parties in contrast to that of the local units. State and local sentiments and loyalties will meet increasing competition from national issues and interests.

33

Public Administration

THE EXPANSION of governmental functions in the United States during the last fifty years has resulted in a greater increase in administrative activity than in legislative or judicial power. The increasing complexity of modern life and the speed with which problems must be solved has necessitated larger numbers of governmental agencies, staffed by men with technical knowledge and specialized skills.

One hundred years after the founding of the government, the United States had eight departments and two commissions, with more than one hundred thousand civil employees. In the succeeding years, two new departments and over three dozen independent agencies were set up, and thousands of new employees were added. At the beginning of the century (1901), there were 256,000 employees in the executive branch of the United States Government. By 1941, the number had increased to 1,358,000.[1] Such agencies as the Reconstruction Finance Corporation, the Securities Exchange Commission, Rural Electrification Administration, and many others have been established to help carry out the increasing functions of the federal government. The executive and administrative branches of state and local governments have also been expanding in scope and importance. Governments are becoming like great businesses in the size and nature of the tasks they undertake.

In the preceding chapter, the future influence of aviation on government in general was presented. In this chapter, we shall

[1] United States Bureau of the Census, *Statistical Abstract of the United States,* 1942. Washington, D.C.: Government Printing Office, 1943, Table 180.

discuss the various ways in which aviation may affect the administrative work of the government.

Regulation of Aviation

Since aviation is a public utility, government will either own it or regulate and control some of its functions, especially with regard to rates and provisions for safety. Under the interstate and foreign commerce clause, Congress passed the Civil Aeronautics Act of 1938. The organizational provisions of this act were later (April 11, 1940) modified by the President in accordance with the Reorganization Act of 1939.

The revised form of this act provides for a Civil Aeronautics Board and an Administrator of Civil Aeronautics, both constituting the Civil Aeronautics Authority within the Department of Commerce.[2]

The Civil Aeronautics Board is composed of five members, appointed by the President for six-year terms. The board deals with the economic and safety regulation of all civil aviation in the United States. It formulates all major policies concerning the development of civil aviation and grants certificates of public convenience and necessity to the airlines, establishes the rate of pay for mail, and controls passenger fares. It promulgates the Civil Air Regulations and sets standards for operation. Its Safety Bureau investigates all civil aircraft accidents in order to prevent future accidents through appropriate action and regulation.

The Administrator of Civil Aeronautics, whose functions are administrative and promotional, has charge of the Civil Aeronautics Administration. This agency, in contrast to the policy-making Civil Aeronautics Board, is an operating agency. It has four main divisions: Federal Airways, Airports, Safety Regulation (enforcing C.A.B. standards), and the War Training Service. The Civil Aeronautics Administration issues certificates to all civil airmen, including not only pilots, but also mechanics, radio operators, traffic controllers, and others connected with aviation ac-

---

[2] *United States Statutes at Large*, 1939-1941, vol. 54, part I, "Reorganizations Plans III and IV." Washington, D.C.: Government Printing Office, pp. 1233, 1235-1236.

tivities. It inspects the designs of all planes and makes flight tests of models. It regulates the airways and acts as a consultant in the development of airports. Neither the Civil Aeronautics Administration nor the Civil Aeronautics Board has jurisdiction over military planes except when they are using federal civil airways or other federal air facilities of peacetime.[3]

There are also other federal agencies which directly concern themselves with aviation. The Administrator of Civil Aeronautics and the Civil Aeronautics Board work in close co-operation with the Special Aviation Assistant to the Secretary of Commerce. Before 1944, the United States Department of State, through its Division of International Communications, was given the responsibility of putting into effect comprehensive and co-ordinated programs of activities involved in the international aspects of various fields, including that of aviation.[4] This division included, among others, sections on aviation and air priorities. On January 15, 1944, the Secretary of State announced a reorganization of this department. The new plan created an Office of Transportation and Communications which included an aviation division. This division has responsibility for promoting policy and action in international aviation and sends representatives to international conferences in regard to aviation.[5]

State governments have aviation commissions or boards chiefly to promote aviation and to look out for the state's interest in aviation. Some states have a division of aeronautics to deal with patrol of aircraft, the prevention of accidents, and so on. Various cities also have authorities or committees whose chief concern is, at present, to plan for landing fields and to promote the extension of aviation services to their cities.

In addition to these governmental agencies which deal with aviation as a form of public transportation, there are special military organizations concerned with the use of military aircraft. These organizations deal not only with bombers and fighter

[3] *Ibid.*; also *The Aircraft Yearbook for 1941*, Howard Mingos, Editor. Aeronautical Chamber of Commerce of America, 1941, pp. 62-65.
[4] United States Office of War Information, Division of Public Inquiries, *United States Government Manual*, Winter, 1943-44, p. 187.
[5] *The Department of State Bulletin*, January 15, 1944, p. 49.

planes, but also with the transportation of men and material in transport planes, gliders, rotary aircraft, and airships, and with the construction and development of new types of aircraft. This last activity was carried on for the most part during wartime through the award of contracts to private companies, with the government in many cases building the factories and supervising the construction of the planes.

Governmental Aid to Aviation

The government has played a very constructive rôle in the development of aviation in the United States. Langley and other early inventors received governmental aid in their experimentation. A considerable amount of research was carried on during World War I. After that war, the government pioneered in the carrying of mail by air. After the air mail routes were successfully developed, they were turned over to private companies and the payments for mail enabled the airline companies to maintain air passenger services, which did not produce enough revenue to be self-supporting. Air mail payments continued to be the financial backbone of the airline companies until World War II.

At the same time, federal, county, and city governments have aided aviation by building and equipping airports. The airports have almost invariably been built by cities or counties, while Congress has appropriated funds to provide the landing facilities, such as radio directional aids, beacons, and markers at the airports. In December, 1943, Congress appropriated $10,000,000 for completing development work on thirty-one airports in the United States. At present the Civil Aeronautics Administration is in charge of a program of construction and improvement of civil airports which may cost over one billion dollars.[6] Airport passenger terminal buildings, hangars, and administration and control buildings have also often been built through federal aid. Both the federal and state governments have built flight strips, which are expected to be used by local lines after the war.

The airways between airports are designated and controlled

[6] *The Aircraft Year Book for 1945*, Howard Mingos, Editor. New York: Lancier, 1945, p. 172.

by the Civil Aeronautics Administration. Along these airways, twenty miles wide in peacetime, bridges, radio towers, high buildings, chimneys, and other obstructions are required, by the Civil Aeronautics Administration, to be lighted. Light beacons along the airways were provided and maintained by the federal government to the number of 2160 in 1944.[7] Approximately 408 intermediate frequency and 143 ultra-high frequency radio range beacons were in operation in 1943 for the guidance of the pilot along the airways. Approach to airports was indicated by 197 radio fan markers in 1943. Traffic at the airports and on the airways is controlled by the Civil Aeronautics Administration. An instrument blind landing system was developed by the administration's experimental station, and a number of airports have been equipped with this system.

The war brought additional radio aids and radar. In 1944, Congress appropriated $46,000,000 for radar and radio developments by the Office of Scientific Research.

Weather observations and forecasting facilities have been greatly expanded to meet the needs of airplane operators. Government-operated teletype wires, totaling 62,545 miles in 1944, connect the weather reporting stations.

One of the most important contributions of the federal government to aviation consists of research on airplanes, engines, propellers, instruments, and other items. The National Advisory Committee for Aeronautics, financed by annual appropriations of Congress, is the chief agency in this research work. It operates three large research laboratories: one at Langley Field, Virginia; another at Moffett Field, California; and one at the Cleveland Municipal Airport. The largest of these is the one at Langley Field, which has some twenty wind tunnels. One wind tunnel for large-sized planes is contained in a building a block long and ten stories high. One of the tunnels is capable of testing planes at a wind speed of seven hundred and fifty miles per hour. There are towing basins for testing seaplanes and hulls, one tank being a half-mile long.

The Cleveland laboratory, testing mainly engines and fuels,

[7] *Ibid.*, p. 434.

has one of the largest refrigeration plants in the world, enabling tests to be made under icing conditions and at the conditions which exist at forty thousand feet altitude in a five hundred-mile wind at 48° below zero.[8]

Important research has also been done by other agencies. The technical division of the Civil Aeronautics Administration studies many phases of safe and efficient airline operation. Navy research has led to the construction and improvement of radial air-cooled engines. The light metal alloys of our metal airliners were also developed by navy research. Army research has been of particular importance in the development of propellers, fuels, lubricants, starters, instruments, and other items. The Air Transport Command under wartime conditions has developed many techniques which will be useful in postwar aviation.

There will be a great postwar recession of governmental activities in the field of aviation, but many of these activities will continue in peacetime. The military aspects of aviation will continue to be important in international policing and national preparedness for quick striking power. No matter how successful the international peace organization may be, it is probable that the sponsorship of military aviation is likely to continue in peace, since force may be needed to prevent wars. The government's promotion of experimental research in aviation through the National Advisory Committee for Aeronautics will continue in peacetime as well as in war.

Governmental assistance to scheduled airline operations is likely to continue. Direct subsidies or subsidies in the form of overpayment for mail may not be necessary for passenger and express operations on the domestic trunk lines, since these had become self-supporting before the war and are expected to expand in traffic. But assistance from the government may be needed for some years for providing mail and passenger service to smaller places and to isolated regions. It is difficult to predict how much assistance the government may give to setting up and maintaining air services to small cities and towns where the amount of air

8 Association of American Railroads, *Initial Study of Air Transportation,* January, 1944, pp. 54-55.

traffic will probably be small. In an isolated region such as Alaska, whose economic and population development rests upon transportation, the government may appropriate special grants to provide mail, cargo, and passenger services. There will undoubtedly be some kind of governmental aid for international aviation, especially on northern and Pacific routes. The competition of other nations for North and South Atlantic trade may also call for special constructive help on the part of the government.

The federal government may be expected to continue to construct new airways and to provide more facilities for instrument flying. There is a possibility that it may provide for the training of some civilian pilots as well as military pilots, although in general the training of civilian pilots will doubtless be a function of private concerns. Local governments will probably be concerned with the financing and building of landing fields and strips as aviation continues to spread.

This brief survey shows the large amount of governmental activity and administration which has resulted from aviation. Seldom, if ever, has a new industry brought forth such a burst of governmental participation along the lines of finance, construction, operation, and regulation. The unusual amount of governmental activity accompanying aviation is likely to continue in the future.

General Effects on Governmental Administration

Our discussion up to this point has dealt with those executive branches of government which were established for, and are solely concerned with, the operation, promotion, and regulation of various aspects of aviation itself. This, however, is not the only influence of aviation on governmental administration. Many other branches of governmental work will also be affected in some way by aviation, such as the government's activities in agriculture, public health, collection of customs, fire-fighting, the administration of public lands, and many others. There are certain general effects which aviation will have on governmental bureaus and departments. We shall discuss these common influences first, and then examine the effects on specific bureaus and departments.

Increased speed of travel by plane will affect all the administrative agencies of the federal government. Since it is located on the east coast rather than centrally, the work of bureaus and departments which conduct many of their activities in Western areas, such as the Departments of the Interior and Agriculture, will be greatly affected by the saving of time spent in travel.

With faster travel, it is possible for an itinerant staff to get more work done per unit of time or for fewer agents to be employed. Air travel might be used, for example, by the Conciliation Service of the Bureau of Labor, whose work requires a large amount of time in travel, enabling this work to be done more efficiently and speedily.

The supervision by governmental bureaus of various agencies and branches scattered over the United States will be facilitated by the use of air travel. For instance, the Farm Credit Association supervises the federal land banks, production credit corporations, federal intermediate credit banks, and district banks for co-operatives. One of each of these organizations is located in Springfield, Massachusetts; Baltimore; Columbia, South Carolina; Louisville; New Orleans; St. Louis; St. Paul; Omaha; Wichita; Houston; Berkeley; and Spokane. Obviously, fast air travel can facilitate the supervision of these credit institutions scattered so widely across the continent.

Travel by air often saves expense, especially in long trips to the Far West where the food and sleeping-car costs of train travel amount to more than the additional costs of airplane tickets. There may also be savings to such agencies as the Office of Indian Affairs, whose work necessitates trips to out-of-the-way spots. Surface means of transportation in such areas are often slow and costly and the use of the airplane will be cheaper.

Another effect of fast transportation upon administration in general is that there is less reliance on the judgment of the men in the field, since more decisions can be made at the central office. The telegraph and the telephone have had the same effect. This influence is especially noticeable in the work of ambassadors, ministers, and consular officers of the State Department. In the days of difficult traveling conditions and less communication by telephone and mail, men in the field had to use their own judgment in making decisions and had a good deal of freedom to act on their own responsibility. It is quite probable that governmental representatives will be brought to Washington more often for consultation when national and international aviation becomes more highly developed. When a governmental bureau has many agents in the field, all of whom are dependent on their own judgment, decisions tend to have greater variability than if they are made in a central office, because of variations of personality and judgment of the field workers. More frequent communication and travel thus tends to make administration more uniform.

In addition to facilitating the work of the administrative agencies of government, aviation in some cases may so increase the work and functions of a bureau that it amounts to a significant enhancement of the bureau's powers. For example, aviation, particularly private aircraft, will probably greatly increase the duties and powers of the United States Secret Service and the Federal Bureau of Investigation. The increasing importance of the federal government in police and detective work has arisen from the inability of local agencies to cope efficiently with the problem of crime in an age of fast transportation, when local and state boundaries are easily and quickly passed. By air, criminals will be able to move still more quickly from one jurisdiction to another, even those very widely separated; but aviation will also enable the federal officers of justice to execute their tasks with greater speed and efficiency. Since aviation is expected to increase police problems and to expedite their solution, it should, in time, bring a considerable expansion of those police and detective agencies of national jurisdiction, magnifying their scope and powers to greater proportions.

Likewise, the National Mediation Board, which governs relations between labor and employer in the railway industry of the country, has had its powers enhanced by aviation. By an act of April 10, 1936, the jurisdiction of the board was extended to carriers by air engaged in interstate commerce or under mail contract.[9]

Immigration and Customs Collection

The work of the Immigration and Naturalization Service and of the Bureau of Customs may be affected after the war by the development of aviation. The Treasury Department has followed the practice of designating as airports of entry only cities or towns along or near international borders. But it has granted landing rights to some international airlines at airports of interior cities. Inland cities have not been designated as points of entry in order to prevent individual planes flying from foreign countries from landing at these ports without stopping first at the border. With inland ports of entry, an individual plane could land between the border and the interior point of entry and discharge illegal goods or persons without reporting it upon arrival at the point of entry. In spite of this, more inland cities will probably be designated as ports of entry for international airlines. Foreign goods and passengers will be examined at the points where they deplane, since the advantages of speed in air travel are lost if the plane has to make an extra stop *en route* at a traditional point of entry. Aviation will mean, then, a multiplication of immigration and customs stations in the United States and other nations.

The process of inspection is likely to be speeded up. Air passengers will feel particularly resentful of long hours of delay for inspection, and there will be pressure to expedite the inspection of foreign goods and the collection of duties. This may be done by simplification of procedure and by the employment of more personnel.

The enforcement of immigration and customs regulations may be made more difficult by the increased ease of smuggling by air. The customs and immigration agencies may need more extensive patrols, especially across Canadian and Mexican borders. The scheduled carriers will not knowingly violate the law, but private

9 *United States Government Manual*, Division of Public Inquiries, Office of War Information. Washington, D.C.: First Edition, 1945, p. 535.

planes and helicopters could land smuggled cargo, or illegal immigrants, at any airport or landing field, where they might pass unnoticed.

Officials of the Bureau of Narcotics in Washington believe that the speed of air travel will increase the smuggling of narcotics and that the problem of inspecting aviation crews will be quite different from present procedures with ordinary seamen.

However, aviation makes closer co-operation between enforcement officers all over the world both possible and more necessary.

Control of Insects and Bacteria

Airplanes introduce new problems of inspection in the control of pests, insects, bacteria, and other menaces to the health of humans, animals, and plants. The dangers of importation are greater with air transportation since planes reach their destinations before insects or parasites have had time to die in transit and in less time than the incubation period for most diseases. The inspection of aircraft and air passengers from foreign countries has expanded the functions of the Bureau of Entomology and Plant Quarantine and the United States Public Health Service, which have had the functions of inspecting trucks, automobiles, ships, and trains. These two agencies, in co-operation with the states, maintain inspection stations at important points of entry into the country and in some cases between sections of the United States. Persons entering the country are examined to determine whether or not they are suffering from or carrying communicable diseases and, if so, they are quarantined for a time before they are allowed to enter, or they may even be sent back to the country from which they came. The Public Health Service sees that all ships are fumigated, if such action is needed, and takes precautions to see that disease is not carried into this country. The Entomology Bureau inspects all plants and produce which enter the United States, and fumigates or rejects them, in an attempt to protect our forests and agriculture. States have sometimes found it necessary — for example, California — to inspect vehicles and persons entering their borders in order to protect their crops and livestock. This rigorous control of pests is vital in view of the fact that about one-half of the important pests in agriculture and forestry of this country are introduced species. Because of the speed of the airplane, even more rigid control and frequent inspection will be required.

Weather Prediction

Another governmental service that has expanded greatly and undergone somewhat of a change because of the demands of aviation is that of the Weather Bureau of the Department of Commerce. Aviation, especially in wartime, has increased the functions, personnel, and volume of work of the Weather Bureau. Many new meteorological stations have been added. In fact, half the total expenditures of the bureau are now for aviation weather studies and forecasts. This development is not wholly a wartime phenomenon, but will continue during peacetime. In addition to the tremendous increase in this service, radically new advances in technique have resulted from research occasioned by aviation. Meteorology is fundamentally a "three-dimensional" science, but the knowledge of weather and climate in the third dimension was severely limited before the development of aviation. Many of the basic phenomena affecting weather occur in the air far above the earth's surface and are not observable from the ground. Aviation has added much to the knowledge of conditions in the earth's atmosphere. It is expected that further researches in the upper air will be even more fruitful in the years ahead. The requirements of airlines following the northerly great-circle courses to the Orient are placing greater emphasis on the necessity of better information for the polar regions. Aviation has, therefore, had a profound effect on meteorology and the governmental service of weather prediction.

Aerial Photography

The development of aerial photography has had almost revolutionary effects on the work of certain executive branches of the government. Foremost among the governmental organizations using aerial photography are the army and the navy. Aerial photographs and the maps made from them played a vital part during the war in the planning and execution of military campaigns. During this period, it is said that more than six million square miles were mapped by aerial photographers, which is about one-ninth of the total land surface of the earth.

Aerial maps are also basic to much peacetime work done in other bureaus. Without them, their work has been retarded and in some cases, as will be shown later, these maps have made possible new types of undertakings. Aerial mapping by the Geological Survey of the Department of the Interior will be especially extensive. Formerly, the work was done by the plane table and level method, a laborious and expensive process. It took over half a century to complete about sixty per cent of the topographical map of the United States. With the use of aerial photographic equipment, the Geological Survey hopes to complete the topographical mapping of the United States in a year or two in the postwar period.

The Agricultural Adjustment Administration has made extensive use of aerial maps in checking crop control. Another important use has been in soil surveys. The quality of the soil is indicated to some extent by the light and dark shades recorded on the film. Soil surveys can be made much more effectively by air when color photography, which is now rather expensive, comes into wider use. Soil surveys are useful for setting up farm programs and for studying various types of land use. Aerial photographs are also extremely useful in making plans for irrigation, water supply, flood control, river and harbor development, and for road, power line, and pipeline constructions, city planning, traffic studies, and tax assessment purposes.[10]

A governmental bureau whose work has been greatly affected by aerial photography is the United States Coast and Geodetic Survey of the Department of Commerce. Its aeronautical charting activities expanded during World War II by some two thousand per cent.

Another important use of these maps has been in connection

[10] S. S. Steinberg, "Mapping from the Air," *Scientific Monthly*, April, 1935, pp. 363-366.

with the statistical work of the United States Bureau of the Census. Aerial maps aid in selecting representative sample, especially samples of rural population and products. Samples properly chosen from aerial maps give results not appreciably different from a complete count, yet the cost is very much less. Also aerial maps are used to insure a full count of all the farms by the enumerators, when the complete census is being taken of an area. Each enumerator works from a map made from the photographs.

The helicopter should make possible a different type of photograph from that taken from a fast-moving plane. The helicopter can fly closer to the ground and hover, making it possible to photograph breeding places of insects, the habitats of wild game, geological conditions, and so on. It can also make better photographs for many engineering projects.

A glance at these activities shows that a great deal of work can go forward faster, cheaper, and better through the use of aerial photographs, especially those using the tri-metrogon system, which shows the third dimension. From the present and future point of view, the United States may be said to have been under-mapped. Aerial surveys can be of much use in the future to a great variety of projects.

The Department of the Interior

The Department of the Interior carries on activities in every state in the Union, and it is administratively responsible for federal contacts with the islands and territories, such as Alaska, the Virgin Islands, Puerto Rico, Hawaii, and the Philippines. The various offices and bureaus of the department, which cover a wide variety of activities, include the Grazing Service, Fish and Wildlife Service, National Park Service, Office of Indian Affairs, Bureau of Mines, Office of Land Utilization, Bureau of Reclamation, Division of Territories and Island Possessions, Geological Survey, General Land Office, Petroleum Conservation Division, and others. Since a great amount of the work of the department is concerned with the natural resources in the Rocky Mountain and Western states, most of the divisions will be affected by the increased speed of air travel. This will be especially true in Alaska.

Alaska is part of the jurisdiction of the Department of the Interior and almost every bureau and division within the department carries on some kind of activity there. Since air transportation is so important in Alaska at present, and for its future development, the governmental administrative units will be particularly affected by aviation. Alaska is expected to increase in population and economic importance after the war, and the importance and volume of work of these agencies will correspondingly increase. The General Land Office of the department administers vast areas of unreserved public domain in Alaska, its duties including co-operation in the development of mineral resources, protection and utilization of timber, planning of town sites, and appropriation of agricultural and other suitable lands for permanent settlement. All of these activities will be facilitated by better air transportation within Alaska and between the United States and Alaska, and by the use of aviation in preparation of aerial maps, for patrolling forests, combating forest fires, and so on. During World War II, the Alaskan Branch of the Geological Survey pioneered in the development of photogrammetry. The geologists of this branch have also used airplanes extensively in reconnaissance work. The effects of aviation in Alaska on the administration of the Office of Indian Affairs will be discussed under another section.

Many of the divisions of the Department of the Interior will have their work modified by aviation in particular ways which will be discussed in some of the following sections.

Grazing Service

The Grazing Service of the Department of the Interior administers an enormous area of 266,000,000 acres, of which 142,000,-000 are federal range land. Transportation is an important problem in this area, where roads are often blocked with snow, especially in areas of high altitude. A large proportion of the area is sparsely settled and arid. It is ideally suited to the use of the airplane except in the mountainous areas where it is difficult to build landing fields. Although the helicopter does not function so well at high altitudes, it can be used in these mountainous areas. The work of the Grazing Service depends upon quick travel between central and subordinate headquarters, travel into areas inaccessible to automobiles, and a considerable amount of local and cross-country travel. The helicopter and the plane should be useful for all purposes of transportation in these areas. Both will also be used in the detection and control of fires in the forests of the grazing land, in the counting of livestock and game on the range, and in killing predatory animals. The use of aerial photography in connection with the Grazing Service has already been discussed.

Fish and Wildlife Service

The Fish and Wildlife Service will also make much use of helicopters and airplanes. The planting of fish in lakes which are inaccessible by surface means of transportation has already been done by plane. The use of helicopters is expected to improve the technique of aerial planting of fish and make possible the placing of fish in streams as well as in lakes. Making inventories of waterfowl and the enforcement of fish and game laws can also be done more effectively. Planes have already been used in Alaska for aerial patrol of fish and wildlife resources. In 1942, agents of the Alaska Game Commission (the operating agency in Alaska) traveled 156,384 miles by plane. They found the plane especially effective in spotting illegal fur trapping activities. The Division of Alaskan Fisheries covered about 10,600 miles in fishery patrol activities.

The Fish and Wildlife Service carries on a war against the animal enemies of fish, fowl, game, and sheep, among which the coyote is especially destructive. Planes have been successfully used in the hunting and shooting of coyotes, and the helicopter is expected to be even better, since it can travel slowly.

Aircraft will be used also in surveys of a biological nature and in research affecting streams, lakes, and other waters. Aerial photography and transportation over rough and inaccessible terrain are important means of aiding the Fish and Wildlife Service.

The National Park Service

The National Park Service of the Department of the Interior, unlike the Grazing and the Fish and Wildlife Services, has found aviation an obstacle rather than a help in its work. Legislation concerning the national parks states that they are to be kept in as natural a state as possible for the enjoyment of future generations. The noise and confusion caused by airplanes would violate this requirement, as well as have a most disturbing effect upon the wildlife for which the national parks are sanctuary. Hence the Park Service has not permitted the construction of aviation facilities in the national parks. If such a ruling continues, as it may well do, landing places for aircraft are likely to be placed near-by outside the boundaries of the parks, for it seems probable that aviation will be used by tourists and vacationists wishing to visit the parks.

It is commonly agreed that the automobile has been instrumental in the extraordinary increase in the annual number of visitors to the national parks. Aviation should further increase the number, especially from points some distance away, as from localities east of the Mississippi, since fast air travel enables more of a vacation period to be spent at the location rather than in travel. Air travel to and from national parks will be on the scheduled airlines at first, because it will be some time before many individuals will be using their own planes for vacationing. Regular airline service will take passengers to landing places near the parks, from which points they can complete the journey by local service.

In general, the National Park Service is unique in limiting the use of aircraft, but it may well find the plane and the helicopter useful for fighting fires, finding lost persons, transporting personnel between parks, and carrying supplies and building materials to inaccessible mountain sites.

Office of Indian Affairs

Another branch of the Department of the Interior that will make much use of aviation is the Office of Indian Affairs. Indian reservations are located from Florida to Alaska and are widely scattered in the West, especially in the Southwest, the Dakotas, and Oklahoma. Here, again, the plane will facilitate contacts between headquarters and field operators by providing rapid travel to remote and more or less inaccessible areas. The Commission of Indian Affairs believes that the airplane may eventually bring about a change in the size of the administrative units.

The medical care of the Indians, like that of all peoples in remote areas, will be affected by aviation. Physicians can cover far larger territories more frequently by using aircraft, and the hospitalization of patients is accomplished much more easily and quickly by planes, and, no doubt, will be further facilitated by the helicopter. Under certain conditions, aircraft may enable Indian schools to be more centralized, affording economies of building construction and other benefits.

The jurisdiction of the Office of Indian Affairs extends to Alaska, where the airplane is the established method of transportation. It is thought that the helicopter will be of value in herding reindeer in Alaska and protecting them against predators. On the unfavorable side, it is also possible that, with a wide use of helicopters, non-Indian trappers and hunters might encroach more easily upon Indian hunting territory, and thus seriously interfere with their limited means of support.

The Office of Indian Affairs has an inter-American program of co-operation, which, like all plans for co-ordinated action over large areas, will be favored by aviation. Roads are often bad or nonexistent in much Indian territory, especially in Latin America, and aviation ought to facilitate greater communication.

Bureau of Mines

The Bureau of Mines may not be affected by aviation as much as other bureaus and services of the department. The engineers of the Bureau of Mines have already made effective use of airplanes in their search for metals which were greatly needed during World War II. The use of aviation has been especially great in Alaska and also in other areas outside the continental United States. Another use of aviation by the Bureau of Mines is likely to be in mine rescue work, and in the investigation of explosions where the time element is very important.

The Department of Agriculture

The administrative work of the Department of Agriculture is as far-reaching geographically as that of the Department of the Interior, and hence air travel presents opportunities of savings in travel time and costs, and also of increased contacts between the department in Washington and the field work and its representatives.

The two most important uses of airplanes in agriculture have been for pest control and for aerial photography. The use of aerial photography has already been discussed in this chapter. The problem of pest control has been discussed more fully in the chapter on the influence of aviation on agriculture. Pest control is a function of both private enterprise and government. The government's exact future rôle in the work is not yet determined, nor can it be definitely foreseen.

There are at present about two hundred privately owned planes engaged in dusting work, and very probably the growth of the work of dusting and spraying by private companies will expand. On the other hand, it seems reasonable to think that governmental planes may be used for combating emergency outbreaks of pests, especially where the danger is regional rather than merely local. It is also likely that government will continue to do experimental and research work with different kinds of sprays and for different kinds of pests. Pest control is a problem more far-reaching than that of an individual farm, and effective spraying or dusting by plane can be done only over large areas. Since the interests affected are so much wider and greater than the individual farmer's, it may well be that public opinion will demand a considerable extension of governmental work in this field of a service nature, beyond experimental and research activities.

A related problem of the Bureau of Entomology and Plant Quarantine is the prevention of the introduction of new pests from other lands. This problem has already been discussed above and also in the chapter on agriculture. For some time, studies have been carried on of the insects in the upper air and of the transportation of insects by planes and the methods of fumigation and control. Thorough inspection of planes from foreign lands will be enforced, but, in spite of this precaution, some new pests may be introduced. When a pest is introduced, if the government as a co-ordinated agency can act sufficiently fast, the pest may be exterminated before it can spread and become common.

The Forest Service of the Department of Agriculture has already given much attention to the use of planes for fire-detection, for transporting men and material for fire-fighting either to nearby airports or for dropping them by parachute, for directing firefighters, and in bringing food and first aid to the scene of the fire. The service is looking forward with much interest to the use of the helicopter, which would seem to be especially useful in forestry work because of its ability to hover in the air and to land in small places which are not prepared landing fields.

The use of the airplane and the helicopter for seeding and fertilization has been discussed in the chapter on agriculture. It is not clear, however, what rôle the government may play in rendering such services, aside from some research work in pollinization, tests in distributing fertilizer by air, and in experimentation on aerial seeding.

In considering the function of the government in these fields in the future, it should be recalled that the work of the Department of Agriculture has been phenomenal in its help to farmers; that, for a long time, farmers have had one of the most effective lobbies in Congress; and that, throughout the United States, there is a very strong sentiment toward preserving and sustaining farming as a way of life, especially for the small farmer. Furthermore, there is at present little fear that the government will go into farming and compete for a market at lower prices, as is feared in manufacturing and transportation. Hence this source of sentiment against governmental expansion in aid to farmers does not exist. In general, there is considerable probability that, if aircraft can be used by the government to help farmers, the government will so aid them.

Public Health

We have spoken of how the United States Public Health Service has already had its work affected by aviation in the protection of the health of the population from sources of infection, particularly malaria and yellow fever, on incoming planes from other countries. Some 13,000 airplanes were inspected in 1943 at ports of entry, and 153,881 passengers examined. Naturally, this work will increase with the expansion of international aviation, with a probable decrease in the number of steamships to be inspected by the quarantine officers. The inspection of ships may be speeded by transporting the health officers to the ships by means of helicopters.

The Public Health Service is also charged with suppressing epidemics and the spread of disease. In the case of disasters such as fires, floods, tornadoes, and storms, the speed of the airplane in transporting food, supplies, and medical aid is of distinct advantage. The helicopter will be useful in getting supplies and aid into otherwise inaccessible areas.

The service has very extensive promotional programs, involving co-operation with state health departments and with various civic agencies. Air transportation will be of great help in such co-operative work, as it will also be in the service's administration of hospitals and hospitalization, particularly of merchant seamen, and also with the prompt collection of health records.

Coast Guard

The United States Coast Guard, with a civilian force of five thousand, has charge of patrolling harbors and coast lines, maintaining lighthouses, operating an ice patrol, and inspecting foreign ships. The Coast Guard had, in 1944, ten air stations, fifty planes, and a few helicopters. Its inspection and rescue work will be greatly helped by more extensive use of the helicopter, as also will its work of law enforcement, harbor patrol, supervision of waterways, regattas and boat-races, and checking aids to navigation. With the airplane, the Coast Guard performs rescues at sea, in addition to rescues along the shore. This work has come as a result of the war; but in peacetime, with many civilians being carried by plane across the oceans, particularly between Europe and America, there will be need for some air-sea rescues. The Secretary of the Navy has requested the Coast Guard to establish an air-sea rescue agency to study new equipment, methods, and techniques for such work. Larger and more powerful amphibious aircraft, equipped with electronic equipment, will replace surface vessels to some extent in the work of the Coast Guard in ice observation, Bering Sea patrol, search and rescue work, and fast transportation of personnel and equipment.

The Department of Commerce

Several activities of the United States Department of Commerce have already been reported as being affected by aviation, notably the Coast and Geodetic Survey and the Weather Bureau. The agencies entrusted with the development and regulation of aviation, namely, the Civil Aeronautics Board and the Civil Aeronautics Administration, are also in this department. However, the future organizational nature of the government's sponsorship of aviation is not fixed, and it might well be an independent commission or even a department some time in the future.

Another branch of the department that must take aviation into account in its function and activities is the Bureau of Foreign and Domestic Commerce, particularly as aviation affects foreign trade. The bureau will be affected by some aspects of the future rulings of air transportation and the distribution of goods in domestic and foreign markets. The Bureau of Standards is constantly engaged in researches in materials which are demanded by advancing aviation technology. In the postwar years, the Reconstruction Finance Corporation and the Export-Import Bank will be concerned with long-term credits in the sale of aviation equipment to other nations. Air travel will promote greater co-ordination of the work of all the divisions of the Department of Commerce, particularly those having agents in foreign countries.

Mail

The effects of aviation on the work of the Post Office Department have been discussed in the chapter on air mail. The use of air mail by the administrative agencies will affect many of their particular services. Timeliness, for instance, is an important factor in the publication of index numbers by the United States Bureau of Labor Statistics, in the collection of health records of the United States Public Health Service, in sample reports of the Bureau of the Census, in handling records for the Civil Service Commission, and in collecting records for the Office of Education.

Air Contacts with Other Countries

Various bureaus and services will have their duties affected by increased contacts with other countries. In the work of the Office of the Co-ordinator of Inter-American Affairs, aviation will speed the travel of technicians, students, diplomats, delegates to conferences, and other personnel interested in inter-American affairs from distant points to central areas and back again. It will also facilitate the transportation of films, books, and other educational materials in the Americas. The success of the "Good Neighbor" policy depends to a large extent on mutual understanding, which will be furthered greatly by aviation. Aviation may do for Latin America and for inter-American relations what the Rural Free Delivery did for the United States; that is, acquaint peoples with each other's customs, needs, and commodities and promote better relations.

In the case of the Labor Department, it is interesting to speculate on whether international air travel will mean that labor leaders of the United States will become better acquainted with labor leaders and labor movements in other countries. The International Labor Office at Geneva, prior to World War II, was an effective organization in holding conferences and collecting and publishing data in an effort to promote better labor standards. As trade and travel become more widespread, labor standards in other countries become important factors in competition. The United States Bureau of Labor has been interested for a long time in international labor problems. The airplane may increase its work in the international field of labor.

Aviation will also create closer linkages between the homeland and ambassadors, ministers, chargés d'affaires, commercial attachés, and other representatives of our government in other countries. The cable, telegraph, radio telephone, and fast steamship mail have already served to speed and increase contacts. With aviation, it will be very easy to call an ambassador from his post for conversation with the Secretary of State or the President. These contacts reduce the individual initiative of our representatives abroad, such as that exercised by Franklin and Jefferson when travel was slow, and increase the control from the homeland. A somewhat more unified policy is now possible.

State Governments

The effects of aviation on the governmental activities of each of the forty-eight states need not be reviewed in detail. The administrative branches of the state governments in the United States are much like those of the federal government in structure. In many of these, uses will be made of aviation similar to those of the federal government, and modification of the state governments' work will take place accordingly. However, aviation will not affect state governments as much as it does the federal government, partly because the greatest advantages of the airplane are derived when it is used over large areas for large populations. But helicopters may be used for intrastate travel.

There has already been some use, on a small scale, of aviation by the state governments. For instance, the State Conservation Department of New York has been using airplanes in fighting fires in the state forests and parks, in planting fish, and in making various surveys. Other states have used planes in work on conservation of natural resources and wildlife. But such uses of aircraft have not been as extensive as those of the Department of the Interior of the federal government.

At the present time, the most active interests of state governments are in planning and promoting aviation, from the advantages of which states, like cities and nations, hope to benefit.

They are attempting to promote aviation by passing needed legislation, especially to provide for the laying-out of airports and the securing of other facilities. State aid and advice are often extended to cities and counties in their planning for landing fields. State aviation departments serve as centers of information and hold conferences on aviation problems. In some states, aviation education is sponsored in the schools.

Another activity of states in regard to aviation centers around state ownership of planes. Perhaps a quarter of the states own from one to a dozen planes, which are used for various purposes. In a majority of these states the planes serve various state officials in their work, sometimes on a rental basis to the departments using them. Common uses of state-owned aircraft are for airport inspection, educational work in air safety, for patrolling forests, reporting fires, transporting men and materials in fighting forest fires, stocking waters with fish, making wildlife surveys, and preserving of animals and birds by feeding them and by fighting predators.

In the future, we may expect that aircraft will be used, especially in the large states, to facilitate administration. In New York State, for instance, the Board of Parole spends about three weeks out of every month in travel to and from prisons. Helicopters could materially reduce the traveling time and improve efficiency. State police will find aviation useful in the apprehension of criminals and in traffic control. State boards of health are planning to take advantage of aviation for emergency work, for inspection of health conditions, and for general administration. State departments of agriculture will be able to use aircraft in some of the ways already discussed in connection with federal use. In general, the regulation and supervision of aviation seems likely to remain in the care of the federal government. Individual state regulation would create a great lack of uniformity.

Cities and Towns

Although cities, counties, and minor jurisdictions are too small for much flying within them, they have a major concern in the location, construction, and management of landing fields. This administrative activity of local governments is expected to be an important development in the years to come.

Of the other administrative branches of the city, the police will be most radically affected. The use of aircraft by the police has been more fully discussed in other sections of this book; but here it might be stated that small aircraft will be used somewhat as police automobiles are now used. When equipped with electronic devices, guns, and cameras, and traveling fast at heights that vastly increase the field of vision, they will be important aids to law enforcement. New York City has operated its own planes for the past fifteen years. One use has been for the capture of criminals. Another has been to direct automobile traffic by means of two-way radio, and to enforce the traffic rules for airplanes regarding altitude of flight. In the future, in cities which have many landing places for helicopters some direction in landing will undoubtedly be needed, and regulations about lanes of traffic, direction of movement, height and speed of flight, and so on, will need police use of aircraft. Other uses by the police will be in the rescue of persons and stolen and lost property, as has been the case in New York City. There are likely to be many miscellaneous uses, such as escorting visitors — an early use in some cities — use in crime surveys, in photography, and possibly in quelling riots.

The fire departments of cities should find the helicopter of use in fighting fires because of its ability to fly vertically in narrow quarters or to hover. Helicopters will have sufficient power to lift the necessary weight of equipment for fire-fighting. They will also prove useful in obtaining a quick, comprehensive view of large fires and, equipped with two-way radio, will be of value in directing fire-fighters.

City boards of health will not have as great a need of aircraft as do the state boards or the United States Public Health Service. They may play a rôle in the inspection of planes in conjunction with federal authorities. An occasional use, especially in emergencies, may be for the transportation of dairy inspectors to surrounding milk sheds. The problem of air pollution, especially by smoke, can be attacked by the use of aircraft, making possible the immediate reporting by radio of heavy outpourings of smoke, and by their use in determining the sources, travel, and location of gases, smoke, and fumes in the atmosphere.

Conclusion

The general effect of aviation on the administrative work of government will be to strengthen and to expand it in line with general trends. Aviation is a new industry that is singularly close to government in sponsorship, promotion, financing, regulation, and ownership. In addition, there are many and varied uses to which aircraft will be put by the departments and bureaus of the federal and state governments. In some cases, these uses mean virtually the creation of new activities, as in aerial photography; in other cases, the nature of the activity will be radically altered, as in the transportation of mail. Sometimes, the effect will be to extend the work of the central government into local areas, as in policing and in health measures. Occasionally, quite new problems are created, as in combating diseases of human beings, plants, and animals which are brought in from foreign lands by airplanes. In short, aviation presents to government administration opportunities for greater efficiency and usefulness.

34

International Relations

AVIATION, with its bombers in war and its long-range transports in peace, must necessarily have profound influences on the relations of nations. These possible influences concern important issues. Can aviation be directed as a force to prevent wars, or must wars become more frequent and more destructive? Does the airplane bring the vision of a world state more nearly to realization, or will it accentuate national rivalries? Can we use the increased contacts brought about by air travel to build a spirit of international good will and to develop a feeling of brotherhood among the peoples all over the world? The statement of these possibilities in the form of questions suggests that we do not think of aviation's influence as inevitable, but rather that the airplane represents a force to be directed to serve the great hopes of mankind. In any case, it seems desirable to break the treatment into two parts. This chapter will present the trends in international relations as affected by aviation, assuming that no unusual planning and no exceptional effort will be made to change them. These trends are thought to be the result of the more or less deterministic forces of history. What is likely to be done to bend these trends to our desires will be the subject of the chapter which follows. In that chapter, we shall mention various policies and offer some discussion of the probability of their success.

In this chapter, the trends of international relations are seen largely in terms of the evolution of states in size. In the past, this evolution has been restricted by the limitations of communication systems. Within these limits, increases in the size of nations have often been achieved by conquest. Obviously, the airplane affects this process. But states are not only political and military organizations; they are also societies with many ties binding the members into a social coherence. To have some assurance of endurance, states must become like communities as well as organizations of power. Aviation also has the potentiality of aiding in the knitting of peoples closer together into larger states. Thus, the present size of states and the present status of aviation will be seen at their proper place in the evolution of states. Such is the outline of the chapter.

Increased Contacts Between Nations

Aviation is, of course, a new form of contact between the peoples of different nations and between the political representatives of states. Though it be a new form, the implication does not follow that there will be an increase in contacts, for aircraft may merely take travelers away from steamships and railroads rather than create new traffic. But, in Chapter 13, it was shown that international aviation is likely to increase quickly the actual travel between nations because of the great saving in time over that required by the boat. In later decades, the increase may be very great if the fare is reduced sufficiently. We conclude, therefore, that aviation will multiply the number of contacts between nations.

These contacts vary in nature. Business and tourist travel will be the most common types. The prospects of increased travel for investment and for reasons of business are very good indeed. The trips to other lands of agents of economic organizations may work out to increase strong linkages between nations. Tourism is a business, too; and with tourists the attitudes are often those of good will.

The value of contacts made possible by transportation depends very much on a common language. Not to be able to converse is a serious barrier to contacts between peoples. Hence travel will be selective by nations for linguistic reasons. The values of contact will be the greater for this reason between the United States and Britain than between the United States and the Soviet Union.

It is possible that there will be a growth in the use of Basic English, with its easily learned vocabulary of 850 words.

Friendliness or Friction

The mere multiplication of contacts between peoples may be good or bad, depending upon whether such contacts lead to friendliness or to friction. Statistics on the number of contacts give little idea of their meaning. Thus, the French have had close contacts with both the English and the Germans and have fought each many times.

In analyzing this question, the influence of distance should be removed. For instance, France has fought Germany, with whom she has had many contacts, more often than she has fought China, with whom she has had few contacts. We might, from this illustration, draw the conclusion that many contacts lead to war and few contacts to peaceful relations. But China has been too far away to fight. If China and Germany were equally close to France, the comparison would be more relevant, and even more so if they were of the same size.

One of the keys to the question of whether more frequent contacts lead to co-operation or to conflict is understanding. It is very difficult to understand a stranger, or a people living in isolation. We therefore cannot, in our imagination, put ourselves in the place of others. Understanding in industrial relations is considered by many experienced observers to be the key to the solution of difficulties between capital and labor. The idea is to get representatives of management and of unions sitting around a table, talking out their problem, until they reach an understanding. It must be said that an understanding is not always reached, and strife results. Yet the conference, with its contacts, is held to be a good step toward an understanding.

Friction comes from a conflict of interests, exploitation, a disregard of the rights of others. For interests to conflict, there must generally be some contacts; but, when interests conflict, we do not want to understand, and we rationalize our selfishness by misunderstandings. Hence we can have close contacts and friction.

The travel by aviation, particularly by representatives of business in our times, is likely to be the key to co-operation or conflict. Free trade by individuals between nations is generally credited with leading to peaceful relations; and, even more, to creating bonds that are barriers for war makers to overcome. On the other hand, trading by nations as a group, or by representatives of private concerns strongly backed by governments, is more likely to lead to national conflicts. So, also, are attempts to monopolize natural resources in another land or to close the door of a region to another trading nation. If aviation becomes a tool of national interests in prosecuting trade and investment along monopolistic practices, it would be more likely to lead toward national conflict than if it is used by individual traders.

Regional Contacts

The number of contacts which aviation will bring between peoples is a function of distance. Thus, more persons from the United States will visit Canada by air than will visit the more distant India. By air, it does not take much time to go to Calcutta, but it does cost more money. Though the airplane is our most remarkable transportation invention in conquering distance, yet it is likely to be used much more frequently for relatively short-distance travel. At the present state of the invention, the most common distance traveled in the United States is less than five hundred miles. Distances of twenty-five hundred miles are much less frequently traveled. This general point — that is, that communication inventions increase local contacts more than long-distance ones — was discovered by Malcolm Willey and Stuart Rice [1] in studying the use of the post office, the telephone, telegraph, and cable. For each of these media, just as for the automobile, railroad, and aircraft, there are different definitions of local and long distances.

From this discovery, an important deduction is made for aviation and international relations. It is that the influence of avia-

[1] Malcolm M. Willey and Stuart A. Rice, "The Agencies of Communication," in *Recent Social Trends in the United States; Report of the President's Committee on Social Trends.* New York: McGraw-Hill Book Co., 1933, pp. 201-202.

tion, because of the added contacts it brings, will be felt much
more by neighboring nations than by more distant states.
Willey and Rice showed that, with modern communication
inventions, local contacts increased at a more rapid rate than
did the long-distance ones, even though there was a marked increase in the latter. If this should be the case with aviation, it
seems to have a meaning of great significance, namely, that the
forces of regionalism — that is, of organizing a group of nations in
a region — will be aided by aviation. These increased contacts
within a region may, as previously stated, lead either to co-operation or conflict. But there is reason to think, as will be indicated
more fully later in this chapter, that in some regions, where there
is a large dominating power at the center, integration rather
than disruption is likely to result. Thus, aviation is likely to increase the contacts of the United States with Canada, Mexico,
and the states around the Caribbean, perhaps in such a way as
to lead to a closer integration.

The Evolution of States in Size

Transportation and Area

The growth of states in size has been facilitated by transportation inventions. At one time the many political units were small
and their areas were only a few square miles. Such was the condition among the primitive hunters, who possessed very simple
tools and who had no other means of transportation than human
legs. The dog, the donkey, the ox, the horse, the boat, and the
railroad made possible political domination of larger areas. Today, by comparison, there are large states, such as Russia, which
includes within its domain one-sixth of the land area of the earth.
Over thousands of years, then, we may say that there has been
an evolution of states in size. Over this same period of time there
have been many advances in transportation. That the size of territory administered by a state is dependent upon transportation
seems, in general, a reasonable statement. Now comes the airplane. Will it lead to an increased size of the state?

Reversals in Trends

The question of the evolution in the size of the state must be examined for briefer periods of time than we have been considering and for exceptions to the thesis. At the outset, it should be observed that most movements, of whatever nature, that have been studied do not follow smooth trends. Rather, there are many up-and-down fluctuations around the trend. On this general theory, some periods of history will be expected to show states decreasing in size. Such, indeed, was the case in Europe during the latter part of the nineteenth century and after World War I.

Another apparent exception to the trend toward larger size is the break-up of empires, of which those of Genghis Khan and of Rome are examples. These large political aggregations seem to overreach themselves in size. The social coherence is not enough to maintain the exaggerated size of the total structure. The unity of a segment of an empire seems to become sufficiently strong to enable it to break away from the whole.

The explanation of these reversals of trends in size seems to lie in the weak linkages of communication between the parts of an empire or between the small units of a large state. These are not strong enough to resist the strength of the smaller units in which the linkages of communication have in time become stronger, closer, and more frequent. This explanation will be discussed later.

Conquest

The growth of transportation and communication does not, *ipso facto*, create states of larger size. Nor will aviation do so, alone. Rather, transportation and communication lay the foundation for greater size. The actual creation of more extended boundary lines for political units is often achieved by conquest, though it sometimes occurs by marriage between ruling families or by contract, as was the case of the thirteen states which formed the United States. Even in this instance a war and threats of wars of conquest were factors in bringing about a larger state. The growth in size of political units is not a gradual process of accretion, like the slow building of a sand dune; it is, rather, a series of sudden changes brought about by crises of war.

The airplane may be viewed as a possible agent in creating the crises of conquests. The horse, a transportation agency, promoted conquests in earlier stages of history.[2] This animal was unknown to the American Indians; but, after its introduction by the Spaniards, the range of contacts of Indian tribes was greater, and the impingement of these enlarged circles of travel of the tribes on one another led to much warlike activity.[3] The automobile and the railroad were not the cause of conflicting areas of operation to the same extent as was the boat. The boat and the horse were both tools of war, as well as of peaceful transport. They were particularly effective in war when one side possessed them and the other did not. The airplane has the possibility of conquest and enlargement of jurisdiction over territory, as did the horse and boat. But, since many other factors are involved, it should not be said that aviation will lead inevitably to the enlargement of the state, though there is that possibility.

A World Organization

These analyses raise the question as to how large an organization aviation could make possible. Could it support a world organization? Questions of this nature have been considered by Hornell Hart,[4] who relates size of state or empire to the speed of transportation existing at the time. His measurement in trend lines indicates the possibility of a world government, with the present speeds of flying, by the middle of the present century. If the horse with its speed would support an empire of the extent of that of Genghis Khan, and if the boat and good roads would permit the great size of the Roman Empire, then the speedy airplane would carry an organization very much larger than either, indeed, of world dimensions.

[2] J. L. Myres, *The Dawn of History.* New York: Henry Holt and Co., 1911, p. 105.

[3] Clark Wissler, "The Influence of the Horse in the Development of Plains Culture," *American Anthropologist,* vol. 16, 1914, pp. 1-25.

[4] Hornell Hart, *Can World Government be Predicted by Mathematics?* Ann Arbor, Michigan: Edwards Brothers, 1943, pp. 1-16.

Such a world organization might come about by conquest, in a stupendous war in which one side possessed a great superiority in the flying atomic bomb. Or it could come about by agreement. Indeed, after the World War I, the League of Nations was formed of nearly all the nations of the world. So, again, a United Nations may evolve into an organization comprising all the peoples of the earth.

To state the possibility of a world political organization is different, of course, from saying that it is probable at the present time, though of course there does exist the charter of a United Nations. To discuss, at this point, its probability would take us far afield and bring in many other factors.

Furthermore, the problem of forming a political organization to include all the peoples of the world is different from the problem of making it endure. Large states, empires, and confederations have been formed, but have, in the course of time, broken up. So, also, did the League of Nations, and so may a United Nations or a single world sovereign state. To resist disintegration a large organization must have social coherence within its structure. How this solidarity is affected by aviation is the subject of the next section.

Growth of Social Cohesion of States

The strength of union is a matter with which the peoples of the United States have had much experience. An early saying at the time of the Revolutionary War when we separated from England was, "United we stand, divided we fall." Later, we fought a long and sanguine war to maintain union. We ought not, therefore, to be easily deceived by the allure of world union.

Solidarity

The bases of unity have long been studied by sociologists, notably Herbert Spencer and Franklin H. Giddings.[5] They noted

[5] Herbert Spencer, *The Principles of Sociology.* New York: D. Appleton & Co., 1886; Franklin H. Giddings, *Democracy and Empire.* New York: The Macmillan Co., 1901.

the obstacle of heterogeneity to unity and the facilitation of unity by resemblances and similarities. Peoples who speak the same language have greater solidarity than those confused with the babble of tongues. Particularly is "concerted" action an evidence of unity; it is a manifestation of "like response to stimuli." The threat of a war from European powers upon the weak thirteen colonies after they had won independence from Britain was a stimulus to which they responded, in a like manner, by a concerted action to pool their interests in a single national effort. So, also, we tend to be alike to the extent that similar stimuli play upon us. Dark skin color is found in tropical areas, a like response to the sunlight. Members of occupational classes resemble one another because they are subject to the same stimuli. Then, too, there is the phenomenon of imitation. Children learn by imitation, and if we imitate each other we tend to be alike.

Such, then, are the social psychological bases of group solidarity. They depend, in the last analysis, upon contacts, and very probably the degree of unity is a function of the frequency of these contacts. There is not solidarity between two strange peoples living in relative isolation. These principles are relevant to the size of states and to the airplane's rôle in supplying contacts.

Unity and the Size of States

It is easy to see how a small community of, say, twenty-five families will have many similarities and much unity. They speak the same language, and their children are subjected to like stimuli. There is a communality of interest. They see each other face to face many times a day. In such a small village in New Mexico, El Cerrito, sociologists [6] observed that the number of visits per day was of the order of twenty to thirty among parents in the twenty-five families, and that, if a parent was not seen throughout the day, the assumption would be that he was sick, and he would be visited to see what was the matter. The number of contacts in a small village are many and tend to produce a likemindedness. There is no problem of social coherence.

[6] O. Leonard, and C. P. Loomis, "Culture of a Contemporary Rural Community, El Cerrito, New Mexico." *Rural Life Studies, 1,* United States Department of Agriculture, 1941, p. 42.

The problem of social coherence arises when the area is larger than a village. If there were no other means of transportation than human feet, it is difficult to see how social coherence could extend over a large area. In larger areas, the contacts necessary for social coherence are made by the various means of communication and transportation. These are donkeys, dogs, travois sleds, roads, carts, canals, boats, carriages, printing presses, railroads, libraries, post offices, typewriters, telephones, telegraphs, cables, radio broadcasts, automobiles, and airplanes. With such aids, the same stimuli can be common over a large area, and the solidarity that comes from like response to stimuli may exist for great distances.

For unity to exist over extensive territory, these communication devices must operate frequently and reach large numbers. Thus the same newspapers must be read daily by the whole population. The communication inventions must, then, be in frequent use to attain, over a large area, a social cohesion approximating that of a small village. Along with this idea of the need of frequent contacts, there should also be included a second idea of great importance. It is that of a common language. For, without a common language, contacts have little significance. Without such social cohesion, large states and empires fall apart, for it is easier to obtain political sovereignty over a large area by conquest and with the exploitation of a transportation invention than it is to secure social cohesion. It is easy for political states to become overexpanded. The airplane may favor just that procedure. A world organization will be easier to obtain than will be the social cohesion necessary to hold it together.

Esprit de Corps

In the preceding discussion, the implication seemed to be that frequency of contacts lead to agreements, whereas, actually, they also lead to disagreements, despite similarities of language and habit. The problem of conflicting loyalties and antagonistic interests is a serious one in maintaining the necessary unity to keep a large state together. To this end, there is built up to overcome local interests and lesser loyalties an *esprit de corps* for the whole.

In states, we sometimes call it patriotism. In modern times it is sometimes referred to as nationalism. This collective morale for a large area is in danger from time to time of being superseded by a loyalty to a smaller group or a subsidiary cause. Thus, in China, loyalty to family is said to be an obstacle to nationalism.

Esprit de corps is a function of contacts, and hence of transportation and communication. Such a loyalty for a large group over a great area rests upon transportation agencies. Without these, nationalism is difficult to build. Yet the greatest success in building an *esprit de corps* probably lies in group rivalries. Few methods can equal a war in developing patriotism. Then, local loyalties are readily made subsidiary to the all-pervading nationalism. Even so, the nationalism of warring states will be more successful with radio, newspaper, literacy, and railroads.

So, then, social cohesion of states depends upon the number of contacts occurring through transportation and communication agencies and upon the development of the spirit of nationalism. A high development of both these forces leads to cohesiveness over a very large area.

Nationalism or Internationalism

The airplane flies easily and quickly across the boundary lines that separate nations. May airplanes then some day abolish nations and bring "one world" in their place? Perhaps, at some future time, the transportation and communication inventions may make "one world" possible, but they do not appear as yet to have made possible an adequate nationalism in some states with areas much smaller than the land area of the whole world. Indeed, a very pertinent question is whether the new communication inventions have yet succeeded in building nationalism in the limited areas of some modern states. If the national *esprit de corps* has not yet developed a cohesion in the smaller area of states, how can it cover the area of the whole world?

As an illustration, we may ask whether the curve of nationalism in a large South American state has yet reached its peak, or rather plateau. It is generally agreed that our South American neighbors have been experiencing a growing feeling of nationalism for the past two or three decades. But may not this feeling continue to grow for several more decades in the future? Agencies of transportation and communication are poorly developed in many South American countries. The large mass of Indian population in some of the countries is illiterate. The literate population tends to be concentrated in towns and cities on the coast rather than in the jungles and mountains of the interior. Roadways, other than those along the coast, are poorly developed. For Brazil, aircraft may be the basis for enhancing nationalism, rather than causing it to forsake its sovereignty and develop a spirit of internationalism.

The situation may be different in Belgium or Denmark, which have had good communication systems across their small areas for a long time. For them, the curve of nationalism may have reached its plateau, and they may be willing more readily to become members of a sovereign world state. The airplane links these countries with the world and increases contacts outside their borders. But in China and Russia aircraft may serve to increase the spirit of nationalism more than that of internationalism. In China, there were before the war only two miles of railroad per one thousand square miles, while in the United States there were eighty-four. In Russia there were six.[7] Furthermore, in the Soviet Union and in China there were less than twenty miles of improved highway per one thousand square miles, while in the United States there were four hundred and twenty-six. In these countries, aircraft will provide many of the contacts which the highways and the railroads fail to supply.

The analysis of the airplane's influence on the evolution of states has been based upon peacetime considerations, especially in increasing contacts over a larger area. So, also, has the effect of aviation on the spirit of nationalism and internationalism been considered only for the civilian uses of aircraft. But war makes definite contributions, not only in aviation's effect on the growth of states, but also in their interrelations. These will be discussed in the succeeding section of this chapter.

[7] *World Atlas*, Encyclopedia Brittanica, 1943, pp. 12, 137, 171.

WAR AND REGIONALISM

The air bomber is a very powerful instrument of warfare. Its power is a result of its speed, its long range, its ability to transcend barriers, and its terrible destructiveness on the enemy's cities, factories, transportation, ships, airplanes, and combat forces. With a weapon of such great potentialities in dealing out death and devastation, differentials in the possessions of these weapons may mean speedy victory or defeat. Hence nations are realigned as powers by virtue of their air power. Thus are international relations affected.

The Weakness of Small Nations

Outstanding in this realignment of military might among nations is the widening of the gap between the small and the large nations. The effect of the bomber is to make the big powers bigger and the little nations littler. The reason is that the small nation is helpless against the air attack of a big power. In World War II, air attack was made jointly with armored tanks. With these two types of mechanized war, small nations could withstand for only a few days or a few weeks the attack of a big power. In three days, Germany, with 6500 planes, destroyed most of Poland's 800 planes and all her airfields. In fifteen days, Germany wiped out the nation of Poland. In a similar manner, Germany quickly overran most of the lesser nations of Europe.

The small nations are not able to build an adequate defense against a big air attack. The best defense is fighter planes. But the development of such a defense is a huge undertaking. Nor can they build an adequate retaliating offense. On this subject, Hanson Baldwin says: [8]

> To put 1000 aircraft, mostly four-engined bombers, over Berlin, some 7000 to 12,000 men are required in the air, but at least 50,000 more are needed at the fields from which these bombers fly, plus other thousands on the various staffs, maintenance and

[8] Hanson W. Baldwin, "Air Power: What It Can and Cannot Do," *New York Times Magazine*, March 26, 1944, pp. 5-6.

repair depots, etc., and many, many more thousands training on the home front. If you lose 600 men on a raid over Germany, you must be able to replace them instantly. One formula for air power is planes times men; you must multiply the number of combat planes you want to operate by approximately 150 trained men if you want air power.

Back of the production of an air force is mass production of planes in a country that must be highly industrialized with the "know-how" and the necessary supply of metals and fuel.

The atomic bomb carried in a piloted plane or in a rocket hardly changes the situation on the evidence in hand now. For industrialization, capital, technique, and equipment are needed to produce atomic bombs, too, and also the vehicles to carry them. Furthermore, whatever the small nation can do in producing atomic bombs, the big powers can do as quickly and in much larger quantities.

As air power shows up the relative weakness of the little nation, so does it augment the power of the great powers. The large states, Russia and the United States and the British Empire, come out of World War II as the great powers. After the World War I, France, Italy, and Japan were considered great powers. With Europe as the main arena of war, the powers were not as large as in World War II, fought in two hemispheres.

The Pattern of National Feudalism

The position of the small nation in a war based on air power has been shown to be one of helplessness. How does this fact affect the status of the small state in peacetime? Its status will be different in a world living under the threat of war from what it would be in a world where war is banished. In a world with no thought or threat of war, a small nation could live contentedly and effectively in a state of security. But, if there are dangers of wars, the small nation must of course be aware of its insecurity, especially if it be in the path of the war machine, as were Norway, the Netherlands, and Poland in World War II. The small states of South America were but slightly affected, since they were not between the firing lines, as it was once feared they

might be. Living among these small states are great war powers
who may fight one another and thus start a world war or who
may go out to acquire more territory.

A somewhat analogous situation among individuals existed in
Europe in the age of feudalism. It was a time of insecurity, fighting, stealing, and murder. Property, too, was not safe. The powerful built themselves fortifications on hills where there was
protection. These wealthy farmers and warriors naturally acquired more property. They became more powerful, and the
little fellows weaker. Thus the overlord gave protection to the
little fellow, who bound himself for service to the protector. This
pattern of relationship between the weak and the strong, as
worked out in lawless feudal times, may serve as a model for the
relations of the large powers and the little nations.

The big power wants around its boundaries a zone of security,
into which no other great warlike power will venture. Surrounding these big powers, or near them, are strings or clusters
of lesser states. The big powers not only want these bordering or
near-by lesser states to be free of occupation and also of influences of another warlike power, but they want free and quick
passage through this territory in case of war. They do not wish
to be delayed by opposition, though brief, from neutrals who
may resist passage. Thus the United States does not want enemy
powers occupying South America or having undue influence
there. Russia does not want to be impeded by Poland in case of a
war in the West. If Belgium had been a military ally of France
and England, instead of a neutral, the offensive from France and
England in World War II would have been facilitated.

The situation looks different to the small state. Even though
nationalistic, proud, and sovereign, its weakness is realized. It
would like neutrality; but neutrality is increasingly difficult in
world wars. Even Switzerland had difficulty maintaining its neutrality in World War II. Norway, with its coveted long coast-
line, suitable for submarine bases, had no chance to remain neutral. If neutrality is impossible or highly improbable for the small
nation which lies near to the prospective battle-line, such a nation
wants to be free from invasion. It does not want to be a battle-

ground, nor does it want to be administered by an enemy power. It would like membership in a federation of states, if thereby the danger of war could be removed. But, failing the collective security of a world organization, it is natural that it will want, in a warlike world, to look for security from a power that can afford it the protection it so much desires.

The small nation will examine carefully and realistically the prospects of security's being actually realized in wartime. Poland and Czechoslovakia were not protected by any big power at the beginning of World War II. The small nation should be interested in whether its expected protector is adequately prepared to give protection. Presumably, if the Netherlands wishes help from Britain's navy in protecting her distant possessions, she will be interested in the strength of the British navy.

In feudal times, the small farmer paid for his protection by service. Similarly, the small nation can aid in a small way in its own protection. This can be done by articulating its military force with that of the power from whom it expects protection. Its air force, small though it be, can be joined with that of the big power. Its air fields can be loaned. Such co-operation in time of actual conflict, to be effective, must be extended to co-operation in the long years of preparation before the outbreak of hostilities. But, preparing for war means taxation, loans, construction of factories, as well as fortifications and conferences of military leaders. So, co-operation of economic ministries and state departments is needed, as well as that of war staffs.

The preceding paragraphs have been concerned with tracing the parallel of the big and little states with that of the lord and peasant in feudal times. All analogies break down if pushed far enough. The most obvious criticism of the pattern of feudal protection as being applicable to the present time is the difference in the social atmosphere. In feudal times, it was one of extreme ruthlessness. Threats of fire and sword were frequent. Now, big wars seem widely spaced. We are thought to be more humane, more "civilized." There is the ever present hope that war may be banished, that the whole world will live as friendly neighbors. Wishful thinking about collective security may preview a very close tie-in of big powers and neighboring states. Then, too, there is the resistance of cultural inertia, in the form of sovereignty, of nationalism, of "face saving" policies, of the spirit of freedom and independence. Again, to build up a military unit between the big powers and the near-by lesser states will be viewed by many as merely the preparation for, and even the guaranteeing of, another big world war; whereas we should be planning for peace, creating a spirit of internationalism, and, by giving up nationalism and limiting sovereignty, be dwelling in a collective security which will outlaw any movements toward warlike aggression.

Regionalism

Military aviation, plus other methods of mechanized warfare, has widened the differentials between the big powers and the lesser states as war potentials. The forces generated by preparation for war are driving toward a military union between a big power and the near-by small states. The result may be a military region, larger in area and in population than the big power. Unless the forces generated by the effort to attain a lasting peace become much stronger, then aviation seems to be pointing toward a regional military and political organization. We are interested in inquiring how closely knit this regional organization will be, and how enduring. Is it a step, in the evolution of states, toward greater size? Is this a necessary step in bringing about a well-integrated world state, a true "one world"?

Military alliances have been common in past history. Some have not endured; others have been the basis of larger states. In the case of relations of the central power with the small power, the *raison d'être* seems to be to provide speed of offense and some protection for both the big power and the smaller ones. These reasons rest on geographical position, which is stable. But the meaning is affected by the change of military invention. Thus, during World War II, the relationship between the big powers and the small ones rested in large part on the tank and the infantry, but also to some extent on the bomber.

There is, though, the idea that the next war will be fought

wholly in the air, and that, since planes fly quickly over intervening barriers such as the land area of small states, there is no great concern about the surrounding small states. Thus, the need of military understandings between the great power and the nearby smaller ones may not be necessary, when bombers fly 10,000 miles and rockets speed over great distances, both to drop atomic bombs.

Against this theory, it is remembered that similar claims were made for air power for World War II at its beginning. Yet the navy and the infantry and the tank corps were needed. Air power was added to, rather than used to supplant, other methods. Also, it was shown that, though airplanes could fly long distances, nevertheless the raids were more effective from close bases. Thus, though the military regional arrangements may at some time be outmoded by new inventions, it is by no means clear that such is the case from what we know of the long-range bombers and the rocket.

Another aviational influence that seems to strengthen the arrangements of the military region is the air base. Present plans of war powers call for a series of surrounding air bases.[9] These are of two kinds, those for use in conjunction with navies and those in the interior, away from the ocean. A ring of bases around a power is good for offense, since it places the planes or the rockets nearer the target. For defense, its value for detection is good, and it serves also for a take-off base for fighters in case the attacking air force flies near the base. Obviously, friendly neighboring states with adequate air bases on their outside borders are desirable to a power.

How will one sovereign power be able to have an air base in another sovereign state? It is the various terms making this arrangement possible which promote the integration of a region. These outlying air bases may be secured for use in a war by treaty, or they may be built on leased land, or special territorial rights may be granted. Thus the United States will need air bases in various states to the south, especially around the Caribbean, near the Canal Zone, and on the east coast of South America.

[9] George Weller, *Bases Overseas*. New York: Harcourt, Brace and Co., 1944.

Certainly, the location of bases in these states for use by the
United States in time of war will mean a closer integration of
those states with the United States. Such a step may even be
viewed as some surrender of sovereignty, though perhaps gladly
done.

That these military regional arrangements are not accidental or
dependent on a particular tradition or exceptional sentiment is
evidenced not only by the preceding analysis, but also by the
actual course of events. Russia's foreign policy shows very clearly
her determination to be surrounded by friendly territory. The
United States feels that she must have a neighborly relation with
Canada and Latin America. Indeed, a friendly England and
Western Europe are considered desirable, for regions are not all
circular, and their shapes are affected by travel routes which go
where there is traffic, whether they follow geometrical lines or
not. So, also, Britain is much interested in a friendly zone of
European states, as her statesmen have publicly announced. The
regional groupings are, then, being actively prosecuted.

Military coherence, in general, irrespective of a particular
region, is not enough to indicate emerging larger political organizations in the evolution of states in size. For these regional arrangements, to be enduring, must have a social coherence. Is
aviation in peacetime increasing the integration of regional
states?

During peacetime, a high degree of military co-operation in
planning means also a co-operation between economic, social, and
governmental organizations. Thus, there should be co-operation
in budget-making for military expenditures, in maintaining stable
currencies, and in adequate credits. The foreign policies should
be in harmony. Even the economy of the various states calls for
division of labor. The reason why military co-operation requires
civil co-operation of various institutions is that modern wars are
total wars, involving all social institutions. Another reason is that
preparation for war requires from six to a dozen years of peacetime effort, or longer. So the military co-operation of states, if
effective, necessitates a closer integration of the various non-mil-
itary organizations of a governmental and economic nature.

Aviation also makes possible more contacts between the peoples of near-by states in purely peacetime pursuits without any reference to war and to the preparations for war. A stronger social cohesion of a region is possible because of aircraft through interconnections of trade, business, investment, and travel. It appears, therefore, that the use of aircraft in war, in the preparation for war, and in purely civilian peacetime activities is leading toward a closer regional integration.

The process, however, must not be thought of as being particularly rapid. The trend toward states of larger size has been viewed in this chapter as occurring over great lengths of time. To unify a region, barriers of language and of sovereignty must be overcome. The state of Austria-Hungary never developed much social cohesion. Even in France today, there are provincial loyalties and dialects that hinder the spirit of nationalism. Indeed, in those states where there is much illiteracy and poor roads, the airplane's influence will be more toward aiding in the social cohesion within the state than toward producing a cohesion between states. The evolution of states in size is a slow process, though it is becoming more rapid.

Conclusion

The natural influence of aviation, at this particular time in history, unless counteracted, is to speed the evolution of states into still larger size. The process of the growth of states in size is a slow one and usually proceeds by intermittent crises involving conquests. Aviation may even facilitate a single political organization of the peoples of the world. Empires and very large states have been formed before, to be broken up later. To endure, states need a social coherence as well as a political structure, a social coherence somewhat like that of a village community. The function of the transportation and communication inventions is to enable the peoples of a large area to possess such a solidarity, depending on the degree of development of the use of these inventions. This cohesion is strengthened by an *esprit de corps* which has priority over the separatist's loyalties of smaller units. In general, the size of political units has evolved faster than their solidarity. Aviation will aid in achieving a stronger unity. At present, many states, particularly those with much illiteracy and poor roads, have expanded their size politically so far that the cohesiveness is weak. In these states, the curve of increasing nationalism has not yet reached a plateau. Under such conditions, aviation is likely to develop nationalism more than internationalism. The next immediate step in the evolution of size is that of aviation's aid in organizing the states in a region into a military union, assuming threats of wars in the future. This development will occur because of the increased disparity in military potential between the small states and the big powers. This relationship in the present warlike world tends to follow somewhat the feudal pattern. The near-by small states want protection and the neighboring big power, with the capacity of affording protection, wants a zone of security around it for defense, for speed of offense, and for air bases. Hence, an integration of the military forces of a region is a logical step but for which there are many resistances. Because wars in the future will be total wars, military integration implies some economic, social, and political integration, too. The peacetime uses of aviation tend to aid the cohesiveness of a region on the principle that aviation will increase long-distance contacts less than contacts over shorter distances with neighboring states. Thus the trend is toward large regional organization.

35

International Policies

IN THE PRECEDING CHAPTER, the influence of aviation on the relationship of nations was considered in terms of trends rather than policies. The subject of this chapter is the modification of these trends by planning and control, not in a general sense, but with particular reference to the instruments of aviation. It is impossible to formulate policy completely on a scientific basis because attitudes of individuals, as well as nations, are always affected by subjective factors as much or more than by the objective facts of the phenomena. In following these pages, the reader will be affected by his own personal attitude toward history and social evolution. Some will see social trends as an inevitable march of social forces. Others will have great faith in man's power to make what he wishes of the future under the leadership of great men. We shall consider some of the possible international policies, the forces working for or against them, and some of the results which may be expected from these various policies.

In the preceding chapter, aviation was shown to be a force in the direction of an integration of states into larger units. It is thought that this process will bring about a regional grouping of states bound by numerous ties into a greater unity than among present-day nations. This integration necessarily is slow, taking place by periodical crises of conquests, with a single world community still far in the future. Most important of the ties holding a region together is the desire for protection and power in a world where wars are probable. Aviation encourages this regionalism by widening the gap in power between the large nations and the small ones, and by increasing the bonds between the central big power and the surrounding little states. Before a world state is achieved, there may occur a world government by conquest or by federation, but conflicts of local interests and civil wars are likely to break up such a world empire or federation until a more enduring world community evolves. This will be the trend, if the process takes its natural course with little attempt at conscious control.

Types of Policies

Various attitudes are forming as to the functions and rôle of international aviation. They are the product of views held toward internationalism, toward government, toward war, toward business, toward freedom, and toward rights. These attitudes are grouped about three different policies. To mention these policies briefly will aid in discussing the various proposals and plans, since any one plan can be affected by all three policies; some may be in conflict and some in agreement.

Internationalism versus Nationalism

The attitudes on internationalism center largely around war and the way to prevent it. This desire to avoid war is generally implemented by a plan for a world international organization in which the members will find security by collectively restraining any aggressor from starting a war. The various issues on which there are national differences will be settled by international law. Underlying this structure is, of necessity, a foundation of good will among states, free from racial and national prejudices. In order to attain such an organization the participating states must give up sovereignty, and subordinate national interests which interfere with a collective world effort to maintain peace. The adherents of this attitude would use international aviation to further such a world organization.

In contrast, the attitude of the nationalist is to advocate power and prestige for his own state. He wishes to make his nation powerful enough to successfully defend its people if they are threatened or attacked by another state or an alliance of states. He would use the strength of national organization to promote the economic interests of its citizens in various parts of the world, and is not willing to sacrifice much of this power to a world organization. Most nationalists want to avoid war, but if they cannot, they want their nation to give a good account of itself. Nationalists would use aviation for increasing national power and prestige in international relations, for aiding the economic enterprises of their nationals, and for building military might.

Free Enterprise versus Regulation

Instead of regarding aviation as an instrument of national policy, there are those who consider it as a business enterprise only. The supporters of this policy want aviation to be open for vigorous promotion as are other businesses, unhampered by governmental regulations which would interfere with business procedures. They do not wish political uses of aviation to interfere with it as a business. They want national politicians and international organizations to let them alone, so they can run their business in their own way. This is an attitude which is frequent among American businessmen and which has been extended to international aviation. However, those who view international aviation solely as a business often are not reluctant to accept governmental aid in securing rights and franchises in other countries, or even in giving subsidies.

The opponents of this viewpoint see aviation not only as a public utility but as an instrument which would serve the larger interests of the state's position among nations. Hence, they believe that diplomatic and military policies should take precedence over business considerations. Furthermore, the supporters of the policy of regulation insist that a transportation system serves other businesses, and it should not exploit those businesses in its own interests.

Big Nations versus Small States

A third basic attitude on international aviation policy at the present time concerns the relation between small states and large ones. Power is very unequally distributed among the states of the world, and this inequality of power affects the distribution of responsibility and also of rights. The development of aviation seems to favor nations that have great expanse of territory and industrial wealth or large empires. Small states are at a disadvantage in acquiring the equipment for extensive air transportation systems and in maintaining globe-circling routes. If the sovereignty of small states is to be protected, specific policies to that end will be needed. Discussions of this problem are likely to occur in international aviation conferences and councils in the future. There is some fear of "economic imperialism," or regional domination by the great powers through international aviation. Because of the inequality in power, some small nations have unduly guarded their ownership of the air above them by closing it to travel by great airlines of other countries. Other small countries, desiring the advantages of air service, have welcomed the airlines of the larger nations, and have received the benefits of such service. International regulation of such things as routes and number of flights could be of aid to the small nations. Policies that discourage war and military preparation would be helpful in maintaining the sovereignty of small nations.

Aviation's influence in the relations of states can be guided by policies concerning international co-operation, business, and the status of small states. How greatly it will be modified is a question. Already these attitudes have been evidenced in agreements, conferences, and conventions on civil international aviation. The issues growing out of these meetings have centered around certain propositions and plans which will be considered in the remainder of this chapter. These concern the establishment of the freedom of the air, the formation of international aviation organizations, the practice of competition, and regionalism.

Freedom of the Air

As with nearly all other important inventions, there has been resistance to the adoption of the airplane.[1] One of the greatest obstacles to the development of international aviation has been the refusal of nations to permit airplanes to fly over their territory or to land on it. While we are technically capable of flying

[1] See Chapter 6, pp. 113-115.

anywhere, we are not capable politically of flying where we wish. There are diverse reasons for these restrictions: the desire of some nations to bargain for the right to use the air above them, uncertainty as to what the consequences of granting such freedom may be, fear that an outsider will gain a competitive advantage, traditional attitudes of guarding national possessions, and fear that flights over national territory will disclose information of possible military value.

In Chapter 13, it was predicted that airplanes in the future will fly across oceans and national boundaries wherever there is potential traffic. We are sure that this will happen, but only after a delay occasioned by nationalistic opposition. This lag will be due to the persistence of attitudes which were suitable to another and earlier age, and are not appropriate to the new Air Age.

A definite policy of action is needed to encourage international transportation by air between states. Such a policy would be the simultaneous declaration of the freedom of the air by many states, replacing the old method of making bilateral agreements over various periods of time. An effort was made to put this policy into effect at the International Civil Aviation Conference held in Chicago, November 1 to December 7, 1944. Representatives of fifty-four nations, including all the great Allied powers except the Soviet Union, attended this conference. The freedom of the air was outlined in five points, and the nations were invited to sign one or both of two agreements, the first including two of the points and the second including all five. The first is known as the transit agreement, or the "two-freedoms agreement." It gives the privilege to a foreign airline (1) of flying over a signatory country and (2) of landing for non-traffic purposes. The last three points are called the freedom-to-trade agreement. They include the right of (3) taking on and (4) setting down passengers and goods from and to the home state of the aircraft, and (5) from and to any other contracting country. Signatures of representatives from forty-six countries had been attached to the "two-freedoms agreement" by the autumn of 1945, and twenty-eight states had signed the "five-freedoms agreement." Further confirmations will be necessary and additional signatures will be needed, but obviously a good beginning has been made to free international aviation from nationalistic restrictions.

The granting of the third and fourth freedoms — that is, the right to receive and discharge passengers and goods to and from the home country of the plane — would mean little on most of the long routes, unless accompanied by the fifth freedom which grants the privilege of carrying passengers and goods between contracting parties but not within the boundaries of one nation. The addition of the fifth freedom is necessary because a long airline route cannot be run economically and efficiently unless passengers can be taken on along the way. For instance, on the airline from Miami to Buenos Aires, only 15 per cent of the passengers landing in the Argentine originated in the United States.[2] Schedules over this route would have to be infrequent to carry a full load from the United States to Buenos Aires.

It may be noted that these five freedoms do not include the privilege of cabotage, that is, the carrying of passengers and goods within the boundaries of a nation by a foreign airline. This traffic is reserved for domestic airlines, but bilateral agreements may be made for air traffic to be carried between cities within a country by a foreign company. This may very well be done by a small country without a good airline of its own; although the ambition of all countries, no matter how small, is to have their own airlines. At the Conference the British claimed that even the free granting of the fifth freedom would make impossible the building up of an adequate international traffic by locally-owned airlines in small countries.[3]

The granting of the fifth freedom by many states will probably have the effect of strengthening the big airlines of the large powers, although as the volume of international traffic increases, there will be more opportunity for a small nation to operate a long route. This effect on small nations could be offset by some policy of international allocation of routes, schedules, and traffic which would assign an adequate share to small nations.

[2] William A. M. Burden, "Opening the Sky," *Atlantic Monthly*, March, 1945, p. 52.
[3] *Ibid.*, p. 53.

International Organization to Facilitate Transportation

International aviation requires not only freedom of the air and planes that can fly long distances but also common rules of air navigation. For safe and efficient operation, international airlines must have uniform procedures and technical codes. For instance, planes should not be required to circle from right to left over the airport in one country, and from left to right in another. Ground radio facilities should be standardized so that planes would not need to carry a large number of receivers and transmitters. There should be standardization of markings and of their display, and uniform signals. Uniform codes for reporting meteorological information would facilitate flying across different countries. Similarly, aeronautical maps should carry the same symbols and the same tints for altitudes. More adequate records would be facilitated by the adoption of a uniform system of measurement, such as the metric system. Then too, there should be standards for preventing the spread of diseases by air travel, for the reporting and investigating of accidents, and there should be a sharing of expense in the search for lost planes.

This list indicates some practices which are essential for international air navigation, and they are not difficult to attain for they are removed from national ambitions. For example, uniformity in symbols on aeronautical maps should be easily achieved. Others will take more time; for instance, the adoption of a common metric system, or the establishing of high standards of inspection to prevent the spreading of diseases. But however great or small the difficulty, an international organization is required. At the Chicago Air Conference in 1944, twelve technical annexes of this type were drawn up and provision was made for an international body to administer, and revise or implement them. International agreement on technical codes will probably be the easiest to achieve, since they invoke a minimum of political complications.

International Organization to Regulate Business

International control of practices which affect profits and volume of air transport business, such as the assignment of routes and the regulation of schedules, is more difficult to achieve than the international control of the rules of air navigation. The most radical plan of achieving this control would place all international air business in one corporation of which the various nations of the world would be members. Such a proposal was made by the New Zealand representative at the Chicago Air Conference. A common enterprise of this nature between nations would be a long step toward world co-operation, a step in the direction of a world state. Little consideration was given to the proposal at the conference, for most nations were ambitious to have their nationals operate airlines flying their own flag. On this proposal, nationalism won over internationalism.

At the Conference the British proposed that the air transportation companies of the various nations be regulated by an international governing board similar to the Civil Aeronautics Board of the United States. This Civil Aeronautics Board assigns routes to the various airlines or denies them, determines the amount of pay for carrying the mail, and decides whether there shall be mergers of airline companies or competition between them. An international Civil Aeronautics Board would have similar powers. However, it would be difficult to establish an impartial board which would not be influenced by the purely national interests of the various states. The representatives on such a board would probably not be chosen as individuals, on the basis of their personal competence, but rather as representatives of their countries. Hence, the decisions of the board concerning routes, equipment, and schedules would be on the basis of national considerations. At the Chicago Conference the solution of this problem was sought in a formula which would solve automatically the assignment of schedules for the different national airlines. The attempt was not successful. If such a formula had been found, attempts at problem-solving in areas other than schedule-making would have been made. However, automatic formulae which would be impervious to national manipulation — if such could be found — would have limited scope in the management of any business.

The obstacles to organizing such an international regulatory body are not only the problems of national representation, but also an attitude of resentment on the part of business toward such regulation. This seems to have been the feeling of the representatives of the United States at the Chicago Conference. They favored giving American airlines freedom to go out and win as much business as they could without interference by international control. The result was that business and nationalism won over a policy of international co-operation.

International Organization to Control Business

There is also the possibility of another form of international co-operation, a form not favored by those whose objective is the abolition of war and the establishment of international good will. This is the type of co-operation among large business concerns popularly known as cartels, and often sponsored by national governments. International aviation in the first postwar decades may see the survival of a small number of large companies doing business over long routes between densely populated areas. They may enter into vigorous competition or, being few in number, they may come to agreements among themselves on rates, routes and other functions. The latter will be especially likely if the total volume of business should be small. Such understandings are a form of international co-operation, but it will be co-operation among a few nations only, for the many small nations without international airlines of their own will not participate. This co-operation of nations operating extensive airlines would further the business and interests of the particular nations involved, rather than those of smaller nations outside the orbit of these powers.

An Over-All International Organization

That these two far-reaching proposals of international co-operation — a world airline corporation and an international Civil Aeronautics Board — were not adopted at the Chicago International Civil Aviation Conference does not indicate a negation of international co-operation in general, but rather a rejection of two extreme proposals. Some degree of co-operation on the control of aviation through an international body is as inevitable as co-operation on technical air navigation rules. Such a co-operative body will handle matters less purely technical than those found in the annexes drawn up at Chicago, but yet will have little control over dominant national interests. Some of the problems which such a body will deal with are the investigation and reporting of accidents, the investigation and perhaps settlement of disputes, the surveying of the adequacy of facilities, the promotion of research, the filing of information on the various airline companies, possibly the obtaining of information on subsidies as well as on rates and tariffs, and perhaps the holding of conferences to avoid rate wars.

Plans were drawn up at Chicago for a provisional body which would become active when twenty-six states had ratified the Convention on International Civil Aviation. At the close of the war, a meeting of the Council of the provisional body was held in Canada, and a secretariat and a number of committees set up. This provisional body is expected to be replaced eventually by a permanent organization, consisting of an Assembly representing all contracting states, and a Council of twenty-one members. One of the aims of the organization is "to prevent economic waste by unreasonable competition," and the duties of the Council include the collection and publication of information about costs of operation and subsidies. At the request of any member state, the Council may investigate and report on any situation which threatens the development of international air navigation.

From this beginning, international co-operation and control of aviation is expected to increase, although there may be withdrawals and disaffections. Not all nations have joined the organization, and separate agreements between nations may be made outside the framework of the international organization. International co-operation will be most easily developed in standardization of navigation aids, research, investigation and publication, with excursions into the field of costs. Regulations that affect profits, business control, and national interests are more difficult to achieve. There is very little evidence as yet to indicate that any policy to subject nationalistic ambitions in international aviation will be effective, though from collaboration in collection, investigation, and publication there will evolve a co-operation based upon the restriction of nationalism and sovereignty.

Competition

The expected trend in international aviation, unless restrained, is for the large nations to have one, or several, airlines engaged in international transport, and for these national airlines to compete for trade and for the advancement of the business of their respective nations in other countries. Since national prestige is tied up with the international aviation of a country, international competition among airlines becomes national rivalry in addition to the struggle between businesses.

An important element of international aviation is the involvement of government. International airlines are not wholly businesses with the sole aim of making a reasonable profit and maintaining a good service, but tools for achieving national power and prestige. Until the present time, as shown in Chapter 2, both domestic and international aviation have been aided by government, by subsidies, provision of equipment, allotment of routes, engineering development, and the setting up of many different regulations. The international airlines further the interests of government in the promotion of foreign trade and investment in other countries, in acquiring sources of raw material, in the fast delivery of mail, and in the multiplication of ties and contacts with neighboring friendly nations. Because there is such a close relation between an international airline and its national government, a nation takes keen interest in the competition to which the airlines flying its flag are subjected.

One possibility in international air transport competition is a rate war which will bring the charge per unit below costs. Such rate wars have occurred in private business enterprises in the United States. For instance, at one time a railroad lowered the fare from New York to Chicago to one dollar for the purpose of driving competitors to either withdraw or sell out to the victor, who then expected to raise the rates above competitive prices.

In air transport competition between nations, such cut-throat competition which would force the competitor of another nation to consider withdrawing, would take on national significance. Probably many nations would meet the lowered rates by subsidy rather than by withdrawal. If it were foreseen that the inevitable result of such competition would be subsidization for all nations, a competitive war would be avoided, which would reduce rates far below costs for all. This danger is so well anticipated at the present time that such cut-throat competition may never occur. However, competition to attract customers, rather than to drive competitors out of business, may be sufficiently keen to reduce rates below costs, with the deficits made up from national treasuries, either directly or indirectly.

If competition follows this course, the effect may be that the small nation with limited resources will be discouraged from maintaining an international airline, and the large states will be favored. Another result may be that the airlines which are run with subsidies will be a charge on the public purse, and will cease to be motivated — as are most businesses — to keep costs below rates.

It is said that the intensity of competition is a function of the size of the prize to be obtained, other factors being constant. If great rewards are expected, competition will be keener. What are the rewards expected in international aviation? Eventually, airline business is expected to be much larger than that of the steamship lines because of lessened travel time and because air fares will be moderate. However, in the early years of international air travel, the traffic may not be large compared with prewar steamship travel, and there is danger of over-equipment, and hence, of expenses being more than revenues. This danger arises because nations will want to establish international airlines for political reasons, to advance the interests of business, and to be prepared to profit by the heavy traffic when it comes.

The possibility that the various states may be forced by competition to subsidize international air transportation at rates below costs could lead to an agreement of some form of international regulation of schedules. For instance, if planes are traveling with an average passenger load of less than 65 per cent of capacity, they would be required to reduce the number of trips made. The British made this proposal at the Chicago Conference in 1944, but it was not adopted. However, if airlines should be running at great losses there may be more pressure for such regulation by an international body. Otherwise the normal trend toward competition is expected to support the nationalistic ambitions and struggles among states.

In the United States, there has been much discussion of competition in international air transport, not with lines of other nations but between companies flying the flag of the United States. Public sentiment favors competition between several American airlines flying the international routes rather than a single American company in the international service. The Civil Aeronautics Board has given permission for three American companies to fly between the United States and Europe. It remains to be seen how much trade each of these companies will have, and whether subsidies, if they are granted, will be greater with three companies than with one. Even with one company, there would be competition from the airlines of other nations who will also fly these routes between Europe and the United States.

An interesting question is whether American international aviation will be more effective in competition with companies of other nations if there are several competing American companies, or if there is one "chosen instrument." Several competing American companies would probably follow a greater number of routes than one company would and if competition among them lowered fares, the United States would offer more competition to other nations than with a "chosen instrument" policy.

A review of the policy on competition in international aviation indicates that it will probably do little to encourage world cooperation among states, unless competition is made to become a stage on the road to international regulation or international cooperation. This may occur but there is no assurance that it will.

Regionalism

The trend of international aviation is to strengthen the regional grouping of states into a closer relationship. If one of the nations in a regional grouping is a great power and the others are small nations, the tendency in a warlike world is for the small nations to be dominated by the large nation, as was shown in the preceding chapter.

This relationship between the small nations and the large power will be affected by the policy adopted concerning the large power's ownership and operation of domestic airlines within the small countries. For instance, Pan American Airways has operated domestic lines in several South American countries, notably Brazil; and other South American lines are owned by foreign capital. In the past there has been little incentive, as a purely business proposition, for the operation of an airline in a small country since the costs have been high, the passengers few, and subsidies have been the accustomed practice of making up the deficits. But in the future, when a larger public patronizes the airways, domestic business in small countries may become an attractive business proposition, and there may be incentive for large aviation companies of foreign countries to seek franchises in small nations.

An international airline which will make more than one stop on its route through a foreign country, is a type of service which will probably develop. If domestic passengers and cargo can be carried between cities in the same country, it will be economically advantageous to the company, and it will provide additional schedules for the domestic traffic. If such a service is permitted, the international company might expand its operations to include stops off the main through route.

But it is not certain that small countries will want to permit foreign airlines to carry their domestic air traffic. In most of the small countries of the world, the spirit of nationalism has not yet reached its peak. Countries in which a strong spirit of nationalism prevails will want to run their own air transportation within their boundaries and will not look with approval upon operators from other countries. However, if there are friendly relations between the small and the large nations, and if the foreign operator can provide better services at lower fares, it is quite possible that small countries will permit their domestic airlines to be owned and operated by foreign companies.

Where an international aviation company operates a domestic line in another country, the concern of the parent government is very great. The capacities for good or bad relationships between the two nations are much increased. A foreign aviation company which handles the domestic traffic of another nation must have very close relations with the government in matters of rates, schedules, payment for the carriage of mail, employment of personnel, and in many other regulations. The profits of the foreign airline are contingent upon the actions taken by the government on these matters.

This relationship between the foreign airline and the government of a small nation may take on some of the aspects of the relation between public utilities — such as railroads or street cars — and the government in the United States. There has been a struggle for power between these public utilities and the government, which has resulted in a great deal of friction. In some periods, the companies have succeeded in exercising great pressure upon the government concerning rates and franchises. Sometimes this pressure has amounted to a virtual control, so that the government did the bidding of the public utilities. At other times, especially in the case of city governments, the government has dominated the public utility companies. The struggle for power to set rates and award franchises, which determines the vital issue of profits, has frequently been carried to the electorate.

One cannot foresee that such a struggle for power will arise between the government of a small nation and a foreign airline doing a domestic business, but certainly the possibilities do exist. The relationship may be worked out harmoniously in a neighborly way. But the association will be close — a point of importance in regional relationships. Since this close relationship is necessary, small nations which desire to maintain their complete independence will discourage the ownership of domestic airlines by foreign countries, or at least will see that the foreign-owned airlines are operated for the best interests of the small nation and with as little friction as possible.

Another factor which will affect regional relationships between a big power and small nations is the policy concerning military air bases. As discussed in the previous chapter, the trend is for the large central power to ring itself about with air bases some distance from its borders, in territory not previously under the rule of the central power. This demand for friendly neighboring states may be lessened by the potential use of atomic explosives carried in long range airplanes or rockets. In such an eventuality, the bordering states would not serve as protection, and their opposition as neutrals would not hinder the flight of airplanes or rockets over their country. However, the longer the distance a bomber must travel, the less effective it will be, and atomic warfare is not likely to supplant all other types of warfare for some time. Rather it will be added to navies, infantry, and tanks. So it is likely that an outlying ring of air bases could still be demanded, thus forcing the small nations into the orbit of the large powers.

This trend would be changed by the adoption of a policy of collective security on a world basis, such as the Organization of the United Nations. Such an organization could, it is argued, be strengthened by the airplane — through an air police force. Indeed, there are those who think that aviation, by this means, could be instrumental in breaking up regional trends and furthering world organization. On the surface, such a policy looks plausible. But it must be remembered that in a world organization of collective security, there will be strong local or regional interests and power systems centered around great nations. These interests will determine how large such an air police force shall be in relation to the size of the air forces of the powers, when and against whom it shall be directed. In other words, the large nations could render futile the power of a world police force if it were directed against a great power.

The control of aviation by a world-wide international organization might also make air bases unnecessary. A single aviation corporation might be formed in which the various nations would be stockholders. A suggestion of this type was made at the Chicago International Civil Aviation Conference, but the proposal was given little serious discussion at that time. These policies, which would make air bases unnecessary, involve the partial surrender of national sovereignty of the big powers which, of course, makes their adoption difficult.

Conclusion

The direction and control of trends in international civil aviation by policy are most successful under two conditions. First, policy is most effective in breaking down resistance to the rights of transit and trade when the old attitudes toward freedom of the seas and trade have survived into the Air Age. Second, policy is most easily achieved in setting up technical aids and rules to expedite flying. There are obstacles of language, different systems of measurement, and so on, but policy is facilitated by the relative absence of political implications. On the other hand, aviation policies are more difficult to effect within the near future which run counter to national rivalries and competition, which rest on organizations of collective security, which strengthen the position of small states, and which oppose regionalism and the evolution of the power of large states. In the long run policy in international aviation will prove more successful than now in developing co-operation in world government.

★ ★ ★

Bibliography

BOOKS

Air Age Education Series, Aviation Education Research Group, Teachers College, Columbia University. New York: The Macmillan Company, 1942. Especially

> *Human Geography in the Air Age,* George T. Renner.
> *Social Studies for the Air Age,* Hall Bartlett.
> *Globes, Maps, and Skyways,* Hubert A. Bauer.
> *Flying High,* Rose N. Cohen.
> *Wings for You,* E. A. Cross.
> *The Air We Live In,* George T. Renner and Hubert A. Bauer.
> *The Airport,* Charles K. Arey.
> *The Biology of Flight,* Frederick L. Fitzpatrick and Karl A. Stiles.
> *Mathematics in Aviation,* George Osteyee.
> *Education for the Air Age,* N. L. Engelhardt, Jr.
> *Geographic Education for the Air Age,* George T. Renner.
> *Aeronautics in the Industrial Arts Program,* Gordon O. Wilber and Emerson E. Neuthardt.
> *Physical Science in the Air Age,* J. G. Manzer, M. M. Peake, J. M. Leps.

Armstrong, Harry G., *Principles and Practice of Aviation Medicine.* Baltimore: Williams and Wilkins Company, 1939.
Bruno, Harry, *Wings Over America.* New York: Robert M. McBride and Company, 1942.
Burden, William A. M., *The Struggle for Airways in Latin America.* New York: Council on Foreign Relations, 1943.
Cleveland, R. M., and L. E. Neville, *The Coming Air Age.* New York: Whittlesey House, McGraw-Hill Book Company, 1944.
Daggett, S., *Principles of Inland Transportation,* 3d edition. New York: Harper and Brothers, 1941.
David, Paul T., *The Economics of Air Mail Transportation.* Washington, D.C.: The Brookings Institution, 1934.

Davy, M. J. B., *Air Power and Civilization.* London: George Allen and Unwin Ltd., 1941.

Frederick, John H., *Commercial Air Transportation.* Chicago: Richard D. Irwin, Inc., 1943.

Gemmill, Chalmers L., *Physiology in Aviation.* Charles C. Thomas, 1943.

Gilfillan, S. C., "The Prediction of Inventions," in *Technological Trends and National Policy.* Washington, D.C.: National Resources Planning Board, 1937.

Gilfillan, S. C., *The Sociology of Invention.* Chicago: Follett Publishing Company, 1935.

Gregory, H. F., *Anything a Horse Can Do: The Story of the Helicopter.* New York: Reynal and Hitchcock, 1944.

Grow, Malcolm Cummings, and Harry G. Armstrong, *Fit to Fly.* New York: D. Appleton-Century Co., 1941.

Hershey, Burnet, *The Air Future.* New York: Duell, Sloan and Pearce, 1943.

Johnston, S. Paul, *Wings After War.* New York: Duell, Sloan and Pearce, 1944.

Josephson, Matthew, *Empire of the Air.* New York: Harcourt, Brace and Company, 1944.

Kincheloe, Samuel C., *The American City and Its Church.* New York: Friendship Press, 1938.

Langewiesche-Brandt, Wolfgang Ernst, *Stick and Rudder.* New York: Whittlesey House, 1944.

Leonard, V. A., *Police Communications Systems.* Berkeley: University of California Press, 1938.

Ley, Willy, *Bombs and Bombing.* New York: Modern Age Books, 1941.

Lissitzyn, Oliver J., *International Air Transport and National Policy,* Studies in American Foreign Relations, no. 3. New York: Council on Foreign Relations, 1942.

Lyon, L. S., and L. C. Sorrell, editors, *Prospects and Problems in Aviation.* Chicago Association of Commerce, 1945.

Macauley, C. B. F., *The Helicopters Are Coming.* New York: McGraw-Hill Book Company, 1944.

Mingos, Howard, editor, *Aircraft Yearbook.* Aeronautical Chamber of Commerce of America, annual publication since 1918.

Morris, C. L., *Pioneering the Helicopter.* New York: McGraw-Hill Book Company, 1945.

National Institute of Municipal Law Officers, *Airports and Airplanes and the Legal Problems They Create in Cities.* Chicago, 1939.

Noel-Brown, S. J., *Economics of Air Transportation*. New York: Pitman Publication Corporation, 1937.

Puffer, Claude E., *Air Transportation*. Philadelphia: The Blakiston Company, 1941.

Recent Social Trends in the United States. New York: McGraw-Hill Book Company, 1933.

Reeves, Earl, *Aviation's Place in Tomorrow's Business*. New York: B. C. Forbes Publishing Company, 1930.

Rosen, S. McKee, and Laura Rosen, *Technology and Society*. New York: The Macmillan Company, 1941.

Ross, D., and D. Weld, *Aviation, Manufacturing — Transportation*. New York: White, Weld and Company, 1940.

Spencer, Francis A., *Air Mail Payment and the Government*. Washington, D.C.: The Brookings Institution, 1941.

Steiner, Jesse F., *Americans at Play*. New York: McGraw-Hill Book Company, 1933.

Van Zandt, J. Parker, *Civil Aviation and Peace*. Washington, D.C.: The Brookings Institution, 1944. (Vol. II in the series, *America Faces the Air Age*.)

Van Zandt, J. Parker, *The Geography of World Air Transport*. Washington, D.C.: The Brookings Institution, 1944. (Vol. I in the series, *America Faces the Air Age*.)

Van Zandt, J. Parker, "Air Transport," *Transportation and National Policy*, Part II, Section I, National Resources Planning Board. Washington, D.C.: Government Printing Office, 1942.

Weller, George, *Bases Overseas*. New York: Harcourt, Brace and Company, 1944.

White, Leonard D., *Trends in Public Administration*. New York: McGraw-Hill Book Company, 1933.

Wood, John Walter, *Airports*. New York: Coward-McCann, 1940.

Zim, Herbert S., *Man in the Air; The Effects of Flying on the Human Body*. New York: Harcourt, Brace and Company, 1943.

ADDRESSES, MONOGRAPHS, AND PAMPHLETS

Air Cargo, Inc., *Air Cargo Potential in 33 Selected Industries*. New York: 233 Broadway, New York, 7, March, 1945.

Air Transport Association of America, *Little Known Facts About the Scheduled Air Transport Industry*, 6th edition, September 1, 1944.

American Medical Association, Council on Medical Education and Hospitals, *Growth and Distribution of Hospital Facilities in the United States*, July, 1938.

Ardussi, Wallace F., *The Aero Hydro Pickup*, Civil Aeronautics Board Investigation of Local Pickup Air Service, Docket no. 857. Exhibit presented by Foote Brothers, Gear and Machine Corporation, Chicago, September 21, 1943.

Association of American Railroads, *Initial Study of Air Transportation*, January, 1944.

Braniff Airways, Inc., *Trade Area Airline Service*, October, 1943.

Brenner, Melvin A., *Post-War Prospects of the Aircraft Industry*. Washington, D.C.: National Resources Planning Board, April, 1943.

Burden, William A. M., *The Place of the Private Airplane in our Aviation Future*. Address delivered before the Los Angeles Chamber of Commerce, July 29, 1943.

Burden, William A. M., *Reconversion and Air Power*. Address to National Industrial Conference Board, September 21, 1944.

Civil Aeronautics Administration, *Air Conditioning Young America*. Washington, D.C., 1942.

Civil Aeronautics Board, *Annual Reports*. Washington, D.C.: Government Printing Office.

Civil Aeronautics Board, Transcript of Testimony of Witnesses offered by Greyhound Corporation, *Investigation of Local Feeder and Pickup Services*, Docket 857. October 21, 22 and 23, 1943.

Civil Aeronautics Board, Economic Bureau, *Survey of United States Overseas Mail*, September, 1943.

Coad, B. R., E. Johnson, and G. L. McNeil, *Dusting Cotton from Airplanes*. Washington, D.C.: United States Department of Agriculture, Department Bulletin 1204, January, 1924.

Crowell-Collier Publishing Company, *Tomorrow's Customers for Aviation*, August, 1944.

Crozier, F. H., *Overseas Air Service Patterns, Civil Aeronautics Board*, Economic Bureau, Research and Analysis Division, Washington, D.C.
    Trans-Atlantic Areas, September, 1943.
    Trans-Caribbean and Off-Shore Island Areas, August, 1944.
        Appendix I and Appendix II.
    Trans-Pacific Areas, vols. 1, 2, 3.
    Travel Distribution and Composition — All Areas, December, 1944.

Curtiss-Wright Corporation, *Air Transportation in the Immediate Post-War Period*, Report BR-69, Airplane Division. Buffalo, New York, March, 1944.

Davies, W. W., *Air Transports, Past and Future*. Paper read before the American Society of Mechanical Engineers, April 27, 1943.

Frederick, John H., Statement before Civil Aeronautics Board, Local, Feeder, Pickup Hearings for Southwest Feeder Airlines, October, 1943.

Geisse, John H., and Samuel C. Williams, *Postwar Outlook for Private Flying*. A Report to W. A. M. Burden, 1943.

Graddick, C. P., *Air Cargo Expectancy*. Speech before First National Clinic of Domestic Aviation Planning, Oklahoma City, November, 1943.

Hart, Hornell, *Can World Government Be Predicted by Mathematics?* Ann Arbor: Edwards Brothers, 1943.

Hershey, Burnet, *Skyways of Tomorrow*. Headline Series, Number 47, Foreign Policy Association, August, 1944.

Hibbard, Hall L., *Jet Propulsion — for War and Peace*. Lecture at the University of California, May 15, 1945.

Husman, Chester N., *A Hopper and Mechanism for Distribution of Bait and Dust by Airplanes for Insect Control*. Washington, D.C.: United States Department of Agriculture, Agricultural Research Administration, Bureau of Entomology and Plant Quarantine, July, 1943.

Illinois Central System, *Air Freight*. Research and Development Bureau, May 19, 1942.

Kaempffert, Waldemar, *The Airplane and Tomorrow's World*. Public Affairs Pamphlets 78, 1943.

International Civil Aviation Conference. Final Act, Part I, Docket 488, GD/70.

Kuznets, Simon, *National Income, 1919-1938*. New York: Occasional Paper 2, National Bureau of Economic Research, April, 1941.

Kuznets, Simon, *National Product, War and Prewar*. New York: Occasional Paper 17, National Bureau of Economic Research, February, 1944.

Kuznets, Simon, *Uses of National Income in Peace and War*. New York: Occasional Paper 6, National Bureau of Economic Research, March, 1942.

Larsen, Spencer A., *Air Cargo Potential in Fresh Fruits and Vegetables*. Detroit: Wayne University Studies in Air Transport, Number One, Wayne University Press, 1944.

Loening, Grover, *Air Cargo Shipping*. Address before Foreign Commerce Club, May 20, 1942.

Loening, Grover, *The Helicopter's Limited Future*. Lecture before Brooklyn Institute of Arts and Sciences, December 3, 1943.

Madden, William J., and Albert Beitel, Examiners, *Investigation of Local-Feeder Pick-up Air Service.* Civil Aeronautics Board, Docket 857, February, 1944.

Malcolmson, J. D., *Air Cargoes.* Pamphlet published by Robert Gair Company, 1943.

Mayer, Joseph, *Postwar National Income.* Washington, D.C.: Pamphlet 55, The Brookings Institution, 1944.

National Industrial Conference Board, Inc., *Measuring and Projecting National Income.* New York: Studies in Business Policy, no. 5, 1945.

National Planning Association, *National Budgets for Full Employment.* Washington, D.C.: Planning Pamphlets 43 and 44, March 16, 1945.

Patterson, W. A., *The Airplane in the Scheme of Postwar Transportation.* Address delivered before National Industrial Conference Board, New York, November, 1942.

Patterson, W. A., *Prospective Expansion of Airline Routes and Services In the United States.* Address delivered at the Chicago Forum on Aviation, Chicago Association of Commerce, April 24, 1945.

Pogue, J. Welch, *Air Cargo Today and Its Influence in the Postwar World.* Speech before University Club, New York, December 12, 1942.

Pogue, J. Welch, *Merchandising by Air.* Address delivered at Oklahoma City before meeting sponsored by the Oklahoma City Chamber of Commerce and National Aeronautics Association, August 2, 1943.

Post Office Department, *A Brief History of the Air Mail Service.* Washington, D.C.: Division of Air Mail Service.

Sheehan, J. V., *The Economics of Post-War Carriage of Air Cargo.* Paper presented before Air Cargo Engineering Meeting of the Chicago Section of Society of Automotive Engineers, December 8, 1942.

Sillcox, L. K., *Flying Freight.* Lecture at Graduate School of Business Administration, Harvard University, December 15, 1942.

Sonne, Hans Christian, *A Preview of National Budgets for Full Employment, "Model T."* Address before National Planning Association, Washington, D.C., June 8, 1944.

Sorrell, L. C., and Harry A. Wheeler, *Passenger Transport in the United States, 1920-1950.* Railway Business Association, 1944.

Southwest Airways Company, *Area Airlines and the Air Age,* 1944.

Stewart, Paul W., and associates, *Survey of Travel in 1941 and Potential Market for Helicopter Service.* Prepared for the Greyhound Corporation, August, 1943.

Stovall, Dr. W. R., *Trends in Civil Aviation Medicine.* Address at Fifteenth Annual Convention of the Aero Medical Association, October 26, 1943.

Stringer, Harry R., editor, *A Headline History of the Air Pick-up, 1939-1942.* All American Aviation, Inc., Wilmington, Delaware.

United Air Lines, Inc. Exhibits before the Civil Aeronautics Board, Dockets 152, 1345, 1346.

United States Department of Agriculture, Forest Service, *Use of Aircraft in Forestry.*

United States Department of Commerce, *Civil Aviation and the National Economy,* September, 1945.

United States Department of Commerce, *Markets After the War,* March, 1943.

United States Surgeon General's Office, Technical Manual 8-310, *Notes on Physiology in Aviation Medicine.* Washington, D.C.: War Department, 1940.

Van Zandt, J. Parker, *European Air Transport on the Eve of the War — 1939.* James Jackson Cabot Lecture, no. 5, Norwich University, Northfield, Vermont, 1940.

Warner, Edward, *Air Transportation Prospects.* Address before Engineering Society of Detroit, December 15, 1943.

Whidden, Howard P. Jr., *New Horizons in International Air Transport.* Foreign Policy Reports, vol. 19, no. 8, July 1, 1943.

Williams, Ernest W. Jr., *The Outlook for the Railroad Industry.* Washington, D.C.: National Planning Association, Planning Pamphlet 22, October, 1943.

Woytinsky, W. S., *Economic Perspectives, 1943-48.* Washington, D.C.: Bureau Memorandum 52, Federal Security Agency, Social Security Board, Bureau of Research and Statistics, October, 1943.

Wright, T. P., *Aviation's Place in Civilization.* The Thirty-Third Wilbur Wright Memorial Lecture delivered in London, May 31, 1945.

MAGAZINE ARTICLES

Air Age Education News. New York: Published by Air Age Education Research, 100 East 42nd Street, New York 17.

Armstrong, Harry G., "A Special Form of Functional Psychoneuroses Appearing in Aviation Pilots," *Journal of American Medical Association*, 1936, p. 1347.

Ashby, Lyle W., "Education for the Air Age," *Journal of the National Education Association*, vol. 32, no. 3, March, 1943, p. 74.

Baldwin, Hanson W., "Air Power: What It Can and Cannot Do," *New York Times Magazine*, March 26, 1944, pp. 5-6.

Bauer, Lt. Col. L. H., "The Development of Commercial Aeronautics and of the Airplane Ambulance," *The Military Surgeon*, February, 1930, vol. 66, no. 2, p. 165.

Bauer, George F., "How Air Cargo Will Affect Four Basic Factors in Distribution, No. 1 — Effect of Time Savings on Turnover," *D and W*, October, 1943, p. 45. "No. 3 — Weight in Post-War Shipping," *D and W*, December, 1943, p. 27.

Berle, Adolph A., Jr., "Freedoms of the Air," *Harper's Magazine*, March, 1945, pp. 327-34.

Bernière, André, "Why You Get Airsick," *Flying*, February, 1945, p. 39.

Bourne, Ray, "Aerial Photography of Rural Areas," *Journal of the Ministry of Agriculture*, January, 1937, vol. 43, pp. 929-31.

Breech, E. R., "After the War — What?" *Tenth Fortune Round Table*, November, 1941.

Burden, William A. M., "Airports of Tomorrow," *Flying*, April, 1944, p. 48.

Burden, William A. M., "The Future of Air Transport," *Atlantic Monthly*, December, 1943, pp. 51-62.

Burden, William A. M., "Opening the Sky," *Atlantic Monthly*, March, 1945, pp. 50-54.

Burgess, George W., "Local Airlines," *Flying*, June, 1944, p. 70.

Chitale, L. M., "Air Menace Spurs Spacious Planning," *American City*, April, 1944, p. 49.

Cole, George E., "Development of Tractor and Airplane Transportation in Manitoba," American Institute of Mining and Metallurgical Engineers, *Transactions*, vol. 153, Metal Mining and Milling Methods, 1943, p. 143.

Corddry, Charles, Jr., "Should Surface Carriers Operate Airlines?" *Flying*, April, 1944, p. 30.

Crichton, Kyle, "Birds Without Feathers," *Collier's*, October 5, 1935, p. 19.

Curry, R. J., "Airport Discipline Means Safety," *Flying*, February, 1945, p. 41.

Darby, Lt. Col. T. E., "Airplane Ambulance Evacuation," *The Military Surgeon*, August, 1932, pp. 162-71.

David, Joan, "Let Your Airport Go to Grass," *Flying*, February, 1945, pp. 42-43.

Deake, Standish, "Streamlining General Science for an Air-Minded Generation," *School Science and Mathematics*, vol. 43, 1943, pp. 567-71.

The Detroiter, "Detroit Tackles Air Cargo Research," December 21, 1942, p. 5.

Doman, Carl T., "Engines for Private Planes," *Flying*, November, 1944, p. 51.

Dove, W. E., "Control of Destructive Insects by Aircraft," *Scientific Monthly*, October, 1942, pp. 382-86.

Drake, C. J., and G. C. Decker, "The Rôle of the Airplane in Grasshopper Control," *Journal of Economic Entomology*, vol. 25, pp. 189-96.

Eliel, Leon T., "Aerial Reconnaissance and Contour Mapping in Mining," American Institute of Mining and Metallurgical Engineers, *Transactions*, vol. 126, Metal Mining and Mining Geology, 1937, p. 560.

Engineering and Mining Journal, November, 1935, vol. 136, no. 11. Entire issue deals with the development of the use of the airplane in the mining industry.

Evans, Ray, Jr., and Eleanor M. Johnson, "Aviation: Its Place in Tomorrow's Curriculum," *Education*, March, 1945, p. 442.

Fedden, Sir A. H. Roy, *Aircraft Power Plant — Past and Future*. A Wilbur Wright Memorial Lecture for 1944, London, Aeronautical Reprint no. 99.

Foster, John, Jr., "The Personal Plane Sales Target," *Aviation*, January, 1944, p. 116.

Foster, John, Jr., "Here Are Your Markets," *Aviation*, May, June, and July, 1944.

Frederick, John H., "Should Motor Carriers Fly Air Cargo?" *D and W*, October, 1943.

Frederick, John H., "How Air Transportation May Affect Marketing and Production Development," *Journal of Marketing*, January, 1944, p. 274.

Froesch, Charles, "Short Haul Transports," *Air Transport*, September, 1943, pp. 32-35.

Fuller, Curtis, "Was Air Power a Success?" *Flying*, August, 1945, p. 21.

Geisse, John H., "Before I Buy a Plane," *Flying*, February, 1945, p. 30.

Geisse, John H., "A Landing-Gear Yardstick for Postwar Airport Layouts," *Aviation*, January, 1944, p. 120.

Geisse, John H., "Suggestions for Furthering Private Flying," *Aeronautical Engineering Review*, August, 1944, p. 47.

Gilbert, Milton; Hans Staehle, and W. S. Woytinsky, with a reply by Simon Kuznets, "National Product, War and Prewar, Some Comments on Professor Kuznets's Study," *The Review of Economic Statistics*, August, 1944, p. 109.

Goldenweiser, E. A., and E. E. Hagen, "Jobs After the War," *Federal Reserve Bulletin*, May, 1944, p. 424.

Grant, Lt. Col. David N. W., "Airplane Ambulance Evacuation," *The Military Surgeon*, March, 1941, p. 238.

Greeves-Carpenter, C. F., "The Flying Ambulance," *Trained Nurse and Hospital Review*, March, 1938, p. 263.

Gregory, Col. H. F., "The Army's Flying Windmill," *Air Force*, March, 1943, p. 6.

Gregory, Col. H. F., "What You Can Believe About the Helicopter," *Saturday Evening Post*, May 27, 1944, p. 22.

Haefner, Ralph, "Air-Age Education Starts in the Elementary School," *The American School Board Journal*, December, 1942, p. 27.

Hagen, E. E., and N. B. Kirkpatrick, "The National Output at Full Employment in 1950," *The American Economic Review*, September, 1944, p. 472.

Hall, William D., "Postwar Private Planes," *Flying*, May, 1944, p. 29.

Jensen, Walter S., "Today and Tomorrow in Aviation Medicine," *Hygeia*, March, 1944, p. 192.

Joint Committee on Public Emergency Ambulance Service, "Outline of a Plan for Public Emergency Ambulance Service," *Hospital Council Bulletin*, November, 1938, p. 10.

Jouett, Col. J., "Jouett Predicts Trends in Aviation's Future," *American Aviation*, November 1, 1941, p. 16.

Journal of the National Education Association, "School Courses in Aviation," November, 1936, p. 256.

Kalam, Harold S., "Coming, the Helicopter Land Boom," *Barron's, National Business and Finance Weekly*, October 18, 1943, p. 3.

Kelly, R. D., and W. W. Davies, "Air Cargo Problems," *Flying*, December, 1942, p. 47.

Kinzel, Robert K., "Looking Ahead to Air Cargo Markets," *Aviation*, Part I, April, 1944, p. 176, and Part II, May, 1944, p. 185.

Langewiesche, Wolfgang, "Airways and Airports of the Future," *American City*, August, 1942, p. 64.

Langewiesche, Wolfgang, "Your Private Airplane," *Harper's Magazine*, January, 1942, pp. 151-60.

Levings, William S., "Aerogeology in Mineral Exploration," *Quarterly of the Colorado School of Mines*, vol. 39, no. 4, October, 1944.

Littrell, Gaither, "New Giant," *Flying,* June, 1944, p. 156.

Lothrop, E. E., "Let's Be Practical About Postwar Plane Markets," *Aviation,* December, 1943, p. 114.

McDonough, F. E., "Aviation Medicine: A Survey," *Proceedings of Mayo Clinic,* April 2, 1941, p. 217.

Masefield, Peter, "The Future of Air Transport: A British View," *Atlantic Monthly,* January, 1944, p. 37.

Meyer, William H., Jr., "Development of Aerial Photographic Equipment," American Institute of Mining and Metallurgical Engineers, *Transactions,* vol. 126, 1937, p. 575.

The Mining Magazine, "Aerial Reconnaissance," May, 1943, p. 309.

Ogburn, William F., "Studies in the Prediction and Distortion of Reality," *Social Forces,* December, 1934, pp. 227-28.

Pack, Harry S., "The Motor Carrier and Air Carrier," *D and W,* November, 1943.

Patterson, W. A., and Ralph S. Damon, "A 'Chosen Instrument' Airline?" *Flying,* September, 1944, p. 26.

Peck, Phillips J., "The Outlook for Feeder Airlines," *Flying,* January, 1945, p. 32.

Pecker, Joseph S., "Basic Drives for Helicopters," *Aviation,* November, 1944, p. 125.

Pendray, G. Edward, "Passenger Flights by Rocket," *Harper's Magazine,* March, 1945, pp. 353-58.

Piper, William Thomas, "Plain Facts About Private Planes," *Atlantic Monthly,* July, 1944, pp. 67-71.

Planck, Charles E., "What Was Wrong with Private Flying?" *Flying,* September, 1944, p. 30.

Rand, Kurt, "Do Runways Limit Plane Size?" *Flying,* January, 1945, p. 69.

Ross, John C., "Airports for Everybody," *Flying,* March, 1945, p. 40.

Rossell, Dr. J. McF., "Flying Doctors in Australia," *Canadian Hospital,* March, 1939, p. 36.

Schnepfe, F., "The Design of Flight Strips," *Roads and Bridges,* February, 1943, p. 25.

Scragg, George H., "Ground Handling Is Essential for Air Cargo," *D and W,* October, 1943.

Shay, Felix B., "Air Transport at Agua Fria," Technical Publication 1156 of the American Institute of Mining and Metallurgical Engineers, published in *Mining Technology,* January, 1940.

Sikorsky, I. I., "Technical Development of the VS-300 Helicopter During 1941," *Journal of the Aeronautical Sciences,* June, 1942, p. 309.

Smith, Frederick H., "What Kind of Instruments for the Personal Plane?" *Aviation,* November, 1944, p. 122.

Staats, W. D., "Aerial Survey of Wheat Acres," *Extension Service Review*, vol. 5, no. 12, pp. 181-82.

Stanton, Charles I., "Air Mail Comes of Age," *Flying*, August, 1944, p. 24.

Stanton, Charles I., "More Airports for the Personal Flyer," *Aviation*, October, 1944, p. 118.

Steinberg, S. S., "Mapping From the Air," *Scientific Monthly*, vol. 40, April, 1935, pp. 363-66.

Stokes, W. E. D., Jr., "Many Aerial Survey Parties Active in 1941, Locating Mineral Areas and Laying Out Pipe Lines," *Mining and Metallurgy*, February, 1942, p. 65.

Thorp, Edward E., "Air Mail Goes RFD," *Aviation*, November, 1944, p. 170.

Tuttle, Col. A. D., and Capt. H. G. Armstrong, "Rôle of Aviation Medicine in the Development of Aviation," *The Military Surgeon*, October, 1939, p. 285.

United States Bureau of Labor Statistics, "Wartime Development of the Aircraft Industry," *Monthly Labor Review*, November, 1944.

United States Bureau of Mines, "Use of Airplanes in Mining and Petroleum Operations," Information Circular 6767, February, 1934.

Van Dusen, William, "Mine Freight by Air in South America," *The Engineering and Mining Journal*, November, 1935, p. 569.

Van Zandt, J. Parker, "International Air Conference," *Flying*, February, 1945, p. 21.

Van Zandt, J. Parker, "The Chicago Civil Aviation Conference," *Foreign Policy Reports*, Foreign Policy Association, February 15, 1945, pp. 290-96.

Warner, Edward, "Postwar Transport Aircraft." The Thirty-First Wilbur Wright Memorial Lecture, May, 1943, reprinted in *Aeronautical Engineering Review*, October, 1943, pp. 7-59.

Warner, Edward, "Requirements of Local Air Transport Service," *Aeronautical Engineering Review*, February, 1944, p. 13.

Warner, Edward, "The Chicago Air Conference," *Foreign Affairs*, April, 1945, pp. 406-21.

Warner, Edward, "Where Next?" *Air Transport*, September, 1944, pp. 32-37, and October, 1944, p. 79.

Weinberger, Julius, "Economic Aspects of Recreation," *Harvard Business Review*, summer, 1937, pp. 448-63.

Welch, E. V., "Insects Found on Aircraft at Miami, Florida in 1938," *Public Health Reports*, United States Public Health Service, vol. 54, no. 14, April 7, 1939, p. 561-66.

Wendt, Dr. G. R., "How to Prevent Air Sickness," *Flying*, April, 1943, p. 58.

Whittingham, H. E., "Preventive Medicine in Relation to Aviation," *Proceedings, Royal Society of Medicine* (United Services Section), vol. 32, pp. 455-72.

Wilber, Gordon O., "Adapting Wood and Metal Shop Facilities to Air-Age Education," *The American School and University*, 1943 Yearbook, p. 321.

Wilber, Gordon O., "Orientation in Aviation Through Industrial Arts," *Education*, October, 1942, pp. 111-16.

Wilmer, Brig. Gen. W. H., "The Early Development of Aviation Medicine in the United States," *The Military Surgeon*, September, 1935, p. 115.

Wilson, Charles Morrow, "The Great Crops Move," *Harper's Magazine*, June, 1943, p. 42-49.

Winters, S. R., "Air War on the Grasshopper," *Flying*, December, 1943, p. 32.

Winters, S. R., "Hospitals on Wings," *Hygeia*, February, 1939, p. 113.

Wissler, Clark, "The Influence of the Horse in the Development of Plains Culture," *American Anthropologist*, vol. 16, 1914, pp. 1-25.

Wright, Marshall S., "The Application of Aerial Photography to Land Use Problems," *Soil Science Society of America, Proceedings, 1936*, vol. 1, pp. 357-60.

★ ★ ★

Index

lation, 41; and coverage, 78; by extrapolation, 36; and fashion, 52; forecast of forecasting, 80; and growth curve, 37, 48; of international travel volume, 299; many results from single cause, 55; by measurement, 36; not based on measurement, 45; of particular invention, 59; of passenger traffic, 118, 120, 136, 145; and planning, 35; for private flying, 263; projection of trends in passenger travel, 117; resistance to use of inventions as factor in, 66; by rough approximation, 35; "slide-rule," 54; of social effect of automobile, 6; of social effect of invention, 58, 68; of social phenomena, popular idea, 32; in social science, possibility of, 8; and social trends, 77; in this book, 57; of unique event, 44; of use of invention, 63; wishful thinking in, 50

Predictions summarized: for agriculture, 616; for air cargo, 190; for air mail, 166; for air passenger travel, 145; for air routes, 288; for airports, 216; for cities, 361; for crime, 441; for education, 463; for family, 339; for forestry, 630; for government, 658; for health, 400; for international policies, 723; for international relations, 705; for international travel, 309; for landing places, 216; for local air service, 241; for manufacturing, 519; for marketing, 536; for mining, 545; for newspapers, 580; for ocean shipping, 498; for population, 329; for private flying, 267; for public administration, 685; for railroads, 486; for real estate, 556; for recreation, 422; for religion, 371; for stock raising, 643; for technological trends in aviation, 112; for transportation of goods, 120

Pressurized cabins for altitude flying, 85, 110, 380

Prisons, administration of, as affected by aviation, 440

Private aircraft: and church attendance, 366; manufacture of, 516; size of postwar market, estimate, 265

Private flying: accidents in, 245; airports for, 206, 248, 350; amount of, 264; and class distinction, 329; as competition to railroad, 483; conclusion, 267; costs, 246; and family expenditures, 335; and family recreation, 334; flying-hours report by Civil Aeronautics Administration, 243; and helicopter, 249; and helicopter, needed improvements, 253; and helicopter, roadable, 262; influence on family, 333; landing places, 248; landing places and real estate values, 549; landing strips, 249; and need for national police, 438; personal reasons for giving it up, 244; prior to World War II, 242; prospect for, 263; reasons for slow development, 243; as recreation, 404; regulation of, 247; and safety, 245; and social classes, 328; speed of, 251; vertical flight, advantages of, 250; for week-end trips, 406; wide social effects of, 242

Projection of curve: amount of air cargo, 180; costs to estimate rates, 131; of international air passenger traffic, 302; factors influencing, 38; of growth of private flying, 265; of trends in plane passenger travel, 117

Prospecting, use of aviation in, 540

Prostitution, effect of aviation on, 428

Public administration, effects of aviation on: Bureau of Mines, 676; cities and towns, 684; Coast Guard, 679; conclusion, 685; control of insects and bacteria, 669; Department of Agriculture, 676; Department of Commerce, 680; Department of Interior, 672; Fish and Wildlife Service, 674; Forest Service, 678; general effects, 665; government aid to aviation, 662; Grazing Service, 673; immigration and customs collection, 668; National Park Service, 675; Office of Indian Affairs, 675; Public Health Service, 679; regulation of aviation, 660; state governments, 682; weather prediction and report, 670

Puffer, C. E., 727

Pullman Company, 483

Pusher propeller for roadable plane, 89

Radar: government aid in develop-